[FINANCE FOR NON-FINANCIAL MANAGERS]

SEVENTH EDITION

[FINANCE FOR NON-FINANCIAL MANAGERS]

SEVENTH EDITION

PIERRE G. BERGERON
University of Ottawa

NELSON

NELSON

Finance for Non-Financial Managers, Seventh Edition

by Pierre G. Bergeron

Vice President, Editorial Higher Education:
Anne Williams

Senior Acquisitions Editor:
Amie Plourde

Editorial Consultant:
Rod Banister

Executive Marketing Manager:
Sean Chamberland

Technical Reviewer:
Ross Meacher

Developmental Editor:
Elke Price

Photo Researcher/Permissions Coordinator:
Lynn McLeod

Senior Content Production Manager:
Imoinda Romain

Production Service:
Integra Software Services Pvt. Ltd.

Copy Editor:
Dawn Hunter

Proofreader:
Jeri Freedman

Indexer:
Integra Software Services Pvt. Ltd.

Manufacturing Manager:
Joanne McNeil

Design Director:
Ken Phipps

Managing Designer:
Franca Amore

Interior Design Modifications:
Cathy Mayer

Cover Design:
Cathy Mayer

Cover Image:
© Buena Vista Images/Getty

Compositor:
Integra Software Services Pvt. Ltd.

Printed and bound in Canada

8 20 19

For more information contact Nelson Education Ltd., 1120 Birchmount Road, Toronto, Ontario, M1K 5G4. Or you can visit our Internet site at nelson.com

Library and Archives Canada Cataloguing in Publication

Bergeron, Pierre G.
Finance for non-financial managers / Pierre G. Bergeron. — 7th ed.

Includes bibliographical references and index.
ISBN 978-0-17-653083-9

1. Business enterprises—Finance. I. Title.

HG4026.B46 2013 658.15
C2012-905660-X

ISBN-13: 978-0-17-653083-9
ISBN-10: 0-17-653083-5

To the memory of my beloved father

Paul E. Bergeron

■

a friend

■

a tutor

■

a motivator

who started me on the trail that
has led to this book, among others,
and introduced me to the measures
of excellence.

[BRIEF CONTENTS]

[CONTENTS]

Chapter 4

FINANCIAL STATEMENT ANALYSIS

Chapter 5

PROFIT PLANNING AND DECISION MAKING

Chapter 6

WORKING CAPITAL MANAGEMENT

Chapter 7

PLANNING, BUDGETING, AND CONTROLLING

Chapter 8

SOURCES AND FORMS OF FINANCING

Chapter 9

COST OF CAPITAL, CAPITAL STRUCTURE, AND FINANCIAL MARKETS

Chapter 10

TIME-VALUE-OF-MONEY CONCEPT

Chapter 11

CAPITAL BUDGETING

Chapter 12

BUSINESS VALUATION

[PREFACE]

Finance for Non-Financial Managers is written for business and non-business students (undergraduates, postgraduates, and graduates), managers, and executives who have a limited background in the field of finance. It is aimed primarily at readers who want to broaden their understanding of financial analysis, improve their decision-making skills, or upgrade old skills in financial management and accounting. It is written at a basic level to help clarify financial terminology, concepts, and techniques, and to help readers apply the theory of finance to solve business problems.

I am convinced that finance is a function that is far too important to be left only to financial specialists. Financial activities should be practised by non-financial managers who are responsible for resources and interested in improving the financial performance and future of their organizations.

Business and non-business students will find this book instrumental in learning the essentials of financial statement analysis and capital budgeting techniques. It can be used for a one-semester course at colleges, for continuing education courses in finance at universities, in business courses for non-business majors, and in small-business management and entrepreneurship courses.

This book will also be useful to (1) managers in all types of organizations who currently work in a non-financial functions, such as marketing, production, human resources, engineering, or research and development; (2) financial analysts who want to adopt more rigid methodologies for solving financial problems; (3) accountants who want to learn how to analyze financial statements in a more comprehensive way and use them as decision-making instruments; (4) entrepreneurs of small- and medium-sized businesses who want to develop fundamental skills in financial control and financial planning; and (5) independent professionals, such as lawyers, engineers, and medical practitioners, who want to understand the financial side of their profession.

The financial topics are presented in a format appropriate for those who supply financial information (accountants) and those who use it (non-financial managers and financial analysts). One of the most important objectives of this book is to make the various topics presented in each chapter understandable to readers at different levels.

Readers will find *Finance for Non-Financial Managers* informative and enjoyable. There is no need to present finance as an abstract subject. Finance can be understood and applied to business situations so that non-financial managers and executives can be more effective. I have presented various financial management concepts and techniques in a simple way, using a practical and common sense approach, supported by many tables, figures, and examples.

Distinctive Features of This Book

A major goal of the seventh edition of *Finance for Non-Financial Managers* is to offer students better ways to learn and understand challenging financial management concepts, theories, and practices. Chapters are grouped under four broad categories to reflect the types of decisions made in organizations: (1) accounting, financial statements, and ratio analysis decisions; (2) operating decisions; (3) financing decisions; and (4) investing decisions.

With a focus on learning, the following features emphasize hands-on activities that capture student interest and guide practical knowledge.

Learning Objectives

Each chapter's learning objectives give structure and coherence to the text content, study aids, and instructor's ancillaries. These numbered objectives are introduced at the beginning of the chapter, at the beginning of each major section, in the end-of-chapter summaries, and in the review questions and learning exercises.

CHAPTER 1

[OVERVIEW OF FINANCIAL MANAGEMENT]

Learning Objectives

After reading this chapter, you should be able to

1 Identify some of the external factors financial managers must consider to improve a company's bottom line.

2 Discuss the role of financial management within a business.

3 Identify the people responsible for the finance function.

4 Explain the four financial objectives of a business.

5 Describe the three major types of business decisions.

6 Examine the issues related to corporate transparency and accountability.

Opening Case

The chapter-opening case profiles the owners of a fictitious company called CompuTech Inc. who are faced with investing, operating, and financing decisions. The case highlights topics covered in the chapter and helps to keep the students engaged. Opening cases are also linked to self-test exercises in each chapter.

OPENING CASE

The Tools and Skills Needed to Start and Manage a Successful Retail Business

After spending 10 years with different organizations, Len and Joan Miller decided to open their own retail business, CompuTech Sales and Service. While Len had worked for several computer retail stores, Joan had been a sales representative for a multinational computer organization. Both felt that their combined experience would be a valuable asset for succeeding in their new venture.

However, before making their final decision, they decided to speak to a long-time friend and entrepreneur, Bill Murray, who had operated his own successful retail business for the past 25 years. They wanted some advice from him before launching their business. Bill had some enlightening ideas to share:

> The two most important factors that make any business successful are its products/services and its management. There must be a demand for the products or services that you want to sell, and you must have the management skills (e.g., planning, organizing, leading, and controlling) and business skills (e.g., merchandising, pricing, sales, and promotion) to realize your vision, objectives, and plans. You will also need operating and financial information to help you gauge the results of your business decisions on an ongoing basis. Although an accountant will help you set up your bookkeeping and accounting systems, you have to make sure that you can analyze your financial statements.
>
> To succeed, your business will have to generate a healthy profit (efficiency) and be able to pay its bills and employees on time (liquidity). In addition, your business must show signs of continuous growth in all segments, such as revenue and profit (prosperity). Most important, be sure that you do not overburden your business with too much debt (stability).
>
> You will be faced with three types of business decisions. The first type is *investing decisions*, such as launching your business. This is not the only investing decision that you will make. If your business prospers, you will have to make decisions about such things as opening new retail outlets, buying equipment, and so on. The second type is *financing decisions*. Once you know exactly how much it will cost you to start your business, you will have to approach investors, such as lenders, for financial support. These different sources of financing bear a cost. Therefore, you have to make sure that your business generates enough profit (return) to pay for financing your business (cost). *Operating decisions* are the third type of business decisions. They have to do with day-to-day operating activities. You will be continually faced with decisions about pricing, advertising, hiring, office expenses, and so on. To maximize your profit (efficiency), you will have to keep your costs as low as possible.

NEL 3

Chapter Overview

Major topics covered in the chapter are highlighted in the chapter overviews. These overviews outline each chapter's key financial management themes.

Figures and Tables

More than 140 figures and tables throughout the book will help students understand the financial topics covered in the text and will help them visualize how these concepts are connected.

Figure 3.1 Westpark Inc.'s Inflows and Outflows of Cash

a reduction in the trade receivables account ($5,000), and a reduction in the cash account ($5,000).

To finance the purchase of these four assets valued at $150,000, Eastpark used $35,000 from internal funding (by withdrawing money from the bank, reducing

Table 3.2 Eastpark Ltd.'s Statements of Financial Position

(in $)	2014	2013	Cash Inflows	Cash Outflows
Assets				
Buildings	400,000	290,000	—	110,000
Machinery	40,000	20,000	—	20,000
Equipment	25,000	15,000	—	10,000
Inventories	30,000	20,000	—	10,000
Trade receivables	10,000	15,000	5,000	—
Cash	5,000	10,000	5,000	—
Total Assets	**510,000**	370,000		
Equity	**150,000**	**125,000**	**25,000**	—
Liabilities				
Mortgage	200,000	130,000	70,000	—
Long-term borrowings	90,000	70,000	20,000	—
Trade and other payables	25,000	15,000	10,000	—
Seasonal loan	20,000	15,000	5,000	—
Short-term borrowings	15,000	10,000	5,000	—
Line of credit	10,000	5,000	5,000	—
Total Liabilities	**360,000**	**245,000**		
Total Equity and Liabilities	**510,000**	**370,000**	150,000	150,000

In The News

This popular boxed feature provides current and real-world examples that show how chapter subject matter affects profit and not-for-profit organizations. With these real-life examples, students are able to see how managers and executives deal with challenging financial decisions and situations.

The $1 million investment in non-current assets generates a 13.2% return.

Managers must also consider whether the investment is worth the risk by relating the return on the investment to both the cost of capital and the investment's inherent risks. For example, let's assume the company is in a 40% tax bracket (it pays 40% of its profit in taxes). If the company borrows the entire amount from lenders at a before-tax cost of 10%, then the after-tax cost of capital is 6%. The company would earn 7.2% (13.2% − 6.0%) more than it cost to borrow the money.

Is a 13.2% return on this investment worth the risk? If this investment were in a high-risk category, such as an investment in an untried product, management might want to earn at least 25% to 30% to justify the investment. However, if the project is low risk, such as the expansion of an existing plant, management will require a much lower return on investment (say, around 10%).

Financing decisions
Decisions related to borrowing from long-term lenders and shareholders.

FINANCING DECISIONS

Financing decisions deal with the accounts listed on the right side of the statement of financial position—that is, funds obtained from long-term lenders and shareholders. Managers examine how best to raise cash from these investors. Financing decisions deal with (1) choosing the most appropriate financing forms and sources of financing when buying assets, (2) determining the **cost of financing** when raising funds, (3) finding the weighted average cost of financing, and (4) establishing the weighted average cost of capital. These topics will be covered in some detail in Chapter 9 (Cost of Capital, Capital Structure, and Financial Markets). In the News 1.2 gives an example about raising cash from investors to bring an idea to life.

Cost of financing
Effective after-tax cost of raising funds from different sources (lenders and shareholders).

In The News 1.2

CONNECTING THE CASH TO THE DREAM

Being creative means dreaming about an idea; being innovative means finding a way to realize the dream. And usually, realizing that dream costs a lot of money. To realize a dream, an entrepreneur has to manufacture and market a product or service in addition to raising cash to finance every step of the process.

That is just what Keller Rinaudo, the 25-year-old founder of Robomotive did after he invented and began marketing a smartphone toy robot. In the process, he raised $1.5 million from various investors (some venture capitalists were even turned away), robot geeks, and customers. This toy is a docking station that turns a smartphone, such as an iPhone, into a robot that can be controlled from another smartphone through a Romo app. Rinaudo is already tinkering with the idea of expanding the smartphone's capabilities, with the intention of conquering the world.

Source: Adapted from Paul Sloane, "Romo the smartphone robot raises $1.5M, seeks world domination," http://news.cnet.com/8301-32973_3-57371451-296/romo-the-smartphone-robot-raises-$1.5m-seeks-world-domination/?tag=mncol;editorPicks, accessed February 5, 2012. For more information about Romo the Smartphone, visit http://romotive.com.

Problem-Solving Examples

More than 80 problem-solving examples with solutions walk students through the processes, step by step. These examples show the students apply the financial concepts and techniques explained in the text and help to prepare them for the self-test exercises and end-of-chapter learning exercises.

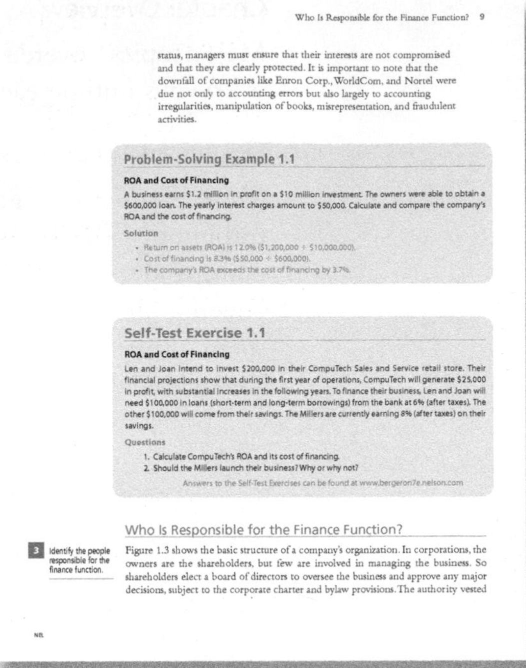

Who Is Responsible for the Finance Function? 9

status, managers must ensure that their interests are not compromised and that they are clearly protected. It is important to note that the downfall of companies like Enron Corp., WorldCom, and Nortel were due not only to accounting errors but also largely to accounting irregularities, manipulation of books, misrepresentation, and fraudulent activities.

Problem-Solving Example 1.1

ROA and Cost of Financing

A business earns $1.2 million in profit on a $10 million investment. The owners were able to obtain a $600,000 loan. The yearly interest charges amount to $50,000. Calculate and compare the company's ROA and the cost of financing.

Solution

- Return on assets (ROA) is 12.0% ($1,200,000 ÷ $10,000,000).
- Cost of financing is 8.3% ($50,000 ÷ $600,000).
- The company's ROA exceeds the cost of financing by 3.7%.

Self-Test Exercise 1.1

ROA and Cost of Financing

Len and Joan intend to invest $200,000 in their CompuTech Sales and Service retail store. Their financial projections show that during the first year of operations, CompuTech will generate $25,000 in profit, with substantial increases in the following years. To finance their business, Len and Joan will need $100,000 in loans (short-term and long-term borrowings) from the bank at 6% (after taxes). The other $100,000 will come from their savings. The Millers are currently earning 8% (after taxes) on their savings.

Questions

1. Calculate CompuTech's ROA and its cost of financing.
2. Should the Millers launch their business? Why or why not?

Answers to the Self-Test Exercises can be found at www.bergeron7e.nelson.com

Who Is Responsible for the Finance Function?

3 Identify the people responsible for the finance function.

Figure 1.3 shows the basic structure of a company's organization. In corporations, the owners are the shareholders, but few are involved in managing the business. So shareholders elect a board of directors to oversee the business and approve any major decisions, subject to the corporate charter and bylaw provisions. The authority vested

NEL

Self-Test Exercises

There are more than 80 self-test exercises, which are directly connected to each chapter's opening case. These exercises will help students apply many of the financial concepts and techniques. Solutions for these exercises are provided on the book's companion site at **www.bergeron7e.nelson.com**.

Chapter Summary

Each chapter includes a concise summary tied to each of the chapter's learning objectives.

Key Terms

A list of financial management terms is provided near the end of each chapter. Each key term, with page reference, appears in bold where first introduced and is defined in the margin. All key terms also appear in the glossary at the end of the book.

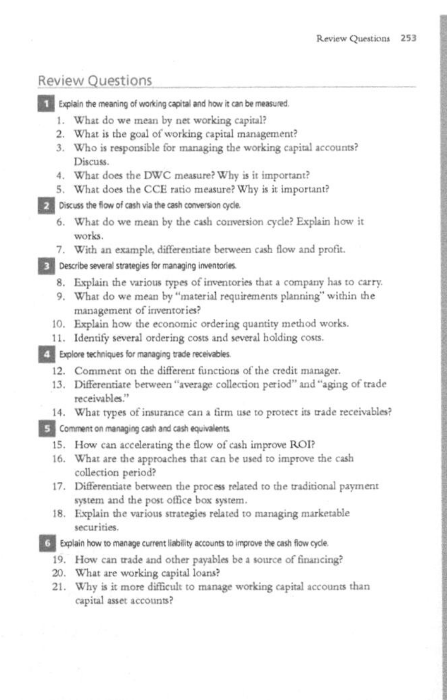

Review Questions 253

Review Questions

1 Explain the meaning of working capital and how it can be measured.

1. What do we mean by net working capital?
2. What is the goal of working capital management?
3. Who is responsible for managing the working capital accounts? Discuss.
4. What does the DWC measure? Why is it important?
5. What does the CCE ratio measure? Why is it important?

2 Discuss the flow of cash via the cash conversion cycle.

6. What do we mean by the cash conversion cycle? Explain how it works.
7. With an example, differentiate between cash flow and profit.

3 Describe several strategies for managing inventories.

8. Explain the various types of inventories that a company has to carry.
9. What do we mean by "material requirements planning" within the management of inventories?
10. Explain how the economic ordering quantity method works.
11. Identify several ordering costs and several holding costs.

4 Explore techniques for managing trade receivables.

12. Comment on the different functions of the credit manager.
13. Differentiate between "average collection period" and "aging of trade receivables."
14. What types of insurance can a firm use to protect its trade receivables?

5 Comment on managing cash and cash equivalents.

15. How can accelerating the flow of cash improve ROI?
16. What are the approaches that can be used to improve the cash collection period?
17. Differentiate between the process related to the traditional payment system and the post office box system.
18. Explain the various strategies related to managing marketable securities.

6 Explain how to manage current liability accounts to improve the cash flow cycle.

19. How can trade and other payables be a source of financing?
20. What are working capital loans?
21. Why is it more difficult to manage working capital accounts than capital asset accounts?

NEL

Review Questions

The end-of-chapter review questions are designed to help students to test their understanding of the chapter's key topics. These questions will also help them review the chapter contents before dealing with the more difficult end-of-chapter learning exercises and cases. The review questions are also directly connected to the learning objectives listed at the beginning of the chapters.

Learning Exercises

End-of-chapter learning exercises give students the opportunity to gain a greater understanding of their own strengths and weaknesses in terms of their financial management competencies and skills. They provide a smooth transition to the more difficult problems contained in the cases. Each learning exercise is also tied to the chapter's learning objectives.

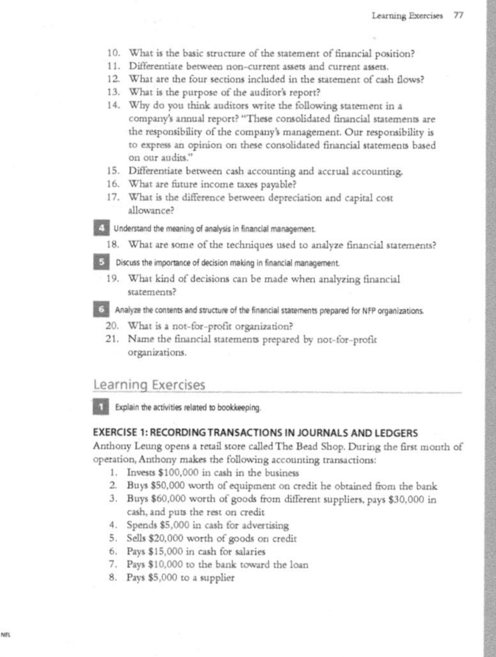

Learning Exercises 77

10. What is the basic structure of the statement of financial position?
11. Differentiate between non-current assets and current assets.
12. What are the four sections included in the statement of cash flows?
13. What is the purpose of the auditor's report?
14. Why do you think auditors write the following statement in a company's annual report? "These consolidated financial statements are the responsibility of the company's management. Our responsibility is to express an opinion on these consolidated financial statements based on our audits."
15. Differentiate between cash accounting and accrual accounting.
16. What are future income taxes payable?
17. What is the difference between depreciation and capital cost allowance?

4 Understand the meaning of analysis in financial management.

18. What are some of the techniques used to analyze financial statements?

5 Discuss the importance of decision making in financial management.

19. What kind of decisions can be made when analyzing financial statements?

6 Analyze the contents and structure of the financial statements prepared for NFP organizations.

20. What is a not-for-profit organization?
21. Name the financial statements prepared by not-for-profit organizations.

Learning Exercises

1 Explain the activities related to bookkeeping.

EXERCISE 1: RECORDING TRANSACTIONS IN JOURNALS AND LEDGERS

Anthony Leung opens a retail store called The Bead Shop. During the first month of operation, Anthony makes the following accounting transactions:

1. Invests $100,000 in cash in the business
2. Buys $50,000 worth of equipment on credit he obtained from the bank
3. Buys $60,000 worth of goods from different suppliers, pays $30,000 in cash, and puts the rest on credit
4. Spends $5,000 in cash for advertising
5. Sells $20,000 worth of goods on credit
6. Pays $15,000 in cash for salaries
7. Pays $10,000 to the bank toward the loan
8. Pays $5,000 to a supplier

NEL

End-of-Chapter Cases

Each case explores a chapter concept or problem faced by members of fictitious companies. The cases provide students with an opportunity to apply the concepts presented in the chapter and can be assigned as individual homework exercises or serve as a basis for class discussion.

Glossary

Each key term, with chapter page reference, is briefly defined at the end of the book. The glossary allows the students to review the more important terms associated with the material covered in the text.

New to the Seventh Edition

This Seventh Edition has been modified to provide a clearer and concise treatment of key financial topics. The theory has been tightened and been made more practical; and examples with solutions and exercises have been added to guide students on their path to success. The main changes to this edition include the following:

- *Problem-solving examples.* More than 80 problem-solving examples and their solutions walk students through the financial concepts. These examples guide the students to apply the financial theory and help to prepare them for the self-test exercises and end-of-chapter learning exercises.
- *Integrated learning system.* Each chapter's learning objectives give structure to the text contents as well as to the student and instructor resources. In addition to

each chapter's learning objectives being directly linked to the chapter content and end-of-chapter summaries, they are now also tied to the review questions and learning exercises.

- *International Financial Reporting Standards.* In January 2011, the *CICA Handbook* was replaced by the *International Financial Reporting Standards.* The text has been updated to reflect the revised structures and contents of the new financial statements, including some of the new terms used to list accounts in various sections of the statement of income, the statement of comprehensive income, the statement of changes in equity, the statement of financial position, and the statement of cash flows. Recommendations made by the International Accounting Standards Board are also covered.
- *In The News.* Most of the In The News boxed features linking the theory to real-life examples, such as RIM, Enbridge Inc., Ottawa Hospital, Caterpillar, Best Buy, and Facebook, have been replaced or updated.
- *Engaging applications.* Exercises in each chapter are presented at four levels. First are the problem-solving examples, which introduce the students to solving simple problems (with solutions) and lead to the second level, the more engaging self-test exercises that are linked to the opening case. The students are subsequently able to work out more intricate end-of-chapter learning exercises and cases at the third and fourth levels.
- *End-of-chapter exercises.* Several end-of-chapters exercises have been added throughout the chapters to give students more practice in using financial calculators or financial spreadsheets.

Instructor Resources

The **Nelson Education Teaching Advantage (NETA)** program delivers research-based instructor resources that promote student engagement and higher-order thinking to enable the success of Canadian students and educators.

Instructors today face many challenges. Resources are limited, time is scarce, and a new kind of student has emerged: one who is juggling school with work, has gaps in his or her basic knowledge, and is immersed in technology in a way that has led to a completely new style of learning. In response, Nelson Education has gathered a group of dedicated instructors to advise us on the creation of richer and more flexible ancillaries that respond to the needs of today's teaching environments.

In consultation with the editorial advisory board, Nelson Education has completely rethought the structure, approaches, and formats of our key textbook ancillaries. We've also increased our investment in editorial support for our ancillary authors. The result is the Nelson Education Teaching Advantage.

NETA Assessment relates to testing materials. Under *NETA Assessment*, Nelson's authors create multiple-choice questions that reflect research-based best practices for constructing effective questions and testing not just recall but also higher-order thinking. Our guidelines were developed by David DiBattista, a 3M National Teaching Fellow whose recent research as a professor of psychology at Brock University has focused on multiple-choice testing. All Test Bank authors receive training at workshops conducted by Prof. DiBattista, as do the copyeditors assigned to each Test Bank. A copy of *Multiple Choice Tests: Getting Beyond Remembering,* Prof. DiBattista's guide to writing effective tests, is included with every Nelson Test Bank/Computerized Test Bank package. (Information about the NETA Test Bank prepared for *Finance for Non-Financial Managers* is included in the description of the IRCD below.)

IRCD

Instructor's Resource CD. Key instructor ancillaries are provided on the Instructor's Resource CD (ISBN 0-17-665292-2), giving instructors the ultimate tool for customizing lectures and presentations. (Downloadable web versions are also available at **www.bergeron7e.nelson.com**.) The IRCD includes the following:

- **Instructor's Manual.** The Instructor's Manual, with solutions, for *Finance for Non-Financial Managers* was prepared by author Pierre Bergeron. It includes learning objectives; lesson summaries and teaching strategies; information about exercises, problems, and cases; and more. This manual has been independently checked for accuracy by Ross Meacher, C.A. It contains the complete solutions to review questions, learning exercises, and cases in the text.
- **NETA Assessment.** The Test Bank was revised by Jake Chazan of Seneca College. It includes more than 625 multiple-choice questions written according to NETA guidelines for effective construction and development of higher-order questions. Also included are true/false, matching, and fill-in-the-blank questions. Test Bank files are provided in Word format for easy editing and in PDF format for convenient printing whatever your system.

  The Computerized Test Bank by ExamView® includes all the questions from the Test Bank. The easy-to-use ExamView software is compatible with Microsoft Windows and Mac OS. Create tests by selecting questions from the question bank, modifying these questions as desired, and adding new questions you write yourself. You can administer quizzes online and export tests to WebCT, Blackboard, and other formats.
- **Microsoft® PowerPoint®.** Key concepts from *Finance for Non-Financial Managers,* Seventh Edition, are presented in PowerPoint format, with generous use of figures and short tables from the text. More than 240 PowerPoint slides for this edition were prepared by Pierre Bergeron.
- **Spreadsheet Templates.** The complete solutions to the financial spreadsheet exercises in Excel® are provided.

- **Image Library.** This resource consists of digital copies of figures, short tables, and photographs used in the book. Instructors may use these jpegs to create their own PowerPoint presentations.
- **DayOne.** DayOne—Prof InClass is a PowerPoint presentation that you can customize to orient your students to the class and their text at the beginning of the course.

Student Resources

Companion Website. Visit **www.bergeron7e.nelson.com** for additional resources, including answers to self-test exercises, web quizzes, Decision Making in Action cases, comprehensive case studies, spreadsheet templates, web links, glossary terms, flashcards, and Excel® templates. Descriptions of some of these resources are listed below.

Answers to Self-Test Exercises

Detailed solutions to the self-test exercises that appear throughout the chapters are provided. The solutions to these exercises have been thoroughly checked by Ross Meacher, C.A., to ensure their accuracy.

Web Quizzes

The interactive quiz questions test students' knowledge of every learning objective in each chapter. Each objective is tested with different types of questions: true/false questions, multiple choice questions, and statement completions.

Decision Making in Action Cases

These cases demonstrate how the theory covered in a chapter can be put into practical use in a specific situation. This helps students understand how financial management concepts are applied within the decision-making process.

Comprehensive Cases

Three comprehensive cases are provided that illustrate how a fictitious company, Micro Tiles Limited, analyzes and makes operating decisions (*Case 1: Look Before You Leap*), investing decisions (*Case 2: Investing for Growth*), and finally funding decisions (*Case 3: Finding Funding*).

Microsoft® Excel® Financial Spreadsheets

The Microsoft® Excel® financial spreadsheets that accompany this revised edition were modified to reflect the presentation format of the financial statements as suggested by the *International Financial Reporting Standards*. The purpose of the spreadsheets is to help readers of *Finance for Non-Financial Managers* perform most financial calculations in this seventh edition, allowing students to devote more time to analytical and decision-making activities and less to number crunching. The spreadsheets include two segments: the first helps to analyze financial statements; the second helps readers make business decisions related to the exercises and cases contained in the book. Readers take just a few moments to input numbers drawn from financial statements into the spreadsheets, which contain more than 30 different financial analytical tools (e.g., 25 financial ratios, economic value added, *Z*-score, sustainable growth rate, DuPont financial calculation, and internal rate of return). Readers can then focus more on interpretation of financial statements and decisions and less on calculations.

Web Links

Relevant Web links for each chapter relate to major themes covered in the chapter and also to major Canadian financial agencies and associations.

[ACKNOWLEDGMENTS]

Although I am the author of this book, the inspiration for the book's structure, content, and style emerged from the questions and discussions that I have had with many executives and managers who have attended my seminars during the past 35 years. They have helped me immensely in writing a pragmatic book in plain language that will surely help many readers understand more thoroughly the intricate discipline of financial management.

At Nelson Education, I am indebted to Herb Hilderley who, some 35 years ago, recognized the need for this type of book and provided me with the opportunity to make the first edition a reality. I also want to thank the world-class team at Nelson Education for the outstanding support they provided while I wrote this book: Amie Plourde, Senior Acquisitions Editor; Rod Banister, Editorial Consultant; Elke Price, Developmental Editor; and Imoinda Romain, Senior Content Production Manager. All were calm, collected, and positive with me and kept things moving smoothly and promptly. I also want to thank Ross Meacher, the technical checker of this book. Special thanks on this team also go to the copy editor, Dawn Hunter, who diligently edited the manuscript and made many suggestions for improving accuracy, and to the proofreader, Jeri Freedman, whose sharp eye found further corrections to make. I am also grateful to Indhumathy Gunasekaran, Project Manager at Integra, for turning things around expeditiously and completing various tasks in a timely fashion. Simply put, everyone at Nelson Education has been great to work with throughout the entire project.

I want to extend my gratitude to the outstanding set of reviewers who provided me with constructive suggestions and whose diligent and thoughtful comments improved this Seventh Edition:

- Cameron Gall, SAIT Polytechnic
- Susan Kelsall, Humber College
- Joseph (Jody) LeBlanc, Eastern College
- Cynthia Duncan, Seneca College of Applied Arts and Technology
- John Trembley, Fanshawe College
- Bruce Weir, Kwantlen Polytechnic University

Finally, *un gros merci* to my wife Pierrette, for having put up with the demands and sacrifices of such an undertaking. As with previous books, Pierrette is always there giving me assistance, encouragement, empathy, and support.

Pierre G. Bergeron
Ottawa, Ontario

[ABOUT THE AUTHOR]

Pierre G. Bergeron is adjunct professor at the Telfer School of Management, University of Ottawa. He was secretary, associate dean (external relations), and assistant dean (undergraduate programs) at the same university. He is president of Budgeting Concepts Inc., an Ottawa-based corporate financial planning consulting firm. He is a highly skilled educator with more than 35 years of experience.

Mr. Bergeron has occupied the position of director in such federal government agencies as Industry Canada (Incentives Division) and Human Resources Canada (Financial Planning Division). In the private sector, he worked at Imperial Oil Limited in the Quebec Marketing Region and at the company's head office in Toronto in market analysis and capital project evaluation. He was also director, corporate financial planning, at Domtar Limited.

Mr. Bergeron is the author of seven books: *Modern Management in Canada*; *Introduction aux affaires*; *Gestion dynamique: concepts, méthodes et applications*; *Finance for Non-Financial Managers*; *Gestion Moderne: Théorie et Cas*; *Planification, Budgétisation et Gestion par Objectifs*; and *Capital Expenditure Planning for Growth and Profit*. The book *Finance for Non-Financial Managers* was adapted by an American publishing company under the title *Survivor's Guide to Finance*. Mr. Bergeron has written extensively on finance, planning, budgeting, and capital budgeting for professional journals, including *CAmagazine*, *CMA Magazine*, *CGA Magazine*, *Banker and ICB Review*, *Financial Post*, and *Optimum*. He is the recipient of the Walter J. MacDonald Award for his series of articles on capital budgeting decisions that appeared in *CAmagazine*.

Mr. Bergeron also collaborated with Industry Canada in developing their Strategis website component called *Steps to Growth Capital*, a program designed to help entrepreneurs raise risk capital funds from venture capital markets. He also participated in producing *Tourism Is Your Business: A Financial Management Program for Canada's Lodging Industry*, and the *ABCs of Financial Performance Measures and Benchmarks for Canada's Tourism Sector*, seven finance-related guides and financial planning spreadsheets for the Canadian Tourism Commission for which he was awarded the J. Desmond Slattery Professional Marketing Award from Clemson University (South Carolina) for excellence.

Mr. Bergeron is a graduate of the University of Ottawa and the University of Western Ontario.

CHAPTER 1

[OVERVIEW OF FINANCIAL MANAGEMENT]

Learning Objectives

After reading this chapter, you should be able to

1. Identify some of the external factors financial managers must consider to improve a company's bottom line.
2. Discuss the role of financial management within a business.
3. Identify the people responsible for the finance function.
4. Explain the four financial objectives of a business.
5. Describe the three major types of business decisions.
6. Examine the issues related to corporate transparency and accountability.

OPENING CASE

The Tools and Skills Needed to Start and Manage a Successful Retail Business

After spending 10 years with different organizations, Len and Joan Miller decided to open their own retail business, CompuTech Sales and Service. While Len had worked for several computer retail stores, Joan had been a sales representative for a multinational computer organization. Both felt that their combined experience would be a valuable asset for succeeding in their new venture.

However, before making their final decision, they decided to speak to a long-time friend and entrepreneur, Bill Murray, who had operated his own successful retail business for the past 25 years. They wanted some advice from him before launching their business. Bill had some enlightening ideas to share:

> The two most important factors that make any business successful are its products/services and its management. There must be a demand for the products or services that you want to sell, and you must have the management skills (e.g., planning, organizing, leading, and controlling) and business skills (e.g., merchandising, pricing, sales, and promotion) to realize your vision, objectives, and plans. You will also need operating and financial information to help you gauge the results of your business decisions on an ongoing basis. Although an accountant will help you set up your bookkeeping and accounting systems, you have to make sure that you can analyze your financial statements.
>
> To succeed, your business will have to generate a healthy profit (efficiency) and be able to pay its bills and employees on time (liquidity). In addition, your business must show signs of continuous growth in all segments, such as revenue and profit (prosperity). Most important, be sure that you do not overburden your business with too much debt (stability).
>
> You will be faced with three types of business decisions. The first type is *investing decisions*, such as launching your business. This is not the only investing decision that you will make. If your business prospers, you will have to make decisions about such things as opening new retail outlets, buying equipment, and so on. The second type is *financing decisions*. Once you know exactly how much it will cost you to start your business, you will have to approach investors, such as lenders, for financial support. These different sources of financing bear a cost. Therefore, you have to make sure that your business generates enough profit (return) to pay for financing your business (cost). *Operating decisions* are the third type of business decisions. They have to do with day-to-day operating activities. You will be continually faced with decisions about pricing, advertising, hiring, office expenses, and so on. To maximize your profit (efficiency), you will have to keep your costs as low as possible.

Len and Joan were convinced that if they put Bill Murray's comments and suggestions into practice, they would stand a good chance of realizing their dream.

THIS CHAPTER WILL SHOW LEN AND JOAN MILLER HOW TO

- Measure the success of their business by using efficiency, liquidity, prosperity, and stability indicators.
- Pinpoint their accomplishments with the aid of three types of business decisions: investing, financing, and operating.
- Be open and transparent with their stakeholders, such as lenders, government agencies, employees, and suppliers.

Chapter Overview

ORGANIZING THE FINANCE FUNCTION

To be successful, an organization needs a structure that shows how its activities are coordinated toward common objectives. This chapter describes the roles of the people responsible for the finance function, their distinct objectives, and the unique types of decisions they make. In particular, it examines six key topics:

- *External environment.* We will examine how external factors, such as the economy, politics, global and open world economies, technological changes, product life cycle, and manufacturing, can affect a company's financial statements.
- *Importance of financial management.* You will learn that the fundamental role of financial management is to manage and control money and money-related matters within a business.
- *Key roles of the treasurer, the controller, and the operating managers.* Operating managers, those responsible for marketing, production, manufacturing, and administration, also play an important role in financial management. They are the ones who make critical business decisions that affect an organization's bottom line.
- *Four financial business objectives.* You will learn that all types of organizations (small and large, for profit and not for profit, manufacturing and service) want to be *efficient* (generate a profit). They also want to be *liquid* in order to pay their bills and employees on time. All organizations also want to *prosper*, that is, continue to grow in terms of revenue and profitability, and pay dividends to their shareholders. Finally, they want to be *stable* by keeping debt in proportion to the owners' equity.
- *Basic types of business decisions: operating, financing, and investing.* Figure 1.1 shows the three types of business decisions and in which chapters they

Figure 1.1 **Business Decisions and Organization of This Text**

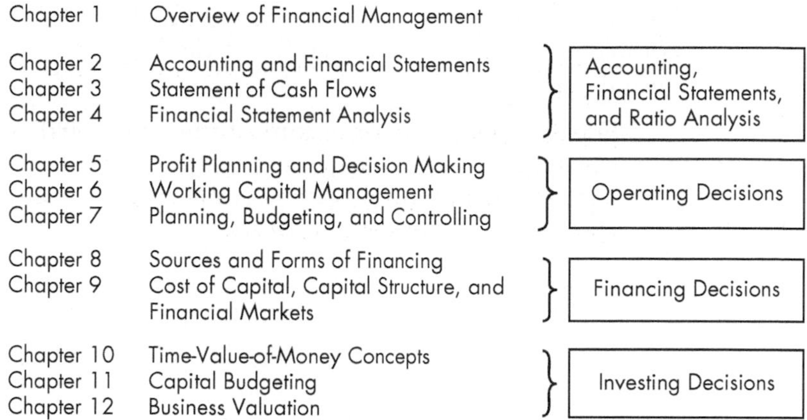

will be covered. *Operating* decisions are made to keep a company's bottom line healthy. *Financing* decisions involve raising money from lenders and shareholders to operate a company. *Investing* decisions relate to the acquisition of non-current assets, such as buying equipment or a business, building a new plant, or modernizing an existing one.

- *Corporate transparency and accountability*. Businesses and government organizations need to have systems in place to prevent fraud. We'll look at government legislation, corporate governance, corporate culture (business ethics), and international accounting.

How the External Environment Drives Financial Performance

1 Identify some of the external factors financial managers must consider to improve a company's bottom line.

Financial management has undergone major changes during recent decades. Initially, finance consisted mainly of raising cash to buy the assets a business needed. When finance emerged as an organizational function in the 1920s, financial management focused almost exclusively on legal matters: acquisitions, corporate offerings, mergers, formation of new businesses, reorganizations, recapitalizations, bankruptcies, and business consolidations. Finance concentrated mostly on the external activities of a business, such as raising cash, rather than on internal activities, such as finding ways to distribute cash effectively within a business. Only in the past several decades has attention been turned to developing analytical and decision-making techniques that can help managers improve the effectiveness of their investing, financing, and operating decisions. Put simply, in the beginning, more attention was devoted to managing one segment of the statement of financial position: raising money from lenders and shareholders.

Although raising money from investors is still important, financial management has focused increasingly on the other segment of the statement of financial position: finding ways to efficiently manage all assets of a business, such as inventories, trade receivables, and cash, and on improving the productivity of assets. Improving a company's bottom line (its profit or earnings) is a major managerial challenge for several reasons:

- *Economic front.* The recessions of the early 1980s and the early 1990s were considered by many economists to be deeper and broader than any other downturns since the Great Depression. As a result, the cost of operating businesses came under intense scrutiny. During the 1980s, managers began to realize that the North American economy was not only undergoing another shift in the business cycle but had also reached a certain level of maturity. Managers began to downsize their organizations in an effort to make them more efficient, responsive, and productive. Even today, businesses face extraordinary challenges in view of the economic slowdown. The acute slump in world economies has caused many governments (e.g., Canada, the United States, the United Kingdom, Germany) to help (through "stimulus packages") financial institutions, car industries, housing industries, and other industries in an effort to stimulate economic growth. In the meantime, many businesses continue to employ cost-cutting measures (e.g., closing plants, cutting back on production, laying off workers, reducing wages) to sustain their operating activities at a reasonable profit level.
- *Political front.* Governments began to open their borders and push businesses to make themselves into leaders in world markets. Both the *Free Trade Agreement*, which was implemented in 1989, and the *North American Free Trade Agreement*, which took effect in 1994, forced managers to rethink their cost structure, improve their manufacturing capabilities, and sharpen their international marketing strategies.
- *Global and open world economies.* Companies were forced to make structural changes to become more responsive to market demand. Globalization is forcing North American businesses to compete more effectively with those in rapidly growing markets, such as China, Korea, and India.
- *Technological change.* Managers must alter their company's operations dramatically by producing new or better products or services, reducing their operating costs, modifying the size of their plants, and integrating operating activities. Technological change is taking place in all parts of organizations, such as manufacturing (e.g., reengineering), administration (e.g., office automation), and communication (e.g., information technology). Increasingly, companies are making use of the Internet (e.g., websites to advertise and promote products and services).

- *Product life cycle.* A product's life cycle is now measured in months, not in years. When a company introduces a product or service into the market, it must measure its "time risk," that is, how many months it should take to recover the investment. This allows the company to determine a price structure that will generate an acceptable profit and return on its investment.
- *Manufacturing side.* Managers must find more innovative ways to produce their goods and provide services more efficiently while also being concerned about quality. Many Canadian firms have turned to **total quality management** to gauge the quality of their products and services against world standards. The goal is near-perfection in customer satisfaction.

Total quality management
A management approach in which everyone in an organization is responsible for creating customer satisfaction.

All these changes can put a strain on the company's financial statements, particularly the bottom line. When managers make investing, financing, and operating decisions, they have to gauge how these decisions will affect their financial statements.

What Is Financial Management?

2 Discuss the role of financial management within a business.

What was once called *finance* is now referred to as *financial management*, reflecting the current emphasis on the importance of having all managers in a business participate in making important decisions that affect the company as a whole. Financial management ensures that a company uses its resources in the most efficient and effective way: maximizing its profit (or earnings), which ultimately increases the value of a business (its net worth or equity).

Financial management
The activities involved in raising money and buying assets to obtain the highest possible return.

Financial management deals with two things: (1) raising funds and (2) buying and using assets to gain the highest possible return. An important objective of financial management is to ensure that the assets used in business produce a return that is higher than the cost of borrowed funds. For example, suppose an individual borrows money from a bank at, say, 6% interest and lends the money to a friend. He would certainly charge his friend more than 6%. In this example, we have two transactions. First, the individual *borrows* money from a bank. Second, the person *lends* it to a friend, creating an investment. Businesses function in the same way. Managers borrow money from lenders and invest it in business assets to earn a profit.

As shown in Figure 1.2, the objective of financial management is to ensure that the return on assets (ROA) generated by a business (here, 10%) is higher than the cost of money borrowed from investors—that is, lenders and shareholders (here, 7%). The statement of financial position has two sides. On the left, it lists the assets, such as non-current assets (e.g., cars, buildings, equipment) and current assets (e.g., inventories, trade receivables), that a business owns; on the right, it shows the money raised from investors, such as equity (shareholders), non-current liabilities (long-term borrowings), and current liabilities (line of credit). In this example, if the business invests $100,000 in assets (left side) and generates $10,000 in profit, it has earned a 10%

Figure 1.2 **Relationship between ROA and Cost of Financing**

Statement of Financial Position

Assets • Non-Current assets • Current assets	Equity and Liabilities • Equity • Non-Current liabilities • Current liabilities
Return on assets 10%	Cost of financing 7%

return ($10,000 ÷ $100,000). If the business borrows the $100,000 and pays $7,000 in interest for it, the cost of financing is 7% ($7,000 ÷ 100,000).

Financial management must answer five important questions:

1. *How are we doing?* Everybody—managers, short- and long-term lenders, shareholders, suppliers, and so on—wants to know about a company's financial performance in terms of its profitability, liquidity, prosperity, and stability.
2. *How much cash do we have on hand?* How much cash a company has on hand determines its liquidity and its ability to pay its bills (suppliers, employees, and short-term lenders) on time.
3. *What should we spend our money on?* Money can be spent on (a) operating activities, such as salaries, advertising, freight, promotions, and insurance, including current assets, such as inventories and trade receivables; and (b) investing activities, that is, non-current assets, such as property, plant, machinery, and equipment.
4. *Where will our funds come from?* Once managers have identified how much money the business needs and how much cash it has, they have to determine where more cash can be obtained. Suppliers? Bankers? Long-term investors, such as shareholders, venture capitalists, or mortgage companies?
5. *How will our business be protected?* One of the most important responsibilities of managers is to protect the investors' interests. Managers are employed by shareholders and should therefore act on their behalf. However, managers have to reconcile the legal and sometimes conflicting objectives of various interest groups (e.g., unions, lenders, employees, customers, suppliers, communities, and government agencies). Because shareholders have a unique legal

status, managers must ensure that their interests are not compromised and that they are clearly protected. It is important to note that the downfall of companies like Enron Corp., WorldCom, and Nortel were due not only to accounting errors but also largely to accounting irregularities, manipulation of books, misrepresentation, and fraudulent activities.

Problem-Solving Example 1.1

ROA and Cost of Financing

A business earns $1.2 million in profit on a $10 million investment. The owners were able to obtain a $600,000 loan. The yearly interest charges amount to $50,000. Calculate and compare the company's ROA and the cost of financing.

Solution

- Return on assets (ROA) is 12.0% ($1,200,000 ÷ $10,000,000).
- Cost of financing is 8.3% ($50,000 ÷ $600,000).
- The company's ROA exceeds the cost of financing by 3.7%.

Self-Test Exercise 1.1

ROA and Cost of Financing

Len and Joan intend to invest $200,000 in their CompuTech Sales and Service retail store. Their financial projections show that during the first year of operations, CompuTech will generate $25,000 in profit, with substantial increases in the following years. To finance their business, Len and Joan will need $100,000 in loans (short-term and long-term borrowings) from the bank at 6% (after taxes). The other $100,000 will come from their savings. The Millers are currently earning 8% (after taxes) on their savings.

Questions

1. Calculate CompuTech's ROA and its cost of financing.
2. Should the Millers launch their business? Why or why not?

Answers to the Self-Test Exercises can be found at www.bergeron7e.nelson.com

Who Is Responsible for the Finance Function?

3 Identify the people responsible for the finance function.

Figure 1.3 shows the basic structure of a company's organization. In corporations, the owners are the shareholders, but few are involved in managing the business. So shareholders elect a board of directors to oversee the business and approve any major decisions, subject to the corporate charter and bylaw provisions. The authority vested

Figure 1.3 **Responsibility of Financial Management**

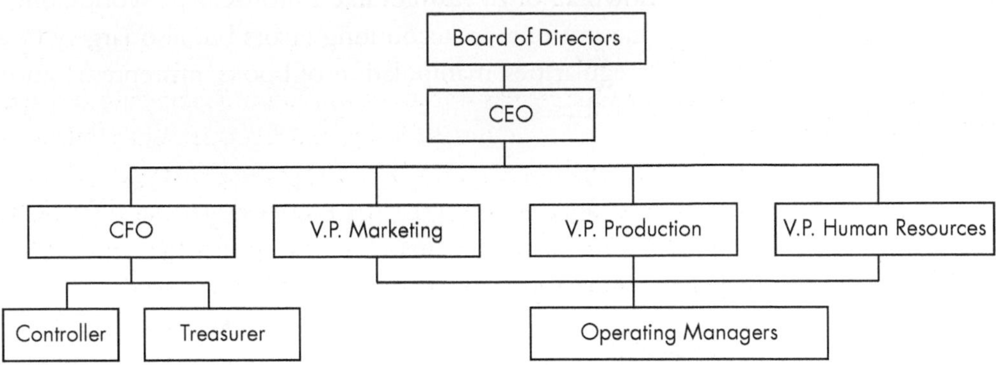

Chief executive officer (CEO) The person who plays a major role in the complete management process and is responsible for creating and implementing strategic plans.

Chief financial officer (CFO) The person in charge of the finance function and responsible for all accounting functions and external activities.

in the board of directors is assigned to a **chief executive officer (CEO)** who is personally accountable to the board and to the shareholders for the company's performance. The CEO is usually the president or the chair of the board of directors and is probably the most important individual in any organization. CEOs play a major role in the complete management process and are responsible for creating and implementing strategic plans.

The **chief financial officer (CFO)** and the vice-presidents report to the CEO. The CFO is the executive in charge of the finance function and is responsible for all accounting functions and external activities. The title *vice-president of finance* is sometimes used instead. In the News 1.1 profiles the important role of a CFO.

In The News 1.1

THE CFO: NOT JUST A FINANCIAL GATEKEEPER

Any organization that values cash, profit margins, and risk mitigation needs a CFO who is more than just a financial gatekeeper. It requires a strategic partner and adviser to the CEO, an active participant in shaping or challenging the organization's strategy. This role is vital particularly when financial markets go through high levels of instability. A CFO must be level headed, strong, shrewd, and intelligent.

These are the skills Mike Bell brought to the role when he joined Manulife (Canada's largest life insurer) as CFO in 2009. During his tenure at Manulife, he helped the company recover from losses, despite the turbulence in the financial markets. One of his key accomplishments at Manulife was to bring greater transparency to an environment that can be described as "intricate."

However, despite his efforts, the company suffered a fourth quarter loss in 2011 of $69 million, compared with a profit of $1.8 billion in the previous year. This was due to the ongoing record low interest rates.

Source: Adapted from John Greenwood, "Manulife posts Q4 loss, announces departure of CFO," http://business.financialpost.com/2012/02/09/manulife-posts-q4-loss/, accessed February 10, 2012. For more information about Manulife, visit http://www.manulife.ca/canada/canada1.nsf/public/prepare.

The finance activities are carried out by the controller, the treasurer, and the operating managers. Both the controller and the treasurer report to the chief financial officer (refer back to Figure 1.3).

CONTROLLER

Controller
The person responsible for establishing the accounting and financial reporting policies and procedures.

The **controller** establishes the accounting and financial reporting policies and procedures; maintains the accounting, auditing, and management control mechanisms; and analyzes financial results. Together with the operating managers, the controller prepares annual budgets and financial plans and determines financial objectives and standards to ensure efficiency and adequate returns. This controllership function deals with how funds are expended and invested to satisfy both consumer needs and shareholder interests.

TREASURER

Treasurer
The person responsible for raising funds and regulating the flow of funds.

The **treasurer**—the person responsible for raising funds—looks after investors, plans investment strategies, analyzes tax implications, and gauges the impact of internal and external events on a firm's capital structure, or the relationship between liabilities and equity. The treasurer also regulates the flow of funds, determines dividend payments, recommends short- and long-term financing strategies, and cultivates relations with investors. In short, the treasurer is responsible for the liability and shareholder equity accounts shown on the statement of financial position.

Table 1.1 lists typical finance activities under the jurisdiction of the controller (controllership functions) and the treasurer (treasury functions).

OPERATING MANAGERS

Operating managers
The people in charge of organizational units, such as marketing, manufacturing, and human resources, and responsible for making operating and investing decisions.

Financial management is also a responsibility of **operating managers** (persons responsible for line and staff functions) in various organizational units, such as

Table 1.1 The Functions of the Controller and the Treasurer

Functions of the Controller	Functions of the Treasurer
• General accounting	• Raising of capital
• Cost accounting	• Investor relations
• Credit and collection	• Short-term borrowings
• Management information system	• Dividend and interest payments
• Trade and other payables	• Insurance
• Corporate accounting	• Analysis of investment securities
• Internal auditing	• Retirement funds
• Budgets and analysis	• Property taxes
• Payroll	• Investment portfolio
• Systems and procedures	• Cash flow requirements
• Planning	• Actuarial decisions
• Controlling	• Underwriting policy and manuals
• Interpreting financial reports	• Tax administration

marketing, manufacturing, human resources, research and development, and general administration. These managers report to various vice-presidents (marketing, production, human resources, etc.; see Figure 1.3) and are responsible for analyzing operating and financial data, making decisions about asset acquisitions, and improving the operating performance of their own organizational units and of the company as a whole.

People often think of finance as a function performed only by accountants, bookkeepers, treasurers, controllers, or financial analysts. Although these people play key roles in financial management and in the financial planning process, *all managers* are accountable for their decisions because they may affect, directly or indirectly, the financial performance of their business unit or organization.

Business decisions of all types cut across all business functions, such as marketing, manufacturing, administration, human resources, research and development, and after-sales services. Operators of businesses make many of these decisions every day. For example, some of these decisions may include hiring an employee, increasing the selling price of one or two product lines or services, cutting some operating expenses, adding a bigger share of the budget to promotion and advertising, buying new equipment to increase efficiency, and providing a better service to customers. These decisions have one thing in common: they affect a business's *financial performance* (statement of income) and *financial structure* (statement of financial position). These two financial documents inform operators of business establishments about the outcome of their decisions. Operating managers who have difficulty reading or interpreting financial statements are unable to effectively gauge how well their business has done, is currently doing, or will do in the future.

A business is much like an aircraft: someone has to fly it. Aircraft pilots are in the best position to control their airplane (whether it is a small or large aircraft) for three reasons.

- They understand the operating environment.
- They know exactly where they want to go.
- They have an appreciation about what needs to be done to reach the destination.

Aircraft pilots do not delegate this most important activity. They may ask for advice or help, but in the end, they make critical decisions based on their analysis and the input from others. The same applies for businesses. It is the operating manager (CEO, vice-presidents, directors, managers) who is ultimately responsible for making important decisions and for determining the financial destiny of an organizational unit or business as a whole.

Finance is a business function that is far too important to be left only to financial specialists or consultants. It is important that all managers (top, middle, or first level) responsible for resources or budgets become familiar with the language of finance and with the different tools available for analyzing business performance and making vital business decisions. A manager who lacks these skills will not be able to contribute fully and effectively to improving the operational and financial performance of the business unit and the organization.

Financial Objectives

4 Explain the four financial objectives of a business.

As mentioned earlier, finance involves managing money. There is no question that all organizations—small or large, public or private, manufacturing or service, government agencies or Crown corporations, for profit or not for profit (NFP)—must manage money to function properly. All these want to be *efficient*, they need to be *liquid* to pay their current bills on time, they do their best to *prosper*, and they want to secure a certain level of *stability*. Let's examine these four important financial objectives.

EFFICIENCY

Efficiency The relationship between profit (outputs) generated and assets employed (inputs).

For a business, **efficiency** means how productive its assets are, or the relationship between the profit generated and the assets employed. In the language of finance, this is referred to as return on assets (ROA), return on equity (ROE), and return on revenue (ROR). The objective of any organization is to ensure that a business's resources are used efficiently to produce an acceptable return. High profits satisfy investors and indicate that the assets of an organization are working hard. The more profit a business earns, the more cash it can invest in operations to finance its growth and to purchase non-current assets, such as machinery and equipment. The notion of efficiency applies not only to for-profit enterprises but also to NFP organizations. Churches, hospitals, colleges, and universities also want to ensure they use their resources efficiently. When businesses deduct all costs from revenue, they call this "profit." An NFP organization may choose to call it a "surplus" or "excess of revenues over expenses."

Let's examine the meaning of efficiency. Figure 1.4 shows a business that generates $100,000 in revenue and earns $8,000 in profit, meaning the company is earning

Figure 1.4 **Return on Revenue**

Statement of Income (in $)

		%
Revenue	100,000	100.0
Cost of sales	(70,000)	(70.0)
Gross profit	30,000	30.0
Other costs	(15,000)	(15.0)
Profit before taxes	15,000	15.0
Income tax expense	(7,000)	(7.0)
Profit for the year	8,000	8.0

Return on Revenue

$0.08 for every revenue dollar. This is commonly referred to as *return on revenue* or *ROR*. If another business generates $10,000 in profit with the same amount in revenue, it may be more efficient since it is earning $0.10 for every revenue dollar.

Let's now explore what this business can do with the $8,000 of profit or $0.08 for each revenue dollar. Figure 1.5 explores some of the options. The $8,000 could be reinvested in the business through retained earnings (say, $5,000 or $0.05 per revenue dollar). Retained earnings are simply the money that will be kept by the business to reinvest. The company could use $3,000 or $0.03 to purchase non-current assets, for example, equipment and machinery, and $2,000 or $0.02 could be used for current assets, or working capital accounts, such as inventories and trade receivables (day-to-day operating expenses). The balance of the original $8,000 cash ($3,000 or $0.03) could be used for external purposes. Here, the shareholders would receive $2,000 or $0.02 in dividends to compensate for the investment they have made in the business. The final $1,000 or $0.01 will be used to repay the principal on the business's debt. You can see that if the $8,000 or $0.08 ROR shrank to, say, $6,000 or even $3,000, the company would have less money to invest internally to help its growth, to invest in assets, and to satisfy its shareholders.

LIQUIDITY

Liquidity
The ability of a firm to meet its short-term financial commitments.

Liquidity is a company's ability to meet its short-term financial commitments. If a business increases its revenue, it will inevitably increase its working capital accounts, such as inventories, trade receivables, and the cash needed to pay its employees, suppliers, and creditors on time. For the business described in Figure 1.5, $2,000 or $0.02 for each revenue dollar is invested in working capital accounts (shown there as current assets). Suppose this business wanted to grow but its ROR performance fell to less than $0.08 per revenue dollar, the business would have less cash from

Figure 1.5 Return on Revenue Objective

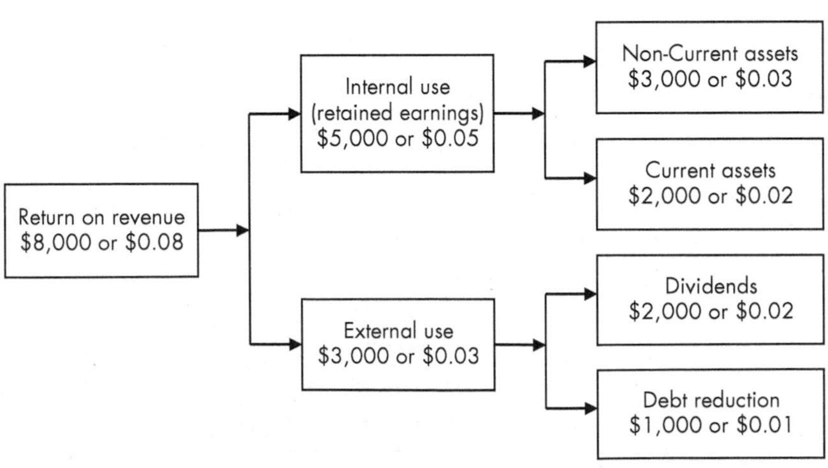

internal operations (retained earnings) to invest in working capital accounts, and it may have to rely on short-term borrowings to keep growing. Additional borrowings reduce a company's profit (because of increased finance costs) and further reduce its ROR.

PROSPERITY

Prosperity
The ability of a firm to grow (i.e., revenue, profit, and equity).

Prosperity means growth in all segments of a business: revenue, profit, dividend payments, non-current assets, equity, and working capital. If a company's ROR falls, it may not be able to finance its growth through internally generated cash. Consequently, it would have difficulty investing in non-current assets, such as equipment and machinery, to expand its operations and improve its productivity. The business would have to borrow from long-term lenders and shareholders to finance the purchase of non-current assets.

STABILITY

Stability
Relationship between debt and equity.

Stability refers to the financial structure of a business. Here, financial management ensures a balance between the cash provided by creditors and that provided by shareholders (the relationship between debt and equity). If a business continues to borrow from lenders, it may have a high debt-to-equity ratio, creating instability. As a result, the business may not be able to meet its short- and long-term debt obligations, particularly if there is a business slowdown caused by economic conditions. If the company's ROR is adequate, it will have enough cash to pay dividends and reduce the principal on its debt. If the ROR is not adequate, the company may have to borrow more from lenders, affecting negatively its stability.

To maintain or improve its stability, a company must never lose sight of the first objective: to earn a suitable ROR. Profit (or retained earnings) can then be used to increase working capital, purchase non-current assets, pay dividends, and reduce debt.

Problem-Solving Example 1.2

Distribution of Profit

A business's owners want to reinvest 80% of their $100,000 after-tax profit in their business and use the rest to repay the principal on their loan. The business's revenue for the year was $1,700,000. They intend to reinvest 40% in working capital and 60% in non-current assets. What is the company's ROR? Calculate the distribution of the after-tax profit.

Solution

- The company's ROR is 5.9% ($100,000 ÷ $1,700,000) or $0.059 for each revenue dollar.
- $80,000 ($100,000 X 80%) will be reinvested in the business.
- $32,000 (40% of $80,000) will be spent on working capital.
- $48,000 (60% of $80,000) will be spent on non-current assets.

Self-Test Exercise 1.2

Distribution of Profit

Len and Joan want to reinvest 70% of their $25,000 profit (look back to Self-Test Exercise 1.1 on page 9) in their business and use the rest to repay the principal on their loan. They expect to invest 50% of the retained earnings in working capital and 50% in non-current assets. CompuTech's 2013 revenue is estimated to be $350,000.

Question

Calculate, as a percentage of revenue, how much the Millers would keep in the business for growth (i.e., working capital and the purchase of non-current assets), and how much would be used to repay the principal on their loan.

Answers to the Self-Test Exercises can be found at www.bergeron7e.nelson.com

Business Decisions

5 Describe the three major types of business decisions.

Figure 1.6 breaks down the three major types of business decisions: investing decisions, financing decisions, and operating decisions. If managers invest $1 million in non-current assets (an investing decision), the cash to buy these assets would be provided by (1) internal activities (an operating decision) and (2) external activities (a financing decision). First, managers provide internal cash by making operating decisions. The outcome of these decisions is shown as profit for the year on the statement of income, and any improvement in the management of current asset and current liability accounts is shown on the statement of financial position. Second, shareholders and long-term lenders, acquired through financing decisions, provide external funds. In our example in Figure 1.6, the company provides $500,000 from internal operations and is able to obtain the rest from investors ($500,000), so the $1 million in non-current assets (an investing decision) would be financed equitably.

Ideally, a business wants to finance as much of the purchase of non-current assets as possible with internally generated cash. For example, by purchasing the assets ($1 million) with $800,000 of internally generated cash, the company relies less on external financing and is able to enhance its financial stability.

Internal financing Cash provided from retained earnings, depreciation/amortization, and a reduction in working capital accounts.

Internal financing is provided from retained earnings—that is, the profit generated by the business—plus the depreciation/amortization that appears on the statement of income as a non-cash expense, and by reducing current asset accounts, such as trade receivables and inventories. (The consideration of depreciation/amortization as a non-cash expense is explained in Chapter 2 on page 51.) In Figure 1.6, the working capital box (current assets and current liabilities) is shaded because managers can obtain cash only if they can reduce such accounts as inventories and trade receivables. An increase in these accounts is considered an outflow of cash.

Figure 1.6 Business Decisions

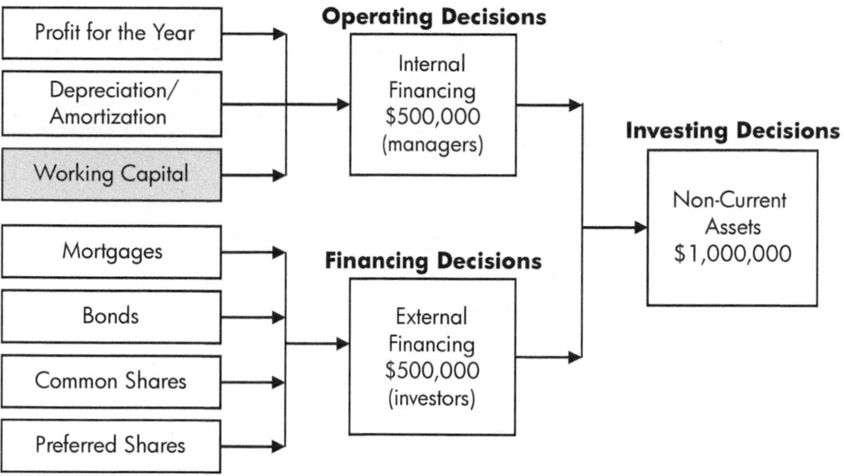

Figure 1.7 illustrates how the three types of business decisions appear on the statement of financial position. On the left are investments in non-current assets, such as buildings, machinery, and equipment, and other assets or intangible assets, such as research and development, goodwill, and patents. These two investing decisions or activities appear in boxes with vertical shaded lines and have a capital I next to them.

External financing Cash obtained from investors (long-term lenders and shareholders).

On the right side of the statement of financial position are the **external financing** decisions related to funds obtained from long-term lenders and shareholders. The two financing decisions or activities appear in boxes with horizontal shaded lines and have a capital F next to them. One is a portion of equity and the other is non-current liabilities. Obtaining funds from these two sources is the responsibility of the CFO or the treasurer.

Managers can provide cash to a business through two sources: (1) profit for the year and (2) an improvement in working capital accounts. The centre of the statement of financial position shows to what extent operating decisions affect retained earnings (statement of income). In Figure 1.7, the statement of income is added at the centre of the statement of financial position strictly for presentation purposes. It shows how profit for the year increases the equity on the statement of financial position.

Operating decisions are the responsibility of all managers and include decisions that affect *every* account shown on the statement of income. If managers make prudent operating decisions in marketing, manufacturing, production, administration, human resources, and so on, they will help generate higher profit (shown in the box with an O beside it) and ultimately improve ROR. As noted, higher profit lets managers pay dividends and reinvest in the business through retained earnings (shareholders' equity). Profit for the year (the shaded box in the middle of Figure 1.7) is reinvested in the business as retained earnings, and a portion of the equity composes retained earnings (also shaded).

Figure 1.7 Business Decisions and the Financial Statements

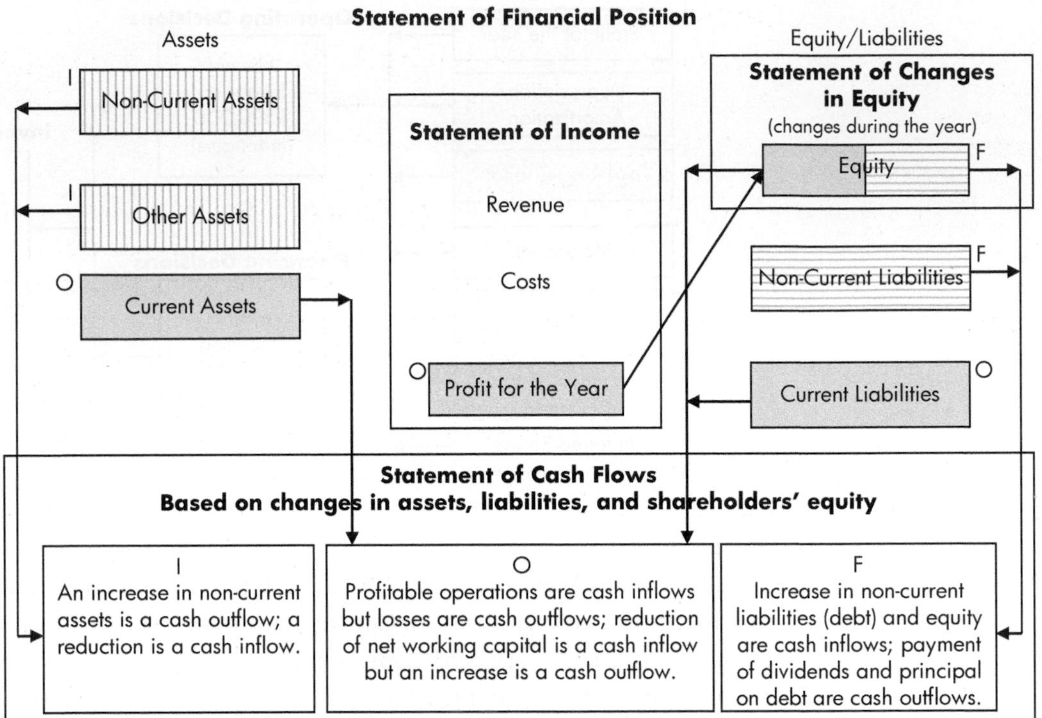

Source: Erich A. Helfert. *Techniques of Financial Analysis: A Guide to Value Creation*. 6th edition. 2000. Fig. 1.9, Page 18. Irwin/McGraw Hill. Reprinted with permission.

Managers are also responsible for the management of working capital accounts (current assets and current liabilities) that appear in the lower portion of the statement of financial position in shaded boxes. The more efficient they are in managing these items (trade receivables, inventories, and trade and other payables), the more cash the business will have (O).

The cash generated by the business (O) and obtained from investors (F) will be used to purchase non-current assets and other assets (I).

The lower portion of Figure 1.7 shows how these three types of business decisions affect a company's cash position. For instance, a decrease in the non-current asset accounts (e.g., through selling an asset, such as a truck) is an inflow of cash. An increase in liability and equity accounts (through borrowing from banks or the injection of additional funds from shareholders) is also an inflow of cash, as is profit generated by a business.

The next sections give an overview of how these three types of business decisions can affect favourably the financial performance (statement of income) and financial structure (statement of financial position) of a business. These three types of business decisions will be covered in more detail in Chapter 3, Statement of Cash Flows.

INVESTING DECISIONS

Investing decisions Decisions related to the acquisition of non-current assets.

Non-current assets Statement of financial position accounts, such as land, buildings, equipment, and machinery.

As mentioned earlier, **investing decisions** deal with the acquisition of non-current assets (e.g., machinery, equipment). Acquiring non-current assets drains a company's cash and is an outflow of cash. Conversely, a reduction in such assets, such as the sale of unproductive capital assets, is an inflow of cash.

Decisions about **non-current assets** (also called *capital* or *fixed assets*) involve the purchase of equipment or machinery and more critical decisions, such as plant expansion, plant modernization to increase productivity, or investment in new facilities. These types of decisions are usually made during the capital budgeting process. Here, management examines the relationship between the cash invested in such assets and the anticipated cash that can be generated in the future by these assets. For example, if someone invests $100,000 in Canada Savings Bonds and earns $5,000 in interest, that person earns 5%. The same applies when managers invest in non-current assets. They want to measure two things: the expected ROA and how it compares with the cost of capital.

Let's look at an example of how investing decisions in non-current assets are calculated. Suppose a company invests $1 million in the following assets:

Land	$ 100,000
Buildings	500,000
Machinery and equipment	400,000
Total investment	$1,000,000

Let's also assume that this investment produces $132,000 in profit each year. The following shows the calculation:

Revenue	$ 2,000,000
Cost of sales	(1,200,000)
Gross profit	800,000
Other costs	(560,000)
Profit before taxes	240,000
Income tax expense	(108,000)
Profit for the year	$ 132,000

Managers can use capital budgeting techniques to gauge how desirable such investments will be. For example, the ROA calculation relates profit for the year to investment in non-current (or capital) assets:

$$\frac{\textbf{Profit for the year}}{\textbf{Investment in non-current assets}} = \frac{\$132{,}000}{\$1{,}000{,}000} = 13.2\%$$

The $1 million investment in non-current assets generates a 13.2% return.

Managers must also consider whether the investment is worth the risk by relating the return on the investment to both the cost of capital and the investment's inherent risks. For example, let's assume the company is in a 40% tax bracket (it pays 40% of its profit in taxes). If the company borrows the entire amount from lenders at a before-tax cost of 10%, then the after-tax cost of capital is 6%. The company would earn 7.2% (13.2% − 6.0%) more than it cost to borrow the money.

Is a 13.2% return on this investment worth the risk? If this investment were in a high-risk category, such as an investment in an untried product, management might want to earn at least 25% to 30% to justify the investment. However, if the project is low risk, such as the expansion of an existing plant, management will require a much lower return on investment (say, around 10%).

Financing decisions Decisions related to borrowing from long-term lenders and shareholders.

Cost of financing Effective after-tax cost of raising funds from different sources (lenders and shareholders).

FINANCING DECISIONS

Financing decisions deal with the accounts listed on the right side of the statement of financial position—that is, funds obtained from long-term lenders and shareholders. Managers examine how best to raise cash from these investors. Financing decisions deal with (1) choosing the most appropriate financing forms and sources of financing when buying assets, (2) determining the **cost of financing** when raising funds, (3) finding the weighted average cost of financing, and (4) establishing the weighted average cost of capital. These topics will be covered in some detail in Chapter 9 (Cost of Capital, Capital Structure, and Financial Markets). In the News 1.2 gives an example about raising cash from investors to bring an idea to life.

In The News 1.2

CONNECTING THE CASH TO THE DREAM

Being creative means dreaming about an idea; being innovative means finding a way to realize the dream. And usually, realizing that dream costs a lot of money. To realize a dream, an entrepreneur has to manufacture and market a product or service in addition to raising cash to finance every step of the process.

That is just what Keller Rinaudo, the 25-year-old founder of Robomotive did after he invented and began marketing a smartphone toy robot. In the process, he raised $1.5 million from various investors (some venture capitalists were even turned away), robot geeks, and customers. This toy is a docking station that turns a smartphone, such as an iPhone, into a robot that can be controlled from another smartphone through a Romo app. Rinaudo is already tinkering with the idea of expanding the smartphone's capabilities, with the intention of conquering the world.

Source: Adapted from Paul Sloane, "Romo the smartphone robot raises $1.5M, seeks world domination," http://news.cnet.com/8301-32973_3-57371451-296/romo-the-smartphone-robot-raises-$1.5m-seeks-world-domination/?tag=mncol;editorPicks, accessed February 5, 2012. For more information about Romo the Smartphone, visit http://romotive.com.

Weighted average cost of capital Composite weighted after-tax cost of raising funds from long-term investors (bonds, mortgages, common shares, preferred shares).

The **weighted average cost of capital** deals with the accounts shown on the right side of the statement of financial position. It involves the more permanent forms of financing, such as mortgages, bonds, and preferred and common shares. These are referred to as *capital funds*, thus, their cost is known as *cost of capital.* In the earlier example of a $1 million investment in non-current assets, managers would have to determine the cost of each loan and the weighted cost of capital. For instance, if the business borrows $400,000 from a mortgage company at 12%, $300,000 from bondholders at 13%, and the rest ($300,000) from shareholders at 15%, the weighted average cost of capital would be 9.29%. (The 15% is what shareholders could earn if they were to invest their funds elsewhere; it is sometimes referred to as the *opportunity cost.*) Because finance costs on mortgasge and bond financing are tax-deductible and the company is in a 45% tax bracket, these financing sources are more attractive than equity financing, as dividends are paid with after-tax profit. The calculation is as follows:

Sources	Amount ($) (1)	Proportion (%) (2)	Before-Tax Cost (%) (3)	After-Tax Cost (%) (4)	Weighted Cost of Capital (%) (5) (2) × (4)
Mortgage	400,000	0.40	12.0	6.60	2.64
Bonds	300,000	0.30	13.0	7.15	2.15
Common shares	300,000	0.30	15.0	15.00	4.50
Weighted average cost of capital	1,000,000	1.00			9.29

Note: The after-tax cost is calculated by subtracting the tax cost from the before-tax cost interest charges (e.g., 12.0% – 5.4% [or 45% × 12.0%] = 6.6%).

Problem-Solving Example 1.3

Cost of Financing and Weighted Average Cost of Capital

Owners of a small business want to expand their operations. They intend to borrow the following: share capital ($300,000), mortgage ($400,000), trade and other payables ($50,000), and a line of credit ($80,000). The owners would receive 6% if they were to invest their money in investment securities. The after-tax cost of capital for the line of credit is 7% and for the mortgage, 6%. Calculate the after-tax cost of financing and the after-tax weighted average cost of capital.

Solution

The cost of financing is 5.74% and the weighted average cost of capital is 6.00%

(continued)

Problem-Solving Example 1.3 (continued)

Cost of Financing	Amount	Proportion	After-Tax Cost	Weight
Share capital	$300,000	0.36	6%	2.16
Mortgage	400,000	0.48	6%	2.88
Line of credit	80,000	0.10	7%	0.70
Trade payables	50,000	0.06	0%	0.00
Total	$830,000	1.00		5.74

Cost of Capital	Amount	Proportion	After-Tax Cost	Weight
Share capital	$300,000	0.43	6%	2.58
Mortgage	400,000	0.57	6%	3.42
Total	$700,000	1.00		6.00

Self-Test Exercise 1.3

Cost of Financing and Weighted Average Cost of Capital

CompuTech needs to raise $212,000 from the following four sources. Assume that the company's income tax rate is 33%.

Source	Amounts ($)
Share capital	100,000
Long-term borrowings (mortgage)	60,000
Trade and other payables	17,000
Short-term borrowings (term loan)	35,000

The bank charges 12% (before tax) for the term loan and 11% for the mortgage. The Millers expect to earn 8% on their savings.

Questions

1. Calculate the company's after-tax cost of financing.
2. Calculate the company's weighted average cost of capital.

Answers to the Self-Test Exercises can be found at www.bergeron7e.nelson.com

OPERATING DECISIONS

Operating decisions Decisions related to accounts appearing on the statement of financial position (current assets and current liabilities) and the statement of income (e.g., revenue, cost of sales, distribution costs).

Operating decisions deal with many accounts appearing on both the statement of income, including revenue, cost of sales, distribution costs, and administrative expenses, and on the statement of financial position, such as current assets and current liabilities (we'll look at both kinds of statements in depth in Chapter 2).

Operating Decisions Related to the Statement of Financial Position

Let's now examine how working capital decisions affect a company's cash flow.

Working capital accounts Statement of financial position accounts, such as inventories, trade receivables, and cash (current assets), and trade and other payables and short-term borrowings (current liabilities).

Working capital accounts are statement of financial position accounts, such as cash, trade receivables, and inventories (called current assets), and trade and other payables and short-term borrowings (called current liabilities).

Managing working capital means accelerating the positive movement of cash in a business. The faster inventories are turned over and trade receivables are collected, the more cash and profit a business earns.

Decisions related to *inventories* deal with reducing raw materials, unfinished goods, and finished goods. Turning over inventory rapidly can improve a company's cash position and, ultimately, its profitability and return on investment. Companies want to invest as little as possible in inventory because it is a non-productive asset. To illustrate, let's assume that managers can reduce inventory levels from, say, $400,000 to $325,000; this means that the company will have an extra $75,000 in cash with which to work.

Decisions related to *trade receivables* deal with collecting receivables from customers as quickly as possible. For example, if managers are able to reduce the level of trade receivables from, say, $300,000 down to $250,000, it means that the company will have an extra $50,000 in cash with which to operate.

Operating Decisions Related to the Statement of Income

Operating decisions can increase a company's profitability in many ways. Some decisions cut across all organizational functions and activities affecting the statement of income, such as improving employee productivity, reducing waste, and eliminating useless activities. Profitability can be improved at three profit levels: gross profit, profit before taxes, and profit for the year.

Gross profit The difference between revenue and cost of sales.

Decisions that affect the **gross profit** are revenue and cost of sales (refer back to Figure 1.4 during this discussion). Revenue decisions affect the number of units sold and the selling price. Decisions affecting revenue (marketing decisions) have to do with sales output and market share performance. Effective marketing decisions can improve a company's sales performance and, ultimately, its revenue.

For manufacturing businesses, cost of sales is a substantial percentage (as much as 80%) of a company's total costs. For this reason, a great deal of attention is devoted to making a company's manufacturing operations more efficient by modernizing its plants (mechanization or automation), reducing waste, improving employee morale, and empowering workers.

Profit before taxes The difference between gross profit and costs related to distribution and administration.

Decisions affecting **profit before taxes** have to do with other costs, such as distribution costs and administrative expenses. Many techniques, such as cutting useless activities, productivity measures, and empowering workers, can improve profit before taxes.

Profit for the year The difference between profit before taxes and income tax expense.

An account that affects profit for the year is income tax expense. **Profit for the year** is the difference between profit before taxes and income tax expense.

Problem-Solving Example 1.4

Cash Flow Provided by Operating Activities

The owners of a small retail store have prepared their projected financial statements. They projected (1) an increase from $20,000 to $25,000 in profit for the year, (2) a reduction in inventories from $95,000 to $85,000, and (3) an increase in trade receivables from $60,000 to $65,000. Calculate the amount of cash the business would generate from operating activities.

Solution

$30,000 would be generated from operating activities.

(1) Profit for the year			$25,000
(2) Inventories	$95,000	$85,000	10,000
(3) Trade receivables	$60,000	$65,000	(5,000)
Net increase in cash			$30,000

Self-Test Exercise 1.4

Cash Flow Provided by Operating Activities

With the following information, calculate CompuTech's cash flow generated by the business. Between 2013 and 2014, inventories increased from $50,000 to $65,000, and trade receivables increased from $35,000 to $45,000. The company also realized an increase in profit from $25,000 to $33,000.

Answers to the Self-Test Exercises can be found at www.bergeron7e.nelson.com

Corporate Transparency and Accountability

6 Examine the issues related to corporate transparency and accountability.

The Bre-X, Enron, WorldCom, Madoff, and Nortel scandals brought cries from all types of stakeholders and the public for greater levels of corporate transparency and accountability. **Transparency** is how visible and open to inspection by stakeholders a business's processes and related information resources, assets, and outcomes are.

Transparency
The extent to which business processes and related information resources, assets, and outcomes are visible and open to inspection by stakeholders.

More than ever, organizations need (1) corporate senior executives (in public and private sector organizations) who have the ability to establish "social architectures" for openness, and (2) a new branch of management theory and practice called "transparency and accountability management."

Both governments and businesses have made far-reaching efforts to achieve that goal through legislation, effective governance, more entrenched corporate culture, and international accounting and financial reporting. Let's look at each one.

LEGISLATION

As a reaction to the financial scandals, in 2002 the U.S. government enacted the *Sarbanes-Oxley Act*. The purpose of this legislation was to set new standards for all public company boards, management, and public accounting firms. The act contained 11 sections, ranging from additional corporate board responsibilities to criminal penalties, and required the Securities and Exchange Commission to implement rulings on requirements to comply with the new law. This was not the first time that the U.S. government (the ultimate gatekeeper of public confidence in public markets) had introduced legislation to (1) build a stronger framework for effective governance, (2) establish high standards and healthy board dynamics, (3) set up guidance for effective corporate communications, and (4) show how red flags can signal the need for prompt investigation and action. Several powerful pieces of related legislation have been enacted in the United States in the past 100 years, including the following:

- the *Sherman Antitrust Act* (1890) on monopolies
- the *Clayton Antitrust Act* (1914) on unfair business practices
- the *Securities Act* on corporate transparency and the *Banking Act* on unfair banking practices, both enacted in 1933
- the *Securities Exchange Act* (1934) on regulating the securities market
- the *Investment Company Act* and the *Investment Advisers Act* (both in 1940) on abusive investment company practices
- the *Foreign Corrupt Practices Act* (1977) on bribery
- the *Financial Institutions Reform, Recovery and Enforcement Act* (1989) on restoring confidence in savings-and-loan institutions
- the *Comprehensive Thrift and Bank Fraud Prosecution and Taxpayer Recovery Act* (1990) on strengthening federal regulators' authority to combat financial fraud
- the *Sarbanes-Oxley Act* (2002) for greater agent and gatekeeper accountability for financial reporting

Despite the enactment of all these laws to prevent accounting irregularities, investigations of corporate fraud are alive and well (e.g., Conrad Black, Bernard Madoff, and the billions of dollars in bonuses paid to Merrill Lynch & Co. executives). It appears that government legislation of high ethical standards in the corporate arena is not enough. Corporate governance, corporate culture, and, now, international accounting and financial reporting are financial and management practices that have been introduced and are being reinforced in many for-profit and not-for-profit organizations.

CORPORATE GOVERNANCE

Because boards of directors have the ultimate authority over and accountability for an organization's affairs, much attention has focused on how board members should *govern* their organizations. Individuals involved in governance include the regulatory body (e.g., CEO, the board of directors, management, and shareholders) and other stakeholders (suppliers, employees, creditors, customers, and the community at large). **Governance** is the process by which decisions are implemented (or not implemented).

Governance
The process by which decisions are implemented (or not implemented).

The fundamental elements of effective corporate governance include honesty, trust and integrity, openness, performance orientation, responsibility and accountability, mutual respect, and commitment to the organization. A key responsibility of effective directors and top-level managers is to *develop* a model of governance that aligns and implants these values throughout their organization and to *evaluate* the model periodically for its effectiveness.

The more commonly publicized principles of effective corporate governance include the equitable treatment of shareholders, respect for the interests of other stakeholders, the role and responsibilities of the board, the integrity and ethical behavior of all members of the organization, and full disclosure of corporate documents and transparency of information and conduct.

CORPORATE CULTURE

In the early 1980s, an important management wave emerged. When North American managers began to realize that they were losing ground to other countries, such as Japan, France, Germany, and England, they wanted to know why and the study of comparative management was born. Today, not only are countries comparing their management approaches, but they are also searching for the "magic of management" that makes one organization more successful than another. It all started with Ouchi's *Theory Z: How American Business Can Meet the Japanese Challenge*,[1] which compared the North American style of management with the Japanese style, which was followed by Peters and Waterman's book *In Search of Excellence*.[2] The lesson was clear. Excellent companies had one thing in common:

---

1. Ouchi, William G., *Theory Z: How American Business Can Meet the Japanese Challenge*, Don Mills, Ontario: Addison-Wesley Publishing Company, 1981, p. 4.

2. Peters, Thomas J., and Robert H. Waterman, *In Search of Excellence*, New York: Harper & Row Publishers, Inc., 1982.

Corporate culture A shared system of values and beliefs within an organization.

a strong sense of shared values, norms, and beliefs about people, products, services, and innovation. A strong **corporate culture**, a shared system of values and beliefs within an organization, was the foundation of a company's success. North American organizations have now caught up in clarifying the meaning and significance of organizational culture and how strong corporate values can be adapted within their own organizations. Many top-level managers now focus on the enforcement of ethical standards within their organizations. In the News 1.3 gives an example of RONA's values and rules.

In the News 1.3

VALUES AND RULES OF ETHICS THAT GUIDE BEHAVIOUR

If an organization wants to practise good behaviour, all it has to do is write, communicate, and live by its code of ethics.

RONA is a classic example of how a company goes through the process of adapting to exceptional working habits. As pointed out by Robert Dutton, president and CEO of RONA Inc., "It is desirable to draw up a set of written rules to which we can refer."

From the start, RONA's employees have drawn strength by adhering to their shared vision and living out deeply entrenched values. Here are some of the terms to which employees hold fast: service, honesty, integrity, professionalism, unity, respect, search for the common good, and sense of responsibility. To many employees, "living" these words that are part of the company's Code of Ethics represents a commitment at two levels: collective and individual. The bottom line is that everybody wins—customers, investors, suppliers, and business partners. Above all, every stakeholder appears to trust RONA.

Source: Adapted from RONA, "Corporate governance guidelines," http://www.rona.ca/corporate/corporate-governance, accessed February 5, 2012. You can download RONA's complete document of the Code of Ethics in PDF version by visiting their site.

INTERNATIONAL ACCOUNTING AND FINANCIAL REPORTING

International Financial Reporting Standards (IFRS) Accounting standards issued by the IASB.

Another way to improve transparency and accountability is by introducing a common international accounting and financial language. This is the role and purpose of the International Accounting Standards Committee (IASC), which was established in 1973. Up until 2001, it had published only 41 **International Financial Reporting Standards (IFRS)**. In the early 2000s, problems started to emerge when multinationals had to prepare financial statements with different standards for different jurisdictions, making cross-country comparisons difficult. It was then that the International Organization of Securities Commissions (IOSCO) asked IASC to review and reinforce global standards and to standardize financial instruments. The IASC's key objective was to put in place "global convergence."

International Accounting Standards Board (IASB) Organization that develops, in the public interest, a single set of high-quality, understandable, and enforceable global standards that require transparent and comparable information in general-purpose financial statements.

In April 2001, the IASC became the **International Accounting Standards Board (IASB)** and was given exclusive responsibility for the IFRS. The basic mandate of the IASB was to develop, in the public interest, a single set of high-quality, understandable, and enforceable global standards that require transparent and comparable information in general-purpose financial statements. For updates on the IASB's work, visit its website at www.iasb.org.

A new era in global conduct of business emerged in 2005 when worldwide adoption of reporting rules and standards took hold. As a consequence, most national generally accepted accounting principles (GAAP) standards were phased out or reduced in importance as countries began to adopt the IFRS. Canada adopted the IFRS in January 2011.

Chapter Summary

1 Identify some of the external factors financial managers must consider to improve a company's bottom line.

Financial statements can be affected by many factors in the external environment. They include factors related to the economy, politics, global and open world economies, technological changes, product life cycle, and manufacturing.

2 Discuss the role of financial management within a business.

The role of financial management is not limited to raising capital dollars; it also extends to finding ways to use funds more effectively within a business. It focuses on answering the following questions: How are we doing? How much cash do we have on hand? What should we spend our funds on? Where will our funds come from? How will our business be protected?

3 Identify the people responsible for the finance function.

The finance functions are usually divided between the *controller*, who is responsible for the internal financial activities of a business, and the *treasurer*, who is responsible for the external financial activities. For financial management to be effective, *operating managers* should also perform this function.

4 Explain the four financial objectives of a business.

Financial management focuses on four basic objectives: *efficiency* (the productivity of assets), *liquidity* (the ability to meet current debt commitments), *prosperity* (improvement in such activities as revenue, profit, payment of dividends), and *stability* (an appropriate balance between the funds provided by the shareholders and by long-term lenders).

5 Describe the three major types of business decisions.

Business decisions can be grouped under three broad categories: investing, financing, and operating. Investing decisions deal with such accounts as non-current assets (e.g., machinery and equipment). Financing decisions deal with such accounts as non-current liabilities and equity. Operating decisions deal with the accounts appearing on the statement of income, such as revenue, cost of sales, distribution costs, and administrative expenses (profit for the year). Operating decisions also deal with the management of working capital accounts (current assets and current liabilities).

6 Examine the issues related to corporate transparency and accountability.

Following recent financial scandals, all types of stakeholders and the public have demanded greater corporate transparency and accountability. Both government and business have made far-reaching efforts to achieve that goal through legislation, corporate governance, corporate culture, and international accounting and financial reporting.

Key Terms

Review Questions

1 Identify some of the external factors that financial managers must consider to improve a company's bottom line.

1. Explain the key difference between what financial management focused on in the past versus today.
2. What factors of the external environment have an impact on a company's financial statements?

2 Discuss the role of financial management within a business.

3. Define financial management.
4. Why is it important for managers to ask such questions as "How are we doing?" and "How will our business be protected?"

3 Identify the people responsible for the finance function.

5. Differentiate between the role of the treasurer and the role of the controller.
6. Why should operating managers be responsible for the finance function?

4 Explain the four financial objectives of a business.

7. What are the four financial objectives? What do they mean?
8. Comment on the importance of the "return on revenue" financial objective.

5 Describe the three major types of business decisions.

9. Differentiate between internal financing and external financing.
10. What are investing decisions and financing decisions?
11. What are non-current assets?
12. What are working capital accounts?
13. What accounts in the statement of income and the statement of financial position are included in (a) investing decisions, (b) financing decisions, and (c) operating decisions?
14. What is the weighted average cost of capital?
15. What is an operating decision? Give some examples.
16. What is gross profit?
17. Why is it important for operating managers to understand the fundamentals of financial management?

6 Examine the issues related to corporate transparency and accountability.

18. What is transparency?
19. Differentiate between legislation and corporate governance.
20. Will the finance function be more important in the future than it was in the past? Discuss.

Learning Exercises

2 Discuss the role of financial management within a business.

EXERCISE 1: RETURN ON ASSETS AND COST OF FINANCING

Non-current assets	$ 1,260,000
Current assets	250,000
Profit for the year	170,000
Cost of debt (after tax)	12%
Cost of equity	12%

Questions

1. If managers want to earn a 12% ROA, how much profit must the company generate?
2. If managers want to earn a 15% ROA, how much profit must the company generate?

4 Explain the four financial objectives of a business.

EXERCISE 2: STATEMENT OF INCOME AND STATEMENT OF FINANCIAL POSITION

With the following data, prepare a statement of income and a statement of financial position. You will have to fill in the missing financial statement accounts.

Cost of sales	$ 700,000
Profit for the year	65,000
Share capital	500,000
Long-term borrowings	800,000
Total current assets	500,000
Gross profit	300,000
Distribution costs	200,000
Total equity	1,100,000
Total assets	2,500,000
Total current liabilities	600,000

EXERCISE 3: DISTRIBUTION OF THE PROFIT FOR THE YEAR

Assume that a company earns $280,000 in profit for the year on $3 million in revenue. The board of directors decides to keep half to pay for dividends and to reinvest the rest in the company. Sixty percent of the retained earnings are invested in non-current assets and the rest, in working capital for growth.

Questions

1. Calculate, as a percentage of revenue, how much would be kept in the company for growth (i.e., working capital and non-current assets) and how much would be used to pay dividends.
2. Explain who is responsible for deciding how much to retain in the business and how much to pay in dividends.
3. What do you think the board of directors would do if the profit for the year increased to $350,000?

5 Describe the three major types of business decisions.

EXERCISE 4: BUSINESS DECISIONS

List the following accounts under their respective type of business decisions:

Change in long-term borrowings
Profit for the year
Acquisition of a business
Depreciation/amortization
Share capital issue

Change in trade receivables
Net change in short-term borrowings
Sale of non-current assets
Change in trade and other payables
Additions to property, plant, and equipment

EXERCISE 5: COST OF BORROWING AND COST OF CAPITAL

Sources	Amounts
Trade and other payables	$200,000
Short-term borrowings	250,000
Mortgage	500,000
Long-term borrowings	250,000
Share capital	300,000
Retained earnings	800,000

The before-tax bank charges are 11.0% for the short-term borrowings, 10.0% for the long-term borrowings, and 10.5% on the mortgage. The shareholders expect to earn 16%. Assume that the company's income tax rate is 50%.

Questions

1. Calculate the company's after-tax cost of borrowing.
2. Calculate the company's weighted average cost of capital.

EXERCISE 6: CASH FLOW FROM INTERNAL OPERATIONS

Owners of a business are contemplating investing $550,000 in non-current assets in early January 2014. They are exploring ways to finance it. In 2012, the company had $250,000 in trade receivables, an amount that it expects will increase to $275,000 in 2013. The inventory level for 2012 was $430,000 and, having introduced a new inventory management system, the owners expect to be more efficient in managing it. They forecast a level of $370,000 in inventories by the end of 2013. They expect a substantial increase in revenue, which will increase their profit from $150,000 in 2012 to $230,000 in 2013.

Questions

1. How much cash will be generated from internal operations by the end of 2013?
2. Will the owners have to borrow money from investors to finance the expansion? If yes, how much?

Case

PACKARD INDUSTRIES INC.

In 2013, the management committee of Packard Industries Inc. is considering investing $800,000 to purchase machinery and equipment to increase the productivity of its plant. In 2012, the company's revenue was $2,800,000, goods purchased from suppliers totalled $600,000, and the profit for the year was $280,000. The company's 2012 statement of financial position is as follows:

Packard Industries Inc.
Statement of Financial Position
As at December 31, 2012

(in $)	
Assets	
Non-current assets	1,000,000
Current assets	
Inventories	300,000
Trade receivables	400,000
Cash and cash equivalents	20,000
Total current assets	720,000
Total assets	**1,720,000**
Equity and liabilities	
Equity	
Share capital	200,000
Retained earnings	700,000
Total equity	900,000
Long-term borrowings	500,000
Current liabilities	
Trade and other payables	170,000
Short-term borrowings	150,000
Total current liabilities	320,000
Total liabilities	820,000
Total equity and liabilities	**1,720,000**

In 2013, management expects revenue to increase by 10%. With cutbacks in different segments of their business activities, ROR is expected to improve to 12%. Cost of sales as a percentage of revenue is expected to improve and decline to 20%.

Management also expects improvements in the working capital accounts. The company's objective is to lower trade receivables to $370,000, with inventory levels expected to reach $280,000.

Questions

1. Calculate the company's return on total assets for 2012.
2. How much cash will be provided by internal operations in 2013, in particular by the following?
   - Retained earnings
   - Inventories
   - Trade receivables

3. How much will management have to raise from external activities (shareholders and lenders) to proceed with an $800,000 investment in non-current assets?

FINANCIAL SPREADSHEETS: EXCEL®

You can download financial spreadsheets from the Companion Website for this book at www.bergeron7e.nelson.com. Use the spreadsheets to perform most financial calculations (simple or complicated) in this text. In fact, most calculations done for this text and the Instructor's Manual were done with the help of these spreadsheets.

The spreadsheets allow you more time for analyzing financial statements by eliminating some "number crunching." The Companion Website includes Read Me Notes that explain how to use the spreadsheets. As we go through the chapters of this text, some brief comments will be made regarding the application and the type of analysis that can be done with these spreadsheets.

The spreadsheets are divided into two parts: (1) Financial Statement Analysis and (2) Decision-Making Tools.

CHAPTER 2

[ACCOUNTING AND FINANCIAL STATEMENTS]

Learning Objectives

After reading this chapter, you should be able to

1 Explain the activities related to bookkeeping.

2 Describe the accounting function and outline the four financial statements.

3 Examine the contents and the structure of the statement of income and the statement of comprehensive income, the statement of changes in equity, and the statement of financial position.

4 Understand the meaning of analysis in financial management.

5 Discuss the importance of decision making in financial management.

6 Analyze the contents and structure of the financial statements prepared for NFP organizations.

OPENING CASE

Financial Statements: Vital Tools for Analysis and Decision Making

After their discussion with Bill Murray, Len and Joan did some additional homework. They felt that Bill's advice about pinpointing operational and financial objectives was critical for formulating operational plans that would help them succeed.

Len and Joan also felt that it was important for them to learn how to set up a bookkeeping and accounting system. They knew that relevant and timely information was critical for analyzing all aspects of their retail operations and making key decisions. They asked Bill if he knew an accountant. He suggested May Ogaki, a chartered accountant with experience in counselling small business owners.

During their first meeting, Len and Joan told May that they were looking for an integrated information system that would provide them with different types of operational and financial data. They would need a cash register that could generate reports about their sales, purchases, inventories, costs, and so on. Len made the following comments:

> The cash register should be the most important information instrument in our business. It should provide us with daily, weekly, and monthly operational data. Anything that we buy and sell will go through the cash register. With a good, integrated software program, we should know exactly what products are moving and when, how much inventory we have in stock at all times, when we should be ordering goods from suppliers, how much profit we make on each product line, how much in sales each salesperson in the store makes, and so on. In addition, we need an accounting software program that can provide us with financial statements, such as the statement of income, the statement of financial position, and the statement of cash flows. This software should also help us prepare our monthly operating budget.

May understood and therefore recommended that an accounting software program, such as Simply Accounting, would provide the type of financial information they needed. She would investigate further. However, before leaving, May asked Len and Joan to think about the type of accounts or ledgers they wanted on their financial statements. As May pointed out,

> This is the first step in the bookkeeping and accounting process. Once you know the information that will help you make your decisions, it will be easy for me to determine the type of customized operational and financial reports that should be produced by your software program.

May also recommended they take a basic course in accounting to understand some of the fundamentals of accounting and financial terms and concepts. Although it was important to have an accountant prepare the financial statements annually for income tax purposes, Len and Joan should be able to read and analyze their own financial statements.

THIS CHAPTER WILL SHOW LEN AND JOAN MILLER HOW TO

- Set up bookkeeping and accounting systems.
- Identify the information needed to analyze all aspects of their financial statements.
- Understand how financial statements can lead to effective decisions.

Chapter Overview

FROM SCOREKEEPING TO FINANCIAL STATEMENTS

Financial management embraces four broad activities: bookkeeping, accounting, analysis, and decision making. This chapter explores these four activities within six key topics:

- *Bookkeeping.* As shown in Figure 2.1, bookkeeping systematically records, electronically or manually in sets of journals and ledgers, the daily financial transactions incurred by a business. These transactions are first recorded in books of original entry known as *journals* and subsequently recorded in books of final entry known as *ledgers*.
- *Accounting.* The accounting activity involves the preparation of the four financial statements: (1) the two-statement report, which includes the statement of income and the statement of comprehensive income; (2) the statement of changes in equity; (3) the statement of financial position; and (4) the statement of cash flows.
- *Structure and contents of these financial statements.* The financial statements presented in this text are based on the set of rules established by the International Accounting Standards Board (IASB)'s International Financial Reporting Standards (IFRS).

Figure 2.1 The Bookkeeping and Accounting Process

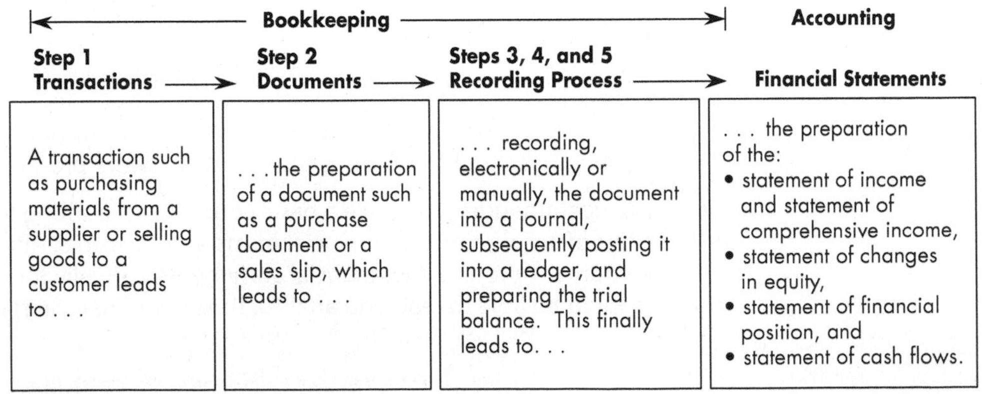

- *Analysis.* Interpreting financial statements is part of analysis. The information presented on financial statements should be not merely be considered as statistics but should be examined carefully to see how well (or badly) a business is doing.
- *Decision making.* It is not enough to record, arrange, and analyze data; the information must be used to make decisions.
- *Contents and structure of financial statements prepared by not-for-profit (NFP) organizations.* The NFP organizations' financial statements include the statement of financial position, the statement of operations, the statement of changes in net assets, and the statement of cash flows.

Bookkeeping

1 Explain the activities related to bookkeeping.

Bookkeeping involves collecting, classifying, and reporting daily transactions that occur in all departments of a business. Some transactions take place in the sales department, others in the trade receivables department or manufacturing plant. All business transactions are recorded under five broad categories or headings of accounts:

Bookkeeping
The activity that involves collecting, classifying, and reporting accounting transactions.

- *Assets*, or what a business owns
- *Equity*, or what it owes to shareholders
- *Liabilities*, or what it owes to creditors
- *Revenue*, or how much it earned from selling its goods or services
- *Costs (or expenses)*, or how much it costs to produce and sell its goods or services

Chart of accounts
A set of categories by which accounting transactions are recorded.

Bookkeeping begins with the preparation of a **chart of accounts**, which establishes the categories by which transactions of the business are recorded. The number of accounts that a business sets up depends largely on management's needs.

We'll look at the bookkeeping process under three headings: the accounting equation, the accounting cycle, and the trial balance.

THE ACCOUNTING EQUATION

Double-entry bookkeeping
A system for posting financial transactions so that the accounting equation remains in balance.

Each time a business transaction takes place, at least two accounts are affected, resulting in two account entries. This is referred to as **double-entry bookkeeping**. For example, when a business buys a truck with borrowed funds from a bank, both the asset and liability accounts are affected. If a business pays its mortgage with cash, both its asset and liability accounts are affected. If shareholders invest money in a business, and the funds are used to buy a truck, the asset and equity accounts are affected.

Accounting equation
Assets = Equity + Liabilities or Assets − Liabilities = Equity

When all the double-entry transactions are complete, the business's statement of financial position can be expressed by the **accounting equation**:

Assets = Equity + Liabilities

It can also be expressed in the following way:

Assets − Liabilities = Equity

The basic structure of the statement of financial position is based on this accounting equation. One side of the statement lists all the asset accounts (e.g., trade receivables, equipment), and the other side lists all the equity and liability accounts (e.g., share capital, trade and other payables). Both sides must be equal, that is, they must balance. For this reason, the statement of financial position is also called the *balance sheet*.

THE ACCOUNTING CYCLE

Bookkeeping and accounting cycle The steps involved in processing financial transactions for preparing financial statements.

Five steps, called the **bookkeeping and accounting cycle,** occur from the time that a business transaction is processed to the time that the transaction is reported on a financial statement. Step 1 has to do with transactions, step 2 with the preparation of documents, and steps 3 to 5 with electronic or manual recording and posting in addition to the preparation of the trial balance (refer back to Figure 2.1).

Step 1. The first step is a business transaction (e.g., investing money in a business, buying a truck, selling goods or services, paying salaries).

Step 2. Each transaction is accompanied by a document (e.g., a deposit slip from the bank, a sales slip, a purchase document, a cheque stub).

Step 3. Through the bookkeeping system, each transaction is recorded in different sets of books: journals and ledgers. By recording business transactions by using the double-entry system, accountants can be assured that the total of all accounts are in balance. Errors are instantly made obvious by a lack of balance. Some transactions are recorded on the left side of an account; these are called **debit** entries. Other transactions are recorded on the right side of an account; these are called **credit** entries. The asset and cost accounts have debit balances and the equity, liability, and revenue accounts have credit balances (see Figure 2.2).

Debit Accounting entries recorded on the left side of an account.

Credit Accounting entries recorded on the right side of an account.

Some basic rules determine whether a transaction should be a debit or a credit:

	Assets	Equity	Liabilities
Debit	Increases	Decreases	Decreases
Credit	Decreases	Increases	Increases

Debits and credits can also be registered in revenue and cost accounts. For these accounts, the credit and debit rules are as follows:

	Revenue	Costs
Debit	Decreases	Increases
Credit	Increases	Decreases

As shown in Figure 2.2, when the revenue and cost accounts are tabulated, there is usually a surplus called profit. The arrow shows that this profit (costs deducted from revenue) is transferred into the equity account in the statement of financial position and called retained earnings. A credit in equity or revenue accounts increases the wealth of a business. Conversely, a debit in the cost or equity accounts reduces the wealth of a business.

Figure 2.2 **Debits and Credits**

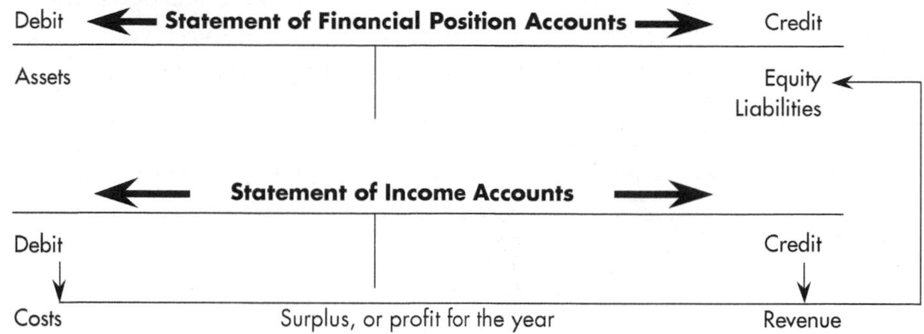

Journals (books of original entry) The books used to record accounting transactions in chronological order.

Journalizing The process of recording, electronically or manually, transactions in a journal (e.g., sales journal, salaries journal).

Ledger (books of final entry) Books that show all amounts debited and credited in individual accounts (e.g., trade receivables, revenue, inventories and salaries), including a running balance.

Posting The process of transferring recorded transactions from the journals to the appropriate ledger accounts (e.g., revenue, trade receivables).

Trial balance A statement that ensures that the general ledger is in balance (debit transactions equal credit transactions).

The books used to record accounting transactions are journals and ledgers. **Journals**, sometimes referred to as the **books of original entry**, are used to record transactions in a chronological order—that is, as they happen. Businesses often have several types of journals, such as the sales journal, the purchases journal, and the salaries journal. The process of recording transactions, electronically or manually, in the journals is called **journalizing**.

Step 4. The fourth step in the bookkeeping and account cycle is to transfer the amounts from the journals into ledgers. Journals do not show the balance of each account after each transaction. This occurs in a second set of books called ledgers. A **ledger** (or **books of final entry**) is very much like a chequebook. It shows all amounts debited and credited in each account, including its running balance. Ledgers for a home would include, say, hydro, credit card, mortgage, salary, and food accounts. To know how much he or she owns or owes, a person would look at the outstanding balance for each of these accounts. To know how much salary he or she earned, or the expenses incurred for telephone, groceries, or entertainment during a given year, the person would look at the separate accounts for the answers.

A business operates with similar accounts. All transactions recorded in journals are transferred to the appropriate ledger accounts in a process called **posting**. Ledgers provide a running balance for each account. Ledger accounts are usually given a number to speed the process of recording the transactions.

THE TRIAL BALANCE

Step 5. The fifth and final step in the bookkeeping and accounting cycle is called *closing the books.* It is done at the end of an accounting period (i.e., the end of a month or the end of a fiscal year). To ensure that all transactions recorded during the period are error free—that is, that the sum of all debits equals the sum of all credits—the outstanding account balances are listed under their appropriate column in the **trial balance**.

Let's look at Table 2.1, which shows the trial balance for 2013 for a company called Eastman Technologies Inc. A trial balance lists, in parallel columns, the debit and credit balances for each account or ledger. For our purposes, Table 2.1 also identifies

Table 2.1 **Trial Balance**

Eastman Technologies Inc.
Trial Balance
As at December 31, 2013
(in $)

	Debit		Credit	
Cash	22,000	SFP		
Revenue			2,500,000	SI
Prepaid expenses	60,000	SFP		
Finance costs	35,000	SI		
Cost of sales	1,900,000	SI		
Retained earnings (beginning of year)			205,000	SCE
Trade receivables	300,000	SFP		
Accrued expenses			20,000	SFP
Sales salaries	140,000	SI		
Income tax expense	97,500	SI		
Taxes payable			80,000	SFP
Advertising expenses	20,000	SI		
Long-term borrowings			800,000	SFP
Inventories	218,000	SFP		
Trade and other payables			195,000	SFP
Notes payable			150,000	SFP
Non-current assets (at cost)	1,340,000	SFP		
Depreciation	40,000	SI		
Accumulated depreciation			140,000	SFP
Share capital			300,000	SFP
Office salaries	170,000	SI		
Dividends	47,500	SCE		
Lease	20,000	SI		
Other income (from investments)			20,000	SI
Total	4,410,000		4,410,000	

SCE = Statement of Changes in Equity

SFP = Statement of Financial Position

SI = Statement of Income

the financial statement on which each account will appear: the statement of income and the statement of comprehensive income (SI), the statement of changes in equity (SCE), and the statement of financial position (SFP). The debit and credit columns are then totalled. If the debit column equals the credit column, it means all accounts are in balance and no arithmetic errors were made.

It's important to do a trial balance because the ledger accounts will be used to prepare the financial statements. Any errors can be caught and corrected before these statements are prepared. The accounts shown in this trial balance will be used to prepare Eastman Technologies Inc.'s statement of income and the statement of comprehensive income, the statement of changes in equity, and the statement of financial position. We'll return to these in later sections.

Some common errors that will cause inequality in a trial balance include the following:

- One of the columns was added incorrectly.
- An amount was improperly reported.
- A debit balance that should have been recorded as a credit (or vice versa) was omitted.
- One side of an account was computed incorrectly.
- An erroneous amount was reported as a debit or as a credit in an account.
- A debit entry was recorded as a credit, or vice versa.
- A debit or a credit entry was omitted.

With some other errors, the debit column will still be equal to the credit column in the trial balance:

- Failure to record an entire transaction.
- Recording the same erroneous amount for both the debit and the credit.
- Recording the same transaction more than once.
- Recording one part of a transaction in the wrong account.

Problem-Solving Example 2.1

Journal Entries and Trial Balance

The accountant of a restaurant noted the following transactions: (1) purchased on credit a computer for $3,500, (2) made a $2,000 payment on a credit account, (3) sold on credit $3,000 worth of merchandise, (4) paid an advertising agency $1,200 for services rendered. For these four transactions, prepare the journal entries and the trial balance.

Solution

(1) Journal entries	Debits	Credits
Transaction 1: Equipment	$3,500	
Trade and other payables		$3,500
Transaction 2: Trade and other payables	2,000	
Cash		2,000
Transaction 3: Trade receivables	3,000	
Revenue		3,000
Transaction 4: Services	1,200	
Cash	—	1,200
Total	$9,700	$9,700

(continued)

Problem-Solving Example 2.1 (continued)

(2) Trial balance	Debits	Credits
Equipment	$3,500	
Trade and other payables		$1,500
Cash		3,200
Trade receivables	3,000	
Revenue		3,000
Services	1,200	
Total	$7,700	$7,700

Self-Test Exercise 2.1

Journal Entries, Ledgers, and Trial Balance

After opening their computer sales and service store, the Millers completed the following four transactions:

1. They invested $100,000 in cash in the business.
2. They purchased on credit $10,000 worth of goods from several suppliers.
3. They sold on a cash basis $13,000 worth of products and services.
4. They paid $3,000 for salaries.

Use the above information to prepare the following:

1. Journal entries
2. Ledgers
3. Trial balance

Answers to the Self-Test Exercises can be found at www.bergeron7e.nelson.com.

Accounting

2 Describe the accounting function and outline the four financial statements.

Managers, owners, lenders, and investors want to know the financial health of the firms they deal with. The financial performance of a business is presented under four **financial statements**:

- The two-statement report called the statement of income and the statement of comprehensive income, also known as the statement of operations, the profit and loss statement, or the statement of earnings
- The statement of changes in equity
- The statement of financial position, also referred to as the balance sheet or the statement of financial condition
- The statement of cash flows

Financial statements Financial reports, which include the two-statement report called the statement of income and the statement of comprehensive income, the statement of changes in equity, the statement of financial position, and the statement of cash flows.

The financial statements are included in annual reports. This chapter examines the contents and the structure of the first three financial statements. Chapter 3 explains the statement of cash flows.

Businesses make many transactions every day: Goods are sold on a cash or credit basis; materials are purchased; salaries, rent, and hydro bills are paid; and goods that were purchased on credit are paid for. Financial statements permit managers to know, on a daily, monthly, or yearly basis, the financial results of all these transactions. **Accounting**, considered the language of business, is the process used to logically and methodically record and summarize business transactions on a company's financial statements.

The IASB, via the IFRS, sets out the structure of the statement of income and statement of comprehensive income, the statement of changes in equity, the statement of financial position, and the statement of cash flows (Figure 2.3).

Figure 2.3 Financial Statements

Statement of Income and Statement of Comprehensive Income

1.	Revenue – Cost of sales = Gross profit
2.	– Distribution costs, administrative expenses, and finance costs, plus other income = Profit before taxes
3.	– Income tax expense = Profit for the year
4.	+ Other comprehensive income/(loss) for the year, net of tax = Total comprehensive income/(loss) for the year

Statement of Changes in Equity

1. Beginning of year • Share capital • Contributed surplus • Retained earnings • Accumulated other comprehensive income/(loss)
2. Transactions made during the year • Share capital (e.g., shares issued) • Contributed surplus (e.g., options exercised) • Retained earnings (profit less dividends) • Accumulated other comprehensive income/(loss) for the year (e.g., currency translation)
3. End of year • Share capital • Contributed surplus • Retained earnings • Accumulated other comprehensive income/(loss)

Statement of Financial Position

1. Non-Current assets	3. Equity
	4. Non-Current liabilities
2. Current assets	5. Current liabilities

Statement of Cash Flows

1. Operating Activities • Profit for the year • Adjustments
2. Financing Activities
3. Investing Activities
4. Cash Balance

Accounting
The process of recording and summarizing business transactions on a company's financial statements.

Statement of income
A financial statement that shows a summary of revenue and costs for a specified period.

Statement of comprehensive income
A financial statement that shows items of income and expense that are not in the statement of income.

Total comprehensive income/(loss)
Transactions and other events (e.g., asset revaluation) that affect the equity account.

Statement of changes in equity
A statement that represents the interest of the shareholders of a business, showing the cumulative net results in equity with respect to share capital, contributed surplus, retained earnings, and accumulated other comprehensive income/(loss) for the period.

Statement of financial position
A financial statement that shows a "snapshot" of a company's financial condition (assets, equity, and liabilities).

The **statement of income** shows the flow of revenue earned and costs incurred by a business during a given period (e.g., one month or one year). It shows three levels of profitability (boxes 1 to 3): gross profit, profit before taxes, and profit for the year. The **statement of comprehensive income** includes other income or loss, net of tax (*net* here means "after"), and highlights income and expenses that are not included in the statement of income, such as foreign exchange differences, assets that are available for sale, and revaluation of property, plant, and equipment and intangible assets. The statement of comprehensive income shows a fourth level of performance (box 4): **total comprehensive income/(loss)**, which is the change in equity during the period (e.g., asset revaluation).

The **statement of changes in equity** represents the interest of the shareholders of a business. It shows the cumulative net results in equity with respect to share capital (money invested in a business by shareholders), contributed surplus (money earned from sources other than its profits, such as by issuing shares at a price greater than their book value), retained earnings (the portion of net earnings that over the years that has not been paid out as dividends to the shareholders), and accumulated other comprehensive income/(loss) for the year (including changes in currency translation and in property valuation). The statement shows the carrying amount of these four components of equity at the beginning and end of the period. For retained earnings, for example, the statement shows (1) the amount of profit that was not distributed to shareholders since the business was started, (2) the profit earned and dividends paid during the current operating period, and (3) the amount of earnings remaining at the end of the period. (Note that the words *profit* and *earnings* mean the same thing and will be used interchangeably throughout this text.)

The **statement of financial position** is a "snapshot" of a company's financial condition at that moment. This statement is divided into five sections (look back at Figure 2.3). The left side shows what the business owns, or its assets. Asset accounts are grouped under two headings: non-current assets and current assets.

The right side shows what a business owes to its shareholders or owners (equity) and creditors (lenders). Debts are grouped under two headings: non-current liabilities and current liabilities.

The **statement of cash flows** shows where the cash came from (cash inflows) and where it went (cash outflows) between accounting periods. This statement is divided into four sections: (1) operating activities (the main revenue-generating activities and changes or adjustments in the balances of working capital accounts, such as trade receivables and inventories), (2) financing activities (changes in the size of equity and long-term borrowings), (3) investing activities (the buying or selling of long-term assets or non-current assets, such as buildings and equipment), and (4) cash balance (changes in the balance of cash on hand and cash equivalents).

Figure 2.4 Relationship between the Statement of Financial Position and the Statement of Income

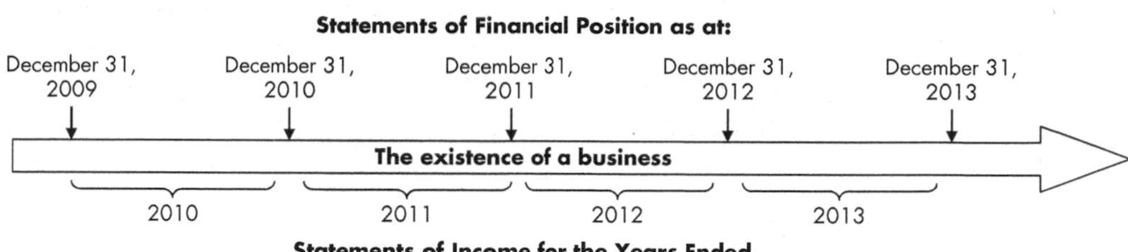

Statement of cash flows
A financial statement that shows where funds came from (cash inflows) and where they went (cash outflows).

Figure 2.4 shows the relationship between the statement of financial position and the statement of income. Because the statement of financial position shows a "snapshot" of a business's financial condition of a business at a given point (say, December 31), the statement reads "as at December 31." Conversely, the statement of income is more like a "movie" of what went on during an operating period (say, from January 1 to December 31), so the statement of income reads "for the period ended December 31."

Financial statements can be reported in one of two ways: the cash method and the accrual method.

Cash method
An accounting method that records business transactions when cash is received or disbursed.

The **cash method** keeps a record of cash receipts from sales and from payments of bills. In this case, the business recognizes revenue when cash or its equivalent is received, no matter when the goods or services are delivered. Costs are treated in a similar way. At the end of an accounting period, the costs are deducted from revenues, and the difference gives the profit or loss for the period. This accounting method is limited to small businesses (such as variety stores) for which most transactions are on a cash basis. For this reason, all financial reports or statements discussed in this book, unless otherwise stated, use the accrual method.

Accrual method
An accounting method that considers sales when made and costs when incurred, regardless of when the cash transaction takes place.

The **accrual method** records revenue when goods are sold or services rendered. For example, if a business makes a sale, whether on a cash or credit basis, or buys goods with cash or credit, it assumes that the revenues and the costs have been incurred. Although a sale is made on credit (and cash has not been received) or goods are purchased from suppliers on credit (and payment has not been made), the statement of income shows the revenue and cost transactions in the accounts. The most important accounts that differentiate cash basis from accrual basis are the trade receivables and trade and other payables.

The accrual method is used to evaluate business operations by assigning to each fiscal period the appropriate revenue and costs. In accounting, this process is called *matching expenses with revenues,* and it is the best way to see the "true" profit generated during a particular operating period.

Financial Statements

3 Examine the contents and the structure of the statement of income and the statement of comprehensive income, the statement of changes in equity, and the statement of financial position.

Let's now examine the contents and structure of these financial statements in more detail, using Eastman Technologies Inc. as our example. The company's statement of income and the statement of comprehensive income are shown in Table 2.2, the statement of changes in equity in Table 2.3, and the statement of financial position in Table 2.4. The information contained in these financial statements is drawn from the trial balance (look back at Table 2.1). Eastman's statement of cash flows will be explained in Chapter 3.

STATEMENT OF INCOME

Everyone associated with a business wants to know if it is making a profit and, if so, how much. The statement of income tells them. This financial statement summarizes the revenue and costs for a period (one month, six months, or a year). All cost and expense figures are bracketed and all revenue or income figures are without brackets (Table 2.2). Eastman's statement of income for the year ended December 31, 2013, shows three levels of profitability: (1) gross profit,

Table 2.2 **The Statement of Income and the Statement of Comprehensive Income**

Eastman Technologies Inc.
Statement of Comprehensive Income
For the year ended December 31, 2013
(in $)

Revenue		2,500,000	
Cost of sales		(1,900,000)	
Gross profit		600,000	Level 1
Other income		20,000	
Distribution costs:			
Sales salaries	(140,000)		
Advertising expenses	(20,000)		
Total distribution costs		(160,000)	
Administrative expenses:			
Office salaries	(170,000)		
Lease	(20,000)		
Depreciation	(40,000)		
Total administrative expenses		(230,000)	
Finance costs		(35,000)	
Total other income and costs		(405,000)	
Profit before taxes		195,000	Level 2
Income tax expense		(97,500)	
Profit for the year		97,500	Level 3

(continued)

Table 2.2	The Statement of Income and the Statement of Comprehensive Income (continued)	
Eastman Technologies Inc. **Statement of Comprehensive Income** **For the year ended December 31, 2013** **(in $)**		
Profit for the year	97,500	
Other comprehensive income/(loss)	—	
Exchange differences on translating foreign operations	—	
Gain or loss on property revaluation	—	
Actuarial gains (losses) on defined benefit pension plans	—	
Total other comprehensive income/(loss) for the year	—	
Total comprehensive income	97,500	Level 4

(2) profit before taxes, and (3) profit for the year. The accounts shown on the statement of income are grouped in two distinct sections:

1. The *operating section*, which shows the gross profit and the profit before taxes.
2. The *owners' section*, which shows the profit for the year or the amount left for the shareholders.

A company has two main sources of income: the major one is the revenue from the sale of its products and services; the second source is income not from sales, such as interest received from investments. The more important costs associated with a business are cost of sales, distribution costs, and administrative expenses. These costs are directly linked to the ongoing operating activities of a business. Finance costs are less significant but are also included in the statement of income.

Operating Section

Operating section
Section of the statement of income that shows a company's gross profit and profit before taxes.

The **operating section** of the statement of income includes two levels of profitability: the gross profit and the profit before taxes.

Gross profit (or gross margin) is the difference between revenue and cost of sales. It is the profit a business makes after paying for the cost of producing the goods.

Revenue	$2,500,000
Cost of sales	(1,900,000)
Gross profit	$ 600,000

It is called gross profit because no other costs have been deducted (*gross* here means "whole" or "total"). It is the amount of money left to pay for other general expenses, such as distribution costs and administrative expenses. Gross profit is the starting point for evaluating the profitability of a business.

Revenue
What a business earns from the sale of its products and services.

Revenue (also referred to as net sales) is what a business earns from the sale of its products and services. It represents items actually delivered or shipped to customers during the fiscal period. Revenue is the amount a company has received or expects to receive after allowing for discounts, returns, and other deductions from the original sale price. Sales taxes (GST/HST) are not included in the revenue amount. Essentially, revenue is the amount that a business receives to cover all operating costs or expenses and to generate a profit. Revenue is an important figure because it is used to determine the financial soundness of a business. For example, revenue is used to calculate a company's level of productivity (the relationship between revenue and total assets) and efficiency (the relationship between revenue and profit for the year). Although annual reports show only one level of revenue, internal reports show two levels of revenue, gross revenue and net revenue, which are presented below:

Gross revenue	$2,700,000
Less: discounts, returns, and allowances	(200,000)
Net revenue	$2,500,000

Cost of sales
The cost incurred in making or producing goods that are sold.

Cost of sales (also known as cost of goods sold or COGS) is the amount it cost to make or produce the goods that were sold. It is by far the largest expense in the statement of income for a manufacturer (in many cases, it may represent as much as 80% of a company's total costs). It includes three major items: materials purchased from suppliers, transportation cost or freight-in for goods shipped from suppliers to the company's plants, and all costs associated with the manufacturing process, such as wages and depreciation on the plant's equipment and machinery. For a retailer, the goods purchased from suppliers and the freight-in for goods shipped from suppliers are considered cost of sales. Service-based industries, such as motels, bowling alleys, advertising agencies, and recreational services, do not have manufacturing costs; instead, cost of sales is all costs or expenses associated with the delivery of the services. Gross profit is the difference between revenue and cost of sales.

Other income
Revenue that is not directly related to the central operations of a business.

Other income is revenue whose source is not directly related to the central operations of a business. It includes, for example, interest earned on investments (e.g., short-term deposits) and rental income for renting parts of a building not needed for business operations.

Distribution costs
Money spent by a business to promote, sell, and distribute its goods and services.

Distribution costs are amounts spent by a business to promote, sell, and distribute goods and services. These costs include advertising, sales salaries, sales commissions, trade shows, sales supplies, delivery expenses, and sales promotions.

Administrative expenses
Expenses that are not directly related to producing and selling goods or services.

Administrative expenses are all other expenses not directly related to producing, distributing, or selling goods. They include costs in such areas as human resources, accounting, legal, finance, computers, consultants, insurance, and depreciation (a non-cash expense) on machinery and equipment. Office equipment is usually a capital expenditure when it is purchased. For a capital expenditure, its useful life is estimated (e.g., five or ten years) and the equipment is then depreciated (reduced in value) over that time. The cost is amortized, or spread, over that same time. Assets that are typically capitalized include factory equipment, computers, tools, machinery, and buildings.

Depreciation
An allocation of the cost of a non-current asset against revenue over the asset's life and an estimated decrease in the value of non-current assets through wear and tear or obsolescence.

Depreciation is a matching of the cost of a non-current asset (e.g., plant, equipment, machinery) to the revenue it helps produce over that asset's life. It also involves an estimated decrease in the value of the asset through wear and tear or obsolescence. Depreciation expenses can be shown in any section of the statement of income where non-current assets are used, including cost of sales, distribution costs, and administrative expenses. For example, a truck (distribution costs) may last seven years; a building (manufacturing costs), 40 years; and furniture (administrative expenses), 15 years. Although a non-current asset may be paid for with cash, the business will apportion the cost over the asset's useful life because it will be used for a number of years.

There are different ways of calculating depreciation. The two most widely used methods are straight-line depreciation and accelerated depreciation. Let's examine how these two depreciation methods work.

Straight-line depreciation. This method is the most popular and the simplest to calculate. It amortizes an equal portion of the non-current asset each year over its estimated useful life. It is calculated as follows:

$$\textbf{Depreciation} = \frac{\textbf{Purchase cost} - \textbf{Scrap/salvage value}}{\textbf{Estimated useful life in years}}$$

For example, suppose a non-current asset, such as a semi-trailer truck, costs $100,000. It has a useful life of five years and no salvage value. The yearly depreciation amount would be $20,000:

$$\textbf{Depreciation} = \frac{\$100{,}000}{5} = \$20{,}000$$

Accelerated depreciation. One way to use the accelerated depreciation method is by applying the sum-of-the-years'-digits method of calculation. This method shifts depreciation forward in an asset's life. It increases charges in the first few years and reduces those in later years of the asset's life. The sum-of-the-years'-digits calculation uses the estimated life of an asset as the common denominator. The numerators of the fractions are the years in the asset's life. We'll use the same $100,000 cost to illustrate this method of calculation:

1. If the life of the asset is five years, each year would be listed as 1, 2, 3, 4, and 5; if it is ten years, the list would go from 1 to 10.
2. The sum of the digits for each year would be added:

$$1 + 2 + 3 + 4 + 5 = 15$$

3. A fraction is identified for each year: 1/15, 2/15, 3/15, 4/15, and 5/15. Each fraction, starting with the last year, is multiplied by the original $100,000 investment. For each year, the calculation to find the depreciation is therefore done in the following way:

$$\textbf{Cost} \times \frac{\textbf{Number of years of depreciation remaining}}{\textbf{Sum of total digits of the asset's useful life}}$$

Year	Fraction		Cost of the Assets		Depreciation	Net Book Value	Depreciated (%)
1	5/15	×	$100,000	=	$ 33,333	$ 66,667	33.3
2	4/15	×	100,000	=	26,667	40,000	60.0
3	3/15	×	100,000	=	20,000	20,000	80.0
4	2/15	×	100,000	=	13,333	6,667	93.3
5	1/15	×	100,000	=	6,667	—	100.0
Total					$100,000		

Profit before taxes is the difference between gross profit and all costs (distribution costs, administrative expenses, and finance costs) plus other income. Sometimes hundreds of expenses are included in these categories, ranging from salaries (a large amount) to legal fees (usually a small amount). Managers are directly accountable for this level of profitability (through their decisions about cost of sales, distribution costs, and administrative expenses, for example). Here is the calculation:

Gross profit		$ 600,000
Plus other income		20,000
Sub-total		620,000
Less: distribution costs	(160,000)	
administrative expenses	(230,000)	
finance costs	(35,000)	
Total		(425,000)
Profit before taxes		$ 195,000

Managers are always watching that number, trying to find ways to improve profitability and satisfy their shareholders. In the News 2.1 gives an example about how radical cost-cutting measures can improve profitability.

In The News 2.1

ONE WAY TO BOOST THE BOTTOM LINE

There are many ways to improve efficiencies, that is, the bottom line. For example, you can (1) increase revenue and maintain costs at the same level, (2) introduce innovation and new technology, (3) improve employee productivity, or (4) take radical and extreme measures by eliminating jobs and closing plants.

Caterpillar, a manufacturer of earth movers, mining equipment, and other machinery, took the fourth option when they announced the closing of their plant and elimination of about 450 jobs in London, Ontario, in February 2012. As pointed out by company officials, globalization, a fragile recovery from the recession, and the rising value of the Canadian dollar were the main causes for the shutdown. A company spokesperson added: "The cost structure of the operation was not sustainable and efforts to negotiate a new, competitive collective agreement were not successful."

Source: "Caterpillar Pulls Plug on London Plant." *Globe and Mail.* Retrieved from http://www.theglobeandmail.com/globe-investor/caterpillar-pulls-plug-on-london-plant/article2325356/, accessed February 5, 2012. To learn more about Caterpillar, go to www.caterpillar.com.

Owners' section
The section of the statement of income that shows the amount of money left for shareholders (i.e., profit for the year).

Owners' Section

The **owners' section** of the statement of income deals with the money left for shareholders, that is, "the bottom line." A company's shareholders are its owners, and they are entitled to receive a share of the company's earnings. The profit for the year belongs to the shareholders.

In our Eastman example in Table 2.2, the company earned $97,500 in profit. The board of directors must decide how much of this amount will be paid to the shareholders in dividends and how much will be left in the business as retained earnings. The portions paid to shareholders and retained in the business both appear on the statement of changes in equity under retained earnings.

Income tax expense
The total amount of taxes due to federal and provincial or territorial governments on the taxable income earned by the business during the current fiscal accounting period.

Income tax expense is the total amount of taxes due to federal and provincial or territorial governments on the taxable income earned by the business during the current fiscal accounting period. The amount is calculated by multiplying the taxable income for the period by the appropriate tax rate (we'll use a 50% income tax rate for our example). Income tax expense does not include other types of taxes, such as payroll and property taxes, which are included in cost of sales and other costs and expenses.

Profit before taxes	$195,000
Income tax expense	(97,500)
Profit for the year	$ 97,500

Corporate income tax expense calculations use the appropriate tax rate for a particular corporation, costs and expenses, and business losses (if any). Here is a brief description of these three elements.

Income tax
A percentage of taxable income paid to the provincial or territorial and federal governments based on taxable income less certain tax deductions.

Corporate and other income tax rates. **Income tax** is a percentage of taxable income paid to the provincial or territorial and federal governments. The tax is charged on taxable income, less certain tax deductions. Provincial and territorial tax rates vary across jurisdictions, and a number of abatements or special deductions exist. For instance, the deductions are large on small-business income, income from manufacturing and processing businesses in Canada, and income from the production of minerals, oil, and gas.

All *costs* and *expenses* incurred by a business, such as salaries, purchases, and advertising, can be claimed against revenue, which reduces a business's taxable income. Finance costs, rent, and lease payments are also considered business expenses and are generally deductible. However, repayment of principal on a loan and dividends on both common and preferred shares are not deductible and are part of the profit or earnings for the year.

Business losses from past years are also tax deductible. For example, when a company incurs a loss, it may carry it back over the three previous years, or it may carry it forward and deduct it from the taxable income of the next twenty years. The *Income Tax Act* provides detailed explanation of tax-deductible losses.

In arriving at its taxable income, businesses may deduct *capital cost allowance (CCA)* on non-current assets (e.g., trucks, buildings). This topic is discussed on page 59.

Through CCA, businesses can recover, over some period, the original amount invested in non-current assets without having to pay tax on a portion of the investments. In the News 2.2 tells how financial statements can be read.

In The News 2.2

PROFILING THE STATEMENT OF INCOME

Several documents can be used to gauge the financial health of an organization. An important one is the income statement. It tells people how a business has done in terms of its revenue, its expenses, and, more importantly, its bottom line, that is, its "profit." This statement shows the direct results (good or bad) of regular business operations.

Just a few numbers revealed De Beers's 2011 income statement performance in both growth and efficiencies for one of its divisions: rough diamond sales increased by 27 percent and earnings, by 21 percent.

Source: "De Beers: Rough Diamond Sales Rise 27 Per Cent, Earnings by 21 Per Cent." *Canadian Business*. Retrieved from http:// www.canadianbusiness.com/article/70409–de-beers-rough-diamond-sales-rise-27-per-cent-earnings-by-21-per-cent, accessed February 10, 2012. To read more about De Beers, visit www.debeers.com.

Problem-Solving Example 2.2

The Statement of Income

With the following accounts, prepare the statement of income: revenue ($200,000), gross profit ($80,000), other income ($10,000), distribution costs ($25,000), administrative expenses ($30,000), finance costs ($10,000), income tax expense ($10,000). What is the profit for the year?

Solution

Profit for the year is $15,000.

Revenue		$200,000
Cost of sales		(120,000)
Gross profit		80,000
Other income	$10,000	
Distribution costs	(25,000)	
Administrative expenses	(30,000)	
Finance costs	(10,000)	
Total other income and costs		(55,000)
Profit before taxes		25,000
Income tax expense		(10,000)
Profit for the year		$15,000

Self-Test Exercise 2.2

The Statement of Income

With the following accounts, prepare CompuTech's statement of income for the year ended December 31, 2013:

Purchases	$ 175,000
Sales salaries	80,000
Advertising	3,000
Travelling	2,000
Revenue	350,000
Finance costs	10,000
Freight-in	2,000
Income tax expense	13,000
Sales commissions	2,000
Depreciation/amortization	38,000

Answers to the Self-Test Exercises can be found at www.bergeron7e.nelson.com.

STATEMENT OF COMPREHENSIVE INCOME

A business can present the statement of comprehensive income for a given period as part of the statement of income or as a separate statement.

Comprehensive income includes all parts of *profit or loss* and of *other comprehensive income/(loss)*. Other comprehensive income/(loss) includes the following:

- Changes in revaluation (property, plant, and equipment)
- Actuarial gains and losses on recognized defined benefit plans (these are the actual amounts a company pays on its pensions compared with previous estimates)
- Gains and losses on the exchange rate from translating the financial statements of foreign operations
- Gains and losses on the value of assets available for sale

Eastman Technologies Inc.'s statement of comprehensive income, in the lower portion of Table 2.2, shows a profit for the year of $97,500. This is drawn from the statement of income and other accounts (but in this example, there are no additional transactions). The total comprehensive income for the year was $97,500 (profit level 4).

STATEMENT OF CHANGES IN EQUITY

The owners' (shareholders') equity is the result of changes in certain accounts, such as share capital, contributed surplus, retained earnings, and other comprehensive income/(loss), for the year.

The statement of changes in equity shows the following for each account:

- The amounts at the start of the fiscal or accounting period; these amounts should agree with the equity figures on the previous year's statement of financial position.
- The changes in the current operating year.
- The amount left in equity at the end of the fiscal year; this amount determines the equity figure that will appear on the current year's statement of changes in equity.

Table 2.3 shows Eastman's statement of changes in equity for 2013 and 2012. A $15,000 change occurred in the share capital account. The retained earnings section shows the $97,500 profit for the year, which was drawn from the statement of income in Table 2.2. An amount of $47,500 was paid out in dividends. The $255,000 amount

Table 2.3 **The Statement of Changes in Equity**

Eastman Technologies Inc.
Statements of Changes in Equity
For the years ended December 31
(in $)

	2013	2012
Share capital		
Balance at beginning of year	285,000	285,000
Common shares issued	15,000	—
Dividend reinvestment and share purchase plan	—	—
Shares issued on exercise of stock options	—	—
Balance at end of year	300,000	285,000
Contributed surplus		
Balance at beginning of year	—	—
Stock-based compensation	—	—
Options exercised	—	—
Balance at end of year	—	—
Retained earnings		
Balance at beginning of year	205,000	205,000
Profit applicable to common shareholders	97,500	—
Dividends paid to shareholders	(47,500)	—
Balance at end of year	255,000	205,000
Total other comprehensive income/(loss) for the year		
Balance at beginning of year	—	—
Change in currency translation	—	—
Change in property revaluation	—	—
Balance at end of year	—	—
Total equity	555,000	490,000

in retained earnings as at December 31, 2013, is the same as the amount shown on the statement of financial position (look ahead to Table 2.4). The total equity amounts for 2013 ($555,000) and 2012 ($490,000) are also the same as the amounts shown on the statement of financial position.

STATEMENT OF FINANCIAL POSITION

Table 2.4 shows Eastman's statement of financial position (also called the balance sheet); it gives a "position statement" of the company as at December 31 for 2013 and 2012. The statement of financial position gives a picture of each major account at a particular moment; it does not show changes in accounts from the previous year's financial statement. The statement of financial position gives a report about the health of a business at the close of an accounting period. Each separate item reported on this statement is called an account. Every account has a name and a dollar amount, which is the balance reported at the end of the accounting period. We'll begin by discussing the meaning and significance of the major statement of financial position classification of accounts.

Table 2.4 **The Statement of Financial Position**

Eastman Technologies Inc.
Statements of Financial Position
As at December 31
(in $)

	2013	2012
Assets		
Non-current assets		
Property, plant, and equipment	1,340,000	1,050,000
Accumulated depreciation	(140,000)	(100,000)
Total non-current assets	1,200,000	950,000
Current assets		
Inventories	218,000	185,000
Trade receivables	300,000	280,000
Prepaid expenses	60,000	55,000
Cash and cash equivalents	22,000	18,000
Total current assets	600,000	538,000
Total assets	1,800,000	1,488,000
Equity and liabilities		
Equity		
Share capital	300,000	285,000
Contributed surplus	—	—
Retained earnings	255,000	205,000
Total other comprehensive income/(loss)	—	—
Total equity	555,000	490,000

(continued)

Table 2.4 **The Statement of Financial Position (continued)**

	2013	2012
Non-current liabilities		
Long-term borrowings	800,000	600,000
Current liabilities		
Trade and other payables	195,000	175,000
Short-term borrowings	150,000	135,000
Accrued expenses	20,000	18,000
Taxes payable	80,000	70,000
Total current liabilities	445,000	398,000
Total liabilities	1,245,000	998,000
Total equity and liabilities	1,800,000	1,488,000

The statement of financial position is made up of assets, equity (also known as net worth), and liabilities. As shown on Eastman's statement of financial position, the total of all assets for each year equals the total for all equity and liabilities. Usually, the statement of financial position's assets, equity, and liability accounts are grouped under several sub-accounts, namely, non-current assets, investments, intangible assets, share capital, retained earnings, non-current liabilities, and current liabilities.

Assets

Assets
Resources that a business owns to produce goods and services (e.g., buildings, equipment, trade receivables, inventories).

Assets are the physical (or tangible) items or rights (intangible) owned by a business. Assets have a monetary value and usually appear under two headings: non-current assets and current assets. Some businesses with other assets, such as investments and intangible assets, will show them separately.

NON-CURRENT ASSETS

Businesses have two types of non-current assets: property, plant, and equipment (previously called *capital assets* or *fixed assets*); and intangible assets. Note that the term *capital assets* will be used interchangeably with the term *property, plant, and equipment* throughout this text.

Property, plant, and equipment
The types of assets that are considered permanent and are used over an extended time, that is, many years (previously called capital assets or fixed assets).

Property, plant, and equipment are considered permanent and to be used over time (usually many years). The word "used" is important because it characterizes the major difference between non-current assets and current assets. Non-current assets have either a limited lifespan (buildings, equipment, machinery) or an unlimited one (land). They are usually listed on the statement of financial position at the price they were purchased for, at "book value" (which is historical cost less accumulated depreciation, the sum of all annual depreciation since the purchase of the non-current assets). However, a company may experience significant changes in the value of some assets and will consequently "write up," or increase, their value. In other instances, the company will "write down" an asset (decrease its value). These adjustments are shown in the statement of comprehensive income. For example, a write-up would take place when the value of a piece of land appreciated significantly; a write-down would be done when a non-current asset suddenly became obsolete, that is, not useful to the company.

Non-current assets (other than land) have a finite lifespan and wear out. As discussed earlier, because of this, a company will depreciate the asset each year. For example, if a building with an original cost of $2,000,000 has a 20-year lifespan, $100,000 will be allocated as an expense in each of those years. Although this $100,000 is not a cash outlay, it is an expense. If the building has been used for four years, the statement of financial position will show an accumulated depreciation of $400,000 deducted from the original or price of the building. The difference between non-current assets (at cost) and the accumulated depreciation is called *net non-current assets*, or *book value*.

Intangible assets
Assets that cannot be seen, touched, or physically measured and are included in the non-current asset section of the statement of financial position.

The second category of non-current assets is **intangible assets**, that is, those assets that cannot be seen, touched, or physically measured. Intangible assets have two primary forms. First are the legal intangibles, also known as intellectual property, such as trade secrets, customer lists, copyrights, patents, trademarks, and goodwill. These types of assets generate legal property rights defensible in a court of law. Second are the competitive intangibles, such as knowledge activities. Human capital (workers) is the primary competitive intangible.

Capital cost allowance (CCA)
A tax deduction that Canadian tax laws allow a business to claim for the loss in value of non-current assets through wear and tear or obsolescence.

As you've learned, depreciation is a usage rate businesses use when calculating profit. **Capital cost allowance (CCA)**, which we touched on earlier, is a deduction established by Canada Revenue Agency and used by all businesses for different categories of assets when calculating income tax expense. The income tax rules stipulate that all businesses must use these rates to calculate their income tax expense, even though the same asset may become obsolete after five years in one business but last ten years in another business. Businesses may deduct CCA on non-current assets.

We noted earlier that CCA allows businesses to recover, over some period, the original amount invested without paying tax on the depreciated portion of the investments. Regardless of the depreciation rate or method businesses use, Canada Revenue Agency establishes a set of percentages for more than 30 different asset categories. Maximum CCA rates, ranging from 4% to 100% per year, are set for each class. For example, the CCA rate for general machinery, which falls in class 8, has a maximum rate of 20%. Buildings that fall in class 1 have a maximum CCA rate of 4%. These rates are applied against declining asset balances in each class, similar to the sum-of-the-years'-digits method. (CCA never brings down the value of the asset to zero.) The CCA for each year is the maximum rate allowed (e.g., 50%) multiplied by the beginning-of-the-year balance.

Using the $100,000 example from above and assuming no disposal of the asset in year five, the CCA at a rate of 50% is calculated as follows:

Year	Value at the Beginning of the Year	CCA Rate	CCA	Value at End of Year
1	$100,000	50% ÷ 2*	$25,000	$75,000
2	75,000	50%	37,500	37,500
3	37,500	50%	18,750	18,750
4	18,750	50%	9,375	9,375
5	9,375	50%	4,687	4,688

*Income tax regulations allow only half of the CCA rate for the first year.

Problem-Solving Example 2.3

Depreciation and Capital Cost Allowance

Everest Inc. purchased a truck for $40,000. The rate of depreciation (straight-line) and CCA for this asset are 20% and 40%, respectively. Calculate the amount of depreciation and CCA for this truck for the first two years and the ending balances.

Solution

Years	Beginning Balance	Depreciation @ 20%	Ending Balance	Beginning Balance	CCA @ 40%	Ending Balance
1	$40,000	$8,000	$32,000	$40,000	$8,000	$32,000
2	32,000	8,000	24,000	32,000	12,800	19,200

Self-Test Exercise 2.3

Depreciation and Capital Cost Allowance

On its statement of financial position, CompuTech shows equipment purchased for $125,000 and a vehicle purchased for $35,000. The rate of depreciation (straight-line) and CCA for these non-current assets are as follows:

	Straight-line depreciation	Capital cost allowance
1. Equipment	25%	40%
2. Vehicle	20%	30%

Question

For the first five years of operation, calculate the amount of depreciation and CCA for the non-current assets.

Answers to the Self-Test Exercises can be found at www.bergeron7e.nelson.com.

Miscellaneous assets
Assets, such as bonds and shares, purchased from other businesses.

Miscellaneous assets are similar to marketable securities, except that they are invested for a longer period. They include such items as cash surrender value of life insurance; amounts due from directors, officers, and employees of the company; bonds and shares purchased from other companies; and investments or advances made to subsidiary and affiliated companies.

Intangible assets. As mentioned earlier, intangible assets are assets that cannot be touched, weighed, or measured. They represent values of trademarks, goodwill, franchises, and patents. These items are not tangible but do have value to the owners of a business. Goodwill, for example, arises when a firm purchases another firm for a price that is higher than the value of the tangible assets. This difference represents the potential earning power resulting from its name or reputation. Also, company trademarks, such as Coca-Cola, McDonald's arch, Apple, and Microsoft, are worth millions of dollars. Usually, intangible assets have little value if a business goes bankrupt.

CURRENT ASSETS

Current assets
Assets, such as inventories and trade receivables, expected to be turned into cash, usually in one year or less.

Current assets are cash or other assets expected to be turned into cash, usually in one year or less, that is, during the operating cycle. Current assets include inventories, trade receivables, prepaid expenses, notes receivables, and cash and cash equivalents.

Inventory
The monetary value a company places on the material it has purchased or goods it has manufactured.

The **inventory** account shows the monetary value a company places on the material it has purchased or goods it has manufactured. Usually, a manufacturer has three types of accounts under inventories:

- *Raw materials*, which are the goods purchased from suppliers to be used for manufacturing.
- *Work-in-process*, which includes the goods or materials in various stages of production, somewhere between raw materials and finished goods.
- *Finished goods*, which are the products ready for sale.

Because inventories are not a source of profit, management tries to keep them at low levels or to move them quickly. Inventories are recorded at cost, not at the price at which the firm hopes to sell them.

Trade receivables
Money owed to the company by its customers for the purchase of goods or services.

Trade receivables are money owed to the company by customers who have purchased goods or services, which can be collected within a reasonable time (usually between 30 and 90 days). To reduce the cash tied up in this account, some businesses have credit policies and collection procedures that minimize the time it takes to turn receivables into cash. Of course, some customers won't pay their bills, so an account called *allowance for doubtful accounts* is created. It holds the amount estimated by management of how much is not expected to be collected. Because this account is a negative asset account, it will be deducted from the regular trade receivables. Usually, allowance for doubtful accounts is not shown separately on the statement of financial position as it is assumed that a reasonable amount has been set. This is how the calculation is done:

Trade receivables before allowance for doubtful accounts	$ 330,000
Allowance for doubtful accounts	(30,000)
Trade receivables	$ 300,000

Prepaid expenses Payments made for services that have not yet been received.

Prepaid expenses are payments made and recorded for services that have not yet been received. Rent, insurance, office supplies, or property taxes are examples. For example, Eastman may pay $8,000 for its insurance premium on June 30. If this is a one-year insurance policy and Eastman's accounting cycle closes on December 31, half of the premium, $4,000, will be recorded as a prepaid expense. This amount will be charged to the next year's accounting period. If Eastman decides to cancel its policy on December 31, the insurance company will owe Eastman $4,000, which is why such items are considered assets. Another example is office and computer supplies bought in bulk and then gradually used up over several months. If annual property taxes are paid at the start of the taxation year, these amounts should be allocated over all the months covered by the property taxes.

Notes receivable are written promises that have a maturity date. A note receivable may be the result of the settlement of an account by a customer that does not have the cash to pay according to the company's credit terms.

Cash and cash equivalents include all funds, such as bills, coins, and cheques, that are on hand or readily available from the bank account. Some cash is usually kept on hand to pay current bills and to take advantage of specific opportunities, such as cash discounts. Cash equivalents include *marketable securities*, such as term deposits or shares that can be readily converted into cash (in less than one year). Because the company will obtain a greater return on these types of assets than on its bank account, the company will buy securities.

Equity

Equity Funds provided by shareholders, that is, share capital, plus contributed surplus, retained earnings, and total other comprehensive income/(loss).

Equity is an important source of funds for financing a business. This money comes from the owners or shareholders in the form of a capital account (if it is a sole proprietorship), partners' account (if it is a partnership), or share capital (if it is a corporation). The money paid by shareholders is called *share capital*. It also includes contributed surplus, retained earnings, and total other comprehensive income/(loss).

Share capital Amount of money that is put into the business by the shareholders.

Share capital is the money put into the business by the shareholders. These could be common shares (certificates of ownership in a company) or preferred shares (shares that rank ahead of common shares in their claims on dividends and in their claim on assets in the event of liquidation).

Contributed surplus, also called *paid-in capital* (*PIC*), is the difference between a share's value and what shareholders paid.

Retained earnings The profit generated by the business that the owners have not received in dividends.

Retained earnings are the profit generated by the business that the owners have not received as dividends. This is the profit for each year that has been accumulated and reinvested into the business to finance the purchase of non-current or current assets or to repay the principal on the debt. If a company makes a profit during the year and pays no dividends, the amount in the retained earnings account shown on the current year's statement of financial position is greater than the amount shown on the previous year's statement. Conversely, if the company incurs a loss, the retained earnings account drops.

As discussed earlier, *total other comprehensive income/(loss)* comprises such items as revaluation of property, plant, and equipment, and the gains and losses on valuing assets available for sale.

Liabilities
The debts of a business.

Liabilities

Liabilities are the debts of a business. They are the credit that people or other businesses (other than the shareholders) have extended to a business to help it buy assets. Liabilities are divided into two distinct groups: non-current liabilities and current liabilities.

NON-CURRENT LIABILITIES

Non-current liabilities
Debts that are not due for at least one year.

Non-current liabilities are accounts that are not due for at least one year. They include such items as mortgages, contracts, or long-term notes and loans, such as bonds. These items are often used to finance the purchase of non-current assets. A mortgage is a long-term borrowing for which a company has pledged non-current assets (such as land and buildings) as collateral. This assures lenders that an asset of equal or greater value will be made available to them if the company ceases to operate or if it is sold or liquidated. A long-term note is similar to notes payable (current liabilities) except that this item is to be repaid beyond a one-year period.

Future income taxes payable
Future tax liability resulting from the difference between depreciation and CCA.

Future income taxes payable. Because companies use depreciation rates that are different from the CCA rate for calculating income tax expense, in many instances businesses pay less tax than they otherwise would, particularly during the first several years of the asset's use. This future tax liability is a result of a temporary difference between the book (accounting) value of assets and liabilities and their tax value. These are referred to as **future income taxes payable**, previously called deferred taxes.

Using the $100,000 example, the five-year straight-line depreciation rate (20%), and the 50% CCA rate, the future income taxes payable would be calculated as follows:

Years	CCA @ 50%	Internal Depreciation @ 20%	Difference between CCA and Depreciation	Annual Future Taxes Payable (tax rate @ 50%)	Cumulative Future Taxes Payable
1	$25,000	$20,000	$ 5,000	$2,500	– $ 2,500
2	$37,500	$20,000	$17,500	$8,750	– $11,250
3	$18,750	$20,000	– $ 1,250	– $ 625	– $10,625
4	$ 9,375	$20,000	– $10,625	– $5,312	– $ 5,313
5	$ 4,687	$20,000	– $15,313	– $7,656	$ 2,343

Using the above depreciation and CCA rates, let's now produce the first year's statement of income (Table 2.5). Depreciation is an expense, while CCA is used to calculate the company's income tax expense. The first column is used to calculate the company's income tax expense by using CCA. Column 3 shows an internal company's document called the "profit and loss statement" for the year that uses the company's five-year depreciation rate (or 20%). Column 2 shows the company's statement of income, that is, the statement that is included in the annual report. The depreciation expense, the income tax expense paid in that year, and the amount of future income taxes payable owed to the government all appear in the statement.

Table 2.5 **The Statement of Income and the Profit and Loss Statement (in $)**

	1 Accountant's Worksheet	2 Statement of Income	3 P & L Statement
Revenue	300,000	300,000	300,000
Cost of sales	(150,000)	(150,000)	(150,000)
Gross profit	150,000	150,000	150,000
Operating costs	(50,000)	(50,000)	(50,000)
CCA/depreciation	(25,000)	(20,000) ←	(20,000)
Total costs	(75,000)	(70,000)	(70,000)
Profit before taxes	75,000	80,000	80,000
Income tax expense			
- Current (50%)	(37,500) →	(37,500)	(40,000)
- Future income tax payable	(2,500) →	(2,500)	—
	(40,000)	(40,000)	(40,000)
Profit for the year	35,000	40,000	40,000

The profits for the year in columns 2 and 3 are the same ($40,000); the only difference between the two columns is the timing of payment of the taxes. The company paid $2,500 less in taxes because of a higher CCA rate. Therefore, the company owes this amount to the government in the form of future income taxes payable. It is like an interest-free loan.

Problem-Solving Example 2.4

Future Income Taxes Payable

Use the information in Problem-Solving Example 2.3 to calculate Everest Inc.'s future income taxes payable. Assume that the company's income tax rate is 25%.

Solution

The difference in the cumulative future taxes payable at the end of two years is $1,200.

Years	CCA	Internal Depreciation	Difference between CCA and Depreciation	Annual Future Taxes Payable (@25% tax rate)	Cumulative Future Taxes Payable
1	$ 8,000	$ 8,000	—	—	—
2	12,800	8,000	4,800	$1,200	$1,200

Self-Test Exercise 2.4

Future Income Taxes Payable

Use the information in Self-Test Exercises 2.2 and 2.3 to calculate CompuTech's

1. Future income taxes payable during the first five years.
2. Statement of income using year two of the CCA and depreciation rates.

CURRENT LIABILITIES

Current liabilities
Debts that a business must pay within one year (i.e., trade and other payables).

Current liabilities are what a business has to pay its creditors, monies that are owed within a short time (less than one year). Normally, such debts are used to finance the current assets. Current liabilities include trade and other payables, short-term borrowings, the current portion of long-term debt, accrued expenses, and current income taxes payable.

Trade and other payables
Money owed to suppliers of goods or services that were purchased on credit.

Trade and other payables are usually the most current debts of a business. This is the money owed to suppliers of goods or services that were purchased on credit.

Notes payable are written promises to repay money within a short period (usually less than one year). However, notes payable can also be recorded as a non-current liability, depending on their term.

Current income taxes payable are taxes to be paid to the government within the current operating year.

Current portion of long-term debt is the amount of long-term borrowings that the company will have to pay within the current operating year (e.g., mortgage).

Accrued liability
Represents what a company owes for services it has received and not yet paid or an expense that has been incurred but not recorded.

Accrued liability accounts are what a company owes for services received but not yet paid or an expense that has been incurred but not recorded. These liabilities are the opposite of prepaid expenses. Normally, a business records expenses as soon as the invoices are received, even though it doesn't pay the invoice until several weeks later. However, certain unrecorded expenses must be identified when a business closes its books. For instance, if employees are paid every second week and the company closes its books on December 31, it may have to record that it owes (as a liability) its employees salaries for the unpaid period up to December 31. The following are typical examples of accrued liabilities:

- Accumulated vacation and sick leave pay
- Interest on debt that has not come due by year end
- Property taxes for the year that have not been paid yet
- Warranty and guarantee work that will be done during the following year on products already sold

Problem-Solving Example 2.5

Statement of Financial Position

Use the following accounts to prepare the statement of financial position: trade receivables ($70,000), inventories ($100,000), property, plant, and equipment ($350,000), accumulated depreciation ($100,000), share capital ($70,000), retained earnings ($30,000), non-current liabilities ($250,000), trade and other payables ($50,000), and short-term borrowings ($20,000).

Solution

Total assets are $420,000, and total equity and liabilities, $420,000.

Assets		
Non-current assets		
Property, plant, and equipment	$350,000	
Accumulated depreciation	(100,000)	
Total non-current assets		$250,000
Current assets		
Inventories	100,000	
Trade receivables	70,000	
Total current assets		170,000
Total assets		$420,000
Equity and liabilities		
Equity		
Share capital	$70,000	
Retained earnings	30,000	
Total equity		$100,000
Non-current liabilities		250,000
Current liabilities		
Trade and other payables	50,000	
Short-terms borrowings	20,000	
Total current liabilities		70,000
Total liabilities		320,000
Total equity and liabilities		$420,000

Self-Test Exercise 2.5

Statement of Financial Position

Use the following accounts to prepare CompuTech's statement of financial position as at December 31, 2013.

Trade receivables	$35,000
Cash and cash equivalents	15,000

(continued)

Self-Test Exercise 2.5 (continued)

Short-term borrowings	30,000
Share capital	100,000
Non-current liabilities	60,000
Property, plant, and equipment	170,000
Prepaid expenses	5,000
Current portion of long-term borrowings	5,000
Retained earnings	25,000
Accumulated depreciation/amortization	38,000
Trade and other payables	17,000
Inventories	50,000

Answers to the Self-Test Exercises can be found at www.bergeron7e.nelson.com.

ANNUAL REPORTS

The main source of financial data about publicly traded companies is included in their annual report. This report is the main way management communicates with a company's shareholders. An **annual report** contains two statements. First is a letter from the president explaining management's opinion of the company's operating results during the past year and its prospects (development and strategies) for the future. Second are the four financial statements: the statement of income and the statement of comprehensive income, the statement of changes in equity, the statement of financial position, and the statement of cash flows. Both the letter and the statements provide an overview of the company's operating activities and financial performance. Annual reports are sent to the shareholders, and most companies publish them on their websites. Each year, the CEOs of publicly owned corporations present their annual report to their shareholders, who can then ask questions of senior managers.

Annual report
A report issued annually by corporations to their shareholders that contains the financial statements and management's opinion of the company's past year's operations and prospects for the future.

Canadian federal corporate law requires every federally incorporated limited company to appoint an auditor to represent shareholders and report to them annually on the company's financial statements. In Canada, the **auditor's report** includes the following:

Auditor's report
A report prepared by an independent accounting firm that is presented to a company's shareholders.

1. The auditor's opinion on the financial statements.
2. A statement that generally accepted accounting principles have been used to prepare the financial statements, on a basis consistent with that of the preceding year.
3. A description of the audit itself. The auditor's report usually comments on the auditing procedures and any tests made to support the accounting records and shows that they were made in accordance with generally accepted auditing standards.

A typical annual report contains the following sections: financial highlights, reports to the shareholders (one from the CEO and the other from the auditors), review of operations, financial statements, management's discussion and analysis, footnotes and supplementary information, a summary of significant accounting policies, five-year summary of financial and statistical data, and the names of the board of directors and corporate officers.

Footnotes are an integral part of an annual report. Writing the footnotes is necessary but difficult as the management has to explain sometimes complex issues in a small space. Footnotes disclose relevant information that shareholders need to make informed decisions and protect their interests. The two types of footnotes disclose

- The main accounting methods used by the business.
- Information that cannot be included in the main body of the financial statements (e.g., details regarding share ownership, long-term operating leases, maturity dates, interest rates, collateral, or other security provisions, lawsuits, and employees' retirement and pension plans).

Analysis

4 Understand the meaning of analysis in financial management.

Once the financial statements have been prepared, the information can be analyzed and interpreted. Many techniques exist for analyzing financial statements. What is important is ensuring that the right type of information has been gathered and that it is presented in a way that will help managers, lenders, and shareholders to analyze it in a meaningful way.

We'll look at some typical analytical techniques in Chapters 3 and 4:

- *Statement of cash flows*, which shows the changes between two consecutive statements of financial position, that is, where the funds came from (inflows of cash) and where they went (outflows of cash)
- *Horizontal analysis*, which shows the company's historical growth pattern regarding its financial structure and profitability
- *Vertical analysis*, which helps financial analysts compare different numbers on a statement of income and a statement of financial position (through ratios) in a more meaningful way
- *Ratio analysis*, which expresses different sets of numbers contained in financial statements as ratios: liquidity ratios, debt-coverage ratios, asset-management ratios, and profitability ratios
- *Break-even analysis*, which shows the relationship between revenues, expenses (fixed and variable), and profits
- *Operational analysis*, which uses information contained in financial statements and management information reports to evaluate the efficiency, effectiveness, and productivity of a business

Decision Making

5 Discuss the importance of decision making in financial management.

This last activity of financial management gets to the heart of the management process—decision making. Bookkeeping, accounting, and analysis are the key steps in financial management because they provide important information to management that will assist in making sensible decisions. We'll review some decision-making techniques in later chapters. The information contained in financial statements and the analysis of this data provides answers to the following questions:

- How much money should we borrow?
- Should we borrow on a short-term or a long-term basis?
- How much inventory should be kept on hand?
- Should we buy or lease an asset?
- Should we invest in this project? Expand this operation? Modernize our plant?
- How much credit should we extend?
- How quickly should our company grow?
- What size of capital commitments should our company tackle this year? Next year?
- What level of risk does this project have?
- How should we administer our current assets and current liabilities?
- What is the optimal level of capital structure?
- What price should we set for our products?
- How can we compare the financial viability of different projects coming from various divisions, and how can we rate them?

Business decisions affect a company's financial statements. A company that decides to invest in a major undertaking, such as building a new manufacturing facility, launching a new product line, or buying another business, would see a change in just about every account on its financial statements (e.g., revenue, cost of sales, finance costs, non-current assets, current assets, equity, non-current liabilities, and current liabilities). In the News 2.3 gives an example of such a critical decision.

In The News 2.3

IMPACT OF A STRATEGIC DECISION ON FINANCIAL STATEMENTS

It sometimes takes hundreds of tactical and operational decisions to stop a company from going bankrupt; but it takes only one bold strategic decision to help make it happen.

This is what Kodak had to do in 2011 when it sought bankruptcy protection from creditors for a $6.7 billion debt load. Kodak was founded more than 130 years ago and well known for its iconic cameras, such as the Brownie and the Instamatic, but these products became obsolete when digital cameras were introduced in the marketplace, and now, more and more digital pictures are being taken by using smartphones and cellphones.

(continued)

In The News 2.3 (continued)

Through the 1990s, Kodak invested $4 billion developing the photo technology inside most of today's cellphones and digital devices and waited until 2001 to bring its own digital cameras to the consumer market. But it was too late to face strong competitors, such as Sony and Canon. Kodak is now getting out of the digital camera line to help cut losses by about $100 million a year as it struggles to stay out of bankruptcy.

Source: "Kodak to Stop Making Cameras, Digital Frames." *Canadian Business*. Retrieved from http://www.canadianbusiness.com/article/70362--kodak-to-stop-making-cameras-digital-frames, accessed February 7, 2012. To learn more about the history of Kodak, visit www.kodak.com.

Not-for-Profit (NFP) Organizations

6 Analyze the contents and structure of the financial statements prepared for NFP organizations.

The not-for-profit (NFP) industry in Canada is huge. Universities, religious institutions, research centres, museums, hospitals, and social service agencies, such as public charities help communities and people in need. These types of organizations manage a variety of programs, ranging from infant daycare programs to antipoverty programs. Most NFPs operate like a business, with a system that is reinforced by NFP accounting rules. People responsible for managing these programs are held accountable for realizing the organization's mission and objectives.

Corporations are formed to operate these programs. Just as in the private sector, NFP organizations are legal entities distinct from the individuals who have created them. These corporations have their own set of responsibilities, powers, and liabilities.

Not-for-profit organizations Organizations that operate exclusively for social, educational, professional, religious, health, charitable, or any other NFP purpose.

The Canadian Institute of Chartered Accountants (CICA) defines **not-for-profit organizations** as "entities, normally without transferable ownership interests, organized and operated exclusively for social, educational, professional, religious, health, charitable or any other not-for-profit purpose. A not-for-profit organization's members, contributors and other resource providers do not, in such capacity, receive any financial return directly from the organization."[1] Section 4400 of the *CICA Handbook* describes how accounting should be practised by NFP organizations.

Just like the for-profit organizations, NFP organizations have to prepare financial statements that normally include the following:

- Statement of financial position
- Statement of operations
- Statement of changes in net assets
- Statement of cash flows

The sections that follow give a brief description of the structure and contents of the first three financial statements for a fictitious NFP organization called Ontario Foundation for Community Care. The statement of cash flows for NFP organizations will be explained in Chapter 3.

[1] The Canadian Institute of Chartered Accountants, "Accounting Recommendations," *CICA Handbook*, July 2003, p. 4012.

STATEMENT OF FINANCIAL POSITION

The statement of financial position (also known as the balance sheet) shows on one side the resources needed by an organization to function properly, called *assets*, and on the other side, the claims of outsiders against those resources, known as *liabilities* and *net assets*. The main purpose of this statement is to show the NFP organization's economic resources (assets), its financial obligations (liabilities), and its net assets as of a specific date. The accounting equation for an NFP organization and the Ontario Foundation for Community Care for 2013 are as follows:

Assets	=	Net assets	+	Liabilities
$410,000	=	$200,000	+	$210,000

In the case of for-profit organizations, the total amount of assets equals equity plus liabilities. As shown above, for NFP organizations, equity is called *net assets*, fund balances, or accumulated surplus or deficit. The statement of financial position for the Ontario Foundation for Community Care is as follows:

Ontario Foundation for Community Care
Statement of Financial Position
As at December 31
(in $)

	2013	2012
Assets		
Non-current assets		
Buildings and equipment (net)	300,000	222,000
Investments	40,000	13,000
Total non-current assets	340,000	235,000
Current assets		
Trade receivables	30,000	15,000
Grants receivable	10,000	5,000
Cash and term deposits	30,000	25,000
Total current assets	70,000	45,000
Total assets	410,000	280,000
Net assets and liabilities		
Net assets		
Net assets invested in capital assets	140,000	100,000
Net assets restricted for endowment	60,000	20,000
Total net assets	200,000	120,000
Liabilities		
Long-term borrowings	150,000	115,000
Current liabilities		
Trade and other payables	40,000	30,000
Accrued liabilities	10,000	8,000
Current mortgage payable	10,000	7,000
Total current liabilities	60,000	45,000
Total liabilities	210,000	160,000
Total net assets and liabilities	410,000	280,000

The first section of the asset part of the statement of financial position is called non-current assets and includes two subsections: buildings and equipment, and investments. *Non-current assets* are investments in land, buildings, and equipment, and these items are normally shown at the cost of buying them less the appropriate depreciation. These *investments* are recorded in the books at the lower of cost and market value. Non-current asset purchases are made for either investment purposes or operational purposes. The second section is called current assets, and it includes trade receivables, grants receivable, and cash and term deposits. Just like the for-profit business's statement of financial position, *trade receivables* are money owed to the NFP organization for goods and services by its users; *grants receivable* are money pledged by individuals, foundations, corporations, and government agencies that will be received during the current operating year; and *cash and term deposits* are money readily available to the organization. As shown, the total assets for 2013 were $410,000.

The first section of the net assets and liabilities side of the statement is called net assets. *Net assets* are the amounts left after deducting all debts used to purchase these assets. It shows the net resources the organization can use to function properly and provide its services efficiently and effectively. The $200,000 amount in net assets includes the following:

- The net book value invested in capital assets of $140,000, which is made up of non-current assets ($300,000) less the sum of the mortgage payable ($160,000)—current in the amount of $10,000 and long-term borrowings of $150,000.
- Net book assets from endowments (long-term donations) of $60,000. An *endowment contribution* is a contribution that will be used over many years that is given with conditions on its use. These endowment funds are usually held in securities controlled by a professional money manager who has been given specific instructions from the board of directors of the NFP organization.

On the liability section of the statement, we have long-term borrowings, which is the money loaned to the NFP organization to buy or renovate its building or equipment. This section may also include *deferred contributions* in the form of restricted contributions and unrestricted contributions related to expenses of future periods. A *contribution* is a gift made to an NFP organization. Such gifts may be cash, other assets, or the cancellation of a debt. Government funding is considered a contribution. A *restricted contribution* is a gift that has stipulations (rules for use) imposed by the donor that specify the purpose of the gift (e.g., purchase of a specific asset or the development of a specific program). An *unrestricted contribution* has no specific rules for its use. The lower portion of the statement of financial position has the three current liabilities, *trade and other payables*, *accrued liabilities*, and *current mortgage payable*, which are amounts the NFP organization has to pay within the current operating year. These are the most immediate claims against assets, amounting to $60,000. The total liabilities for the Ontario Foundation for Community Care is $210,000, and the total net assets and liabilities for 2013 are $410,000.

STATEMENT OF OPERATIONS

The statement of operations shows the revenues earned and expenses incurred by the NFP organization. The purpose of this statement is to show how much surplus (or deficit) was generated during an operating year. It also shows the level of efficiencies of the organization. The statement of operations lists the sources of revenues (grants, contributions, investment income, and other income from services provided by the organization) for the Ontario Foundation for Community Care. After deducting the total expenses from revenue, the organization had a $40,000 surplus, also called excess of revenues over expenses.

Ontario Foundation for Community Care
Statement of Operations
For the year ended December 31, 2013
(in $)

Revenues		
Contributions, gifts, grants	25,000	
Direct public support	115,000	
Investment income	10,000	
Program service revenue (e.g., seminars)	200,000	
Government grants (federal)	50,000	
Government grants (provincial)	40,000	
Total		440,000
Expenses		
Services (salaries, benefits, materials)	(320,000)	
Depreciation of non-current assets	(20,000)	
Interest on mortgage	(10,000)	
Fundraising activities	(50,000)	
Total		(400,000)
Excess of revenues over expenses		40,000

STATEMENT OF CHANGES IN NET ASSSETS

The statement of changes in net assets shows the changes in fund balances and gives information about the net resources the NFP has to provide its services (for-profit businesses use the statement of retained earnings). This statement on the following page shows the accumulation of the organization's net assets for endowments and capital assets.

Ontario Foundation for Community Care
Statement of Changes in Net Assets
For the year ended December 31, 2013
(in $)

Net assets	
Balance, beginning of year	120,000
Excess of revenues over expenses	40,000
Endowment contributions	40,000
Balance, end of year	200,000

Chapter Summary

1 Explain the activities related to bookkeeping.

Bookkeeping involves collecting, classifying, and reporting the business transactions that take place each day in all departments. Bookkeeping begins with the preparation of a chart of accounts. Each time a business transaction takes place, at least two accounts are affected (debit and credit); this is called double-entry bookkeeping. The bookkeeping and accounting process includes five steps: (1) a business transaction, (2) preparation of documents and recording and posting transactions in (3) journals and (4) ledgers, and (5) the preparation of the trial balance. In its simplest form, the financial picture of a business can be expressed by the following formula:

Assets = Equity + Liabilities

2 Describe the accounting function and outline the four financial statements.

The main purpose of accounting is to prepare the financial statements, namely, the statement of income and the statement of comprehensive income, the statement of changes in equity, the statement of financial position, and the statement of cash flows.

3 Examine the contents and the structure of the statement of income and the statement of comprehensive income, the statement of changes in equity, and the statement of financial position.

Four key financial statements were reviewed. The *statement of income* presents the operating results, that is, revenues, expenses, and profit for a given period. The *statement of comprehensive income* shows items of income and expense that are not recognized in the statement of income. The *statement of changes in equity* represents the interest of the business's shareholders and shows the cumulative net results in equity for share capital, contributed surplus, retained earnings, and accumulated other comprehensive income/(loss).

The *statement of financial position*, which describes a company's financial position at a given moment, contains a list of the assets (what a company owns), equity (owners who have a claim on the assets), and liabilities (creditors who have a claim on the assets). Canadian federal corporate law requires that every federally incorporated limited company appoint an auditor to represent shareholders and report to them annually on the company's financial statements. The more important areas that auditors examine include corporate income tax rates, small-business deductions, business expenses and deductions, business losses, and CCA. *Depreciation* is an accounting entry allocating the cost of a non-current asset against the revenue it helps create over the asset's estimated lifespan. There are several ways of calculating depreciation, and we discussed two: the straight-line method and the sum-of-the-years'-digits (the accelerated) method. *Capital cost allowance* is the rate of depreciation set by Canada Revenue Agency and is used by all businesses for calculating their income taxes. Because companies use depreciation rates that are different from the CCA rate to calculate income taxes, in many instances businesses pay less tax than they otherwise would, particularly during the first several years of the asset use. This means that the company owes taxes (liability) to the government. These are called future income taxes payable.

4 Understand the meaning of analysis in financial management.

Once the financial statements have been prepared, the information can be analyzed and interpreted. Some of the more popular analytical tools include analyzing the statement of cash flows, horizontal and vertical analysis, ratio analysis, and break-even analysis.

5 Discuss the importance of decision making in financial management.

Decision making is the process of using information to improve the financial performance of a business. Some of the more important decisions made by managers include the following: How much money should we borrow? Should we buy or lease? Should we invest in this project? What level of risk does this project present?

6 Analyze the contents and structure of the financial statements prepared for NFP organizations.

NFP organizations operate exclusively for social, educational, professional, religious, health, charitable, or any other NFP purpose. For their annual reports, these organizations must also prepare financial statements: the statement of financial position, the statement of operations, the statement of changes in net assets, and the statement of cash flows.

Key Terms

Accounting p. 45
Accounting equation p. 39
Accrual method p. 47
Accrued liability p. 65
Administrative expenses p. 50
Annual report p. 67
Assets p. 58
Auditor's report p. 67
Bookkeeping p. 39
Bookkeeping and accounting cycle p. 40
Capital cost allowance (CCA) p. 59
Cash method p. 47
Chart of accounts p. 39
Cost of sales p. 50
Credit p. 40

Current assets p. 61
Current liabilities p. 65
Debit p. 40
Depreciation p. 51
Distribution costs p. 50
Double-entry bookkeeping p. 39
Equity p. 62
Financial statements p. 44
Future income taxes payable p. 63
Income tax p. 53
Income tax expense p. 53
Intangible assets p. 59
Inventory p. 61
Journalizing p. 41
Journals (books of original entry) p. 41
Ledger (books of final entry) p. 41
Liabilities p. 63
Miscellaneous assets p. 60
Non-current liabilities p. 63
Not-for-profit organizations p. 70
Operating section p. 49
Other income p. 50
Owners' section p. 53
Posting p. 41
Prepaid expenses p. 62
Property, plant, and equipment p. 58
Retained earnings p. 62
Revenue p. 50
Share capital p. 62
Statement of cash flows p. 46
Statement of changes in equity p. 46
Statement of comprehensive income p. 46
Statement of financial position p. 46
Statement of income p. 46
Total comprehensive income/(loss) for the year p. 46
Trade and other payables p. 65
Trade receivables p. 61
Trial balance p. 41

Review Questions

1 Explain the activities related to bookkeeping.

1. What activities are involved in bookkeeping?
2. Explain the accounting equation.
3. What are journals and ledgers?
4. What is the purpose of a trial balance?

2 Describe the accounting function and outline the four financial statements.

5. What are financial statements and what do they include?
6. Explain the different sections of the statement of income.
7. What does the statement of changes in equity show?
8. What is the connection between the retained earnings amount shown in the statement of changes in equity and the statement of financial position?

3 Examine the contents and the structure of the statement of income and the statement of comprehensive income, the statement of changes in equity, and the statement of financial position.

9. Is there a difference between the book value of accounts shown on the statement of financial position and market value? Explain.

10. What is the basic structure of the statement of financial position?
11. Differentiate between non-current assets and current assets.
12. What are the four sections included in the statement of cash flows?
13. What is the purpose of the auditor's report?
14. Why do you think auditors write the following statement in a company's annual report? "These consolidated financial statements are the responsibility of the company's management. Our responsibility is to express an opinion on these consolidated financial statements based on our audits."
15. Differentiate between cash accounting and accrual accounting.
16. What are future income taxes payable?
17. What is the difference between depreciation and capital cost allowance?

4 Understand the meaning of analysis in financial management.

18. What are some of the techniques used to analyze financial statements?

5 Discuss the importance of decision making in financial management.

19. What kind of decisions can be made when analyzing financial statements?

6 Analyze the contents and structure of the financial statements prepared for NFP organizations.

20. What is a not-for-profit organization?
21. Name the financial statements prepared by not-for-profit organizations.

Learning Exercises

1 Explain the activities related to bookkeeping.

EXERCISE 1: RECORDING TRANSACTIONS IN JOURNALS AND LEDGERS

Anthony Leung opens a retail store called The Bead Shop. During the first month of operation, Anthony makes the following accounting transactions:

1. Invests $100,000 in cash in the business
2. Buys $50,000 worth of equipment on credit he obtained from the bank
3. Buys $60,000 worth of goods from different suppliers, pays $30,000 in cash, and puts the rest on credit
4. Spends $5,000 in cash for advertising
5. Sells $20,000 worth of goods on credit
6. Pays $15,000 in cash for salaries
7. Pays $10,000 to the bank toward the loan
8. Pays $5,000 to a supplier

9. Pays $13,000 for some merchandise that he had purchased on credit
10. Pays a salary of $3,000

Questions

Prepare the following:

1. The journal entries
2. The ledgers
3. The trial balance

2 Describe the accounting function and give an outline of the four financial statements.

3 Examine the contents and the structure of the statement of income and the statement of comprehensive income, the statement of changes in equity, and the statement of financial position.

EXERCISE 2: PREPARING THE STATEMENT OF INCOME

At the end of December 31, 2012, Cougar Inc.'s accounts are as follows:

Office salaries	$30,000
Finance costs	3,000
Depreciation (administration)	2,000
Cost of sales	300,000
Income tax expense	35,000
Sales salaries	40,000
Interest income	6,000
Gross revenue	520,000
Advertising	10,000
Lease (administration)	3,000
Promotional expenses	2,000
Sales discounts	20,000
Travel expenses	3,000
Rental charges	5,000

Question

Prepare Cougar's statement of income for the year ended December 31, 2012.

EXERCISE 3: DEPRECIATION AND CAPITAL COST ALLOWANCE

On its statement of financial position, a company shows buildings purchased for $700,000, equipment purchased for $350,000, and machinery purchased for $170,000. The depreciation and capital cost allowance rates for these non-current assets are as follows:

	Capital Cost Allowance	Straight-Line Depreciation
1. Buildings	5%	7%
2. Equipment	20%	25%
3. Machinery	15%	30%

Question

For the first five years of operation, calculate the amount of depreciation and capital cost allowance for the non-current assets.

EXERCISE 4: FUTURE INCOME TAXES PAYABLE

ABC Inc.'s revenue and costs for the current year were the following:

Revenue	$500,000
Cost of sales	300,000
Gross profit	200,000
Operating expenses	100,000

The company's statement of financial position shows the gross value of non-current assets as $100,000. The company's straight-line depreciation rate for the asset is 15%, and the CCA rate is 30%. The company's income tax rate is 50%.

Questions

1. Calculate the company's future income taxes payable during the first five years.
2. Prepare the statement of income by using year two of the CCA and depreciation rates. Assume the same operating results as the current year.

EXERCISE 5: PREPARING THE STATEMENT OF FINANCIAL POSITION

At the end of December 31, 2012, Cougar Inc.'s accounts are as follows:

Accumulated depreciation	$100,000
Current income taxes payable	5,000
Long-term borrowings	25,000
Inventories	90,000
Trade receivables	60,000
Non-current assets (at cost)	300,000
Trade and other payables	40,000
Mortgage	130,000
Accrued expenses	10,000
Future income taxes payable	5,000
Share capital	100,000
Prepaid expenses	10,000
Intangible assets	20,000
Cash and cash equivalents	25,000
Retained earnings	80,000
Short-term borrowings	10,000

Question

Prepare Cougar Inc.'s statement of financial position as at December 31, 2012.

EXERCISE 6: PREPARING FINANCIAL STATEMENTS

An accountant employed by Zimmerman Electronics Inc. was reviewing the following balances shown in the company's ledgers for 2012:

Mortgage	$80,000
Prepaid insurance	2,000
Marketable securities	5,000
Sales returns	50,000

Cash and cash equivalents	5,000
Advertising	50,000
Trade receivables	15,000
Gross revenue	650,000
Trade and other payables	12,000
Buildings (net)	100,000
Cost of sales	300,000
Short-term notes payable	10,000
Retained earnings (December 31, 2011)	40,000
Finance costs	10,000
Land	25,000
Office salaries	70,000
Share capital	15,000
Lease	20,000
Insurance	10,000
Depreciation (Administration)	20,000
Income tax expense	10,000
Dividends paid	10,000
Interest income	15,000
Inventories	20,000
Sales salaries	100,000

Questions

1. Prepare the following financial statements:
   a. Statement of income
   b. Retained earnings (section of the statement of changes in equity)
   c. Statement of financial position
2. Calculate the company's cash flow for the year.

EXERCISE 7: PREPARING FINANCIAL STATEMENTS

Prepare the following four financial statements for Linden International Inc. for 2012:

1. Statement of income
2. Statement of comprehensive income
3. Statement of changes in equity
4. Statement of financial position

Income tax expense	$ 600,000
Decrease in property revaluation	35,000
Current assets	6,500,000
Cost of sales	7,500,000
Distribution costs	900,000
Common shares issued	895,000
Accumulated other comprehensive income/(loss) beginning of year	—
Finance costs	90,000
Stock-option compensation	40,000
Profit before taxes	1,750,000
Retained earnings (end of year)	5,000,000

Dividends paid	150,000
Other income	40,000
Gross profit	3,500,000
Share capital (end of year)	3,395,000
Contributed surplus (beginning of year)	60,000
Non-current liabilities	5,000,000
Change in currency translation (income)	40,000
Retained earnings (beginning of year)	4,000,000
Administrative expenses	800,000
Total liabilities	8,000,000
Total assets	16,500,000

6 Analyze the contents and structure of the financial statements prepared for NFP organizations.

EXERCISE 8: PREPARING FINANCIAL STATEMENTS FOR AN NFP ORGANIZATION

Prepare the following two financial statements for Housing Association Inc. for 2012.

1. Statement of operations
2. Statement of financial position

Direct public support	$ 7,500,000
Non-current assets	32,000,000
Net assets invested in capital assets	21,400,000
Trade and other payables	3,000,000
Services (salaries, etc.)	21,000,000
Current assets	14,500,000
Current mortgage payable	2,500,000
Government grants	1,000,000
Long-term borrowings	18,000,000
Finance costs	2,000,000
Net assets restricted for endowment	1,600,000
Depreciation	4,000,000
Program service revenue	21,000,000

FINANCIAL SPREADSHEETS: EXCEL®

The financial spreadsheets available from this book's Companion website at www.bergeron7e.nelson.com include three input templates: the statement of income, the statement of comprehensive income and the statement of changes in equity, and the statement of financial position. These templates have two types of cells: protected cells (non-shaded) and unprotected cells (shaded). Most cells on these three templates are unprotected because the analyst will want to input data from an organization's financial statements for three consecutive years. The templates are linked to one another as some data is automatically transcribed. For example, the profit for the year shown on the statement of income is copied in the appropriate line on the statement of changes in equity and the total retained earnings (end of year) is transcribed onto the statement of financial position under equity. Most cells on templates 4 to 15 are protected because they are output documents (analytical documents) used to analyze a company's financial performance from different angles (ratios, vertical analysis, horizontal analysis, DuPont system, cash flow, the economic value added, sustainable growth, and the Z-score). Most financial ratios used in this book are calculated by using these spreadsheets; they can save many hours of tedious calculations—time that can be better used in analysis and decision making.

CHAPTER 3

[STATEMENT OF CASH FLOWS]

Learning Objectives

After reading this chapter, you should be able to

1 Explain the importance of managing cash flows.

2 Analyze cash flows by comparing two consecutive statements of financial position.

3 Describe the basic structure of the statement of cash flows.

4 Discuss the structure of the statement of cash flows for not-for-profit organizations.

OPENING CASE

Cash, the Financial Ingredient That Helps Growth and Profitability

In February 2013, Len and Joan Miller started their computer retail business. During the first months of operations, sales objectives were realized, and expenses were in line with their budget. The Millers' original plans included opening a second retail outlet and then opening several retail outlets in different cities over the next 10 years. They understood, however, that in any start-up venture, business survival was a primary focus. They realized that any cash invested in CompuTech Sales and Service had to "return a suitable level of profit." They also recognized that some of the cash required to open new retail stores would have to come from their existing business. They remembered Bill Murray's advice about maintaining stability by not relying on cash from lenders as the only source of growth funds; they needed to rely on cash the business generated from internal operations (profit for the year). The Millers believed that the key was to minimize operating expenses during the first few years of operations and spend a reasonable amount of cash on products and services to generate decent revenue.

The Millers' goal for 2013 and 2014 was to develop a good understanding of their customers' needs, their supplier arrangements, and their day-to-day operating activities. They understood the importance of cash flows. They had often heard from course instructors and long-time business entrepreneurs that "cash is king." They remembered vividly an instructor saying that having money when you need it is as important as being able to predict when you'll get it.

In line with their cash flow strategy, the Millers didn't plan to open a second retail outlet until 2015. Their intention was to generate as much cash as possible from CompuTech during 2013 and 2014, invest a minimal amount of cash for the purchase of some equipment during these two years, and reduce their debt to prepare themselves for future growth.

Opening a new retail outlet in late 2015 would cost an estimated $350,000. They had to implement a cash flow strategy that could lead them successfully toward their expansion program. They wanted to ensure that they had a balanced financing package. They were aiming for a 20% increase in revenue in 2014 and a 90% increase in 2015. CompuTech's key financial figures are summarized on the next page. The investment in property, plant, and equipment is expected to be minimal in 2014 (only $40,000) with a substantial increase ($350,000) in 2015. Cash from business operations will pay for these investments. Part of the cash, $73,000 ($33,000 + $40,000) in 2014 and $157,000 ($77,000 + $80,000) in 2015, would come from profit and depreciation. Long-term borrowings would provide $150,000 in 2015. Appendix A at the end of this text presents CompuTech's financial statements: the statements of income, the statements of comprehensive income, the statements of changes in equity, and the statements of financial position for 2013 to 2015.

(in $000s)	2013	2014	2015
Revenue	$350	$420	$800
Profit for the year	25	33	77
Depreciation/amortization	38	40	80
Purchase of property, plant, and equipment	170	40	350
Increase (decrease) in long-term borrowings	60	(10)	150

THIS CHAPTER WILL SHOW LEN AND JOAN MILLER HOW TO

- Manage cash flows effectively.
- Finance the opening of new stores by using internally generated cash.

Chapter Overview

CASH FLOW: MOVEMENT OF MONEY INTO AND OUT OF A BUSINESS

The statement of income runs like a movie, the statement of financial position is like taking a snapshot, and the statement of cash flows places emphasis on change—undoubtedly the reason it used to be called the "statement of *changes* in financial position." This chapter examines four topics:

- *Importance of cash flow.* We'll look at the reasons that it is important to examine the flow of cash between two accounting periods and what is meant by "cash is king."
- *Meaning and rules of cash flows.* You will learn the meaning of cash flows and the basic rules you can apply to determine whether a change in an account between two accounting periods is a *cash inflow* or a *cash outflow.*
- *Structure and contents of the statement of cash flows.* We'll examine the basic structure and contents of the statement of cash flows for profit-motivated organizations and the various accounts of the statement of financial position that are included in the statement of cash flows, called *adjustments in non-cash working capital accounts.*
- *Structure and contents of the statement of cash flows for an NFP organization.* This topic looks at the statement of cash flows for organizations with different goals, the not-for-profit (NFP) organizations.

Why Analyze Cash Flows?

1 Explain the importance of managing cash flows.

The previous chapter examined the contents and structure of the statement of income and the statement of comprehensive income, the statement of changes in equity, and the statement of financial position.

- The *statement of income* and *the statement of comprehensive income* show the amount of revenue earned and expenses incurred between two dates or during a given period.
- The *statement of changes in equity* tells how much profit (earnings) has been accumulated by a business since it began its operations, the amount of dividends paid to its shareholders during the current operating year, the amount of profit retained in the business, and the amount of cash that was invested in the business by shareholders.
- The *statement of financial position* shows what a business owns and what it owes to creditors and shareholders at a given time.

These financial statements each have a specific purpose, giving important information about the financial performance and financial condition of a business. However, they do not show the cash flows, or changes, that take place between two consecutive accounting periods; this is what the *statement of cash flows* does.

To illustrate the meaning of change, let's examine six accounts drawn from Nandini's personal statements of financial position for 2013 and 2014. The columns 2014 and 2013 below show what Nandini owns and what she owes at the end of these two accounting periods. Only by listing the accounts of two consecutive statements of financial position side by side can you see these changes. Each change produces either a cash inflow or a cash outflow.

(in $)	2014	2013	Cash Inflows	Cash Outflows
1. Bank loan	20,000	5,000	15,000	—
2. Mortgage payable	140,000	100,000	40,000	—
3. Visa loan	2,000	1,000	1,000	—
4. Watch	1,000	—	—	1,000
5. Car	30,000	5,000	—	25,000
6. House	180,000	150,000	—	30,000
Total			56,000	56,000

Let's examine the significance of these changes. In 2013, Nandini owed $5,000 to the bank; in 2014, she owed $20,000. This means that Nandini borrowed an additional $15,000 from the bank in 2014. Because she borrowed (or received) money from the bank, this change is called a *cash inflow*. To find out what she did with the money, we have to look at other statement of financial position accounts; these will be identified later. The mortgage account shows a $40,000 increase between the two accounting periods (from $100,000 to $140,000). This means that Nandini borrowed an additional amount from a mortgage company. This loan is also considered a cash inflow. Again, we're not sure yet what Nandini did with the cash. Nandini's Visa loan account shows a $1,000 change, meaning that Nandini borrowed $1,000 on her credit card. The changes in these three accounts show that Nandini took in $56,000. Now, let's see what she did with this cash.

By examining the other accounts in the statement of financial position, we see that Nandini purchased a $1,000 watch because the 2013 watch account on the statement of financial position had a nil balance, and a $1,000 amount is shown in 2014. This acquisition is a purchase and therefore a *cash outflow*. We can assume that Nandini used the $1,000 from Visa to make that purchase. In 2014, Nandini's car account increased by $25,000. In 2013, this account showed $5,000, which increased to $30,000 in 2014. This means that Nandini purchased a car. We can assume that she used the bank loan ($15,000) and some of the mortgage money ($40,000) to buy the car. Also in 2014, Nandini had a $30,000 solarium installed in her house. As shown, in 2013, Nandini's house account was $150,000; it increased to $180,000 in 2014. To make this addition to her house, she must have used what was left over from the mortgage after the car purchase.

These examples show the changes in various accounts that took place between Nandini's two accounting periods, that is, where she got the money from (cash inflows) and where it went (cash outflows). Nandini obtained $56,000 from three different sources (bank loan, mortgage, and Visa), purchased a watch and a car, and made some renovations to her house. The examples throughout this chapter will demonstrate that the total of all cash inflows and cash outflows must *always be equal.* In other words, when adding all the changes between two statements of financial position from the asset, equity, or liability accounts, the sources always equal the uses. This makes sense, because each time a transaction takes place, it affects two accounts, a cash outflow (e.g., purchase of a car) and a cash inflow (e.g., bank loan).

Financial analysts, lenders, investors, and managers are all interested in the flow of cash within a business and, more importantly, the year-to-year changes in cash-related activities. They often say that "cash is king" because businesses need cash to function. For example, they need cash to pay their bills on time and to invest in non-current assets, such as machinery and equipment, to modernize or expand. They want to know where cash came from (provided by cash inflows) and what it was spent on (used in cash outflows). More importantly, they want to know how much the company will spend in future years and how it will be provided. If a company wants to invest $1 million in capital assets (property, plant, and equipment) during the next budget year (cash outflows), management will want to know where the cash needed to finance these assets will be coming from (cash inflows).

Cash flows
Obtaining (cash provided by) and allocating (cash used in) cash.

This type of analysis and decision-making process is the heart of financial management: obtaining and allocating cash. This process is referred to as **cash flows**. Changes in various accounts of the statement of financial position indicate the flows of cash resulting from management decisions. The statement of cash flows shows the amount of cash invested in (used in) non-current asset accounts and where these funds are obtained (from lenders or shareholders) or come from (cash inflows).

Look back to Figure 1.6. It shows that a business purchased $1 million worth of assets (investing decisions). One-half of the funds used to finance these investments was provided by internal sources (operating decisions), that is, by the business itself; the other half was provided by external sources (financing decisions), that is, investors (shareholders and long-term lenders).

To explain how this works, let's examine two consecutive statements of financial position (as at December 31) of two businesses: Westpark Inc. (Table 3.1) and Eastpark Ltd. (Table 3.2). Table 3.1 shows that Westpark Inc. obtained $80,000 from different sources (cash inflows) and used $80,000 (cash outflows) to purchase assets and pay several loans. The inflows of cash equal the outflows of cash.

The Cash Inflows column shows that Westpark Inc. reduced its trade receivables by $15,000 and borrowed money from a bank: $10,000 (long-term borrowings) and $5,000 (seasonal loan). However, the major portion of the cash inflow was provided by equity ($50,000), which is the profit for 2014.

As shown in the Cash Outflows column, the company invested in buildings, machinery, equipment, and inventories. In addition, the company reduced its mortgage, trade and other payables, and line of credit. Westpark Inc. spent $40,000

Table 3.1 Westpark Inc's Statements of Financial Position

(in $)	2014	2013	Cash Inflows	Cash Outflows
Assets				
Buildings	340,000	325,000	—	15,000
Machinery	35,000	20,000	—	15,000
Equipment	20,000	15,000	—	5,000
Inventories	30,000	25,000	—	5,000
Trade receivables	15,000	30,000	15,000	—
Cash	20,000	10,000	—	10,000
Total assets	**460,000**	**425,000**		—
Equity	200,000	150,000	50,000	
Liabilities				
Mortgage	150,000	160,000	—	10,000
Long-term borrowings	50,000	40,000	10,000	—
Trade and other payables	30,000	35,000	—	5,000
Seasonal loan	15,000	10,000	5,000	—
Short-term borrowings	10,000	10,000	—	—
Line of credit	5,000	20,000	—	15,000
Total liabilities	**260,000**	**275,000**	—	—
Total equity and liabilities	**460,000**	**425,000**	**80,000**	**80,000**

to buy different assets—buildings ($15,000), machinery ($15,000), equipment ($5,000)—and increase its inventories ($5,000). Westpark also increased its cash account ($10,000), reduced its mortgage ($10,000), lowered its credit from suppliers or trades payable ($5,000), and paid down its line of credit ($15,000) for another $40,000 in cash outflows.

To finance the purchase of these assets, Westpark Inc. used $55,000 from internal sources (operating activities), such as the profit for the year (Figure 3.1). The company was able to purchase $40,000 worth of assets and still reduce its overall outstanding debt by $15,000:

Internal Cash Flows	**Provided by**	**Used in**	**Difference**
Trade receivables	$15,000	—	
Cash	—	$10,000	
Equity (profit for the year)	50,000	—	
Total	$65,000	$10,000	$ 55,000
External Cash Flows (from debt)			
Mortgage	—	10,000	
Long-term borrowings	10,000	—	
Trade and other payables	—	5,000	
Seasonal loan	5,000	—	
Short-term borrowings	—	—	
Line of credit	—	15,000	
Total	$15,000	$30,000	(15,000)
Net cash inflows			$ 40,000

Eastpark Ltd.'s financial position, shown in Table 3.2, gives a different picture. The asset accounts show a net increase of $140,000 between 2013 and 2014, from $370,000 to $510,000, with a corresponding total increase in the equity and liability accounts. This is $50,000 more than Westpark's $460,000 in total assets for 2014. The main difference, however, lies in the way that Eastpark Ltd. financed the purchase of the assets. Eastpark Ltd. needed $150,000 to buy the following: building renovation ($110,000), additional machinery ($20,000), new equipment ($10,000), and an increase in inventories ($10,000). Eastpark Ltd.'s inflows of cash were obtained from a mortgage company ($70,000), a bank for an increase in its long-term borrowings ($20,000), suppliers for an increase in trade and other payables ($10,000), a seasonal loan ($5,000), an increase in short-term borrowings ($5,000), and, finally, an increase in its line of credit ($5,000) for a total of $115,000. The remaining $35,000 was obtained from equity, or profit for the year ($25,000),

Figure 3.1 **Westpark Inc.'s Inflows and Outflows of Cash**

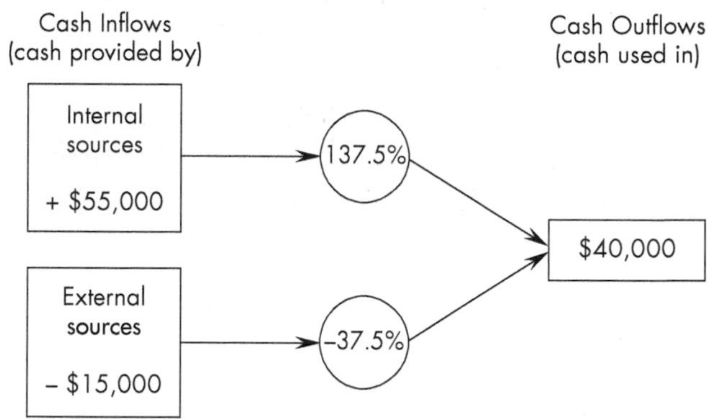

a reduction in the trade receivables account ($5,000), and a reduction in the cash account ($5,000).

To finance the purchase of these four assets valued at $150,000, Eastpark used $35,000 from internal funding (by withdrawing money from the bank, reducing

Table 3.2 **Eastpark Ltd.'s Statements of Financial Position**

(in $)	2014	2013	Cash Inflows	Cash Outflows
Assets				
Buildings	400,000	290,000	—	110,000
Machinery	40,000	20,000	—	20,000
Equipment	25,000	15,000	—	10,000
Inventories	30,000	20,000	—	10,000
Trade receivables	10,000	15,000	5,000	—
Cash	5,000	10,000	5,000	—
Total Assets	**510,000**	370,000		
Equity	**150,000**	**125,000**	**25,000**	—
Liabilities				
Mortgage	200,000	130,000	70,000	—
Long-term borrowings	90,000	70,000	20,000	—
Trade and other payables	25,000	15,000	10,000	—
Seasonal loan	20,000	15,000	5,000	—
Short-term borrowings	15,000	10,000	5,000	—
Line of credit	10,000	5,000	5,000	—
Total Liabilities	**360,000**	**245,000**		
Total Equity and Liabilities	**510,000**	**370,000**	150,000	150,000

Figure 3.2 **Eastpark Ltd.'s Inflows and Outflows of Cash**

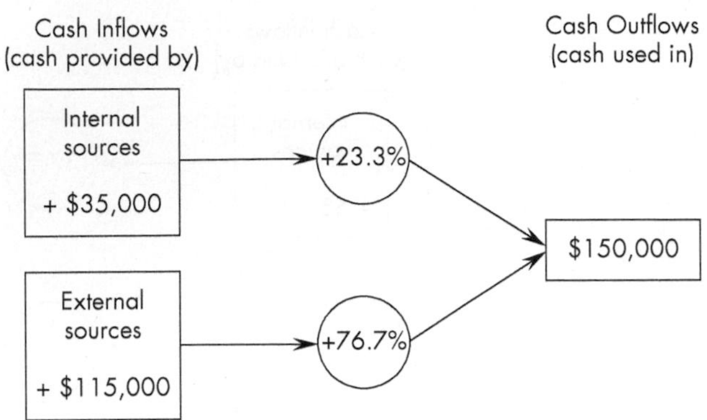

its trade receivables, and using equity, that is, profit for the year) $115,000 (or 76.7% of the total) from external sources or lenders (Figure 3.2). If the company continues this practice year after year, it will soon find itself in a severe financial crunch.

Internal Cash Flows	Provided by	Used in	Difference
Trade receivables	$ 5,000	—	—
Cash	5,000	—	—
Equity (profit for the year)	25,000	—	—
Total	$ 35,000	—	$ 35,000
External Cash Flow (from debt)			
Mortgage	$ 70,000	—	
Long-term borrowings	20,000	—	
Trade and other payables	10,000	—	
Seasonal loan	5,000	—	
Short-term borrowings	5,000	—	
Line of credit	5,000	—	
Total	$115,000		115,000
Net cash inflows			$150,000

Problem-Solving Example 3.1

How to Pinpoint the Inflows and Outflows of Cash

Which of the following are inflows and which are outflows of cash? What are the total outflows and total inflows? (1) Profit increased from $100,000 to $120,000; (2) trade receivables increased from $20,000 to $35,000; (3) cash account went from $15,000 to $12,000; (4) share capital went from $150,000 to $140,000; and (5) inventories went from $45,000 to $35,000.

(continued)

Problem-Solving Example 3.1 (continued)

Solution

Total cash inflow ($133,000) and total cash outflow ($25,000).

	Cash Inflows	Cash Outflows
(1) Profit	$120,000	
(2) Trade receivables		$15,000
(3) Cash account	3,000	
(4) Share capital		10,000
(5) Inventories	10,000	
Total	$133,000	$25,000

Self-Test Exercise 3.1

Identifying the Inflows and Outflows of Cash

Use CompuTech's financial statements to identify whether the following changes are cash inflows or cash outflows.

	2014	2013	Cash Inflows	Cash Outflows
Property, plant, and equipment	$210,000	$170,000	________	________
Trade receivables	45,000	35,000	________	________
Cash and cash equivalents	21,000	15,000	________	________
Long-term borrowings	50,000	60,000	________	________
Short-term borrowings	35,000	30,000	________	________

Answers to the Self-Test Exercises can be found at www.bergeron7e.nelson.com.

Cash Flow Analysis

2 Analyze cash flows by comparing two consecutive statements of financial position.

Before presenting the structure of the statement of cash flows, let's examine the key drivers of cash inflows and outflows and some of the basic rules that can help determine what constitutes a cash inflow and a cash outflow.

CASH FLOW DRIVERS

As shown in Table 3.3, some of the more important cash inflows are profit for the year, sale of non-current assets, sale of investment securities, increase in long-term borrowings, increase in share capital, and decrease in working capital accounts (e.g., trade receivables and inventories). Cash outflows take place when a company experiences a loss, purchases non-current assets, buys investment securities, reduces its long-term borrowings, increases its working capital accounts, or pays dividends.

Table 3.3 Key Cash Flow Drivers

Cash Inflows (cash provided by)	Cash Outflows (cash used for)
• Profit for the year	• Loss for the year
• Proceeds from sale of non-current assets	• Purchase of non-current assets
• Proceeds from sale of investments	• Purchase of investments
• Proceeds from long-term borrowings	• Payment of long-term borrowings
• Proceeds from issue of share capital	• Purchase of share capital
• Decrease in working capital accounts	• Increase in working capital accounts

COMPARATIVE STATEMENTS OF FINANCIAL POSITION

Consecutive statements of financial position Two statements of financial position occurring in succession between two periods or in logical sequence; comparing them helps to determine whether a change in each account is a cash inflow or a cash outflow.

Table 3.4 presents Eastman Technologies Inc.'s **consecutive statements of financial position** for 2013 and 2012 (as at December 31). By placing these two consecutive statements of financial position side by side, we can analyze Eastman's cash inflows and cash outflows, or the cash flow changes that took place between these two accounting periods.

All cash inflows and cash outflows in Eastman's asset, equity, and liability accounts, showing how the cash flows emerged, are listed in Table 3.4. Eastman obtained $352,000 from different accounts and used it to purchase assets and increase some of the working capital accounts. These working capital accounts (current assets and current liabilities) are shaded and we'll explain later (page 101) (1) the accounts included in the *adjustments in non-cash working capital accounts*, and (2) why they are part of *operating activities*. The next section looks at the significance and meaning of each change in cash flows shown in Eastman's financial statements. But first, let's examine some guidelines that can help determine whether a change in a statement of financial position account is a cash inflow or a cash outflow.

Cash inflow guidelines A cash inflow takes place when there is a decrease in an asset account or an increase in an equity or liability account.

Cash outflow guidelines A cash outflow takes place when there is an increase in an asset account or a decrease in an equity or liability account.

GUIDELINES FOR IDENTIFYING CASH INFLOWS AND CASH OUTFLOWS

Cash inflows and cash outflows are associated with specific types of changes in a statement of financial position. Figure 3.3 shows some basic **cash inflow and cash outflow guidelines** to determine whether an asset, an equity, or a liability account is a cash inflow or a cash outflow.

Cash inflows (or cash provided by) take place when there is

- a decrease in asset accounts;
- an increase in the equity accounts (share capital or retained earnings increase from profit from operations); or
- an increase in liability accounts.

Table 3.4 **Comparative Statements of Financial Position**

Eastman Technologies Inc.
Cash Inflows and Cash Outflows
(in $)

Assets	2013	2012	Cash Inflows	Cash Outflows
Non-current assets (at cost)	1,340,000	1,050,000	—	290,000
Accumulated depreciation	(140,000)	(100,000)	40,000	—
Non-current assets (net)	1,200,000	950,000		
Current assets				
Inventories	218,000	185,000	—	33,000
Trade receivables	300,000	280,000	—	20,000
Prepaid expenses	60,000	55,000	—	5,000
Cash and cash equivalents	22,000	18,000	—	4,000
Total current assets	600,000	538,000	—	—
Total assets	1,800,000	1,488,000	—	—
Equity				
Share capital	300,000	285,000	15,000	—
Retained earnings	255,000	205,000	50,000	—
Total equity	555,000	490,000		
Liabilities				
Long-term borrowings	800,000	600,000	200,000	—
Current liabilities				
Trade and other payables	195,000	175,000	20,000	—
Notes payable	150,000	135,000	15,000	—
Accrued expenses	20,000	18,000	2,000	—
Taxes payable	80,000	70,000	10,000	—
Total current liabilities	445,000	398,000		
Total equity and liabilities	1,800,000	1,488,000		
Total cash inflows and outflows			352,000	352,000

Note: Here is the reason why the inflows = the outflows: if you buy something, you need to get the same amount of cash from somewhere!

Cash outflows (or cash used for) take place when there is

- an increase in asset accounts;
- a decrease in equity accounts (dividends paid or retained earnings decrease from loss from operations); or
- a decrease in liability accounts.

Figure 3.3 Guidelines for Identifying Cash Inflows and Cash Outflows

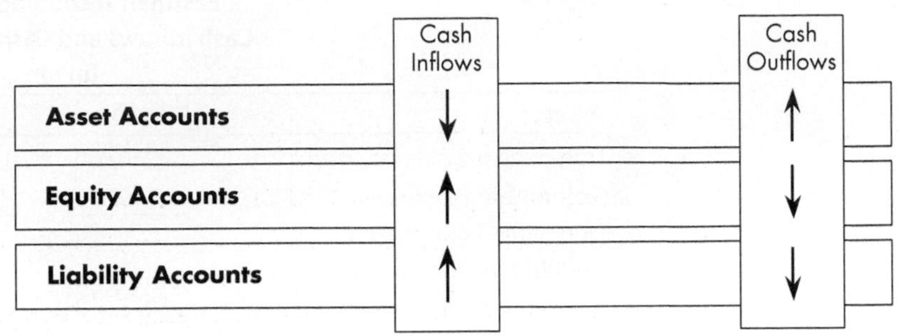

By applying these guidelines to Eastman Technologies Inc.'s financial statements for 2013 and 2012 (from Table 3.4), we can determine the company's cash inflows and cash outflows. Table 3.5 shows that Eastman obtained $352,000 worth of cash from eight different accounts (e.g., increase in share capital, long-term borrowings, trade and other payables) and used the cash for five different accounts (e.g., increase in non-current assets, inventories, trade receivables).

Table 3.5 Cash Inflows and Cash Outflows

Eastman Technologies Inc.
For the year ended 2013
(in $)

Cash Inflows	
Increase in depreciation	40,000
Increase in share capital	15,000
Increase in retained earnings	50,000
Increase in long-term borrowings	200,000
Increase in trade and other payables	20,000
Increase in notes payable	15,000
Increase in accrued expenses	2,000
Increase in taxes payable	10,000
Total cash inflows	352,000
Cash Outflows	
Increase in non-current assets	(290,000)
Increase in inventories	(33,000)
Increase in trade receivables	(20,000)
Increase in prepaid expenses	(5,000)
Increase in cash and cash equivalents	(4,000)
Total cash outflows	352,000

Now that you understand the meaning of cash inflows and cash outflows and how they can be identified, let's look at how the statement of cash flows is prepared.

Problem-Solving Example 3.2

Identifying Cash Inflows and Cash Outflows

With the following accounts, calculate (1) total inflows by the asset accounts, (2) total outflows by the asset accounts, (3) total inflows by the liability accounts, (4) total outflows by the liability accounts, (5) inflows and outflows by the equity account. Changes from 2013 to 2014 are mortgage 1 (from $210,000 to $200,000), RRSP (from $10,000 to $12,000), car loan (from $25,000 to $20,000), house (from $280,000 to $300,000), cottage (from $190,000 to $200,000), bank account (from $2,000 to $3,000), line of credit (from $2,000 to $5,000), MasterCard (from $1,000 to $2,000), furniture (from $10,000 to $14,000), savings (from $4,000 to $3,000), mortgage 2 (from $100,000 to $125,000), and equity (from $158,000 to $180,000).

Solution

1 and 2	From asset accounts:	inflows	$ 1,000	outflows	$37,000
3 and 4	From liability accounts:	inflows	29,000	outflows	15,000
5	From equity account:	inflows	22,000	outflows	—
	Total inflows and total outflows:		$52,000		$52,000

	2014	2013	Cash Inflows	Cash Outflows
Asset accounts				
RRSP	$ 12,000	$ 10,000	—	$ 2,000
House	300,000	280,000	—	20,000
Cottage	200,000	190,000	—	10,000
Bank account	3,000	2,000	—	1,000
Furniture	14,000	10,000	—	4,000
Savings	3,000	4,000	$ 1,000	—
Total assets	$ 532,000	$496,000	$ 1,000	$37,000
Liability accounts				
Mortgage (1)	$ 200,000	$210,000	—	10,000
Mortgage (2)	125,000	100,000	25,000	—
Car loan	20,000	25,000	—	5,000
Line of credit	5,000	2,000	3,000	—
MasterCard	2,000	1,000	1,000	—
Total liabilities	352,000	338,000	29,000	15,000
Total equity	180,000	158,000	22,000	—
Total liabilities and equity	$ 532,000	$496,000	$51,000	$15,000

Self-Test Exercise 3.2

Pinpointing the Cash Inflows and Cash Outflows

On Len and Joan Miller's personal statements of financial position shown below, identify whether each account is a cash inflow or a cash outflow.

	2014	2013	Cash Inflows	Cash Outflows
Assets				
House	$205,000	$136,000	______	______
Car	22,000	6,000	______	______
Furniture	8,500	7,000	______	______
RRSPs	30,000	20,000	______	______
Savings bonds	5,000	4,000	______	______
Short-term deposits	2,000	2,000	______	______
Total assets	$272,500	$175,000	______	______
Equity	$111,000	$ 80,000	______	______
Liabilities				
Mortgage	112,000	79,000	______	______
Car loan	24,000	3,000	______	______
BMO Bank of Montreal loan	21,000	11,000	______	______
Amex	4,500	2,000	______	______
Total liabilities	161,500	95,000	______	______
Total equity and liabilities	$272,500	$175,000	$______	______

Answers to the Self-Test Exercises can be found at www.bergeron7e.nelson.com.

Statement of Cash Flows

3 Describe the basic structure of the statement of cash flows.

Cash budget
A treasury function that determines the cash flow of a business at the microlevel to control the level of liquidity.

We can examine cash flows on two levels: micro and macro. At the *micro level*, cash flows are reviewed through short-term operating statements, such as the monthly cash receipts and payments. The **cash budget** is the financial tool used to determine cash flows at this level, and it is a treasury function. The cash budget ensures the company has enough cash on hand to pay its bills (e.g., salaries, purchases, advertising) and current borrowings. Conversely, if the company has more than enough reserves in cash, the treasurer will invest the surplus in short-term securities. This type of analysis and decision making has to do with liquidity. (Recall from Chapter 1 that liquidity is a company's ability to meet its short-term financial commitments.)

At the *macro level*, cash flow deals with solvency, that is, having more assets than liabilities and being able to pay its debts, and, just as important, the ability of a business to do the following:

1. Generate cash from its operations (profit for the year plus depreciation/amortization and the adjustments in non-cash working capital accounts)
2. Repay its long-term borrowings and pay dividends
3. Purchase property, plant, and equipment (capital assets included in the capital budget)

The operating cash receipts and payments (or disbursements) show the liquidity performance of a business, and the information about solvency and liquidity appears in the statement of cash flows. This statement helps to assess a company's ability to generate cash internally, repay debts, reinvest in capital assets, and pay dividends. The information is needed for operating activities, financing activities, and investing activities.

Preparing the statement of cash flows is a relatively complex task, but interpreting it is easier and of importance for stakeholders. To prepare this statement, financial information is drawn from (1) the statement of financial position, (2) the statement of income, and (3) the statement of changes in equity (e.g., retained earnings).

The preparation of Eastman Technologies Inc.'s statement of cash flows began with three steps:

1. The cash inflows and the cash outflows were listed (refer back to Table 3.4).
2. The accounts affecting the adjustments of the non-cash working capital accounts (the current asset and current liability accounts) were listed. See the shaded entries in Table 3.4 and those listed in Table 3.7 on page 95.
3. The information from steps 1 and 2 were used to prepare the statement of cash flows (look ahead to Table 3.9 on page 105). The table shows the statement (statement of income, statement of changes in equity, and statement of financial position) from which the accounts producing cash inflows and cash outflows are drawn. These cash inflows and cash outflows are listed under three main headings:
   - Operating activities (including adjustments in non-cash working capital accounts)
   - Financing activities
   - Investing activities

Let's now continue preparing the statement of cash flows presented in Table 3.9.

Operating activities The portion of the statement of cash flows that shows how much cash was provided by the business itself (e.g., profit for the year, depreciation/amortization, and adjustments in non-cash working capital accounts).

OPERATING ACTIVITIES

Operating activities deal with the principal revenue-producing activities generated by a business itself (internally generated cash). This section lists three important cash-generated items: profit for the year, depreciation/amortization, and adjustments in non-cash working capital accounts.

Profit for the Year and Depreciation/Amortization

Eastman Technologies Inc. earned $97,500 in profit in 2013 (see Table 3.6). By adding $40,000 in depreciation to this figure, the company generated $137,500 in cash. Depreciation is added to profit for the year as this account is only a book entry and does not represent a "real" cash outflow like paying expenses, such as salaries and leases. In the News 3.1 gives an example of how a slowdown in business activities has the potential to derail a company's projects and growth.

Adjustments in non-cash working capital accounts The cash flow provided (or used) by working capital accounts, such as trade receivables, inventories, and trade and other payables.

Adjustments in Non-Cash Working Capital Accounts

The statement of cash flows does not usually give a detailed listing of the cash flows generated by a company's individual working capital accounts (current assets and current liabilities). However, because working capital accounts are an important element in the management of a company's cash flow, the company will produce a detailed statement called the **adjustments in non-cash working capital accounts** (see Table 3.7). This statement shows whether all individual working capital accounts (which include all current assets, except cash, and all current liability accounts) are generating cash (cash inflows) or using cash (cash outflows). Although a company's net increase in working capital may not change dramatically, this does not mean that all accounts are under control. These accounts are all drawn from the statement of financial position.

Table 3.6 Statement of Income

Eastman Technologies Inc.
For the year ended 2013
(in $)

Revenue	2,500,000
Cost of sales	(1,900,000)
Gross profit	600,000
Other income/expenses (net)	(15,000)
Expenses	(350,000)
Depreciation	(40,000)
Total	(405,000)
Profit before taxes	195,000
Income tax expense	(97,500)
Profit for the year	97,500

In The News 3.1

GROWING SMART AVOIDS A CASH SQUEEZE

Cash flow is like a reservoir: There are inflows and outflows of cash, and a tap regulates the speed. At times, management has to open or close the tap, depending on how fast business activities can generate funds to start or complete capital projects or research and development activities.

This is what is happening at Research In Motion (RIM), a leader in wireless innovation. Today, RIM is struggling. During the last three months of 2011, the smartphone market grew by 47.3% while the BlackBerry showed a 10.7% decline. Critically, the delay in launching its BlackBerry10 platform further compromised its ability to retain current users.

When a company has difficulty competing effectively in the marketplace and is showing signs of weakness in reversing a negative sales trend, it is easy to imagine the effect this will have on the company's current and future cash flow performance.

Source: "RIM 'Struggling' in Smartphone Market as Apple, Samsung Vie for Lead." *Financial Post*. Retrieved from http://business.financialpost.com/2012/02/15/rim-struggling-in-smartphone-market-as-apple-samsung-vie-for-lead/, accessed February 15, 2012. For more information and updates about RIM's performance, visit www.rim.com.

Table 3.7 Adjustments in Non-Cash Working Capital Accounts

Eastman Technologies Inc.
For the year ended 2013
(in $)

Cash Inflows			
Increase in trade and other payables	20,000		Drawn from working capital accounts in the statement of financial position, that is, current assets and current liabilities
Increase in notes payable	15,000		
Increase in accrued expenses	2,000		
Increase in taxes payable	10,000	47,000	
Cash Outflows			
Increase in inventories	(33,000)		
Increase in trade receivables	(20,000)		
Increase in prepaid expenses	(5,000)	(58,000)	
Adjustments in non-cash working capital accounts		(11,000)	

Problem-Solving Example 3.3

Preparing the Adjustments in Non-Cash Working Capital Accounts Statement

Use the following accounts to prepare the adjustments in non-cash working capital accounts statement: increase in trade and other payables ($14,000), increase in inventories ($15,000), increase in notes payable ($20,000), profit for the year ($18,000), and decrease in taxes payable ($13,000).

(continued)

Problem-Solving Example 3.3 (continued)

Solution

Adjustments in Non-Cash Working Capital Accounts Statement

Cash Inflows		
Notes payables	$ 20,000	
Trade and other payables	14,000	
Subtotal		$34,000
Cash Outflows		
Inventories	$(15,000)	
Taxes payable	(13,000)	
Subtotal		(28,000)
Adjustments in non-cash working capital accounts		$ 6,000

Note: Profit for the year is not a working capital account.

Self-Test Exercise 3.3

Preparing the Adjustments in Non-Cash Working Capital Accounts Statement

With the following accounts, drawn from CompuTech's statement of financial position, (1) identify the *working capital accounts* and (2) prepare the adjustments in non-cash working capital accounts statement.

Accounts	2014	2013
Trade and other payables	$ 20,000	$ 17,000
Retained earnings	58,000	25,000
Long-term borrowings	50,000	60,000
Trade receivables	45,000	35,000
Property, plant, and equipment	210,000	170,000
Inventories	65,000	50,000
Cash and cash equivalents	21,000	15,000
Accumulated depreciation/amortization	78,000	38,000
Short-term borrowings	40,000	35,000
Prepaid expenses	5,000	5,000

Answers to the Self-Test Exercises can be found at www.bergeron7e.nelson.com.

The seven working capital accounts shown in Table 3.7 are drawn from the statement of financial position (the shaded rows in Table 3.4) and show a net cash outflow of $11,000. This means that the business used $11,000 over the past 12 months for day-to-day business operations. By adding depreciation ($40,000) to the profit for the year ($97,500), the statement of income shows $137,500 in cash. The upper portion of the statement of cash flows under the heading Operating Activities in Table 3.9 shows that the total cash generated from the business's operations is $126,500, the difference of inflows and outflows.

FINANCING ACTIVITIES

Financing activities The portion of the statement of cash flows that shows how much cash was provided (or used) from external sources (e.g., proceeds from the issue of shares or borrowings, repaying long-term debt, or payment of dividends).

Financing activities deal with the money from the sale of shares, the repayment of long-term borrowings, the borrowing of long-term debt, and the payment of dividends. With the exception of the payment of dividends, which is obtained from the statement of changes in equity (retained earnings), this information comes from the statement of financial position. Cash inflows and cash outflows under financing activities deal with the *long-term financing transactions*, that is, those appearing on the middle section of the statement of financial position under the heading Equity and Non-Current Liabilities. In Table 3.9 under the heading Financing Activities, Eastman Technologies Inc. had $167,500. First, the company paid $47,500 in dividends (see Table 3.8); second, it borrowed $200,000 from its long-term lenders; and finally, the shareholders invested $15,000 in the business.

All accounts appearing under operating and financing activities generated $294,000 in cash. What did Eastman do with this money? The next section answers this question.

Table 3.8 Statement of Retained Earnings

Eastman Technologies Inc.
For the year ended 2013
(in $)

Retained earnings (beginning of year)		205,000
Profit for the year	97,500	
Dividends	(47,500)	(50,000)
Retained earnings (end of year)		255,000

In The News 3.2

VENTURE CAPITAL FOR START-UP BUSINESSES

Cash for financing a business can be secured from different sources. One source of funding that is ideal for start-up and risky businesses is venture capital (VC). VC is not new. It has been around for more than 70 years, going back to 1938 when Laurance S. Rockefeller helped finance the creation of both Eastern Air Lines and Douglas Aircraft. But it was in 1946 with the American Research and Development Corporation, founded by Georges Doriot, the "father of venture capitalism" (and former dean of Harvard Business School), that true private equity investment began to emerge.

Today, entrepreneurs of start-up ventures can benefit from venture capital. According to Thomson Reuters, venture capital firms in Canada invested $1.5 billion in 444 companies last year. According to Canadian Venture Capital & Private Equity Association, Canada's venture capital firms posted strong growth in small business financing in 2011, with 34% more money going to 24% more firms than the year before.

Source: "Venture Capital Hikes Investment in Small Business." *Financial Post*. Retrieved from http://business.financialpost.com/2012/02/14/venture-capital-hikes-investment-in-small-business/, accessed February 14, 2012. For more information about venture capital funds, visit www.cvca.ca.

Investing activities The portion of the statement of cash flows that shows how much cash was provided (or used) to buy or sell non-current assets (e.g., purchase or proceeds from the sale of a building).

In the News 3.2 illustrates how venture capital funds can be an excellent source of external funds for start-up businesses.

INVESTING ACTIVITIES

Investing activities deal with the buying (acquisition) and selling (disposal) of assets, shown in the upper portion of the statement of financial position (non-current assets). Table 3.9 shows that Eastman invested $290,000 to buy non-current assets. In the News 3.3 gives an example about how an important business investing decision can be put on hold as a result of one political decision.

In The News 3.3

POLITICAL DECISIONS CAN AFFECT BUSINESS DECISIONS

Putting investing decisions on hold is not necessarily an internal decision (one that originates from the board of directors or management committee).A recession-driven economy and a political decision can also delay a high-priority capital investment decision.

This is the situation that TransCanada Corp. (a Calgary-based energy company) faced during the early part of 2012 when President Barack Obama rejected the permit application of the Keystone Pipeline system to transport synthetic crude oil from the Athabasca oil sands in Hardisty, Alberta, to the Gulf Coast of Texas refineries in Houston, Texas. The reason: Concerns that the pipeline could pollute air and water supplies and harm migratory birds and other wildlife.

The cost of the pipeline, which would transport 1.1 million barrels per day, was estimated at $5.2 billion with the Keystone XL expansion slated to cost an additional $7 billion. Although TransCanada Corp. was free to reapply in the future, the rejection certainly created a massive change in the company's cash flow projections.

Source: "Customers Push for Construction of Keystone's Southern Leg." *Globe and Mail*. Retrieved from http://www.theglobeandmail.com/globe-investor/transcanada-pushes-back-keystone-start-up-date/article2337539/, accessed February 14, 2012. For an update on this project, visit www.transcanada.com.

Table 3.9 **Statement of Cash Flows**

Eastman Technologies Inc.
For the year ended 2013
(in $)

		Source Document
Operating activities		
Profit for the year	97,500	Statement of income
Depreciation	40,000	Statement of income
Adjustments in non-cash working capital	(11,000)*	Statement of financial position
Net cash from operating activities	126,500	
Financing activities		
Payment of dividends	(47,500)	Statement of changes in equity
Long-term borrowings	200,000	Statement of financial position
Share capital	15,000	Statement of financial position
Net cash from financing activities	167,500	
Investing activities		
Purchase of non-current assets	(290,000)	Statement of financial position
Increase in cash	4,000	Statement of financial position
Cash at beginning of year	18,000	
Cash at end of year	22,000	

* Numbers with brackets are an outflow of cash.

Problem-Solving Example 3.4

Identifying the Statement of Cash Flow Activities

Identify the activities the following accounts belong to in the statement of cash flows: depreciation/amortization, revenue, trade receivables, share capital, trade and other payables, sales salaries, profit for the year, mortgage, equipment, and cash.

Solution

Statement of Cash Flow Activities

Operating activities
Profit for the year
Depreciation/amortization
Trade receivables
Trade and other payables

Investing activities
Equipment

Financing activities
Share capital
Mortgage

Change in the cash account
Cash

Note: revenue and sales salaries are not part of this statement.

Self-Test Exercise 3.4

Identifying the Statement of Cash Flows Activities

Indicate under which activity (operating, financing, or investing) the following accounts belong in the statement of cash flows:

	Activity
Notes receivable (short-term)	______________
RRSP	______________
Computers	______________
Long-term borrowings	______________
Profit for the year	______________
Notes payable (short-term)	______________
Depreciation/amortization	______________
Inventories	______________
Car	______________

Answers to the Self-Test Exercises can be found at www.bergeron7e.nelson.com.

Problem-Solving Example 3.5

Profiling the Statement of Cash Flows

Use the following accounts to prepare a statement of cash flows: increase in trade and other payables ($10,000); increase in investment in plant, property, and equipment ($300,000); decrease in trade receivables ($10,000); profit for the year ($200,000); increase in long-term borrowings ($65,000); increase in inventories ($20,000); increase in depreciation/amortization ($25,000); cash balance at the beginning of the year ($40,000); and cash balance at the end of the year ($30,000).

Solution

Statement of Cash Flows

Cash flow from operations	
Profit for the year	$200,000
Depreciation/amortization	25,000
Trade receivables	10,000
Trade and other payables	10,000
Inventories	(20,000)
Cash flow from operating activities	225,000
Cash flow from investing activities	
Property, plant, and equipment	(300,000)
Cash flow from financing activities	
Long-term borrowings	65,000
Decrease in cash	10,000
Cash at beginning of year	40,000
Cash at end of year	30,000

Self-Test Exercise 3.5

The Statement of Cash Flows

From the following financial statements, prepare CompuTech Sales and Service's statement of cash flows for 2014.

CompuTech Sales and Services
Statement of Income
For the year ended 2014
(in $)

Revenue	420,000
Cost of sales	(209,000)
Gross profit	211,000
Other income	5,000
Costs/expenses	(156,000)
Finance costs	(14,000)
Total	(165,000)
Profit before taxes	46,000
Income tax expense	(13,000)
Profit for the year	33,000

CompuTech Sales and Services
Statements of Financial Position
As at December 31
(in $)

	2014	2013
Non-current assets		
Property, plant, and equipment	210,000	170,000
Accumulated depreciation/amortization	(78,000)	(38,000)
Total non-current assets	132,000	132,000
Current assets		
Inventories	65,000	50,000
Trade receivables	45,000	35,000
Prepaid expenses	5,000	5,000
Cash and cash equivalents	21,000	15,000
Total current assets	136,000	105,000
Total assets	268,000	237,000
Equity		
Share capital	100,000	100,000
Retained earnings	58,000	25,000
Total equity	158,000	125,000
Long-term borrowings	50,000	60,000

(continued)

Self-Test Exercise 3.5 (continued)

Current liabilities		
Trade and other payables	20,000	17,000
Short-term borrowings	35,000	30,000
Current portion of long-term borrowings	5,000	5,000
Total current liabilities	60,000	52,000
Total equity and liabilities	268,000	237,000

Answers to the Self-Test Exercises can be found at www.bergeron7e.nelson.com.

For Eastman Technologies, both operating and financing activities generated $294,000, and the company spent $290,000 buying the non-current assets as shown in the investing activities section. The net amount from these three activities was a surplus of $4,000. As shown in the company's 2013 and 2012 statements of financial position (Table 3.4), the cash and cash equivalents account increased from $18,000 to $22,000.

Statement of Cash Flows for Not-for-Profit Organizations

4 Discuss the structure of the statement of cash flows for not-for-profit organizations.

Chapter 2 covered the structure and contents of the statement of financial position, statement of operations, and statement of changes in net assets for the fictitious NFP organization Ontario Foundation for Community Care. The following paragraphs describe the fourth financial statement, the statement of cash flows.

The NFP's statement of cash flows reports the total cash from its operations and the elements of cash flows that took place in financing and investing activities. This statement complements the other financial statements. In the Ontario Foundation for Community Care's statement of cash flows below, the first segment shows the inflows and the outflows of cash generated by operations. The Ontario Foundation for Community Care had a net cash inflow of $52,000. This includes the $40,000 surplus and $20,000 in depreciation; both amounts are drawn from the statement of operations (see page 73). The net cash inflows also include $8,000 for adjustments in non-cash working capital accounts. This amount comes from the following accounts shown on the statement of financial position (see page 71):

Cash outflows		
Increase in trade receivables	$(15,000)	
Increase in grants receivable	(5,000)	$(20,000)
Cash inflows		
Increase in trade and other payables	$ 10,000	
Increase in accrued liabilities	2,000	12,000
Net cash outflows		$ (8,000)

The statement of cash flows illustrates the organization's ability to generate cash internally to continue operations (providing its services and meeting its contractual obligations). The segment dealing with cash flows from financing and investing activities ($47,000) shows the cash flows received from external sources ($38,000 and $40,000) that were used to finance the acquisition of buildings and equipment ($98,000) and investments ($27,000).

Ontario Foundation for Community Care
Statement of Cash Flows
For the year ended December 31, 2013
(in $)

Cash flows from operating activities	
Excess of revenues over expenses	40,000
Depreciation of buildings and equipment	20,000
Adjustments in non-cash working capital accounts	(8,000)
Net cash generated through operating activities	**52,000**
Cash flows from financing and investing activities	
Purchase of buildings and equipment	(98,000)
Purchase of investments	(27,000)
Long-term borrowings	38,000
Contributions from cash endowments	40,000
Net cash used in financing and investing activities	**(47,000)**
Net increase in cash and term deposits	**5,000**
Cash and term deposits, beginning of year	25,000
Cash and term deposits, end of year	30,000

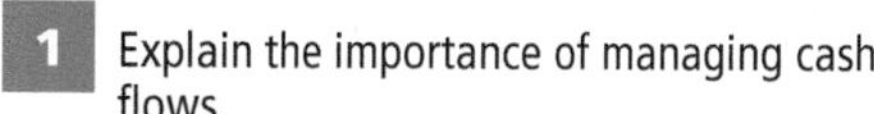

Chapter Summary

1 Explain the importance of managing cash flows.

Because the statement of income shows only the revenue earned and expenses incurred between two dates, and the statement of financial position gives a picture only of the financial condition of a business at a particular time, managers, owners, and creditors want to examine consecutive statements of financial position to have a better picture of the business's financial performance in terms of cash flows. The more important cash inflows are profit for the year, depreciation/amortization, the sale of investment securities, and a long-term loan or new equity. Major cash outflows result from a loss from operations, the purchase of non-current assets, or the repayment of a loan.

2 Analyze cash flows by comparing two consecutive statement of financial position.

To identify the cash inflows and cash outflows (first step in the process of preparing the statement of cash flows) and see the changes in cash flow for each account, two consecutive statements of financial position must be viewed side by side. *Cash inflows* occur when there is a decrease in asset accounts, an increase in equity accounts (share capital or retained earnings increase due to profit), or an increase in liability accounts. *Cash outflows* occur when there is an increase in asset accounts, a decrease in owners' equity (dividends paid or retained earnings decrease through loss from operations), or a decrease in liability accounts.

3 Describe the basic structure of the statement of cash flows.

The statement of cash flows gives a complete picture of the cash inflows and cash outflows of a business under three distinct headings: operating activities, financing activities, and investing activities. It also shows the changes in the cash and cash equivalents between two accounting periods.

4 Discuss the structure of the statement of cash flows for not-for-profit organizations.

NFP organizations also produce a statement of cash flows. Unlike a for-profit organization, an NFP organization's statement of cash flows sometimes contains just two headings: (1) operating activities and (2) financing and investment activities.

Key Terms

Adjustments in non-cash working capital accounts p. 100
Cash budget p. 98
Cash flows p. 88
Cash inflow guidelines p. 94
Cash outflow guidelines p. 94
Consecutive statements of financial position p. 94
Financing activities p. 103
Investing activities p. 104
Operating activities p. 100

Review Questions

1 Explain the importance of managing cash flows.

1. Why is it important for managers to analyze changes in the flow of cash between two consecutive accounting periods?
2. Differentiate between cash inflows and cash outflows.
3. What are internal sources of financing?
4. What are external sources of financing?

2 Analyze cash flows by comparing two consecutive statements of financial position.

5. Identify some of the key cash inflows and cash outflows.
6. Why is depreciation/amortization considered a cash inflow?

7. Why are working capital accounts part of the operating activities shown on the statement of cash flows?
8. Comment on the key guidelines that can be used to identify whether a change in the accounts shown on a statement of financial position between two consecutive accounting periods is a cash inflow or a cash outflow.

3 Describe the basic structure of the statement of cash flows.

9. Identify the basic structure of the statement of cash flows.
10. What is the purpose of the statement of adjustments in non-cash working capital accounts?
11. Comment on the important accounts usually shown under the operating activities section in the statement of cash flows.
12. What financial statements are used to prepare the statement of cash flows?
13. What important accounts are usually shown under the financing activities section in the statement of cash flows?
14. Comment on the important accounts usually shown under the investing activities section in the statement of cash flows.
15. How does the statement of cash flows complement the statement of income and the statement of financial position?
16. How can managers use the statement of cash flows to make important business decisions?

4 Discuss the structure of the statement of cash flows for not-for-profit organizations.

17. How does the statement of cash flows prepared for not-for-profit organizations differ from that prepared for profit-motivated businesses?
18. Give a few examples of accounts shown in the two main sections of the statement of cash flows for a not-for-profit organization.

Learning Exercises

1 Explain the importance of managing cash flows.

EXERCISE 1: SOURCES OF CASH FLOWS

Identify, under the appropriate heading, whether the following changes are an inflow of cash or an outflow of cash. What amounts and percentages were used by internal and external sources to finance the purchase of the assets?

(in $)	This Year	Last Year	Cash Inflows	Cash Outflows
House	134,600	130,000	______	______
Trailer	12,000	—	______	______
Furniture	5,600	4,000	______	______
Salary in excess of expenses	5,000	—	______	______
Mortgage	75,000	60,000	______	______
RRSP	23,000	20,000	______	______
Loan made to a friend	—	5,000	______	______
Car loan	12,000	8,000	______	______
Visa	1,250	600	______	______
The Bay	—	450	______	______
Cash in the bank	3,000	2,000	______	______
Marketable securities	12,000	10,000	______	______
Total			$______	$______

2 Analyze cash flows by comparing two consecutive statements of financial position.

EXERCISE 2: IDENTIFYING CASH INFLOWS AND CASH OUTFLOWS

From Vicky Subbarao's statements of financial position shown below, identify whether each account is an outflow of cash or an inflow of cash.

	This Year	Last Year	Cash Inflows	Cash Outflows
Assets				
House	$145,000	$136,000	______	______
Cottage	65,000	—	______	______
Land	—	40,000	______	______
Car	12,000	6,000	______	______
Computers	7,500	3,000	______	______
Savings bonds	5,000	4,000	______	______
RRSP	20,000	16,000	______	______
Cash	2,000	4,000	______	______
Total assets	$256,500	$209,000		
Equity	$105,000	$ 92,000	______	______
Liabilities				
Mortgage	112,000	99,000	______	______
Bank of Montreal	21,000	11,000	______	______
Bank loan	14,000	3,000	______	______
Visa	1,500	2,000	______	______
Sears	3,000	2,000	______	______
Total liabilities	151,500	117,000	______	______
Total equity and liabilities	$256,500	$209,000	$______	$______

3 Describe the basic structure of the statement of cash flows.

EXERCISE 3: MATCHING ACCOUNTS TO BUSINESS ACTIVITIES

Indicate under which activity (operating, financing, investing) the following accounts belong in the statement of cash flows:

	Activity
Trade receivables	____________
Land	____________
Mortgage payable	____________
Profit for the year	____________
Trade and other payables	____________
Depreciation/amortization	____________
Inventories	____________
Prepaid expenses	____________
Share capital (common)	____________
Buildings	____________
Accrued expenses	____________
Current taxes payable	____________
Equipment	____________
Long-term borrowings	____________
Purchase of a company	____________
Dividends	____________
Share capital (preferred)	____________

EXERCISE 4: WORKING CAPITAL ACCOUNTS

For the following accounts, identify the working capital accounts and prepare the adjustments in non-cash working capital accounts statement.

Accounts	This Year	Last Year
Trade receivables	$230,000	$210,000
Non-current assets	550,000	450,000
Inventories	350,000	290,000
Prepaid expenses	50,000	40,000
Accumulated depreciation	210,000	180,000
Dividends	40,000	32,000
Trade and other payables	240,000	190,000
Revolving loan	90,000	100,000
Mortgage payable	120,000	110,000
Accrued expenses	20,000	30,000
Share capital	50,000	40,000
Short-term borrowings	82,000	34,000
Profit for the year	48,000	39,000

EXERCISE 5: THE ADJUSTMENTS IN NON-CASH WORKING CAPITAL ACCOUNTS AND THE STATEMENT OF CASH FLOWS

With the following financial statements, prepare

- the adjustments in non-cash working capital accounts statement, and
- the statement of cash flows.

Statement of Income
For the year ended December 31, 2013
(in $)

Revenue	550,000
Cost of sales	(200,000)
Gross profit	350,000
Other income	10,000
Costs/expenses	(210,000)
Total	200,000
Profit before taxes	150,000
Income tax expense	(60,000)
Profit for the year	90,000

Statement of Changes in Equity
For the year ended December 31
(in $)

	2013	2012
Retained Earnings		
Balance at beginning of year	210,000	210,000
Profit for the year	90,000	—
Dividends	(70,000)	—
Balance at end of year	230,000	210,000
Share Capital		
Balance at beginning of year	71,000	71,000
Shares issued	—	—
Balance at end of year	71,000	71,000

Statements of Financial Position
As at December 31
(in $)

	2013	2012
Non-current assets		
Property, plant, and equipment	400,000	350,000
Accumulated depreciation	(100,000)	(65,000)
Property, plant, and equipment, net	300,000	285,000

Current assets		
Inventories	300,000	230,000
Trade receivables	250,000	200,000
Cash and cash equivalents	3,000	4,000
Total current assets	553,000	434,000
Total assets	853,000	719,000
Equity		
Share capital	71,000	71,000
Retained earnings	230,000	210,000
Total equity	301,000	281,000
Liabilities		
Non-current liabilities		
Long-term borrowings	200,000	122,000
Current liabilities		
Trade and other payables	200,000	178,000
Accrued expenses	32,000	38,000
Short-term borrowings	120,000	100,000
Total current liabilities	352,000	316,000
Total liabilities	552,000	438,000
Total equity and liabilities	853,000	719,000

4 Discuss the structure of the statement of cash flows for not-for-profit organizations.

EXERCISE 6: THE STATEMENT OF CASH FLOWS

Use the following accounts to prepare a statement of cash flows for a not-for-profit organization:

Long-term borrowings	$ 50,000
Purchase of equipment	110,000
Excess of revenue over expenses	35,000
Purchase of investments	20,000
Depreciation/amortization	10,000
Contributions from cash endowments	50,000
Increase in adjustments in non-cash working capital accounts	5,000
Cash at beginning of year	20,000
Net increase in cash account	10,000

Cases

CASE 1: AUSTIN INDUSTRIES

In 2013, the management committee of Austin Industries Inc. would like to invest $75,000 in property, plant, and equipment. The board of directors would like to approve the decision, but first they must find out how much cash will be generated by the operations in 2013. The members of the board also have the options of raising more funds from the shareholders and increasing their long-term borrowings.

From the information shown on Austin Industries Inc.'s 2013 projected statement of financial position, identify the cash inflows and the cash outflows for the year 2013.

Austin Industries Inc.
Statements of Financial Position
As at December 31
(in $000s)

	2013	2012
Non-current assets		
Property, plant, and equipment	150	75
Accumulated depreciation/amortization	(41)	(26)
Total non-current assets	109	49
Current assets		
Inventories	75	53
Trade receivables	30	22
Term deposits	—	11
Cash	7	15
Total current assets	112	101
Total assets	221	150
Equity		
Share capital	64	38
Retained earnings	95	67
Total equity	159	105
Non-current liabilities		
Long-term borrowings	26	8
Current liabilities		
Trade and other payables	18	15
Notes payable	3	15
Other current liabilities	15	7
Total current liabilities	36	37
Total liabilities	62	45
Total equity and liabilities	221	150

In 2013, management of Austin Industries Inc. expects to generate $38,000 in profit. The board of directors will pay $10,000 in dividends to the shareholders.

Questions

Prepare the following statements:

1. The adjustments in non-cash working capital accounts statement for 2013
2. The statement of cash flows for 2013

CASE 2: GRANT ELECTRONICS INC.

The management committee of Grant Electronics Inc. was studying a report prepared by its economics department about the expansion of a plant to increase their production capacity. The CEO, Jim Smart, indicated that the expansion program would cost approximately $5.6 million in non-current assets (property, plant, and equipment) and that he was hoping that at least half of the funds would be financed through internally generated cash. The investment would take place during the early part of 2013.

He therefore asked his management team to prepare a summary report about how much cash they expected to generate within their respective operations during the remaining six months of 2012. He wanted to review their plans in 30 days.

At the meeting, Jim asked each team member to make a brief statement of much cash he or she would be able to generate before the end of 2012. The vice-president of marketing said that despite the economic slowdown, the company would be able to increase its revenue by 3.2% over 2011. She also added that the introduction of two new product lines and better after-sales service would help the company increase its market share a little. She stated that the industry would grow by only 1.5%. She believed, based on her forecasts, the company would reach $102.0 million in revenue in 2012.

The vice-president of production gave a breakdown of the plant and equipment that would be included in the capital budget proposal. He emphasized that the modernization program would save money in manufacturing, which was included in a 4.1% return on revenue goal for the year 2012.

The chief financial officer said that the projected financial statements included $1.3 million for depreciation/amortization and that she had asked the manager of the trade receivables department to update her about the receivables that would be shown in the statement of financial position by the end of the year. She also mentioned that although there was a three-day improvement in the average collection period, receivables outstanding would show a $700,000 increase.

The vice-president of production indicated that all managers responsible for the production and manufacturing sectors of the company had looked at every possibility to improve the inventory turnover. Despite that, the levels of inventories would increase by $800,000.

The treasurer was asked how much cash could be raised. He replied that $400,000 could be raised from the bank to finance the increased levels of trade receivables and inventories and that he had approached several long-term lenders who were willing to finance part of the capital expenditure project for $1.2 million. He also pointed out that Grant Electronics would continue to pay its common shareholders their annual dividends of $600,000 but that he would be able to raise $500,000 from them by issuing new common shares. The treasurer also noted that the cash in the bank would increase from $600,000 to $782,000 by the end of 2012. He added that because of some changes in the accounting procedures, the current taxes payable would increase by $100,000.

The manager of the trade and other payables department said that she had approached several suppliers about extending the time before paying their bills. Despite the increased amount of purchases that the company would make before the end of the year, she was able to extend its trade and other payables by $200,000.

Questions

1. Use the above information to prepare
   a. the adjustments in non-cash working capital accounts for the year 2012, and
   b. the statement of cash flows for the year 2012.
2. Can the company raise more than half the cash from internally generated funds (as mentioned by the CEO) to finance the capital budget proposal?

FINANCIAL SPREADSHEETS: EXCEL®

Financial spreadsheets can help you prepare projected statements of cash flows. Although accountants produce historical statements of cash flows and include them in annual reports or in other financial documents, financial spreadsheets can produce two projected cash flow documents (output documents). The first document, called the statement of sources and uses of funds, presents a list of cash inflows and cash outflows for individual accounts between two consecutive statements of financial position for a period of two years. The second document is the statement of cash flows. It shows the cash inflows and the cash outflows grouped under four headings: operating activities, financing activities, investing activities, and the changes in the cash account for a period of two years.

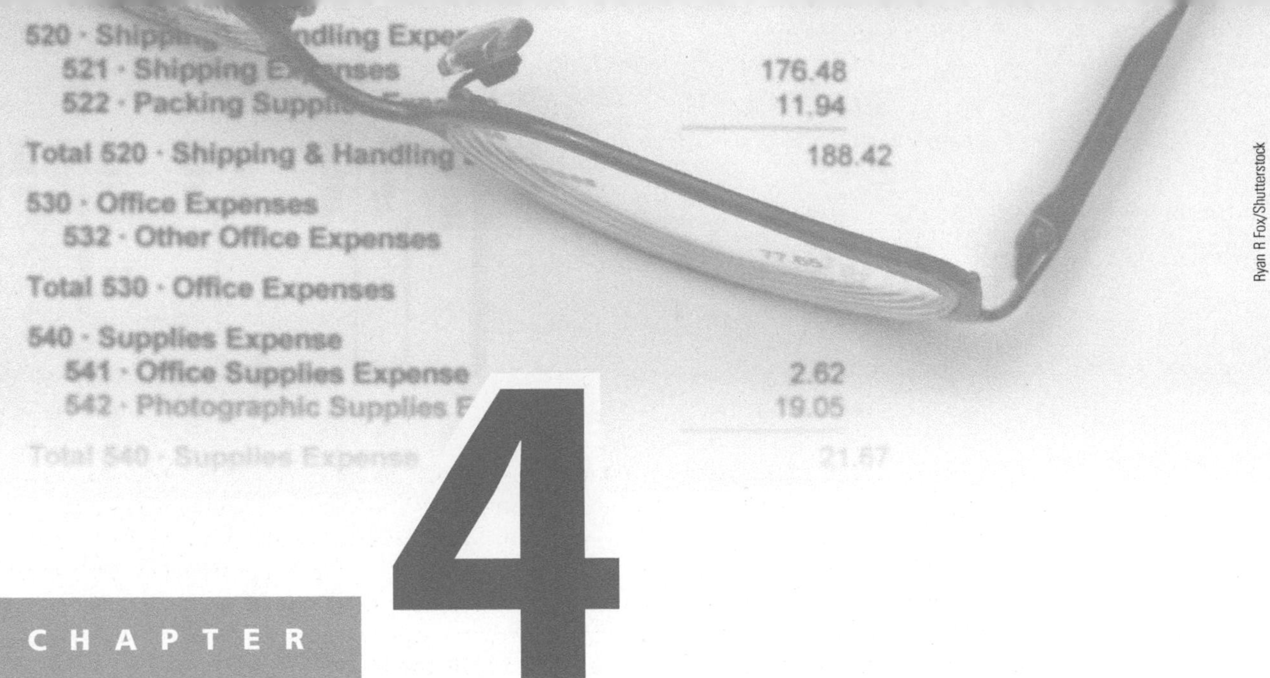

Ryan R Fox/Shutterstock

CHAPTER 4

[FINANCIAL STATEMENT ANALYSIS]

Learning Objectives

After reading this chapter, you should be able to

1. Explain why financial statements need to be analyzed.
2. Evaluate a company's statement of financial position and statement of income by using vertical and horizontal analysis.
3. Analyze financial statements by using meaningful ratios.
4. Describe how financial ratios can be used to measure and improve a company's financial performance.
5. Examine financial statements by using the DuPont financial system.
6. Discuss the limitations of financial ratios.

OPENING CASE

Ratios Measure the Limitless Financial Proportions

Since starting CompuTech Sales and Service, the Millers have received their company's financial statements from accountant May Ogaki each month. The data in the financial statements allow the Millers to analyze their financial performance on a continual basis.

May had explained that the financial statements are critical for measuring the results of past decisions and determining what has to be done. The Millers also remembered the points made by Bill Murray about how to keep a business efficient, liquid, prosperous, and stable.

The Millers' first objective for long-term growth and success is *profitability* (*efficiency*), or the level of profit CompuTech generates compared with revenue, assets, and equity. The Millers know that making effective investment and operating decisions will maximize profitability. A high profit is a sign of efficiency. In 2014, the Millers earned 7.9 cents for every revenue dollar ($33,000 ÷ $420,000), and they believe a good return on revenue is an important financial objective. By increasing revenue and being cautious about spending (e.g., cost of sales and expenses), they can improve their profitability. The Millers know that the more profit the business earns, the more expansion can be funded with the internally generated cash, with less needed from external sources (e.g., lenders).

The second objective is to pay their current bills on time, that is, to be *liquid*. In 2014, CompuTech bought $209,000 worth of goods from suppliers. The Millers always paid their invoices on time (usually within 30 days). They felt maintaining a good relationship with suppliers was important. Having cash on hand (being in a favourable liquid position), also meant the business could take advantage of cash and trade discounts. The business had $90,000 in bank loans (short- and long-term borrowings), and to maintain their banker's trust, the Millers made all debt payments on time.

The third objective is *stability* or maintaining a level of debt that CompuTech can afford. The more debt a business carries, the more costly it is. The Millers realized that a heavy debt load would reduce profits, particularly if finance costs increased, even by 1% or 2%. Also, the Millers' strategy in 2014 was to keep their debt as low as possible (even reducing it) to allow them more leverage to finance the opening of a new store by 2015.

The fourth objective is *productivity*, or generating the highest level of revenue with the least amount of resources (assets). For example, the Millers know that dollars invested in inventories and trade receivables, although necessary, don't generate profit, so they wanted the working capital accounts as low as possible. CompuTech had $268,000 invested in assets in 2014, and each dollar generated $1.57 in revenue ($420,000 ÷ $268,000). To find out whether CompuTech was productive, the Millers needed information from different sources (e.g., banks, industry associations, Dun & Bradstreet) to compare their firm's performance against the industry and other competing firms.

THIS CHAPTER WILL SHOW LEN AND JOAN MILLER HOW TO

- Analyze their financial statements to measure performance in different sectors of their operations.
- Use financial ratios to make critical decisions related to profitability, liquidity, growth, and stability.

Chapter Overview

USING FINANCIAL RATIOS AS DIAGNOSTIC TOOLS

Financial ratio
A comparison of the relationship between numbers on financial statements.

Financial statement analysis is not limited to assessing cash inflows and cash outflows. Another important tool used to gauge the financial health of a business is ratio analysis. A **financial ratio** is the comparison of the relationship between two or more numbers on a statement of financial position or a statement of income. This relationship is usually expressed as a ratio or a percentage. This chapter examines six topics related to statements and ratios.

- *Reasons for analyzing financial statements.* Financial statement analysis through ratios ensures that a business (1) preserves a certain level of liquidity; (2) maintains its solvency, that is, keeps a reasonable level of debt compared with equity; (3) uses its assets in the most productive way; (4) maximizes its return on its investments; and (5) secures long-term prosperity.
- *Approaches to analyzing financial statements.* The two broad approaches to analyzing financial statements are (1) vertical analysis of financial statements, a technique that converts all the elements on the financial statements to percentages, and (2) horizontal analysis of financial statements, an approach that compares the results of a period to previous or future years.
- *Financial ratios.* Ratios are used by businesses to measure a company's financial performance. They can be grouped under five categories: (1) liquidity ratios, (2) debt/coverage ratios, (3) asset-management ratios, (4) profitability ratios, and (5) market-value ratios.
- *Comparative analysis.* A company's financial statements can be compared with external financial results. This topic focuses on financial benchmarks, comparing a company's financial performance with that of successful competitors and with its industry as a whole.
- *DuPont financial system.* The DuPont financial system can be an effective way of measuring the overall financial performance of a business. This system measures a company's return on total assets, taking into account the non-current asset turnover and the profit before taxes.

- *Limitations of financial ratios.* While ratios are important management tools for assessing the performance of a business, they should be used with caution.

Why Analyze Financial Statements?

1 Explain why financial statements need to be analyzed.

Managers, suppliers, investors, and market analysts do not look at the cosmetic parts of financial statements. Just because a statement of financial position balances, or is prepared by professional accountants and audited by a renowned accounting firm, does not mean that a business is in a healthy financial position. Being able to read financial statements tells stakeholders whether a business is financially sound.

As discussed in Chapter 2, the purpose of the first two steps in financial management (bookkeeping and accounting) is to prepare financial statements. The next two steps involve the *analysis* of business performance to assess financial strengths and weaknesses, and make operating, financing, and investing *decisions.*

Ratios are diagnostic tools. Just as a doctor measures various characteristics of the blood, someone evaluating a company measures the relationships of numbers shown on financial statements. Just as a blood test can show symptoms of a disease, the study of numbers on financial statements reveals symptoms of problems or of management errors that require correction.

A ratio compares one account with another and expresses the size of one in relation to the size of the other. For instance, to describe how sunny a month was, you could calculate the ratio of sunny days to rainy days. Dividing the number of sunny days (say, 15) by the number of rainy days (say 15) gives a ratio of 1. Alternatively, you could work out the ratio of sunny days to total days. In this case, you divide the number of sunny days in the month (15) by the total number of days in the month (30), which gives 0.50 or 50%.

Here are a few examples of how numbers shown on financial statements can be compared and for what reasons:

Compare	**to see whether the**
• current liabilities to current assets	• company is able to meet its payroll and pay its suppliers on time
• trade receivables to revenue	• company is collecting its receivables quickly enough
• inventories to cost of sales	• company's inventory is turning over quickly enough
• finance costs to profit	• business can service its debt
• total debts to total assets	• company has too much debt
• total assets to revenue	• company's assets are productive
• profit to revenue	• company as a whole is efficient

Ratio analysis
A method to help readers of financial statements assess the financial structure and performance of a business.

Ratio analysis helps readers of financial statements assess the financial structure and profitability of a business by answering the following questions:

- Is this company able to meet its current debt obligations?
- Are the company's assets being managed efficiently (doing things right) and effectively (doing the right things)?
- Are the business's trade receivables and inventories at suitable levels?
- Will the company be able to meet its long-term borrowing commitments?
- Can the company service its debt comfortably?
- Is the company profitable?
- How do the company's financial structure and profitability compare with those of others in the same industry?
- Is the shareholders' return on investment satisfactory?

Managers analyze financial statements for two main reasons. First, they want to examine the past to gauge how well a business met its financial objectives. Second, they want to set goals and strategies that will improve the company's future financial performance. Financial ratios can make financial analysis and decision making useful and clear.

Analyzing financial statements through ratios helps managers, market analysts, or investors find out what is good or bad about a business. While ratios give only signals about what is wrong or right, they can easily trigger a process that can help managers dig deeper to find answers, solve problems, or improve performance.

It is important to analyze financial statements for five reasons: (1) to ensure liquidity, (2) to maintain solvency, (3) to improve the productivity of assets, (4) to maximize return, and (5) to secure long-term prosperity. Let's examine the relevance of these five objectives.

ENSURE LIQUIDITY

In business, being liquid is just as important as generating an adequate return. Businesses must attract customers every day so that employees and bills can be paid on time. To operate with some degree of comfort, a business must have enough cash (liquidity) to pay its day-to-day expenses and pay off other liabilities on schedule. An important ratio that can test a company's liquidity position is the relationship between all current asset accounts, such as trade receivables and inventories, and all current liability accounts, such as trade and other payables and short-term borrowings, that must be paid within a reasonable time (e.g., a year).

Stakeholders who are interested in liquidity are short-term lenders, suppliers, employees, and owners.

Businesses that want to improve their profit performance (maximize return) can use these strategies to manage cash effectively:

- Speed up billing and collection.
- Delay spending to maximize the use of cash.

- Reduce working capital needs (e.g., inventories and trade receivables).
- Monitor the operating cycle (i.e., the number of days between buying inventory and collecting from customers).

Some of the financial ratios that can provide answers to these concerns include the cash ratio, the current ratio, the quick ratio, the working capital ratio, and the cash conversion cycle.

MAINTAIN SOLVENCY

Solvency
The ability to service or pay all debts (short and long term).

Solvency can be defined as a company's ability to pay its debts. Solvency ratios determine whether a business has too much debt and help identity whether a firm can pay the principal on its debt, finance costs, lease payments, and other fixed obligations. Cash flow performance and capital structure (the proportion of debt to equity) help a company determine its solvency and avoid getting into financial trouble. Maintaining solvency is essential for any business. If a business can't pay back what it owes, this can cause legal problems, strain day-to-day activities, and even derail its operations.

Both managers and investors know that insolvency applies to both current and longer-term operating conditions. This can be examined from two angles:

- *Financial structure* examines whether a company has too much debt compared with what owners have invested in the business (equity).
- *Debt-paying ability* examines whether a business has the ability to service its debt with relative ease. Here, solvency is examined from two angles:
  a. *Short-term solvency* tests (i.e., quick ratio, current ratio)
  b. *Long-term solvency* tests (i.e., debt-service coverage ratio, fixed-charges coverage ratio)

These financial ratios can determine the financial profile of a firm in terms of its creditworthiness and whether it will have enough cash to repay its loans (interest and principal) and pay dividends on time.

IMPROVE THE PRODUCTIVITY OF ASSETS

Productivity
A measure of performance in how resources are used.

Productivity is a measure of performance in how resources are used. It relates goods or services sold (outputs) and the resources used to make them (inputs). At the micro-level, a productivity measure for a manufacturing department could be the relationship between the number of units produced (say, 100,000 widgets) and the resources required (people, equipment, materials) to produce them (say, $100,000). In this case, it would cost the company $1.00 for each widget. If it costs company A $1.00 and company B $1.10, company A is considered more productive.

Financial statements can also be used to estimate the overall productivity of a business, that is, at the macro level. Comparing revenue (outputs) to total assets (inputs) measures productivity. For instance, if company A sells $5 million worth of goods and services and uses $2.5 million worth of assets, it means that for every dollar's worth of assets, the company generates $2 worth of goods and services. If company B sells $5 million worth of goods and services and uses $5 million worth of assets, it uses

$1 worth of assets to produce $1 worth of goods and services. It would therefore be considered less productive than company A.

Of course, management wants to use the least amount of resources to produce the maximum amount of goods or services (revenue). Think of it this way: in business waters, managers want to manage a speedboat, one that moves quickly and is agile, rather than a barge that moves slowly and awkwardly. Managers can use four ratios to measure productivity: average collection period, inventory turnover, capital assets turnover (property, plant, and equipment), and total assets turnover. Both current assets (inventories and trade receivables) and non-current assets (property, plant, and equipment) are used to measure productivity.

MAXIMIZE RETURN

Return
Adequate cash and profit to finance a company's growth.

In business, the word *return* is equal to survival. To survive, a business must earn enough profit and cash flow that will in turn provide a good **return** to investors. A business must also provide enough cash to finance its working capital requirements and to buy non-current assets. Such ratios as return on revenue (ROR), return on assets (ROA), and return on invested capital can show whether a business is generating enough profit to meet its day-to-day operating needs and longer-term financial plans.

Profitability can be improved by a combination of the following:

- Increasing sales volume or unit selling price (or both)
- Reducing expenses (e.g., cost of sales, distribution cost, or administrative expenses)
- Reducing the use of borrowed funds (finance costs)
- Cutting back non-productive assets (e.g., working capital and non-current assets)

Using financial ratios and vertical analysis (which we'll cover later in this chapter) of the statement of income can help set the stage for improved profitability and return performance. The first step is to convert all numbers in the statement of income from dollar figures to percentages (or ratios). Each line on the statement of income is then compared with revenue. Once the percentages or ratios have been calculated, they can be used to analyze past performance and can be compared with those from competitors and with industry-wide statistics. This analysis can help managers see operating efficiencies (or inefficiencies) and profitability:

Sales Revenue	2012 (%)	2013 (%)	Goal for 2014 (%)
Revenue	100.0	100.0	100.0
Cost of sales	80.0	81.0	79.0
Gross profit	20.0	19.0	21.0
Costs/expenses	15.0	16.0	15.0
Profit before taxes	5.0	3.0	6.0

As shown on the previous page, return on revenue (ROR), or for every dollar's worth of revenue, fell from 5 cents to 3 cents between 2012 and 2013. Managers have to find out why. More importantly, they will have to set financial goals for each line on the statement of income (e.g., 79 cents in cost of sales and 15 cents in costs/expenses for 2014), and they will have to figure out ways to meet those goals and improve their gross profit and profit before taxes. To illustrate the importance of this simple analysis, suppose the revenue goal for 2014 is $10 million. A 6% ROR would generate $600,000 in profit before taxes. If the ROR performance stays at the 2013 level (3.0%), the profit before taxes would be reduced to $300,000. Vertical analysis helps to identify what should be done for each account on the statement of income to improve profitability (here, by an extra $300,000) and return. Look ahead to Table 4.1 and Table 4.2 to see Eastman Technologies' vertical analysis for its statements of financial position and statements of income for 2012 and 2013.

Return on assets (ROA) also measures the level of profitability. For example, if profit before taxes increases from $300,000 to $600,000 between 2013 and 2014, with a corresponding growth in total assets from $3 million to $4 million, the company's return would be increased from 10% ($300,000 ÷ $3,000,000) to 15% ($600,000 ÷ $4,000,000).

SECURE LONG-TERM PROSPERITY

If a company can meet the four fundamental financial goals just described, it is more likely to realize its long-term objective: prosperity, or a business's ability to grow smoothly, which is a concern for all stakeholders. Stakeholders typically ask the following questions:

- Do we have enough resources to grow (physical, financial, human)?
- Where will growth funds come from? Internal sources? External sources? How much?
- Do we have enough borrowing power to finance our growth?
- Will we have enough cash to service the new debt and equity (finance costs and dividends)?
- Will the incremental ROR or profit be positive? If yes, to what extent?

Horizontal analysis shows the growth patterns (past and future) for various accounts on financial statements. Look ahead to Table 4.3 and Table 4.4 for Eastman Technologies' horizontal analysis of the company's statements of financial position and statements of income for 2012 and 2013. These financial statements reveal, for example, that an 11.1% increase in revenue for 2013 generated a 30% increase in profit. The company will also need a 21% increase in total assets, with the growth funds coming from an increase of 13.3% in equity (new capital from shareholders and/or an increase in retained earnings), a 33.3% increase in long-term borrowings, and an 11.8% increase in current liabilities. These numbers let managers and investors decide whether the growth rate for each element is feasible.

Now that you understand why ratios are important to analyzing financial statements and to making important operating, financing, and investing decisions, let's examine how financial statements can be analyzed. We will first look at vertical analysis and horizontal analysis, and then examine the more commonly used financial ratios, what they measure, and how they are calculated.

Two Views of Financial Statements

2 Evaluate a company's statement of financial position and statement of income by using vertical and horizontal analysis.

As explained in the previous section, financial statements can be examined from two perspectives: a vertical one or horizontal one.

VERTICAL ANALYSIS

Vertical Analysis
Listing (1) all numbers on the statement of financial position as percentages of total assets, and (2) all numbers on the statement of income as percentages of revenue.

One of the most frequently used ways of examining statements of financial position and statements of income is to convert the dollar amounts to percentages. This is called **vertical analysis**, *common-size ratios*, or *common-size statement analysis.*

In Table 4.1, each entry related to assets on Eastman's statements of financial position is expressed as a percentage of total assets. Each entry related to equity and liabilities is expressed as a percentage of total equity and liabilities. Vertical analysis is useful for comparing the performance of one business with another or one division with another, because it ignores the difference in the size of the individual accounts. All elements are compared on the same terms—percentage.

Vertical analysis also reveals the change between parts of a statement of financial position and between consecutive statements of financial position. For example, Table 4.1 shows that, in 2012, current assets represented 36.16% of every asset dollar. In 2013, this ratio was reduced to 33.33%. Inventories, trade receivables, and prepaid expenses all decreased in percentage terms. The same analysis can be performed for each part of the equity and liability accounts.

Vertical analysis of the statement of income provides the same type of information. In Table 4.2, each component of Eastman's statement of income is converted to a percentage of revenue. Eastman's profit improved between the accounting periods; in 2013, for every dollar of revenue, it made 3.9% (or cents) compared with 3.3% (or cents) in 2012. Although the overall profit of the company improved, some accounts improved and others deteriorated. For example, cost of sales went from 77.5% to 76.0%, which improved the company's gross profit from 22.5% to 24.0%. Salary and lease accounts improved, while depreciation showed an increase.

This analysis enables management to compare financial statements from one year to the next between companies or operating divisions. It also lets management answer the following questions:

- Is our company's financial structure in line with that of the industry?
- Is the ratio of the company's current assets to total assets favourable?
- Is the investment in property, plant, and equipment (capital assets) in the right proportion?
- Are the manufacturing costs too high?
- Are the costs or expenses too high?
- Is the ratio of profit to revenue adequate?

Table 4.1 **Vertical Analysis of the Statement of Financial Position**

Eastman Technologies Inc.
Statements of Financial Position
As at December 31
(in $)

Assets	2013	%	2012	%
Non-current assets				
Property, plant, and equipment	1,340,000	74.44	1,050,000	70.56
Accumulated depreciation	(140,000)	(7.77)	(100,000)	(6.72)
Total non-currents assets	1,200,000	66.67	950,000	63.84
Current assets				
Inventories	218,000	12.11	185,000	12.43
Trade receivables	300,000	16.67	280,000	18.82
Prepaid expenses	60,000	3.33	55,000	3.70
Cash and cash equivalents	22,000	1.22	18,000	1.21
Total current assets	600,000	33.33	538,000	36.16
Total assets	1,800,000	100.00	1,488,000	100.00
Equity				
Share capital	300,000	16.67	285,000	19.15
Contributed surplus	—	—	—	—
Retained earnings	255,000	14.16	205,000	13.78
Total other comprehensive income/(loss)	—	—	—	—
Total equity	555,000	30.83	490,000	32.93
Liabilities				
Non-current liabilities				
Long-term borrowings	800,000	44.45	600,000	40.32
Current liabilities				
Trade and other payables	195,000	10.83	175,000	11.76
Short-term borrowings	150,000	8.33	135,000	9.07
Accrued expenses	20,000	1.11	18,000	1.21
Taxes payable	80,000	4.45	70,000	4.71
Total current liabilities	445,000	24.72	398,000	26.75
Total liabilities	1,245,000	69.17	998,000	67.07
Total equity and liabilities	1,800,000	100.00	1,488,000	100.00

Table 4.2 Vertical Analysis of the Statement of Income

Eastman Technologies Inc.
Statements of Income
For the year ended December 31
(in $)

	2013	Sales (%)	2012	Sales (%)
Revenue	2,500,000	100.0	2,250,000	100.0
Cost of sales	(1,900,000)	(76.0)	(1,743,000)	(77.5)
Gross profit	600,000	24.0	507,000	22.5
Other income	20,000	0.8	18,000	0.8
Distribution costs:				
Sales salaries	(140,000)	(5.6)	(128,000)	(5.7)
Advertising expenses	(20,000)	(0.8)	(19,000)	(0.9)
Total distribution costs	(160,000)	(6.4)	(147,000)	(6.6)
Administrative expenses:				
Office salaries	(170,000)	(6.8)	(155,000)	(6.9)
Lease	(20,000)	(0.8)	(20,000)	(0.9)
Depreciation	(40,000)	(1.6)	(30,000)	(1.3)
Total administrative expenses	(230,000)	(9.2)	(205,000)	(9.1)
Finance costs	(35,000)	(1.4)	(23,000)	(1.0)
Total other income and expenses	(405,000)	(16.2)	(357,000)	(15.9)
Profit before taxes	195,000	7.8	150,000	6.6
Income tax expense	(97,500)	(3.9)	(75,000)	(3.3)
Profit for the year	97,500	3.9	75,000	3.3

Problem-Solving Example 4.1

Efficiency Performance Using Vertical Analysis

Company A generated $4,500,000 in revenue and earned $200,000 in profit for the year. Company B made $26,700,000 in revenue and made $1,100,000 in profit. Use the vertical analysis technique to calculate the ROR for each and determine which company is the most efficient.

Solution

Company A is more efficient since it generated 4.4 % or $0.044 for every revenue dollar compared to 4.1% or $0.041 for Company B.

Company A	Revenue	$ 4,500,000	
	Profit for the year	$ 200,000	4.4%
Company B	Revenue	$26,700,000	
	Profit for the year	$ 1,100,000	4.1%

Self-Test Exercise 4.1

Vertical Analysis of Financial Statements

Use CompuTech's financial statements in Appendix A at the end of the text to prepare a vertical analysis of the company's (1) statements of financial position and (2) statements of income for 2013 to 2015. For the statements of financial position, do the calculations only for total non-current assets, total current assets, total equity, total long-term borrowings, total current liabilities, and total liabilities. For the statements of income, do the calculations only for gross profit, profit before taxes, and profit for the year.

Answers to the Self-Test Exercises can be found at www.bergeron7e.nelson.com.

HORIZONTAL ANALYSIS

Horizontal analysis
A method of analysis that shows the percentage change of accounts on two consecutive financial statements.

Horizontal analysis is done by reviewing two consecutive financial statements and then comparing the differences between the two periods. The comparison shows the growth or decline in each part of a financial statement, both in absolute dollars and as percentages. For example, if two consecutive statements of income show $900,000 in 2013 and $990,000 in 2014, horizontal analysis will show the $90,000 increase and 10% growth.

Tables 4.3 and 4.4 show horizontal analyses for Eastman's statements of financial position and statements of income. In Table 4.3, Eastman's statements of financial position show significant changes in some accounts. For example, total non-current assets show 26.3% growth while total current assets increased by 11.5%. The lower part of the statements of financial position shows an increase of 13.3% in Eastman's equity, an increase of 33.3% in its long-term borrowings, and an 11.8% increase in current liabilities.

Table 4.3 Horizontal Analysis of the Statement of Financial Position

Eastman Technologies Inc.
Statements of Financial Position
As at December 31
(in $)

Assets	2013	2012	Amount of Change	Change (%)
Non-current assets				
Property, plant, and equipment	1,340,000	1,050,000	290,000	27.6
Accumulated depreciation	(140,000)	(100,000)	(40,000)	40.0
Total non-currents assets	1,200,000	950,000	250,000	26.3
Current assets				
Inventories	218,000	185,000	33,000	17.8
Trade receivables	300,000	280,000	20,000	7.1
Prepaid expenses	60,000	55,000	5,000	9.1
Cash and cash equivalents	22,000	18,000	4,000	22.2
Total current assets	600,000	538,000	62,000	11.5
Total assets	1,800,000	1,488,000	312,000	21.0
Equity				
Share capital	300,000	285,000	15,000	5.2
Contributed surplus	—	—	—	—
Retained earnings	255,000	205,000	50,000	24.4
Total other comprehensive income/(loss)	—	—	—	—
Total equity	555,000	490,000	65,000	13.3
Liabilities				
Non-current liabilities				
Long-term borrowings	800,000	600,000	200,000	33.3
Current liabilities				
Trade and other payables	195,000	175,000	20,000	11.4
Short-term borrowings	150,000	135,000	15,000	11.1
Accrued expenses	20,000	18,000	2,000	11.1
Taxes payable	80,000	70,000	10,000	14.3
Total current liabilities	445,000	398,000	47,000	11.8
Total liabilities	1,245,000	998,000	247,000	24.7
Total equity and liabilities	1,800,000	1,488,000	312,000	21.0

Table 4.4 **Horizontal Analysis of the Statement of Income**

Eastman Technologies Inc.
Statements of Income
For the years ended December 31
(in $)

	2013	2012	Amount of Change	Change (%)
Revenue	2,500,000	2,250,000	250,000	11.1
Cost of sales	(1,900,000)	(1,743,000)	(157,000)	9.0
Gross profit	600,000	507,000	93,000	18.3
Other income	20,000	18,000	2,000	11.1
Distribution costs:				
Sales salaries	(140,000)	(128,000)	(12,000)	9.4
Advertising expenses	(20,000)	(19,000)	(1,000)	5.3
Total distribution costs	(160,000)	(147,000)	13,000	8.8
Administrative expenses:				
Office salaries	(170,000)	(155,000)	(15,000)	9.7
Lease	(20,000)	(20,000)	—	—
Depreciation	(40,000)	(30,000)	(10,000)	33.3
Total administrative expenses	(230,000)	(205,000)	(25,000)	12.2
Finance costs	(35,000)	(23,000)	(12,000)	52.2
Total other income and expenses	(405,000)	(357,000)	(48,000)	13.4
Profit before taxes	195,000	150,000	45,000	30.0
Income tax expense	(97,500)	(75,000)	(22,500)	30.0
Profit for the year	97,500	75,000	22,500	30.0

Table 4.4 shows a 30% increase in profit. Accounts that have contributed to this significant increase include revenue, which shows a larger increase than the cost of sales (11.1% versus 9.0%). Although sales salaries increased by only 9.4%, there was a hefty 52.2% increase in finance costs.

In the News 4.1 describes how a company's financial statements can be profiled from different angles: from year-to-year (horizontal analysis) and by comparing figures of the same year (vertical analysis).

In The News 4.1

PROFILING A COMPANY'S FINANCIAL PERFORMANCE

Profiling a company's financial statements is more than just looking at numbers or understanding what they mean. It has to do with who is analyzing the numbers and what information should be looked at. For example, a 1.7 times liquidity ratio is of little or no interest to investors. However, this number is critical to a banker who has to decide whether a line of credit should be extended to a business.

Different types of numbers are presented in newspapers and websites to profile the financial performance of Enbridge Inc. Here are samples of some numbers that relate to vertical and horizontal analysis about Enbridge's financial performance in the fourth quarter: (1) it had a 3% rise in fourth-quarter profit (horizontal); (2) it earned $335 million, or 44 cents a share, in the October-December quarter (vertical), up from $326 million (horizontal); (3) revenue rose 31% to $5.44 billion (horizontal); analysts on average had expected earnings of 39 cents a share, on revenue of $4.41 billion (vertical); and (4) shares went down 3.5% early Friday to $37.80 (horizontal).

Source: "Enbridge achieves better profit on higher volumes." *Calgary Herald*. Retrieved from http://www.calgaryherald.com/business/Enbridge+achieves+better+profit+higher+volumes/6169383/story.html, accessed February 24, 2012. For more information about Enbridge Inc. visit www.enbridge.com.

Problem-Solving Example 4.2

Growth Performance Using Horizontal Analysis

Retail sales for a business grew from $4,500,000 to $5,152,500, while profit for the year jumped from $200,000 to $224,600. Use horizontal analysis to calculate the change for revenue and profit in absolute dollars and on a percentage basis.

Solution

			Change	
	Last year	*This year*	*In dollars*	*In %*
Revenue	$4,500,000	$5,152,500	$652,500	14.5%
Profit for the year	$ 200,000	$ 224,600	$ 24,600	12.3%

Self-Test Exercise 4.2

Horizontal Analysis of Financial Statements

Use CompuTech's financial statements in Appendix A at the end of the text to prepare a horizontal analysis of the company's (1) statements of financial position and (2) statements of income for 2014 and 2015. For the statements of financial position, do the calculations only for total non-current assets, total current assets, total equity, total long-term borrowings, and total liabilities. For the statements of income, do the calculations only for revenue, gross profit, profit before taxes, and profit for the year.

Answers to the Self-Test Exercises can be found at www.bergeron7e.nelson.com.

Financial Ratios

3 Analyze financial statements by using meaningful ratios.

In this section, we examine 16 ratios that can be grouped under three categories:

- *Statement of financial position ratios* relate two accounts shown on the statement of financial position.
- *Statement of income ratios* show the relationship between two accounts on the statement of income.
- *Combined ratios* relate numbers on the statement of financial position to numbers on the statement of income.

These ratios can also be regrouped in five other categories to measure a company's financial performance. We'll use these groups in this chapter:

- *Liquidity ratios* measure the ability of a firm to turn assets into cash to meet its short-term cash obligations.
- *Debt/coverage ratios* evaluate the capital structure, that is, the proportion of funds a business borrows from creditors and owners to finance the purchase of assets, and the firm's ability to service its debt.
- *Asset-management ratios* evaluate how efficiently managers use the assets of a business.
- *Profitability ratios* measure the overall effectiveness of a business by comparing profit levels with revenue, assets, and equity.
- *Market-value ratios* assess the way investors and stock markets react to a company's performance.

The 16 ratios listed in Table 4.5 will be defined and examined within the context of Eastman Technologies Inc.'s statements of income and statements of financial position from Table 2.2 and Table 2.4 in Chapter 2.

Table 4.5 Commonly Used Financial Ratios

Liquidity Ratios	9. Capital assets turnover (times)
1. Current ratio (times)	10. Total assets turnover (times)
2. Quick ratio (times)	**Profitability Ratios**
Debt/Coverage Ratios	11. Profit margin on revenue (%)
3. Debt-to-total assets (%)	12. Return on revenue (%)
4. Debt to equity (times)	13. Return on total assets (%)
5. Times-interest-earned (times)	14. Return on equity (%)
6. Fixed-charges coverage (times)	**Market-Value Ratios**
Asset-Management Ratios	15. Earnings per share ($)
7. Average collection period (days)	16. Price/earnings (times)
8. Inventory turnover (times)	

LIQUIDITY RATIOS

Liquidity ratios
Measures of a firm's ability to meet its cash obligations.

Liquidity ratios examine the current accounts on the statement of financial position, that is, the relationship between current assets and current liabilities. Together, these accounts are referred to as working capital. By using Table 2.4, we can calculate Eastman's net working capital in 2013 as follows:

Current assets	\$600,000
Current liabilities	445,000
Net working capital	\$155,000

Liquidity ratios measure short-term solvency and help one judge whether liquid assets will be enough to meet short-term obligations. The \$155,000 in net working capital is the money Eastman has to operate with on a day-to-day basis—to pay its trade and other bills, short-term bank borrowings, and weekly operating expenses, such as salaries, on time. Some businesses are profitable on paper but may have trouble paying bills as they come due.

The most commonly used liquidity ratios are the current ratio and the quick ratio.

Current Ratio

Current ratio
A test of general business liquidity.

The **current ratio**, also called the working capital ratio, is calculated by dividing current assets by current liabilities. It is an excellent way to measure liquidity because it measures to what extent current assets exceed current liabilities.

Eastman's current ratio is computed as follows:

$$\frac{\textbf{Current assets}}{\textbf{Current liabilities}} = \frac{\$600{,}000}{\$445{,}000} = \textbf{1.35 times}$$

This means that Eastman has \$1.35 of current assets for every dollar of current liabilities. One weakness of the current ratio is that it ignores the *composition* of the current asset accounts, which may be as important as their relationship to current liabilities. Before judging a business's liquidity, we should always look at other factors, such as the ratio of the industry in which it operates, the composition of the current assets, and the season of the year. For example, a business that has a 2 to 1 current ratio with 80% of its current assets in inventories is not as liquid as a company in the same industry that has a 1.5 to 1 ratio with only 30% of its current assets in inventories. Current ratio analysis must be looked at with other working capital ratios, such as the quick ratio.

Rule of thumb. A commonly used practical rule says that an acceptable current ratio is around 2 to 1, that is, every dollar's worth of current liabilities should be backed up by at least two dollars' worth of current assets. This makes sense because if the firm sold its current assets and received only half the values on the statement of financial position, it would still have enough money to pay all current liabilities. Nevertheless, a general standard for this ratio is not useful because different types of business will have different ratios, and even then the ratios might vary with different operating cycles. Industry averages make more sense than overall standards. For example, for distilleries, it may take several years before raw materials become finished products. Consequently, these businesses need a large amount of working capital. In other industries, such as meat packers, the production process is shorter. Businesses are able to receive cash from sales much more quickly and have money available to pay their bills. These companies can operate with less working capital.

Quick Ratio

Quick ratio
A measure of the relationship between the more liquid current assets and all current liabilities.

The **quick ratio**, also called the acid-test ratio, measures the relationship between the more liquid current asset accounts, such as cash, marketable securities, and trade receivables, and the current liability accounts. This ratio complements the current ratio because the problem in meeting current liabilities may result from delays in or even an inability to convert inventories into cash, particularly during economic downturns. The quick ratio is a more precise measure of a business's ability to pay its bills because the least-liquid current asset (inventories) is not included in the calculation. The quick ratio does assume that trade receivables will be converted into cash over the next 12 months.

Eastman's quick ratio, which includes trade receivables ($300,000), prepaid expenses ($60,000), and cash and cash equivalents ($22,000), is calculated as follows:

$$\frac{\textbf{Quick assets}}{\textbf{Current liabilities}} = \frac{\textbf{\$382,000}}{\textbf{\$445,000}} = \textbf{0.86 times}$$

Rule of thumb. An acceptable quick ratio is about 1 to 1; this means that Eastman's second liquidity position also does not appear to be good enough. However, before

Problem-Solving Example 4.3

Liquidity Ratios

With the following financial statement accounts, calculate the company's (1) net working capital, (2) current ratio, and (3) quick ratio: trade receivables ($300,000), inventories ($500,000), share capital ($340,000), trade and other payables ($280,000), salaries ($350,000), and short-term borrowings ($210,000).

Solution:

Current assets:	Trade receivables	$300,000	
	Inventories	500,000	$800,000
Current liabilities	Trade and other payables	$280,000	
	Short-term borrowings	210,000	490,000
(1) Net working capital:			$310,000
(2) Current ratio:	1.63 ($800,000 ÷ $490,000)		
(3) Quick ratio	0.61 ($300,000 ÷ $490,000)		

Self-Test Exercise 4.3

Liquidity Ratios

Use CompuTech's financial statements in Appendix A at the end of the text to calculate the company's (1) net working capital, (2) current ratio, and (3) quick ratio for 2014.

Answers to the Self-Test Exercises can be found at www.bergeron7e.nelson.com.

passing final judgment on Eastman's liquidity, we should evaluate the company's historical working capital performance and compare it with industry standards.

DEBT/COVERAGE RATIOS

Debt/coverage ratios
Measures of the capital structure of a business and its debt-paying ability.

Debt/coverage ratios deal with debt: the money borrowed by a business to buy assets. Two questions are usually asked about debt. First, what mix of funds from lenders and the owner is the best to buy assets (debt ratios)? Second, will the business be able to pay the finance costs (interest) and principal each month (coverage ratios)? The most commonly used debt/coverage ratios are debt-to-total-assets ratio, debt-to-equity ratio, times-interest-earned ratio, and fixed-charges coverage ratio.

Debt-to-Total-Assets ratio

Debt-to-total-assets ratio
A measure of how much debt a business uses to finance all assets.

The **debt-to-total-assets ratio** (also called debt ratio) measures the proportion of all debts (current and long-term) to all assets on the statement of financial position. The more debt a firm has, the more highly leveraged it is. This ratio is calculated by dividing total debt by total assets.

This ratio is important to lenders because they want to ensure that shareholders put enough money into the business to spread the risk more evenly. For Eastman, the 2013 ratio is computed as follows:

$$\frac{\textbf{Total liabilities}}{\textbf{Total assets}} = \frac{\$1{,}245{,}000}{\$1{,}800{,}000} = 69\%$$

This means that 69% of Eastman's assets are financed by debt, and thus lenders bear the greatest portion of risk. This suggests that creditors may have trouble collecting their loan if the business goes bankrupt or into liquidation.

Rule of thumb. Usually when this ratio is higher than 50%, creditors are reluctant to make loans. However, as with all other ratios, it is important to look at the type of assets owned by the business. The book value of assets (how much the business paid), for example, may be much less than their market value (how much they could be sold for). Also, a business may obtain more funds from lenders to build a plant in an industrial park in a large metropolitan area than for one located in an economically depressed region. Furthermore, non-current assets, such as property, plant, and equipment, may have little value except to an ongoing business; for this reason, some find this ratio to have no practical use.

Debt-to-Equity Ratio

Debt-to-equity ratio A measure of the proportion of debt and of equity used to finance all assets.

The **debt-to-equity ratio** is redundant if the debt-to-total-assets ratio is used: the two ratios tell us the same information. The debt-to-equity ratio is explained here because financial publications that provide industry average ratios often cite the debt-to-equity ratio instead of the debt-to-total-assets ratio. This ratio also shows whether a company is using debt carefully or has too much debt. The proportion of lenders' claims compared with ownership claims is used as a measure of debt exposure. Companies with debt-to-equity ratios above 1 are probably relying too much on debt.

In the case of Eastman, the 2013 ratio works out to

$$\frac{\textbf{Total debt}}{\textbf{Total equity}} = \frac{\$1{,}245{,}000}{\$555{,}000} = 2.24 \textbf{ times}$$

Eastman uses more than two dollars in borrowed funds for each dollar provided by shareholders. The debt-to-equity ratio shows that a considerable amount of assets is being financed by debt rather than by equity. The company would find it difficult to borrow more without first raising more equity capital. Borrowing more could put the firm at risk of bankruptcy. Eastman's management should start trying to lower total debt or increase owners' equity over the next year.

Times-Interest-Earned Ratio

Times-interest-earned ratio (TIE) A measure of a business's ability to pay the interest charges on debt.

The **times-interest-earned ratio (TIE)** measures the business's ability to pay its interest charges (or finance costs, as they are called on the statement of income). Suppose someone wanted a loan to buy a $200,000 house. The bank wants to know not just the value of the house and how much of a down payment the homebuyer has, but also the buyer's ability to repay the loan each month. An acceptable ratio is around 30%, that is, for every dollar's worth of gross salary, the loan repayment should not exceed 30 cents. For example, if a homebuyer earns $5,000 a month and is in the 40% tax bracket, $1,500 (or 30%) would go against the loan, $2,000 would be used to pay income taxes, and the remaining $1,500 would be left for monthly living expenses. The higher the loan repayment in proportion to the buyer's gross salary, the less the buyer would have left for ongoing living expenses.

Earnings before interest charges and taxes The profit before taxes and finance costs shown on the statement of income.

This is what the TIE ratio reveals for a business. It is determined by dividing **earnings before interest charges and taxes** (EBIT) by interest charges. The ratio measures the extent to which profit before taxes can decline before the business is unable to meet its annual interest charges.

This ratio shows the number of dollars of EBIT available to pay each dollar of interest. Adding the earnings before taxes ($195,000) and interest charges ($35,000) and dividing the sum by interest charges gives the ratio. This $230,000 is like the homebuyer's $5,000 gross salary. A higher ratio makes lenders more certain that the business will be able to pay all interest charges on time.

The calculation is always done on a before-tax basis because interest charges are a tax-deductible expense. Using information from Table 2.2, Eastman's ratio is computed as follows:

$$\frac{\textbf{Earnings before taxes + Interest charges}}{\textbf{Interest charges}} = \frac{\$195{,}000 + \$35{,}000}{\$35{,}000} = 6.57 \text{ times}$$

This means that the company has $6.57 of EBIT available for each dollar of interest charges to pay the interest charges and taxes. Because interest charges and taxes amount to only $3.78 ($1.00 + $2.78), the rest is profit. Here is another way of describing this ratio:

EBIT	$6.57
Interest charges	(1.00)
EBT	5.57
Income tax expense	(2.78)
EAIT	$2.79

With each $6.57 EBIT, Eastman pays $1.00 toward the interest charges and is left with $5.57 in earnings before taxes. Because the company is in the 50% tax bracket, Eastman pays $2.78 in income taxes and is therefore left with $2.79 to

- Pay dividends
- Pay the principal on the debt
- Reinvest the rest in the business as retained earnings

The lower the ratio, the riskier it is to make a loan. To illustrate, if the TIE ratio is reduced to 3.0, it means that the company would be left with only $2.00 (after paying the interest charges) to pay income taxes, the principal on the loan, and dividends, and to reinvest profit (retained earnings) in the business. This ratio gives additional information about the company's ability to pay its debt.

Rule of thumb. A comfortable TIE ratio is about 4.0 to 5.0. An acceptable ratio in each of the past five fiscal years is at least 3.0 to 4.0 for industrial businesses and 2.0 for utilities. Utilities have little or no competition, and rate boards set rates that allow them to make an acceptable return on their investment, while an industrial company's profit for the year is more uncertain and thus requires a higher safety margin.

Fixed-Charges Coverage Ratio

The times-interest-earned ratio does not present a complete picture. The larger question is whether the company can meet its commitments to all creditors. Another ratio based on all fixed charges, called the fixed-charges coverage ratio, is more inclusive and recognizes that many firms have long-term debts with scheduled rental or lease payments. The total of those obligations, lease payments plus interest charges, compose a firm's total annual fixed charges. The **fixed-charges coverage ratio** is calculated by dividing the sum of the earnings before taxes and all fixed charges by fixed charges. Fixed charges include such items as lease payments, interest charges, principal repayments, and sinking funds (the annual payment required to amortize a bond). These types of payments are unavoidable. The Eastman 2013 ratio is computed as follows:

Fixed-charges coverage ratio
A measure of the extent to which a business can pay all its fixed charges (e.g., interest charges, leases).

$$\frac{\textbf{Earnings before taxes + Interest charges + Lease}}{\textbf{Interest charges + Lease}}$$

$$= \frac{\$195{,}000 + \$35{,}000 + \$20{,}000}{\$35{,}000 + \$20{,}000} = 4.54 \text{ times}$$

Other fixed charges, such as lease payments, reduce the margin of error in Eastman's operating results. This ratio is being used more often because of the increasing popularity of long-term lease agreements. It shows how much earnings before taxes is left to pay for all fixed charges.

In the News 4.2 describes how an organization can be driven to the edge when revenues are less than expenses, it faces a heavy debt load, and it is functioning in a weak economy.

In The News 4.2

COURTING THE EDGE OF A FINANCIAL CLIFF

Whether you are a salaried employee, a millionaire, a not-for-profit organization, a government organization, or a for-profit business, if you spend more than you earn year after year, face a soaring and heavy debt load, and do business in a tough economy, you are unquestionably heading for difficult times.

This was basically the financial profile of the Ontario government as at the start of 2012. A 543-page report by Don Drummond (chair of the commission on public-service reform) recommended that the Government of Ontario consider implementing 362 cost-cutting actions if the government wanted to restore its financial health. The report indicated that the government had a \$16 billion deficit (equivalent to a loss for a business) and a \$250 billion debt, was operating in a feeble economy with a weak job market, and was facing the possibility of a credit rating downgrade. If no actions were taken, the size of the deficit (or loss) could rise to \$30.2 billion by year 2017–18. The prescription needed to make the financially anemic organization healthy again was to massively slash programs and costs.

Source: "Drummond Report: New roadmap for Ontario includes higher hydro bills, larger school classes." *Toronto Star*. Retrieved from http://www.thestar.com/news/canada/politics/article/1131820—drummond-report-higher-hydro-bills-more-user-fees-urged-insweeping-report, accessed February 24, 2012.

Problem-Solving Example 4.4

Debt-Coverage Ratios

With the following accounts, total liabilities ($140,000), interest charges ($18,000), total assets ($320,000), lease payments ($4,000), earnings before taxes ($40,000), and equity ($180,000), calculate the company's (1) debt-to-total assets ratio, (2) debt-to-equity ratio, (3) times-interest-earned ratio, and (4) fixed-charges coverage ratio.

Solution

1. $$\frac{\text{Total liabilities}}{\text{Total assets}} = \frac{\$140,000}{\$320,000} = 43.75\%$$

2. $$\frac{\text{Total liabilities}}{\text{Total equity}} = \frac{\$140,000}{\$180,000} = 0.78 \text{ times}$$

3. $$\frac{\text{EBT} + \text{Interest charges}}{\text{Interest charges}} = \frac{\$40,000 + \$18,000}{\$18,000} = 3.22 \text{ times}$$

4. $$\frac{\text{EBT} + \text{IC} + \text{Lease}}{\text{IC} + \text{Lease}} = \frac{\$40,000 + \$18,000 + \$4,000}{\$18,000 + \$4,000} = 2.82 \text{ times}$$

Self-Test Exercise 4.4

Debt/Coverage Ratios

Use CompuTech's financial statements in Appendix A at the end of the text to calculate the company's debt-to-total-assets ratio, debt-to-equity ratio, times-interest-earned ratio, and fixed-charges coverage ratio for 2014.

Answers to the Self-Test Exercises can be found at www.bergeron7e.nelson.com.

ASSET-MANAGEMENT RATIOS

Asset-management ratios
Measures to evaluate how efficiently managers use the assets of a business.

Asset-management ratios, sometimes called activity ratios, operating ratios, or management ratios, measure the efficiency with which a business uses its assets or resources (i.e., inventories, trade receivables, non-current assets) to earn a profit. The intent of these ratios is to answer one basic question: Does the amount of each category of asset shown on the statement of financial position seem too high or too low in view of what the firm has accomplished or wants to do in the future? The more commonly used asset-management ratios are the average collection period, the inventory turnover, the capital assets (or property, plant, and equipment, as named in the statement of financial position) turnover, and the total assets turnover.

Average Collection Period

Average collection period (ACP)
How many days it takes for customers to pay their bills.

The **average collection period (ACP)** measures how long a firm's average sales dollar (revenue) remains in the hands of its customers. A longer collection period automatically creates a larger investment in assets and may indicate that the firm's credit terms are too generous. However, management must offer similar credit terms to those of competitors to avoid losing sales. Investment in trade receivables has a cost, and a high level of trade receivables means that too much debt or equity is being used by the business. If so, the business is not as capital efficient as it could be.

The average collection period is calculated in two steps. The first step is calculating the average daily sales, which is done by dividing the total annual revenue by 365 days. Eastman's average daily sales for 2013 were $6,849 ($2,500,000 ÷ 365). The second step is dividing the average daily sales into trade receivables. Eastman's average collection period is 44 days and is calculated as follows:

$$\frac{\textbf{Trade receivables}}{\textbf{Average daily sales}} = \frac{\textbf{\$300,000}}{\textbf{\$6,849}} = \textbf{44 days}$$

If Eastman could collect its receivables within 30 days, the company would reduce its trade receivables by $95,886 ($6,849 × 14 days). That amount could be invested in more productive assets. The question for Eastman is, How long should credit be extended? The manager responsible has to decide whether the average collection period is too long. If it is, the company needs to shorten credit terms, refuse any more credit to slow payers, or step up collection efforts.

Inventory Turnover

Inventory turnover
The number of times a year a company turns over its inventories.

Inventory turnover (also called the inventory utilization ratio) measures the number of times a company's investment in inventories is turned over during a year. An inventory item "turns" each time a firm buys another similar item for stock. The number of times that the cycle recurs during the year is that product's annual turnover rate. A company's statement of financial position does not show individual items, of course, so this ratio looks at the total average annual turnover rate. The higher the turnover ratio, the better, because a company with a high turnover has a smaller investment in inventories than one producing the same level of revenue with a low turnover rate. Company management has to be sure, however, to keep inventories at a level that is just right in order not to miss sales.

While both revenue and cost of sales could be used in the calculation, they give different results because revenue is higher than the cost of sales by the amount of the gross profit. Cost of sales (not revenue) should be used as the numerator because the denominator (inventories) is valued at cost, and the purpose is to assess the physical turnover of that inventory.

Because a company's revenue is earned over 12 months (moving-picture concept) but inventory is computed at a specific point (still-photography concept), it is more appropriate to use the average inventory for the year. Usually, we can calculate that by taking the beginning plus ending inventory and dividing by two. Quarterly, and even monthly, inventories can also be used.

This ratio shows how efficiently inventory is turned over, and it can be compared with those of other companies in the same industry. It also provides some clues about whether the company has enough inventory for the volume of sales. If a company has an inventory turnover rate above the industry average, it has a better balance between inventories and cost of sales. There will be less risk of the business being caught with a high level of inventories if the price of raw materials or finished products drops. Here is how Eastman's 2013 inventory ratio is calculated:

$$\frac{\textbf{Cost of sales}}{\textbf{Inventories}} = \frac{\$1{,}900{,}000}{\$218{,}000} = 8.7 \text{ times}$$

Eastman turns the average item carried in its inventory 8.7 times during the year. Of course, not every item in the company's stock turns at the same rate, but the overall average is a logical starting point for inventory management. If Eastman were able to turn over its inventory faster, say, up to 10 times a year, it would reduce its inventories from $218,000 to $190,000 ($1,900,000 ÷ 10) and thus add an extra $28,000 to the company's treasury.

Capital Assets Turnover

Capital assets turnover ratio A measure of how intensively a firm's capital assets are used to generate revenue.

The **capital** (or property, plant, and equipment, as named in the statement of financial position) **assets turnover ratio** (also called the fixed assets utilization ratio) measures how intensively a firm's capital assets, such as property, plant, and equipment, are used to generate revenue. A low capital assets turnover implies that a firm has too much investment in non-current assets relative to revenue; it is basically a measure of productivity.

The following shows how Eastman's 2013 capital assets turnover ratio is calculated:

$$\frac{\textbf{Revenue}}{\textbf{Capital assets}} = \frac{\$2{,}500{,}000}{\$1{,}200{,}000} = 2.1 \text{ times}$$

The company generates $2.10 in revenue for every dollar invested in capital assets. If a competing firm generates $3.00, it implies it is more productive. If a business has a weak ratio, its plant may be operating below capacity, and managers should consider selling the less-productive assets.

Using the capital assets turnover for comparisons has one problem. If the capital assets turnover ratio of a firm with assets it bought many years ago is compared with a company that has recently, for example, automated its operations to make them more efficient or productive, the more modern firm may have a lower capital assets turnover ratio simply because of the increased amount of capital assets.

Total assets turnover ratio A measure of how intensively a firm's total assets are used to generate revenue.

Total Assets Turnover

The **total assets turnover ratio** measures the turnover or use of all of a firm's assets, both non-current assets and current assets. It also indicates the efficiency with which assets are used; a low ratio means that too many assets are used to generate revenue or that some assets (non-current or current assets) should be liquidated or reduced. This ratio is very useful as a first sign of a problem with revenue or an excessive amount of assets. When this ratio is too low, managers may have to modify their revenue objectives and plans, examine the growth in the marketplace and of competitors, or determine if their asset base is too large. Eastman's 2013 total assets turnover is as follows:

$$\frac{\textbf{Revenue}}{\textbf{Total assets}} = \frac{\$2{,}500{,}000}{\$1{,}800{,}000} = 1.4 \text{ times}$$

Eastman produces $1.40 of revenue for every dollar invested in total assets. If Eastman can reduce its investment in trade receivables and inventories or sell a division or some non-current assets, it would increase the total assets turnover ratio and be more productive.

Problem-Solving Example 4.5

Asset-Management Ratios

With the following accounts, capital assets ($210,000), trade receivables ($45,000), interest charges ($8,000), cost of sales ($310,000), revenue ($400,000), equity ($130,000), total assets ($320,000), and inventories ($65,000), calculate the company's (1) average collection period, (2) inventory turnover, (3) capital assets turnover, and (4) total assets turnover.

Solution

1. $$\frac{\text{Trade receivables}}{\text{Average daily sales}} = \frac{\$45{,}000}{\$1{,}096} = 41.1 \text{ days}$$

2. $$\frac{\text{Costs of sales}}{\text{Inventories}} = \frac{\$310{,}000}{\$65{,}000} = 4.8 \text{ times}$$

3. $$\frac{\text{Revenue}}{\text{Capital assets}} = \frac{\$400{,}000}{\$210{,}000} = 1.9 \text{ times}$$

4. $$\frac{\text{Revenue}}{\text{Total assets}} = \frac{\$400{,}000}{\$320{,}000} = 1.25 \text{ times}$$

Self-Test Exercise 4.5

Asset-Management Ratios

Use CompuTech's financial statements in Appendix A at the end of the text to calculate the company's average collection period, inventory turnover, capital assets turnover, and total assets turnover for 2014.

Answers to the Self-Test Exercises can be found at www.bergeron7e.nelson.com.

Problem-Solving Example 4.6

Improving a Company's Cash Flow

Using the information in Problem-Solving Example 4.5, calculate the additional amount of cash if management was able to improve (1) its average collection period to 35 days, and (2) its inventory turnover to six times.

Solution

The company would increase its cash flow by $19,973.

(1) Trade receivables:	Existing		$45,000	
	Target	$1,096 × 35 =	38,360	
	Additional cash flow			$ 6,640
(2) Inventories:	Existing		$65,000	
	Target	$310,000 ÷ 6 =	51,667	
	Additional cash flow			13,333
	Total additional cash flow			$19,973

Self-Test Exercise 4.6

Using Financial Ratios as a Management Tool to Improve Cash Flow

The Millers are trying to find ways to improve their cash flow during 2014. After looking closely at their working capital accounts, they feel that additional cash could be generated internally if they managed trade receivables and inventories more efficiently. Calculate how much cash CompuTech could generate within the next six months if the Millers were able to improve (1) the average collection period to 30 days, and (2) the inventory turnover to 4.5 times.

Answers to the Self-Test Exercises can be found at www.bergeron7e.nelson.com.

Problem-Solving Example 4.7

Improving a Company's Cash Flow

Use the information in Problem-Solving Example 4.6 and the following accounts, accumulated depreciation ($96,000), equity ($130,000), profit for the year ($34,000), and depreciation ($10,000), to calculate the amount of cash that the company would generate in a year.

(*continued*)

Problem-Solving Example 4.7 (continued)

Solution

The company would generate $63,973 in cash.

Profit for the year	$34,000	
Depreciation	10,000	$44,000
Trade receivables		6,640
Inventories		13,333
Total cash flow		$63,973

Self-Test Exercise 4.7

Cash Flow Forecast

Use the company's statement of income shown in Appendix A at the end of the text and the information from Self-Test Exercise 4.6 to calculate the amount of cash that CompuTech would generate by December 31, 2014.

Answers to the Self-Test Exercises can be found at www.bergeron7e.nelson.com.

PROFITABILITY RATIOS

Profitability ratios Measures of the overall efficiency and effectiveness of a business.

Profitability ratios deal with bottom-line performance and measure how successful a business is in generating profit relative to revenue, assets, and equity. These ratios show the level of business efficiency and effectiveness, and measure the results of many policies and decisions. Profitability ratios show the combined effects on operating results of liquidity, asset management, and debt management. The most commonly used profitability ratios are profit margin on revenue, return on revenue, return on total assets, and return on equity.

Profit Margin on Revenue

Profit margin The profit before tax, after adjusting for non-operating accounts, such as other income and finance costs.

Profit margin can be defined as the profit before taxes, adjusted for non-operating accounts, such as other income and finance costs. For Eastman, here is how profit margin is calculated for 2013:

Profit before taxes		$195,000
Other income	− 20,000	
Finance costs	+35,000	+15,000
Profit margin		$210,000

Profit margin on revenue A measure of the operating efficiency of a business.

Profit margin on revenue, or net operating margin (operating income), is computed by dividing profit margin by revenue. This ratio is an excellent measure of a firm's ability to make financial gains because the calculation excludes non-operating items, such as finance costs and other income, which are not part of the operating activities of a business. The main purpose of this ratio is to assess how effective management is in generating operating income.

Eastman's profit margin on revenue is as follows:

$$\frac{\textbf{Profit margin}}{\textbf{Revenue}} = \frac{\$210{,}000}{\$2{,}500{,}000} = 8.4\%$$

Eastman generates 8.4 cents in operating margin for every dollar's worth of revenue.

Return on Revenue

Return on revenue A measure of a company's overall ability to generate profit from each revenue dollar.

Return on revenue is an important measure of a company's financial performance after its finance costs and income taxes have been paid. This ratio gauges the firm's ability to squeeze profit from each revenue dollar. It measures the overall profitability of a business and is calculated by dividing profit for the year by revenue. Profit-seeking businesses want to maximize their return on revenue as this bottom-line figure represents funds either distributed to shareholders as dividends or retained and reinvested in the business (look back to Figure 1.5).

Eastman's 2013 ROR is calculated as follows:

$$\frac{\textbf{Profit for the year}}{\textbf{Revenue}} = \frac{\$97{,}500}{\$2{,}500{,}000} = 3.9\%$$

For every dollar's worth of revenue, Eastman earns 3.9 cents in profit. The higher the ratio, the better for the wealth of the business and its shareholders. This ratio should also be compared with historical company performance, used as a platform for planning, and compared with the industry average or those of competing firms in the industry.

The limitation of the return on revenue ratio is that it is based on profit after deducting finance costs. If the company has increased its debt substantially, the result may be a decrease in profit because of the finance costs deduction. The profit margin on revenue overcomes this problem and provides another view of profitability.

Return on Total Assets

Return on total assets A measure of the performance of assets used in a business.

The **return on total assets** ratio measures profit performance in relation to all assets. This ratio might be viewed as a measure of the efficiency or productivity of total asset usage. It is calculated by dividing profit for the year by total assets. Eastman's 2013 return on total assets is computed as follows:

$$\frac{\textbf{Profit for the year}}{\textbf{Total assets}} = \frac{\$97{,}500}{\$1{,}800{,}000} = 5.4\%$$

This ratio should be compared with the industry average or with those of competing firms. Another way of measuring the effectiveness of this ratio is by comparing it with the company's weighted average cost of capital. Look back to Figure 1.2.

Return on Equity

Return on equity A measure of the yield shareholders earn on their investment.

The **return on equity** ratio relates profit to equity. This ratio is critical to shareholders because it shows how much they earn on their investment (the yield).

It also allows shareholders to judge whether the return is worth the risk. Eastman's 2013 return on equity ratio is calculated as follows:

$$\frac{\textbf{Profit for the year}}{\textbf{Equity}} = \frac{\$97{,}500}{\$555{,}000} = 17.6\%$$

For every dollar invested by the shareholders, 17.6 cents is earned. By most standards, this profit for the year is relatively good.

Problem-Solving Example 4.8

Profitability Ratios

Use the following accounts, equity ($140,000), total assets ($330,000), profit for the year ($15,000), revenue ($440,000), and operating income ($30,000), to calculate the (1) profit margin on revenue, (2) return on revenue, (3) return on total assets, and (4) return on equity.

Solution

1. $$\frac{\text{Profit margin}}{\text{Revenue}} = \frac{\$30{,}000}{\$440{,}000} = 6.8\%$$

2. $$\frac{\text{Profit for the year}}{\text{Revenue}} = \frac{\$15{,}000}{\$440{,}000} = 3.4\%$$

3. $$\frac{\text{Profit for the year}}{\text{Total assets}} = \frac{\$15{,}000}{\$330{,}000} = 4.5\%$$

4. $$\frac{\text{Profit for the year}}{\text{Equity}} = \frac{\$15{,}000}{\$140{,}000} = 10.7\%$$

Self-Test Exercise 4.8

Profitability Ratios

Use CompuTech's financial statements in Appendix A at the end of the text to calculate the company's profit margin on revenue, return on revenue, return on total assets, and return on equity for 2014.

Answers to the Self-Test Exercises can be found at www.bergeron7e.nelson.com.

MARKET-VALUE RATIOS

So far, we have examined *financial statement ratios*, which are calculated by using information from financial statements. The next two ratios are market-value ratios, which are used to analyze the way investors and stock markets are reacting to a company's performance.

Market-value ratios
Measurements of how investors react to a company's market performance.

Market-value ratios relate the data on a company's financial statements to financial market data and provide insight into how investors view a business as a whole, including its strength in securities markets.

We can't calculate these ratios for Eastman or for any company whose stock is not traded on the stock market (e.g., the Toronto or New York stock exchange). Only publicly traded companies have to report market-value ratios at the bottom of their financial statements. If a company's liquidity, asset-management, debt/coverage, and profitability ratios are all good, its market ratios are usually excellent, and its share price is usually high. The more commonly used market-value ratios are earnings per share and the price/earnings ratio.

Earnings per Share

Earnings per share (EPS)
A measure of how much profit is available to each outstanding share.

Earnings per share (EPS) is calculated by dividing the profit for the year after preferred dividends are paid—that is, profit for the year available to common shareholders—by the number of common shares outstanding. If Eastman had 40,000 outstanding shares in 2013, the calculation would be as follows:

$$\textbf{Earnings per share} = \frac{\textbf{Profit for the year}}{\textbf{Number of shares outstanding}} = \frac{\$97,500}{40,000} = \$2.44$$

EPS is a measure that both management and shareholders pay attention to because it is widely used to value common shares and is often the basis for setting strategic goals and plans. Normally, market analysts do not have to calculate the results as they are readily available in the financial pages of daily newspapers.

Price/Earnings Ratio

Price/earnings ratio (P/E)
A measure of how much investors are willing to pay per dollar of reported profits.

The **price/earnings ratio (P/E)** is one of the most widely used and understood ratios. The P/E ratio shows how much investors are willing to pay per dollar of reported profits. The P/E ratio is the market price of common shares divided by the earnings (profit) per common share. For Eastman, we assume here that in 2013, the company's common share market price was $30.00. Daily newspaper stock market pages include EPS and the P/E ratio, which are the primary stock valuation criteria. This ratio is probably the most useful and widely used financial ratio because it combines all other ratios into one figure.

The price/earnings ratio for Eastman is calculated as follows:

$$\textbf{Price/earnings ratio} = \frac{\textbf{Price per common share}}{\textbf{Earnings per common share}} = \frac{\$30.00}{\$2.44} = \textbf{12.3 times}$$

Eastman's P/E ratio of 12.3 is more meaningful when compared with the P/E ratios of other companies. If a competitor is generating a P/E ratio of 10, then Eastman's P/E ratio is higher, suggesting that it may be somewhat less risky as an investment or have better growth prospects or both.

Table 4.6 summarizes Eastman's 16 important financial ratios that were calculated in this chapter.

Table 4.6 Eastman Technologies Inc.'s 2013 Financial Ratios

Liquidity Ratios

1. Current Ratio

$$\frac{\text{Current assets}}{\text{Current liabilities}} = \frac{\$600{,}000}{\$445{,}000} = 1.35 \text{ times}$$

2. Quick Ratio

$$\frac{\text{Quick assets}}{\text{Current liabilities}} = \frac{\$382{,}000}{\$445{,}000} = 0.86 \text{ times}$$

Debt Coverage Ratios

3. Debt-to-Total-Assets Ratio

$$\frac{\text{Total liabilities}}{\text{Total assets}} = \frac{\$1{,}245{,}000}{\$1{,}800{,}000} = 69\%$$

4. Debt-to-Equity Ratio

$$\frac{\text{Total debt}}{\text{Total equity}} = \frac{\$1{,}245{,}000}{\$555{,}000} = 2.24 \text{ times}$$

5. Times-Interest-Earned Ratio

$$\frac{\text{Earnings before taxes} + \text{Interest charges}}{\text{Interest charges}} = \frac{\$195{,}000 + \$35{,}000}{\$35{,}000} = 6.57 \text{ times}$$

6. Fixed-Charges Coverage Ratio

$$\frac{\text{Earnings before taxes} + \text{Interest charges} + \text{Lease}}{\text{Interest charges} + \text{Lease}} = \frac{\$195{,}000 + \$35{,}000 + \$\ 20{,}000}{\$35{,}000 + \$20{,}000} = 4.54 \text{ times}$$

Asset-Management Ratios

7. Average Collection Period

$$\frac{\text{Trade receivables}}{\text{Average daily sales}} = \frac{\$300{,}000}{\$6{,}849} = 44 \text{ days}$$

8. Inventory Turnover

$$\frac{\text{Cost of sales}}{\text{Inventories}} = \frac{\$1{,}900{,}000}{\$218{,}000} = 8.7 \text{ times}$$

9. Capital Assets Turnover

$$\frac{\text{Revenue}}{\text{Capital assets}} = \frac{\$2{,}500{,}000}{\$1{,}200{,}000} = 2.1 \text{ times}$$

10. Total Assets Turnover

$$\frac{\text{Revenue}}{\text{Total assets}} = \frac{\$2{,}500{,}000}{\$1{,}800{,}000} = 1.4 \text{ times}$$

Profitability Ratios

11. Profit Margin on Revenue

$$\frac{\text{Profit margin}}{\text{Revenue}} = \frac{\$210{,}000}{\$2{,}500{,}000} = 8.4\%$$

12. Return on Revenue

$$\frac{\text{Profit for the year}}{\text{Revenue}} = \frac{\$97{,}500}{\$2{,}500{,}000} = 3.9\%$$

13. Return on Total Assets

$$\frac{\text{Profit for the year}}{\text{Total assets}} = \frac{\$97{,}500}{\$1{,}800{,}000} = 5.4\%$$

14. Return on Equity

$$\frac{\text{Profit for the year}}{\text{Equity}} = \frac{\$97{,}000}{\$555{,}000} = 17.6\%$$

Market-Value Ratios

15. Earnings per Share

$$\text{Earnings per share} = \frac{\text{Profit for the year}}{\text{Number of shares outstanding}} = \frac{\$97{,}500}{40{,}000} = \$2.44$$

16. Price/Earnings Ratio (P/E)

$$\text{Price/earnings ratio} = \frac{\text{Price per common share}}{\text{Earnings per common share}} = \frac{\$30.00}{\$2.44} = 12.3 \text{ times}$$

External Comparisons

4 Describe how financial ratios can be used to measure and improve a company's financial performance.

Financial ratios are useful for comparing financial performance of companies in the same industry. When using external comparisons, it is also important to ensure that the financial ratios are calculated in the same way. For example, it would be meaningless to compare the inventory turnover of a company that calculates this ratio by using cost of sales to another business that uses revenue. We'll look at external comparisons in this section in four areas: financial benchmarks, comparing a company to specific competitors, comparing a company to the industry, and trend analysis.

FINANCIAL BENCHMARKS

Financial statements become valuable tools when managers or analysts make the connection between accounts or groups of accounts on the statement of income and the statement of financial position. This information can be revealing when compared with that of competitors and industry norms that can be used as **benchmarks** (excellent industry norms to which a business's own financial ratios can be compared).

Benchmarks Excellent industry norms to which a business's own financial ratios can be compared

An effective way to learn from others is benchmarking. **Benchmarking** is the process of searching for the best practices among competitors and non-competitors that have led to their superior performance, and then adapting them to your own company. By aspiring to be as good as the best in the industry, managers can set their own goals and use this tool to catch up to or become better than the benchmarked company.

Benchmarking The process of searching for the best practices by comparing your own business to a competitor's excellent performance.

Benchmarks can be grouped under four categories. *Process benchmarks* focus on work processes and operating systems, such as the effectiveness of an operating service, customer billing, the way orders are filled and goods received, employee recruitment programs, or even management's planning process. They can help managers to focus on improving efficiencies, lowering costs, or increasing revenues, which can all improve the bottom line.

Performance benchmarks focus on products and services and how effective a business's strategies are related to prices, technical quality, product or services features, speed, and reliability.

Strategic benchmarks (also called outside-of-industry benchmarks) let operators see how competitive their business is within the industry by using excellent results achieved by businesses outside their own industry (e.g., a hotel versus a restaurant). These benchmarks influence the long-term competitive patterns of a business.

Internal benchmarks look at a company's own excellent operating systems to then apply processes and systems throughout its operations. For example, a business that has five restaurants will determine which one has the best operating results so that the others can learn from it. These excellent business units are referred to as "champions." This method can also be used for comparing similar operating systems in different functions, such as in the marketing department and the human resources department.

Financial benchmarks
Financial performance ratios calculated by using dollar amounts on the statement of income and statement of financial position to find areas of excellent financial performance.

Financial benchmarks are ratios that can be calculated by using the dollar amounts on the statement of income and statement of financial position to find areas of excellent financial performance. An operator can use these as the standard of excellence against which to compare their performance.

Financial benchmarks can also be grouped under four categories: liquidity, debt/coverage, asset management, and profitability. Some financial benchmarks should be interpreted cautiously. For example, an excellent return on revenue or debt-to-total-assets performance for one business in a specific industry could be marginal to others in a different industry. Because of this, we'll categorize financial benchmarks in three groups: hard financial benchmarks, soft financial benchmarks, and self-regulated financial benchmarks.

Hard financial benchmarks
Financial targets that can be applied to any business or industry to measure financial performance.

Hard financial benchmarks are financial targets that can be applied to just about any business and industry to measure performance. For example, the ability to service debt can be used as a measurement tool in any sector or business establishment. To illustrate, a person who is looking for a mortgage to finance a house must demonstrate an ability to make (or service) the monthly payments. Banks calculate this ratio for everyone applying for a mortgage, whether the person works for a small or large business establishment, a government organization, or a retail store.

Soft financial benchmarks
Most financial benchmarks fall in this category and should be used with some degree of caution.

Most financial benchmarks are **soft financial benchmarks** or financial targets that should be used cautiously for two reasons. First, these financial benchmarks vary across industries (depending on the nature of the business). For example, liquidity ratios for manufacturers are different from those of service establishments, where inventories are not an important part of working capital. Second, soft financial benchmarks can vary across businesses depending on the nature of certain accounts on a business's financial statements. Here are two examples.

- A business that sells perishable goods to food stores or restaurants will want to collect its payments more quickly than one selling durable goods, such as computers to wholesalers or retailers. The average collection period would be different.
- A business that operates with depreciated assets will show a higher level of productivity (related to revenue) than a manufacturing plant that is highly automated and only two or three years old.

Self-regulated financial benchmarks
Financial targets that are determined by a business's own policies and practices and other financial measures.

Self-regulated financial benchmarks are ratios that are contingent on (1) a company's own policies and practices or (2) other financial performance measures. For example, a business that offers a 2%/10-day net 30 (giving a 2% discount on the invoice amount if the customer pays within 10 days, and charging the full amount if the customer pays on the 30th day) will probably show a better average payment collection than a business that has a different credit policy.

Reading industry and trade journals and attending trade shows and public symposia keeps managers and employees aware of what others are doing and gives them ideas for how to improve their own company's practices.

Table 4.7 summaries our discussion of financial ratios and benchmarks and shows how they are categorized.

COMPARING A COMPANY TO SPECIFIC COMPETITORS

The first step in benchmarking is to use trade journals or periodicals to select companies with the best financial results in their industries (e.g., current assets, trade receivables, capital assets turnover).

For example, Standard & Poor's Compustat Services, Inc., produces all types of historical and current financial ratios about individual firms and industries. If a company wants to improve its working capital accounts, debt structure, or profit

Table 4.7 Financial Benchmarks

Financial Ratios	Category	Benchmark	Reasons
A. Liquidity Ratios			
1. Current ratio (times)	S SR	1.5 times	S • Aging of trade receivables and nature of inventories (i.e., perishable) • Composition of working capital accounts (e.g., inventories versus trade receivables) SR Depends on cash needs, credit policies, and agreement with suppliers
2. Quick ratio (times)	S SR	1.0 times	S Aging of trade receivables SR Depends on cash needs and credit policies
B. Debt/Coverage Ratios			
3. Debt to total assets (%)	S	50%	Type of assets and location of business
4. Debt to equity (times)	S	1 to 1	Type of assets and location of business
5. Times-interest-earned (times)	H	4–5 times	
6. Fixed charges coverage (times)	H	4–5 times	
C. Asset-Management Ratios			
7. Average collection period (days)	SR	N/A	Depends on credit policies
8. Inventory turnover (times)	S	N/A	Level of profit margin and type of inventories (i.e., perishable)
9. Capital assets turnover (times)	S SR	N/A	S Nature of industry, age of capital assets SR Automated versus labour-intensive plant
10. Total assets turnover (times)	S SR	N/A	S Nature of industry, age of capital assets SR Depends on cash needs, credit policies agreement with suppliers, and automated versus labour-intensive plant
D. Profitability Ratios			
11. Profit margin on revenue (%)	S	N/A	Nature of business
12. Return on revenue (%)	S	N/A	Nature of business
13. Return on total assets (%)	SR	N/A	Depends on cost of capital
14. Return on equity (%)	S	N/A	Level of risk

S = soft H = hard SR = self-regulated

performance, it should refer to the Report Library and look for companies that excel in these areas. The next step is to analyze and ask questions about why that company's performance is superior.

Table 4.8 shows a partial list of the type of financial information that can be drawn from the Compustat Report Library on a company and industry-wide basis.

Table 4.8 **Benchmarking the Corporation**

Partial List of Financial Information That Can Be Drawn from Standard & Poor's Compustat Services, Inc., Library Report

Statement of Income Reports
- Annual Statement of Income—11 Years
- Comparative Statement of Income
- Comparative Composite Statement of Income
- Trend Statement of Income
- Common Size Statement of Income
- Quarterly Common Size Statement of Income
- 12-Month Moving Statement of Income

Statement of Financial Position Reports
- Annual Statement of Financial Position—11 Years
- Annual Statement of Financial Position—With Footnotes
- Composite Historical Annual Statement of Financial Position
- Trend Statement of Financial Position
- Common Size Statement of Financial Position
- Quarterly Trend Statement of Financial Position

Statement of Cash Flows
- Statement of Cash Flows (Annual and Quarterly)
- Cash Statement by Source and Use (Annual and Quarterly)
- 12-Month Moving Statement of Cash Flows
- Working Capital Statement (Annual and Quarterly)

Ratio Reports
- Annual Ratio
- Quarterly Ratio
- Comparative Annual Ratio

Market Reports
- Daily Market Date—Seven Days
- Daily Adjusted Prices

Summary Reports
- Profitability
- Trend—Five Years

Graphics Library
- Fundamental Financial Data
- Six-Month and One-Year Daily Price
- Company Segment Pie Chart
- Geographic Segment Pie Chart
- Ten-Year Monthly Price/Earnings

COMPARING A COMPANY TO AN INDUSTRY

The ratios of any business should be compared with those in the sector or industry in which the business operates. To illustrate how ratios can be used as measurement tools, let's examine Table 4.9 and compare Eastman's 16 ratios with those of the industry.

Table 4.9 shows whether Eastman's management should be satisfied or concerned about the financial structure and profitability position of the business. The arrows beside the ratios indicate the better financial performance.

On *liquidity*, Eastman appears to be worse than the industry. There may be no reason for concern if the company can meet its current commitments on time. If the current ratio were too high, say 3.5 or 4.0, it could mean that the company had money tied up in assets that had low earning power, because cash or marketable securities are low profit generators. A high liquidity ratio could also mean that

Table 4.9 Comparative Ratio Analysis of Eastman Technologies Inc. with Industry

Ratios	Eastman Technologies		Industry	
A. Liquidity Ratios				
1. Current ratio (times)	1.35		2.00	←
2. Quick ratio (times)	0.86		1.25	←
B. Debt/Coverage Ratios				
3. Debt-to-total-assets (%)	69		55	←
4. Debt-to-equity (times)	2.24		1.52	←
5. Times-interest-earned (times)	6.6	←	6.0	
6. Fixed-charges coverage (times)	4.5	←	4.12	
C. Asset-Management Ratios				
7. Average collection period (days)	44	←	53	
8. Inventory turnover (times)	8.7	←	6.3	
9. Capital assets turnover (times)	2.1		4.3	←
10. Total assets turnover (times)	1.4		2.1	←
D. Profitability Ratios				
11. Profit margin on sales (%)	8.4	←	6.2	
12. Return on sales (%)	3.9	←	2.4	
13. Return on total assets (%)	5.4	←	4.4	
14. Return on equity (%)	17.6	←	14.3	
E. Market-Value Ratios				
15. Earnings per share ($)	2.44	←	2.11	
16. Price/earnings ratio (times)	12.3	←	10.0	

management should reduce inventories and trade receivables and put the money to more productive uses.

The company appears to be in a worse position than the industry for *debt/coverage*. This means that its creditors face more risk. Although Eastman has a higher debt ratio, its fixed debt commitments are slightly better than the industry (6.6 compared with 6.0). Nevertheless, the high debt-to-total-assets ratio and debt-to-equity ratio suggest that Eastman has reached, if not exceeded, how much it should borrow.

Eastman is doing a good job with the *asset management* of its current assets but shows signs of weakness in capital and total assets. Both the average collection period and the inventory turnover indicate that management is keeping the trade receivables and inventories at minimum levels. These ratios are also in line with the liquidity ratios that deal with the current assets on the statement of financial position. The capital assets turnover and total assets turnover show that, overall, the business has too many assets (mainly capital assets) for the level of revenue. It also means that the capital assets are not working hard enough. The only way to correct this is by increasing revenue or by selling (if possible) some of its capital assets.

On *profitability*, Eastman is doing well on all counts. Profit margin and profit for the year in relation to revenue, assets, or equity are healthy. The profit level is particularly encouraging, despite the fact that capital assets and debt burden are higher than the industry.

Eastman is also doing well on *market value*. Both the EPS and price/earnings ratio exceed those of the industry. Although Eastman is not a publicly owned company, these ratios are shown here for illustration.

TREND ANALYSIS

Comparing one set of figures for a year with those of the industry gives a good picture of the financial structure and profitability level of a business. However, this analysis does not give a full picture of the situation, because it does not take time into account. Comparative analysis gives a snapshot of the financial statements at a given point; it is like still photography. For a more complete picture, ratios of one company should be compared with those of the industry over several years, like a motion picture; this will show whether the financial statements are improving or deteriorating.

Trend analysis
Analyzing a company's performance over a number of years.

Trend analysis is illustrated in Figure 4.1. Four of Eastman's ratios are compared with the industry over four years (from 2011 to 2014); they are the current ratio, debt to total assets, capital assets turnover, and return on total assets.

Eastman's *current ratio* has always been inferior to that of the industry. The gap widened between 2011 and 2012, and reached a 0.65 spread in 2014 (1.35 versus 2.00). The company decreased the level of receivables and inventories or increased its current liabilities. Although the current ratio is a good indicator of current asset management, management and creditors may want to learn more about individual current asset accounts by looking at average collection period and inventory turnover.

Figure 4.1 Trend Analysis

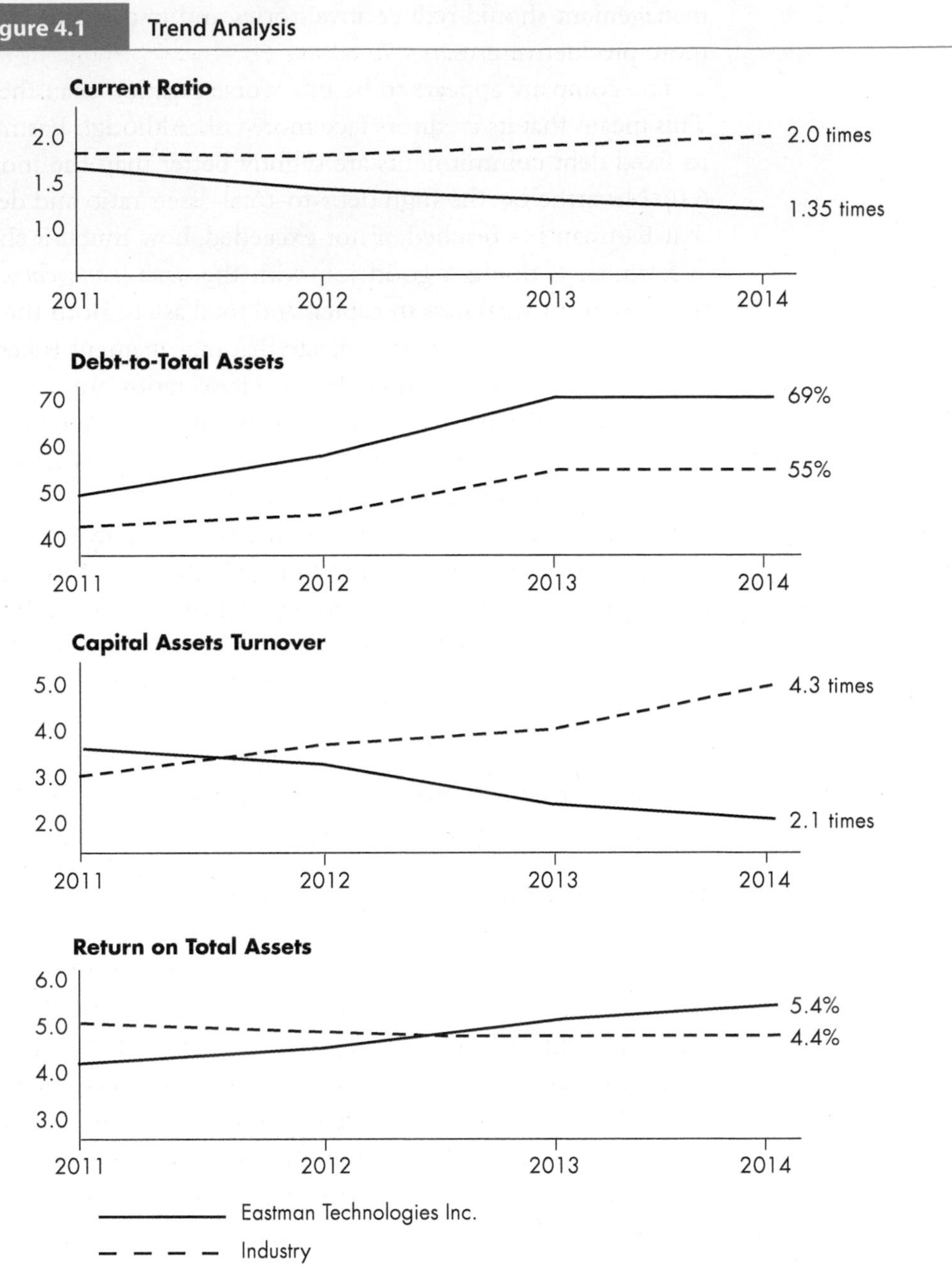

The *debt-to-total-assets* ratio has weakened over the years. While Eastman finances 69 cents of each asset by debt, the industry is at only 55 cents. The debt-ratio position was weak in 2011 and continued to get worse. The company probably invested large sums of money in capital assets that, as seen in the capital assets turnover, are not very productive in relation to the industry.

Eastman's *capital assets* turnover dropped from 4.0 to 2.1 between 2011 and 2014, meaning that Eastman's capital assets are less productive. Not only has the management of current assets been marginal over the past four years, but the acquisition of capital assets during 2011 to 2014 also seems to indicate that Eastman has a surplus of non-productive capital assets. Eastman's management should examine closely all capital asset accounts to see what can be done to improve the ratio. If management sees a growth trend in sales, it might not want to change anything; however, if sales are projected to improve only a little, it may have to sell some of the capital assets to make all assets work at full capacity.

Return on total assets shows a strong position for Eastman. It is operating at a level one point higher than the industry (5.4 versus 4.4). The profitability of Eastman passed that of the industry in 2012; the industry's trend declined over the four years, while Eastman's profit performance during the same period improved considerably. In short, Eastman's profitability is healthy despite the fact that the debt ratio and the capital assets turnover are weaker than the industry.

In the News 4.3 gives an example of a company that was doing exceptionally well for years but suddenly had to make tough decisions to avoid failure.

In The News 4.3

RESTORING FINANCIAL HEALTH

Even if a business has been doing exceptionally well for years or even decades, it may eventually face a bumpy road and have to make difficult or even unpopular decisions to avoid failure. It may not be the internal operations that are the problem but an external environment that forces management to match the business operations with its environment.

This happened to Mike Wilson, CEO of Atlantic Industries Ltd., in Dorchester, N.B., a manufacturer of corrugated steel pipes. His father built a thriving business beginning in the 1950s, and everything was going well when Mike took the reins later as CEO; but, in 1990, he had to turn the company around by streamlining operations and laying off 75 employees, shutting down a plant, and charting a new strategy. The strategic decisions proved to be successful; Atlantic Industries became a world leader in innovative engineered solutions in corrugated metal structures, retaining walls, modular steel bridges, and corrugated pipe; the bold move saved his business from on-going losses and even bankruptcy.

Source: "Company turns it around after laying off 75." *Globe and Mail.* Retrieved from http://www.theglobeandmail.com/report-onbusiness/small-business/sb-growth/success-stories/company-turns-it-around-after-laying-off-75/article2355229/, accessed March 3, 2012. For more information about AIL, visit www.ail.ca/en/home/aboutus/contactus/default.aspx.

The Dupont Financial System

5 Examine financial statements using the DuPont financial system.

The **DuPont financial system** has achieved international recognition. DuPont brought together the key financial ratios in a logical way to assist management in measuring return on assets (ROA). The system shows the various parts that affect return on assets, such as profit for the year, non-current assets and current assets, and the most

DuPont financial system
The presentation of financial ratios in a logical way to measure ROA.

important figures on the statement of income and the statement of financial position. Figure 4.2 shows a modified and simplified version of the DuPont financial system.

The numbers in the upper portion of the diagram deal with the statement of financial position and show how current assets (inventories, trade receivables) and non-current assets are used. To calculate the total assets turnover, we divide revenue by total assets.

Figure 4.2 **The DuPont Financial System**

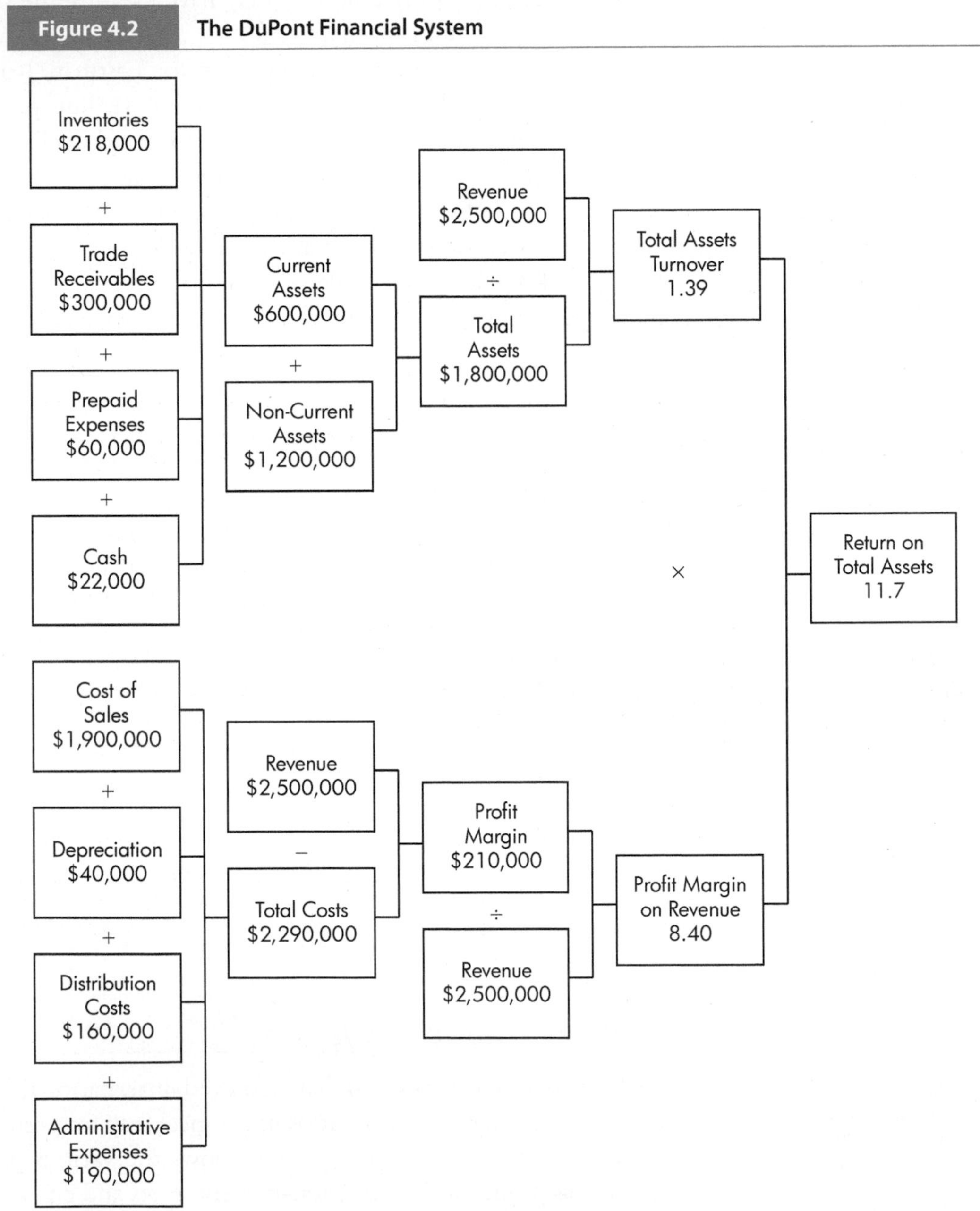

The numbers in the lower portion of the diagram deal with statement of income accounts. They give the profit performance in relation to revenue. By multiplying the total assets turnover by the profit margin on revenue, we find the ROA of 11.7%. See page 147 for an explanation of how the profit margin is calculated. For Eastman, the calculation is as follows: before-tax profit ($195,000) + finance costs ($35,000) − other income ($20,000) = profit margin ($210,000). By dividing the profit margin by revenue, we get 8.40 ($210,000 ÷ $2,500,000).

Eastman's 2013 ROA was calculated by multiplying the 1.39 total assets turnover ratio by the 8.4 profit margin on revenue. This gives an 11.68% ROA. If the company wants to increase this ratio, it will have to improve the capital assets turnover ratio and/or the profit margin on revenue.

The upper portion of the DuPont formula deals with the *productivity* of assets. As shown, it deals with assets and revenue; it indicates that every dollar's worth of assets triggers $1.39 worth of revenue. The more efficient the assets, the higher this ratio, and the more impact it will have on the ROA ratio. The lower portion of the DuPont formula deals with *efficiencies*. The formula deals with costs and revenue; the higher the margin relative to revenue, the higher the ratio. In this case, every dollar of revenue generates 8.40 cents of margin. The higher the profit margin ratio, the higher the ROA ratio. If both ratios (total assets turnover and profit margin on revenue) show an increase, it magnifies the ROA ratio.

Problem-Solving Example 4.9

Calculating the ROA by Using the DuPont Financial System

Use the following accounts, trade receivables ($200,000), non-current assets ($800,000), revenue ($2,000,000), distribution costs ($30,000), cash ($25,000), administrative expenses ($35,000), and cost of sales ($1,800,000), to calculate the company's ROA by using the DuPont financial system.

Solution

ROA is 13.16% (note: the underlined numbers are found by adding figures in the formula)

Step 1: Total assets

Trade receivables	+	Cash	=	Current assets	+	Non-current assets	Revenue	÷	Total assets		
$200,000	+	$25,000	=	$225,000	+	$800,000	$2,000,000	÷	$1,025,000	=	1.95

Step 2: Profit margin

Admin. expenses	+	Distrib. costs	+	Cost of sales	Revenue	−	Total costs	=	Profit margin	÷	Revenue
$35,000	+	$30,000	+	$1,800,000	$2,000,000	−	$1,865,000	=	$135,000	÷	$2,000,000 = 6.75

1.95 × 6.75 = 13.16%

Self-Test Exercise 4.9

Calculating the ROA Using the DuPont Financial System

Use CompuTech's financial statements in Appendix A at the end of the text to calculate the following:

1. The company's 2014 ROA by using the DuPont financial system.
2. The company's 2015 ROA by using the DuPont financial system.

Is there an improvement? Why or why not?

Answers to the Self-Test Exercises can be found at www.bergeron7e.nelson.com.

Limitations of Financial Ratios

6 Discuss the limitations of financial ratios.

Although financial ratios can be effective tools for measuring financial performance and managerial success, they are only one instrument in the management tool kit. A financial ratio gives an indication of the weak and strong points in a business. Ratios will not say why something is going wrong or what to do in a particular situation; they only show where a problem exists. For example, the inventory turnover may have gone from 10 to 7 over three years, and the industry average may be at 9; management will have to investigate to find out what is going wrong and what to do about it.

Another limitation of financial ratios emerges when comparing ratios to other businesses or industry averages. Although there are accepted accounting principles and conventions for constructing financial statements, several different numbers can be used to calculate a ratio. When calculating inventory turnover, for example, one business may use the cost of sales as the numerator, while another may use revenue. Even though both companies are part of the same industry, and are equally efficient in the management of inventory, they will show different ratios. Another example occurs when a business uses the profit margin to calculate its total assets turnover, while another uses the profit for the year. It is important to remember that before comparing ratios, some of the numbers on the financial statements may have to be adjusted.

Different ways of running a business may make the comparison of financial ratios irrelevant. For instance, one business might lease most of its assets while another owns them. In this situation, some of the ratios, such as debt-to-total-assets ratio, TIE ratio, total assets turnover ratio, and return on total assets, would be unrelated.

Another limitation is inflation. Inflation can make the ratio of a particular business look good or bad when yearly trends are examined. For example, inventory turnover may have deteriorated over three years, but the problem might be due to a substantial increase in the cost of sales and not to an increase in inventory. Also, an increase in return on total assets may not mean that the company is more efficient; it may reflect the fact that sales prices (and not volume) have increased rapidly and that the capital assets, which are shown on the financial statements at cost, have remained unchanged.

Finally, statements of financial position reflect the financial situation of a business at a particular time, usually at the end of a fiscal period (e.g., as at December 31), and this may result in a weak ratio. That might not be the case if the same calculation were done by using the June numbers.

Although financial ratios have limitations, a business operator should not shy away from using them. As long as managers know how to use them, understand their limitations, and accept the fact that they are just one of many management tools, they will be in a better position to use them wisely, effectively, and cautiously.

Chapter Summary

1 Explain why financial statements need to be analyzed.

Financial statements should be analyzed to ensure liquidity, maintain solvency, improve the productivity of assets, generate a maximum return, and secure long-term prosperity.

2 Evaluate a company's statement of financial position and statement of income by using vertical and horizontal analysis.

Analysts examine financial statements from different angles. *Vertical analysis* converts all the elements on the financial statements to percentages. *Horizontal analysis* compares the financial results of a particular period to those of previous periods in terms of absolute dollars and percentages.

3 Analyze financial statements by using meaningful ratios.

Financial ratios can be grouped under five main categories. *Liquidity ratios*, such as the current ratio and quick ratio or acid test, measure a company's ability to meet its short-term debts. Second, the *debt/coverage ratios*, such as debt-to-total-assets, debt-to-equity, TIE, and fixed-charges coverage, can measure the extent to which a business is financed by debt as opposed to equity and how it is able to service its debt. Third, the *asset-management ratios*, such as average collection period, inventory turnover, capital assets turnover, and total assets turnover, measure how effectively managers use the assets or resources of a business. Fourth, the *profitability ratios*, such as profit margin on revenue, return on revenue, return on total assets, and return on equity, measure management's overall effectiveness. Finally, *market-value ratios* compare the data on a company's financial statements with financial market data and include earnings per share and the price/earnings ratio.

4 Describe how financial ratios can be used to measure and improve a company's financial performance.

To get the most value from financial ratios, management should compare its standards of performance with those of other companies in the same industry or with industry averages. Financial benchmarks, that is, businesses with superior financial performance, should be examined closely to see how well they are doing and how to apply similar practices in a business's own operations. Also, because financial statements give the financial picture of a company at a particular time, financial trends should be assessed to find out whether financial structure and profitability are improving or deteriorating.

5 Examine financial statements by using the DuPont financial system.

The DuPont system provides an effective way of measuring the overall financial performance of a business. The system measures a company's return on total assets, taking into account the capital assets turnover and the profit margin on revenue.

6 Discuss the limitations of financial ratios.

Although financial ratios are important management tools for assessing the performance of a business, they should be used with caution. Ratios tell where a particular operation is or is not doing well; they do not say why or what to do about a specific situation.

Key Terms

Review Questions

1 Explain why financial statements need to be analyzed.

1. Why is it important to use ratios to analyze financial statements?
2. What does management want to achieve when it tries to "ensure liquidity" and "maintain solvency"?

3. Financial ratios are analyzed by four groups of individuals: managers, short-term lenders, long-term lenders, and equity investors. What is the primary emphasis of each group in evaluating ratios?

2 Evaluate a company's statement of financial position and statement of income by using vertical and horizontal analysis.

4. What is the purpose of vertical analysis and horizontal analysis?
5. What does vertical analysis try to reveal?
6. What does horizontal analysis try to reveal?

3 Analyze financial statements by using meaningful ratios.

7. What do liquidity ratios reveal?
8. Differentiate between the current ratio and the quick ratio.
9. Is it possible for a firm to have a high current ratio and still have difficulty paying its current bills? Why or why not?
10. Is the inventory ratio more important to a grocery store than to a hardware store? Why or why not?
11. What is the purpose of the debt/coverage ratios?
12. What is the purpose of the times-interest-earned ratio?
13. What is the purpose of the asset-management ratios?
14. Explain the purpose of the inventory turnover ratio.
15. Profitability ratios try to indicate the financial performance of a business in terms of revenue, total assets, and equity. Explain.

4 Describe how financial ratios can be used to measure and improve a company's financial performance.

16. What is a financial benchmark and what is it used for?
17. What is the difference between a soft financial benchmark and a hard financial benchmark?
18. Why do managers examine trends when looking at financial statements?

5 Examine financial statements by using the DuPont financial system.

19. Explain what the DuPont financial system tries to reveal.
20. What grouping of financial statement accounts are used to calculate the ROA ratio by using the DuPont financial system?

6 Discuss the limitations of financial ratios.

21. What are the limitations of financial ratios?
22. Why are financial ratios so critical to managers when evaluating business performance?
23. Explain why some companies can influence many of their ratios simply by choosing their fiscal year-end. In what type of industries do you think this might be a particular problem?

Learning Exercises

1 Explain why financial statements need to be analyzed.

EXERCISE 1: FINANCIAL RATIOS

Ian Stoddart was reviewing his company's 2013 year-end financial estimates, and he was not satisfied with the overall performance. He asked his management team to prepare their detailed operational plans for 2014 and provide their operating budgets to the controller so that he could consolidate the budgets and present, in the latter part of November, the company's financial projections for 2014.

As he pointed out to his team, "The financial projections should be better than the year-end 2013 estimates. We have to achieve four basic financial objectives related to liquidity, solvency, and productivity, and our return on revenue (profitability) should be at least 4% and return on total assets more than 6%.

"The specific objectives for 2014 that I have in mind are as follows:

- Regarding liquidity, our current ratio should not be less than 1.5 times.
- For solvency, our debt-to-total-assets ratio should be maintained at no more that 50% and times-interest-earned should be more than 5.0 times.
- The productivity of our total assets should be 1.5 times, the average collection period for our trade receivables should be maintained at less than 45 days, and our inventory turnover should be more than 4 times;
- With respect to profitability, our return on revenue should be at least 4% and return on total assets over 6%."

During the second week of November, the controller presented the projected 2014 financial statements to the management committee.

Projected Statement of Financial Position
As at December 31, 2014

Non-current assets		Equity	$ 800,000
Property, plant, and equipment	$ 800,000	Non-current liabilities	
Current assets		Long-term borrowings	300,000
Inventories	400,000	Current liabilities	
Trade receivables	300,000	Trade and other payables	250,000
Cash	20,000	Short-term borrowings	170,000
Total current assets	720,000	Total current liabilities	420,000
		Total liabilities	720,000
Total assets	$1,520,000	Total equity and liabilities	$1,520,000

Projected Statement of Income For the year ended December 31, 2014		
Revenue	$2,000,000	
Cost of sales	(1,200,000)	
Gross margin		800,000
Other expenses	(600,000)	
Finance costs	(25,000)	
Total expenses		(625,000)
Profit before taxes		175,000
Income tax expense		(65,000)
Profit for the year		$110,000

Question

Should Ian Stoddart be satisfied with the 2014 financial projections?

2 Evaluate a company's statement of financial position and statement of income by using vertical and horizontal analysis.

EXERCISE 2: CASH FLOW CALCULATION

Fauquier Resources Inc.'s current revenue is $20 million, and the sales and marketing department expects that it will reach $30 million by next year. At the moment, trade receivables are $3.5 million; inventories, $4.5 million; and non-current assets, $6 million. The company expects these assets to increase at the same percentage rate as that of revenue.

Based on his calculations, the treasurer anticipates a $2.5 million increase in the company's cash balance and that trade and other payables will increase from $5 million to $7 million. According to the company's operational plans, the pre-tax profit for the year is expected to reach $4 million, and the board of directors has approved a $1.5 million dividend payout. The company's income tax rate is 40%.

Question

Will the company require any external cash flows next year? If yes, how much?

3 Analyze financial statements by using meaningful ratios.

EXERCISE 3: DEBT/COVERAGE RATIOS

Helen Wiseman, owner of a convenience store, is meeting her banker and hopes to increase her working capital loan. She figures that an additional loan would increase her finance costs by an extra $10,000. Before seeing her banker, she asks her accountant to determine whether she would have difficulty servicing her debt with the additional finance costs.

With the following information, calculate the company's TIE ratio and fixed-charges coverage ratio. If you were the banker, would you approve the loan? Why or why not?

Statement of Income		
Revenue	$ 600,000	
Cost of sales	(200,000)	
Gross profit		400,000
Expenses		
Sales salaries	(150,000)	
Rent	(20,000)	
Office salaries	(90,000)	
Advertising	(23,000)	
Finance costs	(30,000)	
Total expenses		(313,000)
Profit before taxes		87,000
Income tax expense		(25,000)
Profit for the year		$ 62,000

EXERCISE 4: USING FINANCIAL RATIOS TO CALCULATE CASH FLOW PROJECTIONS

After being in business for six years, Graham Mason, owner of a small retail store, is considering buying a new information system that would provide him with better operating and financial information. Graham feels that the new system would give him better control over his inventories so that he would be able to manage his purchases more wisely. He is also interested in renovating his store.

After going through some detailed calculations, he determines that he would have to invest around $250,000 in early January 2014. Graham is considering borrowing some money from the bank. However, before meeting his banker, he asks his accountant to figure out how much cash he could squeeze from his operations (internally) to help him finance his two projects.

Graham feels that he can improve his average collection period to 40 days and turn his inventory three times a year by December 31, 2013 (industry averages). With the following partial information, calculate how much cash Graham could raise internally by December 2013.

Partial Statement of Financial Position
As at December 31, 2013
(in $)

Inventories	200,000	Trade and other payables	150,000
Trade receivables	100,000	Notes payable	50,000
Cash	20,000	Future taxes payable	50,000
Total	320,000	Total	250,000

Statement of Income For the year ended December 31, 2013 (in $)		
Revenue	500,000	
Cost of sales	(300,000)	
Gross profit		200,000
Other expenses	(135,000)	
Depreciation/amortization	(15,000)	
Total expenses		(150,000)
Profit before taxes		50,000
Income tax expense		(25,000)
Profit for the year		25,000

4 Describe how financial ratios can be used to measure and improve a company's financial performance.

EXERCISE 5: USING FINANCIAL RATIOS TO IMPROVE WORKING CAPITAL ACCOUNTS

Mary Pascal is having some problems with her cash flow. She asks her accountant to find a way to generate more cash from her working capital. The accountant says that if Mary were to manage her trade receivables and inventories more efficiently, she would be able to improve her cash flow performance. With the following information, calculate how much cash Mary could generate within the next four months if she were able to improve her average collection period to 35 days and the inventory turnover to six times.

Revenue	$2,500,000
Cost of sales	1,700,000
Trade receivables	300,000
Inventories	400,000

5 Examine financial statements by using the DuPont financial system.

EXERCISE 6: CALCULATING ROA USING THE DUPONT FINANCIAL SYSTEM

The following accounts are included in Eva's retail store financial statements:

Cost of sales	$2,300,000
Administrative expenses	170,000
Prepaid expenses	60,000
Inventories	300,000
Depreciation/amortization	25,000
Cash	25,000
Trade receivables	250,000
Revenue	3,000,000
Non-current assets	1,700,000
Distribution costs	200,000

Questions

1. Calculate her ROA by using the DuPont financial system.
2. What impact would there be on the ROA if the revenue account changed to $3,200,000?

Cases

CASE 1: PICKWICK RESTAURANTS

Jaclyn Hargrove is the owner of six Pickwick Restaurants. For the past 10 years, she has always relied on her accountant to analyze her financial statements. Jaclyn feels that if she were able to understand her financial statements, she would be able to improve her financial performance. More importantly, she would be able to make better decisions that touch on all aspects of her business, from the management of working capital to making investments.

Jaclyn has just purchased accounting software that can provide her with monthly, quarterly, and yearly financial statements and, more importantly, all types of ratios that would help her improve her analysis and decisions.

Jaclyn asks you for some advice in understand the meaning of her financial statements. She shows you her December 31, 2013, statement of financial position and statement of income and asks you to calculate and explain the meaning of the more important financial ratios.

To help Jaclyn understand financial ratios, calculate the financial ratios by using the 2013 statement of financial position and statement of income, and explain to her the meaning and significance of each ratio:

a. current ratio
b. quick ratio
c. debt-to-total-assets ratio
d. debt-to-equity ratio
e. times-interest-earned ratio
f. fixed-charges coverage ratio
g. average collection period
h. inventory turnover ratio
i. capital assets turnover ratio
j. total assets turnover ratio
k. profit margin on revenue ratio
l. return on revenue ratio
m. return on total assets ratio
n. return on equity ratio

Statement of Financial Position
As at December 31, 2013
(in $)

Non-current assets		**Equity**	
Property, plant, and equipment	2,600,000	Preferred shares	100,000
Accumulated depreciation	(700,000)	Common shares	500,000
Total non-current assets	1,900,000	Retained earnings	560,000
		Total equity	1,160,000
		Long-term borrowings	1,640,000
Current assets		**Current liabilities**	
Inventories	1,100,000	Trade and other payables	710,000
Trade receivables	900,000	Notes payable	250,000
Term deposits	120,000	Accruals	260,000
Cash	90,000	Current income taxes payable	90,000
Total current assets	2,210,000	Total current liabilities	1,310,000
Total assets	4,110,000	Total equity and liabilities	4,110,000

Statement of Income
For the year ended December 31, 2013
(in $)

Revenue		4,500,000
Cost of sales		(3,300,000)
Gross profit		1,200,000
Other income		20,000
Expenses		
Distribution costs	(350,000)	
Rent	(100,000)	
Administrative expenses	(345,000)	(795,000)
Finance costs		(120,000)
Depreciation		(50,000)
Total other income/costs		(945,000)
Profit before taxes		255,000
Income tax expense		(127,500)
Profit for the year		1 27,500

CASE 2: IMPERIAL ELECTRONICS LTD.

Imperial Electronics Ltd. is a publicly owned company with 100,000 common shares outstanding. At the last executive committee meeting, Sandra Redgrave, CEO of the company, informed the board members of the economic slowdown that she anticipated during the next several years. She also told them that several U.S. firms were considering becoming more aggressive in the industry, particularly in the Canadian market.

Because of these external threats, management of Imperial Electronics Ltd. anticipates difficult times ahead. Company management is now watching its financial ratios closely to keep the firm under control.

On the basis of the information contained in the company's financial statements, calculate and comment on Imperial Electronics Ltd.'s December 31, 2012, financial ratios by comparing them with the industry average. The common shares are valued on the stock market at $120.

a. current ratio
b. quick ratio
c. debt-to-total-assets ratio
d. debt-to-equity ratio
e. times-interest-earned ratio
f. fixed-charges coverage ratio
g. average collection period
h. inventory turnover ratio
i. capital assets turnover ratio
j. total assets turnover ratio
k. profit margin on revenue ratio
l. return on revenue ratio
m. return on total assets ratio
n. return on equity ratio
o. earnings per share
p. price/earnings ratio

In July 2013, management of Imperial Electronics Ltd. is planning to invest $3,000,000 to modernize its capital assets and expand. The management committee is considering borrowing funds from external sources. However, before meeting the investors, the committee wants to examine the amount that could be generated internally before June 30, 2013.

Industry financial ratios are as follows:

a. current ratio	1.95 times
b. quick ratio	1.03 times
c. debt-to-total-assets ratio	55%
d. debt-to-equity ratio	1.21 times
e. times-interest-earned ratio	6.43 times
f. fixed-charges coverage ratio	4.51 times
g. average collection period	35.00 days
h. inventory turnover ratio	7.00 times
i. capital assets turnover ratio	5.10 times
j. total assets turnover ratio	2.90 times
k. profit margin on revenue ratio	9.10%
l. return on revenue ratio	2.10%

m. return on total assets ratio 6.00%
n. return on equity ratio 21.00%
o. earnings per share $8.50
p. price/earnings ratio 10.30 times

Assuming that the company is just as efficient as the industry in managing its inventories and trade receivables, calculate the amount of cash it would generate by June 30, 2013. Also, assume that in 2013 revenue will increase by 9%, return on revenue will be 5%, depreciation will increase to $400,000, and cost of sales in relation to revenue will improve to 72%.

Imperial Electronics Ltd.
Statement of Income
For the year ended December 31, 2012
(in $)

Revenue		30,000,000
Cost of sales		(23,000,000)
Gross profit		7,000,000
Expenses:		
Distribution costs	(2,500,000)	
Lease	(125,000)	
Depreciation	(300,000)	
Administrative expenses	(1,700,000)	
Total expenses		(4,625,000)
Finance costs		(400,000)
Total		(5,025,000)
Profit before taxes		1,975,000
Income tax expense		(900,000)
Profit for the year		1,075,000

Imperial Electronics Ltd.
Statement of Financial Position
As at December 31, 2012
(in $)

Non-current assets		Equity	
Property, plant, and equipment	8,200,000	Common shares	2,500,000
Accumulated depreciation	(2,000,000)	Retained earnings	3,300,000
Total non-current assets	6,200,000	Total equity	5,800,000
		Long-term borrowings	4,200,000
Current assets		Current liabilities	
Inventories	4,100,000	Trade and other payables	2,500,000
Trade receivables	3,500,000	Notes payable	1,600,000
Prepaid expenses	250,000	Accruals	220,000
Term deposits	200,000	Current income tax payable	80,000
Cash	150,000	Total current liabilities	4,400,000
Total current assets	8,200,000	Total liabilities	8,600,000
Total assets	14,400,000	Total equity and liabilities	14,400,000

CASE 3: ADC PLUMBING AND HEATING LTD.

Albert Ellis owns a small plumbing and heating business. His main activities consist of installing and repairing piping systems, plumbing fixtures, and equipment, such as water heaters, particularly for the residential market. His accountant and adviser prepared his financial statements for the current year. The statement of financial position and the statement of income for the year 2012 are presented below.

ADC Plumbing and Heating Ltd.
Statement of Financial Position
As at December 31, 2012
(in $)

Non-current assets		Equity	
Property, plant, and equipment	300,000	Shares held by Albert	130,000
Accumulated depreciation	(50,000)	Retained earnings	150,000
Total non-current assets	250,000	Total equity	280,000
		Long-term borrowings	150,000
Current assets		Current liabilities	
Inventories	10,000	Trade and other payables	200,000
Trade receivables	330,000	Short-term borrowings	50,000
Cash	90,000	Total current liabilities	250,000
Total current assets	430,000	Total liabilities	400,000
Total assets	680,000	Total equity and liabilities	680,000

ADC Plumbing and Heating Ltd.
Statement of Income
For the year ended December 31, 2012
(in $)

Revenue		1,500,000
Cost of sales		(750,000)
Gross profit		750,000
Expenses:		
Distribution costs	(350,000)	
Lease	(25,000)	
Depreciation	(30,000)	
Administrative expenses	(200,000)	
Total expenses		(605,000)
Finance costs		(30,000)
Total		(635,000)
Profit before taxes		115,000
Income tax expense		(40,000)
Profit for the year		75,000

Albert and his accountant are considering making a few decisions that will affect the financial statements.

Questions

1. If Albert were to use $80,000 of his cash from the business to pay off some of his trade and other payables, how will this alter his current ratio, quick ratio, and debt-to-total-assets ratio?
2. Albert is trying to keep his inventories at a minimum with only $10,000. However, another plumbing and heating contractor is going out of business and is selling his inventories, valued at $100,000, for only $60,000.
   (a) Albert's son, who is not presently an owner of the business, is considering buying the inventory for cash and, in return, would gain a part ownership in the business. How would this transaction modify the company's current ratio, quick ratio, and debt-to-total-assets ratio?
   (b) Instead of having his son become a shareholder of the business, Albert borrows a working capital loan from the bank for $60,000 at 10% interest. How would that decision affect the ratios identified in (a), as well as the times-interest-earned ratio?
   (c) If Albert were to borrow the $60,000 on a long-term basis, how would this decision alter the ratios identified in (a), as well as the times-interest-earned ratio?

FINANCIAL SPREADSHEETS: EXCEL®

The financial spreadsheets that complement this text calculate most financial ratios covered in this chapter. Once the financial data is inputted into the three input documents (statement of income, statement of changes in equity, and the statement of financial position), the spreadsheet calculates financial ratios on output documents that are presented on six templates focusing exclusively on financial ratios:

- Vertical analysis of the statement of income
- Horizontal analysis of the statement of income
- Vertical analysis of the statement of financial position
- Horizontal analysis of the statement of financial position
- Financial ratios (26 ratios covered under four categories: liquidity, debt-coverage, asset-management, profitability)
- DuPont system

These financial spreadsheets can calculate ratios for a period of three years. The two key benefits of these spreadsheets are the following:

1. An analyst can spend more time analyzing a company's historical financial performance.
2. A manager can spend more time making decisions and finding ways to improve the financial performance of a business's operations from different angles (liquidity, debt-coverage, asset-management and profitability) and less time on number crunching.

CHAPTER 5

[PROFIT PLANNING AND DECISION MAKING]

Learning Objectives

After reading this chapter, you should be able to

1 Identify how break-even analysis can help to maximize profitability.

2 Describe the cost concepts related to break-even analysis, such as fixed and variable costs, the relationship between revenue and costs, the contribution margin, the relevant range, and the relevant costs.

3 Draw the break-even chart and calculate the break-even point, the cash break-even point, and the profit break-even point, and explain how they can be applied in different organizations.

4 Differentiate between different types of cost concepts, such as committed and discretionary costs, controllable and non-controllable costs, and direct and indirect costs.

OPENING CASE

Break-Even Analysis: A Decision Tool That Uses Simple Math

The Millers have been in business for close to two years, and they are continually faced with operating and investing decisions:

- Should we increase our advertising budget? By how much?
- Should we hire more part-time or full-time sales associates? Should we let some go? How many?
- Should we launch a new product line?
- Should we open a new retail outlet?
- Should we reduce our selling price for a product line? Increase it? By how much?
- Should we introduce a new service?

The Millers realize that the determining factor is whether the increase in revenue will generate enough profit. For example, if they spend an additional $2,000 in advertising, how much more revenue should it generate to pay for this cost and make a profit? Although the Millers had been making some of these decisions by using their instinct and good judgment, they needed a reliable decision-making tool. Len had heard about break-even analysis (also called operating leverage) and decided to meet with May Ogaki, the Millers' accountant, to learn more about it and how they could use it to improve the effectiveness of their decisions. During the meeting, May made the following comments:

> Break-even analysis is a valuable decision-making aid and is very easy to apply. You will have to draw on your cost accounting knowledge and skills. However, before using this tool you need to carefully separate your store's fixed and variable costs. Some costs are relatively easy to classify. For example, such costs as the goods you buy from suppliers and sales commissions vary directly with revenue and, for this reason, they are considered variable. The more you sell, the more you buy goods from suppliers. However, such costs as leasing and office salaries do not vary with the level of sales activities (revenue). For that reason, they are considered fixed.
>
> Other costs, however, are more difficult to differentiate; for example, you may want to classify some of your sales associates' salaries as fixed and some as variable. Advertising could also be considered fixed or variable. It all depends on how you look at these costs. For instance, should you set a fixed budget for advertising a product line, or should you increase your advertising budget if you sell more of a certain product line? Once you have determined whether each account (e.g., advertising, sales salaries) in your operating budget is fixed or variable, you can make the break-even calculation rather quickly and easily.
>
> The allocation of your store's overhead costs to each department is also important to include when calculating the break-even point for product

> lines. For example, how will you charge your finance costs, your depreciation expense, and office salaries against each product line? You will have to go through a cost accounting allocation process to get the full benefit of the break-even technique.

Len felt that the break-even calculation would be an excellent tool. He was willing to invest some time and effort in understanding cost accounting if it meant making more effective decisions.

THIS CHAPTER WILL SHOW LEN AND JOAN MILLER HOW TO

- Prepare a cost system that will help them better analyze their business activities.
- Use break-even analysis as a powerful decision-making tool.

Chapter Overview

BREAK-EVEN ANALYSIS: A BAROMETER OF PROFITABILITY

This is the first chapter related to operating decisions (refer back to Figure 1.1). Break-even analysis deals with day-to-day managerial decisions that can affect (favourably or unfavourably) a company's bottom line. This tool can also be useful for managers when making capital investment decisions (investing decisions), such as modernizing a plant or investing in a new facility.

This chapter focuses on four topics:

- *Usefulness of break-even analysis.* We will first determine the business circumstances in which break-even analysis can be applied.
- *Cost concepts related to break-even analysis.* This topic explains the meaning of fixed costs, variable costs, and semi-variable costs and how these various costs affect a company's bottom line. It also clarifies the meaning of the contribution margin concept and its importance, the relevant range, and the relevant costs.
- *Break-even analysis.* This section examines how the break-even chart can be drawn and how the break-even point is calculated. It also explains the cash break-even point, the profit break-even point, and the relevance of sensitivity analysis. It looks at how break-even analysis can be applied to different areas of an organization, such as company-wide, in a district or sales territory, in a service centre, and in a retail store. This segment also clarifies the relevance of break-even wedges.
- *Other cost concepts.* We will differentiate other cost concepts, such as committed versus discretionary costs, controllable versus non-controllable costs, and direct versus indirect costs.

Using Break-Even Analysis as a Decision-Making Tool

1 Identify how break-even analysis can help to maximize profitability.

If a business operated without fixed costs (e.g., rent, salaries), its managers would not have to be concerned about incurring a loss. In fact, managers of this unusual type of business would not have to go through detailed calculations to set prices for different products nor evaluate the risk associated with the business. If variable costs (e.g., purchases, sales commissions) were the only element to be deducted from revenue to arrive at a profit, profit planning would be relatively simple; all that would be required would be to deduct, say, a $5 variable cost from a $7 price per unit to obtain a $2 profit. Irrespective of whether a business sold 20 or 100,000 widgets, it would make a $2 profit on each unit. The absence of fixed costs would not only simplify the preparation of profit plans and detailed operating budgets but also allow the business to operate at minimal or no risk. Under these operating conditions, chances of a loss would be virtually nonexistent.

However, businesses don't operate under such favourable conditions. Because fixed costs must be paid, managers must know the number of widgets they need to sell. In addition, they need to know the price at which each product should be sold, the cost of producing each widget, and the total costs to the business if x or y number of widgets are sold.

If managers are to plan their profit and measure precisely the risk they are prepared to take, they need to calculate, analyze, and compare the projected sales volume, the unit selling price for each product, and all costs associated with running the business. If managers can't accurately forecast their costs and revenue, the chances of a favourable profit are small.

Break-even analysis is a powerful tool that can help managers make decisions that affect many business activities. Here are a few examples:

- For *pricing decisions*, break-even analysis helps to analyze the effect that changing the prices and volumes will have on levels of profit.
- For *new product, new plant, new sales representative, new sales office*, or *new advertising campaign decisions*, break-even analysis helps determine the sales revenue needed to justify the investment or increased costs.
- For *modernization* or *automation decisions,* break-even analysis reveals the effect on profit. All it requires is to determine the extent to which variable costs (e.g., direct labour) can be replaced by fixed costs (e.g., finance costs or depreciation).
- For *expansion decisions,* it helps answer critical questions such as, Will the volume and cost levels have a positive (or negative) effect on profitability? Because expansion programs affect variable costs, fixed costs, economies of scale, and profitability, break-even analysis helps to analyze the interplay between these variables.

- For *profit decisions,* break-even analysis clarifies what a business needs to do to achieve a certain level of profit. For example, if a business wants to meet a profit objective, say, 10% return on assets, this tool can help management answer the following questions:
  - How many units should we sell? At what price should we sell our product or service?
  - What should our fixed costs be?
  - What should each unit variable cost be?
  - Which product or service should we push?

Cost Concepts Related to Break-Even Analysis

2 Describe the cost concepts related to break-even analysis, such as fixed and variable costs, the relationship between revenue and costs, the contribution margin, the relevant range, and the relevant costs.

Calculating the profit generated by a business, a product, or a service at different levels of production requires knowing how volume, price, product mix, and product costs relate to one another. That knowledge comes from a tool called **cost–volume–profit analysis**, which helps managers determine the interrelationships among all costs affecting profits. The next three sections in this chapter related to cost concepts examine (1) *cost behaviour*, that is, the meaning of fixed and variable costs; (2) the *anatomy of profit*, that is, the relationship of costs to changes in the level of profit; and (3) some basic *break-even concept* terminology, that is, the meaning of the break-even point, contribution margin, PV ratio, relevant range, and relevant costs.

COST BEHAVIOUR

Cost–volume–profit analysis A tool for analyzing how volume, price, product mix, and product costs relate to one another.

All costs included in statements of income and budgets fall into two distinct groups: fixed costs and variable costs.

Fixed Costs

Costs that remain constant at varying levels of production are called **fixed costs**, also known as *period costs, time costs, constant costs*, or *standby costs.* These costs have an element of constancy and must be paid on a regular basis. Such costs do not change with different levels of production. Some of these costs are inescapable because they are essential for operating. Typical examples of fixed costs include rent or lease payments, finance costs, property insurance, property taxes, office salaries, depreciation, security, telephone, and professional fees.

Fixed costs Costs that remain constant at varying levels of production.

Variable Costs

Variable costs Costs that fluctuate directly with changes in volume of production.

Costs that vary with fluctuations in production levels are referred to as **variable costs,** also known as *direct costs, out-of-pocket costs,* or *volume costs.* As the volume of a business increases, so do these costs. For example, if a business produces and sells 100 widgets at a per-unit cost of $0.10 for material A and $0.20 for material B, its total variable cost would be $30. If it produces and sells 1,000 units, the cost would increase to $300.

Such costs are called variable because they vary almost automatically with volume. Typical examples of variable costs include sales commissions, direct labour, packing materials, freight-in or freight-out, overtime premiums, equipment rentals, materials, and fuel.

In the News 5.1 describes how variable costs (in this case, raw materials) can have an impact on the most vulnerable figure in the statement of income, profit.

In The News 5.1

WHEN RAW MATERIALS COSTS MOVE UPWARD, PROFITS START TO PLUMMET!

The most vulnerable number on the statement of income is profit. It can be altered by many accounts, such as falling prices, lower sales volume, or increases in cost of sales, distribution costs, and administrative expenses. Organizations must always protect profit.

One problem that BASF SE, a German-based chemical, plastics, and oil company, experienced during the final months of 2011 was the rising prices of raw materials, which held back fourth-quarter profits. The company decided to offset the rising costs by increasing its prices and sales volume across its divisions. The strategy paid off, and revenues rose by 10%. The company was able to sustain its level of profitability and even increase its dividends.

Source: "Profits at German chemical firm BASF held back by higher raw material costs." *Winnipeg Free Press*. Retrieved from http://www.winnipegfreepress.com/business/revenues-rise-on-higher-materials-prices-at-chemical-firm-basf-profits-lag-on-weakdemand-140267513.html, accessed February 25, 2012. For more information about BASF, visit http://corporate.basf.com/en/investor/se/.

Semi-Variable Costs

Semi-variable costs Costs that change disproportionately with changes in output levels.

While some costs vary directly and proportionately with volume, others have characteristics of both fixed and variable costs; these costs, called **semi-variable costs** (or semi-fixed costs), have different degrees of variability, or they change in a disproportionate way with changes in output levels.

Let's consider four examples. First, homeowners pay for electricity. They pay a basic fixed cost each month (say, $100) even if they don't use any electricity; in fact, an owner could be away on holidays for several months and still receive a $100 monthly bill from the hydro company. However, owners pay additional costs if they are at home, using electrical equipment (e.g., stove, toasters, heaters, dryers). This cost varies based on which electrical appliances are used and how often.

Second, a business owner may have a fixed lease payment on equipment to use up to a certain volume. When that level is reached, the owner may have to increase the usage of the equipment (and the lease payment) to meet the demands of increased production. These costs would be considered fixed for a specific period or up to a certain capacity or range of production.

Third, a business owner may pay a set price for raw materials, but if production increases and the company can buy and use more, the price may be lower because of volume discounts.

Fourth, if a business owner wants to produce an extra volume of units with the same production crew after regular hours, time-and-a-half or double-time wages may have to be paid. These direct or variable costs would not vary proportionately with volume increments and would not fit the linear cost pattern.

It is important to separate fixed and variable costs for different levels of volume (see Figure 5.1). This helps in preparing accurate operating budgets. Once the costs are separated, they can be related to specific levels of volume.

Figure 5.1 **Relationship of Costs to Volume**

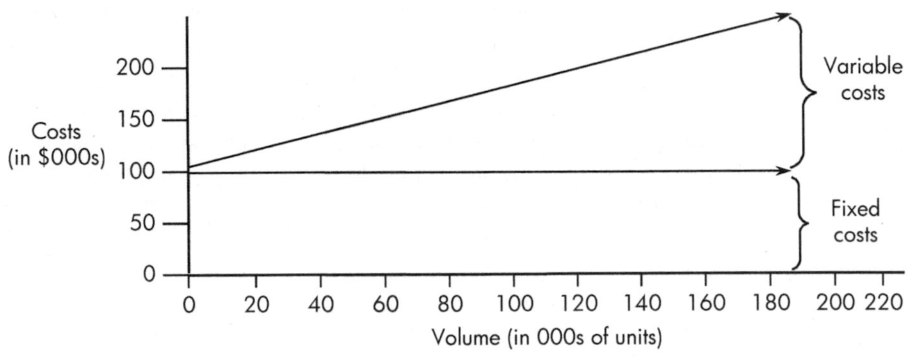

Problem-Solving Example 5.1

Setting Costs Apart

List the following monthly home budget accounts under the headings fixed, variable, and semi-fixed costs. Find the total fixed costs, the total variable costs, and the total costs. The percentages are the portion of the cost that is variable: mortgage, $1,300; municipal taxes, $150; mobile phone, $55 (10%); cable TV, $90 (10%); water, $40 (15%); food, $200; entertainment, $100; car and house insurance, $140; heating, $100 (30%); payment for car loan ($125); gasoline, $100 (50%); hydro, $75 (20%); and alarm system, $30.

Solution

			Semi-Fixed	
	Fixed	Variable	Fixed	Variable
Mortgage	$1,300			
Municipal taxes	150			
Car/house insurance	140			
Car payment (loan)	125			
Alarm system	30			

(continued)

Problem-Solving Example 5.1 (continued)

			Semi-Fixed	
	Fixed	Variable	Fixed	Variable
Food		$200		
Entertainment		100		
Mobile telephone			$ 50	$ 5
Cable TV			81	9
Water			34	6
Heating			70	30
Gasoline			50	50
Hydro			60	15
Total	$1,745	$300	$ 345	$115
Total fixed	$2,090			
Total variable		$415		
Total costs			$2,505	

Self-Test Exercise 5.1

Fixed and Variable Costs

CompuTech's statement of income shows the following cost items: purchases (included in cost of sales), sales commissions, salaries (distribution), advertising, travel, salaries (administration), leasing, finance costs, depreciation/amortization, and freight-in (included in cost of sales). Which of these costs are fixed and which are variable?

Answers to the Self-Test Exercises can be found at www.bergeron7e.nelson.com.

ANATOMY OF PROFIT

If operating costs changed in the same proportion as revenue, or if profits had a linear relationship with costs or revenue, this chapter would be irrelevant. However, as indicated earlier, costs behave in a variety of ways with respect to revenue. To prepare budgets and profit plans accurately, management must know how costs change within specific periods, at different levels of production, and even with changes in methods of operation.

Analyzing the relationships among costs, volume, and profit helps a manager to answer basic questions:

- How much volume do we need to sell before hiring another employee?
- At what sales volume should we change our method of operation; for example, should we maintain the existing warehouse or should we move to a larger one?

- Which products require streamlining, from a cost point of view, if we are to improve our profit performance?
- Should we change our product mix?
- When should we purchase another piece of equipment?
- Should we reduce the level of output of product A and increase that of product B?

In the News 5.2 describes how, for one company, selling prices have a direct impact on profitability.

In The News 5.2

SELLING PRICE AND PROFIT: A LINEAR CONNECTION

The figure that has the most direct impact on profit is the selling price, and profit is the most sensitive to changes in selling prices. If sales volume goes down, so does cost of sales, which, to some degree, offsets the damage to profit. Selling prices act differently. A decrease in selling prices has an immediate, direct, and absolute impact on profit. There are no twists; the connection is straight to the bottom line.

This is what happened to Wal-Mart Stores Inc., the world's largest retailer, during the latter part of 2011. Falling prices reduced profits by 12% (from \$1.70 a share to \$1.50). To contain the damage and preserve its profit, Wal-Mart's response was swift and effective, and it included pulling greeters from store lobbies to help with customer service.

Source: "Falling prices mean sliding profits for Wal-Mart." February 22, 2012, *Ottawa Citizen*, p. D6. For more information about Wal-Mart, go to www.walmart.ca/en.

BREAK-EVEN CONCEPT

Break-even point The level of production at which revenues equal total costs.

Cost behaviour can be understood more easily in a cost–volume–profit relationship when break-even analysis is used. It deals with the **break-even point**, the point at which, at a specific level of revenues, a business begins to make a profit. In other words, it is at that level of operation at which profit levels stand at zero, or where total revenues equal total costs. Before explaining the break-even chart, let's examine several important concepts, namely, the contribution margin, relevant range, and relevant costs. These concepts will help you understand how break-even analysis works.

Contribution Margin Analysis

Contribution margin The difference between revenues and variable costs.

The difference between revenues and variable costs is called the **contribution margin**. The contribution margin is the level of profit that "contributes" to paying for fixed costs and, eventually, making a profit. For example, assume that Jin's monthly fixed expenses for his house are \$2,000 (mortgage, hydro, insurance, etc.). Let's also assume that Jin works on a commission basis (say, a job in direct marketing) and earns, on average, \$25 an hour. It would take 80 hours for Jin to pay his fixed expenses

($2,000 ÷ 25 hours). In other words, every hour of work (or $25) contributes toward the fixed expenses. If Jin works 81 hours, the money that he would earn during the last hour would contribute toward a surplus (profit). If Jin works 40 hours a week (or 160 hours a month), he would make a $2,000 surplus [(160 hours × $25 = $4,000) – $2,000]. Contribution margin is also known as *marginal contribution, profit pick-up, cash margin*, or *margin income.*

Rearranging the expense accounts shown on a statement of income can help identify (or calculate) the contribution margin. Table 5.1 shows how contribution margin relates to revenue, fixed and variable costs, and profit before taxes.

The contribution margin can also be expressed on a per-unit basis, as the difference between unit selling price and unit variable cost. This information is valuable for decision making. If the contribution margin is positive, management knows how much money is earned on each unit sold, which will contribute to paying fixed costs and making a profit. The contribution can also be expressed by a ratio called the *marginal contribution ratio, contribution ratio*, or *marginal income ratio.* The term that will be used in this chapter is **profit-volume (PV) ratio**.

Profit-volume (PV) ratio
The contribution margin expressed on a per-unit basis.

Table 5.2 shows how to calculate the contribution by using the PV ratio for various volume levels. The difference between revenue and variable costs gives a contribution margin of $250,000 or a PV ratio of 0.25 ($250,000 ÷ $1,000,000). If revenue increases by 25%, to $1,250,000, the contribution becomes $312,500, and the PV ratio stays at 0.25 ($312,500 ÷ $1,250,000). If revenue drops to $600,000 and produces a contribution of $150,000, the PV ratio is still 0.25 ($150,000 ÷ $600,000).

The contribution margin approach makes it easy to look at pricing alternatives. Management can readily determine the effect each increase or decrease in price has on volume, revenue, and profit; this analysis helps streamline production and lower costs as much as possible.

Table 5.1 The Statement of Income and the Contribution Margin

Revenue		$1,000,000
Less variable costs:		
Direct material	$(500,000)	
Direct labour	(250,000)	
Total variable costs		(750,000)
Contribution margin		250,000
Less fixed costs:		
Manufacturing	(150,000)	
Administration	(50,000)	
Total fixed costs		(200,000)
Profit before taxes		$ 50,000

Table 5.2 **Calculating the Contribution by Using the PV Ratio**

	Base Case	Ratio	Increased Revenues	Decreased Revenues
Revenue	$1,000,000		$1,250,000	$600,000
Variable costs	(750,000)	0.75	(937,500)	(450,000)
Contribution margin	250,000	0.25 (PV)	312,500	150,000
Fixed costs	(200,000)		(200,000)	(200,000)
Profit/(loss) before taxes	$ 50,000		$ 112,500	$ (50,000)

Problem-Solving Example 5.2

Contribution Margin and the PV Ratio

Using the expense accounts shown in Problem-Solving Example 5.1, and assuming that Jin's salary is $3,500 a month, calculate (1) his contribution margin and, (2) his PV ratio.

Solution

Contribution margin is $3,085 and the PV ratio is 0.88.

	Salary	$3,500
	Variable costs	(415)
(1)	Contribution margin	$3,085
(2)	PV ratio	0.88 ($3,085 ÷ $3,500)

Self-Test Exercise 5.2

The Contribution Margin and the PV Ratio

Use the following information to calculate CompuTech's (1) profit before taxes, (2) contribution margin, and (3) PV ratio.

Purchases (cost of sales)	$205,000	Salaries (administration)	$38,000
Freight-in (cost of sales)	4,000	Revenue	420,000
Salaries (distribution)	60,000	Depreciation/amortization	40,000
Commissions	3,000	Leasing	7,000
Travel	3,000	Finance costs	14,000
Advertising	5,000		

Answers to the Self-Test Exercises can be found at www.bergeron7e.nelson.com.

Relevant Range

Changes in the operating variable costs alter the PV ratio, which in turn affects the profit level. As was indicated earlier, fixed costs can change from period to period or from one level of output to another. These kinds of costs (fixed and variable) that apply to a certain

Figure 5.2 Example of Relevant Range

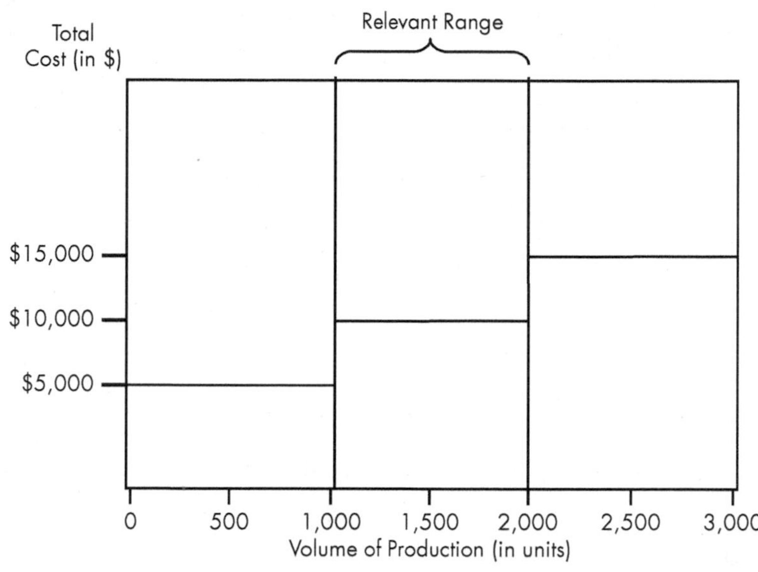

Relevant range
Costs (fixed and variable) that apply to a certain level of production.

level of production are referred to as **relevant range**. Costs within a specific period must be evaluated within a specific range of volumes. If management decides to increase its manufacturing capacity, more costs (fixed costs) will be incurred or overtime pay (variable costs) at time-and-a-half or double time will have to be included. Figure 5.2 shows an example of relevant range. In this case, the cost information used to budget for the year would apply to volumes of production within the 0 to 1,000 range ($5,000), the 1,000 to 2,000 range ($10,000), and the 2,000 to 3,000 range ($15,000).

Relevant Costs

Relevant costs
Cost alternatives that managers can choose from to operate a business.

Relevant costs arise when management can choose among several cost alternatives. Cost variations among the options are called *differential costs.* For example, if management is spending $20,000 in operating costs to sell $50,000 worth of goods, they can look at two cost options for making a plant more cost efficient and increasing profit. Option A in Table 5.3 shows that an additional $10,000 in variable costs and $15,000 in fixed costs would be incurred. Option B shows an additional $14,000 in variable costs (less efficient than option A) and $13,000 in fixed costs (more efficient than option A). The table shows the differential (the difference) between the two options. The $20,000 already spent for selling $50,000 worth of goods is not taken into account in this analysis because it has already been spent. These costs are sometimes called "sunk costs." The only costs that are relevant here are the uncommitted or unspent amounts, which are $25,000 for option A and $27,000 for option B. These options should be analyzed because of the $2,000 cost differential. As shown in the table, option A gives a $5,000 profit compared with $3,000 for option B.

Table 5.3 Differential Costs between Two Cost Options

	Option A	Option B	Differential
Revenue	$50,000	$50,000	—
Current costs	(20,000)	(20,000)	—
Variable costs	(10,000)	(14,000)	$4,000
Fixed costs	(15,000)	(13,000)	(2,000)
Total relevant costs	(25,000)	(27,000)	2,000
Total costs	(45,000)	(47,000)	2,000
Profit	$5,000	$3,000	$2,000

The net cost or profit advantage of choosing option A is $2,000.

Break-Even Analysis

3 Draw the break-even chart and calculate the break-even point, the cash break-even point, and the profit break-even point, and explain how they can be applied in different organizations.

Break-even chart
A graphic that shows the effect of change in both revenue and costs on profit.

The next four sections look at break-even analysis, in particular (1) the break-even chart, (2) how various break-even points (regular break-even, cash break-even, and profit break-even) are calculated, (3) where break-even analysis can be applied, and (4) the break-even wedges.

THE BREAK-EVEN CHART

The **break-even chart** is a relatively simple way of picturing the effect of change in both revenue and costs on profit. Figure 5.3 shows the break-even chart for a firm that sells widgets. The break-even chart has several parts:

- Revenue — line OD
- Revenue zone — area OED
- Fixed-cost line — line AB
- Fixed-cost zone — area AOEB
- Total-cost line — line AC
- Total-cost zone — area AOEC
- Profit zone — area ZCD
- Loss zone — area AOZ

The number of units sold are on the horizontal axis, while total revenue and total costs are on the vertical axis.

Fixed costs (line AB) are shown parallel to the volume-in-units line (the horizontal axis). Fixed costs are $100,000 and remain unchanged, whether at 0,600, or 1,600 units.

Revenue (line OD) slopes upward at an angle. As the company sells more units, revenue increases proportionately.

Total costs (line AC) has a gradual slope and intersects the revenue line at 1,000 units. The line begins at $100,000 (fixed costs), and slopes at an angle that is less steep than the revenue line.

Figure 5.3 **The Break-Even Chart**

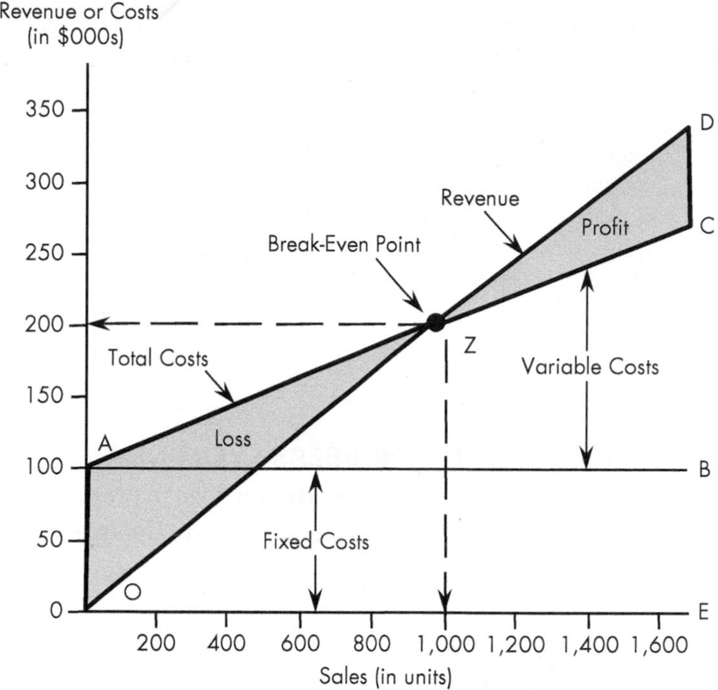

The *loss zone* (area AOZ) shows the losses if the company sells less than 1,000 units. If the company's unit selling price is maintained at $200 and fixed costs and variable costs stay the same, losses range from $100,000, at 0 unit sales, to $100 at 999 units.

The *profit zone* (area ZCD) shows the profits made by the company. Any volume of sales over 1,000 units (horizontal axis) or $200,000 in revenue (vertical axis) produces a profit.

The profit and cost schedule in Table 5.4 was used to construct Figure 5.3. The table shows the profit at different levels of sales—from 200 to 1,600 units. For example, at 200 widgets with an average selling price per unit of $200, revenue is $40,000. At any level of sales volume, the company's fixed costs remain unchanged at $100,000. If the unit variable costs are $100, the total variable cost is $20,000 at the 200-unit volume. At that level, total costs (fixed and variable) are $120,000 and the company losses $80,000.

At 400 units, the loss is reduced to $60,000; at 1,000 units, revenue is $200,000, fixed costs remain at $100,000, and variable costs reach $100,000, for a total cost of $200,000. At that point, the company has neither a loss nor a profit, as costs equal revenue. This is the general break-even point. Additional sales will improve the company's profit. At sales of 1,400 and 1,600 units, the company generates profits of $40,000 and $60,000, respectively.

Table 5.4 The Profit and Cost Schedule

Sales Units	Unit Price	Revenue	Fixed Costs	Variable Costs	Total Costs	Profit (Loss)
0	$200	0	$(100,000)	0	$(100,000)	$(100,000)
200	200	$ 40,000	(100,000)	$ (20,000)	(120,000)	(80,000)
400	200	80,000	(100,000)	(40,000)	(140,000)	(60,000)
600	200	120,000	(100,000)	(60,000)	(160,000)	(40,000)
800	200	160,000	(100,000)	(80,000)	(180,000)	(20,000)
1,000	200	200,000	(100,000)	(100,000)	(200,000)	—
1,200	200	240,000	(100,000)	(120,000)	(220,000)	20,000
1,400	200	280,000	(100,000)	(140,000)	(240,000)	40,000
1,600	200	320,000	(100,000)	(160,000)	(260,000)	60,000

CALCULATING THE BREAK-EVEN POINTS

The break-even chart gives a visual presentation of the variables affecting profit. However, if managers need to know the quantity and revenue break-even points, and they know the variables, such as sales units, fixed costs, and unit variable costs, then they can find the solution algebraically. The following information is needed for an algebraic solution:

SP = **selling price per unit**
VC = **variable cost per unit**
FC = **fixed costs**
N = **quantity of units sold at break-even**

By definition, we know that, at break-even, total revenue equals total cost. If

$$\textbf{Total revenue} = SP \times N$$

and

$$\textbf{Total costs} = (VC \times N) + FC$$

then break-even is:

$$(SP \times N) = (VC \times N) + FC$$

The break-even formula can also be presented in the following ways:

$$N(SP - VC) = FC$$

or

$$N = FC/(SP - VC)$$

By using the information from Table 5.4, we get:

$$FC = \$100{,}000$$
$$SP = \$200$$
$$VC = \$100$$

The contribution margin ($SP - VC$) is \$100 (i.e., \$200 minus \$100).

Break-Even Point Calculations

Unit break-even point
The number of units that must be sold to cover total costs.

By applying the information shown above to the break-even formula, we get the following break-even results for quantity and for revenue. The **unit break-even point** is

$$\text{BEP} = \frac{\text{Fixed costs}}{\text{Price per unit} - \text{Variable costs per unit (or Unit contribution)}}$$

$$\text{BEP} = \frac{\$100{,}000}{\$200 - \$100} = \frac{\$100{,}000}{\$100} = 1{,}000 \text{ units}$$

Revenue break-even point
The revenue that must be reached to cover total costs.

The **revenue break-even point** is calculated in two steps:

Step 1: Find the PV ratio or unit contribution:

$$\text{PV} = \frac{\text{Unit contribution}}{\text{Unit selling price}} = \frac{\$100}{\$200} = 0.50$$

Step 2: Find the revenue break-even point:

$$\text{BEP} = \frac{\text{Fixed costs}}{\text{PV}} = \frac{\$100{,}000}{0.50} = \$200{,}000$$

If the break-even volume is multiplied by the unit selling price, we get the same answer: 1,000 units × \$200 = \$200,000.

Problem-Solving Example 5.3

Break-Even Calculation

Peter is considering opening a stand at a weekend fair. The information about his project is as follows: (1) number of widgets that he expects to sell (15,000), (2) variable costs (\$60,000), (3) fixed costs (\$20,000), (4) unit selling price (\$6.00). With this information, calculate (1) the contribution margin, (2) the profit, (3) the break-even point in units, and (4) the break-even point in revenue. Should Peter proceed with the weekend fair project? Why?

(continued)

Problem-Solving Example 5.3 (continued)

Solution

Peter should go ahead with his project since he will break-even at 66.7% ($60,000 ÷ $90,000) of his revenue target.

Revenue	$6.00	×	15,000 units	=	$90,000
Variable costs	($4.00)	×	15,000 units	=	(60,000)
(1) Contribution margin	$2.00				30,000
Fixed costs					(20,000)
(2) Profit					$10,000

(3) Break-even point in units: 10,000 units ($20,000 ÷ $2.00)

(4) Break-even point in revenue: $60,000 (10,000 × $6.00)

Self-Test Exercise 5.3

The Break-Even Point

The Millers are thinking of introducing a new product line in their store. For this exercise, assume the following:

- Total fixed costs for the line are estimated at $15,000.
- Total number of units they expect to sell are 10,000, based on a market study.
- Total variable costs are $20,000.
- Unit selling price is $4.50.

Based on the information, answer the following questions:

1. What is the break-even point in units?
2. What is the break-even point in revenue?
3. Should they go ahead with their plan?

Answers to the Self-Test Exercises can be found at www.bergeron7e.nelson.com.

Cash Break-Even Point Calculations

Cash break-even point
The number of units or revenue that must be reached to cover total cash fixed costs (total fixed costs less depreciation/amortization).

The break-even model can also be used to solve cash-management problems. Most costs, such as rent, salaries, hydro, insurance, raw materials, or telephone, are paid with cash (they are cash outlays). Other costs, however, are non-cash items, such as depreciation/amortization; even though they are treated as expenses, they do not entail an actual outflow of cash.

If we use the revenue and cost information in Table 5.4 and assume that the $100,000 fixed cost includes an amount of $25,000 for depreciation, the fixed cash outlays would be $75,000. The **cash break-even point** is the number of units or revenue that must reached to cover total cash fixed costs.

The cash break-even point for both quantity and revenue is calculated as follows:

(1) Quantity (or unit) break-even point:

$$\textbf{Cash BEP} = \frac{\textbf{Fixed costs} - \textbf{Depreciation}}{\textbf{Price per unit} - \textbf{Variable costs per unit}}$$

$$= \frac{\$100{,}000 - \$25{,}000}{\$200 - \$100} = \frac{\$75{,}000}{\$100} = 750 \textbf{ units}$$

(2) Revenue break-even point:

$$\textbf{Revenue cash BEP} = \frac{\textbf{Fixed costs} - \textbf{Depreciation}}{\textbf{PV}}$$

$$= \frac{\$75{,}000}{0.50} = \$150{,}000$$

Profit Break-Even Point Calculations

Profit break-even point
The number of units or revenue that must be reached to cover total costs and meet a profit goal.

Companies are interested in more than just breaking even. Some set profit goals to determine how many sales units are needed to reach it. To do this, all that is needed is to modify the break-even formula. The **profit break-even point** is the number of units or revenue that must be reached to cover total costs and meet a profit goal.

We'll use the data in Table 5.4 again, and assume that $10,000 is the goal. We can calculate the profit break-even points for both quantity and revenue as follows:

(1) Quantity (or units) break-even point:

$$\textbf{Profit BEP} = \frac{\textbf{Fixed costs} + \textbf{Profit objective}}{\textbf{Price per unit} - \textbf{Variable costs}}$$

$$= \frac{\$100{,}000 + \$10{,}000}{\$200 - \$100} = 1{,}100 \textbf{ units}$$

(2) Revenue break-even point:

$$\textbf{Profit BEP} = \frac{\textbf{Fixed costs} + \textbf{Profit}}{\textbf{PV}}$$

$$= \frac{\$110{,}000}{0.50} = \$220{,}000$$

The quantity and revenue break-even points are summarized below:

	Quantity (in units)	Revenue
Regular break-even	1,000	$200,000
Cash break-even	750	$150,000
Profit break-even	1,100	$220,000

Sensitivity Analysis

Any change in revenue, whether from an increased unit selling price, a change in product mix, or a reduction in fixed or variable costs, will effect a company's profit. For example, using the data in Table 5.4, a reduction of $20,000 in fixed costs (to $80,000) would reduce the break-even point to 800 units or $160,000 in revenue. Similarly, reducing variable costs to $80 (with fixed costs staying at $100,000) would reduce the break-even point to 833 units [$100,000 ÷ ($200 − $80)]. A simultaneous decline of both costs would improve the company's profit substantially and reduce the break-even point to 667 units [$80,000 ÷ ($200 − $80)].

If, for instance, the company faces a $20 per unit variable cost increase, and it wants to maintain its break-even point at 1,000 units, it would have to increase the unit selling price by $20 to $220. Obviously, this assumes that the increase in unit selling price would not decrease the units sold. The opposite takes place if fixed and variable costs are increased. A change in unit selling price a profit.

Sensitivity analysis A technique that shows to what extent a change in one variable (e.g., selling price, fixed costs) affects the break-even point.

Before deciding to change the methods of operation or to buy new equipment, it is important to make a **sensitivity analysis** of different break-even points for changes in units sold, selling price, unit variable costs, and fixed costs.

Problem-Solving Example 5.4

Cash and Profit Break-Even Calculations

Use the numbers in Problem-Solving Example 5.3 to calculate (1) the cash break-even point in units and in revenue, and (2) the profit break-even point in units and in revenue. Assume that fixed costs include $2,000 for depreciation and that Peter wants to earn $4,000 in profit.

Solution

(1) Cash break-even points:

in units: 9,000 units ($18,000 ÷ $2.00)
in revenue: $54,000 (9,000 × $6.00)

(2) Profit break-even points:

in units: 12,000 units ($24,000 ÷ $2.00)
in revenue: $72,000 (12,000 × $6.00)

Self-Test Exercise 5.4

Cash and Profit Break-Even Points

The Millers have been approached by a supplier to sell a new product line. Based on the supplier's estimates, CompuTech could sell as many as 1,500 units. The suggested retail price for each unit is $14.50. The purchase price for each unit is $7.00. The fixed costs for that department is $6,000, which includes $1,000 for depreciation. On the basis of this information, calculate the following:

1. Contribution margin
2. PV ratio

(continued)

Self-Test Exercise 5.4 (continued)

3. Revenue break-even by using the PV ratio
4. Cash break-even point in units and in revenue
5. Profit generated
6. Profit break-even point in units and in revenue

Answers to the Self-Test Exercises can be found at www.bergeron7e.nelson.com.

Problem-Solving Example 5.5

Sensitivity Analysis

Begin with the information in Problem-Solving Example 5.3. If fixed costs were increased by $10,000, variable costs reduced by $1.00 per unit, and unit selling price remained unchanged, what would be the new (1) unit contribution, (2) profit, (3) break-even point in units, and (4) in revenue? Should Peter still go ahead with the weekend fair project?

Solution

Peter should still go ahead with his project since he will break-even at 66.7% ($60,000 ÷ $90,000) of his revenue target.

Revenue	$6.00	×	15,000 units	=	$90,000
Variable costs	($3.00)	×	15,000 units	=	(45,000)
(1) Contribution margin	$3.00				45,000
Fixed costs					(30,000)
(2) Profit					$15,000

(3) Break-even point in units: 10,000 units ($30,000 ÷ $3.00)

(4) Break-even point in revenue: $60,000 (10,000 × $6.00)

Self-Test Exercise 5.5

Sensitivity Analysis

Begin with the information in the Self-Test Exercise 5.3. If fixed costs were increased by $5,000 and variable costs and unit selling price remained unchanged, what would be the new PV ratio and break-even point in units and in revenue?

Answers to the Self-Test Exercises can be found at www.bergeron7e.nelson.com.

WHERE THE BREAK-EVEN POINT CAN BE APPLIED

The break-even system can be applied in just about any type of business or any area of a company's operations where variable and fixed costs exist and where products or services are offered. For example, a break-even chart can be used in any of the following areas: company-wide, district or sales territory, service centre, retail store, plant, production centre, department, product division, or machine operation.

Let's examine how the break-even points can be used company-wide, in district or sales territory, in a service centre, and in a retail store.

Company-Wide

Figure 5.4 shows a company-wide break-even chart. It includes all the parts that make up the total cost line. The company's revenue is $470 million. Total variable costs are $305 million and include variable distribution costs ($70 million), variable production costs ($100 million), direct material ($70 million), and direct labour ($65 million). Total fixed costs are $125 million, made up of cash fixed costs of $90 million and $35 million for non-cash costs (depreciation). The company's profit before taxes is $40 million. On the basis of this information, the company's break-even point is $356 million and cash break-even point is $256 million. The calculations are as follows:

Figure 5.4 **Company-Wide Break-Even Chart**

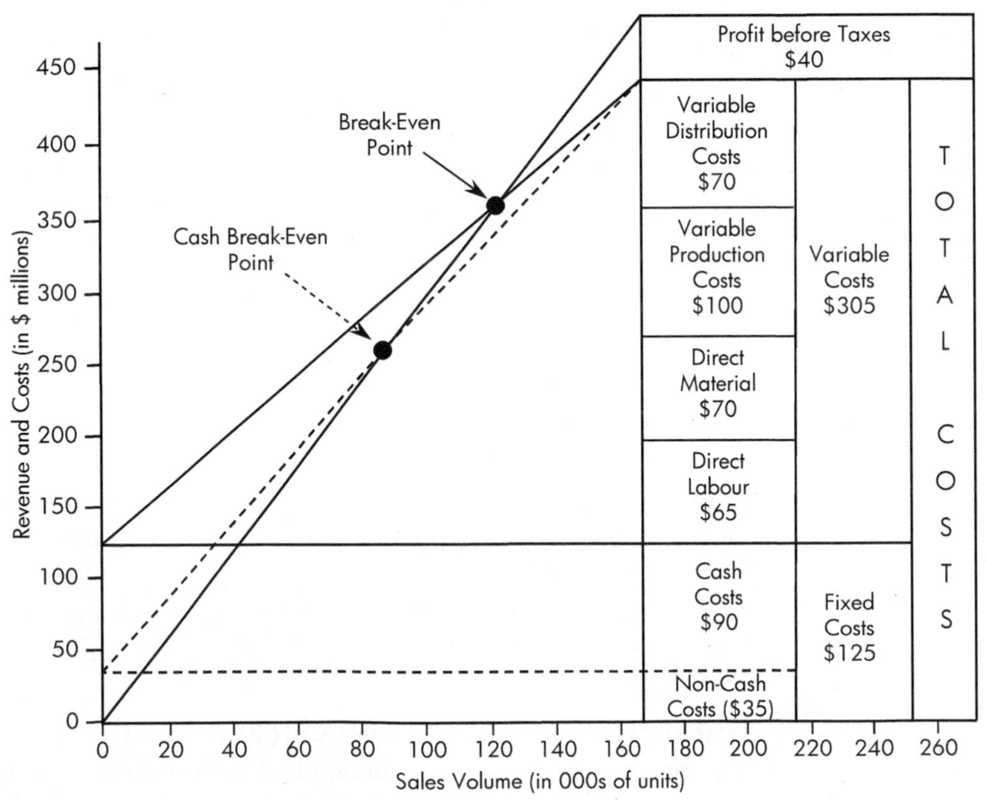

	(in $000s)
Revenue	470,000
Total variable costs	(305,000)
Contribution margin	165,000
Total fixed costs	(125,000)
Profit before taxes	40,000

The PV ratio is 0.351 ($165,000,000 ÷ $470,000,000).
The company's break-even point is $356 million ($125,000,000 ÷ 0.351)
The company's cash break-even point is $256 million ($90,000,000 ÷ 0.351).

Problem-Solving Example 5.6

Company-Wide Break-Even Point

Calculate the company-wide (1) profit, (2) revenue break-even point, and (3) cash break-even point with the following information: revenue ($800,000), cost of sales ($600,000 of which 80% is variable), distribution costs ($130,000 of which 20% is variable), and administrative expenses ($50,000). A depreciation expense of $50,000 is included in cost of sales as fixed costs.

Solution

Revenue	$ 800,000	
Cost of sales	(600,000)	
Gross margin		200,000
Distribution costs	$(130,000)	
Administrative expenses	(50,000)	
Total costs		(180,000)
(1) Profit		$ 20,000
Revenue		$800,000
Variable costs		
Cost of sales (80%)	$(480,000)	
Distribution costs (20%)	(26,000)	
Total variable costs		(506,000)
Contribution margin		294,000
Fixed costs		
Cost of sales (20%)	(120,000)	
Distribution costs (80%)	(104,000)	
Administrative expenses	(50,000)	
Total fixed costs		(274,000)
Profit		$ 20,000

(continued)

Problem-Solving Example 5.6 (continued)

PV ratio: 0.3675 ($294,000 ÷ $800,000)

(2) Break-even point: $745,578 ($274,000 ÷ 0.3675)

Cash fixed costs: $224,000 ($274,000 − $50,000)

(3) Cash break-even point: $609,524 ($224,000 ÷ 0.3675)

Self-Test Exercise 5.6

Company-Wide Break-Even Point

With the information about CompuTech below, calculate the following:

1. Contribution margin and profit before taxes
2. Revenue break-even point
3. Cash break-even point

Purchases (cost of sales)	$ 205,000	Salaries (administration)	$ 38,000
Freight in (cost of sales)	4,000	Revenue	420,000
Salaries (distribution)	60,000	Depreciation/amortization	40,000
Commissions	3,000	Leasing	7,000
Travelling	3,000	Finance costs	14,000
Advertising	5,000		

Answers to the Self-Test Exercises can be found at www.bergeron7e.nelson.com.

District or Sales Territory

The break-even point is also useful for analyzing whether to open a sales office in a particular area. In this case, the fixed costs are rental charges, clerical staff, hydro, depreciation of office equipment, and so on. Fixed costs would also include a portion of head-office fixed expenses. The variable costs would include sales commissions, travel, and living allowances.

The break-even analysis may be useful for determining whether a sales office should be located in a business district, where fixed costs would be high and variable costs minimized, or in an area remote from the city core, where fixed costs are lower and variable costs higher. In weighing the two choices, the manager would have to consider the market potential, the market share objectives, and the revenue for the short and medium term.

Let's take the example of a company that is thinking about opening a sales office with a small staff. The initial market study indicates that the company could take a reasonable share of the market if it has sales staff there. The sales department estimates

$5.0 million in revenue during the first year and expects variable costs to be 45.5% of revenue. As shown below, the district office fixed cost is estimated at $1.6 million. However, because some headquarters staff would provide services (administration, computers, etc.) to the sales office, $625,000 in overhead costs would be allocated to the sales office. Management's first-year goal is a $500,000 profit before taxes. Based on this information, the sales manager is quite enthusiastic about the new sales office and is prepared to go ahead with the decision.

(in $000s)			
Revenue		5,000	
Office variable costs		(2,275)	
Contribution margin		2,725	PV = 0.545
District office overhead costs	(1,600)		
Head office fixed costs	(625)		
Total fixed costs		(2,225)	
Profit before taxes		500	

The break-even point with head office allocation is $4,082,569 ($2,225,000 ÷ 0.545) or 82% ($4,082,569 ÷ $5,000,000) of the revenue goal, and the break-even point without head office allocation is $2,935,780 ($1,600,000 ÷ 0.545) or 59% ($2,935,780 ÷ $5,000,000) of the revenue goal.

Problem-Solving Example 5.7

New Department

Bill wants to add a new department in his store. He predicts that it would add $180,000 revenue to his store operations. The store will incur $600,000 in variable costs, which includes 20% for the new department, and $300,000 in fixed costs, which includes 10% in overhead for the new department. What would be Bill's (1) profit and (2) break-even point for the new department? Should he go ahead with his plan?

Solution

Bill should go ahead with his plan since he would break even at 50.5% ($90,909 ÷ $180,000) of his revenue goal.

Revenue	$180,000	
Variable costs	(120,000)	($600,000 × 20%)
Contribution margin	60,000	
Fixed costs	(30,000)	($300,000 × 10%)
(1) Profit	$ 30,000	
(2) Break-even point	$90,909	
	($60,000 ÷ $180,000 = 0.33)	
	($30,000 ÷0.33 = $90,909)	

Self-Test Exercise 5.7

Product Line Analysis Using the Break-Even Point

With the following information, calculate the break-even point in sales dollars for CompuTech's product lines A, B, and C.

- Revenue

Product line A	$ 45,000
Product line B	$ 21,750
Product line C	$ 35,000

- Cost of sales for the three product lines is 45%, 50%, and 52% of revenue, respectively.
- Fixed costs are estimated at $32,000.

Answers to the Self-Test Exercises can be found at www.bergeron7e.nelson.com.

Service Centre

Break-even analysis works well for activities that produce specific units of output. Here, fixed costs and direct costs can be related to specific levels of operation. Like a retail store, a service unit does not produce specific production units; while fixed costs can be readily identified, variable costs cannot be related to a specific level of operation. The break-even concept can be applied to service operations but with subtle differences.

As shown below, if the variable costs were 50% of revenue, variable costs would increase by a factor of 0.50 every time a dollar sale is made. The service department breaks even at $62,000 ($31,000 ÷ 0.50). This is based on $100,000 revenue generated by the service, a 50% cost directly related to providing the service ($50,000), and $31,000 in fixed costs. The service department's profit before taxes is $19,000.

Revenue	$ 100,000	
Variable costs	(50,000)	
Contribution margin	50,000	PV = 0.50
Fixed costs	(31,000)	
Profit before taxes	$ 19,000	

Retail Store

The break-even point can also be calculated for a retail store (Table 5.5). First, we must determine the number of products that would be sold and the unit selling price for each. The total revenue forecast is $500,000. Based on that forecast, variable costs, which include purchases and commissions, are $275,000 and $25,000, respectively. By deducting total variable costs from total revenue, we find the store's contribution margin is $200,000. This margin contributes to paying for the $100,000 in fixed costs; the remaining $100,000 is profit before taxes. The store breaks even at $250,000 or 50% of its revenue forecast.

Table 5.5 **Retail Store Break-Even Point**

	Suits	Jackets	Shirts	Ties	Socks	Overcoats	Total
Number of units	800	200	700	900	2,400	500	
Unit price	$ 300.00	$150.00	$ 50.00	$ 30.00	$ 7.50	$ 300.00	
Revenue subtotal	$240,000	$30,000	$35,000	$27,000	$18,000	$150,000	
Revenue							$ 500,000
Variable costs							
Purchases							(275,000)
Commissions							(25,000)
Total variable costs							(300,000)
Contribution margin							200,000
Fixed costs							(100,000)
Profit before taxes							$ 100,000

$$\frac{\text{Contribution margin}}{\text{Sales revenue}} = \frac{\$200{,}000}{\$500{,}000} = 0.40 \text{ or } \$\,0.40$$

$$\text{BEP} = \frac{\text{Fixed costs}}{\text{PV ratio}} = \frac{\$100{,}000}{0.40} = \$\,250{,}000$$

BREAK-EVEN WEDGES

Managers have different ways of structuring the cost profile of their businesses (a cost profile is all the costs associated with a business). They make their decisions based on two major factors: the level of risk they are prepared to take, and the level of expected sales volume. Some managers may favour a high volume and a low PV ratio; others, a low volume and a high PV ratio. Some may prefer high fixed costs and low variable costs, while others prefer low fixed costs and high variable costs. Figure 5.5 shows some possibilities. The **break-even wedge** is the tool that helps managers to determine the best way of structuring these operating costs (fixed versus variable).

Break-even wedge
A tool that helps managers to determine the best way of structuring operating costs (fixed versus variable).

For example, with an extremely high and stable level of sales, Company A should build a highly automated plant with high fixed costs and low unit variable costs. Management of Company B is not as optimistic about sales levels; it would therefore go for a plant that is not as highly automated (lower fixed costs), but it would have to pay higher unit variable costs (direct labour). Company A would therefore have a competitive advantage over Company B if the economy is strong and there is a large demand for the product. Profits are larger after the company has reached its break-even point. If, however, the economy is weak and production levels are low, Company B would have a distinct competitive advantage over Company A, because its fixed costs would be lower.

Figure 5.5 shows four companies with different cost structures and PV ratios. Each company has a different profit wedge. We know that companies A and B have the same break-even points, but Company A has higher fixed costs and a higher PV ratio

Figure 5.5 **Break-Even Wedges**

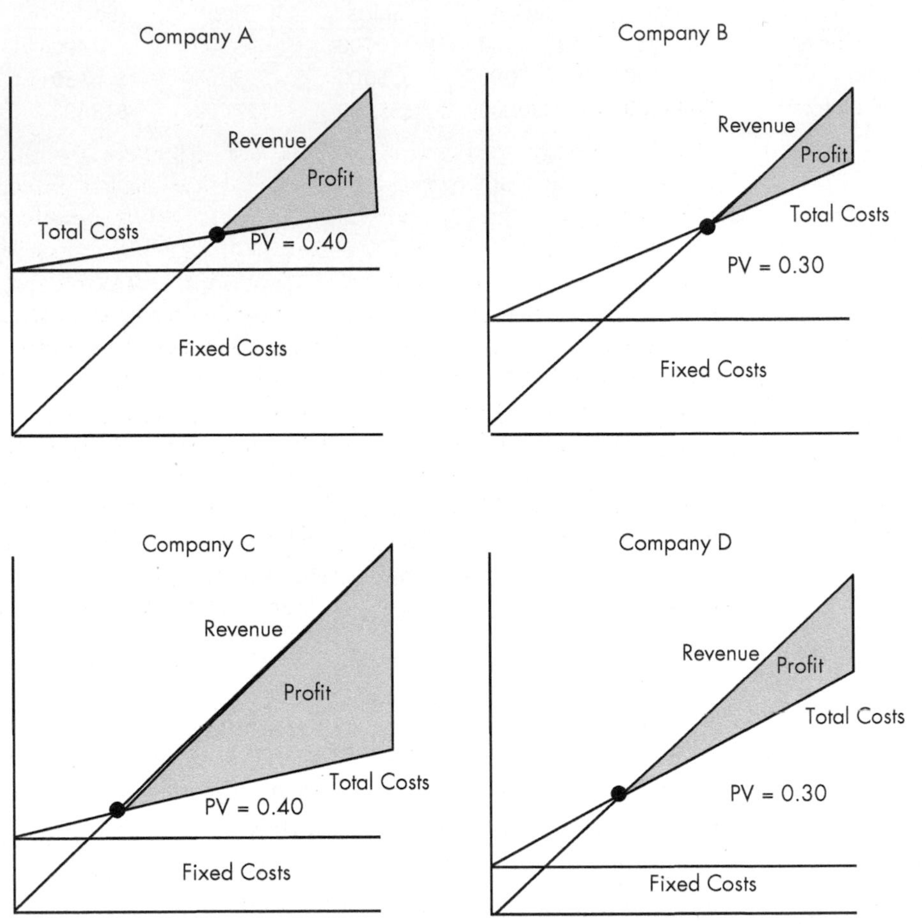

than Company B. Although Company A's profits are increased after the break-even point, it is more vulnerable if sales volume falls short of the break-even point. The loss zone is more pronounced for Company A than for Company B.

Companies C and D have lower fixed costs. The revenue line is the same as those of Companies A and B, but the profit levels are reached earlier. For example, Company C's profit structure (PV ratio) is similar to that of Company A, but Company C generates a profit on each sales dollar at a lower level of production. Profits made by Companies B and D follow a similar pattern.

The major advantage of Companies A and C is that profits increase faster once they have reached the break-even point (producing a wider wedge or bigger PV ratio). These companies are, however, more vulnerable to losses in a slow economy. Companies B and D have similar revenue and variable-cost patterns (the slope of the lines are identical), which produce a similar wedge in the profit zone.

In the News 5.3 explains what a company can do to sustain their bottom line.

In The News 5.3

THINKING OUTSIDE THE BOX

When things go completely wrong and you have no control of the situation, sometimes you have to do things that are a bit out of the ordinary. To keep a reasonable level of profitability, some companies will increase their selling prices, others will increase their advertising budget, and some will cut their costs.

The growing popularity of online shopping was having an adverse effect on RONA's bottom line, and buying online is a trend that is expected to accelerate over the next few years. This will force some retailers to undersize their operations and, most important, become leaner. Reasons for buying online include more informed consumers, a wider range of products, and saving gas. So, RONA decided, during the early part of 2012, to shift toward smaller stores instead of the big-box outlets—a totally new strategy. The company closed 10 of the underperforming large stores, downsized 13 others, and added 25 smaller shops. The strategy is to rethink the concept of big-box stores and squeeze more business into fewer aisles. These changes are based on consumer buying habits: making fewer shopping trips, using shops that are closer to home, and having more personal contacts with sales associates. The goal is to maintain customer satisfaction and loyalty and, ultimately, preserve the integrity of the bottom line.

Source: "RONA believes it's doing it right by closing stores." *Winnipeg Free Press*. Retrieved from http://www.winnipegfreepress.com/business/rona-believes-its-doing-it-right-by-closing-stores-140272843.html, accessed February 24, 2012. For more information about RONA, go to www.rona.ca/content/home.

Other Cost Concepts

4 Differentiate between different types of cost concepts such as committed and discretionary costs, controllable and non-controllable costs, and direct and indirect costs.

Managers classify costs in different categories. So far, we have made the distinction between fixed and variable costs and have shown that there are also costs that can be classified as semi-fixed or semi-variable. Let's examine other cost concepts and see how they can be used for analysis and control.

COMMITTED VERSUS DISCRETIONARY COSTS

Fixed costs can be grouped in two distinct categories: committed and discretionary.

Committed fixed costs
Costs that must be paid to operate a business.

Discretionary fixed costs
Costs that can be controlled by managers.

Committed fixed costs are those that cannot be controlled and that must be paid to operate a business. They include depreciation on buildings and equipment and salaries paid to managers.

Discretionary fixed costs can be controlled by managers from one period to another, if necessary. For example, costs for research and development, training programs, advertising, and promotional activities can be increased or decreased from one period to the next.

It is important to recognize the difference between committed and discretionary fixed costs in cost–volume–profit analysis. As shown in Figure 5.6, when planning for a period they anticipate will be challenging, management may decide to cut some discretionary fixed costs to bring the break-even point from B to A.

Figure 5.6 Committed versus Discretionary Fixed Costs

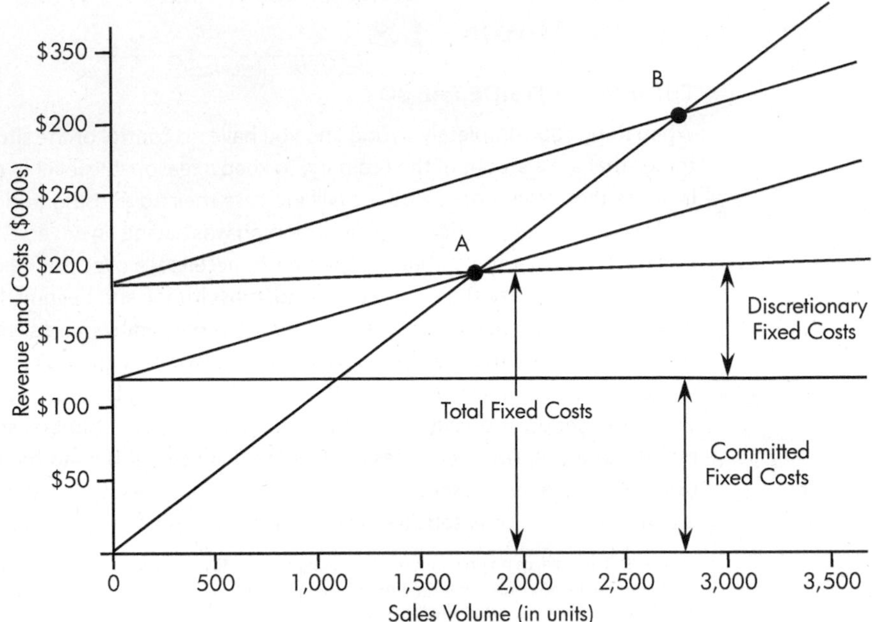

CONTROLLABLE VERSUS NON-CONTROLLABLE COSTS

Accountability is important in the management process, so it is vital to separate costs that managers can control from those they cannot.

Controllable costs
Costs that operating managers are accountable for.

Non-controllable costs
Costs that are not under the direct control of operating managers.

Budgets are allocated to individual managers, and they have to report on whether they operate within that budget. If costs over which managers have control exceed the budget, managers must explain why. Typical **controllable costs** for plant managers are maintenance, production supplies, overtime, waste, and equipment. Other costs are incurred over which they have no control, such as the example given earlier about the opening of a district or sales office (see page 200). In that instance, the district manager would not have to account for the head-office cost allocations. Typical **non-controllable costs** are depreciation, insurance, a supervisor's salary, and other overhead costs (e.g., allocated costs).

On the manager's budget reports, costs should be grouped into these two categories, and managers should be expected to account only for amounts over which they have control.

Direct costs
Materials and labour expenses that are directly incurred when making a product.

DIRECT VERSUS INDIRECT COSTS

Costs can be direct or indirect. **Direct costs** are directly related to a specific activity, product, program, project, or goal. These costs are avoided if the activity is eliminated or incurred if the activity is performed.

Indirect costs
Costs that are necessary in production but that cannot be clearly allocated to specific products or services.

Indirect costs are not associated with a specific activity, product, program, project, or goal. Typical indirect costs include overhead (e.g., head-office allocation), which is usually shared among operating or production units. For example, Table 5.6(a) shows a company that produces three different products, each with its own direct costs. A total of $90,000 in indirect costs or overhead costs is split equally ($30,000) among the products. As shown, products A and B are producing positive net results while product C has a $5,000 loss. Management may think about no longer making product C. If it does, the $90,000 overhead (if these costs cannot be reduced by getting rid of product C) would be split between products A and B. As shown in Table 5.6(b), this would reduce the profits of these two products and even produce a negative result for product B. In addition to apparently losing money on product B, the company would reduce its overall profit from $45,000 to $20,000. The company would, therefore, be in a better position if it continued to manufacture product C.

Table 5.6(a) Direct and Indirect Costs

	Product A	Product B	Product C	Total
Revenue	$100,000	$90,000	$75,000	$265,000
Direct costs	(25,000)	(55,000)	(50,000)	(130,000)
Indirect costs	(30,000)	(30,000)	(30,000)	(90,000)
Total costs	(55,000)	(85,000)	(80,000)	(220,000)
Profit	$ 45,000	$ 5,000	$ (5,000)	$ 45,000

Table 5.6(b) Direct and Indirect Costs

	Product A	Product B	Total
Revenue	$100,000	$ 90,000	$190,000
Direct costs	(25,000)	(55,000)	(80,000)
Indirect costs	(45,000)	(45,000)	(90,000)
Total costs	(70,000)	(100,000)	(170,000)
Profit	$ 30,000	$(10,000)	$ 20,000

Chapter Summary

1 Identify how break-even analysis can help to maximize profitability.

Break-even analysis can be used in business to make different types of decisions, such as pricing decisions, new product decisions, modernization decisions, and expansion decisions.

2 Describe the cost concepts related to break-even analysis, such as fixed and variable costs, the relationship between revenue and costs, the contribution margin, the relevant range, and the relevant costs.

To make the right decision, management must have a complete knowledge of its business's operating cost structure.

Cost–volume–profit analysis studies show the interrelationships among volume of production, fixed costs, and variable costs. Fixed costs remain constant and do not vary with different levels of production. Variable costs vary in direct proportion to changes in level of output. There are also semi-fixed or semi-variable costs that vary at different levels of production. Break-even analysis is the tool that helps management determine at what point profit or loss takes place. The break-even point is the level of output at which a business stops incurring a loss and begins to make a profit. The contribution margin is the difference between revenue and variable costs. This difference is used to pay for fixed costs and to earn a profit. Relevant range has to do with costs (fixed and variable) that apply to a certain level of production. Relevant costs have to do with alternative ways that managers can choose from to operate a business.

3 Draw the break-even chart and calculate the break-even point, the cash break-even point, and the profit break-even point, and explain how they can be applied in different organizations.

The break-even chart gives a visual presentation of the interrelationships between revenues, variable costs, fixed costs, and total costs. The *break-even point* is calculated by using the following formula:

$$N = FC \div (SP - VC)$$

The *cash break-even point* determines how much revenue a business must generate to pay for its cash costs. The *profit break-even point* determines the revenue a business must generate to meet a profit goal. Sensitivity analysis is used to find the various break-even points when there are changes in any one of the variables, such as unit selling price, volume of production, fixed costs, or variable costs. Break-even analysis can be used in many areas, including sales territories, retail stores, plants, departments, product divisions, production centres, service centres, and machine operation. The break-even wedge is a tool that helps managers determine the most appropriate way to structure operating costs (fixed versus variable).

4 Differentiate between different types of cost concepts, such as committed and discretionary costs, controllable and non-controllable costs, and direct and indirect costs.

Costs can also be broken down into committed fixed costs versus discretionary fixed costs, controllable versus non-controllable costs, and direct versus indirect costs.

Key Terms

Review Questions

1 Identify how break-even analysis can help to maximize profitability.

1. Why do fixed costs create an element of the unknown in the decision-making process?
2. In what types of decisions can break-even analysis help managers?
3. How can break-even analysis help in making pricing decisions?

2 Describe the cost concepts related to break-even analysis, such as fixed and variable costs, the relationship between revenue and costs, the contribution margin, the relevant range, and the relevant costs.

4. What is the relevance of break-even analysis?
5. Differentiate between fixed and variable costs.
6. Why are some costs called semi-fixed?
7. Explain the meaning and significance of the contribution margin.
8. Comment on the more important elements that affect profit levels.
9. What do we mean by relevant range?
10. What do we mean by relevant costs?

3 Draw the break-even chart and calculate the break-even point, the cash break-even point, and the profit break-even point, and explain how they can be applied in different organizations.

11. Draw a hypothetical break-even chart.
12. What is a PV ratio?
13. Why would someone use the PV ratio instead of the unit contribution margin?
14. Why should managers be interested in calculating the profit break-even point?
15. How is the contribution margin calculated?
16. Differentiate between the break-even point and the cash break-even point.
17. What is the significance of calculating the cash break-even point?
18. What is the usefulness of sensitivity analysis?
19. "The major factor that will underlie the cost structure of a business is the level of risk that managers are prepared to take and the level of expected sales volume." Explain.

20. What is the significance of using the break-even wedge analysis when analyzing the break-even point?
21. How can break-even analysis help managers make pricing decisions? Give an example.

4 Differentiate between different types of cost concepts, such as committed and discretionary costs, controllable and non-controllable costs, and direct and indirect costs.

22. Differentiate between committed fixed costs and discretionary fixed costs.
23. What is the difference between direct costs and indirect costs? Give an example of each.

Learning Exercises

2 Explain cost concepts related to break-even analysis, such as fixed and variable costs, the relationship between revenue and costs, the contribution margin, the relevant range, and the relevant costs.

EXERCISE 1: BREAK-EVEN POINT IN UNITS AND IN REVENUE

For this exercise, use the following information:

- Total fixed costs are estimated at $100,000.
- Total units expected to be sold are 50,000.
- Total variable costs are $300,000.
- Unit selling price is $8.00.

Calculate the following:

1. Break-even point in units
2. Break-even point in revenue

EXERCISE 2: CONTRIBUTION MARGIN, PV RATIO, AND BREAK-EVEN POINT

A company expects to sell 75,000 widgets at a price of $10.00.The unit variable costs are estimated at $8.00, and the fixed costs are estimated at $125,000. On the basis of this information, calculate the following:

1. Contribution margin
2. PV ratio
3. Revenue break-even by using the PV ratio
4. Profit generated

EXERCISE 3: BREAK-EVEN POINT IN UNITS AND IN REVENUE

Using the information in Exercise 1, if rent were increased by $25,000 and variable costs and unit selling price remained unchanged, what would be the new PV ratio and break-even point in units and in revenue?

EXERCISE 4: IDENTIFYING FIXED AND VARIABLE COSTS AND CALCULATING THE CONTRIBUTION MARGIN AND THE PV RATIO

Parkway Travel Tours is organizing a five-day trip from Toronto to Branson, Missouri, a family town with all types of attractions and theatres. Although it is a small town (around 10,000 people), Branson attracts millions of visitors every year.

Branson hosts more than 100 live shows in 52 state-of-the art theatres. For this particular five-day trip, it will cost the agency the following:

Buss and driver	\$2,500/day
Travel guide	\$500/day
Advertising	\$1,000 (brochure and newspapers)
Meals per person/day	\$5.00 (4 breakfasts)
	\$20.00 (5 dinners)
Hotel rooms (night)	\$60.00 (4 nights)
Events/attractions	\$40.00 (per event for a total of 7 events)
Other fixed costs	\$1,000
Miscellaneous variable costs	\$100 (per person)
Price per client	\$1,700

Questions

With the above information, calculate the following:

1. Total fixed costs
2. Variable costs (per client)
3. Contribution margin (per client)
4. PV ratio
5. The number of clients needed to break-even
6. The number of clients needed if Parkway wants to generate a \$5,000 profit

3 Draw the break-even chart and calculate the break-even point, the cash break-even point, and the profit break-even point, and explain how they can be applied in different organizations.

EXERCISE 5: CALCULATING THE BREAK-EVEN POINT

With the following information, calculate the break-even point in sales dollars for a retail store:

- Revenue

Product line A	\$ 100,000
Product line B	\$ 200,000
Product line C	\$ 600,000

- Cost of sales for the three product lines is 50%, 45%, and 55% of revenue, respectively.
- Fixed costs are estimated at \$350,000.

EXERCISE 6: CALCULATING THE PV RATIO AND THE BREAK-EVEN POINT

With the information outlined below, calculate the following:

1. Profit
2. Break-even point in revenue
3. Cash break-even point

Depreciation	$ 30,000
Plant direct wages	100,000
Plant supervision	60,000
Advertising	30,000
Plant insurance	20,000
Sales commissions	100,000
Office supplies	3,000
Revenue	550,000
Overtime	30,000
Rent	35,000
Property taxes	10,000
Raw materials	100,000

EXERCISE 7: CALCULATING THE REGULAR AND CASH BREAK-EVEN POINTS

The owner/manager of a beverage and food retail outlet intends to invest $400,000 in another retail store. He wants to make at least $75,000 in profit before taxes, or 18.75% return on his investment. Based on his market study, he estimates selling 200,000 coffees, 100,000 donuts, 75,000 sandwiches, and 75,000 soups.

The unit selling prices for these products are $1.75 for coffee, $1.00 for donuts, $2.25 for sandwiches, and $1.75 for soups. Based on current purchasing costs from existing suppliers, his cost of sales are estimated at 15%, 20%, 40%, and 25% of revenue for coffee, donuts, sandwiches, and soups, respectively. His other annual costs include rent ($100,000), salaries ($235,000), heating and hydro ($45,000), municipal taxes ($35,000), and a variety of other costs ($40,000).

Questions

1. With the above information, (a) construct the statement of income and (b) calculate the owner/manager's break-even point in dollars.
2. Based on his forecast, should he go ahead with the project?
3. If his cost of sales was reduced by 10%, how would that affect his break-even point?
4. If his rent and salaries increase by $25,000 and $50,000, respectively, how would these changes affect his break-even point (assume that the variable costs remain at the original estimate)?
5. If the changes in both 3 and 4 above take place simultaneously, how would these changes affect his break-even point?

6. If the owner/manager wants to make a $150,000 profit before taxes based on his original cost estimates, how much revenue must his retail outlet generate?

EXERCISE 8: SENSITIVITY ANALYSIS

Company A and Company B are both selling $2.5 million worth of goods. Company A's PV ratio is 0.40 while B's is 0.60. Company B's fixed costs are $1 million, which puts the business at a competitive disadvantage versus A, which has $500,000 in fixed costs.

Questions

1. On the basis of the above information, if revenues were to increase by 20% for both businesses next year, how much profit before taxes would each generate?
2. On the basis of the above information, if revenues were to decrease by 20% for both businesses next year, how much profit before taxes would each generate?
3. Because of the varying cost structures, discuss the implications that the PV ratio has on both companies' profit performance.

Cases

CASE 1: QUICK PHOTO LTD.

Tony Kasabian was ready to put the finishing touches on a business plan he wanted to present to a local banker for financing for his new venture, Quick Photo Ltd. The investment proposal contained a marketing plan designed to capture a good share of the southern Ontario digital print market. Tony was interested in buying several new high-technology digital film printers manufactured in Japan and capable of providing online photo finishing and processing of top-quality prints from digital camera cards and CDs. His retailing plan consisted of operating digital print processors in kiosks in several Ontario high-traffic malls, including locations in Don Mills, Ottawa, Windsor, London, and Kingston. He felt that his business concept was in line with the trend of developing high-quality photo finishing services.

However, he realized that his banker would be asking him many questions about market size, his competitors, his revenue targets for the next several years, and, most important, his marketing assumptions backing up his sales forecast. Therefore, before finalizing his business plan, Tony asked his friend, a recent commerce graduate, to help him calculate the number of prints that he would have to process each year to cover his fixed costs and earn a reasonable profit.

On average, Tony figured out that he would charge $0.32 per print, a price consistent with competitors' charges for work of similar quality; most prints would be

4 × 6 and some would be 5 × 7 or 8 × 10. Quick Photo's projected statement of income for the first year of operations is as follows:

Number of prints developed		5,000,000
Revenue		$1,600,000
Cost of sales		
Direct materials	$(250,000)	
Direct labour	(265,000)	
Depreciation	(78,000)	
Supervision	(80,000)	
Total cost of sales		(673,000)
Gross profit		927,000
Operating expenses		
Distribution costs		
Salaries	(230,000)	
Sales commission	(110,000)	
Advertising	(25,000)	
Subtotal		(365,000)
Administration expenses		
Salaries	(185,000)	
Insurance	(20,000)	
Rent	(60,000)	
Depreciation	(33,000)	
Subtotal		(298,000)
Finance costs		(35,000)
Total		(698,000)
Profit before taxes		229,000)
Income tax expense		(101,000)
Profit for the year		$ 128,000)

Questions

1. Calculate Tony's break-even point in revenue and the cash break-even point in revenue.
2. How many prints a year and what level of revenue must Tony reach if he wants to earn $275,000 in profit before taxes?
3. Calculate Tony's annual revenue break-even point by using the PV ratio if he is to meet the $275,000 profit before tax goal.
4. If he increases his advertising budget by $20,000, what would be Tony's new yearly break-even point in prints and in revenue? How many additional prints must Tony develop to increase his revenue to cover the incremental advertising budget?

5. If Tony reduces his direct material costs for processing the prints by $25,000, what would be his new break-even point in units and in revenue?

CASE 2: V & A CARPET CLEANING SERVICES

In March 2003, Vincent and Anne-Marie Finney started their carpet-cleaning services business in Toronto. The business was geared primarily at young couples, a market that they felt was growing rapidly. Vincent and Anne-Marie had worked during the previous 10 years as salaried employees for different types of organizations. They were frustrated with the fact that their future was in the hands of employers, so they decided to start V & A Carpet Cleaning Services. After 10 years of tremendous success in the business, the couple decided to launch a franchise.

They placed advertisements in different daily newspapers across Canada promoting the franchise business. Bill and Jill Robinson of Ottawa saw the advertisement and called V & A for information about the economics and advantages of managing a carpet-cleaning franchise operation. The Finneys provided the following information:

- Average revenue for cleaning carpets in each household is $120.
- A 20% sales commission per contract is secured by a sales representative.
- Machine operators receive $30 for cleaning the carpets in each household.
- Average costs for gas and maintenance for trucks for each household is $5.50.
- Maintenance charges are $400 per machine for each 100 houses cleaned.
- Monthly rental charges for office and small warehouse for inventories is $1,200.
- Annual depreciation for the equipment is $500.
- Monthly salary paid to Bill and Jill would total $3,500.

Other costs include the following:

- A $1,400 monthly salary for office employees.
- A $500 yearly expense for various insurance policies.
- A $125 monthly expense for utilities and telephone.
- A yearly $10,000 fee for the franchise.
- A $5.00 franchise fee for each household cleaned.

Questions

On the basis of the above information, calculate the following:

1. How many carpets would Bill and Jill have to clean each year to start making a profit?
2. How much revenue would they have to earn each year in order to break even?
3. How many carpets would they have to clean each year if they want to earn a yearly profit of $45,000 before tax?
4. Prepare a statement of income on the basis of earning $45,000 in profit before tax.

FINANCIAL SPREADSHEETS: EXCEL®

Templates 1 and 2 of the decision-making tools of the financial spreadsheets accompanying this book can calculate the break-even points by using the contribution margin and the PV ratio. Template 1 (Break-Even Analysis Using the Contribution Margin) calculates the break-even point, in units and in revenue, of a business decision by using the contribution margin. Template 2 (Break-Even Analysis Using the PV Ratio) calculates the revenue break-even point by using the PV ratio. The break-even point for these two templates can be done for three consecutive years.

Joel Blit/Shutterstock and Bank of Canada

CHAPTER 6

[WORKING CAPITAL MANAGEMENT]

Learning Objectives

After reading this chapter, you should be able to

1 Explain the meaning of working capital and how it can be measured.

2 Discuss the flow of cash via the cash conversion cycle.

3 Describe several strategies for managing inventories.

4 Explore techniques for managing trade receivables.

5 Comment on managing cash and cash equivalents.

6 Explain how to manage current liability accounts to improve the cash flow cycle.

OPENING CASE

Managing Working Capital Accounts to Maximize Earnings

During the third year of operation, the Millers spent more time managing their working capital accounts, such as inventories and trade receivables. In the early years of any business, a large amount of funds are invested in working capital. The following shows the evolution of CompuTech's current assets, net working capital, total assets, and revenue between the years 2013 and 2015.

(in $000s)	2013	2014	2015	% Increase
Current assets	105	136	235	124%
Current liabilities	52	60	132	154%
Net working capital	53	76	103	94%
Total assets	237	268	637	169%
Revenue	350	420	800	129%

The Millers' current assets increased by 124% between 2013 and 2015, while current liabilities grew by 154%. Revenue increased by 129%. To improve their financial performance, the Millers recognize that they have to be cautious in managing their working capital accounts.

Len and Joan have realized that managing working capital accounts is more complex and time consuming than managing non-current assets (e.g., capital assets). For the capital assets (e.g., investing in a new store), they went through a detailed capital budgeting process, using investment yardsticks to launch their first store. However, once that decision was made, nothing much could be done. They had to live with the consequences, good or bad. Conversely, managing working capital accounts is a painstaking daily activity.

The Millers know that they have to maintain a certain amount of inventories in their store, and sell goods and services on credit, which results in accounts receivable. These working capital accounts are essential investments and must be made to generate revenue. However, the Millers also realize that they have to be wise in the way that they spend their cash in these unproductive but necessary accounts. As Len pointed out,

> Too much investment in inventories and trade receivables drains CompuTech's cash flow and can even lower the return on our assets. The more that we have to invest in these accounts, the more we will have to borrow from short-term lenders. And of course, the larger the loan, the more finance costs CompuTech has to pay, which ultimately reduces profitability.

The Millers must ensure that just enough cash is invested in working capital accounts to meet their day-to-day operating needs and maximize earnings, but not so much that such unproductive assets are a cash drain. The Millers need to know how much cash to invest in current assets, such as trade receivables and inventories, and how much cash they need from short-term lenders.

THIS CHAPTER WILL SHOW LEN AND JOAN MILLER HOW TO

- Squeeze cash out of working capital accounts to improve financial performance.
- Make decisions related to managing inventories, trade receivables, and trade and other payables.

Chapter Overview

ROADMAP TO MEASURE WORKING CAPITAL ACCOUNTS' EFFICIENCIES

This is our second chapter dealing with operating decisions. This chapter covers how current asset and current liability accounts should be managed to maximize profit. The accounts that we will examine in this chapter are inventories, trade receivables, cash, and marketable securities under current assets; and trade and other payables, and working capital loans under current liabilities. Working capital management will be examined under six topics:

- *Management of working capital.* We will look at how to manage working capital accounts and how to measure efficiencies related to inventories, trade receivables, cash, and current liabilities.
- *Cash conversion cycle.* We will then explore the cash conversion cycle and how cash flows within the operating cycle of a business.
- *Inventory management.* We will explain four decision models used to manage inventories: materials requirements planning (MRP), just-in-time inventory, the economic ordering quantity, and inventory replenishment.
- *Trade receivables management.* We will explore strategies used for managing trade receivables, particularly setting credit terms, granting credit to customers, billing customers, monitoring payments made by customers, collecting trade receivables, and having adequate credit insurance.
- *Management of cash and cash equivalents.* We will analyze how cash and cash equivalents can be made productive, ways to improve cash collection, and strategies to manage near-cash accounts, such as marketable securities.
- *Management of current liabilities.* We will explore how current liabilities, such as trade and other payables, and working capital loans can help improve profitability if managed appropriately.

Management of Working Capital

1 Explain the meaning of working capital and how it can be measured.

This section looks at working capital and how working capital can be measured.

MEANING OF WORKING CAPITAL

In Chapter 1, *working capital* referred to all accounts listed in the current accounts of the statement of financial position, that is, current assets and current liabilities. In the early years of financial management, working capital included only current asset accounts, such as inventories, trade receivables, and cash and cash equivalents. These assets are essential for operating a business. Although inventories and trade receivables, money in the bank to pay bills, and money in marketable securities, such as short-term investments, are not productive assets, some cash must be tied up in these types of accounts. But it's important for a business to ensure that a minimum amount of funds is tied up in these current asset accounts: just enough for day-to-day operations and to maximize profitability, but not so much that it affects the business's activities. Managing current assets is critical, as they are a major portion (in many cases, about half) of a company's total assets.

Today, working capital is defined more broadly to include current liabilities, such as trade and other payables, notes payable, other accruals, or all loans that are due within 12 months. Table 6.1 lists the typical working capital accounts. A current liability, such as trade and other payables, is interest free, and it's worthwhile for a business to use this type of short-term liability to finance its business activities. However, a business should be careful not to risk its position by not being able to meet its short-term obligations.

Net working capital The difference between current assets and current liabilities.

Net working capital is the difference between current assets and current liabilities. In Table 6.1, for instance, the company's current assets total $1,420,000 and its current liabilities are $720,000, so its net working capital is $700,000 (current ratio of 1.97 times).

Table 6.1 Working Capital Accounts

Current Assets		Current Liabilities	
Inventories	$ 755,000	Trade and other payables	$400,000
Trade receivables	500,000	Accrued wages	50,000
Prepaid expenses	40,000	Taxes payable	20,000
Cash and cash equivalents	125,000	Notes payable	50,000
		Bank loan	200,000
Total current assets	$1,420,000	Total current liabilities	$720,000

Working capital management Managing individual current asset and current liability accounts to ensure proper interrelationships among them.

Working capital management refers to all aspects of managing individual current asset and current liability accounts, and ensuring proper interrelationships among all current asset accounts, all current liability accounts, and other statement of financial position accounts, such as non-current assets and long-term borrowings.

It takes more time to manage working capital accounts than non-current assets, such as land, buildings, machinery, and equipment. The level of investment in each of the working capital accounts usually changes daily, and to effectively manage the business, managers must always know how much cash needs to be in each of these accounts. Mismanagement of current accounts can be costly; excess current assets can reduce profitability and be a source of undue risk. Not enough current assets, conversely, may cause revenue loss; for example, a shortage of inventories may send customers to your competitors.

Goal of working capital management Accelerating the cash flow cycle after sales have been made.

The **goal of working capital management** is to accelerate the cash flow cycle after sales have been made. The faster the cash moves, the more profitable it is to the business because it means that a company has less cash tied up in unproductive (but necessary) assets. Let's use Table 6.1 as an example. If inventories and trade receivables were reduced by $100,000 and $75,000, respectively, the company would be able to invest $175,000 in investment securities, say, at 4% (before tax), and earn $7,000 in interest annually. Instead, managers would probably want to invest this excess cash in more productive assets, such as plant modernization or new equipment, which would generate a 20% return on the assets each year, as long as the inventories and trade receivables were kept at the new level.

In the News 6.1 confirms that a company must be in top financial shape and know how to accelerate its cash flow cycle if it is going to grow responsibly over the long term.

In The News 6.1

GROWING SMART AVOIDS A CASH SQUEEZE

To sustain growth for the long term, a business must balance its business plan with its cash flow. These are the major drivers that help keep all accounts on your statement of financial position healthy and stable.

As an example, look at the growth pace of Frogbox, a company that rents stackable, sturdy, green plastic bins to customers for residential and commercial use. After a successful appearance on *Dragon's Den*, entrepreneur Doug Burgoyne received $200,000 from investors for a 25% stake. His business exploded: in the first 10 days, he received 500 franchise applications, and the company went from 3 locations to 21 in just seven months. But, as Alec Morley, a senior vice-president with TD Canada Trust pointed out, "To grow fast, your business must be in tip-top financial shape, while a lot of people over-extend themselves and confuse top-line revenue growth with bottom-line profitability." He also added, "Banks can help you manage the cycle, but they want to see that the company has a lot of working capital and a profitable bottom line."

Source: "Canadian firm prepares for U.S. expansion." *Toronto Star*. Retrieved from http://www.thestar.com/business/smallbusiness/article/1069920-canadian-firms-prepare-for-u-s-expansion, accessed March 4, 2012. To learn more about Frogbox, visit http://frogbox.com./

MEASURING EFFICIENCIES IN WORKING CAPITAL ACCOUNTS

Days of working capital (DWC)
The number of DWC a business holds to meet average daily sales requirements.

Two broad approaches are used to measure the productivity of working capital accounts: days of working capital and cash conversion efficiency. **Days of working capital (DWC)** measures the number of days of working capital a business has to meet its average daily sales requirements. The fewer the days, the more efficient a business is in managing its working capital. Consider, for example, Eastman Technologies Inc., which was introduced in Chapter 2. The company shows 47.2 DWC for 2013. This ratio is calculated as follows:

$$\frac{\textbf{(Inventories + Trade receivables) − Trade and other payables}}{\textbf{Revenue ÷ 365}}$$

The information used to calculate Eastman's days of working capital is drawn from the statement of income (refer back to Table 2.2) and the statement of financial position (refer back to Table 2.4):

$$\frac{(\$218{,}000 + \$300{,}000) - \$195{,}000}{\$2{,}500{,}000 \div 365} = \frac{\$323{,}000}{\$6{,}849} = 47.2 \text{ days}$$

Cash conversion efficiency (CCE)
A measure of how quickly a business converts revenue to cash flow.

The **cash conversion efficiency (CCE)** calculation measures how quickly a business converts revenue to cash flow. The financial data used for calculating Eastman's cash conversion efficiency ratio is drawn from Table 3.9, the statement of cash flows, and Table 2.2, the statement of income.

$$\frac{\text{Operating activities (cash flow)}}{\text{Revenue}} = \frac{\$126{,}500}{\$2{,}500{,}000} = 5.1\%$$

Eastman Technologies' cash performance ratio does not mean much unless it is compared with previous years' ratios and with industry standards. The higher the ratio, the more efficient a company is in generating cash. Our results mean that for every sales dollar, Eastman produces 5.1 cents in operating cash flows. If the company were to increase its cash flows to $200,000 with the same level in revenue, the ratio would be 8.0%, or 8 cents.

Managing working capital accounts means reducing costs related to them by keeping inventories and trade receivables as low as possible, investing excess cash for a short term, and increasing trade and other payables. Increasing revenue is not the only way to improve profitability; all accounts that are affected by revenue must be closely managed.

An important criterion for measuring overall financial performance is return on assets (ROA). The accounts appearing under current assets are in the denominator of the ROA equation, so if working capital accounts are minimized, ROA improves.

Problem-Solving Example 6.1

Measuring the Working Capital Accounts

With the following information, calculate the company's (1) days of working capital and (2) cash conversion efficiency ratio: revenue ($4,500,000), cash flows from operating activities ($270,000), trade and other payables ($100,000), trade receivables ($260,000), and inventories ($500,000).

Solution

1. Days of working capital: $\frac{(\$500{,}000 + \$260{,}000) - \$100{,}000}{\$4{,}500{,}000 \div 365} = \frac{\$660{,}000}{\$12{,}329} = 53.5 \text{ days}$
2. Cash conversion efficiency ratio: $\frac{\$270{,}000}{\$4{,}500{,}000} = 6.0\%$

Self-Test Exercise 6.1

Measuring Working Capital Efficiencies

Use CompuTech Inc.'s financial statements in Appendix A to calculate the following:

1. For 2013 and 2014, the company's days of working capital
2. For 2014, the company's cash conversion efficiency ratio

To calculate the CCE ratio for 2014, refer to Self-Test Exercise 3.5 (The Statement of Cash Flows) in Chapter 3.

Answers to the Self-Test Exercises can be found at www.bergeron7e.nelson.com.

2 Discuss the flow of cash via the cash conversion cycle.

Cash conversion cycle
The movement of cash through working capital accounts, such as inventories, trade receivables, and trade and other payables.

Cash Conversion Cycle

An important concept related to the management of working capital accounts is the **cash conversion cycle** (Figure 6.1). It can be defined as the movement of cash through working capital accounts, such as inventories, trade receivables, and trade and other payables. This includes decisions related to credit, delivery of raw materials, manufacturing, shipment, and so on. Working capital accounts can be displayed on a wheel, and the faster the wheel turns, the faster and more effectively management can use the cash generated from revenue. The goal is to find and reduce the number of days it takes to perform each activity shown on the wheel. If, overall, it takes 95 days for cash to circulate in a business, the goal may be to reduce it to, say, 80 days.

HOW CASH FLOWS WITHIN THE CASH CONVERSION CYCLE

Figure 6.2 shows that the flow of cash is like a boomerang. Business activities start with cash and eventually end with cash. The company buys inventories and pays wages to employees in its plant to transform raw materials into finished goods for

Figure 6.1 **The Cash Conversion Cycle**

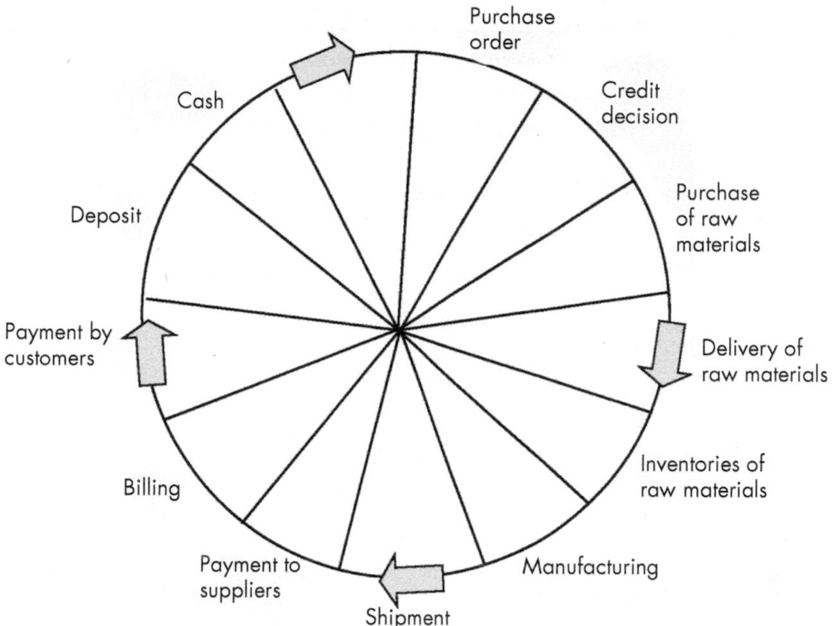

shipment to customers (revenue). Customers usually buy goods on credit (trade receivables); when collected, the business once again has cash, which is then used to buy more inventories, produce more goods, and the process continues. Some of the cash collected from customers is used to buy other things, such as non-current assets (capital assets) or to pay the principal on a debt, income taxes, and even dividends.

Table 6.2 shows how Eastman Technologies' cash conversion cycle for the years 2012 and 2013 were calculated. Both inventories and trade receivables are used to

Figure 6.2 **Cash Flow of Working Capital Accounts**

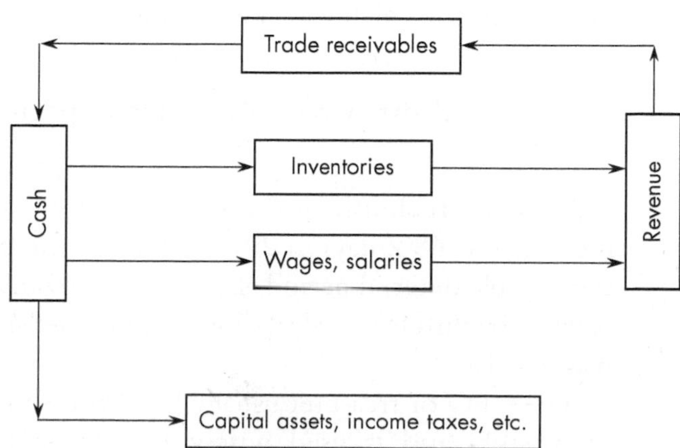

Table 6.2 **Eastman Technologies' Cash Conversion Cycle**

	2013	2012
Liquidity ratios		
Current ratio	1.35	1.35
Quick ratio	0.86	0.89
Cash conversion cycle		
Inventory conversion period	41.9 days	38.7 days
Receivables conversion period	43.8 days	45.4 days
Operating cycle	85.7 days	84.1 days
Less: Trade and other payables deferral period	37.5 days	36.6 days
Cash conversion cycle	48.2 days	47.5 days

Operating cycle
The number of days inventories and trade receivables take (in days) to be converted into cash.

calculate the company's operating cycle. Essentially, the **operating cycle** represents the number of days that both inventories and trade receivables take to be converted into cash. Here is how the conversion periods for both accounts are calculated:

$$\textbf{Inventory conversion period} = \frac{\textbf{Inventories}}{\textbf{Cost of sales} \div \textbf{365}}$$

$$\textbf{Trade receivables conversion period} = \frac{\textbf{Trade receivables}}{\textbf{Revenue} \div \textbf{365}}$$

The operating cycle shown in Table 6.2 for 2013 is 85.7 days. But it is reduced by the trade and other payables deferral period of 37.5 days. The trade and other payables deferral period calculation is as follows:

$$\textbf{Trade and other payables deferral period} = \frac{\textbf{Trade and other payables}}{\textbf{Cost of sales} \div \textbf{365}}$$

Eastman Technologies' cash conversion cycle in 2012 was 47.5 days, and it increased to 48.2 days in 2013. Although the operating cycle increased by 1.6 days, the payable deferral period also increased by 0.9 days (the company was able to delay paying for purchases a little longer). The net increase in the cash conversion period was 0.7 days.

The CFO or treasurer usually handles cash management, ensuring that cash flows in quickly and is used wisely. Using the numbers from Table 3.9, Eastman's statement of cash flows, Figure 6.3 shows the ways cash flows into and out of a business. At the centre of the system is the cash pool; all money comes from and flows back into this pool. The right side of the figure shows operating activities: customers pay for goods or services (inflow), and Eastman pays suppliers for goods purchased, wages to employees, and income taxes to the government (outflows). The left side shows financing activities and investing activities. Lenders and shareholders provide money to Eastman (inflows), and shareholders receive dividends and lenders receive repayment of loans (outflows). Cash does flow in and out of investing activities, but usually cash flows out because businesses continually buy non-current assets, such as equipment and machinery. An inflow would be created if, for example, Eastman sold some non-current assets. Overall, Eastman generated $126,500 in cash (operating activities), received $167,500 from external sources (financing activities), and invested $290,000 in capital assets (investing activities).

Figure 6.3 The Flow of Cash at Eastman Technologies Inc.

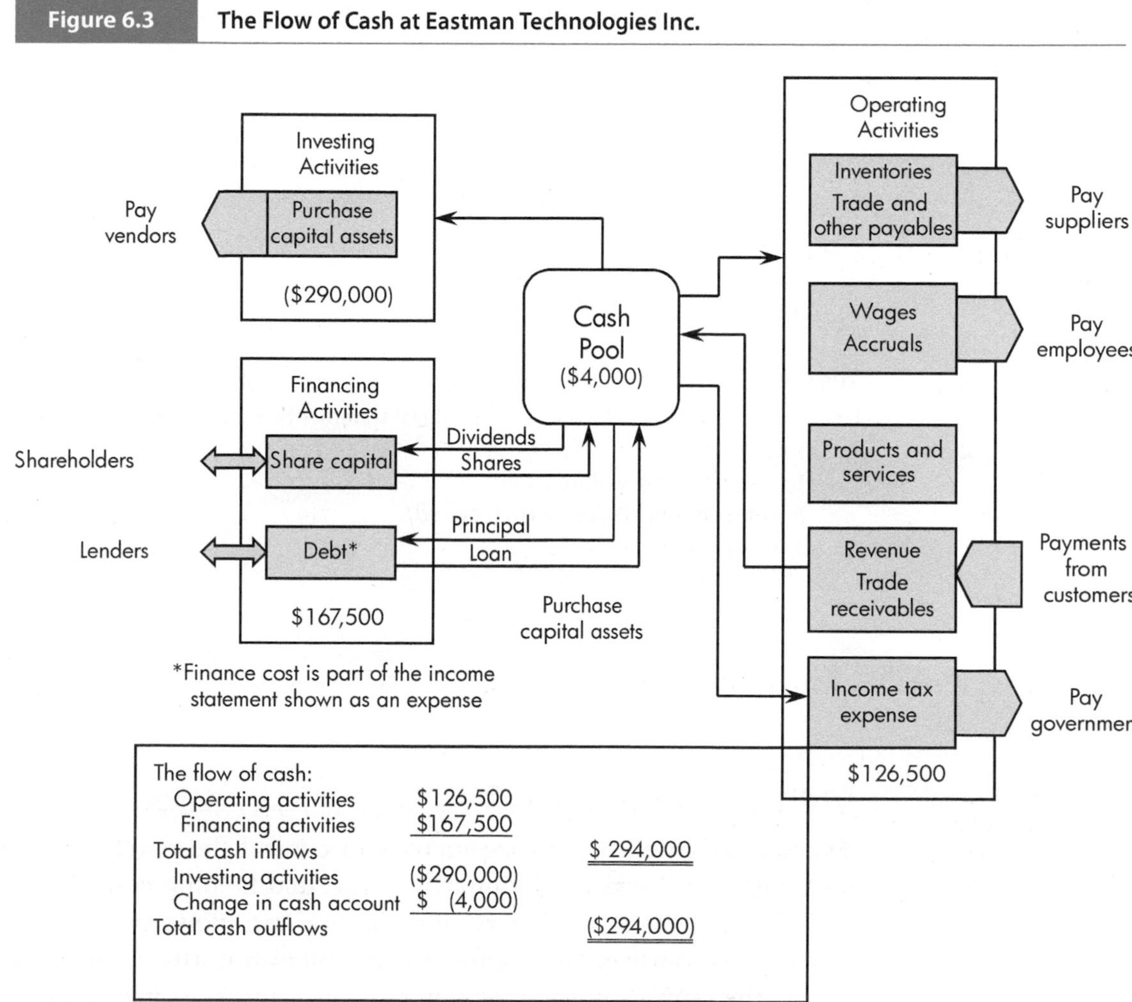

Problem-Solving Example 6.2

The Cash Conversion Cycle

With the following information, calculate the company's (1) inventory conversion period, (2) trade receivables conversion period, (3) trade and other payables deferral period, (4) operating cycle, and (5) cash conversion cycle: revenue ($2,800,000), inventories ($400,000), trade and other payables ($180,000), trade receivables ($230,000), and cost of sales ($2,000,000).

Solution

1. Inventory conversion period: 73.0 days
   $400,000 ÷ ($2,000,000 ÷ 365) = $400,000 ÷ $5,479
2. Trade receivables conversion period: 30.0 days
   $230,000 ÷ ($2,800,000 ÷ 365) = $230,000 ÷ $7,671
3. Trade and other payables deferral period: 32.8 days
   $180,000 ÷ ($2,000,000 ÷ 365) = $180,000 ÷ $5,479
4. Operating cycle

Inventory conversion period	73.0
Trade receivables conversion period	30.0
Operating cycle	103.0

5. Cash conversion cycle

Less: Trade and other payables	32.8
Cash conversion cycle	70.2

Self-Test Exercise 6.2

The Cash Conversion Cycle

Use CompuTech Inc.'s 2013 and 2014 financial statements in Appendix A to calculate the following for the company:

1. Inventory conversion period
2. Trade receivables conversion period
3. Operating cycle
4. Trade and other payables deferral period
5. Cash conversion cycle

Answers to the Self-Test Exercises can be found at www.bergeron7e.nelson.com.

3 Describe several strategies for managing inventories.

Managing Inventories

The goal of inventory management is to control the purchase, storage, and use of inventories or stocks to minimize the order and holding costs.

Turning inventories more rapidly improves cash flows, profit, and ROA. One way for a firm to analyze management is by calculating the annual inventory turnover rate, or the number of times a business sells (or turns) its investment in inventories in a year. The turnover rate relates an investment in inventory directly to sales volume (for a retail or wholesale business) or cost of sales (for a manufacturer).

The turnover rate is significant because it has a direct relationship to cash flows and profit: the faster the inventories turn over, the lower the investment in inventories. To calculate the inventory turnover rate, the annual cost of sales or revenue is divided by the average investment in inventories.

Maintaining the right level of inventories can be compared to maintaining the right level of water in a bathtub. If water flows out of the tub more rapidly than into it, the tub will soon be empty. However, if more water is let in than out, the tub will overflow. The same principle applies in inventory management. On one side, inventories are used continually to produce manufactured goods and, on the other, raw materials keep flowing into the storage area. A manager needs to determine two things: (1) the level of investment needed in inventories and (2) how much should be purchased, and at what interval, to maintain the right level of stock.

A delay in shipping goods lengthens the cash conversion period and slows cash flows. To avoid delays, a firm should have a well-organized shipping process.

An inventory control system should meet two essential needs:

- Maintaining a current record of the amount of each inventory item held in stock
- Locating that stock

Accountants refer to this system as *perpetual inventory*. The sale and purchase of each item in inventory is logged on a computerized stock sheet. At any time, managers can see the total inventory of each item held in stock. The computer system should show the location of the items, which saves employees from searching and prevents shipping delays. The perpetual inventory system also helps to determine the reorder points for each item.

A periodic count of every item in stock is the first rule of good inventory management. The physical count serves two primary purposes:

- It lets a business check how accurate its accounting procedures are that keep track of inventory. As the amount of each item in stock is verified, it confirms the value of the investment in inventory.
- It provides the basic data needed to perform an item analysis of the inventory.

Item analysis gives a firm control over its investment in inventories. This analysis compares the amount of investment in each stock item against the amount actually needed, based on the firm's recent sales. It shows where a company may have overinvested in its inventories.

In the News 6.2 describes the importance of inventory management, the impact that customer demand has on inventory levels, and how it can influence selling prices and, ultimately, profitability.

In The News 6.2

MANAGING INVENTORIES: A BALANCING ACT BETWEEN INVENTORY LEVELS AND CUSTOMER NEEDS

Sometimes, all it takes to boost sales in a slow economy is one annual activity or event. It can lead a business or an industry to start selling, shrinking inventory levels and generating revenue, profit, and, most importantly, cash.

This is what happens every fall when students go back to school. In August 2009, U.S. retailers took advantage of the "back-to-school" bounce as students and their parents began to stock up on school supplies and children's clothing. Retail Metrics, a market research company, indicated that despite a retail sales decline of 2.3% in August, after the prolonged 12-month drop, it was the smallest drop in revenue since September 2008. Even though the back-to-school event helped retailers to sell more, they are still going through difficult times. Because of the previous 12-month economic downturn, retailers had to keep inventories low. This meant offering fewer choices to parents and students, fewer designs, colours, and sizes. Maintaining low inventory levels and, at the same time, enticing buyers to buy more is a balancing act.

Source: Adapted from Alexandra Frean, "U.S. retailers benefit from back-to-school bounce." *The Times*, London © Times Newspapers Ltd. 2009. To read more about Retail Metrics, visit www.retailmetrics.net/corp.asp.

The next two sections cover types of inventories and inventory decision models.

TYPES OF INVENTORIES

Types of inventories Raw materials, work-in-process, and finished goods.

The three most important **types of inventories** for most manufacturing operations are raw materials, work-in-process, and finished goods.

Raw material inventories consist of goods purchased to use in manufacturing other goods. This type of inventory is influenced by the level of production, the reliability of suppliers, and how well purchases are scheduled and produced.

Work-in-process inventories consist of partially assembled or incomplete goods. These inventories are not ready for sale.

Finished inventories are the products that are ready to be sold and shipped to customers.

INVENTORY DECISION MODELS

Four models can be used to manage inventory: material requirements planning, just-in-time inventory management, economic ordering quantity, and inventory replenishment.

Material Requirements Planning

Material requirements planning (MRP) A method of scheduling that coordinates the use of resources in production.

Material requirements planning (MRP) schedules production to coordinate and use resources (materials, people, and equipment) more effectively. Companies with many types and varieties of products, and those with expensive inventories, use computer software to help them manage production-related information. MRP can also link individual departments to the production flow; to plan material requirements, managers need to know when each department will need inventory and how long the production cycle is in each department.

Just-In-Time Inventory Management

Just-in-time inventory management
An inventory management technique that obtains supplier materials just when they are needed.

Using **just-in-time inventory management** helps to reduce inventories, speed the cash conversion cycle (refer back to Figure 6.1), and increase profits. Just-in-time (JIT) management includes frequent (even daily) deliveries of parts or supplies, which help to keep inventory levels low. This system relies on suppliers to deliver goods on time, free of defects, and in the quantities ordered. With JIT, manufacturers don't need to hold stock in case they run short. To keep JIT running smoothly, suppliers are encouraged or sometimes even required to have plants very close to their customer's plants. JIT can dramatically reduce in-process inventories, improve product quality, reduce the need for inspection, and increase output per day.

Economic Ordering Quantity

Economic ordering quantity (EOQ)
A method that determines the best quantity of goods to order each time.

The **economic ordering quantity (EOQ)** model minimizes total inventory costs. Inventory decisions are based on the reorder point, which is the inventory on hand when a new order is placed, and the reorder quantity, which is the quantity ordered each time. Before examining the EOQ model, let's look at the two types of costs associated with inventory: ordering costs and holding costs.

Ordering costs
The costs associated with buying goods (e.g., receiving, inspecting, and accounting).

Ordering costs include the following:

- The administrative costs of scheduling, entering, and receiving an order
- The labour costs of receiving, inspecting, and shelving each order
- The cost of accounting and paying for the order

Because buying inventory creates costs that rise as a business places more orders, order frequency should be minimized. Everyone knows the direct cost of buying inventory: the purchase price. However, many overlook other ordering costs and the negative impact it has on the level of investment in inventories.

The administrative, accounting, and labour costs associated with any order are higher than many people realize. The ordering costs from numerous orders can push earnings down significantly. These costs remain about the same regardless of the size of the order.

Holding costs
The costs associated with storing goods in inventories (e.g., insurance, rent).

Holding costs are the costs for storing goods in inventory. This is the cost most people associate with inventories. Included in this category are the following:

- The costs of maintaining and managing warehouses or other storage facilities
- The costs of safety or alarm systems
- The costs of inventory shrinkage that can occur from spoilage, theft, or obsolescence
- The costs of company funds tied up in inventory (opportunity costs or finance costs)

Holding costs rise as the size of inventory increases, so each part of these costs should be examined and kept at a minimum. In contrast to ordering costs, holding costs are variable: holding more units in inventory increases these costs. Therefore, as inventory levels increase, warehouse costs also increase because the firm needs more space to store more inventories. As the investment in inventory grows, so too will insurance and maintenance costs and expenses from deterioration or obsolescence. Estimates of holding costs often range from 20% to 30% of the value of the inventories.

The basic EOQ equation shows the ideal reorder quantity:

$$\textbf{EOQ} = \sqrt{\frac{\textbf{2} \times \textbf{Ordering cost} \times \textbf{Yearly demand}}{\textbf{Annual carrying cost for 1 unit}}}$$

If a business sells 5,000 units of product per year, the ordering costs are $50.00 per order, and the carrying costs are $0.80 per unit per year, the company should reorder 791 units each time it places an order:

$$\textbf{EOQ} = \sqrt{\frac{\textbf{2} \times \textbf{\$50.00} \times \textbf{5,000}}{\textbf{\$0.80}}} = \textbf{791 units}$$

Table 6.3 shows the total ordering and holding costs for ordering different quantities during the year, now that we know the EOQ is 791 units. Column 1 shows the number of orders the company can place during the year (1 to 10). Column 2 presents the number of units it has to order each time. For example, with five orders, the company would order 1,000 units each time. Column 3 lists the annual cost for placing the orders. For instance, ordering five times costs the company $250.00 ($50.00 × 5). Column 4 shows the average number of units that the company would have in its warehouse. If only one order of 5,000 units is placed during the year, the company would average 2,500 units (5,000 ÷ 2) in stock. Column 5 presents the average dollar investment. If the holding cost per unit is $5.35, the average dollar investment if the company places one order each year is $13,375

Table 6.3 The Economic Ordering Quantity

Number of Orders (1)	Order Quantity (units) (2)	Annual Ordering Cost ($50.00 per order) (3)	Average Unit Inventories (column 2 ÷ 2) (4)	Average Dollar Investment (column 4 × $5.35) (5)	Annual Holding Costs (column 5 × 15%) (6)	Ordering Cost + Holding Cost (column 3 + column 6) (7)
1	5,000	$50	2,500	$13,375	$2,006	$2,056
2	2,500	100	1,250	6,687	1,003	1,103
5	1,000	250	500	2,675	401	651
6	833	300	416	2,226	334	634
8	625	400	312	1,669	250	650
10	500	500	250	1,337	200	700

(2,500 × $5.35). Column 6 shows the annual holding costs, which can be calculated in two ways. The first is to multiply the average dollar investment by 15%, which is the annual holding cost ($13,375 × 15% = $2,006). The second is to multiply the annual holding costs per unit ($0.80) by the average unit inventory ($0.80 × 2,500 = 2,000, with the difference being rounding). Column 7 shows the sum of column 3 (ordering costs) and column 6 (annual holding costs). For this business, 833 units (which is the closest to 791) is the combination that costs the least ($634).

Problem-Solving Example 6.3

The Economic Ordering Quantity

A purchasing agent for a retail store estimated the demand for a certain product will increase from 28,000 to 30,000 next year. He figured out that the ordering costs for each unit would be $2.00 and predicted that the purchase price for each unit would increase by 10% and reach $10.00. After a lengthy analysis, he estimated that the per unit annual carrying costs will be $0.75. How many units should the purchasing agent order each time?

Solution

He should order 400 units each time.

$$\sqrt{\frac{2 \times \$2.00 \times 30{,}000}{\$0.75}} = 400 \text{ units}$$

Self-Test Exercise 6.3

The Economic Ordering Quantity

The Millers are thinking of marketing one of their products more aggressively. Current sales are 2,000 units per year, and they expect them to increase by 25%. Current carrying costs are $0.23 per unit, and order costs are $1.50. The Millers want to minimize their inventory costs. Calculate CompuTech's economic ordering quantity for the expected increased sales volume.

Answers to the Self-Test Exercises can be found at www.bergeron7e.nelson.com.

Inventory Replenishment

Inventory replenishment The decision of when to order goods from supplier.

The final inventory decision model is **inventory replenishment**. Suppose the company decides to order 791 units each time. The next decision is to decide how frequently to order. Figure 6.4 shows the key factors that are considered when replenishing (or restocking) inventories:

- The minimum and maximum levels of inventories the business wants to have in stock before placing a new order
- The time it takes from the purchase to the receipt of the goods (LT)
- When the order should be placed (RP)

Figure 6.4 **Inventory Replenishment**

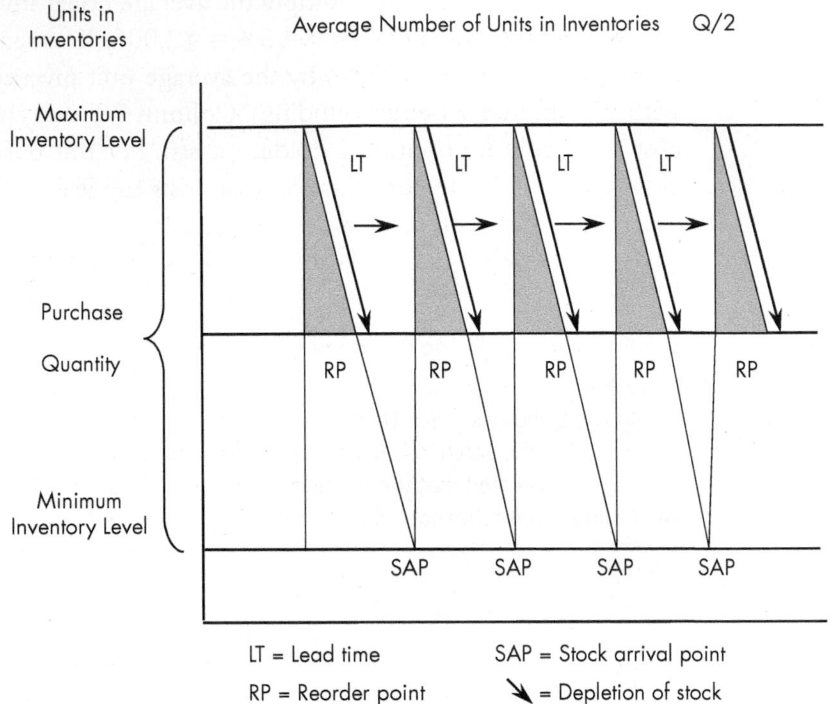

Problem-Solving Example 6.4

Monthly Inventory Replenishment

A purchasing agent wanted to know how many orders she would have to make each month when buying a particular product from a supplier. She knew the number of units ordered per year (12,000), the ordering costs per order ($8.00), and the holding cost per unit ($0.60). How many orders should she make on average each month?

Solution

The EOQ is 566 units, 21 orders per year, or 1.75 orders per month.

$$\text{EOQ} = \sqrt{\frac{2 \times \$8.00 \times 12{,}000}{\$0.60}} = 566 \text{ units}$$

Orders per year: 12,000 ÷ 566 = 21 orders per year
Orders per month: 21 ÷ 12 = 1.75 orders per month

Self-Test Exercise 6.4

Monthly Inventory Replenishment

The Millers have decided to increase their advertising to push one of their product lines. The current sales of 2,500 units per year are expected to increase by 60% next year. Current carrying costs are $0.10 per unit, and the ordering costs are $3.50. The Millers want to minimize their inventory costs.

Questions

1. What is the new economic ordering quantity?
2. How many orders should they place each month once the new sales level is reached?

Answers to the Self-Test Exercises can be found at www.bergeron7e.nelson.com.

4 Explore techniques for managing trade receivables.

Managing Trade Receivables

Most firms sell on credit, and for most of them, credit sales are the bulk of their revenue, making it important to manage trade receivables well. The level of trade receivables is determined in two ways: by the volume of sales made on credit and by the time it takes for customers to pay off their accounts.

The credit manager sets credit terms, grants credit to customers, bills customers, monitors payments made by customers, collects trade receivables, and ensures the company has enough credit insurance.

SET CREDIT TERMS

Credit terms
The conditions under which credit is extended, especially how quickly the customer is expected to pay the account.

The credit manager decides what **credit terms** a firm should adopt, although these terms are influenced by the firm's industry. One basic part of credit terms is the length of time customers are given to pay their accounts.

Trade discounts can help a company's cash flow, but they do so at the expense of profit. For some companies, that may be a good trade-off. For example, a business may give a 2% discount off the original price of goods if a customer pays the invoice within 10 days of shipment. If the customer pays between 11 and 30 days, the full amount is charged. On an invoice, these terms would appear as "2/10, N/30." However, before deciding to offer trade discounts, the credit manager estimates the costs and benefits of various combinations by exploring the following points.

First, the credit manager measures the benefits. When a customer uses the discount, it shortens a company's average collection period and speeds up cash flow. At the same time, the investment in trade receivables is reduced, as are the costs of carrying that investment. Cash discounts benefit both parties in the transaction: the customers save money, and the seller enjoys a better cash flow and a lower investment in trade receivables.

Second, the credit manager calculates the price when offering a discount and must recognize how it affects the company's profit. Let's assume that a company sells products with an average unit selling price of $400.00. The cost of manufacturing or buying materials from suppliers is $250.00. In this industry, customers typically pay 60 days after purchase. As shown below, if the cost of money (the finance cost) is 10%, the firm should offer 2/10, N/30: the profit generated when customers pay in 10 days is $146.69, compared with $145.89 if they pay in 60 days.

Line		10-Day Payment	60-Day Payment
1.	Effective selling price	$392.00	$400.00
2.	Purchase (or manufacturing) costs	(250.00)	(250.00)
3.	Finance cost (10 and 60 days)	(0.68)	(4.11)
4.	Interest on investment (50 days)	5.37	—
5.	Profit	$146.69	$145.89

If the customer takes the 2% discount, the company would receive $392.00 ($400.00 × 98%) instead of $400.00 (line 1). Whether the company offers a 2% discount or not, line 2 shows that the company pays $250.00 to manufacture the product or to buy it from a supplier. Line 3 shows the finance costs for both options. The company would pay $0.68 [$250.00 × 10% × (10 ÷ 365)] to finance the $250.00 purchase if payment is received in 10 days, and $4.11 [$250.00 × 10% × (60 ÷ 365)] if payment is received in 60 days. In line 4, we see that the company would make $5.37 [$392.00 × 10% × (50 ÷ 365)] if the $392.00 is deposited in the bank for the remaining 50 days and earns 10%. Line 5 tells us that there is an advantage to offering the 2% discount.

Problem-Solving Example 6.5

Should a 1% Trade Discount Be Offered?

A wholesaler sells goods to retailers for $500, and they pay in 70 days. The cost of the product is $300, the finance cost is 6%, and interest from the bank is 3%. Should the wholesaler offer a 1% trade discount (1/10, N/30)?

Solution

There would be an advantage ($0.40) to offering the 1% trade discount.

	10-Day Payment	70-Day Payment
Effective selling price	$495.00	$ 500.00
Purchase costs	(300.00)	(300.00)
Finance costs (10 versus 70 days)	(0.49)	(3.45)
Interest on investment (60 days)	2.44	—
Profit	$196.95	$ 196.55

Self-Test Exercise 6.5

Trade Discount Policies

CompuTech sells goods with an average retail sales price of $250.00 to industrial customers. These customers usually pay 65 days after the date of purchase. Cost of sales for each unit is $110.00. If CompuTech's cost of borrowing is 11%, should the Millers offer 1/10, N/30 to these accounts?

Answers to the Self-Test Exercises can be found at www.bergeron7e.nelson.com.

GRANT CREDIT TO CUSTOMERS

Credit managers can also grant credit. Two questions are asked: Should credit be granted to a customer? If yes, how much? The criteria used by firms to rate borrowers are the six C's of credit: character, collateral, capacity, capital, circumstances, and coverage. We will discuss these in more depth in Chapter 8.

To shorten the cash conversion cycle, the credit decision should be made as soon as a purchase order is received. Therefore, it is important to approve in advance lines of credit for major customers. In other words, the credit manager should anticipate customers' needs before they exceed their credit limits.

Little is lost if a customer does not use all the credit available. However, sales will move faster and customers will receive their orders quicker if credit is pre-approved. Pre-approved credit aids in the completion of a sale and improves a firm's services. A faster response inevitably offers a competitive advantage.

The same approach can be used for new customers. It is better to check the creditworthiness of a new customer before receiving a larger order. Gathering the information for a credit check—bank checks, supplier checks—can take several days and could lengthen the cash conversion cycle. If the delay is too long, the business risks losing the sale to a competitor with a more efficient credit-decision process.

However, credit analysis should not be sacrificed for the sake of speedy approval. Even a modest increase in bad-debt losses (if some customers do not pay their bills) can wipe out the benefits from a faster cash conversion cycle. Any part of the administrative process that delays a sale hampers the smooth flow of cash into a business.

Let's look at the types of credit analysis that businesses use when granting credit to consumers and businesses.

Consumer Credit

Credit-scoring system
A system used to determine the creditworthiness of potential customers.

Credit-scoring systems are often used to judge the creditworthiness of potential customers. The system has specific guidelines for rating a potential customer as a good or bad risk and is used by businesses that offer credit cards to thousands of consumers (e.g., retail stores and banks). Table 6.4 shows a typical credit-scoring system. Several variables are examined (in this case, age, marital status, occupation, time on last job, annual income, residence, home ownership, and telephone), and each is given a weight. The weights have been determined by looking at a sample of existing customers and finding the factors that distinguish those who pay their accounts promptly from those

Table 6.4	Credit-Scoring System			
Variable	**Measurement**	**Value**	**Weight**	**Weighted Value**
Age	In years as reported	36	0.4	14.4
Marital status	Coded 1 (yes) or 0 (no)	1	20.0	20.0
Occupation	Coded 1 to 5 for different professions	4	4.3	17.2
Time on last job	In years as reported	6	0.9	5.4
Annual income	In thousands of dollars as reported	45.0	0.6	27.0
Residence	Coded 1 to 5 for different postal zones	3	4.6	13.8
Home ownership	Number of years owned as reported	4	1.2	4.8
Telephone	Coded 1 (yes) or 0 (no)	1	15.0	15.0
Total credit score				117.6

who are slow payers. In our example, the credit score is 117.6, but what does it mean? That depends on the guidelines, which may say that if the score is less than 60 points, credit will be denied; if it is between 61 and 80, the customer will be investigated further; and if it is 81 or greater, credit will be granted. Under these guidelines, the consumer in our example would be granted credit.

Business Credit

Granting credit to commercial customers requires a different type of analysis, which includes gathering information about the companies' credit standing. Sometimes, the firm will ask for a business credit report, such as one from Dun & Bradstreet or Standard & Poor's. The information typically provided by credit reporting agencies is summarized in Table 6.5.

Based on the information it receives, the firm will specify the type of account to be granted (an open account or another arrangement), the credit period (when payment is due), the size of the discount, and the discount period.

Table 6.5	Information Shown on Business Credit Reports
Summary	Classification code for line of business, year business started, rating, principal executives (owners)
Report information	Payments, sales worth, number of employees, trends
Payments	How business pays its bill (i.e., amounts owing, amounts past due, terms of sales, manner of payments, and supplier comments)
Finance	Financial conditions and trend of business (statement of financial position and statement of income)
History	Names, birthdates, and past business experience of the principals or owners; affiliations; ownership; outside interests of the principal owners
Operations	Nature of the premises, neighbourhood, size of floor space, production facilities

Credit policy
A decision about the extent of credit that should be extended to customers.

A firm's **credit policy** determines the extent of credit to be provided to customers. If a business has a restrictive credit policy, it will likely sell less, have less invested in inventories and trade receivables, and have fewer bad debts. Conversely, as a firm relaxes its credit terms, it sells more goods to a wider range of customers, including those that are poorer credit risks; this, in turn, increases bad debts.

Because there is a close connection between selling and credit, changing a credit policy requires an integrated management analysis (The sales department's information should be in sync with the accounts receivable department's information). Most firms do not really have a choice of selling on credit or for cash, so the decision to change the firm's credit policy is an important one. ROI is used to compare the credit alternatives, including cash discounts, potential revenue and operating profit, and bad debt expenses. The decision to extend credit depends on the trade-off between (1) the cost of carrying the investment in trade receivables and (2) the benefits of a larger sales volume.

Some links and relationships need to be considered when changing credit terms:

- Credit terms and policy and the firm's total marketing effort
- Credit policy and the inventory level
- Credit policy and production capacity
- Credit policy and the efficiency of the firm's operations

To set the right credit policy, the credit manager must examine how the level of operating income generated and the extra investment in trade receivables and inventories would change. Table 6.6 shows how to calculate the changes in operating profit

Table 6.6 Establishing a Credit Policy

	Existing Terms	Proposed Terms
Expected volume (units)	500,000	550,000
Expected revenue ($10.00 per unit)	$5,000,000	$5,500,000
Expected operating profit before bad debts (10% of revenue)	$ 500,000	$ 550,000
Expected bad debt expense*	$ 25,000	$ 55,000
Expected operating profit (after bad debts)	$ 475,000	$ 495,000
Incremental operating profit	—	$ 20,000
Expected collection period (days)	31	38
Average trade receivables	$ 425,000	$ 575,000
Inventories	$ 850,000	$ 900,000
Incremental investment	—	$ 200,000

* A 0.5% factor is used for calculating bad debts for existing credit terms and a 1.0% factor for the proposed terms.

$$\text{Return on investment} = \frac{\$20{,}000}{\$200{,}000} = 10\%$$

and investment resulting from a change in credit terms. In this case, if the firm's cost of capital is 12%, it will not go ahead with the proposed credit policy.

The levels of inventories and trade receivables are affected by the proposed change in the credit policy. It is important to calculate the effect each change in credit policy has on working capital accounts.

Problem-Solving Example 6.6

Should the Company Change Its Credit Policy?

A manufacturing firm is studying different approaches to increase its return on investment. One way is to change its credit policy. The company's sales revenue is now $2 million and would (according to the sales manager) increase to $2.5 million if a more relaxed credit policy is adopted. Currently, the company's return on revenue is 4.0%, but the change in credit policy would reduce it to 3.5%. The trade receivables manager estimates that trade receivables would jump from $350,000 to $425,000 with the change, since the current net 30 days, which is respected by most customers, would move to 40 days. What should the company do if management wants to make a 15% return on their investment?

Solution

There are no benefits to changing the credit policy. The company would earn less (10%) than their objective (15%).

(in $000s)	Net 30 Today	Net 40 Proposed	Change
Revenue	$2,000	$2,500	$500
Profit for the year (4% versus 3.5%)	80.0	87.5	7.5
Trade receivables	350	425	75

Return on investment: $\frac{\text{Incremental profit}}{\text{Incremental investment}} = \frac{\$7,500}{\$75,000} = 10\%$

Self-Test Exercise 6.6

Establishing a Credit Policy

In 2013, CompuTech sells on terms of net 30 days and is considering a change to net 45 days. The Millers want to invest the extra funds in their new retail store, hoping that this will generate a return on investment greater than 20%. The expected effect of the change in credit is summarized below. Should the Millers make the change?

(in $000s)	Net 30 Today	Net 45 Proposed	Change
Revenue	$420	$450	$30
Profit for the year	33	36	3
Trade receivables	45	65	20

Answers to the Self-Test Exercises can be found at www.bergeron7e.nelson.com.

BILL CUSTOMERS

The invoice lists the merchandise sold, the shipment date, and the amount due from the purchaser. Promptly completing and sending an invoice is an important part of the cash cycle for two reasons. First, few purchasers will pay for merchandise before getting the invoice. In most businesses, the invoice typically triggers the payment process in the accounting system. Second, the invoice date is usually the date that the payment period begins, as defined by a firm's selling terms.

Completing and sending an invoice increases available cash and earnings. A firm should not provide a monthly statement of account to trigger payment. This is a costly and time-consuming administrative process, and often causes customers to ignore invoices and wait for the monthly statement. Allowing customers to pay in response to monthly statements, rather than to invoices, adds from 1 to 30 days to the cash conversion cycle. Issuing the invoice to complete a sale is the final step in the administrative process.

MONITOR PAYMENTS MADE BY CUSTOMERS

Credit collection must be monitored continually to measure how effective the policy is and how well it is applied. Two common approaches to gauging effectiveness, monitoring payment behaviour, and taking action on overdue accounts are (1) the average collection period (in days) and (2) the aging of accounts receivable.

The *average collection period* is the average time it takes for customers to pay their accounts after sales have been made on credit. Look back at Chapter 4 for a recap. Let's examine how the average collection period works when monitoring customer payments. Assume that a business sold \$3 million in goods last year and the same amount this year. However, the trade receivables increased from \$450,000 to \$500,000. This indicates that customers paid their accounts more slowly over the past 12 months. The calculation is done as follows:

$$\textbf{Last year's average collection period} = \frac{\$450{,}000}{\$3{,}000{,}000} \times 365 = 54.8 \textbf{ days}$$

$$\textbf{This year's average collection period} = \frac{\$500{,}000}{\$3{,}000{,}000} \times 365 = 60.8 \textbf{ days}$$

Aging of accounts receivable
A report showing how long trade receivables have been outstanding; it gives the percentage of receivables past due for one month, two months, or other periods.

The company's average collection period is now six days longer.

Six days may seem like a small increase, but the credit manager may want to look closely at the **aging of accounts receivable** by preparing an aging schedule that shows the percentage of each month's sales still outstanding at the end of successive months. An example is shown in Table 6.7. The aging of accounts receivable is grouped by age category and by the percentage of receivables outstanding that fall in each age category. The aging process is an essential part of the trade receivables analysis.

Table 6.7 Aging of Accounts Receivable

	As a percentage of total receivables	
Receivables (%)	Last Year	This Year
Under 31 days old	60.4	54.2
Between 31 and 60 days	24.4	23.8
Between 61 and 90 days	7.2	10.4
Between 91 and 120 days	6.5	8.3
Over 120 days	1.5	3.3

Problem-Solving Example 6.7

Should the Company Change Its Credit Terms?

A firm is considering changing its credit terms. Customers pay within the 45-day limit, but the revised terms would increase the average payment to 60 days. The company's revenue is $3.0 million and would increase to $3.5 million. The current profit after bad debts would decrease from 5.0% to 4.8%. Trade receivables would jump from $400,000 to $500,000. The company's tax rate is at 40%. If the management wants to earn 15% on their investment, should they go ahead with the change?

Solution

There are no benefits to changing the credit terms. The company would earn less (10.8%) than their objective (15%).

(in $000s)	Current Terms	Proposed Terms	Change
Revenue	$ 3,000.0	$3,500.0	$500.0
Profit after bad debts (5% versus 4.8%)	150.0	168.0	18.0
Income tax expense (40%)	(60.0)	(67.2)	(7.2)
Profit for the year	90.0	100.8	10.8
Trade receivables	400.0	500.0	100.0

Return on investment $\frac{\text{Incremental profit}}{\text{Incremental investment}} = \frac{\$10{,}800}{\$100{,}000} = 10.8\%$

Self-Test Exercise 6.7

Impact of Revised Credit Policy on ROI

CompuTech is planning to change its credit policy. The product is characterized as follows:

Current selling price	$10.00 per unit
Average cost	$ 7.50 per unit
Current annual sales	4,000 units
Current terms of sale	net 30 days

(continued)

Self-Test Exercise 6.7 (continued)

The Millers want to extend the credit period terms to net 60 days. They expect a reaction from competitors, but they believe such a move would produce the following results:

1. Sales are expected to increase to 5,000 units.
2. Bad debt losses are expected to increase by $2,000 per year.

The cost per unit for the increased number of units produced would be $6.50. The company's income tax rate is 35%, and its required minimum rate of return is 16% after tax.

Question

Would you recommend that the Millers change the company's credit policy?

Answers to the Self-Test Exercises can be found at www.bergeron7e.nelson.com.

COLLECT TRADE RECEIVABLES

Effective credit collection begins by mailing invoices promptly. Once the invoices are mailed, the credit manager must study, on a regular basis, the average collection period and take action if the period is too long. Asking customers for payment usually follows several steps. First, there is the "dunning" approach: mailing a duplicate copy of the original invoice to the customer. Second, the credit manager can call the customer, which can serve as a routine, but stronger, reminder. Third, the credit manager can visit the customer and see whether they can work out a payment schedule. Fourth, the credit manager can send a registered letter, telling the customer that if payment is not received by a certain date, the firm will have to turn the account over to a collection agency. Finally, the most expensive way is to resort to formal legal charges.

BUY CREDIT INSURANCE

Credit insurance protects against the cash drain caused by uncollectible trade receivables (when customers do not pay their bills). Just as a vehicle theft or a warehouse fire disrupt a business, the inability to collect a large receivable can interrupt its cash flow. Not only can credit insurance prevent a cash flow crisis, but it can also lead to higher earnings. Insurance on trade receivables comes in two forms.

Indemnification policy
Insurance that a business takes against a catastrophic loss in cash.

An **indemnification policy** is insurance against a catastrophic loss of cash that might occur when a large receivable becomes uncollectible because the customer has gone bankrupt, the debt has been reorganized by creditors, or another legal process occurs because the debtor is insolvent.

Credit insurance policy
Insurance to cover losses when a firm's trade receivables become uncollectible.

A **credit insurance policy** covers losses when any trade receivables become uncollectible. The coverage has two limits. First, the insurance company can apply a deductible (an agreed amount the company gives up) to each loss. Second, the insurance company can limit the maximum coverage for each debtor. Typically, the limits are tied to ratings established by national credit agencies, such as Dun & Bradstreet. While premiums vary, the coverage may cost 0.25% to 0.5% of annual sales, which is a small price to pay for survival. With this type of insurance, a company can grant credit to higher-risk customers. If they don't pay, the insurance company will compensate the company.

5 Comment on managing cash and cash equivalents.

Managing Cash and Cash Equivalents

Cash
Cash holdings and short-term deposits.

Cash consists of cash holdings and short-term deposits. Paying ongoing bills, such as buying raw materials and paying salaries, is a constant drain on a company's cash pool. However, this cash pool is constantly being replenished by cash sales of inventories and the collection of trade receivables. The first part of this section examines the management of cash; the second part looks at the management of cash equivalents (e.g., marketable securities).

MANAGING CASH

Companies should keep an adequate amount of cash in reserve, look for ways to make cash a productive asset, and have strategies related to cash collection.

Maintaining Liquid Assets

The cash pool must be kept at an appropriate level, and amounts should be assigned to specific purposes (e.g., inventories, marketable securities, trade receivables). Maintaining a balanced cash pool is important for four reasons. First, it lets a business carry out its daily operating transactions, such as paying current bills (e.g., utilities, salaries, supplies, and materials), and partially finance its inventories and trade receivables. Second, cash is needed because forecasting cash receipts and cash outlays is never perfect. Third, having cash on hand means a company can take advantage of opportunities, such as trade discounts. Finally, it can be used to pay bills on time and maintain good credit with short-term lenders and suppliers.

Making Cash a Productive Asset

The main goal of cash management is to have enough cash to pay bills but not so much that profits are affected. One way to increase profitability is to reduce the time between the date a payment is mailed by a customer and the date it is deposited in the company's bank account. For example, if a business can make 12% on short-term securities and $30,000 arrives 20 days late, the company misses the opportunity of making $197.26. The calculation is as follows:

$$\$30{,}000 \times 12\% \times \frac{\text{20-day delay}}{\text{365 days}} = \$197.26$$

If a company has hundreds or thousands of cheques arriving late, it can lose thousands of dollars each year in interest alone. Using electronic payments is an excellent way to reduce the time lag.

Problem-Solving Example 6.8

Earning Interest on Investments (ROI)

How much would a company lose when it receives a \$20,000 cheque 15 days late if management expects to a earn 15% return on investment?

Solution

The business would lose \$123.29.

$$\$20{,}000 \times 15\% \times \frac{\text{15-day delay}}{\text{365 days}} = \$123.29$$

Self-Test Exercise 6.8

Earning Interest on Investments

CompuTech can make 12% by investing its money in a long-term investment. If the Millers receive \$10,000 20 days sooner than expected, how much would the company make?

Answers to the Self-Test Exercises can be found at www.bergeron7e.nelson.com.

Establishing a Minimum Cash Balance

One of the activities of cash management is determining how much cash is needed on hand. To manage cash effectively, a firm must balance its cash inflows with its cash outflows each month. Cash planning can be done through the cash budget (look ahead to Table 7.2 for an example of a monthly cash budget). The cash budget allows a firm to figure out the following:

- The flow of monthly cash receipts
- The flow of monthly cash outlays
- The surplus or shortages of cash at the end of each month
- The amount of cash that should be invested in short-term securities (surplus) or that will be needed from the bank in a loan (shortage)

Cash management aims to set a minimum level of cash that will meet business needs and increase profits but not reduce business activities or risk the business not being able to pay its bills. Cash reserves (including marketable securities) should be enough to meet daily cash expenditures. What a business needs is the following:

- A practical minimum cash balance to operate with
- An amount to cover any unforeseen expenses
- Some money to take advantage of profitable opportunities (e.g., taking discounts on purchases, stocking up on raw materials before a price increase, buying a special piece of equipment at a low price)

Cash needs can be estimated in two steps: (1) determine the average daily cash outlays over recent months, and (2) estimate the cash reserves as a specific number of days of average cash outflow, based on the business's unique characteristics.

For example, if a business spends $300,000 in cash each month, the average daily cash outflow is $10,000 ($300,000 ÷ 30). The treasurer might determine that six days of cash are needed to meet the average expenses under normal business operations. This business would need a $60,000 cash balance ($10,000 × 6 days).

Problem-Solving Example 6.9

Pinpointing the Minimum Cash Reserve

A business spends on average $90,000 a month on such items as salaries and purchases. How much cash should management have on hand for a nine-day period?

Solution

The company should keep $27,000 on hand.

Step 1: Average daily cash expenditures are $3,000 ($90,000 ÷ 30).

Step 2: Cash reserve should be $27,000 ($3,000 × 9).

Self-Test Exercise 6.9

Establishing the Minimum Cash Reserve

Len and Joan are figuring out the best level of liquid funds to have to pay their ongoing bills. Over the past several months, the average monthly expenditures have been $28,000, and they want enough cash on hand for a 10-day period. What should CompuTech's minimum cash reserve be?

Answers to the Self-Test Exercises can be found at www.bergeron7e.nelson.com.

Float
The amount of funds tied up in cheques that have been written but are still in process and have not yet been collected.

Electronic funds transfer (EFT)
A means of transferring funds between customer and supplier by using the Internet or any other electronic medium.

Ways to Improve the Collection of Cash

A firm can speed up cash receipts and make that asset productive in several ways.

A *customer's decision to purchase* goods or services starts the cash conversion cycle. Using the fastest communication process to encourage a customer to quickly place an order is the first step in the cash conversion cycle (look back at Figure 6.1).

A business can *reduce the negative float*. The **float** is the money tied up in cheques that have been mailed to the firm but not yet received. There are three ways to improve a negative float.

The first is electronic communications. An **electronic funds transfer (EFT)** is an effective way to collect payments from customers. EFT eliminates delays caused by the postal system, the administrative structure of a business, or the cheque-clearing process and allows a business to use the collected funds sooner. This process transfers money from the customer's bank account to the firm's bank account in a matter of hours.

Regional banks
Banks where customers pay their accounts and the money is transferred to the seller's bank account.

The second process involves **regional banks**. Customers pay their bills at the bank, and the payment is transferred to the company's account. Firms set up collection accounts at several banks around the country, and customers are encouraged to pay their bills in their region rather than sending payments to a central location.

Post office box
A location to which customers send their cheques, which are then transferred to the seller's bank account.

The third strategy is to use a **post office box** in an area where the firm has many customers. A firm rents post office boxes in different cities and has banks manage and monitor them. The firm tells customers in that region to mail their cheques to the regional post office box instead of to the firm. As soon as cheques from customers arrive, they are verified, checked for completeness, and deposited in the firm's account. Although this system can improve the collection of cash, a business must weigh the bank's fees against the benefits of a shorter cash conversion period. Often, the profit from a faster cash flow can make the cost of the post office box insignificant.

MANAGING MARKETABLE SECURITIES

One of the responsibilities of the CFO (or the treasurer) is to manage the company's cash balance, either by investing excess cash in short-term securities or by borrowing cash through short-term loans.

It is more profitable for a business to invest excess cash, even if it is only for several days, than to leave it in a bank account that does not earn interest. Funds are held in short-term marketable securities or temporary investments for three reasons:

1. To finance seasonal or cyclical operations (temporary working capital)
2. To finance known requirements, such as the purchase of equipment or machinery
3. To invest funds received from the sale of long-term securities (shares or bonds)

Different types of marketable securities are available, and four features of each should be studied carefully before investing. First is *maturity*, the time by which the principal must be paid back to the investor. Second is the *denomination*, the unit of transaction for buying or selling. Third is *marketability*, or the ease with which an investor can sell the marketable security. Finally, there is the *yield determination*, which is the method of earning a return on the investment.

Investment securities
Short-term deposits, such as treasury bills and bank deposits.

There are many types of **investment securities** (or marketable securities), such as Government of Canada treasury bills, bank deposits, commercial paper, finance company paper, Eurodollar deposits, Canadian government bonds, and corporate bonds with different maturity dates and yields. A treasurer has to find the type of security that best fits the business's needs.

Managing marketable securities for a small business is relatively easy. The only requirement is matching the short-term investments with the excess cash in the monthly cash budget. Large businesses, conversely, can have millions of dollars in cash or near-cash accounts, making it very important to use investment strategies that will give them the highest return on investment.

6 Explain how to manage current liability accounts to improve the cash flow cycle.

Managing Current Liabilities

Current liabilities, the credit obligations that fall due within 12 months, are also part of working capital management. A business should always use its trade and other payables as a source of financing, because they are spontaneous and self-adjusting; these accounts can expand and contract with changes in the levels of sales. When more sales are made, trade and other payables increase in roughly the same proportion.

This section deals with short-term leverage, the funds that can be used from suppliers (trade and other payables), and working capital loans from commercial banks.

TRADE AND OTHER PAYABLES

To use credit effectively, managers must follow several guidelines. First, they should prepare a sales budget to find out when the money for raw materials will be needed. Second, they should set the manufacturing budget to determine salary and wage payments. Third, managers should choose suppliers that offer the best products and services with credit terms that meet the company's needs. Finally, they should decide when and how invoices should be paid.

Firms should always take advantage of cost-free funds, such as trade and other payables. They can slow their payments while still ensuring the bills are paid on time. A supplier contributes financing to a firm any time credit is extended. Therefore, its use calls for deliberate cash planning that focuses on four points: (1) the link between trade credit and cash capability (whether the company has enough cash to pay its bills), (2) the benefits to the firm of an alternative supplier's selling terms, (3) the relationship between trade credit and cash flows, and (4) the working relationships with suppliers. Here is a brief explanation for each of these points.

Link between trade credit and cash capability. Trade credit is a significant source of financing for most businesses. If properly managed, it can help a business increase its cash capability and use interest-free single-payment loans.

Benefits from an alternative supplier's selling terms. Delaying payment generates more cash capability in a firm and increases profits. The guiding principle of liability management is that a business should not pay its bills before they are due. However, a business should never abuse a creditor or be late in making a payment.

To calculate the average payable period and to find how it contributes to positive cash flow, trade and other payables are divided by the average daily purchases. For example, if the trade and other payables in a statement of financial position are \$300,000, and the average daily purchases are \$10,000, the average payment period is 30 days. Thus, each dollar of trade credit remains in the bank for 30 days before being paid to the supplier. If the average payment period is extended to 45 days, trade and other payables increase to \$450,000 (\$10,000 × 45 days), which provides an extra \$150,000 in cash.

Two important factors should be considered:

- Payments to suppliers should be made on time to preserve relationships and goodwill.
- Cash discounts should be considered before delaying payments.

Problem-Solving Example 6.10

Slower Payments to Suppliers Mean More Cash

In the current year, a business bought $500,000 worth of goods, materials, and supplies and has $41,100 worth of trade and other payables. Management was able to extend its credit to 40 days. How much cash will the business generate as a result of this change?

Solution

Increasing its average payment from 30 to 40 days earns the business an extra $13,700 in cash.
Average daily purchases $1,370 ($500,000 ÷ 365).
Existing payment practices 30 days ($41,100 ÷ $1,370).

Increased level of trade and other payables would be ($1,370 × 40)	$54,800
Existing trade and other payables ($1,370 × 30)	41,100
Incremental cash	$13,700

Self-Test Exercise 6.10

Slowing the Disbursements to Suppliers

CompuTech bought $209,000 worth of goods and services in 2014. The Millers think they can delay paying their bills up to 50 days without jeopardizing their relationship with suppliers. The company's trade and other payables are $20,000. If the company defers paying its bills to 50 days, how much financing would the company obtain?

Answers to the Self-Test Exercises can be found at www.bergeron7e.nelson.com.

Relationship between trade credit and cash flows. A trade discount increases profit at the expense of cash flows; therefore, the trade-off should be calculated. When a company offers a trade discount, it may mean that its average collection period is long (45, 60, or even 90 days). The trade discount gets its customers to pay faster. This has two benefits: accelerated cash flow and increased profitability.

A business should take advantage of a supplier's trade discount, as long as the cost of borrowing from the bank is less than the supplier discount. Here is the effective cost of various early-payment discounts when annualized (adjusted to reflect a period of a year):

Discounts Allowed for Payment in 10 Days	Annualized Cost to the Supplier
0.5%	9%
1%	18%
2%	37%

This means that if a supplier offers a 2% discount if paid within 10 days, the 2% discount translates into a 37% annual borrowing cost. Figure 6.5 shows how this percentage was calculated.

Figure 6.5 **Annualized Finance Costs**

$$\text{Annualized finance costs} = \left(\frac{\text{Discount percent}}{100 - \text{Discount percent}}\right) \times \left(\frac{365}{\text{Credit limit} - \text{Discount period}}\right) =$$

$$\left(\frac{2\%}{100\% - 2\%}\right) \times \left(\frac{365}{30 - 10}\right) =$$

$$\left(\frac{2\%}{98\%}\right) \times \left(\frac{365}{20}\right) = 37.2\%$$

Working relationship with suppliers. A good working relationship with suppliers directly influences a firm's cash capability. Most businesses eventually establish ongoing relationships with their major suppliers; once these relationships are created, a business should develop and maintain the maximum potential cash capability from each supplier's credit terms.

Two management practices contribute to good supplier relations. First, a consistent payment pattern is a good practice. Erratic payments upset even the most patient suppliers. As long as the supplier knows when to expect payment, even if persistently late, the supplier can feel comfortable with the relationship. Second, lines of communication should always be kept open. The more a supplier knows about a business, the more it can respond to the company's needs. After all, the business's purchases presumably are profitable sales for the supplier. The better the supplier responds to a business's needs, the more it can improve its own bottom line.

WORKING CAPITAL LOANS

Working capital loans
Short-term loans made to finance working capital accounts (e.g., inventories, trade receivables).

Most companies need some sort of **working capital loan**. Management should always match the sources of financing to the appropriate assets. (This topic will be covered in more depth in Chapter 8, under the heading "The Matching Principle.")

Management should use short-term loans (those with a maturity of one year or less) to finance seasonal current assets and use long-term loans to finance non-current assets. Because financing comes in so many different forms and from many sources, management must ensure that they approach a lender that can meet their specific need, such as a line of credit, a short-term loan, a term loan, or revolving credit.

In the News 6.3 gives an example of how a company is able to expand its business by negotiating extended payment terms with suppliers.

In The News 6.3

MANAGING CASH WELL MAKES A BUSINESS LESS DEPENDENT ON BORROWED FUNDS

Managing cash is more than getting your customers to pay fast and turning your inventory over quickly. To complete the cash cycle, you also have to know how to manage your payables by creating a strategy with suppliers in which you earn a reputation of being a slow but dependable payer.

This is how entrepreneur Mark Cahsens, owner of Great Circle Works, a manufacturer of toys and sporting goods, in Oakville, Ontario, helped his business grow from $50,000 in revenues in 2007 to $4 million in 2012. As he points out, "Cash flow can make or break a venture." One of his strategies was to negotiate with suppliers advantageous payment terms (up to 120 days in some cases). He adds, "This way, I'm able to receive money from my customers before I even have to pay my suppliers." This strategy is paying off, and his business has enough working capital to run smoothly without having to go to the bank for help.

Source: "Eight rules to keep small businesses afloat." *Toronto Star*. Retrieved from http://www.thestar.com/business/smallbusiness/article/1069967-eight-rules-to-keep-small-businesses-afloat, accessed March 4, 2012. For more information about Great Circle Works, visit www.greatcircleworks.com.

Chapter Summary

1 Explain the meaning of working capital and how it can be measured.

Working capital management involves managing all current asset and current liability accounts and ensuring a balance between them. Because these types of accounts vary from day to day, managing the current accounts is time consuming. A balanced relationship must also exist with other statement of financial position accounts, such as non-current assets and long-term borrowings. Current assets include inventories, trade receivables, marketable securities, and cash. The purpose of managing working capital accounts is to speed up the cash conversion cycle and the operating cycle. There are two ways to measure the efficiency and effectiveness of working capital management: (1) the DWC, that is, the number of DWC a business holds to meet average daily sales needs; and (2) the CCE, that is, how quickly a business converts revenue into cash flow from its operating activities.

2 Discuss the flow of cash via the cash conversion cycle.

The cash conversion cycle, which is the movement of cash through working capital accounts, such as inventories, trade receivables, and trade and other payables, is an important part of managing working capital accounts.

3 Describe several strategies for managing inventories.

Managing inventories means replenishing stock while keeping associated order and holding costs at a minimum.

Keeping inventories low helps to improve profits. Four methods used to manage inventories are MRP, JIT, EOQ, and inventory replenishment.

4 Explore techniques for managing trade receivables.

Managing trade receivables involves six activities: setting credit terms, granting credit to customers, billing, monitoring payments made by customers, maintaining or reducing the average collection period, and choosing the right credit insurance.

5 Comment on managing cash and cash equivalents.

Managing cash ensures a business has enough cash on hand to conduct its daily operating activities, handle emergencies, and take advantage of opportunities. The preparation of a cash budget helps management find what level of cash is needed and when. Managing marketable securities consists of investing surplus cash in profit-making investments, such as treasury bills, bank deposits, or bonds.

6 Explain how to manage current liability accounts to improve the cash flow cycle.

Management of current liabilities consists of using current debt, such as trade and other payables, and working capital loans, as sources of financing.

Key Terms

Aging of accounts receivable p. 241
Cash p. 244
Cash conversion cycle p. 224
Cash conversion efficiency (CCE) p. 223
Credit insurance policy p. 243
Credit policy p. 239
Credit terms p. 235
Credit-scoring system p. 237
Days of working capital (DWC) p. 223
Economic ordering quantity (EOQ) p. 231
Electronic funds transfer (EFT) p. 246
Float p. 246
Goal of working capital management p. 222
Holding costs p. 231
Indemnification policy p. 243
Inventory replenishment p. 233
Investment securities p. 247
Just-in-time inventory management p. 231
Material requirements planning (MRP) p. 230
Net working capital p. 221
Operating cycle p. 226
Ordering costs p. 231
Post office box p. 247
Regional banks p. 247
Types of inventories, p. 230
Working capital loans p. 250
Working capital management p. 222

Review Questions

1 Explain the meaning of working capital and how it can be measured.

1. What do we mean by net working capital?
2. What is the goal of working capital management?
3. Who is responsible for managing the working capital accounts? Discuss.
4. What does the DWC measure? Why is it important?
5. What does the CCE ratio measure? Why is it important?

2 Discuss the flow of cash via the cash conversion cycle.

6. What do we mean by the cash conversion cycle? Explain how it works.
7. With an example, differentiate between cash flow and profit.

3 Describe several strategies for managing inventories.

8. Explain the various types of inventories that a company has to carry.
9. What do we mean by "material requirements planning" within the management of inventories?
10. Explain how the economic ordering quantity method works.
11. Identify several ordering costs and several holding costs.

4 Explore techniques for managing trade receivables.

12. Comment on the different functions of the credit manager.
13. Differentiate between "average collection period" and "aging of trade receivables."
14. What types of insurance can a firm use to protect its trade receivables?

5 Comment on managing cash and cash equivalents.

15. How can accelerating the flow of cash improve ROI?
16. What are the approaches that can be used to improve the cash collection period?
17. Differentiate between the process related to the traditional payment system and the post office box system.
18. Explain the various strategies related to managing marketable securities.

6 Explain how to manage current liability accounts to improve the cash flow cycle.

19. How can trade and other payables be a source of financing?
20. What are working capital loans?
21. Why is it more difficult to manage working capital accounts than capital asset accounts?

Learning Exercises

1 Explain the meaning of working capital and how it can be measured.

EXERCISE 1: WORKING CAPITAL ACCOUNTS

From the information below,

1. List the working capital accounts.
2. Calculate the net working capital.

Buildings	$100,000
Cash	5,000
Trade receivables	25,000
Trade and other payables	40,000
Inventories	50,000
Cost of sales	150,000
Land	500,000
Wages payable	10,000
Prepaid expenses	12,000
Goodwill	50,000

2 Discuss the flow of cash via the cash conversion cycle.

EXERCISE 2: DAYS OF WORKING CAPITAL

With the following information, calculate the company's DWC for 2012 and 2013.

	2012	2013
Profit for the year	$ 176,000	$ 225,000
Depreciation/amortization	55,000	70,000
Trade receivables	360,000	385,000
Inventories	450,000	490,000
Trade and other payables	400,000	440,000
Revenue	2,200,000	2,500,000

EXERCISE 3: CASH CONVERSION EFFICIENCY RATIO

With the information from Exercise 2, calculate the company's CCE ratio for 2012 and 2013. Assume that in 2011 the company's net working capital was $350,000.

3 Describe several strategies for managing inventories.

EXERCISE 4: ECONOMIC ORDERING POLICY

A company decides to market its products more aggressively. Current sales are 60,000 units per year and are expected to increase by 20%. Carrying costs are $0.50 per unit, and order costs are $10.00. The firm wants to minimize its inventory costs. Calculate the company's current economic ordering quantity.

EXERCISE 5: NUMBER OF ORDERS PER MONTH

A company has decided to market its products more aggressively. Current sales are 30,000 units per year and are expected to increase by 50% next year. Carrying costs are $0.20 per unit, and order costs are $7.00. The firm wants to minimize its inventory costs.

Questions

1. What is the projected economic ordering quantity?
2. What is the projected optimal number of orders per month?

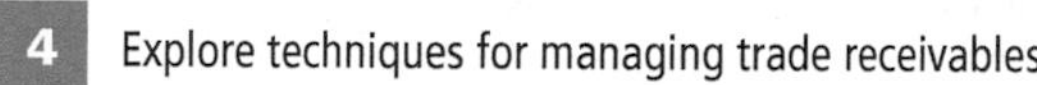
4 Explore techniques for managing trade receivables.

EXERCISE 6: CREDIT COLLECTION POLICY

A firm sells goods with an average retail price of $550.00. Customers usually pay 60 days after the date of purchase. The per unit cost of producing the goods is $125.00. Assume the cost of borrowing is 12%.

Question

Should the company change its credit collection policy to offer 1/10, N/30?

EXERCISE 7: CREDIT POLICY

A company is planning to change its credit policy. The details are as follows:

Current selling price	$5.00 per unit
Average cost	$4.50 per unit
Current annual sales	360,000 units
Current terms of sale	net 30 days

The company wants to extend its credit period to net 60 days. Allowing for the reaction of competitors, it is anticipated that this move would produce the following results:

1. Sales are expected to increase to 420,000 units.
2. Bad debt losses are expected to increase by $6,000 per year.

The marginal cost per unit for the increased number of units to be produced would be $3.00. The company's after-tax rate is 40%, and its required minimum rate of return on such investments is 15% after tax.

Question

Would you recommend that the company adopt this new credit policy?

EXERCISE 8: CREDIT TERMS

A company sells on terms of net 30 days and is considering a change to net 60 days. The firm wants to invest in projects that generate an ROA greater than 20%. The expected effect of the change in credit is summarized below.

	Net 30 Today (in $000s)	Proposed Net 60	Change
Revenue	$1,000	$1,200	$200
Profit for the year	100	120	20
Trade receivables	82	197	115
Total assets	500	630	130

Question

Would you make the change?

5 Comment on managing cash and cash equivalents.

EXERCISE 9: CASH AND CASH EQUIVALENTS

A business can make 15% by investing its money in bonds. If the treasurer receives $20,000 30 days sooner, how much would the company make?

EXERCISE 10: CHANGING PAYMENT TERMS (TRADE PAYABLES)

A company buys $2 million of goods each year. The treasurer of the company thinks it can delay paying bills up to 45 days without jeopardizing its relationship with suppliers. The company's accounts payable are $165,000.

Question

If the company defers paying its bills to 45 days, how much financing would it be able to obtain from that source?

6 Explain how to manage current liability accounts to improve the cash flow cycle.

EXERCISE 11: PURCHASING POLICY

A company's trade and other payables amount to $500,000, and annual purchasing costs for materials from suppliers are $10,000,000. A new purchasing policy states that they should be paid in 30 days.

Question

How much cash would the company generate if it followed the 30-day policy? What if the firm negotiates a 40-day, or even a 60-day, payment term?

Cases

CASE 1: KENT IMPORTS LTD.

Albert Cunningham began his career as a manufacturer's representative in the medical equipment business. Included in his lines were products imported from several European manufacturers. Albert's business gradually evolved into Kent Imports Ltd., a wholesaling business that bought medical equipment from European manufacturers and sold it to retailers through a sales organization. By purchasing medical equipment in large quantities from European manufacturers, Kent Imports was able to negotiate favourable prices and reduce shipping costs substantially. Furthermore, the company was able to ensure delivery to customers because orders could be filled from a Toronto warehouse rather than from a European location. In 2010, Albert retired and turned over his business to his son, David. At that time, revenue had reached $13 million a year and profit for the year was in excess of $400,000.

By late 2012, David could see that revenue for the year was going to be less than $12 million and that profit would be about $200,000. He decided to hire a marketing manager who could boost revenue quickly.

David contacted an executive placement firm, which recommended Ross Belman. Belman had a record of frequent job changes but had produced very rapid revenue increases in each position. He stayed with Kent Imports Ltd. for only 12 months (leaving in November 2013). In that short time, Belman was able to increase revenue from $12 million to more than $18 million. Furthermore, profit for the year soared by 273%. Even when Belman announced his resignation to take another position with a larger company, David felt the decision to hire him had been a good one.

David contacted the executive placement firm once again. This time the firm recommended Helen Tang, a dynamic woman who was currently a district sales manager for another import manufacturer. Helen was very interested in the job because it would give her greater marketing responsibilities. Helen asked David what policy changes Ross Belman had implemented to increase revenue so dramatically. David explained Belman's belief that merchandise availability was the key to medical equipment import sales. Belman had insisted on increases in the amount of inventories carried by Kent Imports and had encouraged medical equipment retailers to carry more by extending more generous credit terms. Specifically, he established an unofficial policy of not pressing for collection as long as the merchandise was still in a store's inventories. The sales representatives—who were paid a commission at the time of sale—were responsible for reporting what inventories the stores actually held. In addition, Belman changed the credit standards so that the company could approve more new stores for credit. He felt that the old policy was biased against these new retail stores because they did not have a track record. Willingness to sell to this group had accounted for nearly half of the total revenue increase.

Helen asked if this policy had weakened the company's trade receivables, particularly the cash flow position. David responded that he had been monitoring the average collection period very closely and there had been only a very slight change. Helen told David that although she was very interested in the position, she could not make a decision until she had looked at the company's financial statements. David was hesitant to show this information to an outsider, but he finally agreed to let her look at the records in the office. He allowed Helen to look at the statements of income and the statements of financial position. She did her own analysis of the company's financial statements in addition to determining to what extent the working capital policies actually helped improve Kent Imports' overall financial performance.

Questions

1. Do you agree with David Cunningham that the quality of the working capital accounts (inventories and trade receivables) showed only a slight change?
2. Comment on the company's overall financial performance for 2012 and 2013, particularly as it relates to the (1) liquidity ratios, (2) debt/leverage ratios, (3) asset-management ratios, and (4) profitability ratios.
3. Did the company's DWC and CCE ratio improve when Ross Belman was the marketing manager?
4. Did David do the right thing by hiring Ross Belman?

Kent Imports Ltd.
Statements of Income
For the year ended December 31
(in $000s)

	2012	2013
Revenue	11,800	18,600
Cost of sales	(8,500)	(13,200)
Gross profit	3,300	5,400
Expenses		
Distribution costs	(1,100)	(1,620)
Administrative expenses	(1,500)	(2,100)
Depreciation/amortization (administrative expenses)	(200)	(300)
Finance costs	(200)	(320)
Total	(3,000)	(4,340)
Profit before taxes	300	1,060
Income tax expense	(110)	(350)
Profit for the year	190	710

Kent Imports Ltd.
Statements of Financial Position
As at December 31
(in $000s)

	2012	2013
Non-current assets (at cost)	2,900	3,700
Accumulated depreciation/amortization	(800)	(1,100)
Non-current assets (net)	2,100	2,600
Current assets		
Inventories	2,100	3,600
Trade receivables	1,600	2,100
Prepaid expenses	100	70
Cash and cash equivalents	160	240
Total current assets	3,960	6,010
Total assets	6,060	8,610
Equity		
Share capital	1,500	1,500
Retained earnings	2,100	2,810
Total equity	3,600	4,310
Long-term borrowings	1,300	1,800
Current liabilities		
Trade and other payables	850	1,400
Short-term borrowings	310	1,100
Total current liabilities	1,160	2,500
Total liabilities	2,460	4,300
Total equity and liabilities	6,060	8,610

Note: In 2011, the company's net working capital was $2,700,000.

FINANCIAL SPREADSHEETS: EXCEL®

The financial spreadsheets that accompany this manual calculate the DWC and the CCE ratio. The financial spreadsheets calculate the CCE ratio from two angles:

- Using the operating activities cash flow
- Using the profit for the year plus depreciation/amortization

The financial spreadsheets also include three decision-making tools for managing working capital. The first spreadsheet (cash discounts) determines whether a cash discount should be given to customers to improve cash receipts for different paying conditions (e.g., 60-day payment terms versus 90 days) and allowing different discounts (e.g., 1%/10, net 30 days, versus 2%/10, net 30 days). The second spreadsheet (credit terms) helps to determine if existing credit terms should be extended to customers. It shows whether the profit earned from increased revenue gives a larger (or lower) return on the investment in trade receivables than the cost of capital. The third spreadsheet (economic ordering quantity) calculates the number of units that a business should buy each time an order is placed with a supplier.

CHAPTER 7

[PLANNING, BUDGETING, AND CONTROLLING]

Learning Objectives

After reading this chapter, you should be able to

1 Comment on the activities that link planning, budgeting, and controlling.

2 Describe the meaning of planning, its process, and how to measure organizational performance.

3 Explain why SWOT analysis and planning assumptions are important for setting goals and preparing plans, budgets, and projected financial statements.

4 Show how budgeting fits within the overall planning process, the different types of budgets, and how to make budgeting a meaningful exercise.

5 Explain the nature of a business plan and its benefits and contents.

6 Describe projected financial statements and how to measure growth and financial health.

7 Discuss the importance of controlling, the control system, and the different types of controls.

OPENING CASE

Framing Financial Success with Plans and Budgets

The Millers have spent several months going over the economics involved in opening a new retail store. They are now preparing their business plan, which they will present to several investors. In 2014, CompuTech reduced its debt and purchased all assets from internally generated funds (see Self-Test Exercise 3.5 in Chapter 3). The Millers were pleased with their financial results in managing their liquidity and debt. The financial statements also revealed that they managed their assets (productivity) well and generated a reasonable return on the company's assets (profitability). Financial statements and financial ratios that were calculated in the Self-Test Exercises in Chapter 4 will be presented to investors.

Based on the Millers' calculations (see Self-Test Exercise 5.6 in Chapter 5), CompuTech's 2014 break-even point shows positive results only two years after the company started, that is, 80.3% ($337,374) of revenue ($420,000). The Millers also know that the new retail outlet that they want to open would be viable; in fact, it shows an excellent internal rate of return of around 25% (this topic will be covered in Chapter 11). Even the financing package that the Millers were considering appeared reasonable. The Opening Case in Chapter 9 shows that of the $449,000 that they need for the new retail store ($350,000 in capital assets and $99,000 in working capital), 35% would be financed from internal operations ($157,000) and about 15% or $70,000 from shareholders. The business and shareholders would therefore provide about 50% of the funds. The Millers are looking for the remaining 50% of the funding from lenders ($150,000 from long-term lenders and $72,000 from short-term lenders).

Everything looked positive, but the work wasn't finished yet. The Millers realized they had to present projected financial statements for the next several years and a detailed cash budget for 2015 to the lenders and to potential shareholders. They also had to prove that they had an accounting and financial reporting system in place that would help them manage their monthly cash budget and pay their bills on time. They also knew that the banks would probably not look at the company's detailed cost structure. However, the Millers planned to show them that through their planning process, they had made informed business decisions and had an effective control system to monitor operating and financial results.

The Millers were prepared to demonstrate that CompuTech could manage its 90% increase in revenue in 2015 and that they were going to more than double their profit for the year, which would help finance their growth (sustainable growth). They also wanted to show that the company's overall financial health position (Z-score) is excellent.

The Millers wanted to prepare a business plan to satisfy not only investors' needs but also their own. They realized that planning and budgeting were a prerequisite for success.

THIS CHAPTER WILL SHOW LEN AND JOAN MILLER HOW TO

- Plan for growth and success.
- Prepare budgets and understand why they play an important role within the strategic planning process.
- Control and check for problems, find the reasons for them, and correct them.

Chapter Overview

FINANCIAL SUCCESS: THE ECHO OF FINANCIAL PLANNING

This is the third and last chapter dealing with operating decisions (look back to Figure 1.1) Planning, budgeting, and controlling are important ongoing operating activities. Organizations cannot be financially successful without goals and plans. This chapter covers the planning-budgeting-controlling process under seven topics:

- *Planning-budgeting-controlling process.* The first section presents a broad view of the planning-budgeting-controlling process. The parts of the process will be covered under four main activities: planning, budgeting, business plans and financial projections, and controlling (see Figure 7.1).
- *Planning and measuring organizational performance.* This section focuses on the meaning of planning, why it is important, the different categories of goals and plans (strategic, tactical, and operational), and how managers measure performance by using standards of efficiency and effectiveness.
- *SWOT analysis and planning assumptions.* We will then turn to SWOT analysis, an acronym for the strengths, weaknesses, opportunities, and threats of an organization. SWOT analysis helps managers identify planning assumptions, which are then used as benchmarks to set priorities, create goals, and prepare plans.
- *Budgeting.* The next section looks at budgeting and the different types of budgets (operating, complementary, and comprehensive) managers use. All managers are responsible for preparing their own budgets. The controller then combines the budgets and prepares the projected financial statements.
- *Business plan.* We will then look at the contents of a business plan. This document gives a complete picture about an organization's goals, plans, operating activities, financial needs, financing requirements, and financial statements; briefly, it is a roadmap the organization follows to reach its goals.
- *Projected financial statements.* We will then examine the part organizational budgets play in projected financial statements. We'll explain two measurement tools: the sustainable growth formula, which shows the rate at

which a company should grow to stay financially stable, and the Z-score formula, which combines five ratios to assess the financial health of an organization.

- *Controlling.* This last section looks at the management function of control, its process, the different types of controls, and who is responsible for controlling.

The Planning-Budgeting-Controlling Process

1 Comment on the activities that link planning, budgeting, and controlling.

Nothing can be changed in financial statements presented in annual reports or in historical financial statements. Shareholders, members of the board of directors, executives, and managers may be pleased or unhappy with the results. Projected financial statements, however, are a different story. They can be properly "framed" by sound operating, financing, and investing decisions.

Successful organizational decisions depend largely on how well plans are developed. What would be the point of managing an organization if goals and plans are not clearly established? How can employees be motivated if goals are not clearly formulated or if organizational units do not plan their activities together? How can managers control their activities if they do not know what to control?

Let's define the three key management concepts covered in this chapter: planning, budgeting, and controlling. *Planning* is the management process that creates the company's goals and how to work toward them. It deals with two elements: (1) where a business wants to be in the future, and (2) the plans needed to get there.

Budgeting is the process of allocating resources, evaluating the financial outcome, and establishing the financial and operational benchmarks the organization's performance will be measured against. This activity helps managers to select the alternative that will help their organization meet its goals and costs effectively and figure out what resources they will need to do this.

Controlling is the function that closes the management loop. For planning to be useful, managers need to know about their accomplishments. Controlling is so closely linked to planning that they can be referred to as the "conjoined twins." Controlling is defined as the process of comparing results with expectations (goals and plans), and if necessary, taking steps to get back on course.

Figure 7.1 shows how the planning-budgeting-controlling activities are linked (A to K). Planning assumptions (A) are used to set goals and prepare plans, budgets, and financial statements. The numbers shown on projected financial statements, such as revenue, cost of sales, expenses, non-current assets, inventories, and trade receivables, are meaningless unless they are supported by planning assumptions. These assumptions are boundaries that determine (1) what a company plans to do, and (2) how the numbers shown on projected financial statements are put together. All goals and plans (D and E) have an impact (positive or negative) on budgets and projected financial statements (F to I).

Figure 7.1 **The Planning, Budgeting, and Controlling Process**

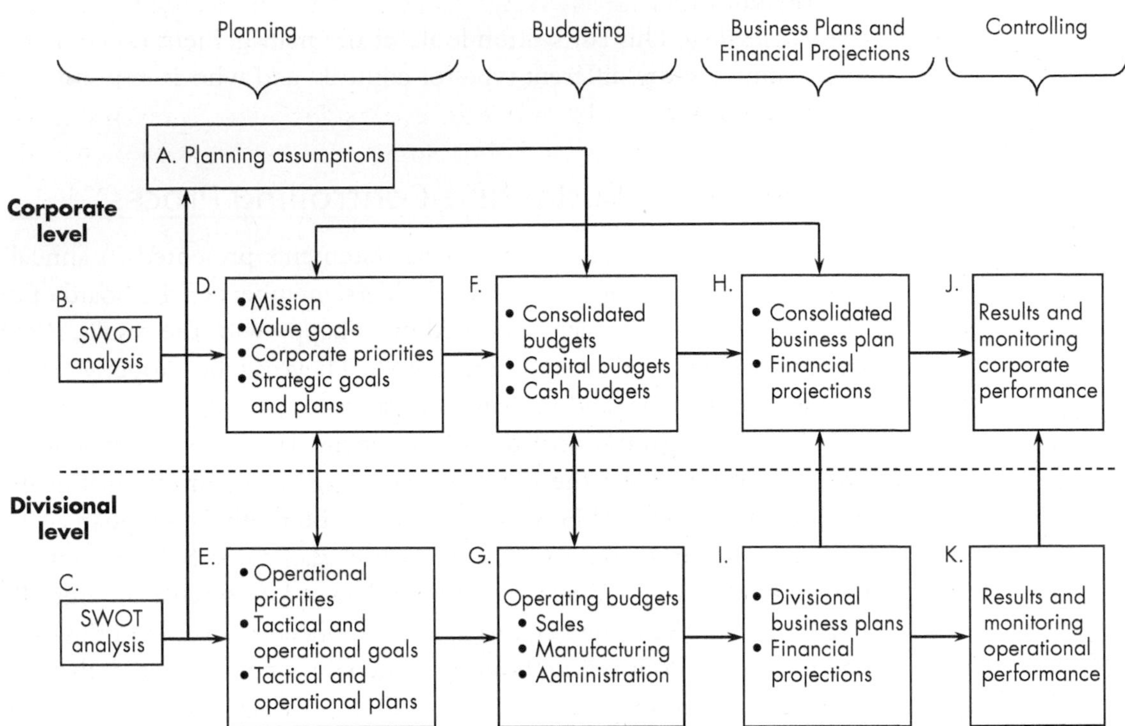

SWOT analysis is used when planning (B and C). The strengths and weaknesses are the company's internal operations (e.g., marketing, production, human resources); opportunities and threats focus on the company's external environment (general and industry). SWOT analysis helps to set goals and plans and to also create planning assumptions.

Budgeting is a crucial part of planning. Creating strategic goals and plans, identifying corporate priorities, developing market/product strategies, and writing detailed operational plans and procedures are all essential steps in planning. Individually, these steps accomplish little; they become meaningful only as part of consolidated projected financial statements. These planning efforts are translated into the common language of business—dollars—through the budgeting process. As Figure 7.1 shows, budgeting does not stand alone within the overall planning and controlling process (F and G). Budgeting involves putting together operating budgets (sales, manufacturing, administration, research and development, etc.) and consolidated budgets, capital budgets, and cash budgets.

Plans and budgets are used to prepare a business plan, which summarizes goals, plans, and financial projections (H and I). A business plan can be prepared by owners

Strategic business unit (SBU)
A unit within a multi-business company.

of a small business interested in approaching lenders or by division managers of a large corporation, showing the future of each **strategic business unit (SBU)**.

Projected financial statements (H and I) are also included in a business plan. They show the impact that the goals and plans are expected to have on a company's future financial performance.

Controlling (J and K) is the feedback system that compares actual performance with predetermined standards. It identifies deviations, measures their significance, and takes any action to assure that all organizational resources are being used effectively and efficiently.

Planning

2 Describe the meaning of planning, its process, and how to measure organizational performance.

Planning
The process of creating goals and outlining action plans to meet those goals.

Planning is the process of setting goals and outlining action plans to meet the goals. It is a decision-making activity. Goals and plans have an impact on budgets and financial projections. The planning process includes five activities, each of which involves decisions that affect a company's projected financial statements and performance (see Figure 7.2). Because plans affect the amount of resources needed to achieve organizational goals, managers must deal with the following questions: Do we have enough resources to meet our goals? If not, what resources should we acquire? How much will the plans cost? Can we afford to buy capital assets? What impact do these goals and plans have on our bottom line?

Figure 7.2 **The Planning Process**

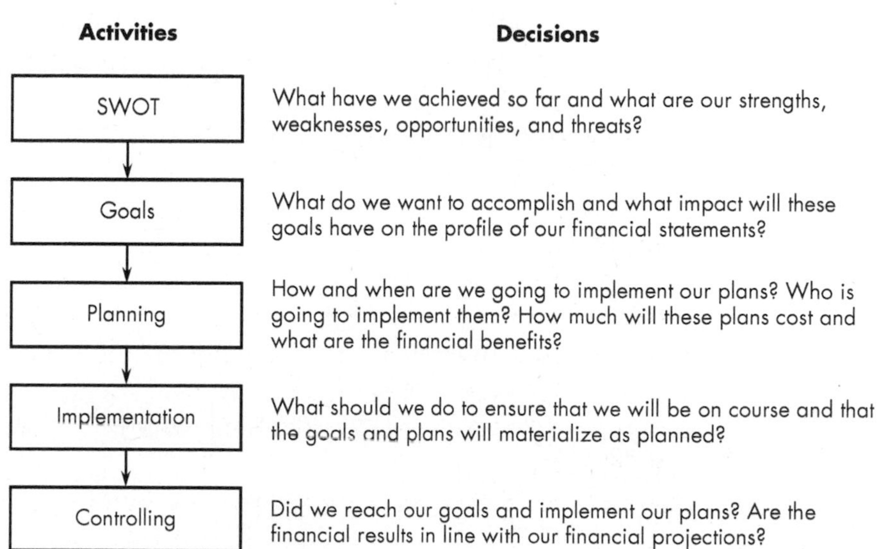

IMPORTANCE OF PLANNING

Effective planning has many advantages. First, it encourages managers to evaluate different options before choosing one. It forces them to be more *creative*, *innovative*, and *resourceful* in how resources are used and how activities should be carried out.

Second, planning helps to integrate short-term (operational) goals with long-term (strategic) goals, leading to *goal congruence* (all smaller goals are working toward the larger organizational goals). Each division prepares a divisional business plan that has short- and medium-term projected budgets and financial statements. These reports are then combined into consolidated budgets and financial statements that are based on meaningful assumptions.

Third, planning provides a *sense of purpose and direction*. Instead of reacting to circumstances, managers can anticipate the future and act in ways to improve the company's profits. Goals tell what should be done; plans show, step by step, where it should be done, how, and by whom.

Fourth, planning enables a business to *cope with change*. Businesses operate in rapidly changing environments; planning makes managers aware of the future environment and helps them develop reasonable and logical plans based on realistic assumptions about what to expect. Managers must therefore anticipate opportunities and threats before they happen.

Fifth, planning *simplifies managerial control*. Having identified the goals and the plans necessary to reach them, managers are in a much better position to monitor and evaluate their fulfillment. Planning allows managers to identify what needs to be done, by whom, and when; controlling points out what was done and not done, and, if necessary, what steps will bring everything back in line. Both budgets and financial statements are excellent documents to use to make such comparisons.

HIERARCHY OF GOALS AND PLANS

Managers at all levels play different roles in the planning process. Table 7.1 lists three types of plans—strategic, tactical, and operational—and who is responsible for them.

Table 7.1 The Hierarchy of Plans

Types of Plans	Management Level	Responsibility	Time Frame*
Strategic goals and plans (consolidated budgets and financial statements)	Top-level managers	Company-wide	5 years and more
Tactical goals and plans (divisional budgets and financial statements)	Middle-level managers	Divisions	1 to 5 years
Operational goals, plans, and budgets	First-level managers	Organizational units	1 year and less

* Time frame varies across industries. In the petroleum industry, long-range plans can span 20 years; in the clothing industry, the span may be one or two years.

A *strategic plan* involves analyzing goals and choosing the mission for an organization, examining the alternatives for achieving the goals, and allocating the resources needed. Strategic planning helps managers bring their organizations into line with their environment by (1) coping well with an organization's external environment (e.g., seizing opportunities and neutralizing threats) and (2) managing its internal environment (e.g., boosting strengths and eliminating weaknesses). Consolidated budgets and projected financial statements clearly demonstrate in quantitative terms how effective strategic plans are.

A *tactical plan* involves preparing goals and plans to help divisional managers carry out long-term strategies. Managers of divisional or functional units prepare their tactical plans, budgets, and medium-range financial statements to show how they will successfully put corporate strategies into practice. Divisional budgets and financial statements also clearly measure the outcome of the plans.

An *operational plan* involves developing detailed short-range plans and operating budgets. These plans identify who is going to do what, when, and where. First-level managers who are accountable for the results prepare operating budgets. The controller uses these operating budgets to prepare the consolidated budgets and the projected financial statements.

Managers must prepare many other plans, including policies, procedures, methods, rules, regulations, programs, schedules, projects, and standards. All these plans affect budgets and financial statements.

PERFORMANCE INDICATORS

Performance indicator
A measurement used to evaluate organizational performance.

All organizations (for-profit or not-for-profit) want to achieve a high level of performance and meet organizational goals by using resources creatively and wisely. Performance indicators are used to evaluate organizations' performance. A **performance indicator** is a measurement used to evaluate organizational performance. For example, the success of the trade receivables department is measured by the *average collection period.*

Performance standards
Benchmarks against which performance is measured.

Performance standards are benchmarks against which performance is measured. These involve numbers. For example, in a trade receivables department, a *35-day average collection period* could be a performance standard. Performance standards can be grouped under four categories: time, output, costs, and quality. These will be explained in more detail later in the chapter, under the heading "The Control System." The financial ratios summarized in Chapter 4, Table 4.6, may be considered performance standards.

Economy
The process for determining the type of resources (human and materials) that should be acquired (the least costly option) and how they should be processed.

Intelligent use of resources requires both economy and efficiency. **Economy** is the process for determining the type of resources (human and materials) that should be acquired (the least costly option) and how they should be processed. This means assessing the alternatives available to reach a goal and selecting the one that is the most economical. Here, costs are linked to benefits. The following are some typical cost–benefit questions:

- Would it be more economical to buy or lease a building or a vehicle?
- Would it be more economical to buy a machine to do our own printing or contract it out?
- Would it be more economical to automate the office and use only three workers or use conventional equipment and six workers?

Efficiency indicators Measures of how well resources (inputs) are brought together to achieve results (outputs); efficiency means doing things right.

Performance indicators can be grouped under two categories: efficiency and effectiveness. **Efficiency indicators** measure the amount of resources needed to produce goods or services. They relate goods and services produced (outputs) to the resources used to make them (inputs). Efficiency means *doing things right.*

There are three types of efficiency indicators. *Unit cost measures* relate the volume of work done to the resources used. The cost per unit could therefore be considered an efficiency indicator and $0.75 per unit, for example, considered the standard. If 200,000 units are processed at a cost of $150,000, the efficiency standard for that item is $0.75. *Productivity measures* relate products and services (outputs) and human resources (person-years). For example, if a credit department employs 100 workers and processes 200,000 documents a year, it has a productivity rate of 2,000 documents per person-year. *Work measurement* shows the output that a worker can produce within a given time period. Here are typical work measurements:

- 20 person-minutes per claim decided (for an insurance company)
- 30 person-minutes per test (for performing X-rays in a hospital)
- 5 person-hours per case (for a social worker employed in a rehabilitation centre)
- 14 person-minutes per call (for sales agents making reservations for an airline company)

Effectiveness indicators Measures of the goal-related accomplishments of an organization; effectiveness means doing the right things.

Effectiveness indicators measure the goal-related accomplishments of an organization. Effectiveness means *doing the right things.* These indicators are often expressed in response time, percentage of mistakes, or number of complaints. Here are a few examples of effectiveness indicators and effectiveness standards:

Indicators	Standards
Telephone response time	15 seconds
Time delay between receipt and completion of an application	4 days
Percentage of mistakes	0.05%
Number of persons attending a seminar	25 persons
Percentage of defects	0.03%

All organizations are trying to reach the highest level of effectiveness (goals) by using the least amount of resources (economy and efficiency). Figure 7.3 shows the relationship between organizational efficiency and effectiveness. An organization can reach its objectives (be effective) yet waste its resources (be inefficient), or it can be extremely cautious in using resources (economy and efficiency) but not use them on the right

Figure 7.3 Organizational Efficiency and Effectiveness

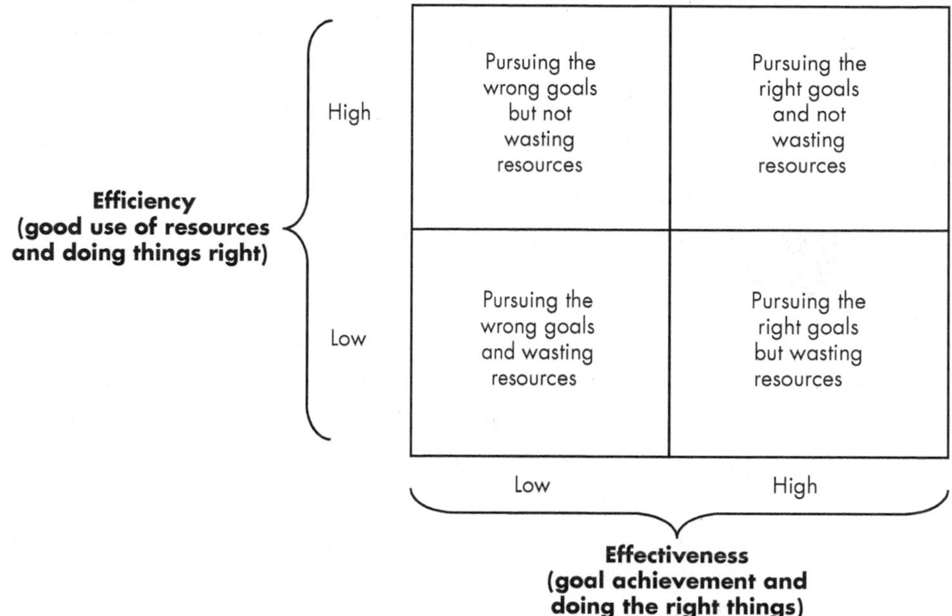

things (ineffective). The ideal situation is to reach the goals (be effective), use the resources sensibly (be economical), and ensure that the work is done rapidly (be efficient).

In the News 7.1 outlines the importance of using quality indicators to measure client satisfaction and performance.

In The News 7.1

MEASURING EXCELLENCE EQUALS LEADERSHIP

Goals or measurement indicators can be a guiding force for anyone. A lack of clearly stated goals makes it difficult for an individual or an organization to focus on results. As the Cheshire Cat told Alice in Lewis Carroll's 1865 book *Alice's Adventures in Wonderland,* "If you don't know where you are going, any road will get you there."

Dr. Jack Kitts, president and CEO of The Ottawa Hospital, understands the principles of goal setting and the use of quality measures as tools to help his hospital succeed. As he once pointed out, "Quality indicators are the benchmarks used to measure patient satisfaction and our performance. Our goal is to be in the top 10% of North America's teaching hospitals, and we are working to make that happen by working to attain greater than 80% hand hygiene compliance before patient contact; decrease the rate of re-admission to 6.7%; reduce the rate of *C. difficile* associated diseases to less than 0.74 per 1,000 patient days; and achieve greater than 74.8% of patients who would 'definitely recommend' our hospital to others."

Source: The Ottawa Hospital "Quality Improvement Plan, 2011-12(short form)." Retrieved from http://www.ottawahospital.on.ca/wps/wcm/connect/46c627804b25aec6b87cfd1faf30e8c1/The+Ottawa+Hospital+-+QIP+-+March+3+2011+Final.pdf?MOD=AJPERES, accessed September 27, 2012.

Let's go back to the trade receivables department and apply a cost–benefit analysis to a managerial decision. For this company, assume that revenue is $30 million and trade receivables is $3,000,000, with average daily sales of $82,192 ($30,000,000 ÷ 365). The average collection period is 36.5 days, and the manager wants to improve performance to 32 days by hiring one additional employee. If the additional employee costs $40,000, should the employee be hired? By reducing the trade receivables from 36.5 to 32 days, the company could generate an additional amount of $369,856 in cash.

Trade receivables	$3,000,000	
Improvement in trade receivables	2,630,144	($82,192 × 32)
Additional cash	$ 369,856	

By investing this additional cash in capital projects and earning, say, 12%, the company would generate $44,383 ($369,856 × 12%). Here we are comparing a cost of $40,000 to a benefit of $44,383. The company would more than break even with this decision. If the manager can reduce the average collection period, hiring the additional employee is economically attractive.

Look back at the vertical analysis of the statement of income shown in Table 4.2. It illustrates the level of efficiencies of Eastman Technologies Inc. at different profit levels (gross profit, profit before taxes, and profit for the year).

Problem-Solving Example 7.1

Performance Indicators

List one efficiency indicator and one effectiveness indicator for each of the following: (1) jail, (2) student, (3) politician, (4) hotel, and (5) school.

Solution

	Efficiency Indicators	Effectiveness Indicators
Jail	Number of inmates per social worker	Rate of reoffending (%)
Student	Number of study-hours for an exam	Results on exam (%)
Politician	Cost per constituent	Votes obtained (%)
Hotel	Cleaning costs per room	Occupancy rate (%)
School	Number of students per teacher	Class average (%)

Self-Test Exercise 7.1

Performance Indicators

List efficiency and effectiveness indicators for each of the following organizational units or activities of CompuTech Inc.:

(continued)

Self-Test Exercise 7.1 (continued)

1. Retail store
2. Company
3. Sales associates
4. Security system
5. Promotional coupons

Answers to the Self-Test Exercises can be found at www.bergeron7e.nelson.com.

SWOT Analysis and Planning Assumptions

3 Explain why SWOT analysis and planning assumptions are important for setting goals and preparing plans, budgets, and projected financial statements.

Projected financial statements are not stand-alone documents. The numbers on projected statements of income or statements of financial position increase or decrease over time for many reasons. The key factors that influence and explain these numbers are planning assumptions. Figures 7.1 and 7.4 demonstrate that planning assumptions come from SWOT analysis. SWOT analysis helps identify what is happening in a company's external environment (general and industry) and the internal elements (e.g., marketing, production) that can help managers prepare a list of planning assumptions. These planning assumptions then help managers create goals, set up their plans, and prepare their budgets and projected financial statements.

SWOT ANALYSIS

SWOT analysis An acronym for a method of identifying a company's strengths, weaknesses, opportunities, and threats.

From Figure 7.1, you learned that the first step in the planning process is looking at a company's external environment and internal elements to identify the company's strengths and weaknesses. Analyzing the external environment and the internal factors is done through **SWOT analysis**, a process that identifies a company's strengths, weaknesses, opportunities, and threats.

Figure 7.4 **Relationship between Planning Assumptions and Projected Financial Statements**

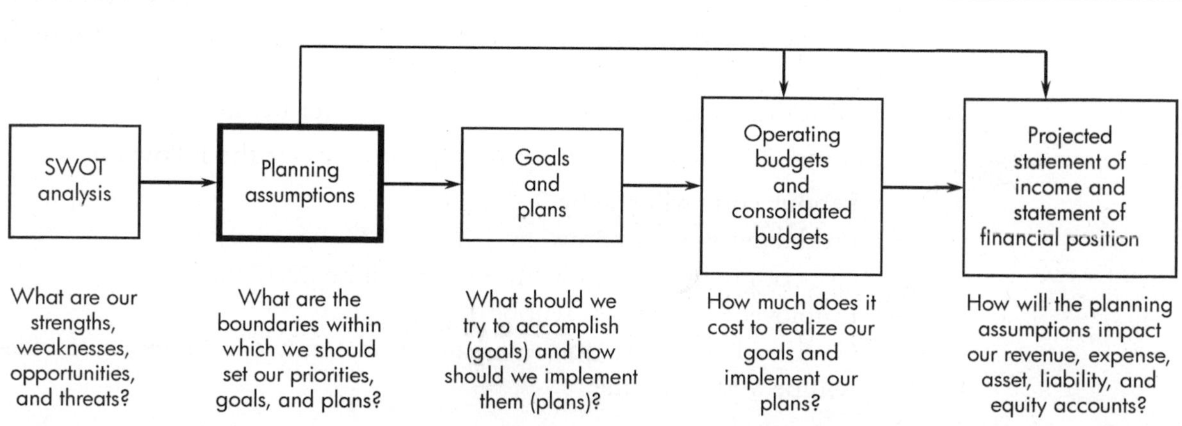

Strengths are things the company is good at or that give an advantage over competing firms. Examples include solid financial resources, strong relationships with suppliers, low cost of raw materials, and a superior sales force. A *weakness* is something that a company does poorly and that puts it at a competitive disadvantage. Examples are high inventory costs, weak after-sales service, high cost of wages, and high investment in working capital.

Opportunities are things in the external environment that offer a company ways to expand, such as economic recovery, a rapid increase in market growth, or a reduction in the interest rate. *Threats* are those parts of the external environment that pose serious problems to the well-being of an organization. Threats can emerge from new foreign competitors entering the marketplace or the introduction of new products or services.

PLANNING ASSUMPTIONS

As shown in Figure 7.4, SWOT analysis helps managers identify their planning assumptions (also known as planning premises).

Planning assumptions
Boundaries on which priorities, goals, plans, budgets, and financial projections are based.

Planning assumptions are important for two reasons. First, they establish the boundaries on which the company's plans and budgets are based. Assumptions about the industry and the company's internal operations help managers to be realistic in their projections. For example, if managers of a home electronics manufacturing company estimate a 4% increase per year in the electronics market over the next five years, the company will use this assumption to set its goals, plans, budgets, and financial projections.

Second, planning assumptions help all division, department, and organizational unit managers to be consistent in developing their goals, plans, budgets, and financial projections because all units use the same assumptions. For instance, if managers of a home electronics manufacturing company estimate a 1% population growth and an increase of 4.5% a year in consumer disposable income, all managers will use this information to set their goals, plans, budgets, and financial projections.

Some planning assumptions can be quantified, while others are stated in general terms. *Quantitative assumptions* are those that can be expressed in specific terms. For example, external quantitative planning assumptions include such statements as the following:

- The Canadian dollar will remain at US$0.99 over the next two years.
- Market growth for Product A will be 3.7% a year over the next three years.
- The federal corporate tax rate will be 45%.
- GNP in real terms will increase by 2.2% over the next year.

Internal quantitative planning assumptions include the following:

- Labour costs will rise by 3.2%.
- Productivity will improve by 1.2%.
- Cost of raw materials for Product Y will be $2.15/unit.
- Employee absenteeism will be 1.5%.
- Overhead cost allocation to organizational units for computer services will be $90 an hour.

Qualitative assumptions are stated in broad terms. For instance, they may include potential changes in government regulations, company image, and employee morale.

Although some planning assumptions are generic, others are more specific and can be linked to accounts on financial statements. Let's now turn to how planning assumptions can help produce the projected statements of income and statements of financial position. Look ahead to Tables 7.4 and 7.6, which will be explained later in the chapter. They show Eastman Technologies Inc.'s projected statement of income and statement of financial position for 2014. Each account is influenced by one or several planning assumptions.

Projected Statement of Income Planning Assumptions

Table 7.4 shows Eastman Technologies Inc.'s statements of income for two years. Revenue is expected to increase by 22% over 2013. After deducting all expenses from revenue, the company expects $264,000 in profit. To prepare a full business plan, Eastman will have to create financial targets for each line shown on the statement of income, and, more importantly, clearly show the assumptions used to reach the revenue and expense estimates.

This section gives a few examples of questions that can help to create the statement of income planning assumptions. Each line on Eastman's statement of income shows a financial goal, the increment over the previous year's (2013) operations, and a percentage related to the revenue line. For example, cost of sales is expected to reach $2,050,000 by 2014. This is a 7.9% increase over the previous year ($2,050,000 – $1,900,000) ÷ $1,900,000). Also, total cost of sales is expected to be 67.2% of revenue ($2,050,000 ÷ $3,050,000), compared with 76% in 2013.

The statement of income shows the company's future revenue, costs, and profit performance. To examine the company's projected financial performance, managers can set goals similar to the ratios we looked at in Chapter 4, and they can use vertical (look back at Tables 4.1 and 4.2) and horizontal analyses (look back at Tables 4.3 and 4.4).

Eastman's 2013 year-end forecast and 2014 budget year operating performance are summarized below. Significant improvements were expected in the cost of sales, which would increase the gross profit and profit for the year. The horizontal analysis (the differences between two consecutive statements of income) is also shown in the last column:

	As % of Sales		
	2014 Budget	2013 Year-End	Increase over 2013 (%)
Revenue	1.00	1.00	22.0
Cost of sales	(0.67)	(0.76)	7.9
Gross profit	0.33	0.24	66.7
Distribution costs	(0.06)	(0.06)	20.0
Administrative expenses	(0.09)	(0.09)	13.9
Profit for the year	0.09	0.04	170.8

The following types of questions can lead to creating the statement of income planning assumptions for revenue and expense accounts:

Revenue

- By how much will the market grow?
- How many units of different product lines will we sell?
- What will be the changes in the selling price for our products and services?

Cost of sales

- What type and quantity of supplies will we buy from each supplier?
- What terms or purchase agreements will we have with existing suppliers?
- Will there be a new collective agreement? Is so, what are the new terms?

Distribution costs

- Will there be a new compensation package offered to our sales staff?
- Will the policies regarding travel and entertainment programs change?
- What products or services will we advertise?

Administrative expenses

- Will there be more employees working in support or overhead units?
- Will there be a change in the equipment that we lease?
- Will we buy new equipment, such as computers and printers, that will affect the depreciation expense?

Projected Statement of Financial Position Planning Assumptions

A similar analysis of planning assumptions can be done for the statement of financial position accounts. Look ahead to Table 7.6, which shows Eastman Technologies Inc.'s projected statement of financial position, including non-current assets, current assets, equity, non-current liabilities, and current liabilities. Eastman Technologies Inc.'s total assets increased by $279,000—from $1,800,000 to $2,079,000—or 15.5%, and the percentage of each account related to total assets changed between 2013 and 2014.

To figure out how this increase took place, we have to examine the key elements of the assets, such as non-current assets, inventories, and trade receivables, as a percentage of total assets. The vertical analysis of the key accounts of Eastman's statement of financial position follows, and the horizontal analysis (differences between two consecutive statements of financial position) is shown in the last column:

	Percentage of Total Assets		
	2014 Budget	2013 Year-End	Increase (%)
Non-current assets	0.68	0.67	17.7
Current assets	0.32	0.33	11.2
Total assets	1.00	1.00	15.5

Percentage of Total Equity and Liabilities			
	2014 Budget	2013 Year-End	Increase (%)
Equity	0.37	0.31	38.6
Long-term borrowings	0.40	0.44	3.8
Current liabilities	0.23	0.25	7.9
Total liabilities	0.63	0.69	5.2
Total equity and liabilities	1.00	1.00	15.5

The following questions can be asked when making the statement of financial position planning assumptions:

Assets

Non-current assets

- What capital assets will we buy next year?
- How much will these assets cost?

Inventories

- How much will we invest in raw materials? Finished goods?
- Will there be a change in insurance premium rates for insuring inventories?

Trade receivables

- What will be the aging of our trade receivables?
- What percentage of our revenue will be made on credit?

Cash and prepaid expenses

- What interest rate will we earn by investing cash in marketable securities?
- How much of our expenses (e.g., insurance) will apply to next year's statement of financial position?

Equity

- What amount will we need to raise from our shareholders?
- How much cash will be retained in the business, and how much will we pay in dividends?

Liabilities

Long-term borrowings

- What percentage of our capital assets will be financed by debt?
- What will be the borrowing rates and agreements for the long-term debt?

Current liabilities

- Are we going to negotiate new credit terms with our suppliers?
- Will there be a change in purchase discounts?

Problem-Solving Example 7.2

Planning Assumptions

A company sells 140,000 units at $4.50 per unit. The average cost for each unit is $2.60. The current distribution costs and administrative expenses are $130,000 and $110,000, respectively. The sales manager expects unit sales to increase by 6% during the budget year and the unit selling price, by 3%. The purchasing manager expects the purchase price per unit to increase by 2%. The vice-president of marketing also predicts that the $130,000 distribution costs will go up by 4%, and the vice-president of administration expects his costs of $110,000 to increase by 3%. On the basis of these assumptions, construct a statement of income for the current year and for the budget year.

Solution

	Current Year	Increase	Budget Year
Number of units	140,000	6%	148,400
Revenue ($4.50)	$630,000	3% ($4.63)	$687,092
Cost of sales ($2.60)	(364,000)	2% ($2.65)	(393,260)
Gross profit	266,000		293,832
Distribution costs	(130,000)	4%	(135,200)
Administrative expenses	(110,000)	3%	(113,300)
Profit before taxes	$ 26,000		$ 45,332

Self-Test Exercise 7.2

Planning Assumptions

With the following information, prepare an operating budget for one of CompuTech's departments for 2014.

The operating results for 2013 for this department are as follows:

Revenue	$32,400
Cost of sales	(21,600)
Gross profit	10,800
Salaries	(8,000)
Profit	$ 2,800

In 2013, the department sold 5,400 units and the retail sales price per unit was $6.00. The purchase price per unit was $4.00. A portion of the salaries, $8,000, was allocated to that department. Both the controller and the sales manager made planning assumptions for the 2014 budget year. They projected a 6% increase in the number of units to be sold and that both the selling price and cost of sales would increase by 2%. Salaries will show an 8% increase.

Answers to the Self-Test Exercises can be found at www.bergeron7e.nelson.com.

Budgeting

4 Show how budgeting fits within the overall planning process, the different types of budgets, and how to make budgeting a meaningful exercise.

Budgeting plays an important role in the overall planning process, fitting right in the middle of activities related to creating goals and plans and preparing the business plan and financial projections. Figure 7.5 shows that operating budgets are used to prepare the projected financial statements, such as the statement of income, the statement of financial position, and the statement of cash flows.

Budgeting is the process by which management shares out or allocates corporate resources, evaluates the financial outcome of its decisions, and sets the financial and operational profile against which future results will be measured. If managers see budgeting as a mechanical exercise or a yearly ritual performed by planning groups or accountants, they will not understand how the company can improve its economic performance.

Budgeting
The process by which management allocates corporate resources, evaluates financial outcomes, and sets systems to control operational and financial performance.

TYPES OF BUDGETS

Because different types of decisions are made in different parts of organizations, managers use different approaches to budgeting. These methods can be grouped into five categories: (1) operating budgets, (2) strategic budgeting, (3) complementary budgets, (4) comprehensive budgets, and (5) capital budgets. Let's examine each.

Operating Budgets

Operating budgets
The budgets prepared by operating managers.

Operating managers prepare **operating budgets**. The budgets used to prepare the projected statement of income are the sales budgets, the manufacturing budgets, and the staff or overhead budgets. The marketing department prepares the sales budget (revenue), the manufacturing department prepares the flexible or variable budgets (cost of sales), and the staff organizations (e.g., human resources, administration) prepare the overhead budgets.

Sales budgets
The budgets prepared by managers in the sales or marketing department.

Sales budgets. **Sales budgets** are prepared by the sales organization (marketing) and are critical because they provide the basis for other sections of the master budget. The sales budget includes the number of units to be sold and the selling price per unit, which becomes the revenue forecast.

Figure 7.5 Relationship between Operating Budgets and Projected Financial Statements

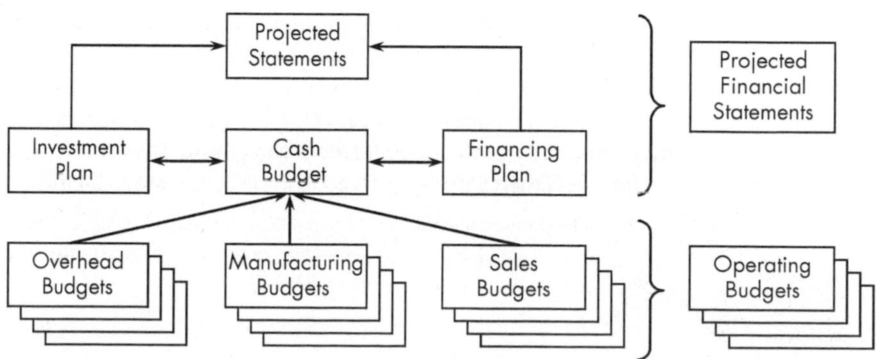

Flexible or variable budgets The budgets prepared by managers in the manufacturing or production department.

Flexible or variable budgets. The manufacturing or production department prepares the **flexible or variable budgets,** where costs of production (standard costs) are used as benchmarks for comparing actual results and identifying price and quantity differences. These benchmarks not only check whether a production unit is within its budget but also whether it is within predetermined standards.

Overhead budgets The budgets prepared by managers responsible for staff units, such as the human resources, finance, or legal departments.

Overhead budgets. Administrative organizational units prepare **overhead budgets**. In many instances, traditional (or incremental) budgeting is used to prepare these budgets. In an incremental budget, projected new expenses for the coming year are added to the previous year's total expenses, and they are expressed as percentages (increments) of the previous year's total. Such a budget might look like this:

		% Increase
Last year's expenses	$350,000	
Inflation	7,000	2.0%
New activities	10,500	3.0%
Increase due to volume	14,000	4.0%
Next year's budget	$381,500	9.0%

The incremental budgeting approach has the following flaws:

- It is difficult to relate the budget to specific goals and plans.
- Past activities may be approved without being tested and justified.
- Corporate priorities may get lost in the shuffle.
- The previous year's figures could have been inflated by one-time special expenses.

In the News 7.2 explains why planning can help small businesses better manage cash flows and be in a better position to grow.

In The News 7.2

GOALS ARE NOT BACKED UP BY DREAMS BUT BY PLANS

Setting goals is one thing; knowing how to reach them is another. Reaching goals requires a plan, a list of actions to take.

This is one rule that entrepreneur Mark Cahsens, owner of Great Circles Works, an Oakville-based manufacturer of toys and sporting goods, also follows. As he points out, "Poor cash-flow management totally can and does sink companies." He makes sure to understand and respect eight basic principles: (1) plan ahead, (2) make better deals, (3) mind your money, (4) ditch deadbeats, (5) get help, (6) borrow early, (7) inspect inventory, and (8) reduce overhead. These principles have helped Great Circle Works to grow from less than $50,000 in revenue in 2007 to close to $4 million in 2012.

Source: Torstar Syndication Services.

Strategic Budgets

Numerous traditional budgeting methods, such as incremental budgeting, have major flaws. For this reason, many organizations, within the marketing, production, and administrative units, use more sophisticated and effective budgeting processes. The two most popular are zero-based budgeting and the balanced scorecard.

Zero-based budgeting. Zero-based budgets (ZBB), pioneered by Peter A. Pyhrr[1] and popularized in the 1970s, are based on the idea that every budget dollar needs justification. Unlike the traditional budgeting approach—whereby expenditures of the previous years are automatically incorporated into the new budget and only increments are looked at and debated—**zero-based budgeting** places all dollars, including last year's authorized expenditures and new requests, on an equal footing. It assumes that a manager has had no previous expenditures. It is much like the redesigning process, in which managers ask, "If we were re-creating this organizational unit or company today, given what we know and given current technology, what would it look like?"

Zero-based budgeting
The process of preparing a budget by using decision packages and the assumption that a new organizational unit will be started.

In the zero-based budgeting process, managers prepare budget proposals called "decision packages." These budget proposals are ranked against one another to compete for scarce corporate resources. Zero-based budgeting is a priority form of budgeting in which all budget proposals are ranked in order of importance. It is an effective way to analyze programs, proposals, or projects and make the best use of a company's resources.

ZBB focuses on input–output relationships. It can be used by overhead organizational units, such as purchasing, marketing, administration, engineering, human resources, legal services, and operations research.

ZBB has three steps:

1. Identifying the decision units (organizational units) in terms of their mission, activities, outputs, and performance indicators (efficiencies and effectiveness)
2. Preparing the decision packages (budget proposals), which contain a description of the objectives, activities, programs, projects, outputs, efficiency and effectiveness standards, resource requirements (person-years, physical, budgets), risk, and time requirements
3. Ranking the decision packages based on corporate priorities and strategies

Balanced Scorecard
A management system that can translate an organization's mission, vision, and strategies into measurable targets and action plans.

Balanced Scorecard. The **Balanced Scorecard** (BSC) is another, more effective and sophisticated planning and budgeting system that emerged in the 1990s. The BSC can translate an organization's mission statement, value goals, vision statement, and strategies into measurable targets and action plans. It can also gauge to what extent

1. Peter A. Pyhrr, *Zero-Base Budgeting*, John Wiley & Sons, Inc., New York, 1973.

Problem-Solving Example 7.3

Zero-Based Budgeting: Levels of Services

Suppose you wanted to prepare your home budget by using zero-based budgeting for two decision units, (say, meat and entertainment). What four levels of service (costs) would help you decide how to spend your budget dollars for these two units? The first level for each is the cheapest and the fourth is the most expensive.

Solution

	Meat Department	Entertainment
Level 1	Hamburger	Rent movies
Level 2	Minute steak	Go to movies
Level 3	Sirloin steak	Go to movies and buy popcorn
Level 4	Filet mignon	Go to movies and restaurant

With eight packages, the next step would be to rank and select the ones (starting with the lowest level) that would best meet your priorities, including other home expenses, such as recreation and clothing, in terms of rank and budget limits.

Self-Test Exercise 7.3

Zero-Based Budgeting: Levels of Services

What factors would you consider when determining the levels of services for CompuTech's retail store?

Answers to the Self-Test Exercises can be found at www.bergeron7e.nelson.com.

overall targets are being met. It has become popular in small, medium, and large businesses, as well as in not-for-profit (NFP) organizations. More than half the Fortune 500 companies use BSC. The *Harvard Business Review* calls BSC one of the most effective management ideas of the twentieth century to help organizations quickly see benefits, such as by increasing financial return, aligning goals, improving communication, and successfully applying strategies. The pioneers of the BSC management process, Robert Kaplan and David Norton,[2] were able to combine many tools to help decision makers measure their organization's performance.

2. Robert S. Kaplan and David P. Norton, *The Balanced Scorecard*, Boston: Harvard Business School Press, 1996.

The BSC looks at strategy through a magnifying glass, from the following four perspectives:

- *Financial perspective*: How should our organization appear to our stakeholders?
- *Customer/client perspective*: How should our organization appear to our customers?
- *Internal process perspective*: What business processes should our organization excel at?
- *Employee learning and growth perspective*: How should our organization maintain its ability to change and improve?

Each scorecard perspective includes four elements: (1) an objective, (2) performance measures, (3) performance targets, and (4) initiatives. Initiatives are specific programs, activities, projects, or actions needed to ensure that an organizational unit meets or exceeds its performance targets. For example, a student's scorecard would read as follows:

Objective:	Complete the introductory finance course
Performance measure:	Grade
Performance target:	80%
Initiatives:	• Complete case study No. 1 by November 30
	• Present research study findings on January 15

Figure 7.6 shows the "building blocks" of the BSC process, which include the mission statement, value goals, vision statement, strategies, objectives, performance measures, performance targets, and initiatives. They all lead to the preparation of the organizational budgets, action plans, and follow-up.

The BSC system represents a balance among the following:

- External measures for shareholders and customers, and internal measures of internal processes, employee learning, and growth
- Targets related to the use of resources (economy and efficiency) required to meet goals (effectiveness)
- Lagging indicators (results from past efforts) and leading indicators (measures that drive future performance)
- Easily measureable outcomes and subjective drivers of the outcome measures

Complementary budgets
Budgets that complement operating budgets, presenting data differently and in more detail.

Complementary Budgets

Complementary budgets are the offspring of operating budgets and present operating budget data differently. They fall into four categories: product budgets, program budgets, item-of-expenditure budgets, and cash budgets.

Figure 7.6 The Balanced Scorecard's Planning, Budgeting, and Controlling Management Process

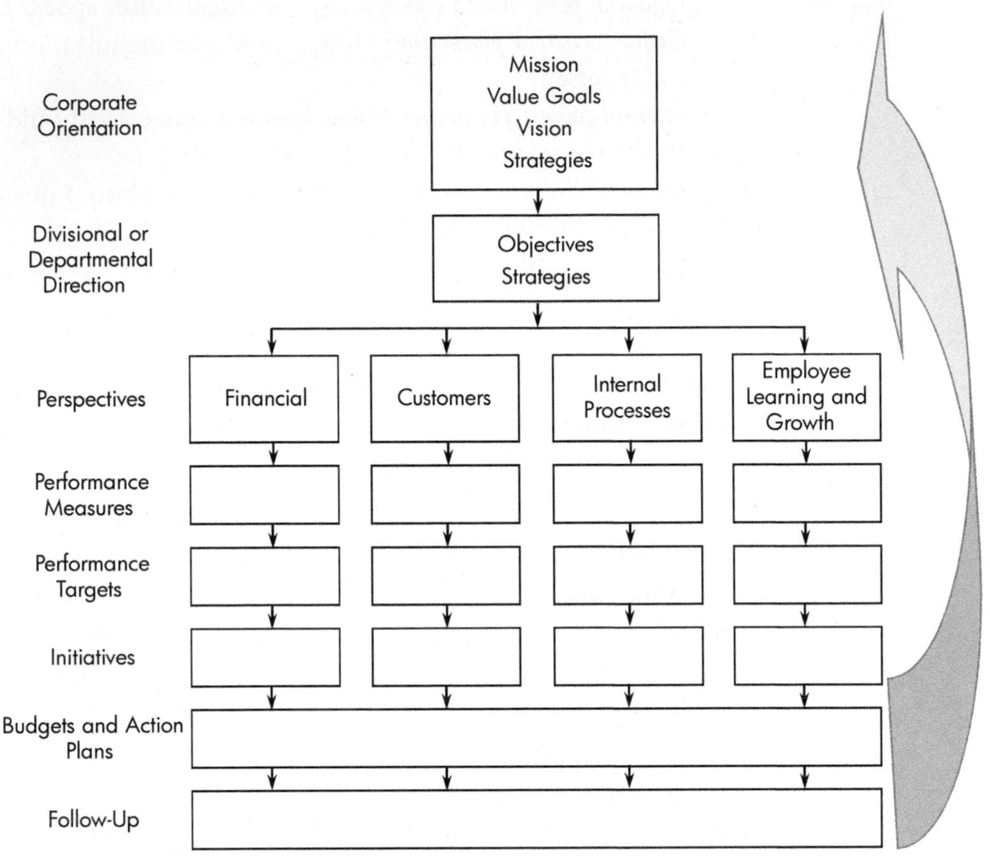

Problem-Solving Example 7.4

Balanced Scorecard

Create an objective, efficiency and effectiveness measurements, and targets and two initiatives for a telephone operators' organizational unit.

Solution

Objective	Operate an efficient and effective organizational unit
Measurement (efficiency)	Average time per call (minutes)
Target (efficiency)	12 minutes
Measurement (effectiveness)	Average response time
Target (effectiveness)	45 seconds
Initiative 1	Training ($15,000)
Initiative 2	Buy new technology ($24,000)

Self-Test Exercise 7.4

Balanced Scorecard

For CompuTech's sales department, create examples of the following:

1. An objective
2. An efficiency measure and an effectiveness measure
3. An efficiency target and an effectiveness target
4. A lagging indicator and a leading indicator
5. Two initiatives

Answers to the Self-Test Exercises can be found at www.bergeron7e.nelson.com.

Product budgets. Product budgets are used by marketing departments to measure the profit of different product lines. For example, the budgets for three products may be prepared in the following way:

	Products		
	A	B	C
Revenue	$500,000	$770,000	$1,300,000
Cost of sales	(250,000)	(300,000)	(600,000)
Gross profit	250,000	470,000	700,000
Marketing budget			
Distribution costs	(50,000)	(75,000)	(100,000)
Advertising	(25,000)	(40,000)	(70,000)
Salaries and commissions	(100,000)	(150,000)	(250,000)
After-sales service	(50,000)	(40,000)	(100,000)
Total marketing budget	(225,000)	(305,000)	(520,000)
Net product margin	$ 25,000	$ 165,000	$ 180,000

From this budget, it is possible to find out how much money will be spent by each department (e.g., distribution, advertising) and on each product. It shows the profitability level of each product line. A business may also calculate the return on investment of each product by identifying, for each, the capital investments and the profit level (after allocating the company's overhead).

Program budgets. Program budgets are used mostly by NFP organizations, including federal, provincial or territorial, and municipal governments. Program budgeting is also called the *planning-programming-budgeting system (PPBS).* This budgeting process has five basic steps:

- The goals of the major activities or programs are created.
- The benefits (or results) to be generated by each activity or program are analyzed.

- The initial outlay and the future costs for each program are estimated.
- The alternatives are examined.
- The budget is prepared on the basis of the first four steps.

Item-of-expenditure budgets. Item-of-expenditure budgets are the most popular budget format. Resources are classified in an entirely different way. For example, expenses might break down into salaries, supplies, equipment, travel, and utilities. A typical item-of-expenditure budget follows:

Items	Amounts
Salaries and wages	$200,000
Transportation and communication	25,000
Information	12,550
Professional services	35,500
Rentals	10,000
Purchases, repairs, and upkeep	5,000
Utilities, materials, and supplies	32,000
Other expenditures	20,000
Total	$340,050

Cash budgets. Cash budgets are planning and controlling tools, and can be used when setting up a line of credit with commercial banks. These budgets trace, on a monthly basis, the funds that will be (1) available and (2) required. In short, cash budgets keep track of the monthly cash balances a business needs, avoiding idle cash and cash shortages. Table 7.2 shows that the cash budget is usually broken down into four sections:

1. Cash receipts
2. Cash disbursements
3. Cash surplus or deficit
4. Financing

The cash budget has two steps. First, for each month all receipts from cash sales and collections are totalled (section 1). Table 7.2 assumes that revenue for November and December were $285,000 and $200,000, respectively, for the previous year. Total receipts for January are $245,000:

	Revenue	Collection Period	Percent Received	January Receipts
January	$ 225,000	within 30 days	10%	$ 22,500
December	$ 200,000	31–60 days	40%	80,000
November	$ 285,000	61–90 days	50%	142,500
Total				$ 245,000

The same calculation is done for February to July.

Table 7.2 The Cash Budget

(in $)	January	February	March	April	May	June	July
1. Cash Receipts Section							
Revenue	225,000	285,000	290,000	300,000	400,000	500,000	600,000
Collections							
Within 30 days (10%)	22,500	28,500	29,000	30,000	40,000	50,000	60,000
In 31–60 days (40%)	80,000	90,000	114,000	116,000	120,000	160,000	200,000
In 61–90 days (50%)	142,500	100,000	112,500	142,500	145,000	150,000	200,000
Total receipts	245,000	218,500	255,500	288,500	305,000	360,000	460,000
2. Cash Disbursements Section							
Cost of sales (purchases)	(115,000)	(125,000)	(100,000)	(150,000)	(200,000)	(250,000)	(300,000)
Payments							
Cash (30%)	(34,500)	(37,500)	(30,000)	(45,000)	(60,000)	(75,000)	(90,000)
30 days (70%)	(70,000)	(80,500)	(87,500)	(70,000)	(105,000)	(140,000)	(175,000)
Total payments	(104,500)	(118,000)	(117,500)	(115,000)	(165,000)	(215,000)	(265,000)
Distribution costs	(52,300)	(50,300)	(50,060)	(50,500)	(38,000)	(56,000)	(55,000)
Administrative expenses	(108,000)	(82,000)	(111,500)	(85,860)	(88,000)	(84,000)	(71,000)
Total disbursements	(264,800)	(250,300)	(279,060)	(251,360)	(291,000)	(355,000)	(391,000)
3. Cash Surplus or Deficit Section							
Total receipts	245,000	218,500	255,500	288,500	305,000	360,000	460,000
Total disbursements	(264,800)	(250,300)	(279,060)	(251,360)	(291,000)	(355,000)	(391,000)
Gain (deficit)	(19,800)	(31,800)	(23,560)	37,140	14,000	5,000	69,000
4. Financing Section							
Beginning bank balance	27,200	7,400	(24,400)	(47,960)	(10,820)	3,180	8,180
Gain (deficit)	(19,800)	(31,800)	(23,560)	37,140	14,000	5,000	69,000
Closing bank balance (loan)	7,400	(24,400)	(47,960)	(10,820)	3,180	8,180	77,180

The second step totals all cash spent on individual expense items (section 2). Cost of sales is done in two stages: 30% within 30 days and 70% within 60 days. We assume that purchases for cost of sales for December of the previous year were $100,000. Total payment for purchases is $104,500:

	Purchases	Payment Period	Percent Paid	January Payments
January	$115,000	cash	30%	$ 34,500
December	$100,000	30 days	70%	70,000
Total				$104,500

The same calculation is done for February to July.

Several departments must participate in the preparation of the cash budget, which requires a certain degree of judgment. For example, the sales department provides the revenue figures, while the credit manager provides a breakdown of the percentage of revenue that will be made on a cash basis, on credit, or paid within 30, 60, or 90 days. Various departmental heads also provide information on operating expenses related to purchases, wages, salaries, lease payments, and so on.

The difference between the receipts and the disbursements gives either a net cash surplus or a shortage (section 3).

The financial officer then determines how much cash should be (section 4)

- Kept in the bank at all times (cash at start of month)
- Invested in short-term securities (surplus cash)
- Required from the bank in the form of a line of credit (outstanding loans)

The cash budget helps managers plan for efficiently getting needed funds and for using short-term investments.

Problem-Solving Example 7.5

Cash Budget

A company has a cash balance of $10,000. Its cash receipts for January, February, and March are $60,000, $70,000, and $65,000, respectively. Its cash disbursements are $45,000, $90,000, and $55,000, respectively. Prepare a cash budget for each month, showing the monthly surplus or deficit and the cumulative surplus or deficit.

Solution

		January	February	March
Opening balance		$10,000	$25,000	$ 5,000
Cash receipts		60,000	70,000	65,000
Cash disbursements		(45,000)	(90,000)	(55,000)
Monthly surplus (deficit)		15,000	(20,000)	10,000
Cumulative surplus (deficit)	$10,000	$25,000	$ 5,000	$15,000

Self-Test Exercise 7.5

Cash Budget

With the following information, prepare a cash budget for January to April 2014.

The marketing department's sales forecast follows:

(continued)

Self-Test Exercise 7.5 (continued)

November (20113)	$50,000
December (2013)	60,000
January (2014)	60,000
February	70,000
March	75,000
April	80,000

The credit manager provides the following information:

- 80% of revenue is on a cash basis.
- 20% is collected after 30 days.
- Cost of sales, which is 50% of revenue, is incurred in the month in which the sales are made.
- These goods are paid for 30 days after the purchases are made.

Monthly selling and administrative expenses are as follows:

Salaries	$12,000
Finance costs	2,500
Leasing	800
Depreciation	3,000
Advertising	1,000

Other expenses are as follows:

- Taxes: $10,000 in February, $10,000 in April, and $10,000 in September
- Purchase of assets: $3,000 in January, $12,000 in February, $20,000 in March, and $3,000 in April
- Cash balance on January 1, 2014, is $3,000

Answers to the Self-Test Exercises can be found at www.bergeron7e.nelson.com.

Comprehensive budget
A set of projected financial statements, such as the statement of income, the statement of financial position, and the statement of cash flows.

Comprehensive Budgets

When the controller has received all revenue forecasts and budgets from the operating managers, the accountants merge them and prepare the projected financial statements as a **comprehensive budget**. The projected financial statements will be discussed later in this chapter, in the section "Financial Projections."

Capital budget
A budget that shows how much will be spent to buy capital assets.

Capital Budgets

A **capital budget** reveals how much needs to be invested in non-current assets (e.g., capital assets). This budget breaks down the capital assets by major category, how much funding is needed and when, the location of the assets, and the reasons for spending. These budgets include investments, such as cost-reduction programs or research and development projects, expansion of a manufacturing operation, replacement of outdated equipment, installation of computer equipment, construction of a warehouse, or even the purchase of another business. Capital projects or capital assets generate benefits (returns, profits, savings) over an extended number of years. Projects that are included in capital budgets are critical because they usually need a large amount of money. The capital budgeting process and the evaluation methods will be discussed in Chapter 11.

RULES FOR SOUND BUDGETING

The following points summarize the rules to follow when preparing budgets, especially operating budgets, such as revenue, flexible, and overhead budgets. These rules are necessary for effective budgeting, and breaking any of them can easily put the budgeting process at risk.

- Decide who is responsible for what (authority and responsibility).
- Integrate all activities (goals, priorities, strategies, plans).
- Insist on enough and accurate information (standards, targets, indicators).
- Encourage participation (get everyone to create their goals and plans).
- Link budgeting to monitoring (follow-up to see if goals and plans are met).
- Tailor budgeting to organizational needs (adapt systems, presentation formats, and needs to the managers' requirements).
- Communicate budget guidelines and planning assumptions (premises and assumptions should be the same in all organizational units).
- Relate costs to benefits (perform cost–benefit analysis to confirm budget needs).
- Establish standards for all units (each unit should set efficiency and effectiveness targets).
- Be flexible (if uncontrollable events take place and are not the fault of the manager, budgets should be adjusted).

Business Plan

5 Explain the nature of a business plan and its benefits and contents.

Business plan
A document that gives a complete picture about an organization's goals, plans, operating activities, financial needs, and financing requirements.

A **business plan** gives a complete picture of an organization's goals, plans, operating activities, financial needs, and financing requirements. It is like a road map showing how an organization will reach its goals. The business plan helps readers (lenders, investors, and other stakeholders) understand the intentions of the management team and what they want to accomplish. Business plans are produced by (1) heads of divisions in large corporations and (2) entrepreneurs managing small businesses. Because large corporations have divisions that operate more or less like independent businesses, each produces its own business plan and all are presented to corporate managers (CEO and vice-presidents) for review and approval. Divisional business plans are then merged into an overall corporate plan. Owners of small businesses prepare business plans for potential lenders and investors to introduce the business and the opportunity to invest in it.

BENEFITS OF THE BUSINESS PLAN

There are many reasons for carefully preparing a business plan. First, the company benefits in several ways:

- The plan shows specifically how management intends to put its plans into action and how it will happen (who will do what and when).
- It forces managers to realistically assess different operating units (strengths and weaknesses).
- It provides managers with a document against which they can compare their results and to take corrective action, if necessary.
- It allows managers to see that all resources of the business are used efficiently and effectively.

To investors, a sound business plan offers many benefits:

- It provides a solid base on which they can judge a company, readily assess its past performance, and find out whether it has enough resources to successfully carry out its plans.
- It assures them that management is aware of both the opportunities and the threats related to the business.
- It shows the company's ability to maintain and repay its debt in the short and medium term and shows the return generated by the projects described in the business plan.
- It identifies all parts of the company's operations, both internal, such as resources (financial, human, physical, technological, material), and external (industry environment, competition, trends).
- It identifies the timing and nature of future cash requirements.
- It enables investors to assess management's ability to plan and organize the use of the resources efficiently and effectively.
- It indicates how much funding is needed, who will provide it, and when it will be required.

CONTENTS OF THE BUSINESS PLAN

The structure of a business plan can vary in style and detail; there is no perfect sequence of contents. Each investor may want to see sections in a different order or see different information emphasized. The length of the business plan depends on the stage of development of a business (start-up versus ongoing) and the amount of funds being sought. A business plan typically has the following sections:

- Executive summary
- Company and ownership
- External environment
- Mission, statement of purpose, and strategy statements
- Products and services
- Management team

- Operations (e.g., marketing, production)
- Financial projections
- Appendices

Table 7.3 describes the contents in each sections of the business plan.

Table 7.3 Contents of a Business Plan

Section	Contents
Cover sheet	Name of business, address, and telephone number
Executive summary	Description of (1) the company's structure and major players; (2) company's purpose in the marketplace, as well as its products and services; (3) management team; (4) financial needs and financing requirements; and (5) key financial results
Company and ownership	(1) Chronological history based on major milestones; (2) form of ownership (public or private company, date of incorporation); (3) names and addresses of founding shareholders and directors; (4) company's major successes or achievements; and (5) location of business
External environment	Description of the company's operating environment and its ability to respond effectively to opportunities and threats in the external environment; four key components: general environment (e.g., economic, political), industry characteristics, market dynamics, and competitive climate
Mission, statement of purpose, and strategy statements	Statement of desired direction or achievement; briefly outlines the overall picture and has several directional statements that lenders and investors use to evaluate management's plans with their required financing
Products and services	Description of products and services; includes key product characteristics, distinctive features, and how they differ from competing firms
Management team	Description of (1) experience and skills of the key members of the management team; (2) key employees; (3) organizational chart; (4) number of employees and labour requirements of the business, including employee benefit package
Operations	Description of important goals and strategies for key functions related to marketing, production, finance, and human resources; *Marketing/distribution plan*: market size, consumer profile, product strategy, pricing strategy, distribution strategy, marketing programs (advertising, promotions), composition of the sales force, sales revenue by product line, market share, product development *Production/operations plan*: physical space, inventory and supplies, distribution system, patented processes, state of technology, type of equipment used, plant capacity, key suppliers and availability of raw materials, labour requirements, capital investment estimates, plant layout, government regulations *Human resources plan*: personnel required by function, number and category of workers, training needs and costs, working conditions, compensation programs, turnover and morale, labour relations
Financial projections	Audited financial statements, projected financial statements (statements of income, statements of financial position, statements of cash flows, cash budget), break-even analysis, and financial returns
Appendices	Results of market research studies, corporate or product brochures, management resumes, summaries of key agreements, credit reports, copy of leases, copy of letters patent or corporate charter and by-laws, detailed plant layout and production process, articles, clippings, special reports, graphs and charts, glossary of terms, references from investors, lenders, trade creditors, and letters of intent from potential customers

Financial Projections

6 Describe projected financial statements and how to measure growth and financial health.

Projected financial statements
Expected results of some assumed events that are part of financial projections (e.g., statement of income, statement of financial position, and the statement of cash flows).

Operating budgets are integrated into projected financial statements, also known as pro-forma financial statements. **Projected financial statements** show the expected results of some assumed events that are part of financial projections. The most important financial statements that managers, owners, lenders, and other interest groups examine to measure the overall financial performance of a business are the statement of income, the statement of financial position, and the statement of cash flows.

STATEMENT OF INCOME

Table 7.4 presents Eastman Technologies Inc.'s projected statement of income for 2014. The statement shows the company's future revenue, costs, and profit performance. Improvements were forecast in the cost of sales, which has a favourable effect on the gross profit and profit for the year. To examine the company's expected financial performance, managers can calculate the ratios we looked at in Chapter 4 (look back at Table 4.6), use vertical analysis of the statement of financial position and the

Table 7.4 Projected Statements of Income

Eastman Technologies Inc.
Statements of Income
For the year ended December 31
(in $)

	2014	2013	Increase or Percentage of Revenue
Revenue	3,050,000	2,500,000	(22.0% increase)
Cost of sales	(2,050,000)	(1,900,000)	(67.2% of revenue from 76.0%)
Gross profit	1,000,000	600,000	(66.7% increase)
Other income	23,000	20,000	
Distribution of costs			
Sales salaries	(158,000)	(140,000)	(5.2% of revenue from 5.6%)
Advertising expenses	(34,000)	(20,000)	
Total distribution costs	(192,000)	(160,000)	
Administrative expenses			
Office salaries	(185,000)	(170,000)	(6.1% of revenue from 6.8%)
Lease	(29,000)	(20,000)	
Depreciation	(48,000)	(40,000)	
Total administrative expenses	(262,000)	(230,000)	
Finance costs	(41,000)	(35,000)	
Total other income and expenses	(472,000)	(405,000)	(16.5% increase, 15.5% of revenue from 16.2%)
Profit before taxes	**528,000**	**195,000**	
Income tax expense	(264,000)	(97,500)	
Net profit for the year	**264,000**	**97,500**	(8.7% of revenue from 3.9%)

statement of income (see Tables 4.1 and 4.2), and use horizontal analysis of the statement of financial position and the statement of income (see Tables 4.3 and 4.4).

STATEMENT OF CHANGES IN EQUITY (RETAINED EARNINGS SECTION)

Table 7.5 shows Eastman's projected statement of changes in equity (retained earnings section) for 2014. The company will pay $50,000 in dividends, retain $214,000 in the business, and have $469,000 in retained earnings.

STATEMENT OF FINANCIAL POSITION

A similar analysis can be done for the statement of financial position. In Table 7.6, Eastman Technologies Inc.'s projected statement of financial position shows non-current assets, current assets, equity, non-current liabilities, and current liabilities, and how these elements are distributed at the end of 2013 and 2014. Eastman Technologies Inc.'s total assets increased by $279,000—from $1,800,000 to $2,079,000.

The projected statement of financial position is created by starting with the statement of financial position for the year just ended and adjusting it, using all activities that are expected to take place during the budgeting period. The more important reasons for preparing a projected statement of financial position include the following:

- To disclose some unfavourable financial conditions that management might want to avoid
- To serve as a final check on the mathematical accuracy of all the other schedules
- To help managers figure out a variety of financial ratios
- To highlight future resources and obligations

To determine where these increments (changes) are recorded, we have to examine the key elements of the assets, such as inventories, trade receivables, and non-current assets as a percentage of total assets.

Table 7.5 Projected Statement of Changes in Equity (Retained Earnings Section)

Eastman Technologies Inc.
Retained Earnings Statement
For the year ended December 31, 2014
(in $)

Retained earnings (beginning of year)		255,000
Earnings	264,000	
Dividends	(50,000)	214,000
Retained earnings (end of year)		469,000

Table 7.6 Projected Statements of Financial Position

Eastman Technologies Inc.
Statements of Financial Position
As at December 31
(in $)

	2014	2013	Increase or Percentage of Revenue
Assets			
Non-current assets			
Property, plant, and equipment	1,600,000	1,340,000	(see capital budget for details)
Accumulated depreciation	(188,000)	(140,000)	
Total non-current assets	1,412,000	1,200,000	
Current assets			
Inventories	230,000	218,000	(0.2 time improvement)
Trade receivables	325,000	300,000	(5-day improvement)
Prepaid expenses	67,000	60,000	
Cash and cash equivalents	45,000	22,000	(Cash to revenue of 1.5% from 0.9%)
Total current assets	667,000	600,000	
Total assets	2,079,000	1,800,000	
Equity			
Share capital	300,000	300,000	(no change)
Contributed surplus	—	—	
Retained earnings	469,000	255,000	(see statement of income and statement of changes in equity for details)
Total other comprehensive income/(loss)	—	—	
Total equity	769,000	555,000	
Liabilities			
Non-current liabilities			
Long-term borrowings	830,000	800,000	
Current liabilities			
Trade and other payables	220,000	195,000	(slightly more than 10% of cost of sales)
Short-term borrowings	140,000	150,000	
Accrued expenses	30,000	20,000	
Taxes payable	90,000	80,000	
Total current liabilities	480,000	445,000	
Total liabilities	1,310,000	1,245,000	
Total equity and liabilities	2,079,000	1,800,000	

STATEMENT OF CASH FLOWS

Table 7.7 presents Eastman's projected statement of cash flows for 2014. Essentially, it shows how much cash will be used to finance the company's capital budget. The investing activities portion of the statement shows that $260,000 will be invested in non-current assets (capital assets). Operating activities will generate $280,000, which will be used to buy the assets and to pay dividends to shareholders.

Table 7.7 Projected Statement of Cash Flows

Eastman Technologies Inc.
Statement of Cash Flows
For the year ended December 31, 2014
(in $)

	Cash Inflows	Cash Outflows
Operating activities		
Profit for the year	264,000	—
Depreciation	48,000	—
Inventories	—	12,000
Trade receivables	—	25,000
Prepaid expenses	—	7,000
Cash and cash equivalents	—	23,000
Trade and other payables	25,000	—
Notes payable	—	10,000
Accrued expenses	10,000	—
Taxes payable	10,000	—
Total	357,000	77,000
Net cash from operating activities	**280,000**	**—**
Financing activities		
Payment of dividends	—	50,000
Long-term borrowings	30,000	—
Share capital	—	—
Total	30,000	50,000
Net cash from financing activities	—	**20,000**
Net cash from investing activities	—	**260,000**
Total	**280,000**	**280,000**

Note: The format of this statement of cash flows is different from the one presented in annual reports, such as the one shown in Table 3.9. This format is used more as a management tool; it lists more details under operating activities, and the cash account is listed under operating activities and not as a separate item.

In the News 7.3 explains why cash flow is the lifeblood of small businesses and how growth should not be limited by a cash flow crisis.

In The News 7.3

CASH IS KING

We sometimes hear people say, "Cash is king" or "Profits are an opinion, but cash is a fact." Positive cash flow is essential to the success of every business. You can lose a customer without doing permanent damage, but a gap in your cash flow that causes you to miss payroll or a payment to a supplier, for example, may tarnish your business's reputation.

Best Buy Co. is currently troubled by a shortage of cash. For that reason, the company is planning to cut $800 million in costs by fiscal 2015. To adjust, the company is now changing its strategy by closing 50 hulking big-box stores and opening 100 small mobile locations in the United States. The shortage of cash is a direct result of a $1.23 billion loss for the period ended March 3, 2012, compared with a profit of $1.28 billion the previous year.

Source: "Best Buy to close 50 U.S. stores." *The Globe and Mail*. Retrieved from http://www.theglobeandmail.com/report-on-business/best-buy-to-close-50-us-stores/article2385378/ Accessed March 29, 2012. For more information about Best Buy, visit http://www.bestbuycanadaltd.ca/experience/headoffice.asp"

FINANCIAL INDICATORS

After management has produced all its budgets and the projected financial statements, it has to answer three key questions:

- What is the company's financial performance?
- Is the company growing within its operating and financial abilities?
- How healthy is the business? Will its financial health improve or weaken?

Financial Ratios

Lenders and investors want to assess the company's liquidity, debt coverage, asset management, and profitability. The ratios we discussed (look back to Table 4.6) for Eastman's performance can also be used to find trends. Eastman's projected financial performance for 2014, compared with 2013 and 2012, continues to improve.

	Actual 2012	Year-End 2013	Budget Year 2014
Liquidity ratios			
Current ratio (times)	1.35	1.35	1.39
Quick ratio (times)	0.89	0.86	0.91
Debt/coverage ratios			
Debt-to-total assets (%)	67.07	69.17	63.01
Times-interest-earned ratio (times)	7.52	6.57	13.88
Fixed-charges coverage ratio (times)	4.49	4.55	8.54

(continued)

	Actual 2012	Year-End 2013	Budget Year 2014
Asset-management ratios			
Average collection period (days)	45.42	43.80	38.89
Inventory turnover (times)	9.42	8.72	8.91
Capital assets turnover (times)	2.37	2.08	2.16
Total assets turnover (times)	1.51	1.39	1.47
Profitability ratios			
Gross profit to revenue (%)	22.53	24.00	32.79
Operating income to revenue (%)	6.89	8.40	17.90
Return on revenue (%)	3.33	3.90	8.66
Return on total assets (%)	5.04	5.42	12.70
Return on equity (%)	15.31	17.57	34.33

Sustainable Growth Rate

Most people equate growth with success, and managers often see growth as something to maximize. Their view is simple: If the company grows, the firm's market share and profit for the year should also increase. However, growing too fast (if growth is not properly managed) may create problems. In some instances, growth exceeds a company's human, production, and financial resources. When that happens, the quality of decision making tends to get worse, product quality suffers, and financial reserves often disappear. If growth is not managed, a business can grow broke.

There are limits on how quickly a company should grow. Growth at any cost can overextend a company administratively and financially, resulting in lower profit, cash shortages, and, ironically, slower growth, as managers repair the damage. Some signs of growing too quickly are large increases in inventories and trade receivables compared with revenue, declining cash flow from operations, and increasing interest-bearing debt.

Sustainable growth rate
The rate of increase in revenue a company can attain without depleting financial resources, borrowing excessively, or issuing new stock.

To understand growth management, we must first define a company's **sustainable growth rate**: the maximum rate at which a company's revenue can increase without using up its financial resources. Managers must look at several options when they figure out the company's sustainable growth rate. In many instances, management should limit growth to conserve financial strength.

If a company wants to grow, it has several options:

- Increase profit for the year on revenue
- Reduce dividends to retain earnings
- Sell new equity
- Increase leverage (more debt versus equity)
- Increase the productivity of assets

The sustainable growth equation can show a company's optimal growth rate:

$$\textbf{Growth} = \frac{(M)(R)(1 + D/E)}{(A) - (M)(R)(1 + D/E)}$$

where

M = ratio of profit for the year to revenue
R = ratio of reinvested profit to profit for the year before dividends
D/E = ratio of total liabilities to equity
A = ratio of assets to revenue

Eastman's 2013 and 2014 sustainable growth rates are 10.1% and 40.7%, respectively. We use the following ratios to arrive at these:

	2013	2014
M = ratio of profit for the year to revenue	0.04	0.09
R = ratio of reinvested profit to profit for the year before dividends	0.51	0.81
D/E = ratio of total liabilities to equity	2.24	1.70
A = ratio of assets to revenue	0.72	0.68

Eastman can grow faster in 2014 than in 2013 because favourable changes are expected in the ratio of profit for the year to revenue. In 2013, the company had only $0.04 in profit for every dollar's worth of revenue to invest in growth, such as investments in capital assets or research and development. This ratio jumped to $0.09 in 2014.

The ratio of reinvested profit to profit before dividends also increased. In 2013, the company's ratio was only 0.51 (with profit for the year of $97,500 and $47,500 in dividends), compared with 0.81 for 2014 (with profit for the year of $264,000 and $50,000 in dividends). This means that the company will have more cash to reinvest in the business to grow.

A similar improvement is taking place in the ratio of total liabilities to equity. In 2013, 69% of the company's total assets were financed by debt. This figure is expected to drop to 63% in 2014. As a result, the ratio of total liabilities to equity will improve from 2.24 to 1.70. This improvement gives the company more flexibility to borrow in the future.

The fourth ratio used in the formula is the total value of assets needed to support every dollar of revenue. In 2013, the company needed $0.72 in assets to produce $1.00 in revenue; in 2014, the company needed only $0.68. This is another improvement.

Because these four ratios have improved, the company will be able to increase its sustainable growth to 40.7%, which compares well with the company's expected revenue growth in 2014 of 22.0%. The company is well within its organizational and financial limits.

Financial Health Score

Let's turn now to measuring Eastman's financial health. In 1962, Edward Altman developed a mathematical model to help financial analysts predict the financial performance of businesses. Altman used a combination of ratios and a statistical tool called *discriminant analysis* to create a way to assess the likelihood that a firm would go bankrupt. The formula includes business ratios and is weighted by coefficients.

Financial health score (Z-score) An analysis in which five measures are weighted to give an overall score for the financial health of a business.

The model combines five financial measures using both reported accounting and stock/variables to give the **financial health score**, or the **Z-score**. The coefficients were estimated by identifying a group of firms that had declared bankruptcy and then collecting a sample of firms that had survived, matching them by industry and approximate size (in assets). If the five ratios give a Z-score of 3.0 or higher, the company is in a healthy financial position or in a safe zone. If the score falls between 1.8 and 3.0, the company is in the grey zone and could go either way. If the score is less than 1.8, the company is in danger of bankruptcy.

Table 7.8 shows Altman's Z-score formula and Eastman's five financial ratios for 2013 and 2014. Eastman scored 2.36 in 2013 (grey zone) and 3.11 in 2014 (safe zone). This tells us that the company was able to take steps to make it more financially sound. Here is a brief explanation for each of these ratios:

- Ratio (a): There was no change in the ratio of net working capital to total assets between the two accounting periods.
- Ratio (b): The relationship between retained earnings and total assets increased substantially in 2014 over 2013 (from 0.14 to 0.23) because of an 84% increase in retained earnings. This reflects a strong profit ($0.09 profit for every dollar of revenue in 2014, compared with $0.04 in 2013), with a small increase in dividend payments.

Table 7.8 Altman's Z-Score

Measuring the Financial Health Zone of Eastman Technologies Inc. for 2013 and 2014

Zone	Range
Safe zone	3.0 and over
Grey zone	1.8 to 3.0
Bankrupt zone	0 to 1.8

$$Z = 1.2\,(a) + 1.4\,(b) + 3.3\,(c) + 0.6\,(d) + 1.0\,(e)$$

				2014	2013
a	=	$\frac{\text{Working capital}}{\text{Total assets}}$	=	0.09	0.09
b	=	$\frac{\text{Retained earnings}}{\text{Total assets}}$	=	0.23	0.14
c	=	$\frac{\text{Earnings before interest and taxes}}{\text{Total assets}}$	=	0.27	0.13
d	=	$\frac{\text{Equity}}{\text{Total liabilities}}$	=	0.59	0.45
e	=	$\frac{\text{Revenue}}{\text{Total assets}}$	=	1.47	1.39
		Z-score		**3.15**	**2.39**

- Ratio (c): The ratio of earnings before interest and taxes to total assets also increased substantially. This reflects a strong profit in 2014 compared with 2013.
- Ratio (d): The equity-to-debt ratio improved in 2014 (0.59 compared with 0.45).
- Ratio (e): The revenue-to-total assets ratio improved in 2014 (1.39 to 1.47).

Problem-Solving Example 7.6

The Z-Score

With the following information, calculate the company's Z-score.

Working capital (WC)	$100,000	Total assets (TA)	$300,000
Retained earnings (RE)	$ 70,000	E.B.I.T.	$ 55,000
Equity (E)	$210,000	Total liabilities (TL)	$130,000
Revenue (R)	$500,000		

Solution

1.2(WC/TA) + 1.4(RE/TA) + 3.3(E.B.I.T./TA) + 0.6(E/TL) + 1.0(R/TA) = Z-score

1.2(0.333) + 1.4(0.233) + 3.3(0.183) + 0.6(1.615) + 1.0(1.667) = Z-score

0.400 + 0.326 + 0.604 + 0.969 + 1.667 = 3.97

Self-Test Exercise 7.6

Financial Indicators

Use CompuTech's financial statements for 2014 in Appendix A to calculate the following:

1. The company's sustainable growth rate
2. The company's Z-score

Answers to the Self-Test Exercises can be found at www.bergeron7e.nelson.com.

Controlling

7 Discuss the importance of controlling, the control system, and the different types of controls.

Controlling is the part of the management process that closes the loop by showing managers the results of their planning and budgeting. Setting strategic and operational control points is crucial to ensuring that goals are met and plans are carried out.

THE CONTROL SYSTEM

Figure 7.7 explains the six steps of an effective control system:

Step 1: Design the subsystem.
Step 2: Establish performance indicators.
Step 3: Determine performance standards.
Step 4: Measure performance.
Step 5: Analyze variations.
Step 6: Take corrective action when necessary.

Design the Subsystem

The first step in creating a control system is to determine the most effective type of subsystem. The control subsystem should fit the organization's culture and be one that managers and employees at all levels will benefit from. Managers in bureaucratic organizations may prefer a bureaucratic control system (with extensive rules and procedures), while democratic organizations may opt for organic controls (employees monitor themselves). Managers should also ask questions, such as How do we want the system to help us? Should the control system be more future oriented (solve the problem before it appears) or reactive (give us information after an event takes place)? Or should we have both systems?

The system should provide the specific inputs (quantity and quality) managers need, when they need the information. Managers will also have a preference for the way output is presented (e.g., online, reports, or presentations).

Figure 7.7 The Control Process

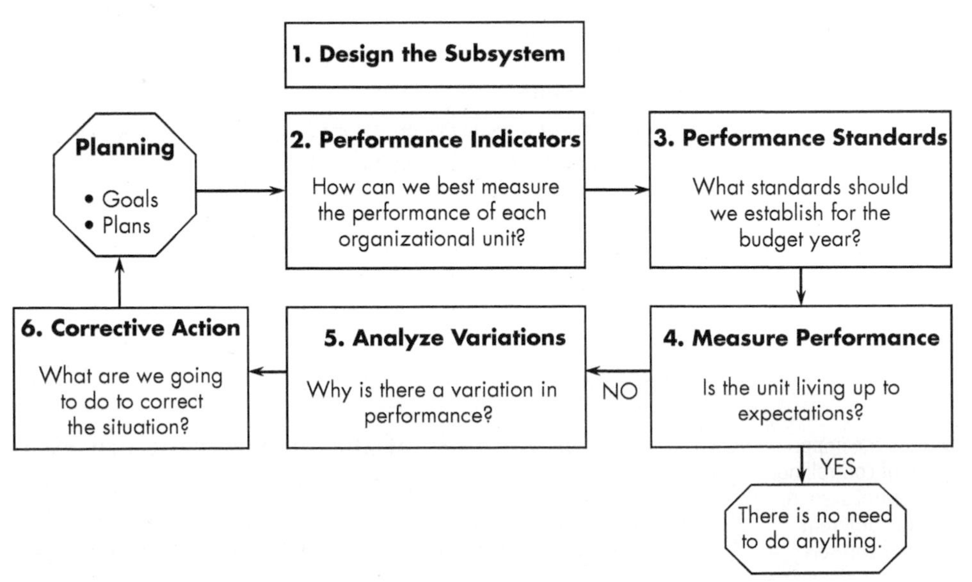

Establish Performance Indicators

The control process is closely linked to the planning activity. Setting operational and financial goals during the planning phase allows managers to determine the type of performance indicators they should use to measure results. The control process allows managers to determine how organizational units should be measured. First, managers determine the key costs and benefits of the organizational units. Second, they determine which elements need to be measured. This is the principle of selectivity (also known as Pareto's principle[3]), which states that often only a small number of important activities account for the largest number of outputs. If the right indicators are not chosen, managers may have a hard time measuring the real organizational performance. For example, return on revenue is an indicator for assessing global company performance, cost per unit is suitable for gauging manufacturing operations, and share of market is excellent for measuring marketing performance. Table 7.9 gives examples of performance indicators (operating and financial) for different organizational units.

Indicators can also be used to measure the performance of specific activities within a department, such as marketing and production, or units, such as sales and quality control. Indicators can also help measure employee performance.

Table 7.9 Standards for Assessing Performance

Organizational Units	Performance Indicators	Standards	Performance	Variations
Company-wide	Return on revenue (%)	7.5	7.7	0.2
Departments				
Marketing	Share of market (%)	12.7	12.4	(0.3)
Production	Cost per unit ($)	2.07	2.05	0.02
Organizational units				
Sales	Number of units sold	200,000	210,000	10,000
Quality control	Number of tests per day per technician	6	6	—
Employees				
Marketing	Number of customers visited per day per sales representative	3	2.5	(0.5)
Production	Number of units produced per hour	35	38	3

3. David Parmenter, *Pareto's 80/20 Rule for Corporate Accountants,* Hoboken, NJ: John Wiley & Sons, Inc., 2007.

Determine Performance Standards

Once performance indicators are chosen, the next step is to decide on the standards for a particular period (day, week, month, or year). These standards are set during the planning phase and serve as benchmarks. There are four broad categories of performance standards: time, output, cost, and quality.

Time standards determine the length of time required to perform a task. For example, the time it takes to serve a customer at a bank or the time between a customer complaint and a company response determines the quality of service offered and, thus, customer satisfaction.

Output standards measure the number of units that should be produced by individuals or groups. Managers of ticket agents for an airline company know the number of calls the agents can respond to each hour or the number of minutes it takes, on average, to provide information to customers. For a telephone company, management knows the number of service calls technicians can respond to each day. At a university, student advisers know how many students they can meet daily.

Cost standards measure the resources needed to produce goods or services. Holiday Inn knows how much it costs to clean its rooms each day, Bic knows how much it costs to make a pen, and Gillette knows how much it costs to produce a can of shaving foam.

Quality standards identify the quality needed to meet customer expectations. The total quality management concept is about whether customers are receiving the quality they expect. For example, the services expected by guests at Holiday Inn or Comfort Inn will be different from those at Westin Hotels or the Four Seasons. It is critical to measure the quality standards expected by customers and to carefully respond to their needs. Table 7.9 gives examples of performance standards.

Measure Performance

Performance can be measured daily, weekly, monthly, or annually. To measure performance, managers need information from five sources: written reports, computer documents, oral presentations, personal observations, and electronic media.

To compare results to standards, managers must analyze information. Table 7.9 shows how results are compared with standards. For example, if the company established a target of 7.5% return on revenue and achieved 7.7%, that is a superior performance.

Analyze Variations

Variations between standards and results must be examined to determine why they happened. Unfavourable variations do not necessarily mean mediocre performance. For example, the credit department may have exceeded its salary budget by $14,000, but if credit officers worked overtime to recover the trade receivables more rapidly and succeeded in reducing the average collection period from 50 to 45 days, the benefits could have exceeded the $14,000 overtime cost.

It is not enough just to look at the column showing variations and judge quickly the performance of an organizational unit. Managers should investigate the reasons for the variations and determine whether they have favourable or unfavourable effects on the overall company performance.

Take Corrective Action

When variations occur and the causes are known, managers then need to solve the problems. They have three options. First, there is the status quo. If a manager is on target or the variation is only minimal, she may decide not to do anything. Second, a manager may want to correct the problem. This is a likely option if the manager sees serious operating trouble and wants to bring operations back in line. Third, the manager may want to change the standard. This may be appropriate if the original standard was set too high or if uncontrollable circumstances have changed the environment dramatically.

TYPES OF CONTROLS

Most control systems are one of three types: preventive controls, screening controls, or feedback controls (see Figure 7.8).

Preventive Controls

Preventive controls A system that helps to guide actions toward intended results.

Preventive controls (also known as feedforward controls, preliminary controls, steering controls, or proactive controls) are used to guide actions toward the

Figure 7.8 Types of Control Systems

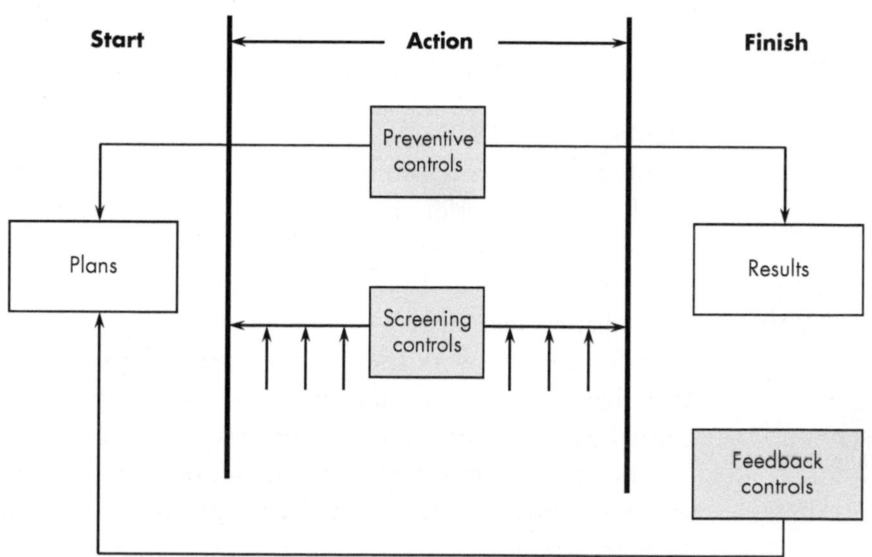

intended results. A recipe for making a cake is a classic example. The recipe will guide the baker to the intended results (the cake). This control system emphasizes the future; a manager knows what he wants and puts in place the necessary means to get the intended results. Let's take two business situations to illustrate how preventive controls work. Before hiring bank tellers, the human resources department identifies the qualifications for the job to ensure that the manager hires good tellers and maintains employee turnover at a low level. The job description prevents managers from hiring unsuitable applicants; that is why this system is called preventive control. Similarly, in a manufacturing operation that makes products, such as soft drinks, coffee, chocolate bars, or hamburgers, management will specify the quality level and the ingredients before production actually begins.

Screening Controls

Screening controls
A system that helps to monitor performance while work is being performed.

Screening controls, also known as concurrent controls, occur as the process takes place. Some screening controls take the yes-no form. This means that the process can either be continued or stopped to make changes. For example, when buying a house, a potential homeowner will say yes or no during each step of the purchase process (visit the house, negotiate the price or other terms, agree with the terms of the mortgage loan) before signing the final purchase agreement.

Screening controls can also be done by using what is called the "steering" mechanism. As the process evolves, small adjustments are made to bring it back into line without actually stopping the process. In an automobile manufacturing plant, for example, control points are established at every critical step of the assembly line. As a car moves along the line, periodic control checks are made to see that each job meets standards before the car moves to the next point. Screening controls reduce unnecessary manufacturing costs (e.g., having to remove the dashboard if the electrical wiring system is improperly installed).

Feedback Controls

Feedback controls
A system that helps to focus on variations of past performance.

Feedback controls, also known as corrective controls or post-performance controls, emphasize past performance, and the manager makes corrections only when comparisons are made and the variations are seen. Managers are reacting to a given situation; for example, if your bank statement shows you are in overdraft, you will immediately take action by making a deposit. In organizations, daily, weekly, and monthly reports work the same way; they inform managers about performance so that they can correct unfavourable situations. Typical feedback controls are report cards, budget reports, and audit reports.

The objective of these three types of control systems is the same—to help managers gauge performance and make corrections to reach the goals.

Chapter Summary

1 Comment on the activities that link planning, budgeting, and controlling.

Planning, budgeting, and controlling are connected, ongoing operating activities that management uses to improve a company's financial position. Planning deals with setting goals and plans, budgeting has to do with allocating resources among operating units, and controlling is the feedback system that compares actual performance to predetermined standards.

2 Describe the meaning of planning, its process, and how to measure organizational performance.

Planning is the process of setting goals and outlining action plans to meet those goals. Planning is important because it (1) helps managers to become more resourceful, (2) integrates their operational plans with strategic plans, (3) provides a sense of purpose and direction, (4) helps them to cope with change, and (5) simplifies managerial controls. Goals and plans can be grouped under three categories: strategic, tactical, and operational. One of managers' priorities is to achieve the highest level of performance with the least use of resources, which means being efficient (doing things right) and being effective (doing the right things).

3 Explain why SWOT analysis and planning assumptions are important for setting goals and preparing plans, budgets, and projected financial statements.

The first step in the planning process is to go through SWOT analysis by looking at a company's internal environment to identify its strengths and weaknesses, and then at its external environment to identify the opportunities and threats. The purpose of SWOT analysis is to create planning assumptions that are benchmarks on which priorities, goals, plans, budgets, and financial projections are based.

4 Show how budgeting fits within the overall planning process, the different types of budgets, and how to make budgeting a meaningful exercise.

Budgeting is a vital element of the management planning and control process. It translates corporate intentions into specific tasks and identifies the resources needed by each manager to carry them out. Budgeting is only part of the planning and controlling framework. An organization may have different types of budgets, which can be grouped under five categories: *operating budgets* (sales, flexible, and overhead budgets), *strategic budgeting* (zero-based budgeting, balanced scorecard), *complementary budgets* (product budgets, program budgets, item-of-expenditure budgets, and cash budgets), *comprehensive budgets* (projected financial statements), and *capital budgets* (capital assets).

5 Explain the nature of a business plan and its benefits and contents.

A business plan is a document that gives a complete picture about an organization's goals, plans, operating activities, financial needs, and financing requirements. Both managers and investors benefit from a carefully prepared business plan. The business plan includes an executive summary, an explanation of the company and its owners, the external environment, its mission and strategy statements, its products and services, its management team, its operations (e.g., marketing, production, human resources), its financial projections, and appendices.

6 Describe projected financial statements and how to measure growth and financial health.

Financial planning merges all budgets into projected financial statements to determine whether the company's financial performance is improving. There are three projected financial statements: the projected statement of income, the projected statement of financial position, and the projected statement of cash flows. Management should also be able to manage the company's growth in a way that doesn't use up its human and financial resources. The sustainable growth formula identifies how fast a company should grow to conserve financial strength. The Z-score formula, which combines five ratios, is used to assess the financial health of a business.

7 Discuss the importance of controlling, the control system, and the different types of controls.

Controlling is the management activity that helps managers determine whether they have met their goals and plans. Establishing a control system involves six steps: (1) design the subsystem, (2) establish performance indicators, (3) determine performance standards, (4) measure performance, (5) analyze variations, and (6) take corrective action, when necessary. Control systems can be grouped into three major categories: preventive controls, screening controls, and feedback controls.

Key Terms

Review Questions

1 Comment on the activities that link planning, budgeting, and controlling.

1. What is the connection between SWOT analysis and planning assumptions?
2. What is the relationship between planning assumptions and budgeting?

2 Describe the meaning of planning, its process, and how to measure organizational performance.

3. What is planning and why is it important?
4. What is the difference between a performance indicator and a performance standard?

3 Explain why SWOT analysis and planning assumptions are important for setting goals and preparing plans, budgets, and projected financial statements.

5. What is the purpose of SWOT analysis?
6. Why are planning assumptions useful?

4 Show how budgeting fits within the overall planning process, the different types of budgets, and how to make budgeting a meaningful exercise.

7. What is budgeting?
8. Why is budgeting so important?
9. Explain budgeting in terms of planning as a whole.
10. What are operating budgets?
11. Differentiate between incremental budgeting and zero-based budgeting.
12. Why is the balanced scorecard so effective as a management tool?
13. What do we mean by complementary budgets?
14. What is the purpose of a cash budget?
15. List the more important rules of sound budgeting.

5 Explain the nature of a business plan and its benefits and contents.

16. What are the benefits of a business plan for a company?

6 Describe projected financial statements and how to measure growth and financial health.

17. What is financial planning?
18. What do we mean by the term "sustainable growth"?
19. Explain Altman's financial health formula.

7 Discuss the importance of controlling, the control system, and the different types of controls.

20. What is controlling?
21. Explain the various steps involved in the control system.
22. Comment on the various types of performance standards.
23. Differentiate between preventive controls and screening controls.
24. Contrast control as a "policing activity" and control as a "steering activity."

Learning Exercises

2 Describe the meaning of planning, its process, and how to measure organizational performance.

EXERCISE 1: EFFICIENCY AND EFFECTIVENESS INDICATORS

Identify efficiency and effectiveness indicators for the following organizational units, individuals, or organizations:

1. Sales department
2. Telephone-answering service
3. Purchasing department
4. Politician
5. Rehabilitation centre
6. Student
7. General insurance company
8. Cleaning department
9. Security department
10. School

3 Explain why SWOT analysis and planning assumptions are important for setting goals and preparing plans, budgets, and projected financial statements.

EXERCISE 2: STATEMENTS OF INCOME AND RETURN ON REVENUE

Nick Strizzi owns and operates a pizza delivery and take-out restaurant. In 2013, he sold 100,000 pizzas at an average selling price of $15.00. The cost to make each pizza is $3.00 for cheese, $2.50 for spices, and $3.75 for the crust and other ingredients. The annual cost of operating the business is as follows:

Rent	$ 55,000
Salaries	$230,000
Insurance	$ 15,000
Advertising	$ 30,000
Car expenses	$150,000

The income tax rate for 2013 was 18%. Nick is preparing a projected income statement for 2014. The planning assumptions are as follows:

Increase in number of pizzas sold	10%
Selling price per pizza	$ 16.00
Increase in cost of cheese	8%
Increase in cost of spices	5%
Increase in cost of crust and other ingredients	9%
Annual rent	$65,000
Increase in salaries	12%
Increase in insurance costs	10%
Advertising costs	$35,000
Increase in car expenses	15%
Income tax rate	17%

Questions

1. Prepare Nick Strizzi's statement of income for 2013 and 2014.
2. Calculate Nick Strizzi's return on revenue ratios for 2013 and 2014.

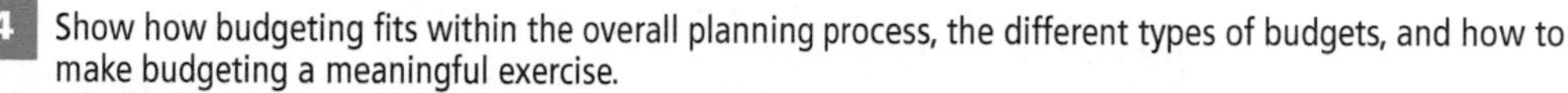
4 Show how budgeting fits within the overall planning process, the different types of budgets, and how to make budgeting a meaningful exercise.

EXERCISE 3: ZERO-BASED BUDGETING

Identify the factors that you would consider when using zero-based budgeting to determine the level of services for the following organizational units:

1. Sanitation department
2. Training department
3. Quality control department
4. Police department
5. Advertising department
6. Telephone-answering service

EXERCISE 4: CASH BUDGET

With the following information about Quantum Plastics Ltd., prepare a cash budget for the months of January to April 2014.

The marketing department's sales forecast follows:

November (2013)	$ 25,000
December	50,000
January (2014)	75,000
February	120,000
March	140,000
April	110,000

The credit manager provides the following information:

20% of sales are on a cash basis.
60% are collected after 30 days.
20% are collected after 60 days.

Cost of sales, which is 50% of sales, is incurred in the month in which the sales are made. These goods are paid for 30 days after the purchases are made.

Monthly selling and administrative expenses are as follows:

Salaries	$22,000
Telephone	1,000
Amortization	500
Rent	2,200
Hydro	1,100
Stationery	500

Other expenses are as follows:

Taxes: $3,000 in February and $3,000 in June.
Purchase of equipment in January for $24,000.
The cash balance on January 1, 2014 is $12,000.

5 Explain the nature of a business plan and its benefits and contents.

EXERCISE 5: THE BUSINESS PLAN

List the key parts of a typical business plan.

6 Describe projected financial statements and how to measure growth and financial health.

EXERCISE 6: THE SUSTAINABLE GROWTH RATE AND THE Z-SCORE

Using Eagle Electronics Inc.'s financial statements below, calculate the following:

1. The company's sustainable growth rate
2. The company's Z-score

Statement of Financial Position
(in $)

Non-current assets	2,000,000	Equity	
Current assets		Share capital	400,000
Inventories	600,000	Retained earnings	850,000
Trade receivables	300,000	Total equity	1,250,000
Cash and cash equivalents	100,000	Non-current liabilities	1,000,000
Total current assets	1,000,000	Current liabilities	
		Trade and other payables	350,000
		Notes payable	100,000
		Bank loan	300,000
		Total current liabilities	750,000
		Total liabilities	1,750,000
Total assets	3,000,000	Total equity and liabilities	3,000,000

Statement of Income and Statement of Retained Earnings (partial)
(in $)

Revenue	3,000,000
Cost of sales	(1,500,000)
Gross profit	1,500,000
Expenses*	(900,000)
Profit before taxes	600,000
Income tax expense	(300,000)
Profit for the year	300,000
Dividends	(100,000)
Increase in retained earnings	200,000

* Includes $ 100,000 of finance costs.

Cases

CASE 1: SEABRIDGE DISTRIBUTORS INC.

Seabridge Distributors Inc. is a distributor of central air conditioners, purifiers, humidifiers, and dehumidifiers. It has the franchise for the distribution, installation, and servicing of products for a well-known national brand in eastern Canada.

In September 2013, Louise Lane, president of the company, asked Bill Vance, general sales manager, to prepare a monthly sales budget for 2014. Lane informed Vance of the importance of a sales budget, giving the following reasons:

1. It helps to set goals for each sales representative and for individual product lines.
2. Manufacturers are told at least six months ahead of time of Seabridge's short-term needs for each product line; this ensures Seabridge receives products in the right quantities at the right time.
3. The bank manager is told of Seabridge's financial needs for each month of the budget year; the bank provides Seabridge with short-term money to finance the company's inventories and is interested in its short-term repayment ability.
4. If Seabridge is to operate effectively, it should not be caught short of products at times when demand is high. Similarly, it would be costly to be left with excessive stock in inventory at the end of a season.

Following this meeting, Bill Vance decided to have a meeting with his four area managers to get the ball rolling. In early October, Bill met with his managers, emphasizing the importance of sound sales budgeting and stressing that the foundation for the preparation of a sound sales budget is sales forecasting.

The four sales managers had sales territories with the following number of sales representatives.

Territory	Number of Sales Representatives
North	4
South	5
East	3
West	4
Total	16

At the meeting, Vance presented some PowerPoint slides showing the industry's demand projections for each product line, the company's 2013 share of market, and what he hoped to achieve in 2014. The figures are shown below.

		Share of Market	
	Total Market (in units)	Estimated	Objective
	2014	2013	2014
Air conditioners	15,000	14%	16%
Air purifiers	2,300	12%	15%
Air humidifiers	83,000	11%	13%
Air dehumidifiers	74,000	9%	11%

He also gave the following percentage breakdown of the number of units sold each month for different products based on the previous five years.

% of Sales by Month				
	Air Conditioners	Air Purifiers	Air Humidifiers	Air Dehumidifiers
January	—	3	1	—
February	—	2	1	—
March	2	2	—	—
April	4	4	—	—
May	10	8	—	5
June	28	22	—	33
July	44	33	—	56
August	12	8	6	6
September	—	6	12	—
October	—	6	38	—
November	—	4	28	—
December	—	2	14	—
Total	100	100	100	100

The average unit selling prices budgeted are as follows:

Air conditioners	$4,700
Air purifiers	650
Air humidifiers	515
Air dehumidifiers	450

At the end of the meeting, the idea of sales objectives was discussed with the area managers. Although the company had not yet set goals for every sales representative, they agreed to set goals to help the company increase its share of the market for 2014.

Questions

1. Using the information available, prepare a monthly sales budget for 2014 for individual and combined product lines.
2. Is there anything wrong with the way that the sales budget and sales objectives were introduced in this company? How would you have approached the situation?

CASE 2: ANDERSON EQUIPMENT LTD.

One day in March 2013, John Sutherland, industrial commissioner for the city of South Elk, received a telephone call from Nick Faranda, president of Anderson Equipment Ltd., who wanted to see him as soon as possible.

When Sutherland arrived at Faranda's office, Faranda was sitting at his desk going over his current year's cash budget. Faranda informed Sutherland that as a result of the revised credit restrictions adopted by his bank, he was being asked to prepare an estimate of his financial requirements for the balance of the calendar year. All major customers of the bank were asked to provide this information.

Faranda also informed Sutherland that he was going to have a meeting with Joanne Armstrong, the lending officer responsible for handling the company's account, and that he wanted to show her his financial requirements for the rest of the calendar year. Consequently, Faranda asked Sutherland to help prepare a budget forecast. On the basis of the information available, Faranda felt that it would not be necessary to borrow funds before July 2013. The budget would therefore be prepared for the period July 1, 2013, to January 31, 2014.

The marketing department provided the following sales forecast:

July	$ 50,000
August	100,000
September	500,000
October	650,000
November	550,000
December	400,000
January	200,000

Ten percent of sales are for cash, 40% of sales are collected after 30 days, and the remaining 50% after 60 days. Purchases, which are 80% of sales, are incurred in the month in which the sales are made. These goods are paid 30% in cash and 70% within 30 days. Distribution and administrative expenses are $10,000 per month, plus 1% of monthly sales. Start-up costs in July are $30,000. Income taxes for the entire operating period are paid in April and are 40% of the profit. The monthly depreciation is $10,000. The company feels that it is necessary to maintain a minimum cash balance of $25,000 during the selling season.

The cash balance on July 1 is $75,000.

Question

Prepare a monthly cash budget from July 1, 2013 to January 31, 2014.

CASE 3: UNITED MANUFACTURERS LTD.

With the financial objectives and assumptions presented below, prepare the following for the company:

a) Projected statement of income for 2014
b) Projected statement of changes in equity for 2014
c) Projected statement of financial position for 2014
d) Projected statement of cash flows for 2014
e) Financial ratios for 2014, comparing them with the 2013 financial results

Also, calculate the following:

f) The company's 2014 sustainable growth rate
g) The company's 2014 Z-score

Financial objectives and assumptions:

1. Related to the statement of income:
   - Revenue will increase by 10.0%.
   - Cost of sales as a percentage of revenue will decline to 51.5%.
   - Distribution costs as a percentage of revenue will improve slightly to 10.5%.
   - General and administrative expenses will drop to 5.7% of revenue.
   - Research and development costs as a percentage of revenue will increase to 2.0%.
   - Depreciation/amortization will be $120,000.
   - Other income will be $6,000.
   - Finance costs will be $35,000.
   - Income tax rate (as a percent of profit before taxes) will be maintained at the 2013 level.
2. Related to the statement of changes in equity:
   - $50,000 in dividends will be paid to shareholders.
3. Related to the statement of financial position:
   a. Non-current asset accounts
      - Investment in new capital assets will be $660,000.
      - Other assets will be increased by $100,000.

   b. Current asset accounts
      - Inventories will improve to 4.9 times.
      - Trade receivables will improve to 44.9 days.
      - Cash and cash equivalents will be 2.0% of revenue.

   c. Equity
      - Shareholders will invest an additional $200,000 in the business.

   d. Non-current liabilities
      - Long-term borrowings will increase by $39,700.

   e. Current liabilities
      - Trade and other payables will increase to 11.31% of cost of sales.
      - Notes payable will increase to $268,685.

United Manufacturers Ltd.
Statements of Income
For the year ended December 31
(in $)

	2012	2013
Revenue	2,900,000	3,100,000
Cost of goods sold	(1,870,000)	(1,880,000)
Gross profit	1,030,000	1,220,000
Other income	4,000	5,000
Distribution, administration, and other expenses		
Distribution	(325,000)	(330,000)
Administration	(220,000)	(210,000)
Research and development	(35,000)	(45,000)
Depreciation/amortization	(95,000)	(105,000)
Total distribution, administration, and other expenses	(675,000)	(690,000)
Finance costs	(27,000)	(30,000)
Total (expenses less other income)	(698,000)	(715,000)
Profit before taxes	332,000	505,000
Income tax expense	166,000	252,500
Profit for the year	166,000	252,500

United Manufacturers Ltd.
Statements of Financial Position
As at December 31
(in $)

	2012	2013
Assets		
Non-current assets		
Capital assets	2,719,000	2,919,000
Accumulated depreciation/amortization	(595,000)	(700,000)
Net capital assets	2,124,000	2,219,000
Other assets (intangible)	100,000	200,000
Total non-current assets	2,224,000	2,419,000
Current assets		
Inventories	256,000	268,000
Trade receivables	420,000	459,000
Cash and cash equivalents	48,000	54,000
Total current assets	724,000	781,000
Total assets	2,948,000	3,200,000
Equity and liabilities		
Equity		
Share capital	800,000	800,000
Retained earnings	652,000	904,500
Total equity	1,452,000	1,704,500
Non-current liabilities	950,000	1,000,000
Current liabilities		
Trade and other payables	140,000	131,600
Notes payable	256,000	263,900
Other current liabilities	150,000	100,000
Total current liabilities	546,000	495,500
Total liabilities	1,496,000	1,495,500
Total equity and liabilities	2,948,000	3,200,000

FINANCIAL SPREADSHEETS: EXCEL®

The financial spreadsheets that accompany this text are exceptional tools for looking at projected financial statements. Once the goals and plans have been set and the financial results entered into the input documents (statements of income, statements of changes in equity, and statements of financial position), analysts and managers can immediately interpret the results by looking at the output documents (vertical and horizontal financial statements, ratios, etc.). The most positive feature about the spreadsheets is that changes made on the financial statements from altered goals and plans can quickly be measured in terms of the impact they have on financial performance (e.g., liquidity, profitability, asset management, debt coverage). The spreadsheets also calculate the more complex ratios, such as sustainable growth rate and financial health score. The spreadsheets also include decision-making tools that can help prepare monthly cash budgets, and sales and manufacturing budgets.

CHAPTER 8

[SOURCES AND FORMS OF FINANCING]

Learning Objectives

After reading this chapter, you should be able to

1 Describe financial needs and financing requirements.

2 Differentiate between internal financing and external financing.

3 Explain the types of risk-related financing options (ownership versus debt).

4 Explain useful strategies for approaching lenders.

5 Discuss the categories of equity financing.

6 Discuss the sources and forms of intermediate and long-term debt financing.

7 Discuss the most important sources and forms of short-term financing.

8 Identify the factors that influence the choice between buying and leasing an asset.

OPENING CASE

Financing Requirements: Just as Important as Financial Needs

The Millers have identified their 2015 financial needs and financing requirements. These are shown below as the difference between the 2015 and 2014 statement of financial position accounts. They have completed their business plan. Now, they are ready to approach investors (shareholders and long-and short-term lenders) to raise funds.

(in $)	Financial Needs (cash outflows)	Financing Requirements (cash inflows)
Property, plant, and equipment	**350,000**	
Internal sources		
Profit for the year		77,000
Depreciation/amortization		80,000
Total internal sources		**157,000**
Working capital		
Inventories	45,000	
Trade receivables	45,000	
Prepaid expenses	5,000	
Cash and cash equivalents	4,000	
Total working capital	**99,000**	
Working capital financing		
Trade and other payables		27,000
Short-term borrowings		40,000
Current portion of long-term borrowings		5,000
Total working capital financing		**72,000**
External sources		
Share capital		70,000
Long-term borrowings		150,000
Total external sources		**220,000**
Total	**449,000**	**449,000**

CompuTech needs $449,000 to finance its existing retail store and to open the new one. The Millers will use $350,000 to open the new store and $99,000 to finance the working capital (inventories, trade receivables, prepaid expenses, and cash).

To help finance part of the $350,000 property, plant, and equipment, the Millers will contact investors and will try to raise $70,000 from shareholders (e.g., friends, family, or private investors) and $150,000 from long-term lenders. Based on the Millers' financial projections for 2015, 35%, or $157,000, will be generated by their existing store (profit for the year and depreciation/amortization), and 16%, or $72,000, will come from suppliers and short-term lenders. The Millers will approach a bank for a $40,000 short-term loan, which is about 45% of the $90,000 required to finance inventories ($45,000) and trade receivables ($45,000).

Although the Millers have identified their financing requirements, they are unsure whether these sources are the best mix to finance their $449,000 financial needs. They analyzed various *sources* of financing and wonder which of the following they should ask for more funds:

- Lenders or shareholders
- Friends or private investors (i.e., angels)
- Banks or government institutions
- Short-term lenders or suppliers
- Leasing or lending institutions

They are wondering about the best *forms* of financing and which of the following they should consider:

- Term loans or conditional sales contracts
- A line of credit or a revolving loan
- Secured loans or unsecured loans
- Seasonal loans or factoring receivables

THIS CHAPTER WILL SHOW LEN AND JOAN HOW TO

- Identify their financial needs.
- Understand their financing requirements.
- Identify the various sources and forms of financing.
- Recognize the difference between short-, medium-, and long-term financing.

Chapter Overview

THE ART AND SCIENCE OF RAISING FUNDS

This is the first chapter dealing with financing decisions (look back to Figure 1.1). It will examine the sources and forms of financing: where, why, and how companies can raise funds and the types of financing available to businesses. Raising funds is both an *art*, that is, drawing on experience, knowledge, and observations, and a *science*, that is, the application of knowledge based on a methodical and logical approach. We'll cover eight topics:

- *Financial needs and financing requirements.* This section explains the difference between financial needs, which are the items a business needs, such as inventories, equipment, and so on, and financing requirements, which are the sources that will provide the money, such as shareholders and lenders.
- *Internal and external financing.* You will learn that financing requirements can come from two broad sources: internal operations and external financing.
- *Risk-related financing options.* We will explore types of risk-related financing options, namely, business risk, financial risk, and instrument risk.

- *Approaching lenders.* We will examine strategies that owners can use when approaching lenders. This has to do with the matching principle, the criteria used by investors to evaluate borrowers, and how a company can become creditworthy.
- *Equity financing.* We will examine how equity financing can come from shareholders, risk capital investors, and government institutions.
- *Sources and forms of intermediate and long-term financing.* This section explains the more important sources and forms of intermediate and long-term financing, such as long-term loans, conditional sales contracts, bonds, mortgages, and subordinated debt.
- *Sources and forms of short-term financing.* We will then turn to the popular forms and sources of short-term financing, such as suppliers, chartered banks, confirming institutions, and factoring companies.
- *Buying or leasing an asset.* This last section looks at the advantages of leasing versus owning, the factors that influence lease-or-buy decisions, and how to calculate the economics of a lease-versus-buy option.

Financial Needs and Financing Requirements

1 Describe financial needs and financing requirements.

Financial needs
The items for which a business needs money.

Selecting the right source and form of financing can improve the long-term financial structure and profitability of a business. Before approaching investors, a chief financial officer (CFO) has to identify what is to be financed (the **financial needs**) and the amount needed. Below are a few examples:

- Purchase of property, plant, and equipment
- More investments in research and development
- The launch of a new product that needs a large cash outlay for promotion and advertising
- Acquisition of another business
- Additional working capital (inventories and trade receivables)

Once the financial needs have been identified, the next step is to think about the source and amount of financing. Figure 8.1 shows the relationship of financial needs to financing requirements. The left side of the figure shows that the company needs $1 million to expand its activities. This could be the purchase of capital assets that will appear on the statement of financial position and operating expense items (e.g., advertising, promotion, salaries for research and development) that will appear on the statement of income. The $1 million could be made up as follows:

Capital assets	$ 600,000
Marketing costs	100,000
Research and development	100,000
Working capital	200,000
Total	$1,000,000

Figure 8.1 **Financial Needs and Financing Requirements**

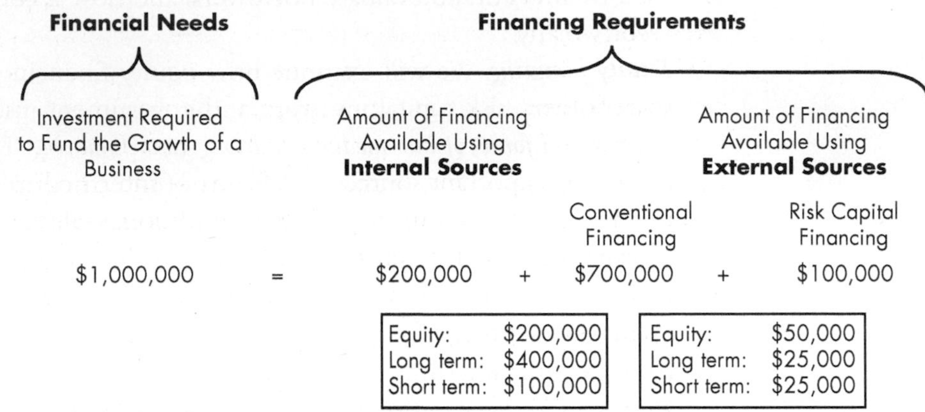

The CFO has to be precise when calculating the financial needs. Lenders want to know that the amounts being asked for are based on reasonable assumptions:

- Are the revenue estimates reasonable relative to the expected market growth?
- Are the levels of inventories and trade receivables in line with the company's sales growth?
- Will the investment in non-current assets produce the estimated number of units and revenue?
- Will the company be able to service its debt with the projected sales growth?
- Are the company expenses for cost of sales, distribution, and administration reasonable and in line with industry standards?

Financing requirements Who will provide the money (shareholders and lenders) to finance a business and in what form (e.g., mortgage, working capital loan).

The right side of Figure 8.1 (equity and debt) shows the **financing requirements**, that is, where the $1million will come from for the expansion. The $1 million financial needs shown in the figure will be financed in the following way:

a. Total internal sources			$ 200,000
b. External sources			
Equity			
Shareholders	$200,000		
Risk capital	50,000	$250,000	
Long-term borrowings			
Conventional	400,000		
Risk capital	25,000	425,000	
Short-term borrowings			
Conventional	100,000		
Risk capital	25,000	125,000	
Total external sources			800,000
Total financing requirements			$1,000,000

You can see that business can raise money from a wide range of sources and in many forms. Sources are institutions that provide funds and include commercial banks, investment bankers, equipment vendors, government agencies, private venture capital investors, suppliers, trust companies, life insurance companies, mortgage companies, individuals (angels), institutional investors, and shareholders. Forms are the financing instruments used to buy assets or to pay for the growth of a business. They include share capital (common and preferred), risk capital, mortgages, bonds, lease financing, short-term loans (secured or unsecured), term or installment loans, and revolving loans.

Table 8.1 groups the forms and sources of external financing into four categories: equity, long-term, intermediate, and short-term financing. When choosing the right form and source of financing, the following should be considered:

- Firm's annual debt commitments or obligations
- Cost of financing
- Risk factors from a slowdown (or acceleration) in economic or market conditions
- Control factors (related to existing shareholders)
- Flexibility to respond to future financing decisions
- Pattern of the capital structure in the industry
- Stability of the company's earnings
- Common shareholders' expectations

Table 8.1 Forms and Sources of Financing

Financial Needs	Forms	Sources
	Equity financing	
Intangible assets: R & D, promotional programs	Retained earnings	Reinvested earnings
	Share capital (common and preferred)	Ownership investment
	Grants and contributions	Institutional investors
		Government-backed corporations
		Private investors
	Long-term debt financing	
Capital assets: Property, plant, and equipment	Leases (services, financial, sale, and leaseback)	Leasing companies
	Bonds	Investment dealers
	Mortgages (secured and unsecured)	Pension, insurance and trust companies, chartered banks
	Subordinated debts	Government agencies
		Venture capitalists/private investors

(continued)

Table 8.1 Forms and Sources of Financing (continued)

	Intermediate financing	
Capital assets: Property, plant, and equipment	Term loans	Chartered banks
	Leases (as above)	Trust companies
		Finance companies
		Leasing companies
	Short-term financing	
Flexible current assets: Inventories	Inventory financing (general lien, floor planning, warehouse financing)	Confirming institutions
	Consignment	Suppliers
Trade receivables	Trade receivables financing	Factoring companies
Cash	Line of credit	Chartered banks
	Seasonal loan	
	Revolving credit	
	Notes payable	
	Single loan	
	Trade credit	Suppliers
Durable current assets: Inventories and trade receivables	Working capital loans	Chartered banks

Problem-Solving Example 8.1

Financial Needs and Financing Requirements

For the following accounts, distinguish between the financial needs and the financing requirements: withdrawal of term deposits ($2,000), car ($22,000), car loan ($18,000), The Bay charge account ($2,500), mortgage ($120,000), computer ($1,300), withdrawal of mutual funds ($50,000), MasterCard ($3,000), television ($1,200), furniture ($5,000), line of credit ($10,000), cottage ($170,000), house renovations ($10,000), and bank loan ($4,000).

Solution

Financing Requirements		Financial Needs	
Term deposits	$ 2,000	Car	$ 22,000
Car loan	18,000	Computer	1,300
The Bay	2,500	Television	1,200
Mortgage	120,000	Furniture	5,000
Mutual funds	50,000	Cottage	170,000
MasterCard	3,000	Renovations	10,000
Line of credit	10,000		
Bank loan	4,000		
Total	$209,500		$209,500

Self-Test Exercise 8.1

Financial Needs and Financing Requirements

For one of their stores, Len and Joan want to invest some cash and are considering obtaining the financing from different sources. With the following information, list Len and Joan's financial needs and financing requirements.

Short-term borrowings	$4,000	Inventories	$8,000
Trade receivables	4,000	Computers	4,000
Furniture	6,000	Depreciation	3,000
Suppliers	2,000	Chartered bank	4,000
Profit for the year	6,000	Len and Joan	3,000

Answers to the Self-Test Exercises can be found at www.bergeron7e.nelson.com.

Internal versus External Financing

2 Differentiate between internal financing and external financing.

Internal sources Funds generated by a business (e.g., profit for the year, depreciation/amortization).

External sources Funds provided by investors (shareholders and lenders).

In Chapter 3, you learned that businesses obtain financing from two sources: internal and external. **Internal sources** are funds generated by the business itself. For example, look back at Table 3.9, which shows the principal sources of internal financing under the heading "Operating activities." These include profit for the year and depreciation/amortization. A decrease in working capital accounts is also a source of internal financing. **External sources** are funds obtained from investors. Under the heading "Financing activities" in Table 3.9 are the two principal sources of external financing: shareholders (equity) and lenders (loans). Equity financing can come from conventional and risk capital investors. Similarly, debt financing can also come from conventional lenders (e.g., banks, suppliers, insurance companies) and risk capital investors (e.g., factoring companies, confirming institutions). This chapter deals primarily with external financing. First, though, let's see how a business can generate its own cash.

Profit for the year and depreciation/amortization are the main sources of internal cash flows. To calculate the amount of cash generated by a business, we look at the statement of income and the statement of changes in equity (retained earnings section). From Eastman Technologies Inc.'s statement of cash flows, also shown in Table 3.9, we find the following:

Profit for the year	$97,500
Depreciation/amortization	40,000
Total cash generated by the business	137,500
Dividends paid to shareholders	(47,500)
Cash retained in the business	$90,000

After Eastman pays income taxes and dividends, $90,000 will be reinvested into the business. These funds can be used to purchase non-current assets, help finance working capital accounts, or reduce the principal on the debt.

Working capital is also an important source of financing. Working capital accounts, such as inventories and trade receivables, usually increase when a business grows. However, if a business is in financial difficulty, it can reduce the level of its net working capital and generate extra funds.

Let's see how a business can generate funds from its inventories and trade receivables accounts. To illustrate the calculation, we'll use Eastman Technologies Inc.'s statement of income and statement of financial position, shown in Chapter 2 in Tables 2.2 and 2.4.

In 2013, Eastman had $218,000 in inventories with an inventory turnover of 8.7 times ($1,900,000 ÷ $218,000). If management sets an inventory target of 10 times, it can reach this by being more efficient with purchasing and using better inventory management control systems. The 10-time ratio would reduce inventories to $190,000 ($1,900,000 ÷ 10), thus generating an additional one-time cash inflow of $28,000.

The statement of financial position also shows trade receivables of $300,000, with an average collection period of 44 days. If management wants to reduce this to 30 days, it needs to do it without lowering sales performance. Management may choose to use a more restrictive credit policy. With an average daily sales performance of $6,849 ($2,500,000 ÷ 365) and a collection period target of 30 days, trade receivables could be reduced to $205,470 ($6,849 × 30) from $300,000. This would produce an additional one-time inflow of cash of $94,530.

Problem-Solving Example 8.2

Cash Inflows from Working Capital Accounts

How much cash would be generated in 2014 if a company's statement of financial position for the year 2013 shows the following balances: inventories ($100,000), trade receivables ($80,000), trade payables ($70,000). In 2014, the account balances are inventories ($80,000), trade receivables ($75,000), and trade payables ($65,000).

Solution

Cash inflow is $20,000.

	2013	2014	Cash Sources
Inventories	$100,000	$80,000	$20,000
Trade receivables	80,000	75,000	5,000
Trade payables	70,000	65,000	(5,000)
Cash inflow			$20,000

Self-Test Exercise 8.2

Raising Cash from Working Capital Accounts

How much additional cash could Len and Joan obtain from their working capital accounts by the end of 2014 if they improved the average collection period by two days and the inventory turnover by 0.5 times? In 2014, CompuTech's inventories account was $65,000 and its trade receivables account was $45,000. The company's 2014 revenue is estimated at $420,000 and its cost of sales is estimated at $209,000.

Answers to the Self-Test Exercises can be found at www.bergeron7e.nelson.com.

Risk-Related Financing Options

3 Explain the types of risk-related financing options (ownership versus debt).

Once the company's financial needs have been identified and the financing requirements are known, the next step is to decide which instruments (or forms) could be used to finance the expansion. Financing forms include conventional financing instruments and risk-capital financing instruments.

It's important to understand that each financing form has different costs. Risk is the key to determining that cost, and there is a direct relationship between risk (the variability of returns, or the chance of losing on the investment) and return (what investors expect to earn). As risk of a project or business increases, the return (or cost of capital) that investors expect on their money will also increase.

Companies face three types of risk: business risk, financial risk, and instrument risk.

Business risk
The uncertainty built into projecting the level of revenue and EBIT.

Business risk is built into a firm's operations. It has to do with the uncertainty of projecting the future revenue and earnings before interest and taxes (EBIT). The industry and economic environment in which a firm operates create business risk. A high-tech firm, for example, faces a great deal more business risk than a food processing business. Future demand and product life cycle for food are easier to predict than for most technology products. General economic cycles and changing industry conditions cause business variations. This is the most important influence on a firm's capital structure (debt versus equity).

Financial risk
The way that a business is financed (debt versus share capital).

Financial risk has to do with a firm's capital structure. In general, the more debt a firm has, the greater the risk of insolvency and hence the riskier it is to finance the business. Financial risk is also placed on common shareholders when management decides to use more debt. Highly leveraged firms (those with a lot of debt) may not have the financial strength to ride out a long sales decline or an economic slowdown. Financial risk can magnify business risk because the company relies on fixed costs (finance costs) or the amount of cash needed to pay for the loans.

Instrument risk
The quality of security available to satisfy investors.

Instrument risk is the quality of the security (the collateral) available to satisfy investors (e.g., secured versus unsecured loans). For example, a first mortgage loan is less risky (because of the guarantees or collateral) than a second mortgage. A conditional sales contract is less risky than financing trade receivables through factoring (having another company buy the trade receivables at a discount).

Figure 8.2 **Risk-Related Financing Options (Risk versus Return)**

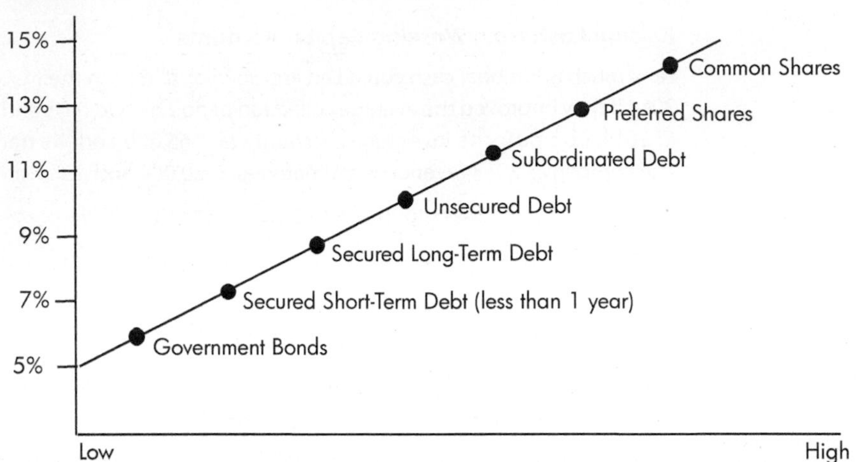

Management must also balance business risk and financial risk. For instance, a firm with a low level of business risk can use more debt financing than a business with a high level of business risk. When risks are high, the financing instruments (common shares versus risk capital) must offer a high rate of return to attract investors. Figure 8.2 shows the risk curve, which is the relationship between risk and return for different financing instruments.

Although equity appears to need a high return, for a growing business, it is often the most stable and appropriate source of capital. Conventional financing, which is generally provided by commercial banks, credit unions, and trust companies, tends to accept a lower return; the risk related to the investment is low because collateral is used to guarantee these loans. Collateral is something of value put up against a loan taken by the lender if the loan is not repaid. In contrast, high-risk investors tend to invest in projects with higher levels of risk and, for this reason, will demand a higher rate of return.

Strategies: Matching Principle, Lender Criteria, and Creditworthiness

4 Explain useful strategies for approaching lenders.

Let's examine the strategies that can be useful when approaching lenders: the matching principle, the criteria used by investors to rate borrowers, and the ways in which a business can make itself creditworthy.

THE MATCHING PRINCIPLE

The matching principle is used to fit the time span of the financial needs to the length of time the funds are required (financing requirements). For example, an individual would use a credit card to buy a watch and a mortgage to buy a house. Similarly, a business would use a line of credit to finance its working capital needs and a mortgage to buy capital assets. This principle considers two factors: cost and risk.

For example, in Figure 8.3, funds are needed to finance capital assets, durable (permanent or fixed) current assets and flexible (or variable) current assets. The matching

Figure 8.3 **Strategies for Financing Working Capital**

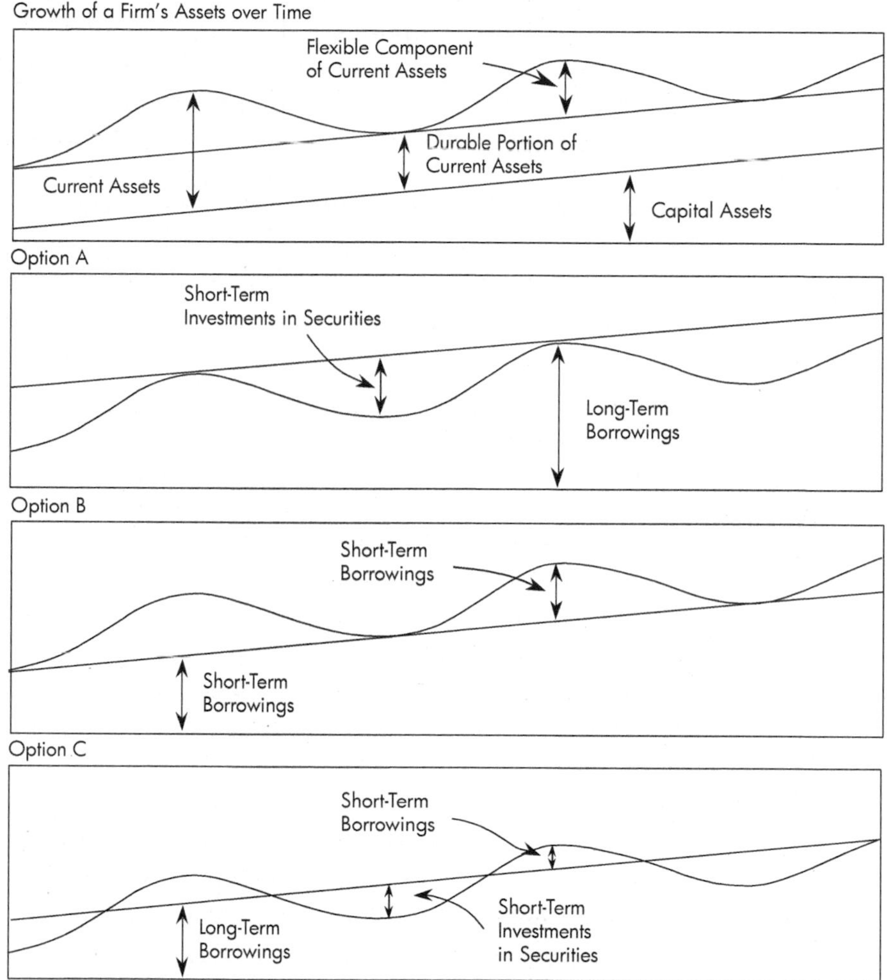

principle says that capital assets should be financed by long-term borrowings and current assets should be financed by short-term credit. The flexible part of the current assets changes depending on the financial needs of a business. Durable current assets are necessary to operate a business, and flexible current assets vary with business conditions.

Three strategies can be used to finance current asset (or working capital) accounts. In the first strategy (option A), all current assets are financed by long-term borrowings; this is the most conservative strategy but the most costly. It is not risky because the business always has enough debt to meet its current needs. However, it is costly because excess cash can be invested only in short-term securities. The return on short-term investments (say, 3%) is far less than the cost of a loan (say, 6%).

In the second strategy (option B), all current assets are financed by short-term borrowings. This option is risky because interest rates may rise when it is time to renew a loan, and the lender may refuse to renew the loan.

The third strategy (option C) is a compromise between the first option (conservative and more costly) and the second (risky and less expensive). In this option, the business uses a small amount of short-term credit to meet peak seasonal working capital requirements. During the off-season, excess cash is kept in marketable securities (recall that marketable securities can be converted into cash quickly). The crests above the line in Figure 8.3 represent short-term borrowings; the troughs below the line represent holdings in short-term securities.

CRITERIA USED BY INVESTORS TO RATE BORROWERS

Investors need certain information before they put money in a business. Some of the information is provided by the business, and investors will obtain the rest through their own research and networking. Investors judge potential borrowers by using six criteria, commonly referred to as the **C's of credit**: character, collateral, capacity, capital, circumstances (or conditions), and coverage.

C's of credit
Factors that investors look at to judge a business's creditworthiness: character, collateral, capacity, capital, circumstances, and coverage.

Character means two things to an investor (lender or shareholder). First, the borrower should have the skills and abilities to manage the business professionally and should be serious, dependable, and accountable. Second, investors look for people who are true to their word and appear to feel morally obligated to pay their debt, dividends, or principal as promised.

Collateral is the pledge offered by a business (particularly to lenders) in exchange for a loan. It is like a form of insurance on physical assets, which will become the property of the lender if a business stops operating or is liquidated. This is vital to lenders because the absence of such security increases their risk. Businesses that have a high credit rating may get an unsecured loan, that is, one given on faith and trust; others, however, are obliged to back their borrowings with collateral.

Capacity means two things to investors. First is the ability of a business to generate enough cash to meet its obligations: repayment of principal, finance costs, and dividends. A close look at a business's cash flow forecast or cash budget can show a business's capacity to meet its financial commitments. Second is how capable the management team is in managing a new project or an expanded operation. Do they have the managerial skills (planning, organizing, leading, and controlling) and technical ability in production, marketing, manufacturing, distribution, finance, and competence to expand a business or make a new operation a real success?

Capital refers to a business's financial structure—the mix between equity and the funds provided by lenders. The more money that shareholders have invested in their business, the more confidence the lenders will have about providing a loan.

Circumstances, or *conditions*, refer to the environment the business operates in, specifically the industry's trends in demand, prices, competition, profitability, and government regulations.

Coverage refers mainly to insurance coverage. Most businesses have losses arising from different sources: death of a principal owner or an important partner; damage to the business property from a fire, explosion, or any violent cause; embezzlement, theft, or any dishonest act committed by a shareholder, an officer, or an employee; and public liability lawsuits. Investors feel less vulnerable when businesses to which they have lent money have enough insurance.

The information about the C's of credit is usually required by investors. If the business can't provide it, investors will seek it elsewhere, such as from business contacts, other investors, suppliers, or credit institutions. It is therefore a good strategy to know, before meeting investors, what they are looking for.

MAKING A COMPANY CREDITWORTHY

Making a company creditworthy is the first step to obtaining funds quickly and at a lower rate. Borrowers should look at their business situation from an investor's perspective when hoping to raise funds. They should anticipate investors' questions and carefully think about how to answer them. Although the specifics are different in every situation, here is a broad range of reasons investors tend to reject investment proposals or loan applications:

Factors related to creditworthiness

- Poor earnings record
- Questionable management ability
- Collateral of unsatisfactory quality or quantity
- Slow and past due in trade or loan payments
- Poor accounting system
- New firm with no established earnings record
- High moral risk (poor character)

Factors related to a bank's overall policies

- Not enough equity
- Requested maturity of the loan too long
- Applicant has no established deposit relationship with the lender
- Type of loan not handled by the lender
- Line of business not handled by the lender
- Loan portfolio for the type of loan already full

The rest of this chapter deals with external forms and sources of financing. We'll look at the features, including the advantages and disadvantages of each source, for (1) equity financing, (2) intermediate and long-term financing, and (3) short-term financing.

Equity Financing

5 Discuss the categories of equity financing.

Equity is the interest an owner holds in a business. If a business is privately owned, the owners can also obtain funds from investors that specialize in small and medium-sized business loans and mortgages. In this case, owners of the privately owned business will prepare a business plan and will go directly to specific individuals and ask them to become shareholders of the business.

For publicly owned businesses, the process is more complicated. The owners have to prepare a **prospectus**, which is a document that discloses the details of a security

Prospectus
A document that discloses the details of a security and the underlying business to prospective investors.

and the underlying business to prospective investors, and then approach an investment dealer to raise funds from the public through a public issue. The investment dealer buys the securities from the firm and sells them to the general public.

The investment dealer plays a key role in raising funds from the public. As discussed, long-term financing can come from two distinct sources: *shareholders*, when funds are raised by issuing shares, and *lenders*, when money is in the form of a loan, such as bonds or mortgages. Investment dealers (or investment bankers) help in the financing of businesses by buying (wholesale) issues of bonds or shares and reselling them (retail) to their clients. Investment dealers borrow the money they need to pay for the issue. Usually, they get it from banks on a very short-term basis, and they repay their lenders when the issue sells out. This process may take a week or two, or it may all be completed in one day.

The cost of public issues of bonds or shares is high because many legal details must be taken care of. The process is long, requiring approval by at least one provincial securities commission, and sometimes by several, depending on where the bonds or shares are issued. Thus, this source of funds can be used only periodically and for large amounts of money. New firms are usually either too small to use investment dealers or find their services (which may cost as much as 10% to 25% of the funds raised) too expensive. Table 8.2 summarizes the steps involved in making a public issue.

Table 8.2	Steps Involved in Making a Public Issue
Step 1	The firm decides to list (or not to list) its issue on an exchange (e.g., Toronto Stock Exchange).
Step 2	The firm selects one or more investment dealers who will be responsible for buying and selling the issue, called the underwriter(s).
Step 3	A meeting takes place between the issuing company and the underwriter(s) to discuss the amount of capital to be raised, the type of security to be issued, and the general terms of the issue.
Step 4	A preliminary prospectus is prepared. The preliminary prospectus discloses important aspects of the issue and forms the basis of the agreement among all parties.
Step 5	A public accounting firm audits the company's financial situation, and management prepares the required financial statements to be included in the preliminary prospectus.
Step 6	After it is signed, the preliminary prospectus is filed with the provincial securities commission. It takes around 15 business days for the staff of the securities commission to read the prospectus, evaluate the accuracy of the data and content, and ensure that nothing is missing or misrepresented in the document.
Step 7	After clearance is given by the securities commission, the final prospectus is prepared and final clearance is given. An underwriting agreement is signed by the issuing company and the underwriter that lays out the date of the issue, the price that the underwriter will pay, and the commission.

Let's now turn to the major sources of equity funds: shareholders, risk capital investors, and government institutions.

SHAREHOLDERS

Shareholders
The owners of a business (common and preferred shareholders).

Funds can come from **shareholders** who buy common shares and preferred shares. The owners (shareholders) of a business provide common share financing. The rights of shareholders of common shares are listed in Table 8.3.

To a company, the advantage of issuing *common shares* is that they do not have fixed charges. Unlike a mortgage payment, dividends are paid only when earnings are generated. Common shares do not have fixed maturity dates and can be sold more easily than debt.

Preferred share financing has some characteristics of both common share and debt financing. The preferred share appears in the equity section of the statement of financial position. Although this type of financing is considered equity, preferred shareholders do not have the same rights as common shareholders.

Equity financing has several advantages: (1) it is low risk, (2) dividends are paid when profit is made, (3) it has no restrictions that could cause a default, and (4) it provides stability and permanency. But it has some significant disadvantages: (1) voting rights or control is extended to additional shareholders, (2) more owners can share the right in profit (which dilutes the equity interest), (3) underwriting cost can be expensive, and (4) dividends are not tax deductible.

RISK CAPITAL INVESTORS

Risk capital investors
Individuals or institutions that provide money to finance a business that entails relatively high risk; these investors seek a high potential return.

Risk capital investors provide equity financing to small or new businesses, thereby absorbing much of the risk that commercial lenders are unwilling to take. Commercial lenders are rarely interested in inventions that need more research, development,

Table 8.3 Shareholders' Collective and Specific Rights

Collective Rights
- Change articles of incorporation
- Adopt and change bylaws
- Elect the directors of the corporation
- Authorize the sale of capital assets
- Authorize mergers and amalgamations.
- Change the number of authorized common and preferred shares
- Alter the rights and restrictions attached to common shares
- Create a right of exchange of other shares into common shares

Specific Rights
- Vote in the manner set out by the corporate charter
- Sell their shares to other parties
- Inspect corporate accounting books (practical limitations)
- Share in residual assets of the corporation (last among the claimants)

and engineering. They have preferences about the companies they want to support. These preferences are usually based on the type, history, and status of the company, and the amount of financing needed.

Conversely, risk capital investors prefer to deal with companies whose products have potential or are already selling well but lack the capital to make the most of their markets. Risk capital investors generally provide equity financing or both equity and long-term debt financing (e.g., subordinated debt).

Risk capital investments are unique in the following ways:

- They apply mostly to fast-growth businesses.
- Usually, several years are required before the risk capital investors can liquidate their investment or make an exit.
- During the early years, there is usually no organized secondary market (also called an aftermarket) in which previously issued financial instruments, such as stocks and bonds, are bought and sold (e.g., a batch of loans are sold by a bank to investors).
- The new firm faces a high risk of failure.
- Several cash injections are usually necessary before the new enterprise begins to show a profit.

Risk capital investment has six categories: embryonic, start-up, development, expansion, turnaround, or buyout. *Embryonic investments* are made in firms developing a new product or process up to the point where it is possible to make a prototype. *Start-up investments* are made in new firms just getting started with a new product or service in an established market. *Development investments* are made in small firms that are already in production and just about to realize profits but do not have enough cash flow to continue operations. *Expansion investments* are made in smaller firms that need additional productive capacity but don't have enough funds of their own. *Turnaround investments* are made in firms that are having financial trouble but have great potential for profit with more capital and better management. *Buyout investments* are made in established firms with a proven track record whose owners want to sell and retire. Usually, employees are the ones who want to buy the firm but don't have the funds to do so.

Risk capital investors include angel investors, private investors, institutional investors, government-backed corporations, and corporate strategic investors.

Angel Investors

Angel investors are professional investors, retired executives with business experience and money to invest, or high-net-worth individuals looking for investment opportunities. **Angel investors** will usually invest between $25,000 and $300,000 in a venture. Many angels are sophisticated investors and will go through the formal due diligence review, that is, a potential buyer investigates and evaluates a company or its assets before investing in it.

Angel investors
High-net-worth individuals looking for investment opportunities.

Venture capital
Risk capital supplied to small companies by wealthy individuals (angels), partnerships, or corporations, usually in return for an equity position in the firm.

Private Investors

Private investors and **venture capital** firms are individuals or groups of professionals with the experience, contacts, and business skills that can help a business become more profitable. The size of their investment can range from $25,000 to $5 million. Investors in this category have their own preferences, strategies, and investment criteria. While some private firms will be interested in investing in the development stage, many will be interested in companies involved in the expansion, acquisition, and buyout stages. These investors include labour-sponsored venture funds (a venture capital company that is created to invest in small and mid-sized businesses), such as GrowthWorks Canadian Fund, Fonds de solidarité, and Canadian Medical Discoveries Fund.

Institutional Investors

Institutional investors provide equity and subordinated risk capital investment (a debt that ranks after other debts should a company fall into liquidation or bankruptcy) to small- and medium-sized businesses. These investors include subsidiaries of commercial banks, investment banks, certain life insurance companies, and pension funds. These companies fund investments that are less than $1 million, as well as larger ones. Canada has a wide range of such organizations, including BMO Capital Markets, RBC Capital Markets, CIBC Wood Gundy Capital Corporation, Penfund, Desjardins Capital de risqué (ID), Roynat, Ontario Teachers' Pension Plan, and TD Capital.

In the News 8.1 shows how entrepreneurs should prepare themselves when meeting angel investors.

In The News 8.1

UNDERSTANDING THE NEEDS OF ANGEL INVESTORS

An estimated 260,500 angels are active in the United States. It is apparently the largest source of seed money available to entrepreneurs. The only problem is knowing how to approach them. If an entrepreneur is overly enthusiastic about the product or service, an angel can lose interest in the first meeting. Entrepreneurs who give vague or evasive answers to questions could turn off the angel. Entrepreneurs need to do their homework before approaching these important sources: seed money from angel investors helped such American icons as Starbucks, FedEx, Amazon, and Google get off the ground.

Three Ottawa-based entrepreneurs who knew how to approach venture capitalists will receive $1.95 million in seed money from the Federal Economic Development Agency for Southern Ontario to start their businesses. Toushay Inc., a software developer working to allow businesses to make and manage mobile applications, will receive $750,000. Protecode Inc., a manufacturer of products to help businesses manage software licenses, will receive $680,000. Bendria Corp., a developer of a new notification system to be used with social media to track down software, will get $517,250.

Source: Vito Pilieci, "Ottawa startups secure $2M in federal money." May 8, 2012, *Ottawa Citizen*, p. D1. For more information about the Federal Economic Development Agency for Southern Ontario, visit www.actionplan.gc.ca/initiatives/eng/index.asp?initiativeId=103. Material reprinted with the express permission of Ottawa Citizen, a division of Postmedia Network Inc.

Government-Backed Corporations

Government-backed corporations invest in smaller, regional communities where mainstream investors are less active. For example, the Atlantic Canada Opportunities Agency provides support to businesses located in the Atlantic provinces. The Business Development Bank of Canada is unique because it offers counselling, training, and mentoring, as well as the following types of financing:

- Venture loans (between $100,000 and $1 million) for expansion and market development projects
- Working capital for growth funding (up to $100,000)
- Patient capital, directed at knowledge-based businesses in the early stages of development; offered on a long-term basis (up to $25,000)
- Micro-business programs for training and counselling to very small companies, along with up to $25,000 for new businesses and up to $50,000 for existing businesses

Corporate Strategic Investors

Corporate strategic investors differ from traditional venture capital companies in that their motivation is more than financial. Their business agreements are referred to as strategic alliances or corporate partnerships. A strategic investor may have a broad range of objectives that include enhancing innovation, gaining exposure to new markets and technologies, identifying companies with the potential to buy, ensuring sources of supply, assisting a client, starting new ventures internally, and spinning off businesses that might be profitable but are not appropriate for the original firm.

GOVERNMENT INSTITUTIONS

Government financing Funds obtained (directly or indirectly) from government or government institutions to finance a business.

Government financing is a direct or an indirect form of financial assistance to businesses offered by a municipal, provincial or territorial, or federal agency to help businesses with capital expenditure projects or expansion. Government financing (or programs) can be grouped into two broad categories: allowances for income tax purposes, and grants (direct and indirect). Federal financing aid can come from non-refundable grants, refundable grants, conditionally refundable grants, equity participation, direct loans, guarantee of loans, remission of tariff (in which the government relaxes or removes import fees on needed goods), export financing, cost sharing, fees for counselling, training grants, and small business loans. Provincial or territorial financing aid can come from forgivable loans, direct loans (mortgage, small business loans), working capital loans, training grants, guarantee of loans, equity participation, inventory financing, leasebacks (in which the business sells an asset and then leases it back long term), and venture capital. Municipal financing aid can come through free land, deferred property taxes, and industrial sites (e.g., infrastructure assistance).

The more important governmental financial institutions include Export Development Canada (EDC), Farm Credit Canada (FCC), the Business Development Bank of Canada (BDC), and provincial or territorial venture capital organizations.

Export Development Canada

Export Development Canada is a Crown corporation that provides a wide variety of financial services, including export insurance, bonds, loans, and lines of credit to both Canadian exporters and foreign buyers of Canadian goods. Canadian exporters can insure their export sales against non-payment by foreign buyers for up to 90% of the value of the shipments. This insurance can cover commercial and political risks of insolvency, default, repudiation by the buyer, cancellation of import licences, blockage of funds, and war. Virtually any export transaction can be insured by EDC, which provides export financing at either fixed or floating interest rates to foreign buyers of Canadian goods. The money is paid in Canada directly to the exporting company, so the export sale is a cash sale for the Canadian firm. EDC can operate either on its own account or for the Canadian government when it would like to help exports in ways that fall outside the more commercial transactions normally made by EDC.

Farm Credit Canada

Farm Credit Canada is a Crown corporation created in 1959 to help individual Canadian farmers to establish, develop, or maintain their farms. The corporation also makes farm loans to groups of farmers organized to share the use of farm machinery, specialized farm buildings, and equipment. Loans made by FCC are usually made at fixed interest rates based on the combined overall cost of funds to FCC. These loans can be for terms of five to 15 years, with amortization as long as 30 years.

An important innovation is the shared-risk mortgage, which was introduced in 1985. The interest rate on this type of loan is adjusted each year. The FCC and the farmer equally share the interest rate increases and decreases, up to a maximum of 2.5%. The normal term of the shared-risk mortgage is six years, and the loan limit is $350,000 for individuals or $600,000 for partnerships.

Another innovation is the commodity-based loan program. Payments are calculated by linking the loan principal amount to a price index of one or two of the major commodities produced on the farm. If prices go up by 5%, for example, then both the principal of the loan and the periodic payments would also increase by 5%. Financial advisory services are also offered to new and existing borrowers.

The Business Development Bank of Canada

The Business Development Bank of Canada is a Crown corporation established in 1975 (under the name Federal Business Development Bank) to promote and assist in the establishment and development of small and medium-sized Canadian businesses. It provides three types of services: financial (loans and loan guarantees), venture capital, and management (counselling, training, information, and financial planning). The BDC concentrates on helping new businesses that cannot obtain funds from other sources. It is, therefore, a supplemental or last resort lender. It tends to concentrate its efforts on helping companies in manufacturing, wholesale and retail trade, and tourism.

The BDC provides loans, loan guarantees, equity financing, or any combination in whatever way best fits the needs of the firm. The BDC provides funds for start-ups, modernization, expansion, change of ownership, or other business purposes to firms unable to obtain financing from other sources on reasonable terms and conditions. Term loans can be used to finance capital assets, such as buildings, land, machinery, or equipment, with the assets used as collateral. In some cases, term loans can also be made to finance working capital needs.

Provincial and Territorial Venture Capital Organizations

Most provinces and territories have legislation allowing private investors to set up small business development companies to supply venture capital. In some provinces, such as Manitoba, the provincial government matches 35% of the capital raised by private investors. In Ontario, the provincial government provides a tax-free cash grant of 30% of the investor's contribution, thus reducing the risk for individual investors. Some provinces have direct financing programs for small businesses that meet the criteria. These programs change frequently.

The Small Business Loans Act

The *Small Business Loans Act* (SBLA) is a federal law intended to help new and existing small businesses obtain financing for capital assets from the chartered banks and other designated lenders (trust companies, credit unions, and caisses populaires) according to normal commercial procedures. The federal government guarantees the loans. The maximum amount is $100,000, and the maximum term is 10 years. The interest rate is usually prime plus and fluctuates as the prime rate changes. SBLA loans are restricted to firms whose gross revenues do not exceed $2 million annually.

Sources and Forms of Intermediate and Long-Term Debt Financing

6 Discuss the sources and forms of intermediate and long-term debt financing.

We will differentiate intermediate financing from long-term debt financing simply by the length of time funds are borrowed. Intermediate financing refers to two- to five-year loans, while long-term financing refers to those of more than five years. We'll first discuss long-term loans for the purchase of capital assets.

CONVENTIONAL INTERMEDIATE AND LONG-TERM DEBT FINANCING

Long-term loan
A loan to finance capital assets for a long period (more than five years).

Intermediate and **long-term loans** usually finance capital (or non-current) assets. These may be straightforward term loans, usually secured by the physical asset itself. Banks, life insurance companies, pension funds, and federal and provincial or territorial government agencies provide longer-term financing on capital assets.

Term Loans

Term loan
A loan made to buy capital assets.

Term loans are a main form of medium-term financing used to buy capital assets. They are usually three to seven years; however, in certain circumstances, the maturity may be as long as 15 years. In a term loan, the borrower agrees to make to the lender a series of interest and principal payments of specific amounts and on specific dates. This differs from a bank line of credit, whereby repayment is at any time (demand) or at a specified time in one lump sum. The key characteristics of a term loan are the following:

- Terms of the loan are tailored to the needs of the borrower.
- Security is usually in the form of a chattel mortgage on equipment or machinery. In a chattel mortgage, the buyer transfers legal ownership of an asset that can be physically possessed (not a building or other immovable property) to the lender. When the loan is repaid in full, the lender transfers ownership back to the buyer.
- In addition to collateral, the lender may place restrictions on the operations of the business (e.g., no additional borrowings and no increase in salaries to the officers of the company without approval of the lender).
- The loan is repaid through systematic repayments over its term.

Let's take an example of a company that wants to borrow $200,000 at 8% over 10 years. The company would have to pay $29,806 each year to amortize the loan. To find the annual loan repayment, divide the principal ($200,000) by the interest factor (6.7101, from Table D: Present Value Interest Factor of an Annuity in Appendix B at the end of this text). The factor is found in the cell at the intersection of column 8% and year 10. Learning how to use interest tables will be covered in Chapter 10.

Problem-Solving Example 8.3

Annual Loan Payments

Suppose you have a $200,000 first mortgage for 25 years at 4%, and a $25,000 second mortgage for five years at 6%. What is the annual loan payments for each? What is the total interest that you will pay over the lifespan of the loans?

Solution

The first mortgage's yearly payment is $12,802.46 and the second's is $5,935.00. The total interest is $124,737. To calculate these loan repayments, refer to Table D (present value interest factor of an annuity) in Appendix B at the end of the text.

Loan repayment

First mortgage

$$\frac{\$200{,}000}{25 \text{ years @ } 4\%} = \frac{\$200{,}000}{15.6220} = \$12{,}802.46$$

Second mortgage

$$\frac{\$25{,}000}{5 \text{ years @ } 6\%} = \frac{\$25{,}000}{4.2123} = \$5{,}935.00$$

(continued)

Problem-Solving Example 8.3 (continued)

Interest charges

First mortgage	$12,802.46 × 25 = $320,062 − $200,000 =	$ 120,062
Second mortgage	$5,935.00 × 5 = $29,675 − $25,000 =	$ 4,675
Total interest		**$124,737**

Self-Test Exercise 8.3

Annual Loan Payments

a) If the Millers borrow $100,000 for five years at 9%, what would their annual loan payment be?

b) If they borrowed $500,000 for 15 years at 14%, what would their annual loan payment be?

Answers to the Self-Test Exercises can be found at www.bergeron7e.nelson.com.

Conditional Sales Contract

Conditional sales contract
An agreement between a buyer and a seller for the purchase of an asset (e.g., a truck) by installments.

A **conditional sales contract** is a written agreement between a buyer and a seller for the purchase of production equipment or other capital assets on a time-payment basis. The seller accepts a down payment, which is usually at least one-third of the value of the asset; the rest is paid by monthly installments. The seller retains legal ownership until the buyer has made all the payments, usually over 12 to 36 months.

Term loans and conditional sales contracts have several advantages: (1) longer repayment terms, (2) easy access, (3) flexibility, and (4) tax-deductible finance costs. They do have some disadvantages: (1) tie up assets, (2) increase financial risk through cash payments of interest and principal, (3) commit the business because it is subject to penalties, and (4) often include penalties.

Bonds

Bond
A long-term loan (10 to 30 years) that can be secured or unsecured.

Bonds are long-term contracts, typically for 10 to 30 years, under which a borrowing firm agrees to pay principal plus interest, usually semi-annually, to the holders of the bond contract. An investor buys a bond (an annuity) and receives regular payments until the maturity date, when the principal amount is repaid. An indenture is a legal document that spells out the rights of both the bondholders and the issuing firm. A trustee, usually a trust company, represents the bondholders and ensures that the firm lives up to its obligations. The firm pays the interest to the trustee as scheduled, and the trustee then pays the bondholders, who are required to clip coupons off the bond and cash them like cheques. Today, though, actual bond coupons are less common. Electronic records are often used instead.

Bonds may be secured or unsecured. *Secured bonds* are essentially long-term promissory notes. Holders of secured bonds have prior claims over the assets and earnings (similar to first, second, and third mortgages). *Unsecured bonds* are called debentures. Only the earning power of the firm backs them up. Bonds may also be converted into shares of the issuing company, or redeemable before the maturity date, at the request of either the bondholder or the firm. Many variations are possible. The firm does not know who buys the bonds, making bonds an impersonal and inflexible financing method, not suitable for all firms. These unsecured bondholders are similar to general creditors; they have a claim on the residual value of all assets that are free of any other creditor claims.

Mortgages

Mortgage
A loan obtained against which specific real property is used as collateral (e.g., a building).

Mortgages are pledges of specific real estate property, such as land or buildings. Mortgages are long-term financing (e.g., 25 years). The amount of the mortgage is based on the market value of the property. For example, 75% of the market value might be common, but a company may find lenders that will finance up to 90% of the value of an asset. These investors prefer long maturity periods. The repayment schedule is usually based on equal blended payments of interest and principal. The interest rate is fixed for a specific term and depends on the market rate, the length of the term, and availability. Insurance companies, pension funds, chartered banks, and trust companies provide this type of financing.

Let's examine the concept of amortized loans, which are similar to home mortgages and car loans. Debt is amortized when the principal is paid off over the life of the loan. Businesses borrow money from lending institutions, and the loans are amortized over time. An amortized loan is normally structured so that there is a fixed payment, which is usually made on a monthly basis. The payment schedule includes interest and an amount (principal) that reduces the outstanding loan. Each successive payment contains larger proportions of principal repayment and smaller amounts of interest.

Let's examine the makeup of a loan amortization schedule for $300,000 with a 10% interest rate paid over 10 years. The annual repayment schedule is shown in the table below. Over the 10-year period, the company pays $488,230, which comprises $188,230 in interest and $300,000 in principal for the repayment of the original loan. Here's how the calculation works: First, the yearly repayment of $48,823 is determined by dividing the $300,000 loan by the factor 6.1446 (column 2). This factor, which represents the 10% interest rate for 10 years, is from Table D in Appendix B. The yearly interest payment is then calculated. During the first year, the $30,000 shown in column 3 is the 10% interest multiplied by the $300,000 original loan (column 1). In the next step, we deduct the $30,000 interest payment from the $48,823 payment to determine the principal that will be paid in that particular year. In year 1, the principal repayment is $18,823 (column 4). Finally, the ending balance (column 5) is calculated by deducting the principal repayment from the beginning balance. As shown, the ending balance in year 1 is $281,177. This figure is used in column 1 for year 2. The same calculations are done for the interest and principal payments for the succeeding nine years (small rounding errors are common in such schedules).

Period	Beginning Balance	Payment	Interest @ 10%	Principal Reduction	Ending Balance
	1	2	3	4	5
1	$300,000	$ 48,823	$ 30,000	$ 18,823	$281,177
2	281,177	48,823	28,117	20,706	260,471
3	260,471	48,823	26,047	22,776	237,695
4	237,695	48,823	23,769	25,054	212,641
5	212,641	48,823	21,264	27,559	185,082
6	185,082	48,823	18,508	30,315	154,767
7	154,767	48,823	15,476	33,347	121,420
8	121,420	48,823	12,142	36,681	84,739
9	84,739	48,823	8,474	40,349	44,390
10	44,390	48,823	4,433	44,390	—
Total		$488,230	$188,230	$300,000	

Mortgage financing has its advantages: (1) a long-term commitment without equity dilution, (2) the maturity matches the long life of the assets, (3) the interest is tax deductible, and (4) it's a relatively inexpensive source of financing. It does have some disadvantages too: (1) it's fairly rigid financing, (2) it increases financial risk because of the fixed stream of interest and principal repayments, and (3) it's subject to penalties if the company misses a payment.

Problem-Solving Example 8.4

Repayment Schedule

Calculate the annual repayment, interest, and principal on the $25,000 second mortgage presented in the Problem-Solving Example 8.3.

Solution

Year	Loan Balance	Loan Payment	Interest (6%)	Principal Reduction
1	$25,000	$ 5,935	$1,500	$ 4,435
2	20,565	5,935	1,234	4,701
3	15,864	5,935	952	4,983
4	10,881	5,935	653	5,282
5	5,599	5,935	336	5,599
Total		$29,675	$4,675	$25,000

Self-Test Exercise 8.4

Repayment Schedule

Calculate the annual repayment, interest, and principal on the $100,000 loan presented in Self-Test Exercise 8.3a.

Answers to the Self-Test Exercises can be found at www.bergeron7e.nelson.com.

RISK CAPITAL LONG-TERM FINANCING

Risk capital investors invest in equity shares and equity-related debt in relatively small or untried businesses, thereby absorbing much of the risk that commercial lenders are unwilling to take. These investors prefer dealing with companies whose products are already selling and are successful but that haven't yet made the most of their markets.

Subordinated debt
A loan that is risky, for which investors charge higher interest rates.

Subordinated debt is a loan for which the lender accepts a higher level of risk than conventional loan sources would. This loan is riskier because it is subordinate to other debt, that is, the creditor is paid last if the company goes bankrupt. These loans have interest rates that typically range from 8% to 12%. However, the overall rate of return to the investor will be higher, even as much as 15% to 25% per year. This type of financing is good only if a business has exhausted secured financing (e.g., term loans based on capital assets, or short-term financing based on current assets, are not available). Subordinated debt is best suited to rapidly growing companies, expansion programs, management and leverage buyouts, and acquisitions. In a leveraged buyout, a significant amount of borrowed money (bonds or loans) is used to make the purchase.

Effectively, these investors can structure the instrument to share in the expected success of the company in a few ways:

- Royalties (percentage of net cash flow generated from operation)
- Participation fees (charging a fee for providing financing)
- Normal cost of common shares
- Warrants or options to purchase shares
- Rights to convert debt into common shares

Subordinated debt repayments can be tailored to individual businesses. With these extra incentives, there is less risk of the borrower defaulting than with conventional long-term financing. Sources of subordinated debt include private-sector venture capital firms, institutional investors, labour-sponsored funds, and government-sponsored corporations.

Subordinated debt financing has some advantages: (1) it is flexible and can be tailored, (2) it is less expensive than equity, (3) there is little dilution of equity, (4) it fills a financing gap, and (5) it offers high leverage availability (more debt than equity). It has some disadvantages as well: (1) it takes time to access, (2) it's expensive relative

Table 8.4 Choosing Long-Term Financing

	Payout of Income	Control	Risk
Common shares	Paid after interest and preferred share dividends; by decision of the board of directors, all or a portion of the remaining funds may be retained by the business or distributed in the form of dividends.	Common shareholders have the legal right to make all major decisions and to elect the board of directors. They have the ultimate control of the corporation.	Because they have the last priority of claims in the event of liquidation, they bear the highest risk of any claimants.
Preferred shares	Dividends are paid before common dividends and may be cumulative if they are not paid during a specific year.	Preferred shareholders sometimes have a right to elect some of the directors on the board of directors (minority).	They have priority over the common shareholders regarding the assets (in the event of liquidation) and earnings for payment of dividends.
Long-term debt	There is a fixed payment of interest, which is made in the form of a sinking fund (periodic repayment of a debt).	Usually, long-term creditors do not have the right to vote. However, if the bond goes into default, the bondholders may be able to take control of the company.	Bondholders have the first claim (secured) over the assets of a company (in the event of liquidation) and earnings.

to other sources of debt financing and set-up costs are high, (3) it does not provide the stability of equity, and (4) restrictive covenants often apply.

The payout of income, control, and risk factors related to common share financing, preferred share financing, and long-term debt are listed in Table 8.4.

In the News 8.2 shows how a capital restructuring program can help an organization in need of cash to bring new products to market.

In The News 8.2

CAPITAL RESTRUCTURING CAN GIVE AN ORGANIZATION A SECOND LIFE

When it takes a long time to bring a product to market, it can have serious effects on cash flow. Some products need a great deal of product development before they gain market acceptance, and that can take years and a considerable amount of cash. Sometimes, financial restructuring or turnaround investments are necessary.

(continued)

In The News 8.2 (continued)

This is where Quebec biotech entrepreneur Dr. Francesco Bellini found himself early in 2012 when he announced a deal to refinance his company after what was to be a blockbuster drug to treat Alzheimer's disease had collapsed in clinical trials. Bellini's Bellus Health Inc. converted most of its $30.4 million debt and preferred shares into common equity and obtained $17 million from Pharmascience Inc., a Montreal-based private generic drug company. This refinancing package will ensure that the company has enough cash to test and market another drug named Kiacta that has the potential to treat a rare kidney ailment.

Source: Sean Silcoff, "Deal buys time to bring kidney disease treatment to market." *Globe and Mail.* Retrieved from http://www.theglobeandmail.com/report-on-business/deal-buys-time-to-bring-kidney-disease-treatment-to-market/article2394583/, accessed April 9, 2012. For more information about Health Inc., visit www.bellushealth.com/english/home.

Sources and Forms of Short-Term Financing

7 Discuss the most important sources and forms of short-term financing.

Short-term financing Financing for less than one year (e.g., trade credit, line of credit).

Supplier credit Financing from suppliers (trade payables).

Short-term financing can come from suppliers (trade credit), chartered banks (trust companies), and specialized lenders that finance current assets, such as inventories (confirming institutions) and trade receivables (factoring companies) on a secured basis for less than one year.

SUPPLIER CREDIT

Supplier credit is also known as trade financing. Almost all businesses use trade credit. When a firm (purchaser) buys goods or services from another firm (supplier), the purchaser does not have to pay for the goods or services immediately. The debt becomes outstanding to the supplier. Invoices for materials, supplies, and services from suppliers are not received until after the materials are delivered or the services are performed. However, if a business can extend its trade payables, it can be an excellent source of financing. For example, if a company pays its bills within 30 days but then arranges to extend payments by an extra 15 days (to 45 days), this could generate more cash inflows. If the company has $195,000 in trade payables and the cost of purchases is $2,372,500, it could generate an extra $97,500 in cash inflows. Here is the calculation:

Existing trade payables	$195,000
Average daily purchases are $6,500 ($2,372,500 ÷ 365)	
New level of trade payables ($6,500 × 45)	292,500
Additional cash from trade credit	$97,500

Problem-Solving Example 8.5

Cash Gain from Supplier Credit

Calculate the additional cash a company could obtain from suppliers with an additional five-day payment extension. The current trade payables are $100,000, and the cost of sales is $1,200,000.

(continued)

Problem-Solving Example 8.5 (continued)

Solution

The company could obtain an additional $16,395 in cash.

Existing trade payables	$100,000
Average daily purchases is $3,288 ($1,200,000 ÷ 365)	
Average payable period is 30.4 days ($100,000 ÷ $3,288)	
Targeted level of trade payables ($3,288 × 35.4)	116,395
Increased cash inflows from trade payables	$ 16,395

Self-Test Exercise 8.5

Cash Inflows from Supplier Credit

How much additional cash could CompuTech obtain from its trade credit in 2014 if can extend its trade credit by an extra 10 days? The company has trade payables of $20,000 and buys $209,000 in goods from various suppliers.

Answers to the Self-Test Exercises can be found at www.bergeron7e.nelson.com.

This type of debt is shown on the statement of financial position as trade and other payables. This is a very attractive form of financing because, in most instances, buyers do not have to pay for the goods or services for 30 days or sometimes 60 days, and it's interest-free. As a business grows, supplier credit also grows. Trade credit is usually offered to buyers who have a good credit rating. However, it can be dangerous for a business that doesn't know how to use this credit instrument. Businesses that abuse their credit limit and have difficulty paying their suppliers can find their reputations damaged.

Supplier credit has some important advantages: (1) it's the least expensive source of financing, (2) limited documentation is required, (3) it's easy to access, and (4) it doesn't need any controls or security. It also has disadvantages: (1) it's very short term, (2) it's not enough to bridge fully the time between paying for supplies and receiving cash from sales, and (3) if the company defaults on payment, the supplier might cut off future supplies.

Chartered bank
An institution that provides short-term loans, such as seasonal loans, operating loans, or working capital loans.

CHARTERED BANKS AND TRUST COMPANIES

The second most important source of short-term financing is **chartered banks** and trust companies. Banks make short-term loans that usually appear on the borrowing firm's statement of financial position as seasonal loans, operating loans, or working capital loans. These loans can change as often as daily to cover expected cash shortfalls.

Borrowers must ask for short-term loans, but they are more flexible than trade credit because the money can be spent on a wider range of business needs. Bank loans can be either unsecured or secured by some form of collateral. Unsecured loans usually cost more.

As a firm's financing needs increase, it usually asks its banker to increase its line of credit. If the bank refuses, the firm may miss out on growth opportunities. Most firms try to choose a bank that is willing to provide service, advice, and counsel; assume some risks; and show loyalty to its customers. A business owner therefore expects to develop a long-term relationship with its banker. When an owner looks for financing, it is best to choose a commercial bank (or branch) that will be an asset, not a liability, to the business. Here are some important attributes to look for when selecting a commercial bank.

Financial counselling. It is a banker's job to know about financial developments, so one of the most valuable jobs that a commercial loan officer can perform for a business is that of external financial expert. Management or owners should look for a bank where the commercial loan officers specialize in businesses of their size and type, and should develop a strong relationship with the person handling the loan.

Loyalty. A commercial bank's loyalty to its customers is very important. Some banks, when times get tough, quickly stop accepting applications for increases in lines of credit (especially for smaller businesses). Other banks will work with a business as much as possible to help ride out the storm.

Degree of loan specialization. It is important that a loan is looked after by the department in the bank that specializes in the business's particular type of loan (e.g., working capital loan, revolving loan).

Understanding the nature of the industry. A banker who knows the industry and its particular financing requirements can be invaluable, save the business time, and provide financial counselling when needed.

Full range of services. Management should choose a bank that offers a full range of banking services.

Reputation. The bank's or branch's reputation for counselling services and providing loans to businesses is also important. Bank loans have much greater variability than other sources of business funds.

Types of bank loans. Most bank loans are short term and self-liquidating; that is, money is lent for a purpose, such as buying inventories, and is repaid from the proceeds of the sale of the inventories. Because firms need to buy inventory before they can sell it, they need to borrow frequently to cover seasonal shortfalls in cash flow (e.g., the pre-Christmas sales season for retailers). Then, at the end of the sales season, they can pay off the loans.

Cost of short-term loans. A typical bank loan might have a maturity of only 90 days. When it is repaid, the bank can lend the money to other firms that have different cash flow patterns. Most of the fixed maturity loans (e.g., 90 days) are made at what is called discount interest, which means that the interest is deducted in advance.

Calculating the cost of financing for the sources of short-term financing is important. The equation used to calculate the annual percentage rate (APR) for short-term loans is as follows:

$$\textbf{APR} = \frac{\textbf{Finance costs}}{\textbf{Loan}} \times \frac{\textbf{365}}{\textbf{Maturity (days)}}$$

To illustrate the use of this equation, let's take the example of a business that borrows $20,000 for six months (182 days) with a $600 finance cost. Assuming that the principal is paid only at maturity, the APR would be 6.02%:

$$\textbf{APR} = (\$600 \div \$20{,}000) \times (365 \div 182) = 6.02\%$$

About half of the outstanding loans of the chartered banks are operating loans, and they are used by businesses to finance inventories and trade receivables. These loans are frequently renewed year after year and basically are quasi-permanent working capital financing. Most of the operating loans are not made on a basis of fixed maturity but on a demand basis. This means that the bank can request payment at any time. Demand loans are risky because if the bank suddenly demands repayment, the company would have no choice but to negotiate another loan with another financial institution. The interest rate on this type of loan is usually floating, not fixed. The floating rate is usually specified as the **prime rate**, which is the rate the banks charge their most creditworthy customers, plus some premium for risk. The cost of bank loans varies for different borrowers at different times because of differences in the risk to the lender. The cost of bank loans also varies over time as economic conditions and interest rates change.

Prime rate
The interest rate that banks charge to their most creditworthy customers.

Because the prime rate is the base interest rate established by the Bank of Canada, commercial banks may charge a slightly higher rate to their customers. Other borrowers pay more, depending on the risk of the loan. A typical operating loan might have a cost stated as prime plus two, meaning that if the prime rate is 3%, the borrower pays 5%. As the prime goes up or down, the loan rate also changes if it is floating. Usually interest is calculated each month and is deducted from the firm's bank account.

Line of Credit

Line of credit
A formal written agreement between a bank and a borrower regarding a loan.

Banks offer different forms of credit to their clients. A **line of credit** is a formal written agreement between a banker and a borrower about the maximum loan that will be made to a business during the year. For instance, a business may estimate that it will need a $20,000 loan during a four-month period to produce goods and to sell them on credit. Although the business may have a high credit rating and may be able to obtain as much as $50,000, the business owner will have to indicate to the loan officer the amount required and when it will be needed. The agreement (based on the cash budget) confirms that the funds will be available as a temporary loan.

A bank line of credit has some advantages: (1) it's fairly quick to access, (2) it's relatively inexpensive and flexible, (3) the loan level changes and maximizes the use of cash, and (4) the interest charges are tax deductible. It has some disadvantages: (1) it increases the financial risk because cash servicing is required, (2) the amount available has a ceiling, (3) if the company experiences problems, the lender can demand/cancel the line and take the security, and (4) the financial risk may be high.

In the News 8.3 illustrates how a single factor, such as higher gas prices, can dampen economic activities, slowing business growth and ultimately reducing debt-seeking activities.

In The News 8.3

ADVERSE RIPPLE EFFECTS ON FUNDRAISING BECAUSE OF HIGHER GAS PRICES

Business owners will put the brakes on expanding their businesses or investing in projects for several reasons; the effects of higher gas prices are one of them. Higher gas prices encourage consumers to change their spending habits by cutting back on travelling, restaurant meals, or big ticket items, such as cars and furniture. Higher gas prices have a ripple effect: (1) gas prices go up, (2) consumers change their buying habits, (3) this puts a squeeze on the economy, (4) businesses sell less, (5) business owners delay capital expenditure investments, and (5) ultimately the need to raise capital dollars from lenders is lessened.

This is the situation Canadian business owners faced early in 2012 when gasoline prices approached record levels. Prices hit $1.40 per litre, up 20 percent. They could go as high as $1.60 or even $1.70 if disruptions take place in the Middle East. As the Bank of Canada Governor Mike Carney points out, higher pump prices are leaving less money for activities that can spur economic growth.

Source: Pain at the pumps starts to squeeze economy. *The Globe and Mail.* Retrieved from http://www.theglobeandmail.com/report-on-business/economy/pain-at-the-pumps-starts-to-squeeze-economy/article2393603/ Accessed April 9, 2012.

Problem-Solving Example 8.6

Average Percentage Rate

Calculate the average percentage rate for a company that wants to increase its inventories by $600,000. It expects the bank to finance at least 70% over four months. The bank's interest charges would be $16,000.

Solution

The average percentage rate would be 11.58%.

		Interest charge	÷	$600,000 (70%)	×	Finance period		
APR	=	($16,000	÷	$420,000)	×	(365 ÷ 120)	=	
		0.0381			×	3.04	=	11.58%

Self-Test Exercise 8.6

The Average Percentage Rate

During the next three months, Len and Joan are considering applying for a bank loan, mostly to finance their inventories. They expect their inventories to increase by $30,000 and hope to obtain 60% financing from the bank. The bank manager said it would cost them $400 in finance costs for three months. What is CompuTech's APR for the three-month loan?

Answers to the Self-Test Exercises can be found at www.bergeron7e.nelson.com.

Cost of pledging trade receivables. A business may want to finance (or pledge) its trade receivables. Here is an example to illustrate how to calculate the APR for financing trade receivables. Let's assume that a bank lends 60% of the trade receivables at 2% above the prime rate of 6%. The bank also charges a 1% service fee of the pledged trade receivables. Both the finance costs and the service fee are payable at the end of each borrowing period. The company's trade receivables total $700,000, and its average collection period is 40 days. As shown below, the percentage rate for financing the trade receivables is 17.1%.

$$\begin{aligned}
\textbf{Loan} &= \textbf{0.60} \times \textbf{pledged trade receivables}\\
&= \textbf{0.60} \times \textbf{\$700,000} = \textbf{\$420,000}\\
\textbf{Finance costs} &= \textbf{(\$420,000} \times \textbf{0.08)} \times \textbf{(40} \div \textbf{365)}\\
&= \textbf{\$3,682}\\
\textbf{Service fees} &= \textbf{\$420,000} \times \textbf{0.01} = \textbf{\$4,200}\\
\textbf{APR} &= \textbf{[(\$3,682 + \$4,200)} \div \textbf{\$420,000]} \times \textbf{(365} \div \textbf{40)} = \textbf{17.1\%}
\end{aligned}$$

Problem-Solving Example 8.7

Cost of Pledging Trade Receivables

Calculate the cost of pledging the trade receivables: trade receivables ($900,000), loan (70% of trade receivables), interest charges (3% over the 4% prime rate), service fees (1.5%); average collection period (45 days).

Solution

The cost of pledging the trade receivables is 13.0%.
Loan = 0.70 of $900,000 = $630,000

Finance costs	=	($630,000 × 0.07)	×	(45 ÷ 365)		
		$ 44,100	×	0.1233	=	$ 5,437
Service fees	=	$630,000	×	0.015	=	9,450
Total						$14,887

(continued)

Problem-Solving Example 8.7 (continued)

Average percentage rate	=	($14,887 ÷ $630,000)	×	(365 ÷ 45)	
		0.024	×	8.111	= 19.5%

Self-Test Exercise 8.7

Cost of Pledging Trade Receivables

During the next six months, Len and Joan will be entering a busy season. They expect their commercial trade receivables to reach $40,000 and want to have the bank finance 70%. The bank charges 9% and an additional 1% service fee of the pledged trade receivables. The average collection period for CompuTech's commercial accounts is 50 days. What is the company's APR for the pledged trade receivables?

Answers to the Self-Test Exercises can be found at www.bergeron7e.nelson.com.

Self-liquidating loan Funds used to finance temporary changes in working capital accounts (e.g., inventories, trade receivables).

Self-Liquidating Loans

Seasonal or **self-liquidating loans** are used by businesses mostly to finance temporary changes in inventories and trade receivables, which are the flexible working capital accounts. For instance, a business that sells ski equipment may have a seasonal borrowing pattern. It may need some financing in July, as inventories begin to accumulate. Once inventories are shipped to retailers in September and October, buyers start to make their payments. Seasonal loans can be secured or unsecured, and interest rates can change over time. Like a demand loan, the bank can call such loans at any time. In most cases, these loans are repaid by installments (amortized over the life of the loan), but they may also be repaid in a lump sum.

Revolving credit The maximum amount of a loan a bank agrees to provide a business (borrower).

Revolving Credit

Revolving credit is similar to a line of credit. In this case, the bank signs an agreement with the borrower (business) to provide credit up to a maximum amount. This type of financing costs a little more because additional fees can be charged by the bank. For instance, if the bank offers a credit limit of $300,000 and the borrower uses only $200,000, the unused portion may be charged a standby fee, say, 0.5%, to compensate the bank for committing itself to the loan.

Interim financing A loan made to a business to help finance a capital project, such as the construction of a new plant, until regular financing is obtained.

Interim Financing

Interim financing, also called bridge financing, is a business loan to help finance a capital project, such as the construction of a new plant or the expansion of an existing one, until regular financing, such as a first mortgage, is received. This financing is called interim because it is used to bridge the time gap (the interim) between the date construction begins and the time the long-term loan is received.

Secured Loan

Firms that can't obtain unsecured credit, such as a line of credit, a seasonal loan, or revolving credit will have to pledge some of their assets as security to obtain a loan. In a **secured loan**, the borrower puts up some assets, such as marketable securities, equipment, machinery, buildings, land, inventories, or trade receivables, as collateral that the lender can claim if the borrower does not follow the loan agreement or if the business is liquidated. Because most of the capital assets are financed by long-term loans (mortgages), short-term lenders will use inventories and trade receivables as collateral to secure short-term loans.

Secured loan
A loan that the borrower guarantees by pledging some assets.

An instrument frequently used by banks is *commercial paper* or *corporate paper*. For larger firms, commercial paper is an alternative to bank loans. The maturity of commercial paper is generally very short but may go as long as one year. When the maturity date arrives, the borrower must pay; extensions are usually not given. Failing to pay on time will damage a firm's reputation and may prevent it from borrowing in the future.

ASSET-BASED FINANCING

Asset-based financing is a form of short-term risk capital financing. Just like a bank line of credit, an asset-based loan has a ceiling amount. It also involves a security pledge of inventories and trade receivables. However, pure asset-based loans differ from bank loans because they rely on collateral rather than being linked to financial forecasts. Therefore, business and financial risk are less of an issue for asset-based lenders than for conventional short-term lenders. However, pricing is higher, and interest charges may range from the prime rate plus 2% to 5% annually.

Asset-based financing
A form of short-term risk capital financing.

Short-term risk capital financing is offered by factoring companies and confirming institutions.

Factoring Companies

In **factoring**, the business sells its trade receivables to finance a business. The customer is told that the invoice has been sold and is asked to make payments directly to the finance company (the factor). This arrangement means the lender takes on all the risk. To reduce the risk, the factor takes over the work of the borrower's credit department. All orders received from customers are sent to the finance company, which does a credit check. Factoring is fairly costly for businesses. It involves a continuing agreement under which the factor purchases trade receivables as they take place. The factor assumes the risk of accounts becoming uncollectable and is responsible for collections. In the past, factoring was used mainly in the apparel, textile, and furniture industries. In other industries, it was considered a sign of poor financial health. Today, factoring appears to be gaining acceptance in many industries.

Factoring
Selling trade receivables to a financial institution.

There are two types of factoring arrangements. In *maturity factoring*, the factor purchases all the business's invoices, paying the face value less a discount or commission. The customer is then told to pay the amount due to the factor by a specific due date, say 30 days. The factor may charge the customer interest on amounts outstanding after the due date.

In *old-line factoring*, the factor becomes a lender of sorts. It will advance funds to the company based on 70% to 90% of the value of an invoice. The factor may charge interest at prime rate plus 2% to 5% annually, as long as the invoice is outstanding. In this case, the company receives cash almost immediately after the sale.

The maximum advance a business can obtain from the factor is limited to the amount of factored trade receivables less the factoring commission, finance costs, and reserve that the factor withholds to cover any returns or allowances by customers.

The factor normally charges a service fee ranging between 1% and 3% of the factored trade receivables to cover the credit-checking costs, collection, and bad debt losses, in addition to the 2% to 5% over the prime rate. These higher costs are partly offset by administrative costs (credit checking, collection, and bad debts) saved by the company selling the trade receivables.

Let's assume that a company has $500,000 in trade receivables with a 60-day average collection period and decides to sell them to a factor. The factor may (1) require a 10% reserve for returns and allowances, (2) charge a 2% factoring commission, and (3) charge an annual interest rate of 3% over prime (assume in this case the prime is 4%). The 10% reserve for returns is not considered a cost of factoring because the factor will return the amount to the company if the customers make no returns or adjustments. Here is the calculation:

Funds advanced by the factor:	
Average level of trade receivables	$500,000
Less: Factoring commission (2%)	(10,000)
Less: Reserve for returns (10%)	(50,000)
Subtotal	440,000
Less: Interest on advance (0.07 × $440,000) × (60 ÷ 365)	(5,063)
Total funds advanced by factor	$434,937
Fees and finance costs calculation:	
Factoring commission	$ 10,000
Finance costs	5,063
Total	$ 15,063

Annual percentage rate = ($15,063 ÷ $434,937) × (365 ÷ 60) = 21.1%

Now, let's assume that the company manages its own trade receivables at a cost of $1,000 a month for administrative fees and clerical costs in addition to $2,000 a month in bad debt losses. This additional information allows the company to determine whether it is worth having a factor handling its trade receivables:

APR = [($15,063 − $6,000) ÷ $434,937)] × (365 ÷ 60) = 12.7%

It costs the company more to use a factor than to administer the trade receivables itself. This calculation is done for a 60-day period. This comparison would be used to make the decision. If the company enters into an agreement with the factor, this type of calculation would be done on a continuous basis.

Confirming Institutions

Confirming institution
An organization that finances inventories.

Inventory is an asset that can serve as excellent security for short-term loans from **confirming institutions**. The major aspect lenders look at before extending inventory financing is the marketability of the inventories. Work-in-process inventories, for example, are poor collateral. Raw materials may be more secure because they can be sold to other manufacturers; finished goods, ready to be shipped to retailers, may not be as good collateral as raw materials. The level of financing on inventories depends largely on the nature of the goods.

Inventories can be financed in a number of ways. First, they can be financed by having a *blanket coverage* or a general lien put on them, such as the one used for trade receivables. Then the lender can claim as collateral a percentage of the business's inventories. This type of arrangement is easy to set up, but the lender takes a risk in that it does not have control over the quality and quantity of the goods in stock.

Second is *floor planning*. This type of financing is used mostly to finance automobile, farm, and industrial equipment dealers. In this case, each product is identified by a serial number and, when the good is sold, a portion of the proceeds is sent to the lender for loan repayment. Each time goods are replenished, the borrower must sign a new agreement of terms and conditions. Sometimes the lender will spot check the quantity and quality of the physical assets.

Third is *warehouse financing*. This type of financing involves an independent third party that controls access to the goods as security for the lender. There are two basic types of warehousing arrangements: *field warehousing* and *public warehousing*. With *field warehousing* the inventories are located on the borrower's property, and the warehousing agent exercises very strict control. In *public warehousing* arrangements, the merchandise is located away from the borrowers' premises, probably in a public warehouse under the control of the warehouse agent.

Fourth, there is *consignment*. A seller delivers goods to a buyer but remains the owner until the goods are then sold to the public. Because the buyer does not actually purchase the goods, the seller may need to obtain short-term loans to finance the product. In this case, the buyer takes no risk. The profit on consigned goods is normally smaller than that on similar non-consigned items.

Asset-based financing has several advantages: (1) it is ideal for growing highly leveraged and turnaround situations, because of the higher level of risk assumed by the lender, (2) the financial agreements are not complicated, (3) the interest is tax deductible, and (4) it lowers the need to raise equity and avoids equity dilution. It has some disadvantages: (1) it increases the financial risk, (2) it's more expensive than conventional short-term financing, and (3) it comes with time-consuming inventory and trade receivables monitoring requirements, sometimes as often as daily.

Lease Financing

8 Identify the factors that influence the choice between buying and leasing an asset.

Almost any physical asset can be purchased or leased. We are all familiar with leasing (renting) an apartment, whereby a lessee (the tenant) gains the right from the lessor (owner) to live in the apartment in return for monthly rental payments.

Leasing is an alternative to traditional financing for many assets, but especially for equipment that has a useful life of three to ten years. The **lessee** or user gets the full use of the assets without the bother of owning them, and frequently this can happen with little or no down payment. The **lessor** is the one who lends the asset to the lessee.

Lessee
One who pays to use an asset without owning it.

Lessor
One who lends an asset to someone (lessee).

TYPES OF LEASES

The three most popular forms of leases are operating leases, financial leases, and sale and leaseback.

Operating Leases

Operating lease
A lease that is cancellable by the lessee at any time upon due notice.

Operating leases provide financing and maintenance of the asset, so they are popular for office equipment and cars as well as highly technical types of equipment, such as computers. The operating lease is an agreement between a lessee and a lessor that can be cancelled by either party with enough notice. Usually, the lease price includes services and repairs. Operating leases are not always fully amortized during the original contract period; the lessor expects to recover the rest of its costs by either leasing the asset again or selling it. If the original lessee believes that the equipment has become obsolete, it is usually possible to cancel the contract at little or no penalty cost before the normal lease expiry date.

Financial Leases

Financial lease
An agreement to lease a specific asset for a specified period.

In a **financial lease,** the lessee agrees to lease a specific asset over a specified period. The lease does not provide for maintenance, is usually fully amortized, and does not normally include a cancellation clause. Financial leases are commonly used for large assets, such as airplanes, office equipment, movable offshore oil drilling rigs, medical equipment, railroad cars, and construction equipment. Lessors generally borrow 80% of the cost of the asset from a third party (or parties). The loan is secured only by the lease payments. Lease periods as long as 15 or 20 years are common. The lessor records on its statement of financial position only the net investment (20%) but can deduct both finance costs on its debt financing and depreciation on the asset; therefore, income for tax purposes is usually negative in the early years of the lease. The lessee may get lower lease payments than would otherwise be the case, and its payments are usually tax deductible. Virtually all financial institutions are involved in leasing, either directly or through subsidiaries.

In a financial lease, three parties are involved: the lessee, the lessor, and a lender. Here is how a typical financial lease works. The company (lessee) chooses the equipment or machinery it needs. The company approaches a leasing company about the asset it wants and the time for which they need it. The leasing company then (1) borrows money from a lender (if necessary), (2) buys the asset from a manufacturer, and

(3) leases it to the company (lessee). Usually, the lease period lasts throughout the useful life of the asset so that the leasing company does not have to lease it to another company. In this lease agreement, the leasing company does not even take physical possession of the asset.

Sale and Leaseback

Sale and leaseback An arrangement to sell an asset to a lessor and then lease it back.

A **sale and leaseback** arrangement can be used only once, because it requires the firm to sell an asset and then lease it back. Thus, it still gets to use the asset while increasing the funds available within a particular period. Lease payments in such arrangements are similar to mortgage payments or payments on a long-term loan. For example, a firm could sell its factory building and land to a financial institution and then lease it back. The selling firm receives the full purchase price of the property, which it can use for any purpose. It is committed to making periodic payments to the financial institution, which is equivalent to paying rent.

LEASE-OR-BUY ANALYSIS

Medium- and long-term financing are generally used to buy capital assets, such as buildings, machinery, and equipment. As long as the assets do the job, a business is not concerned about how assets are financed. Managers' main interest is to see that the assets do that job at the lowest possible cost. To financial managers, however, the choice between owning versus leasing has financial consequences. Their job is to ensure not only that assets are obtained at the lowest possible cost and on the most favourable terms but also that they produce the greatest financial benefits. Although leasing has legal and accounting consequences too, we'll deal here only with the cost factors in choosing whether to lease or buy an asset. Table 8.5 presents a cost comparison between owning and leasing $1 million of assets. This cost analysis makes the following assumptions:

- Life of the assets is 10 years.
- Duration of the lease is 10 years, with annual installments of $162,745 (before tax) and $81,372 (after tax) based on a 10% compounded interest charge.
- Debt agreement is for 100% of the assets; there is a 10-year repayment schedule with a 10% compounded interest charge. (Assets are rarely financed at 100% of value; however, this assumption is made only to illustrate the true economic comparison between the two options.)
- Capital cost allowance is 15%.
- Income tax rate is 50%.
- Residual value of the asset is nil.

As shown in column 1, the annual cost of the lease is $81,372, or $162,745 × 50% (income tax rate). The second column shows the annual payment for the $1,000,000 loan. The $162,745 annual lease payment is obtained by dividing $1,000,000 by the factor 6.1446 (from Table D in Appendix B at the end of the text, at the intersection of column 10% and line 10 years). Columns 3 and 4 show how much will be paid each year for finance costs and principal, respectively. In the first year, with a $1,000,000

Table 8.5 **Comparison of Cost of Owning versus Cost of Leasing**

Computing Net Cost of Owning

Year	Lease Payment after Tax at 50% (1)	Total Payment (2)	Finance Costs (3)	Principal (4)	CCA (5)	Income Tax Deductible Expenses (6)	Tax Shield 50% (7)	Net Cost of Owning (8)	Net Advantage (Disadvantage) versus Lease (9)
		(3) + (4)				(3) + (5)	(6) ÷ 2	(2) − (7)	(1) − (8)
1	$81,372	$ 162,745	$100,000	$ 62,745	$ 75,000	$ 175,000	$ 87,500	$ 75,245	$ 6,127*
2	81,372	162,745	93,725	69,020	138,750	232,475	116,238	46,508	34,865*
3	81,372	162,745	86,823	75,922	117,938	204,761	102,380	60,365	21,008*
4	81,372	162,745	79,230	83,515	100,247	179,477	89,739	73,006	8,367*
5	81,372	162,745	70,880	91,865	85,210	156,090	78,045	84,701	(3,328)
6	81,372	162,745	61,693	101,052	72,428	134,121	67,061	95,685	(14,312)
7	81,372	162,745	51,587	111,158	61,564	113,151	56,576	106,169	(24,796)
8	81,372	162,745	40,472	122,273	52,329	92,801	46,401	116,344	(34,971)
9	81,372	162,745	28,245	134,500	44,480	72,725	36,363	126,383	(45,010)
10	81,372	162,745	14,795	147,950	37,808	52,603	26,302	136,444	(55,071)
	$813,720	$1,627,450	$627,450	$1,000,000	$785,754	$1,413,208	$706,604	$920,850	$(107,125)

* Favours owning
( ) Favours leasing

loan at a 10% interest rate, the finance costs will be $100,000 (column 3) and the principal repayment will be $62,745 (column 4). Column 5 shows the annual capital cost allowance for the $1,000,000 capital assets. Year 1 shows $75,000 [($1,000,000 × 15%) ÷ 2], and the remaining yearly figures are calculated on a declining basis. Column 6 shows the total tax-deductible amount made up of the finance costs (column 3) and capital cost allowance (column 5). Column 7 shows the yearly tax shield. Because the company is in a 50% income tax bracket, it will benefit from an $87,500 (column 6 ÷ 2) tax shield. Column 8 shows the net cost of owning the asset, which is the annual payment of the loan (column 2) less the annual tax shield. Column 9 (net advantage or disadvantage versus lease) shows the net difference between the after-tax lease payment and net cost of owning. As indicated, it is preferable to lease the asset. During the 10-year period, the total cost of owning is $920,850 versus $813,720 for leasing, for a net difference of $107,130. The difference in the totals is due to rounding figures in individual columns. Adding the 10 numbers in column 9 gives $107,125, not $107,130, which is the result of the sum of the 10 numbers appearing in column 1 ($813,720) subtracted from the sum of the 10 numbers in column 8 ($920,850).

In the early years, there is a distinct cash flow advantage to owning the asset; by the fifth year, however, cash flow favours leasing.

Problem-Solving Example 8.8

Lease or Buy a Car

Calculate whether it would be more economical to lease or buy a car: cost of the car ($35,000), term of the lease (5 years @ $7,000), tax shield (40%), CCA allowance (5 years straight-line), residual value (nil), finance costs (8%).

Solution

It would be more economical to lease the car: $21,000 versus $26,300 for the purchase. Here are the calculations.

Lease option:

Year	Payment	Tax Savings	After-Tax Cost
1	$ 7,000	$ 2,800	$ 4,200
2	7,000	2,800	4,200
3	7,000	2,800	4,200
4	7,000	2,800	4,200
5	7,000	2,800	4,200
Total	$35,000	$14,000	$21,000

Purchase option: Payment calculation ($35,000 ÷ 3.9927)

Year	Payment	Interest (8%)	CCA	Tax-Deductible Expenses	Tax Shield (40%)	Cost
1	$ 8,766	$ 2,800	$ 7,000	$ 9,800	$ 3,920	$ 4,846
2	8,766	2,323	7,000	9,323	3,729	5,037
3	8,766	1,807	7,000	8,807	3,523	5,243
4	8,766	1,251	7,000	8,245	3,298	5,468
5	8,766	649	7,000	7,649	3,060	5,706
Total	$43,830	$ 8,830	$35,000	$43,824	$17,530	$26,300

Self-Test Exercise 8.8

Lease or Buy a Truck

The Millers are not sure whether they should buy or lease a truck. A five-year lease could be arranged with annual lease payments of $5,000, payable at the beginning of each year. The tax shield from lease payments is available at year end. CompuTech's tax rate is 35%. The truck would cost $25,000 and has a five-year expected lifespan, and no residual value is expected. If purchased, the asset would be financed through a term loan at 14%. The loan calls for equal payments to be made at the end of each year for five years. Suppose that the truck would qualify for CCA on a straight-line basis over five years.

Calculate the cash flows for each financing alternative. Which alternative is the most economical?

Answers to the Self-Test Exercises can be found at www.bergeron7e.nelson.com.

FACTORS THAT INFLUENCE LEASE-OR-BUY DECISIONS

The comparative cost analysis above does not consider all the cost factors for each option. Many other factors, such as interest rate, residual value, obsolescence, risk factor, increase in financial leverage, extra costs, and capital cost allowance rate, must be considered.

Interest rate. Although the example in Table 8.5 assumes the same interest rate for both leasing and owning, this may not always be true. It is important to compare the lessor's interest rate with lending interest rates. Some leasing firms offer specialized services, and their costs will be included in the leasing charges, complicating the comparison.

Residual value. Most assets have a residual value at the end of a lease period. If a firm owns an asset and sells it at the end of a similar period, the resulting cash inflow would be a reason to favour owning.

Obsolescence. The type of equipment also influences owning versus leasing. If a piece of equipment will soon become obsolete or out of date, leasing may be the better option. Why purchase equipment with a 10-year lifespan that will become obsolete after four years? Some will argue that the higher the obsolescence factor, the higher the cost of the lease. This is not always true, because lessors can often find other users for their equipment; not all users have the same obsolescence rate.

Risk factor. Leasing a piece of equipment with a high rate of obsolescence passes the element of risk to the lessor.

Increase in financial leverage. Leasing often has a double effect on financial leverage. First, more money is usually available to finance assets through a lease than through a loan. Assets can be leased at 100%, but chattel mortgage or conditional sales contracts can be obtained at only 50% or 75%. Second, financing part of a capital asset through leasing leaves room for future financing, if an expansion is needed right after start-up. However, while leasing may seem to promise greater leverage, less risk of obsolescence, and lower cost, lenders are wise to the financial obligations of "off-statement of financial position" financing and take them into account when assessing creditworthiness.

Extra costs. Certain costs, such as legal fees, are not as high for leasing as for debt financing; these should also be considered in the cost comparison.

Capital cost allowance rate. A change in the capital cost allowance rate may alter the decision. For example, if the CCA rate increases from 15% to 25%, this would favour the purchase option.

Problem-Solving Example 8.9

Lease or Buy Office Equipment

A company is choosing between leasing and buying some equipment. The five-year lease option would cost $25,000 per year (before tax). The second option would be to buy the same equipment at a cost of $150,000 and have it totally financed at 8% per year for the same five-year period. If the company buys the equipment, it would cost $6,000 for maintenance and repairs per year.

(continued)

Problem-Solving Example 8.9 (continued)

Assume that the capital cost allowance (straight-line) is 20% and is based on $100,000 ($150,000 less the residual value of $50,000). The company's income tax rate is 30%.

Solution

Both options are equal: $87,500 for leasing and $87,488 for owning.

Year	Lease Payment	Loan Payment (8%)	Finance Cost	Principal Repayment	Maintenance and Repairs	CCA	Tax Ded. Expenses	Tax Savings (30%)	Cost of Owning
1	$17,500	$ 37,568	$12,000	$ 25,568	$ 6,000	$ 20,000	$ 38,000	$11,400	$ 26,168
2	17,500	37,568	9,955	27,613	6,000	20,000	35,955	10,786	26,782
3	17,500	37,568	7,744	29,824	6,000	20,000	33,744	10,123	27,445
4	17,500	37,568	5,359	32,209	6,000	20,000	31,359	9,408	28,160
5	17,500	37,568	2,782	34,786	6,000	20,000	28,782	8,635	28,933
Total	$87,500	$187,840	$37,840	$150,000	$30,000	$100,000	$167,840	$50,352	$137,488
Less (value of equipment)									–50,000
Net cost	$87,500								$87,488

Self-Test Exercise 8.9

Lease or Buy Computers

The Millers are deciding whether to buy or lease several computers (including a cash register) for their new store. The computers can be leased for $8,000 a year or purchased for $30,000. The lease includes maintenance and service. The salvage value of the equipment after five years is $6,000. The company uses the declining balance method for capital cost allowance at a rate of 35%. If the computers were purchased, service and maintenance charges (a deductible cost) would be $300 a year. CompuTech can borrow the entire amount at a rate of 14% if they choose to buy. The tax rate is 35%, and the company's cost of capital is 11%. Which method of financing would you choose?

Use the following capital cost allowance amounts.

Year	Amount
1	$10,500
2	6,825
3	4,436
4	2,884
5	1,875

Answers to the Self-Test Exercises can be found at www.bergeron7e.nelson.com.

Chapter Summary

1 Describe financial needs and financing requirements.

Financial needs are items a business needs to operate, such as inventories and equipment. *Financing requirements* are the forms and sources of financing, such as shareholders and lenders.

2 Differentiate between internal financing and external financing.

Financing can be obtained from two sources. *Internal financing* uses the profit generated by operations, including depreciation, and by managing the current assets more effectively. *External financing* comes from shareholders (through purchase of common or preferred shares) and short-term and long-term lenders.

3 Explain the types of risk-related financing options (ownership versus debt).

External financing can be obtained from different sources and in different forms. Each is used to finance a specific asset, different venture, or business undertaking. A business faces three types of risk. *Business risk* has to do with the uncertainty inherent in projecting future earnings of a business. *Financial risk* deals with a company's financial structure. *Instrument risk* focuses on the type of instrument or tool that should be used to finance a business.

4 Explain useful strategies for approaching lenders.

When considering financing, businesses should attempt to match, as closely as possible, the maturity of the source of funds to the period for which the funds are needed. To do this, both cost and risk need to be considered. Investors use different criteria for assessing the worthiness of prospective clients, including the C's of credit: character, collateral, capacity, capital, circumstances (or conditions), and coverage.

5 Discuss the categories of equity financing.

Equity financing can come from shareholders and risk capital firms. These types of funds can be obtained from private or public sources. If public offerings are made, investment dealers must be used to process the issue. Risk capital firms provide financing for smaller, high-risk firms. They generally provide equity financing or both equity and long-term debt financing. Risk capital investments can be categorized as embryonic, start-up, development, expansion, turnaround, or buyout. Risk capital investors include angel investors, private investors, institutional investors, and government-backed corporations. Government financing is a direct or indirect form of financial assistance to businesses offered by a municipal, provincial or territorial, or federal agency to help businesses carry out capital expenditure projects or expand their activities. The more important governmental financial institutions include Export Development Canada, Farm Credit Canada, the Business Development Bank of Canada, and provincial and territorial venture capital organizations.

6 Discuss the sources and forms of intermediate and long-term debt financing.

Sources of intermediate and long-term financing are commercial banks and trust companies. There are *conventional long-term investors* (e.g., banks, shareholders) and *risk-capital investors*, including government institutions. Intermediate and long-term financing come from conventional institutions and include term loans, conditional sales contracts, bonds, and mortgages. Risk capital funds can also be obtained on subordinated debt for which investors accept a higher level of risk. When considering common share, preferred share, and long-term debt financing, several factors must be considered: the payout of income, control, risk, and the advantages and disadvantages of each.

7 Discuss the most important sources and forms of short-term financing.

The most popular *sources* of short-term financing are suppliers, chartered banks and trust companies, and asset-based financing. The most popular *forms* of short-term financing are trade credit (suppliers) and lines of credit, seasonal or self-liquidating loans, revolving credit, and interim financing offered by chartered banks. Other financing institutions also offer secured loans on inventories and trade receivables. Lenders can offer asset-based loans. These include factoring on trade receivables and general lien, floor planning, warehousing agreements, and consignment to finance inventories.

8 Identify the factors that influence the choice between buying and leasing an asset.

Lease financing is another popular way of acquiring assets. The three major types of leases are operating leases, financial leases, and sale and leaseback. Before deciding on buying or leasing assets, the cost of each option should be evaluated. The factors that will determine the choice are interest rate, residual value, obsolescence factor, risk factor, increase in financial leverage, extra costs, and capital cost allowance rate.

Key Terms

Review Questions

1 Describe financial needs and financing requirements.

1. What is the difference between financial needs and financing requirements?

2 Differentiate between internal financing and external financing.

2. Differentiate between internal and external financing. Give several examples.
3. How can working capital become a source of internal financing?

3 Explain the types of risk-related financing options (ownership versus debt).

4. Discuss the concepts of business risk, financial risk, and instrument risk.

4 Explain useful strategies for approaching lenders.

5. Differentiate between flexible and durable current assets.
6. Explain the meaning of the matching principle.
7. Identify the six C's of credit.
8. Explain the significance of capacity.
9. How can a company become more creditworthy?
10. Is it easier for a big firm to obtain a loan than a small business? Explain.
11. Why is it important for a business to understand the nature of its assets before approaching lenders?

5 Discuss the categories of equity financing.

12. What steps are involved when making a public issue?
13. Differentiate between shareholder collective rights and specific rights. Identify three of each type of right.
14. What is the purpose of a risk capital investor? Comment on some of them.
15. What types of capital investments do risk capitalist firms invest in?
16. How can government agencies help businesses?

6 Discuss the sources and forms of intermediate and long-term debt financing.

17. Differentiate between a secured bond and an unsecured bond.
18. What is the purpose of a subordinated debt?

7 Discuss the most important sources and forms of short-term financing.

19. Why are suppliers considered an important source of financing?
20. What factors should a company consider before selecting a chartered bank as a lender?
21. Differentiate between a seasonal loan and revolving credit.
22. What sort of financing do factoring companies and confirming institutions provide?

8 Identify the factors that influence the choice between buying and leasing an asset.

23. Differentiate between an operating lease and a financial lease.
24. Do you believe that leasing would be as popular if income taxes did not exist? Explain.

25. If you were to provide a term loan to a small business entrepreneur, what provisions would you include in the contract to protect your interest?

Learning Exercises

1 Describe financial needs and financing requirements.

EXERCISE 1: FINANCIAL NEEDS AND FINANCING REQUIREMENTS

A company needs $1.2 million to invest in different types of assets and operating expenses to launch a new line of products. With the following information, make a list of the company's financial needs and financing requirements.

Marketing costs	$55,000	Trade receivables	$175,000
Depreciation	50,000	Equipment	500,000
Shareholders	200,000	Suppliers	250,000
Inventories	350,000	Profit for the year	100,000
Working capital loan	100,000	Equipment vendors	200,000
Research and development	120,000	Commercial bank	300,000

2 Differentiate between internal financing and external financing.

EXERCISE 2: CASH INFLOW FROM WORKING CAPITAL ACCOUNTS

How much additional cash could a company obtain from its working capital accounts if it can improve its inventory turnover by 0.2 times and average collection period by 5 days? The company's inventories are $500,000, and trade receivables are $250,000. The company's revenue is estimated at $1.8 million and cost of sales at $900,000.

EXERCISE 3: CASH INFLOW FROM TRADE PAYABLES

Calculate the amount of additional cash that a company could raise from suppliers if its trade credit is extended by 10 days. Assume that the company's trade payables are $300,000 and that it buys $2,300,000 from various suppliers yearly.

3 Explain the types of risk-related financing options (ownership versus debt).

EXERCISE 4: TYPES OF RISKS

There are three types of risk-related financing options: business risk, financial risk, and instrument risk. List each of the following under the appropriate risk concept:

Bonds	Leverage
Insolvency	More debt
Business variations	Mortgage
Finance costs	Economic environment
Unsecured loans	Common shares
Conditional sales contracts	High-tech businesses
Capital structure	Industry environment
Uncertainty	

4 Explain useful strategies for approaching lenders.

EXERCISE 5: THE C'S OF CREDIT

Match the following words with the six C's of credit: character, collateral, capacity, capital, circumstances, and coverage.

- Business environment
- Security
- Insurance
- Equity versus debt
- Cash flow
- Trust

5 Discuss the categories of equity financing.

EXERCISE 6: SOURCES OF EQUITY FINANCING

Match the following with the following equity investors: shareholders, risk capital investors, and government institutions.

- Venture capitalist
- Common shareholders
- Export Development Canada
- Angel investors
- Preferred shareholders
- Business Development Bank of Canada

EXERCISE 7: SHAREHOLDERS' COLLECTIVE AND SPECIFIC RIGHTS

Which of the following are collective rights? Which are specific rights?

- Amend the articles of the incorporation
- Vote in the manner prescribed by the corporate charter
- Sell a share
- Adopt and amend bylaws
- Inspect corporate books
- Elect the directors
- Authorize the sale of capital assets
- Share in the corporate profits

6 Discuss the sources and forms of intermediate and long-term debt financing.

EXERCISE 8: ANNUAL LOAN PAYMENTS

a) If a company borrows $300,000 for four years at 10%, what would the annual loan payments be?
b) If the company borrows $650,000 for 10 years at 12%, what would the annual loan payments be?

EXERCISE 9: ANNUAL PRINCIPAL AND INTEREST PAYMENTS

Calculate the annual payment, finance costs, and principal repayments on a $300,000 loan with a 10% interest rate over four years.

7 Discuss the most important sources and forms of short-term financing.

EXERCISE 10: AVERAGE PERCENTAGE RATE

During the next four months, a company is considering approaching banks to finance its increased level of working capital. The company expects to increase its working capital needs by $30,000 and hopes to obtain 55% financing from the bank. The bank manager said that it would cost them $700 in finance costs for the four-month period. Based on this information, calculate the company's APR for the four-month loan.

EXERCISE 11: AVERAGE PERCENTAGE RATE FOR PLEDGED TRADE RECEIVABLES

During the next four months, a furniture manufacturer will be entering its holiday season. Management expects commercial trade receivables to reach $900,000 and will be seeking a bank loan that will finance 60% of the receivables. The bank charges 8% and an additional 1% service fee of the pledged trade receivables. The average collection period is 45 days. Calculate the company's APR for the pledged trade receivables.

EXERCISE 12: COLLECTING VERSUS FACTORING TRADE RECEIVABLES

A furniture company is considering using a factor to manage its trade receivables. The company has $1,600,000 in trade receivables with a 70-day average collection period. The factor charges a 10% reserve for returns and allowances, a 2% factoring commission, and an annual interest rate of 4% over prime (assume prime is 5%). If the company manages its own receivables, it would cost $3,000 a month for administrative fees and clerical costs in addition to $4,000 a month in bad debt losses. Based on this information, what would the company's APR be?

8 Identify the factors that influence the choice between buying and leasing an asset.

EXERCISE 13: PURCHASE VERSUS LEASE CALCULATION

In a lease-or-buy decision, a four-year lease could be arranged with annual lease payments of $90,000, payable at the beginning of each year. The tax shield from lease payments is available at year-end. The firm's tax rate is 40%. The machine costs $500,000 and has a four-year expected life, and no residual value is expected. If purchased, the asset would be financed through a term loan at 12%. The loan calls for equal payments to be made at the end of each year for four years. The machine would qualify for accelerated capital cost allowances written off on a straight-line basis over two years.

Calculate the cash flows for each financing alternative. Which alternative is the most economical?

EXERCISE 14: PURCHASE VERSUS LEASE CALCULATION

Hull Manufacturing Co. must decide whether to purchase or lease a new piece of equipment. The equipment can be leased for $4,000 a year or purchased for $15,000. The lease includes maintenance and service. The salvage value of the equipment at the end of five years is $5,000. If the equipment is owned, service and maintenance charges (a tax-deductible cost) would be $900 a year. The firm can borrow the entire amount at a rate of 15% if they buy. The tax rate is 50%. Which method of financing would you choose?

Use the following capital cost allowance amounts.

Year	Amount
1	$4,500
2	3,150
3	2,205
4	1,543
5	1,081

Cases

CASE 1: GRIP CASE INC.

In April 2013, Miriam and Ben Friedman were thinking about starting their own business, Grip Case Inc. Their objective was to produce and market inexpensive attaché cases. It was not their intention to compete directly against expensive cases produced by such companies as Samsonite, Hartmann, Zero Halliburton, or Atlantic. Miriam and Ben felt that if their company produced an inexpensive case (retailing at about $50), they would sell at least 15,000 units during the first year of operation. Of course, to launch Grip Case Inc., they would need to borrow from various lending institutions.

Miriam and Ben intended to approach their venture in three phases. The first phase would be a detailed feasibility study, including legal work for patent registration and additional work on the product design. The second phase would involve the preparation of a detailed investment proposal to seek the financing for the purchase of the capital assets, the working capital requirements, and operating funds needed to market the products effectively. The third phase would be implementation through production and commercialization.

Attaché cases are marketed under private brands or manufacturers' brands. Private brands account for a smaller segment of the Canadian retail market. Most often, private brand cases are manufactured for retail outlets, such as The Bay, Sears, and Wal-Mart. Manufacturers' brand names include Hartmann, Samsonite, Atlantic, SOLO, and Stebco.

After examining dozens of different types of cases, Miriam and Ben found that the four most important parts of the product for consumers are construction, convenience, interior, and exterior. The quality of construction of a case depends on its frame, hinges, handle, feet, latches, and locks. Convenience is determined by what the case offers, such as files and pockets. Miriam and Ben found that cases are available with a wide variety of files and pockets. How the interior of a case is divided also interests buyers. Things that buyers look for are lining, stability, and file compartments. Some attaché cases have pockets for business cards, a calculator, airline tickets, and parking-lot receipts. The exterior comes in different qualities of materials. This factor significantly affects the retail sales price. Cases are made of leather, vinyl, or moulded plastic. Good-quality leather cases are the most expensive, with prices between $250 and $800. Vinyl cases are priced between $75 and $250. The cheapest moulded-plastic case sells for about $70.

Although Miriam and Ben intend to market the three basic types of cases (attaché case, briefcase, and portfolio), they want to market only the attaché cases during the first year of operation to hold down their initial investment and production costs. The type of case that they want to market would retail between $40 and $60. The cost of production and the amount of markup by the middle parties determines the exact price. They will focus primarily on the student markets (secondary, colleges, and universities). They believe that a practical, low-priced model could meet consumers' needs. Grip Case Inc. would sell its products directly to wholesalers and/or retailers. The exact distribution network has not yet been determined.

Grip Case Inc. is to manufacture cases for private brands and sell to retail stores, such as Wal-mart, Zellers, discount stores, and drugstores. It would also sell cases bearing its own brand name: Grip Case. By selling cases at about $25 to wholesalers/retailers, and with 15,000 units, the company would be able to cover its costs and begin to make a profit during the second year of operation. The following shows Grip Case Inc.'s financial needs.

Financial Needs		
Working capital		
Inventories	$60,000	
Trade receivables	40,000	$100,000
Capital assets		
Leasehold improvements	100,000	
Equipment	70,000	
Machinery/truck	80,000	250,000
Research and development		50,000
Marketing/promotion		50,000
Total financial needs		$450,000

Grip Case Inc.'s condensed projected statements of income for the first three years of operations follow:

(in $) Years	1	2	3
No. of units	15,000	20,000	25,000
Unit selling price ($)	25	25	25
Revenue	375,000	500,000	625,000
Cost of sales	(187,500)	(250,000)	(312,500)
Gross profit	187,500	250,000	312,500
Administrative expenses	(85,000)	(95,000)	(110,000)
Distribution costs	(90,000)	(70,000)	(80,000)
Depreciation	(30,000)	(30,000)	(30,000)
Finance costs	(25,000)	(25,000)	(25,000)
Total expenses	(230,000)	(220,000)	(245,000)
Profit before taxes	(42,500)	30,000	67,500
Income tax expense	—	—	(12,000)
Profit for the year	(42,500)	30,000	55,500

Miriam and Ben had saved $150,000 over the past 10 years and were planning to invest the entire amount in the business in the form of equity. They knew that they would have difficulty obtaining debt financing but had a $250,000 house of which 40% could be used as collateral. However, they were prepared to use this option only as a last resort.

Miriam and Ben were determined to adopt a conservative strategy, growing slowly and carefully in starting their business. Rather than investing huge sums of money in expensive equipment and buying a building, they intended to purchase some used equipment and rent a building belonging to Miriam's father. If, after the first three years, the attaché case product line reached the expected level of sales, they would then consider making the briefcase and the portfolio product lines. Depending on the company's financial position three years after start-up, Miriam and Ben might lease a larger building or even build their own.

Although Miriam and Ben were still at the research stage, they had done some costing to calculate how much profit they would make for each case. At 15,000 units, the cost of production would be around $187,500, for a total unit production cost of approximately $12.50. The cost breakdown is as follows: direct materials, $6.30/unit; direct labour, $2.00 (for a total of $124,500 in variable costs); and the rest ($63,000) in fixed manufacturing costs.

Questions

1. What questions do you think lenders will ask Miriam and Ben about their venture?
2. How many units would the company have to sell in the first year of operation to break even? When will the company break even? Is the break-even point in that year reasonable? Why or why not? (The break-even point was discussed in Chapter 5.)

3. What type of investors or lenders should Miriam and Ben approach? Why?
4. What type of collateral would the lenders want to take into consideration?
5. How much do you believe Miriam and Ben will be able to obtain from the different financing sources? Why?

CASE 2: BALDWIN EQUIPMENT INC.

Management of Baldwin Equipment Inc. is considering increasing the productivity of its plant. Management heard from suppliers that a certain piece of equipment could have an after-tax cash flow savings of more than $35,000 a year if it was installed in Baldwin's plant. However, Jim Henderson, the controller of the company, is unsure whether the company should buy or lease the equipment. If the asset is leased for a 10-year period, it would cost the company $45,000 a year (before tax). The company's income tax rate is 50%. If the company buys the asset, it would cost $300,000 and be financed entirely through debt for 10 years at a cost of 10%. The asset's capital cost allowance is 25% (declining basis). On the basis of this information, Jim is now considering whether to purchase or lease the equipment. He is considering doing a sensitivity analysis regarding the two options by modifying some of the data in the information presented above.

Question

On the basis of the following, calculate the effect that each individual change would have on the decision. Changes to the base case (the information given above) are as follows:

- Capital cost allowance would be increased to 40%.
- The interest on the loan would be 8%.
- The company would be able to sell the asset for $50,000 in the tenth year.

FINANCIAL SPREADSHEETS: EXCEL®

Template 8 (Vertical Analysis of the Statement of Financial Position) of the financial statement analysis part of the financial spreadsheets accompanying this text can give a detailed view of the makeup of the various liability and equity accounts over a three-year period. Template 8 (Lease/Buy Decision) of the decision-making tools spreadsheets is designed to calculate the cost of leasing an asset versus the cost of owning an asset.

CHAPTER 9

[COST OF CAPITAL, CAPITAL STRUCTURE, AND FINANCIAL MARKETS]

Learning Objectives

After reading this chapter, you should be able to

1 Describe the relationship between the major components of finance.

2 Explain financial and capital structure, and explain the cost concepts.

3 Explain why the cost of financing is used and how it is calculated.

4 Show how economic value added is used to measure managerial performance related to maximizing shareholder wealth.

5 Describe the parts of the average weighted cost of capital: common shares, retained earnings, preferred shares, and long-term borrowings.

6 Demonstrate the importance of leverage analysis and how operating leverage, financial leverage, and combined leverage are calculated.

7 Discuss financial markets, the stock market, and three theories related to dividend payments.

OPENING CASE

Synchronizing Return on Assets with Cost of Capital

By the end of 2014, the Millers were pleased with CompuTech Sales and Service's financial performance. In fact, they had exceeded their financial expectations. During that year, they decided to incorporate their business. It is now called CompuTech Inc. The Millers were entering an important phase in their business development; they wanted to further expand their retail business. The factor limiting the number of outlets they could open was how much financing they could obtain from investors. They were also considering asking a few friends to invest in their business.

CompuTech Inc. is an attractive investment, in part, because of the quality of its collateral and its ability to service its debt. However, potential shareholders want to invest in a company that can increase its revenue and earnings. The Millers would have to prove they can manage the company well and demonstrate that CompuTech Inc. could generate substantial earnings.

The Millers began to prepare a business plan to present to investors. They wanted to expand the working capital of their existing retail outlet and open another outlet in 2015. The required investment in non-current assets (property, plant, and equipment) was estimated at $350,000. The following shows how the Millers proposed to finance their expansion program.

	Cash Outflows	Cash Inflows
Property, plant, and equipment	$350,000	
Internal financing		$157,000
Share capital		70,000
Long-term borrowings		150,000
Working capital requirements	99,000	
Short-term borrowings	———	72,000
Total	$449,000	$449,000

The Millers remembered that when entrepreneur Bill Murray had advised them, he said, "You have to make sure that your business generates enough cash (or profit) to finance part of its growth." Now that the Millers were facing growth and expansion, they began to realize the significance of Bill's statement. They had to make sure that the business has enough cash to pay finance costs and dividends. They also had to make sure that earnings from their business would be sufficient to reinvest for the purchase of non-current assets (new store, equipment, etc.) and for working capital requirements.

A quick analysis of their projected financial statements for 2015 showed that CompuTech Inc. would generate a 12.1% return on assets (ROA). The Millers had to ensure that the cost of borrowed funds from different financing sources would be less than the ROA. To encourage other shareholders to invest in CompuTech Inc., they had to demonstrate how the business would generate additional wealth for them.

The Millers had more ambitious goals for the longer term. They wanted to go public by 2022, meaning they had six to seven years to show that CompuTech Inc. had real growth potential with powerful earnings. They wanted to start approaching venture capitalists by 2017, asking for substantial sums of money in the form of equity. They realized, however, that these types of investors were looking for a 25% to 35% (if not more) return on their investment. If they wanted to entice these types of investors by 2017, the Millers had to show that CompuTech Inc. had substantial growth and earnings.

THIS CHAPTER WILL SHOW LEN AND JOAN HOW TO

- Make the connection between cost of capital and return on assets.
- Add value to the shareholders' wealth (EVA).
- Increase earnings by using leverage calculations.

Chapter Overview

HOW COST OF CAPITAL SWAYS PROFITABILITY

Chapter 8, the first on financing decisions, covered the sources and forms of financing. This chapter also deals with financing decisions and examines seven topics:

- *Major components of finance.* The three major components of finance—capital structure, cost of capital, and capital budgeting—are interrelated.
- *Cost and structure.* You will learn the broad definitions of *cost* and *structure*, the difference between cost of financing and cost of capital, and the difference between the financial structure and the capital structure.
- *Cost of financing.* We will discuss the importance of cost of financing and describe its purpose and how it is calculated.
- *Economic value added.* The economic value added (EVA) measures managerial performance in terms of increasing shareholder wealth. This section shows how EVA is calculated.
- *Cost of capital.* We will explain the key characteristics of long-term capital financing sources and the cost of capital. **Cost of capital** has to do with the cost of borrowing funds from long-term investors (common shares, retained earnings, preferred shares, and long-term borrowings).
- *Leverage.* **Leverage** is a technique used to find the best operating and financial structure to amplify a firm's operating and financial performance. It focuses on the following questions: Should a business have more fixed costs than variable costs? What would be the right proportion? Should the business have more equity than debt? Again, what would be the best combination or proportion? We'll define operating leverage, financial leverage, and combined leverage.

Cost of capital
The cost of borrowing money from different sources (shareholders or lenders) to finance a business.

Leverage
A technique used to find the most suitable operating and financial structure to amplify financial performance.

Financial markets, stock market, and dividend theories. We will analyze financial markets, the stock market, and dividend theories and dividend payments. The section related to financial markets examines the organizations and the procedures involved in the buying and selling of assets. We will look at different types of markets, such as money markets, capital markets, primary markets, secondary markets, spot and future markets, mortgage markets, consumer credit markets, and physical asset markets. This section also deals with the stock market, the difference between a privately held company and a publicly traded company, and the meaning of an initial public offering and a listed company. It also explains various dividend theories, dividend policy, and dividend payments.

Relationship between the Major Components of Finance

1 Describe the relationship between the major components of finance.

Three components of finance—capital structure, cost of capital, and capital budgeting—have an important connection. *Capital structure* deals with the types of funding sources, which determine, to a large extent, the *cost of capital*, that is, the factor that will set the discount rate used during the *capital budgeting* process. The lower the cost of capital, the more financially attractive the capital projects will look in the capital budgeting process. Figure 9.1 illustrates this interrelationship. This chapter deals with capital structure and cost of capital, and Chapter 11 covers the third component: capital budgeting.

One of the first steps in capital expenditure planning (or capital budgeting) is to determine how much should be borrowed and from whom (capital structure). Let's look at a scenario with two options, A and B, shown on the following page. Suppose a treasurer is asked to raise $1 million. The cost of funds will have to be calculated (cost of capital). The composition of the debt and equity, which is made up of common equity, preferred equity, and long-term borrowings (bonds or mortgages), largely determines the cost of capital. In option A, raising funds from equity costs

Figure 9.1 **Relationship between the Major Components of Finance**

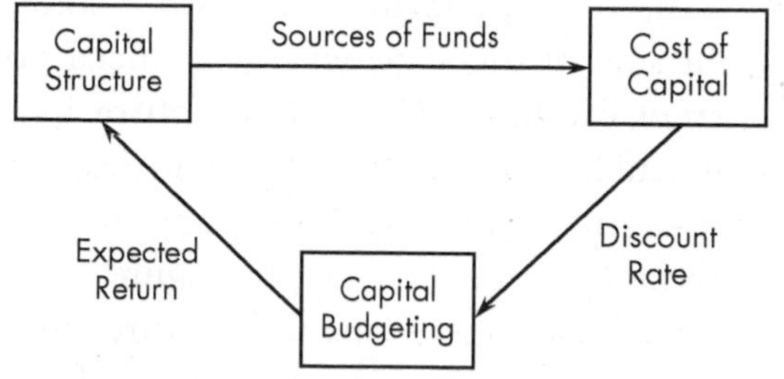

more (12.0%) than from debt (5.0%), and obtaining funds from lenders is more appealing than raising it from shareholders.

Debt-to-equity structures influence the relationship between the cost of capital and ROA. To continue our scenario, suppose the company has $1 million invested in assets, which give a 9.0% ROA. The financial structure shown in option A gives a 9.9% weighted average cost of financing (WACF), while option B gives 7.1%. The **weighted average cost of financing** is the proportion of the cost of each amount financed in a company's financial structure.

Weighted average cost of financing The proportion of the cost of each amount financed in a company's financial structure.

A 9% ROA puts the company in a negative position by 0.9% (9.0% ROA versus a 9.9% WACF) in option A. With option B, a different financial structure, the company's ROA would be more than the cost of financing by 1.9%.

Option A

	Equity		Debt		Total
Amount	$700,000	+	$300,000	=	$1,000,000
Cost of funds	12.0%		5.0%		
Weight	× 0.70	+	× 0.30	=	1.00
WACF	8.40%	+	1.50%	=	9.90%

Option B

	Equity		Debt		Total
Amount	$300,000	+	$700,000	=	$1,000,000
Cost of funds	12.0%		5.0%		
Weight	× 0.30	+	× 0.70	=	1.00
WACF	3.60%	+	3.50%	=	7.10%

Financial structure The way a company's assets are financed by the entire right side of the statement of financial position (long-term and short-term financing).

Structure and Cost Concepts

2 Explain financial and capital structure, and explain the cost concepts.

Let's examine the difference between financial structure and capital structure, and between cost of financing and cost of capital.

Financial structure is the way a company's total assets are financed by the entire right side of the statement of financial position (equity, long-term borrowings, and current liabilities). **Capital structure** includes the more permanent forms of financing, such as equity (common shares, retained earnings, and preferred shares) and long-term borrowings (mortgages, bonds), that are normally used to finance non-current (or capital) assets. In Figure 9.2, the shaded portion represents the capital financial package. Capital structure, therefore, accounts for only a portion of a company's total financial structure and excludes current liabilities.

Capital structure The permanent or long-term financing sources used to buy non-current assets.

Figure 9.2 **Financial Structure and Capital Structure**

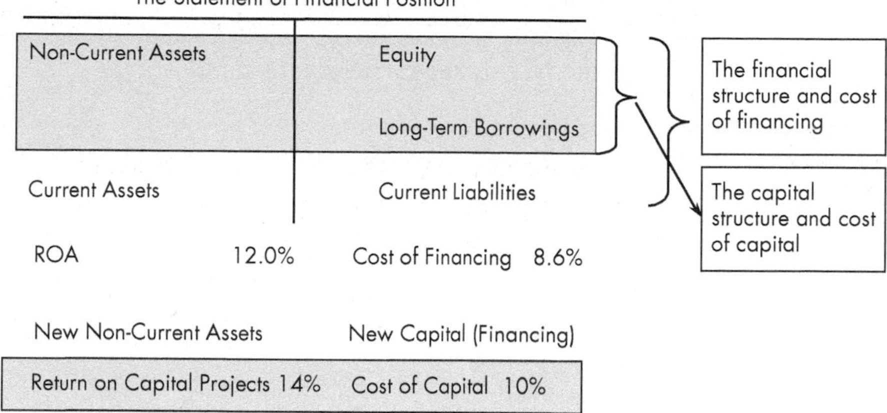

Problem-Solving Example 9.1

Financial Structure and Capital Structure

From the following accounts, choose which would you use to calculate a person's financial structure and which would you use for capital structure: (1) line of credit, (2) The Bay charge account, (3) student loan (six years), (4) second mortgage, (5) bank overdraft, (6) mortgage, (7) Visa account, (8) home repair loan (five years), (9) cash advance, (10) car loan (four years), (11) vehicle repair (MasterCard).

Solution

Financial Structure	Capital Structure
(1) Line of credit	
(2) The Bay charge account	
(3) Student loan	Student loan
(4) Second mortgage	Second mortgage
(5) Bank overdraft	
(6) Mortgage	Mortgage
(7) Visa account	
(8) Home repair loan	Home repair loan
(9) Cash advance	
(10) Car loan	Car loan
(11) MasterCard account	

Self-Test Exercise 9.1

Financial Structure and Capital Structure

From the following financing sources, identify CompuTech's financial structure and capital structure, and calculate the proportion or weight of each.

Sources	Amounts
Share capital	$100,000
Trade and other payables	20,000
Retained earnings	58,000
Long-term borrowings	50,000
Term loan	40,000
Working capital loan	—

Answers to the Self-Test Exercises can be found at www.bergeron7e.nelson.com.

Let's now look at the importance of calculating the cost of financing and the cost of capital. The *cost of financing* is how much a business is charged to finance the assets shown on its statement of financial position. Refer to Figure 9.2 and assume that a company borrows funds from different financial institutions. The funds cost 8.6% and earn 12.0% ROA; in this case, the company's cost of financing is less than what it earns. This produces positive results and makes good business sense. However, if the cost of financing a business is more than its ROA, the shareholders would not be earning enough to justify the investments in total assets.

The *cost of capital* is a different concept, but it is calculated in a similar way. It deals with only the permanent forms of financing and raising new long-term capital to buy new non-current assets. The company raises new capital funds from different financing sources (equity and long-term borrowings) at a cost of 10.0% (cost of capital). These funds are invested in new non-current assets and produce a 14.0% return (capital budgeting). This means that the cost of the newly acquired capital or permanent financing is less than the return to be earned on newly acquired non-current assets. Again, this would make good business sense.

Cost of capital is associated with capital budgets as both have long-term implications. Bonds and mortgages, for example, are borrowed on a long-term basis (say, 15 years) to finance capital projects that also have long lifespans (like 15 years). If the company's cost of capital is 10.0%, and it earns 14.0% ROA, the business will have a 4.0% positive spread (or difference) every year during the next 15 years. If the spread were negative, the shareholders would make less on their investments and therefore management would not proceed with the investment decision.

Problem-Solving Example 9.2

Weighted Average Cost of Capital (WACC)

With the following accounts, calculate the person's cost of capital: (1) student loan ($20,000 at 5.3%), (2) second mortgage ($10,000 at 7.4%), (3) mortgage ($200,000 at 4.2%), (4) home repair loan ($5,000 at 7.0%), (5) car loan ($6,000 at 8.5%).

Solution

The person's weighted average cost of capital is 4.59%.

	Amounts	Weight (%)	Cost	WACC
(1) Student loan	$ 20,000	0.083	5.3	0.440
(2) Second mortgage	10,000	0.041	7.4	0.303
(3) Mortgage	200,000	0.830	4.2	3.486
(4) Home repair loan	5,000	0.021	7.0	0.147
(5) Car loan	6,000	0.025	8.5	0.212
Total	$241,000	1.000		4.588

Self-Test Exercise 9.2

Weighted Average Cost of Financing and Cost of Capital

Use the information in Self-Test Exercise 9.1 and the following costs for individual financing sources to calculate CompuTech's weighted average after-tax cost of financing and cost of capital.

Sources	Cost (%)
Share capital	12
Trade and other payables	0
Retained earnings	11
Long-term borrowings	5
Term loan	7
Working capital loan	6

Answers to the Self-Test Exercises can be found at www.bergeron7e.nelson.com.

In the News 9.1 illustrates one of the reasons why a person or business should be warned not to go overboard in debt financing.

In The News 9.1

THE PERILS OF RACKING UP DEBT

Borrowing plenty of cheap money to buy a house or some capital assets is quite enticing. People can borrow on a long-term basis, say for 25 years, at a variable rate, or at a three- or five- year fixed rate. Both options are sensible, but it's important to realize that an increase in interest rates could easily cause borrowers to become cash strapped or fall behind in their payments, or even file for bankruptcy. Let's take the case of someone who obtains a 25-year $200,000 mortgage at 4%. The mortgage monthly payments would be $1,056. If the borrower makes $4,000 in gross salary a month, 26% of his salary would go to the mortgage payment. This is an acceptable ratio for lending institutions. However, an increase in the interest rate to 6% would bring the mortgage payment to $1,289, and at 10%, to $1,817. In the latter case, 45% of the salary would go to the mortgage payment, far above the 30% cap for most lending institutions or for living comfortably.

Many Canadians would be facing this situation if the Bank of Canada decided to increase the current 1% prime rate. It is kept low for one reason: to stimulate the Canadian economy. But an increase in the inflation rate could justify an increase in the prime rate and, ultimately, in interest rates. According to Mark Carney, governor of the Bank of Canada, this alone would make many Canadian businesses and household consumers "financially vulnerable."

Source: "Ignoring warning, racking up debt." *Winnipeg Free Press*. Retrieved from http://www.winnipegfreepress.com/business/ignoring-warning-racking-up-debt-147282615.html, accessed April 15, 2012. For more information about current interest rates, visit Bank of Canada's website at www.bankofcanada.ca.

Cost of Financing

3 Explain why the cost of financing is used and how it is calculated.

Table 9.1 shows a company that raises $1,200,000 from seven different sources. Equity financing accounts for $450,000 (or 37.5%), long-term borrowings account for $500,000 (or 41.7%), and short-term borrowings or current liabilities account for $250,000 (or 20.8%) of the total financing package. The table also presents the cost of financing for each amount raised, before and after taxes. For example, management raised $50,000 from Source A at a cost of 8.0% before taxes. Assuming the company is in a 40% tax bracket, the after-tax cost of borrowing from Source A would be 4.8%. The same arithmetic is done for all other loans. However, the cost of raising funds from equity is 12%, whether before or after tax, because dividends are paid to shareholders with after-tax profit. The last two columns of Table 9.1 present the WACF. Based on that financing structure, it would cost the company 9.05% before tax to raise funds from different sources, and 7.12% after tax.

The WACF, however, is irrelevant unless it is compared to the return that the company earns on its assets. Table 9.2 gives us this comparison. On the left side of the statement of financial position, the company earns a 14.20% ROA before taxes and 8.52% after taxes. The before-tax return is based on the assumption that the company generated $170,400 in profit before taxes ($1,200,000 × 14.20%) and $102,240 ($1,200,000 × 8.52%) after taxes on total assets of $1,200,000.

Table 9.1 Cost of Financing

	Amounts (in $)	Weight (%)		Cost of Financing Before Tax	Cost of Financing After Tax		Weighted Average Cost of Financing Before Tax	Weighted Average Cost of Financing After Tax
Equity								
Share capital	150,000	12.5	×	12.0%	12.0%	=	1.50%	1.50%
Retained earnings	300,000	25.0	×	11.0%	11.0%	=	2.75%	2.75%
Subtotal	450,000	37.5					4.25%	4.25%
Long-term borrowings								
Mortgage	200,000	16.7	×	7.0%	4.2%	=	1.17%	0.70%
Bond	300,000	25.0	×	7.5%	4.5%	=	1.88%	1.12%
Subtotal	500,000	41.7					3.05%	1.82%
Current liabilities								
Source A	50,000	4.2	×	8.0%	4.8%	=	0.34%	0.20%
Source B	100,000	8.3	×	8.4%	5.0%	=	0.70%	0.42%
Source C	100,000	8.3	×	8.6%	5.2%	=	0.71%	0.43%
Subtotal	250,000	20.8					1.75%	1.05%
Total debt	750,000	62.5					4.80%	2.87%
Total sources	1,200,000	100.0						
Weighted average cost of financing							9.05%	7.12%

Table 9.2 Comparing Cost of Financing to ROA

Statement of Financial Position

				Before tax	After tax
Assets		Equity	$ 450,000	4.25%	4.25%
Non-current	$ 800,000	Liabilities			
Current	400,000	Non-current	500,000	3.05%	1.82%
		Short-term	250,000	1.75%	1.05%
Total	$1,200,000	Total	$1,200,000	9.05%	7.12%

	ROA	Cost
Before tax	14.20%	9.05%
After tax	8.52%	7.12%

Before tax

Debt $750,000	×	14.20% (ROA)	=	$106,500
Debt $750,000	×	7.67% (Cost)	=	(57,525)
Financial leverage				$ 48,975

After tax

Equity financing	15.04%	×	0.375	=	5.64%
Debt financing	4.60%	×	0.625	=	2.88%
Return on assets					8.52%

As noted earlier, the after-tax return assumes the company is in a 40% tax bracket. The spread is positive using the before-tax calculation because the company's assets are generating more than the borrowed funds are costing it (14.20% versus 9.05%). The spread is also positive after taxes (8.52% versus 7.12%). After-tax comparison is typically used for comparing cost of financing to ROA.

Let's push this analysis a little further and calculate how much the company is earning on borrowed funds (see the lower portion of Table 9.2). The company borrowed $750,000 ($500,000 from long-term lenders and $250,000 from short-term lenders) and earned 14.20% (ROA) or $106,500. The WACF from both long- and short-term sources is 7.67%. These amounts are drawn from the sources of financing in Table 9.1.

Sources	Amounts	Weight (%)		Before-Tax Cost		Weighted Cost (%)
Mortgage	$200,000	26.67	×	7.0	=	1.87
Bond	300,000	40.00	×	7.5	=	3.00
Source A	50,000	6.67	×	8.0	=	0.53
Source B	100,000	13.33	×	8.4	=	1.12
Source C	100,000	13.33	×	8.6	=	1.15
Total	$750,000	100.00				7.67%

There is a 6.53% spread (14.20% minus 7.67%) before taxes between the cost of debt financing and the ROA. The company's financial leverage—that is, the amount of money the owners earn by using other people's money—is $48,975 ($750,000 × 6.53%).

The lower portion of Table 9.2 also shows how the shareholders' return can be increased as a result of the company's earnings performance and financial structure. Because the cost of debt financing is 7.67% before taxes, the after-tax cost of financing (assuming the company is in a 40% tax bracket) would be 4.60%. Also, the proportion of the $1,200,000 raised from equity is $450,000, or 37.5%, and the balance, $750,000, or 62.5%, is obtained from debt. Instead of earning an 11.38% return (12% for share equity and 11% for retained earnings), the shareholders are actually getting 15.04%.

Here is how this number is calculated. Debt financing is constant; that is, no matter what happens, the company has to pay the interest—here, 4.60%, which is 2.88% of the total cost of financing. Table 9.2 shows that the company earns an 8.52% after-tax ROA. By subtracting the 2.88% portion of the debt financing from the 8.52% ROA, we get 5.64% (5.64% ÷ 0.375 = 15.04%).

Economic value added (EVA)
A tool that measures the wealth a company creates for its investors.

Economic Value Added

4 Show how economic value added is used to measure managerial performance related to maximizing shareholder wealth.

A financial concept that has gained prominence in the business community to measure after-tax net operating profit relative to cost of capital is the **economic value added (EVA)**. EVA measures how profitable a company is in terms of creating shareholder wealth. Calculating the EVA begins with the company's revenue and then subtracts the expenses incurred in running the business, which results in *net operating profit before* *taxes (NOPBT)*. Then it subtracts income tax expense to obtain *net operating profit after taxes (NOPAT)*. By deducting from NOPAT the cost of all the capital used, we get EVA. Capital assets include buildings, equipment, computers, and vehicles, as well as working capital.

EVA is expressed by the following formula:

EVA = (Return on total assets − Cost of capital) × Capital

In effect, EVA charges the company for the use of the assets at a rate that compensates the lenders and the shareholders for providing the funds. What is left is EVA, and it measures profits after all costs are covered, including the cost of using assets shown on the statement of financial position.

EVA has become the financial tool of choice at leading companies, such as Coca-Cola, AT&T, Walmart, Eli Lilly, and Quaker Oats. At Eli Lilly, for example, EVA was linked to the company's bonus-plan pay system.

The reasons for the increasing popularity of this performance measurement are the following:

- It closely reflects the wealth created for shareholders.
- It promotes management accountability.
- It helps managers to make better decisions.

Table 9.3 shows an example of how EVA is calculated. The company's NOPBT is $1 million. On an after-tax basis, the NOPAT is $550,000. The company here is in a 45% income tax bracket. The company's cost of capital of 10.9% (after tax) to finance the $4,500,000 of capital funds (trade and other payables are excluded from this calculation because suppliers do not charge interest) produces $490,500 in finance costs. The difference between the NOPAT and the cost of capital gives a $59,500 positive EVA. EVA can also be calculated by using the formula:

EVA = (Return on total assets − Cost of capital) × Capital
= (12.22% − 10.9%) × $4,500,000 = $ 59,500 (rounded from $59,400)

Table 9.3 Economic Value Added

	Net Operating Profit	Minus	Cost of Capital	Equals	EVA
NOPBT	$1,000,000	Weighted cost	10.9%*		
Income tax expense	(450,000)	of capital	×		
		Total capital	$4,500,000		
NOPAT	$ 550,000	*MINUS*	$ (490,500)	*EQUALS*	$59,500

*10.9% = 60% of equity at 14.5%, or 8.7%, plus 40% of debt at 5.5%, or 2.2% (8.7 + 2.2 = 10.9%).

These calculations show the importance of comparing the cost of capital with ROA. If the ROA is less than the cost of capital, management must either increase the return on its assets or restructure its financing package differently to improve the EVA or the wealth to its shareholders.

Problem-Solving Example 9.3

Economic Value Added

A company's sources of capital and their respective costs are as follows: equity ($600,000 at 12.0%), long-term borrowings ($700,000 at 8.0%), and short-term borrowings ($100,000 at 9.0%). If the company's net operating profit before taxes is $300,000 and is in the 40% tax bracket, calculate the economic value added.

Solution

The company's economic value added is $68,980.

Step 1: Calculate the cost of capital:

	Amounts	Weight (%)	Cost B.T.	Cost A.T.	WACC
Equity	$ 600,000	0.429	12.0	12.0	5.15
Long-term borrowings	700,000	0.500	8.0	4.8	2.40
Short-term borrowings	100,000	0.071	9.0	5.4	0.38
Total	$1,400,000	1.000			7.93

Step 2: Calculate the economic value added:

Net operating profit before taxes (NOPBT)	$300,000
Income tax expense (40%)	(120,000)
Net operating profit after taxes (NOPAT)	180,000
Cost of capital ($1,400,000 × 7.93%)	(111,020)
Economic value added (EVA)	$ 68,980

Self-Test Exercise 9.3

Economic Value Added

Use CompuTech's 2015 financial statements to calculate the company's EVA.

CompuTech Inc.
Statement of Income
For the year ended December 31, 2015
(in $)

Revenue	800,000
Cost of sales	(406,000)
Gross profit	394,000

(continued)

Self-Test Exercise 9.3 (continued)

Other income	5,000
Distribution costs	(140,000)
Administrative expenses	(110,000)
Finance costs	(30,000)
Total other income/expenses	(275,000)
Profit before taxes	119,000
Income tax expense	(42,000)
Profit for the year	77,000

The company's three major sources of financing are shareholders ($305,000), long-term borrowings ($200,000), and short-term borrowings ($85,000). The equity portion was split between share capital of $170,000 and retained earnings of $135,000.

The cost of capital for these three sources of financing is as follows:

Common share equity	14.0%
Long-term borrowings	11.0%
Short-term borrowings	13.0%

Answers to the Self-Test Exercises can be found at www.bergeron7e.nelson.com.

Cost of Capital

5 Describe the parts of the average weighted cost of capital: common shares, retained earnings, preferred shares, and long-term borrowings.

The cost of capital incurred by businesses is set out in contracts made between a borrowing company and the stakeholders. The key issues are (1) dividends and growth potential expected by the common shareholders (common shareholders and retained earnings), (2) the dividends the company will pay to preferred shareholders, and (3) the amount of interest it will pay to lenders.

This section shows how to calculate the cost of capital for a hypothetical company called Wildwood Inc. Assume that Wildwood's management wants to raise $20 million to invest in different capital projects. We will calculate the cost of capital of four financing sources:

1. Common shares
2. Retained earnings
3. Preferred shares
4. Long-term borrowings

Afterward, we will define the marginal cost of capital. Let's first examine the characteristics of each of these major sources of financing.

Characteristics of long-term financing sources
Payout, risk, voting rights, cost of capital, tax cost, and cost of issue; these characteristics should be considered when raising funds from long-term sources.

CHARACTERISTICS OF LONG-TERM CAPITAL SOURCES

Common share, preferred share, and debt financing have one important common characteristic: They are all obtained from external sources. Retained earnings (that is, profit for the year generated by a business) is the only internal financing source. Table 9.4 summarizes the basic **characteristics of long-term financing sources**

Table 9.4 Characteristics of the Major Sources of Long-Term Financing

	Common Shares	Retained Earnings	Preferred Shares	Debt
Payout	Dividends are paid after debt and preferred dividends.	Reduced payment of dividends leaves more funds in a business; may be unfavourable in the short term but favourable in the long term.	Same as debt; the amount is specified by agreement.	Interest and principal must be paid according to the contract.
	Company is not forced to make payment.		Dividends can be cumulated from year to year.	Bondholders do not participate in superior earnings.
Risk	They do not carry a fixed maturity date.	They increase the value and worth of a business.	They have maturity and are usually callable.	If lenders are not paid according to the agreement, they can force a business into receivership.
			They have prior claim over common shareholders for receiving dividends and other assets if company is liquidated.	
Voting rights (control)	New issue changes the ownership structure (extends voting rights). Holders have a legal right to make major decisions (elect board of directors).	When earnings are retained in a business, existing owners do not have ownership right.	They have limited voting privileges; if they do, it is for minority representation on board of directors.	They have no say in business unless the bond goes into default.
Cost of capital	The rate is more difficult to determine because external factors and the growth potential of a business form part of the cost.	The cost is not easily determinable because of unpredictable growth trends.	The cost is easy to calculate because the source has a maturity date and a stated dividend rate and share price.	The cost is easy to calculate and determinable because the interest rate is stipulated.
Tax cost	Common dividends are not tax deductible.	They are taxed before payments are made to shareholders.	Preferred dividends are not tax deductible.	Interest charges are tax deductible.
Cost of issue	Underwriting and distribution costs are usually higher than preferred share and debt financing.	They avoid the cost of issue.	The flotation cost is expensive.	The underwriting cost is less expensive than the alternatives.

(payout, risk, voting rights or control, cost of capital, tax cost, and cost of a new issue) from an issuing company's point of view.

Payout is the money that a business must pay its stakeholders in exchange for funds. Payout ranges from compulsory payment (debt) of principal and interest to non-obligatory payments, such as dividends on common shares.

Risk refers to the impact each source of financing has on a business if the business is unable to meet its obligations. Debt financing is the riskiest choice, particularly when economic or business conditions are difficult to predict, because bondholders may demand that interest be paid as per agreement. If it is not, they can force the business into receivership.

Voting rights refer to the control that different stakeholders have over a business. Those who have the ultimate control of a company are the common shareholders. The issue of a new bond or preferred shares does not take away the rights of existing shareholders, but the issue of new common shares dilutes common shareholders' voting control. Additional shareholders can force a company to spread earnings more widely and thinly (see the numbers in Table 9.5 for the spread of profit to new and existing shareholders).

Cost of capital includes the costs associated with the borrowing of money, such as payment of dividends for common or preferred shares, interest on debt, underwriting and distribution costs, and taxes. All these elements must be weighted to determine the costs associated with each source of financing. Costs related to preferred shares and debt are more easily determinable and relatively more certain than common share financing.

Tax cost plays an important part in deciding whether to use share or debt financing. Common or preferred share dividends are not tax deductible; interest on bonds is.

Table 9.5 Impact of Debt and Share Financing on Profit

	Common Shares (A)	Preferred Shares (B)	Debt (C)
Profit before taxes	$500,000	$ 500,000	$ 500,000
Financing costs	0	0	(50,000)
Taxable income	500,000	500,000	450,000
Income tax expense (at 45%)	(225,000)	(225,000)	(202,500)
Profit for the year	275,000	275,000	247,500
Preferred dividends	0	(60,000)	0
Profit to common shareholders	275,000	215,000	247,500
Profit to new shareholders	(123,750)	—	—
Profit to existing shareholders	$ 151,250	$ 215,000	$ 247,500

Financing assumptions

A. *Common share financing* of $500,000 raised from new shareholders.
B. *Preferred share financing* of $500,000 raised from investors with a dividend rate of 12%.
C. *Debt financing* of $500,000 raised from lenders with interest rate of 10%.

Table 9.5 shows the impact taxes have on debt and share financing. Alternative C (debt financing) is the least attractive form of financing because the profit after taxes is $247,500, compared with $275,000 for alternatives A and B. However, alternative C is the most lucrative for the existing shareholders because they earn $96,250 ($247,500 − $151,250) more than common share financing and $32,500 ($247,500 − $215,000) over preferred share financing.

Cost of issue includes the charges associated with underwriting and distributing a new issue. Costs of issuing common shares are usually higher because the investigation is more detailed than for preferred share and debt financing. A company that wants to raise funds will examine all the advantages and disadvantages of each source of financing and select the one that best meets its specific needs at the time of the issue.

The main factors that are considered when raising funds are as follows:

- The nature of a company's cash flows
- The company's annual burden of payments (existing debt)
- The cost of financing each type of capital
- The control factor
- The expectations of the existing common shareholders
- The flexibility of future financing decisions
- The pattern of the capital structure in the industry
- The stability of the company's earnings
- The desire to use financial leverage
- The market conditions that can easily dictate the use of one form of capital source over another

CALCULATING THE COST OF CAPITAL

Let's now calculate the cost of long-term capital sources, namely, common shares, retained earnings, preferred shares, and debt.

Common Shares

Both preferred share and debt costs are easily calculated, quite determinable, and certain. They are contracts signed by the company and the shareholders or bondholders.

Cost of common shares
Dividends paid to shareholders, flotation costs, and growth rate.

Calculating the **cost of common shares** is more complicated. The common shareholders know what they want, but it is difficult for the treasurer of a company to estimate the future expected values of the business in terms of growth, retained earnings, and so on, all of which are incorporated in the calculation. Two different approaches are used for calculating the cost of common shares.

The first approach is based on past performance. By looking at trends related to common share prices and dividend payments, the treasurer can price a new issue. For instance, if, during the past five years, the selling price of common shares has been $25 and dividends paid were $2.50, the average investor's rate of return is 10%

(\$2.50 ÷ \$25). If there are no significant changes in shareholders' expectations, interest rates, or investors' attitudes toward risk, the treasurer can assume that the future cost of common shares will be 10%.

The second approach is based on forecasts. Here, the treasurer considers three factors: (1) annual common dividends to be paid, (2) price of the common shares, and (3) expected growth in earnings and dividends. The formula to calculate the cost of common shares is as follows:

$$\textbf{Cost of common shares} = \frac{\textbf{Dividends on common shares}}{\textbf{Market price of the share} - \textbf{Issue costs}} + \textbf{Growth rate}$$

Let's use Wildwood Inc.'s financing package. The company intends to raise \$10 million from common shares. The common share market price is \$100, and the company's current annual common dividend payout is 10% or \$10 per share. Historically, the company's growth performance in earnings, dividends, and share price has been 4% a year, which will presumably continue during the next few years. Using the formula, Wildwood Inc.'s cost of common shares would be 14%:

$$\textbf{Cost of common shares} = \frac{\$10}{\$100} + 4\% = 14\%$$

The flotation cost or the cost of selling a new issue is also considered. If Wildwood Inc.'s flotation costs are 10% on a \$100 common share issue, the company would net \$90. The cost of the new shares would be 15.11%:

$$\textbf{Cost of common shares} = \frac{\$10}{\$100(1-0.10)} + 4\% = 15.11\%$$

The company is showing growth because part of the retained earnings is plowed back into investments. These investments generate additional earnings and have a favourable effect on the company's growth potential. For example, suppose Wildwood Inc. earns 20% on its investments, half of each dollar earned is paid in dividends, and the other half retained in the business, means that each new reinvested dollar produces 10 cents (\$0.50 × 20%). Instead of reinvesting half the earnings into the business, suppose management decides to pay all its earnings in dividends; this may halt the company's growth. The market price of the share may remain at \$100 as the investors would still receive a 14% return. (The payment of dividends will be covered later in this chapter.) Here is how this rate is calculated:

$$\textbf{Cost of common shares} = \frac{\$14}{\$100} + 0 = 14\%$$

Retained Earnings

Wildwood Inc. expects to generate $2 million through its earnings. Some managers may think that retained earnings are "free money"; although the money may be free to them, it is not to the shareholders. Shareholders expect to make a return on their money (equity), because they would expect to earn it if they were to invest the $2 million elsewhere. This is sometimes referred to as **opportunity cost**. Shareholders make a sacrifice by not pursuing the next best investment alternative.

Opportunity cost The income sacrificed by not pursuing the next best investment alternative.

Calculating the **cost of retained earnings** is similar to calculating the cost of common shares, except that issue costs are not incurred. If the company expects to earn $20 a share and pay $10 in dividends during the coming year, and the growth pattern is also 4%, the cost of retained earnings will be 14%.

Cost of retained earnings Dividends and growth rate.

Preferred Shares

Preferred shares are a hybrid of common shares and debt. Like debt, preferred shares carry a fixed contracted commitment for a company to pay—in this case, the dividends due to the preferred shareholders. In the event of liquidation, preferred shareholders take precedence over common shareholders. Dividends are paid to preferred shareholders before the common dividends are paid.

Calculating the **cost of preferred shares** is relatively easy because they carry a maturity date and a stated dividend rate with a current price. For example, if Wildwood Inc. issued preferred shares of $1 million bearing 12%, the cost would be $120,000 annually. If, one year from now, the preferred shares were sold in the market for 90% of their value, say $900,000, the interest rate to be earned by the new preferred shareholders would be 13.33% (12% ÷ 90%). Several factors can influence a decline in the market value of such shares:

Cost of preferred shares Fixed dividends paid to shareholders and the flotation costs.

- The general rise of interest rates, which forces the price of the shares to drop
- A renewed fear of rampant inflation
- A decline in the general value of the business as an investment opportunity

Wildwood Inc. would also have to pay a commission to the investment dealers, and such flotation costs would be included in the calculation.

Assuming that Wildwood Inc. sells 10,000 preferred shares at $100 each, bearing a 12% dividend rate, and the investment dealers charge a selling and distribution commission of $4 a share, Wildwood Inc. would net $96 a share. The formula used for calculating the cost of preferred shares is as follows:

$$\textbf{Cost of preferred shares} = \frac{\textbf{Dividends on preferred shares}}{\textbf{Market value of the share} - \textbf{Flotation costs}}$$

Wildwood Inc.'s cost of the preferred share issue would be 12.5% or $125,000:

$$\textbf{Cost of preferred shares} = \frac{\$12}{\$100 - \$4} = 12.5\%$$

So far, we have calculated the cost of raising $13 million of the $20 million that Wildwood Inc. wants to raise. The remaining $7 million would have to come from debt financing.

Debt

Cost of debt Finance costs less income tax expense.

The **cost of debt** financing is relatively easy to calculate. For example, if a company borrows $100,000 for one year at 10%, the lenders would receive $10,000 in finance costs. Ignoring income tax for the moment, the cost of capital for that source would be 10%.

Debt financing considers two fundamental questions. First, how should the cost be calculated when there are several different types of bonds? Second, because finance cost is tax deductible, how does income tax affect the cost of debt?

First, if there are several bonds with different interest rates, we have to calculate the average rate of interest. For example, let's assume that Wildwood Inc. decides to issue two bonds, a senior bond (like a first mortgage on a house) for $5 million at 7%, and a $2 million subordinated bond (like a second mortgage; it is paid only if the senior bonds are paid) at 9%. The average interest rate is calculated as follows:

$$\textbf{Average cost of bonds} = \frac{(\$5,000,000 \times 7\%) + (\$2,000,000 \times 9\%)}{\$7,000,000} = 7.57\%$$

Second, we must deal with the impact of income taxes on the cost of debt. Because finance costs are tax deductible, we must find the income tax rate to calculate the effective cost of debt. The higher the income tax rate, the lower the effective cost of debt will be. For example, if a company has a 40% income tax rate, the after-tax cost of borrowing $7 million in bonds is 4.54% [7.57% × (1 − 0.40)] or $317,800. If the income tax rate is 25%, the after-tax cost of borrowing would be 5.68% [7.57% × (1.0 − 0.25)] or $397,600. If no taxes are paid, the cost of debt would be 7.57% or $529,900, annually.

The formula used for calculating the after-tax cost of debt follows:

$$\textbf{After-tax cost of debt} = \textbf{Before-tax cost} \times (\textbf{1.0} - \textbf{tax rate})$$

By applying this formula to the $7 million bond issue, and assuming that Wildwood Inc.'s tax rate is 40%, the after-tax cost of the debt would be 4.54%:

$$\textbf{After-tax cost of debt} = 7.57\% \times (1.0 - 0.40) = 4.54\%$$

Weighted Average Cost of Capital

We have now calculated the cost of capital for common shares, retained earnings, preferred shares, and debt. With this information, we can calculate Wildwood Inc.'s weighted average cost of capital. We need to (1) compute the proportion of each source of capital relative to the total capital structure, and (2) multiply this number by the cost of that source of capital. As shown in Table 9.6, Wildwood Inc.'s weighted

Table 9.6 Weighted Average Cost of Capital

Source of Capital	Amount of Capital	Percent of Total		After-Tax Cost of Capital		Proportion of Cost
Common shares	$10,000,000	0.50	×	15.11%	=	7.555%
Retained earnings	2,000,000	0.10	×	14.00%	=	1.400%
Preferred shares	1,000,000	0.05	×	12.50%	=	0.625%
Debt	7,000,000	0.35	×	4.54%	=	1.589%
	$20,000,000	1.00				11.169%

cost of capital is 11.169%. This rate is the approximate value that would be used as the hurdle rate (the lowest acceptable rate of return on an investment) when reviewing potential capital investment projects.

Marginal Cost of Capital

Let's assume that, during the year, Wildwood Inc. wants to raise an extra $2 million to invest in more capital projects. Let's also assume that debt and preferred shares are raised at the same cost, while the cost for raising common shares is higher. By using the common share dividend yield, (say, 12%), a 10% flotation charge, and a 4% growth rate, the new cost of the common share issue would be 17.33%:

$$\textbf{Cost of common shares} = \frac{12.00\%}{0.90} + 4\% = 17.33\%$$

Marginal cost of capital (MCC)
The increased average cost from having obtained new funds at higher rates than previously.

Wildwood Inc.'s new cost of capital is 12.740% (see Table 9.7). The additional dollars raised above $20 million mean that Wildwood Inc. would have a new average cost of capital of 12.740%; this is referred to as the **marginal cost of capital (MCC).** Wildwood Inc.'s MCC, which was 11.169% to raise the $20 million, increases to 12.740% to raise $22 million (an extra $2 million).

Figure 9.3 shows graphically the increased cost of capital from 11.2% to 12.7%, which is due to the additional $2 million raised from common shares. The graph

Table 9.7 New Weighted Average Cost of Capital

Source of Capital	Amount of Capital	Percent of Total		After-Tax Cost of Capital		Proportion of Cost
Common shares	$12,000,000	0.5455	×	17.33%	=	9.454%
Retained earnings	2,000,000	0.0909	×	14.00%	=	1.273%
Preferred shares	1,000,000	0.0454	×	12.50%	=	0.568%
Debt	7,000,000	0.3182	×	4.54%	=	1.445%
	$22,000,000	1.0000				12.740%

Figure 9.3 Marginal Cost of Capital

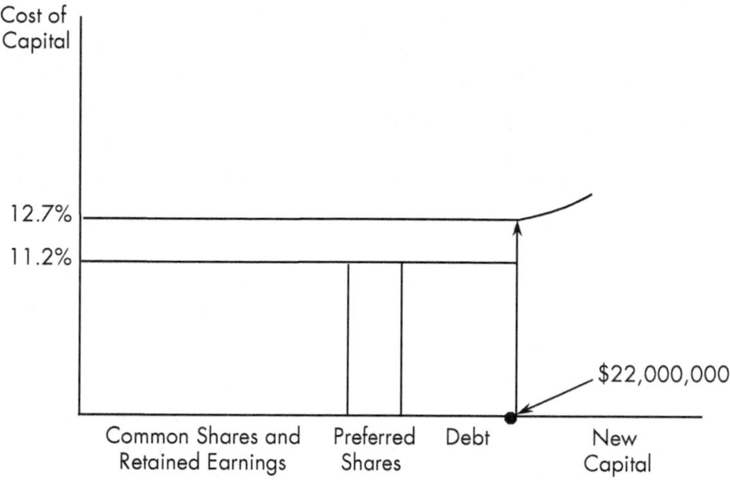

shows that the cost curve is flat up to $22 million; it then moves up gradually and continues to rise. The reason for the rise is that Wildwood Inc. may find it difficult to raise new securities in a short time. If it finds new sources of capital, they will be more expensive because of the higher risk to be borne by the stakeholders and the corresponding higher return they will demand from the company.

Problem-Solving Example 9.4

Weighted Average Cost of Capital

Vincent and Hannah want to buy a cottage. They have accumulated $20,000 in savings, which pays them 3%. The bank is willing to give them a $110,000 first mortgage at 6% and another financial institution will lend them $10,000 on a second mortgage at 7%. Vincent's brother is also prepared to advance them $10,000 at 5%. What would the couple's weighted average cost of capital be?

Solution

The WACC is 5.60%

	Amounts	Weight (%)	Cost (%)	WACC
Savings	$ 20,000	0.133	3.0	0.40
Mortgage	110,000	0.733	6.0	4.40
Second mortgage	10,000	0.067	7.0	0.47
Brother	10,000	0.067	5.0	0.33
TOTAL	$150,000	1.000		5.60

Self-Test Exercise 9.4

Weighted Average Cost of Capital

Len and Joan are considering buying a cottage valued at $175,000. They have a combined savings of $40,000, and the bank approved a $120,000 first mortgage. Len's father agreed to provide them with a $10,000 loan. Also, Joan was lucky enough to win $5,000 at a casino. If Len and Joan invested their money in short-term deposits, they could earn 4.5%. The interest rate offered by the bank on the first mortgage was 10%. Len's father agreed to lend the money at only 5%. Calculate Len and Joan's weighted average cost of capital.

Answers to the Self-Test Exercises can be found at www.bergeron7e.nelson.com.

Using the Marginal Cost of Capital in Capital Budgeting Decisions

The purpose of calculating the MCC is to ensure that the cost of borrowing does not exceed the return that will be earned from capital projects. For example, if it costs 15% to borrow capital dollars, the company will need the aggregate return of all projects to be at least 15%; if it is less, the company will be in a negative return position. Let us examine how this works.

Once the MCC is calculated, the next step is to relate it to capital projects. Using the Wildwood Inc. example, if the company intends to invest $20 million in capital projects giving an 11.2% return, most projects will be accepted. However, if managers submit capital projects that exceed the $20 million level, management will then have to examine all investment opportunities and accept a mix of projects that will maximize the overall value of the business.

The first step is to find the MCC, such as the one shown in Figure 9.4. Second is evaluating projects and determining the rate of return. The capital budgeting technique used to assess the economic attractiveness of capital projects is called the *internal rate of return (IRR)*. This technique is explained in Chapter 11. Using the IRR, the aggregate cash flow of all projects is discounted. The idea is to find the net present value of all projects that will give a zero figure. This happens when the total cash inflow of all projects equals the total cash outflow. In Wildwood Inc.'s case, management can approve a mix of projects that, when discounted by a rate of 11.2%, give $20 million. If the company's aggregate IRR does not equal the cost of capital, we have to proceed to the next step.

The discounted values of the cash flows of all projects are then calculated at various discount rates (say, 35% down to 5%) and the result is plotted on a graph (see Figure 9.4). If the company raises $20 million at a cost of 11.2%, it will approve $20 million worth of capital projects. If more projects are approved, the aggregate IRR will fall below the 11.2% point, and Wildwood Inc. would be in a negative return position.

Figure 9.4 Marginal Cost of Capital and Internal Rate of Return

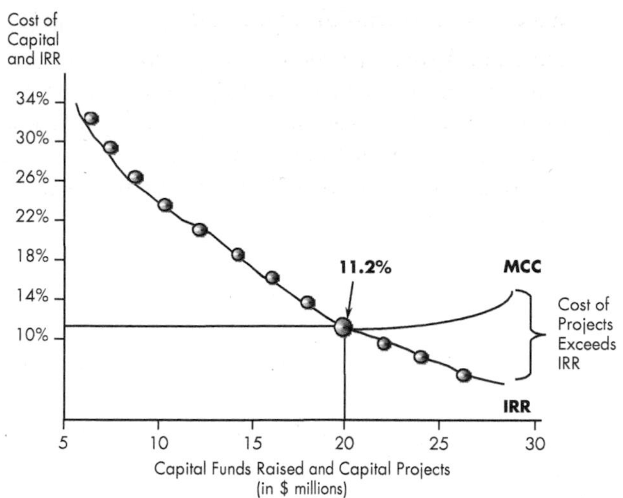

Problem-Solving Example 9.5

Weighted Average Cost of Capital

Calculate the company's weighted average cost of capital with the following information: common shares ($5 million at 11%), retained earnings ($1 million at 8%), and long-term borrowings ($6 million at 7% before tax). The company's income tax rate is 30% and the common share's growth rate is expected to be 3%.

Solution

The WACC is 7.70%.

In millions of $	Amounts	Weight (%)	A.T. Cost (%)	WACC
Common shares	5.0	0.417	11.0	4.59
Retained earnings	1.0	0.083	8.0	0.66
Long-term borrowings	6.0	0.500	4.9	2.45
Total	12.0	1.000		7.70

Self-Test Exercise 9.5

Weighted Average Cost of Capital

Len and Joan are considering investing $1 million to open two other retail outlets in different cities. After reviewing the financial projections with their accountant, May Ogaki, the Millers determined that

(continued)

Self-Test Exercise 9.5 (continued)

the two retail outlets showed a combined 8.5% return on investment. The Millers would be able to obtain the following amounts:

Common shares	$ 250,000
Retained earnings	100,000
First mortgage	500,000
Second mortgage	150,000
Total	$1,000,000

The cost of capital for each source of financing is as follows:

Common shares	14.0%
Retained earnings	14.0%
First mortgage	10.0%
Second mortgage	13.0%

The company's corporate income tax rate is 33%.

Question

1. Calculate the company's weighted cost of capital.
2. Should the Millers go ahead with the project?

Answers to the Self-Test Exercises can be found at www.bergeron7e.nelson.com.

Leverage Analysis

6 Demonstrate the importance of leverage analysis and how operating leverage, financial leverage, and combined leverage are calculated.

Leverage analysis is used to determine the financing package or cost structure that will optimize the worth of a business. The purpose of leverage analysis is to answer one fundamental question: What is the best financing mix or capital structure to use to finance our assets? An example will illustrate how leverage analysis works. Let's assume that a firm borrows $400,000 at 6% after tax to finance projects that cost $500,000 and earn 12% after tax. Here, the owners earn $36,000 (after-tax profit of $60,000 less finance costs of $24,000) on their $100,000 investment, a return on equity of 36%. This compares favourably to the project's return of only 12%. Under these circumstances, where there is a wide spread between the rate of return and the rate of interest, management would use debt rather than equity funds. As mentioned before, debt is cheaper than equity financing.

This example is relatively simple, but it is usually more complicated to determine the leverage factor that produces the greatest financial benefits. To understand leverage, we have to look at the behaviour of revenue, fixed and variable costs, profit before taxes and finance costs, debt charges, and earnings per share (EPS). Figure 9.5 shows the three types of leverage: operating leverage, financial leverage, and total or combined leverage.

Figure 9.5 The Leverage Concept

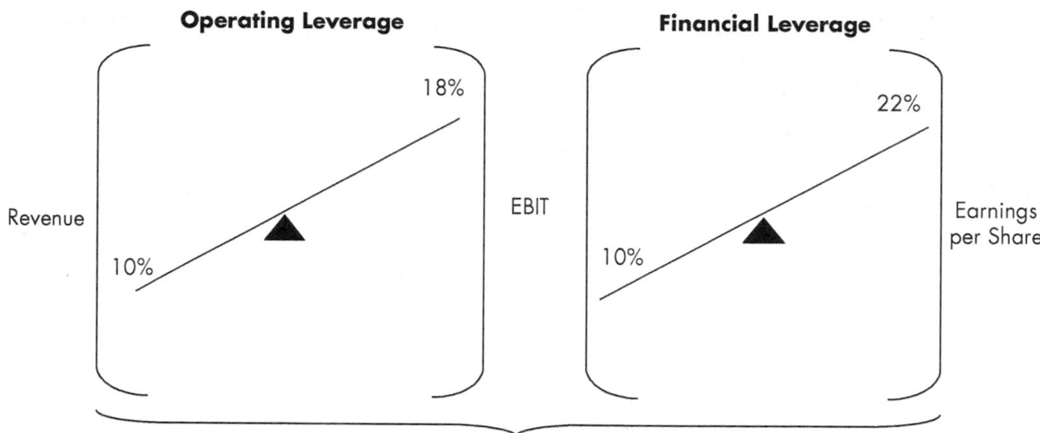

OPERATING LEVERAGE

Operating leverage A financial technique that determines to what extent fixed costs should be used relative to variable costs.

Operating leverage deals with the behaviour of costs at the operating level (e.g., company or plant); it does not consider financing costs. This approach determines the most suitable costs (fixed versus variable costs) that will maximize earnings before the payment of finance costs or dividends.

Operating leverage is based on the break-even analysis concept, a decision-making tool we examined in Chapter 5. It involves the analysis of relationships between three elements: revenue, fixed costs, and variable costs. The idea is to select the cost mix that will maximize earnings under a set of economic or industry considerations. A favourable operating leverage is achieved when a change in revenue generates a larger change in EBIT (earnings before interest and taxes). As shown in Figure 9.5, a 10% increase in revenue produces an 18% increase in EBIT. The element that amplifies the earnings is the relationship between fixed costs and total operating costs.

Here is an example of how operating leverage works. Let's assume that management is thinking of modernizing a manufacturing plant that requires a $700,000 capital expenditure. Management will have to identify the level of sales volume and revenue that will be achieved in the future and the impact that the new technology will have on the company's fixed and variable cost structure.

As shown in Table 9.8, the new technology will change the company's operating cost structure. Under the present cost structure, the company's fixed costs are $200,000, and it earns a $5.00 contribution (an amount that will be used to pay fixed costs). If the company decides to modernize, the cost structure would change and the new fixed costs would increase to $300,000 (an increase of $100,000 over existing operations). However, the unit variable costs will be reduced to $8.00 (from $10.00)

Table 9.8 **Impact of Plant Modernization on Operating Leverage**

	Present Production Methods			Proposed Production Methods		
Fixed costs		$200,000			$300,000	
Selling price		15.00			15.00	
Variable costs		(10.00)			(8.00)	
Contribution		$ 5.00			$ 7.00	
	High	Expected	Low	High	Expected	Low
No. of units	100,000	70,000	40,000	100,000	70,000	40,000
(in $000s)						
Revenue	$1,500	$1,050	$600	$1,500	$1,050	$600
Variable costs	(1,000)	(700)	(400)	(800)	(560)	(320)
Fixed costs	(200)	(200)	(200)	(300)	(300)	(300)
Total costs	(1,200)	(900)	(600)	(1,100)	(860)	(620)
EBIT	$ 300	$ 150	$ –	$ 400	$ 190	$(20)

because of higher productivity. The new contribution margin would increase to $7.00. In other words, the company would earn an extra $2.00 in contribution to pay for the $100,000 fixed cost increment. The question is this: Is the expansion worth the investment? To answer it, the company would have to estimate the sales volume that it expects to achieve in the next year or two. Table 9.8 shows that at sales of 40,000 units, the company would break even with the existing facility, but if management modernizes its plant, the company would incur a $20,000 loss. However, if the company can sell 100,000 units, this new sales level would justify the investment because it would generate $400,000 in EBIT instead of $300,000 with the present production methods.

Essentially, operating leverage measures how much the operating cost structure increases EBIT. A 10% increase in revenue (with the proposed production methods) generates a 17.5% increase in EBIT or a leverage of 1.75 (see Table 9.9).

Table 9.9 **Operating Leverage**

	For the Proposed Production Methods (high)		
Revenue	$1,500,000	$1,650,000	10.00%
Variable costs	(800,000)	(880,000)	10.00%
Contribution margin	700,000	770,000	10.00%
Fixed costs	(300,000)	(300,000)	—
Profit (EBIT)	$ 400,000	$ 470,000	17.50%

$$\frac{\text{Contribution margin}}{\text{Contribution margin} - \text{Fixed costs}} = \frac{\$700{,}000}{\$400{,}000} = 1.75$$

Financial leverage
A financial technique used to determine the most favourable capital structure (equity versus debt).

FINANCIAL LEVERAGE

Financial leverage is used to choose the most favourable capital structure—the one that will generate the greatest financial benefits to the shareholders. Shareholders generally favour projects with return rates that exceed the cost of borrowed funds. Because debt is the cheapest source of funds, shareholders will prefer to borrow as much as possible from this particular source (provided that the projects can generate enough cash to pay off the debt).

Financial leverage can be gauged by looking at one option and changing its capital structure mix to determine by how much the leverage can enhance the EPS position. By excluding the effect of operating leverage from this analysis (Table 9.9), Table 9.10 shows that a 10% increase in EBIT produces a 16% increase in profit before taxes. Here, the financial leverage is 1.6.

Combined leverage
A financial technique used to calculate both operating and financial leverage.

COMBINED LEVERAGE

Combined leverage simply calculates both the operating and financial leverage. As shown in Table 9.11, when revenue increases by 10%, profit for the year (or profit before taxes) shows a 28% increase or a leverage of 2.8. The income tax rate used is 40%.

Table 9.10 Financial Leverage

For the Proposed Production Methods (high)			
EBIT	$ 400,000	$ 440,000	10.0%
Interest	(150,000)	(150,000)	—
Profit before taxes	$ 250,000	$ 290,000	16.0%

$$\frac{\text{EBIT}}{\text{EBIT} - \text{Interest}} = \frac{\$400{,}000}{\$250{,}000} = 1.6$$

Table 9.11 Combined Leverage

For the Proposed Production Methods (high)			
Revenue	$1,500,000	$1,650,000	10.0%
Variable costs	(800,000)	(880,000)	10.0%
Contribution margin	700,000	770,000	10.0%
Fixed costs	(300,000)	(300,000)	—
EBIT	400,000	470,000	17.5%
Finance costs	(150,000)	(150,000)	—
Profit before taxes	250,000	320,000	28.0%
Income tax expense	(100,000)	(128,000)	28.0%
Profit for the year	$ 150,000	$ 192,000	28.0%

$$\frac{\text{Contribution margin}}{\text{EBIT} - \text{Interest}} = \frac{\$700{,}000}{\$250{,}000} = 2.8$$

or

$$1.75 \times 1.6 = 2.8$$

Problem-Solving Example 9.6

Leverages

With the following information, calculate the company's (1) operating leverage, (2) financial leverage, and (3) combined leverage: revenue ($800,000), variable costs ($550,000), fixed costs ($200,000), interest charges ($30,000), income tax rate (30%).

Solution

Operating leverage is 5.0, financial leverage is 2.5, and combined leverage is 12.5.

1. Operating leverage

			Change
Revenue	$800,000	$880,000	10%
Variable costs	(550,000)	(605,000)	10%
Contribution margin	250,000	275,000	10%
Fixed costs	(200,000)	(200,000)	—
Profit before taxes	50,000	75,000	50%
Income tax expense (30%)	(15,000)	(22,500)	50%
Profit after taxes	$ 35,000	$ 52,500	50%

[$250,000 ÷ ($250,000 − $200,000)] = 5.0

2. Financial leverage

			Change
EBIT	$50,000	$55,000	10%
Interest charges	(30,000)	(30,000)	—
Profit before taxes	20,000	25,000	25%
Income tax expense (30%)	(6,000)	(7,500)	25%
Profit after taxes	$14,000	$17,500	25%

[$50,000 ÷ ($50,000 − $30,000)] = 2.5

3. Combined leverage

			Change
Revenue	$800,000	$880,000	10%
Variable costs	(550,000)	(605,000)	10%
Contribution margin	250,000	275,000	10%
Fixed costs	(200,000)	(200,000)	—
EBIT	50,000	75,000	50%
Interest charges	(30,000)	(30,000	—
Profit before taxes	20,000	45,000	125%
Income tax expense (30%)	(6,000)	(13,500)	125%
Profit after taxes	$ 14,000	$ 31,500	125%

[$250,000 ÷ ($50,000 − $30,000)] = 12.5 or 5.0 × 2.5 = 12.5

Self-Test Exercise 9.6

Operating Leverage, Financial Leverage, and Combined Leverage

Use the following information to calculate CompuTech's operating leverage, financial leverage, and combined leverage.

Revenue	$420,000
Variable costs	$212,000
Fixed costs	$148,000
Finance costs	$ 14,000
Income tax rate	33%

Answers to the Self-Test Exercises can be found at www.bergeron7e.nelson.com.

Problem-Solving Example 9.7

Effects of Changes on Leverages

Use the information in Problem-Solving Example 9.6, and assume that the company plans to make the following changes by modifying their plant: reduce variable costs by $40,000, increase fixed cost by $30,000, and increase finance charges by $5,000. Are these changes worthwhile from a leverage point of view?

Solution

The changes would not be advantageous from a leverage point of view: operating leverage would drop from 5.0 to 4.8, financial leverage from 2.5 to 2.4, and combined leverage from 12.5 to 11.6.

1. Operating leverage

			Change
Revenue	$800,000	$880,000	10%
Variable costs	(510,000)	(561,000)	10%
Contribution margin	290,000	319,000	10%
Fixed costs	(230,000)	(230,000)	—
Profit before taxes	60,000	89,000	48.3%
Income tax expense (30%)	(18,000)	(26,700)	48.3%
Profit after taxes	$ 42,000	$ 62,300	48.3%

[$290,000 ÷ ($290,000 – $230,000)] = 4.83

(continued)

Problem-Solving Example 9.7 (continued)

2. Financial leverage

			Change
EBIT	$60,000	$66,000	10%
Interest charges	(35,000)	(35,000)	—
Profit before taxes	25,000	31,000	24%
Income tax expense (30%)	(7,500)	(9,300)	24%
Profit after taxes	$17,500	$21,700	24%

[$60,000 ÷ ($60,000 − $35,000)] = 2.4

3. Combined leverage

			Change
Revenue	$800,000	$880,000	10%
Variable costs	(510,000)	(561,000)	10%
Contribution margin	290,000	319,000	10%
Fixed costs	(230,000)	(230,000)	—
EBIT	60,000	89,000	48%
Interest charges	(35,000)	(35,000	—
Profit before taxes	25,000	54,000	116%
Income tax expense (30%)	(7,500)	(16,200)	116%
Profit after taxes	$ 17,500	$ 37,800	116%

[$290,000 ÷ ($60,000 - $35,000)] = 11.6 or 4.83 × 2.4 = 11.6

Self-Test Exercise 9.7

Effect of Changes in Costs on Operating Leverage, Financial Leverage, and Combined Leverage

Use the data contained in Self-Test Exercise 9.6, and assume that the Millers want to increase the company's automation and are able to reduce the variable costs to $165,000, increase the fixed costs by $20,000 (i.e., to $168,000), and increase the interest charges (finance costs) from $14,000 to $18,000. Calculate the new operating leverage, financial leverage, and combined leverage.

Answers to the Self-Test Exercises can be found at www.bergeron7e.nelson.com.

Financial Markets

7 Discuss financial markets, the stock market, and three theories related to dividend payments.

Financial markets Organizations and procedures involved in the buying and selling of financial assets.

Financial markets are the businesses, individuals, government institutions, and procedures involved in buying and selling financial assets. The objective of financial markets is to match buyers and sellers efficiently and effectively. Organizations and individuals that want to raise money are brought together in the financial markets with those that have a surplus of funds. The financial market system is an important vehicle for the operation of the economy. Given that there is a transfer of funds between sellers (saving units or savers) to buyers (investing units), the latter must pay for the capital supplied by the savers, and the investment activity is highly influenced by the rate of return (cost of capital) that the firm must pay to entice funds from the savers.

Investment dealers (also known as investment bankers) make possible the transfer of funds between sellers and buyers. When the transfer of these securities is done directly between a borrower (or business) and a lender (or saver), they are called *primary claims* (see Figure 9.6).

Trades of securities can also be done by financial intermediaries, which include banks, trust companies, credit unions, insurance companies, and caisses populaires. As shown in Figure 9.6, they differ somewhat from investment dealers in that they issue *secondary claims* (instead of primary claims) to the ultimate lenders. Financial intermediaries help with the indirect transfer of funds between lenders and borrowers and are paid for their services via an *interest rate spread.* For instance, a bank may loan money to an individual or a business at an average of 8% interest, pay depositors (savers) 5%, and earn 3%, which they will use to operate their financial institution (e.g., salaries and other expenses).

TYPES OF MARKETS

There are several categories of financial markets, each consisting of different types of institutions. Each market deals with somewhat different types of securities, services different types of customers, or even operates in a different part of the country.

Figure 9.6 Transfer of Funds Process

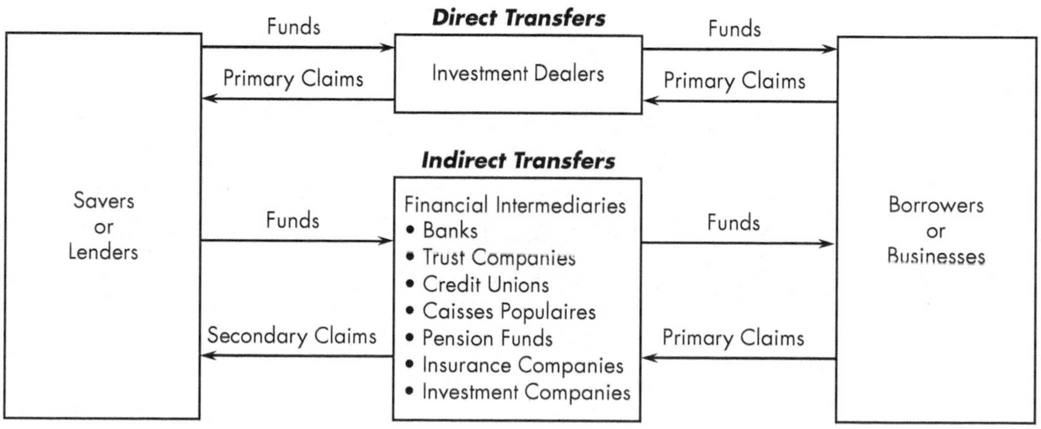

Money markets are the markets for short-term (less than one year) debt securities. Most large corporations participate in the money markets, particularly when they have more cash than they need to run their business. For example, a business might have $100 million in cash and short-term investments. By investing the cash in money market securities, the business can earn interest rather than leaving it in a bank account earning little or no interest.

Capital markets deal with long-term securities, those that have maturities longer than one year. Businesses use these markets for long-term funds, either equity or debt, when they want to raise funds externally. The Toronto Stock Exchange (TSX) and the New York Stock Exchange (NYSE) are examples of such markets.

Primary markets are those in which newly issued securities are bought and sold for the first time. For example, if Rogers Canada or Bell Canada were to sell a new issue of common shares to raise capital, this would be considered a primary market transaction. Each day, in just about every business newspaper, announcements are made about the issuance of new equity or debt securities.

Secondary markets resell existing securities, those that are "used" rather than newly issued shares and bonds. These markets are well established in North America, where shares are traded on a security exchange, such as the TSX.

Spot markets and *future markets* are terms used to identify whether an asset is bought or sold for "on the spot" delivery within days or at a future date (e.g., three months).

Mortgage markets deal with loans on residential, commercial, and industrial real estate.

Consumer credit markets have to do with loans on large items, such as automobiles and appliances, as well as loans to individuals interested in going to university or taking a vacation.

Physical asset markets (also called tangible or real asset markets) deal with real estate, machinery, and so on. While financial markets deal with shares, bonds, and mortgages, physical asset markets deal with real assets.

STOCK MARKET

Stock market
A network of exchanges, brokers, and investors that trade securities.

The **stock market** is a network of exchanges, brokers, and investors that trade securities. It is a place where individuals go to buy and sell shares. The most active stock market in Canada is the TSX, and in the United States, the NYSE, where there are networks of exchanges and brokers.

A *stock exchange* is a physical marketplace where the transfer of securities takes place. A brokerage firm is a company of stockbrokers that generally have the right to trade on an exchange. It employs individuals (the brokers) who are licensed by the government to help people sell and buy securities. While public companies pay fees to the exchange, investors pay fees to the brokers.

In Canada, the securities markets are regulated by provincial and territorial legislation. Depending on the jurisdiction, the securities regulations are established in the *Securities Acts* or consumer affairs legislation, and all jurisdictions require companies to disclose specific information to potential investors when they are about to issue new securities. *Disclosure* means that investors must be given complete and accurate information about the companies behind the shares that are offered for sale.

When someone starts a new business, funds are usually provided by the owner(s), family members, and sometimes friends. Normally, the entrepreneur is the owner of the unincorporated business. Because the business is not incorporated, it is not a corporation and has no shares to sell to the general public. However, if the business is successful and the entrepreneur wants to raise more money for growth purposes, the owner can incorporate and sell shares to others. If the entrepreneur incorporates and sells shares to a small group of individuals without becoming a public entity, the business is a **privately held company**. These corporations can sell shares to a small group of individuals, but this type of transaction is rigorously restricted by provincial and territorial regulations.

Privately held company
A business that can sell shares to a small group of people but not to the general public.

Later, if the business is successful and needs additional funds to expand its operations and seize business opportunities, the entrepreneur can choose to go public and become a publicly traded company. The entrepreneur would approach an investment dealer, who would find out whether a market would welcome the company's offerings and would work on the price of the shares. If the response is positive, the registration procedure would begin with the preparation of a document called a prospectus that discloses the details of a security and the profile of the business in question to prospective investors. The purpose of the prospectus is *disclosure:* it must give a true and accurate picture of the nature of the business and the risks involved.

Publicly traded company
A business that can sell securities broadly, after a prospectus is approved by the securities commission.

Publicly traded companies can sell shares to the general public but require the approval of the provincial or territorial securities commission. Getting approval from and registering with the appropriate securities commission is known as *going public.* Going public requires the help of an investment dealer.

When a prospectus is approved by the securities commission, the investment securities may be offered to the general public. This initial offering is called an **initial public offering (IPO).**

Initial public offering (IPO)
The securities of a company newly established as a public one, offered to the general public for the first time.

If a business continues to grow and is successful, it may want to list its name on the stock market. This makes it easier for investors to buy or trade shares in the secondary market. If, in the future, the company decides to raise more funds from investors, being a **listed company** on the stock exchange would make it easier.

Listed company
A company that is listed and traded on an organized stock exchange.

Share prices are reported each day in financial newspapers, such as the *Globe and Mail* and the *Financial Post,* and on financial websites. Table 9.12 lists the typical financial information shown about companies trading on the stock market. The information includes the stock name, the ticker symbol, the share prices (opening, high, low, and closing prices during the trading day, including the change), the average volume during the trading day, the yield (dividends and percent), the EPS and price/earnings (P/E) ratio, the 52-week stock performance (high and low), and the number of shares outstanding and their value.

In the News 9.2 shows Rogers Communications Inc. financial stock market information as it appeared on the CNX Market link on September 26, 2012.

Table 9.12	Typical Stock Market Information
1. Stock	Abbreviated name of the company (e.g., Rogers for Rogers Communications Inc.)
2. Ticker	The company's tickertape or ticker symbol (e.g., RCI.B for Rogers)
3. Open	Price of the stock when the trading day opened (e.g., 30.00)
4. High	Highest price paid during the trading day (e.g., 33.50)
5. Low	Lowest price paid for the stock during the trading day (e.g., 29.90)
6. Close	Price of the stock at the end of the trading day (e.g., 32.80)
7. Net change	Net change (up or down) from the previous trading day (e.g., 2.80)
8. Average volume	Number of shares that changed hands during the trading day (e.g., 2,100,000 shares)
9. Yield	
• Dividends	Dividends paid (e.g., 0.30)
• Percent	Dividend yield expressed as a percentage (e.g., 3.4%)
10. EPS	Earnings per share (e.g., 1.90)
11. P/E ratio	Price/earnings ratio (e.g., 14.9 times)
12. 52-week high	The highest price paid for the stock during the past year (e.g., 39.00)
13. 52-week low	The lowest price paid for the stock during the past year (e.g., 26.75)
14. Shares out	Number of shares outstanding (e.g., 506.900 million)
15. Quoted market value	Value of the shares on the market (e.g., 15.900 billion)

In The News 9.2

ROGERS COMMUNICATIONS INC.'S STOCK MARKET INFORMATION

Rogers Communications, with headquarters in Toronto, was founded in 1920. It is one of Canada's largest communications companies, particularly in the field of wireless communications and cable television. In 2011, the company employed 28,745 and realized annual revenues of $12.42 billion with net income of $1.74 billion.

Source: Courtesy TMX. ROGERS & MOBIUS Design TM is owned and used with permission of Rogers Communications Inc. For more information about Rogers' stock market performance, visit their official website at www.rogers.com.

DIVIDENDS

Many investors buy shares for the dividends that they expect to receive. As a result, the board of directors pays attention to dividend payouts. Dividend payout also influences a company's cash flow and the level of retained earnings that remains available for reinvestment purposes.

Recall from Chapter 1 that there is a relationship between internal use of cash (retained earnings) and external use of cash (payment of dividends and debt reduction). In cash flow analysis, the amount of cash to be retained in a business for reinvestment purposes has to be balanced with the amount of cash to be paid out as dividends, decisions the board of directors must make. Retained earnings are important for a business if it wants to stimulate growth in future earnings and, as a result, influence future share values. Conversely, if dividends are paid now, shareholders have immediate tangible returns.

Most jurisdictions have laws that regulate the payment of dividends. For example, the Ontario Securities Commission (OSC) is the government agency that administers the *Securities Act* and the *Commodity Futures Act* for Ontario; the OSC also regulates securities and listed futures contract transactions in Ontario. In general, these laws about dividends state the following:

- A company's capital cannot be used to pay dividends.
- Dividends must be paid out of a company's present and past net earnings.
- Dividends cannot be paid when a company is insolvent.

Dividend Theories

Dividend irrelevance theory
A theory suggesting that investors are indifferent to the payment of dividends because the value of lower dividends now is offset by growth-created value in the future.

Dividend preference theory
A theory suggesting that investors prefer instant cash to uncertain future benefits.

The major issue about dividends has to do with how much a company should pay. Does the payment of larger or smaller amounts of dividends have a positive, negative, or neutral effect on a company's share price? Do shareholders prefer current dividends or deferred dividends? There are three major theories regarding the preference of investors for or against dividend payments: the dividend irrelevance theory, the dividend preference theory, and the dividend aversion theory.

The **dividend irrelevance theory** advanced by Miller and Modigliani[1] states that dividends have little effect on share price, because if earnings are kept in the business for growth purposes, the incremental re-invested cash may cause the business to become more profitable or grow faster in the future. That would, in turn, make the future selling price of the shares increase faster and also increase dividend payments in the future.

The **dividend preference theory** advanced by Gordon and Lintner[2] maintains that, in general, investors prefer receiving dividends now compared with not

1. Merton Miller and Franco Modigliani, "Dividend Policy, Growth, and the Valuation of Shares," *Journal of Business 34*, October 1961, pp. 411–433.
2. Myron J. Gordon, "Optimal Investment and Financing Policy," *Journal of Finance*, May 1963, pp. 264–272; and John Lintner, "Dividends, Earnings, Leverage, Stock Prices, and the Supply of Capital to Corporations," *Review of Economics and Statistics*, August 1962, pp. 243–269.

receiving any. The argument is based on the uncertainty factor: What will happen in the future? They argue that investors prefer not to have management use their cash now, in case they cannot make the company grow later. It is a question of trust. The major flaw in this argument is this: If investors are concerned about re-investing their money into the company now, why have they invested their money in that particular company in the first place?

Dividend aversion theory
A theory suggesting that investors may prefer future capital gains to current dividends because of lower tax rates on capital gains.

The **dividend aversion theory** is based on the premise that investors prefer not to receive dividends now to enhance share prices in the future. This argument is based on the assumption that dividends are often taxed at higher rates than capital gains. The decision about receiving versus not receiving dividends has to do with trading immediate dividends for a higher selling price later. The trade-off is in investment income (now) versus the appreciated price that represents a capital gain when the shares are sold. It boils down to one question: Should I receive dividends today or possibly a benefit from a higher price at a later date?

Dividend Policy

Dividend policy is the process in which a business determines what it will pay in dividends. This process deals with two things: the amount to be paid and the pattern under which dividends will be paid. Let's first examine the meaning of the term **dividend payout ratio**, which is the proportion of earnings that a business pays out in dividends. Many businesses have a payout ratio they want to maintain over the long term. The dividend payout ratio is calculated as follows:

Dividend payout ratio
The proportion of earnings that a business pays out in dividends.

$$\textbf{Dividend payout ratio} = \frac{\textbf{Dividend}}{\textbf{Earnings}} = \frac{\textbf{Dividend per share}}{\textbf{EPS}}$$

For example, if a company's dividend per share is \$1.50 and its earnings per share is \$3.50, its dividend payout would be 42.8% (\$1.50 ÷ \$3.50). The business pays a cash dividend of 42.8 cents out of every dollar it earns. Sometimes a business may have trouble paying out its dividends in difficult times or if it has other substantial priorities, such as investing in capital assets or debt repayment.

The second part of dividend policy has to do with the *dividend payment pattern*. Usually, businesses try to pay their dividends on a regular basis. A stable dividend refers to a constant amount of dividend paid at regular intervals and normally increased on a regular basis. A decrease in the amount of dividends carries an unfavourable signal to investors. Consequently, the board of directors makes an effort to keep dividends per share from going down. The objective in the payment of dividends over the long term is to make them grow; sometimes the amount can flatten out but preferably not diminish.

Dividend Payments

At each quarterly meeting, the board of directors evaluates the company's performance and decides the amount of dividends to be paid during the next period. As noted, the board tries to keep the amount of dividends from going down, particularly if the company tries to follow a rigid dividend payment pattern strategy. Most businesses

Problem-Solving Example 9.8

Dividend Payout Ratio

Use the following information to calculate the company's payout ratio: dividends paid ($1,000,000), number of shares outstanding (800,000), profit for the year ($2,500,000).

Solution

The payout ratio is 39.9%.

Dividend per share is $1.25	($1,000,000 ÷ 800,000)
Earnings per share is $3.13	($2,500,000 ÷ 800,000)
Payout ratio is 39.9%	($1.25 ÷ $3.13)

Self-Test Exercise 9.8

Dividend Payout Ratio

Use CompuTech's financial information in Appendix A to calculate the company's payout ratio, for the year 2015. Assume that the company has 40,000 shares outstanding and pays $36,000 in dividends.

Answers to the Self-Test Exercises can be found at www.bergeron7e.nelson.com.

follow a dividend declaration and payment procedure such as the one shown in Figure 9.7. The procedure usually deals with a declaration date, an ex-dividend date, a record date, and a payment date.

The *declaration date* is the day that the board of directors meets to set the quarterly dividend. In our example, February 15 is the declaration date.

The major stock exchanges require two business days before the record date to have enough time to record ownership changes. This is referred to as the *ex-dividend date*, which is the last date on which a share trades without a declared dividend that has yet to be paid. An investor that buys shares on or after this date is not entitled to receive the declared dividends. In this case, if investors buy shares on or after February 26, they are not entitled to receive the dividend that quarter.

The *record date* is the date on which a business makes a list from its stock transfer books of those shareholders who are eligible to receive the declared dividends (February 28 in our example).

Figure 9.7 The Dividend Payment Procedure

The *payment date* is usually about four weeks or so after the record date. In the example in Figure 9.7, the company makes the dividend payments to the shareholders on March 30.

In the News 9.3 indicates that full disclosure when dealing with public funds is not only necessary but an absolute must.

In The News 9.3

RAISING PUBLIC FUNDS REQUIRES FULL FINANCIAL DISCLOSURE

The Canadian Securities Commission and its 13 provincial and territorial counterparts exist for one reason: to protect Canadian investors from unfair, improper, or fraudulent practices. When a company raises capital dollars from the general public, it has to comply with securities regulation, policies, and practices.

Early in 2012, AD Equity Inc., which raised $478,000 for a Halifax software maker, Adventus Inc., had to appear in front of the Nova Scotia Securities Commission. The reason: allegations that it failed to file the requisite continuous disclosures, such as interim financial statements, annual financial statements, and material change reports, for the Bridgewater economic development corporation since 2004, an organization that helped raise the capital funds. The money was raised to help Adventus Inc. finance the development of a sophisticated software engine that would provide immediate, quality feedback when a MIDI piano keyboard is connected to a computer.

Source: "Securities probe targets community development firm." *The Chronicle Herald*. Retrieved from http://thechronicleherald.ca/business/83961-securities-probe-targets-community-development-firm. Accessed April 16, 2012. For more information about Adventus Inc., go to http://www.adventus.com.

Chapter Summary

1 Describe the relationship between the major components of finance.

The finance function deals with three key components: capital structure (or the composition of the sources of funds), cost of capital (which determines how much it costs to raise capital funds), and capital budgeting (which uses the cost of capital, as a discount rate, to determine the attractiveness of capital projects).

2 Explain financial and capital structure, and explain the cost concepts.

Financing decisions consider not only sources and forms of financing but also financial and capital structure, cost of financing, and cost of capital. *Financial structure* is the way a company's total assets are financed by the entire right side of the statement of financial position, long-term and short-term financing. *Capital structure* represents the permanent forms of financing, such as common shares, retained earnings, preferred shares, and long-term borrowings. *Cost of financing* is how much it costs a business to finance all assets shown on a company's statement of financial position. *Cost of capital* means the weighted rate of return a business must provide to its investors in exchange for the money they have placed in a business. Cost of capital is a critical element in the financing decision process because it is the basis for determining the capital expenditure investment portfolio.

3 Explain why the cost of financing is used and how it is calculated.

To calculate the cost of financing requires four steps. First, identify the amount obtained from each source. Second, find the weight or proportion for each amount from each source. Third, identify the cost of each source (before and after taxes). Last, multiply the weight of each source by the after-tax cost of financing and obtain the weighted cost. Adding all individual weighted costs gives the weighted average cost of financing (WACF).

4 Show how economic value added is used to measure managerial performance related to maximizing shareholder wealth.

EVA is a tool that measures how profitable a company is. It is calculated by deducting the cost of using the assets (finance costs) from the net operating profit after taxes (NOPAT).

5 Describe the parts of the average weighted cost of capital: common shares, retained earnings, preferred shares, and long-term borrowings.

The important characteristics of long-term financing are payout, risk, voting rights, cost of capital, tax cost, and cost of issue. The key elements to consider when calculating a company's cost of capital are (1) the amount of funds obtained from each financing source (shareholders and lenders), (2) the proportion of each source, and (3) the after-tax cost of each source. The weighted average cost of capital is arrived at by multiplying each amount calculated in (2) by each cost listed in (3). There is a connection between the cost of capital and investment decisions. Cost of capital tells management how much it costs to raise funds from long-term sources, while techniques in capital budgeting, such as the internal rate of return (IRR), tell management how much each project generates. If a project earns less than the cost of capital, it might be rejected.

6 Demonstrate the importance of leverage analysis and how operating leverage, financial leverage, and combined leverage are calculated.

Leverage analysis is used to determine the financing package or cost structure that will maximize the worth of a business. There are two types of leverage: operating leverage and financial leverage. *Operating leverage* deals with the cost behaviour of an operating unit; it determines the most appropriate cost mix (fixed versus variable) that will maximize profitability under a given set of economic and industry conditions. *Financial leverage* is used to determine the best capital structure—that is, the one that will generate the greatest financial benefits to the shareholders. *Combined leverage* is used to calculate both operating and financial leverage.

7 Discuss financial markets, the stock market, and three theories related to dividend payments.

Financial markets are the organizations and procedures involved in the buying and selling of financial assets. The different types of markets include money markets, capital markets, primary markets, secondary markets, spot and future markets, mortgage markets, consumer credit markets, and physical asset markets. Privately held companies don't trade on a stock market, while publicly traded companies do. Publicly traded companies begin with an initial public offering and become a listed company. Dividend theories, dividend policy, and dividend payments are all important considerations for a publicly traded company.

Key Terms

Capital structure p. 376
Characteristics of long-term financing sources p. 385
Combined leverage p. 399
Cost of capital p. 374
Cost of common shares p. 388
Cost of debt p. 391
Cost of preferred shares p. 390
Cost of retained earnings p. 390
Dividend aversion theory p. 408
Dividend irrelevance theory p. 407
Dividend payout ratio p. 408
Dividend preference theory p. 407
Economic value added (EVA) p. 382
Financial leverage p. 399
Financial markets p. 403
Financial structure p. 376
Initial public offering (IPO) p. 405
Leverage p. 374
Listed company p. 405
Marginal cost of capital (MCC) p. 392
Operating leverage p. 397
Opportunity cost p. 390
Privately held company p. 405
Publicly traded company p. 405
Stock market p. 404
Weighted average cost of financing p. 376

Review Questions

1 Describe the relationship between the major components of finance.

1. Comment on the major components of finance.

2 Explain financial and capital structure, and explain the cost concepts.

2. What do we mean by financial structure?
3. What do we mean by capital structure?
4. What is the difference between weighted average cost of financing and weighted average cost of capital?

3 Explain why the cost of financing is used and how it is calculated.

5. What accounts in the statement of financial position are taken into consideration to calculate the cost of financing?
6. How is the weighted average cost of financing calculated?
7. What is the connection between the weighted average cost of financing and return on assets (ROA)?

4 Show how economic value added is used to measure managerial performance related to maximizing shareholder wealth.

8. What is the meaning of economic value added (EVA)? What does it measure? Why is it important?
9. How is the economic value added formula expressed?

5 Describe the parts of the average weighted cost of capital: common shares, retained earnings, preferred shares, and long-term borrowings.

10. What is the purpose of calculating the cost of capital?
11. What major characteristics should be explored when considering the major sources of long-term financing?
12. What are the major elements of the cost of capital?
13. What is the relationship between the cost of capital and the internal rate of return?
14. Define opportunity cost.
15. Differentiate between debt financing and common share financing.
16. What does the growth factor represent when calculating the cost of common shares?
17. What do we mean by marginal cost of capital?

6 Demonstrate the importance of leverage analysis and how operating leverage, financial leverage, and combined leverage are calculated.

18. Explain the meaning of leverage.
19. What is the objective of using the leverage analysis technique?
20. What is the purpose of operating leverage analysis?
21. What is the purpose of financial leverage analysis?
22. What is the usefulness of combined leverage?
23. How can leverage analysis be used to determine whether a plant should be modified or not?

7 Discuss financial markets, the stock market, and three theories related to dividend payments.

24. What are financial markets?
25. What is the difference between a primary financial market and a secondary financial market?
26. What is the purpose of a stock exchange?
27. What is a prospectus?
28. What does the dividend irrelevance theory suggest?

Learning Exercises

1 Describe the relationship between the major components of finance.

EXERCISE 1: COST OF CAPITAL

A company wants to raise $50 million to finance the following capital expenditure projects, with their respective rates of return.

Project A	8%
Project B	9%
Project C	10%
Project D	11%
Project E	12%
Project F	13%

The various sources and cost of funds are as follows:

In millions of $	Amounts	Cost (after tax)
Common shares	$20	14%
Retained earnings	10	10%
Mortgage	10	6%
Bonds	10	7%

Questions

1. What is the company's cost of capital?
2. What discount rate would you use during the capital budgeting process?
3. What would be the new discount rate if the cost of common shares and mortgage increase to 16% and 7%, respectively?
4. What projects would be approved with and without the change in the cost of capital?

2 Explain financial and capital structure, and explain the cost concepts.

EXERCISE 2: FINANCIAL STRUCTURE AND CAPITAL STRUCTURE

From the following financing sources, identify the company's financial structure and capital structure and calculate the proportion or weight of each.

Sources	Amounts
Retained earnings	$450,000
Share capital	300,000
Trade and other payables	300,000
Long-term borrowings	900,000
Working capital loan	70,000
Short-term borrowings	200,000

3 Explain why the cost of financing is used and how it is calculated.

EXERCISE 3: AVERAGE COST OF FINANCING AND COST OF CAPITAL

Use the information in Exercise 2 and the following costs for individual financing sources to calculate the company's weighted average after-tax cost of financing and cost of capital.

Sources	Cost (%)
Share capital	14
Trade and other payables	0
Retained earnings	12
Long-term borrowings	6
Short-term borrowings	8
Working capital loan	6.5

4 Show how economic value added is used to measure managerial performance related to maximizing shareholder wealth.

EXERCISE 4: ECONOMIC VALUE ADDED

Oscar Lewitt, CEO of Ingram Corporation, had just read in a recent issue of *Fortune* magazine an article entitled "America's Wealth Creators" and noticed several names of corporations he was familiar with, such as Microsoft, General Electric, Intel, Walmart, Coca-Cola, Merck, and Pfizer. These top wealth creators were listed in terms of their market value added (MVA) and economic value added (EVA). Although he knew that some of the MVA and EVA were in the billions of dollars, he noticed in the article two other numbers, return on capital and cost of capital. He felt that if these corporations, despite their size, were able to figure out how much value they were adding to the wealth of their shareholders, it would be possible to calculate the EVA for Ingram Corporation.

At his next management committee meeting, Mr. Lewitt asked his controller to calculate the EVA for Ingram Corporation and to report the information to the management committee at their next meeting for discussion purposes.

After some research about this new financial technique, the controller knew that he had to refer to his financial statements to calculate the EVA. He had to draw several numbers from the statement of income and the statement of financial position to determine the cost of capital and ROA. The company's most recent statement of income and different sources of financing are shown below:

Ingram Corporation
Statement of Income
For the year ended December 31, 2014

Revenue	$1,200,000
Cost of sales	(650,000)
Gross profit	550,000
Expenses	
Distribution costs	(150,000)
Administrative expenses	(125,000)
Depreciation	(50,000)
Finance costs	(45,000)
Total expenses	(370,000)
Profit before taxes	180,000
Income tax expense	(67,500)
Profit for the year	$ 112,500

The company's three major sources of financing are from short-term lenders for $100,000, a mortgage for $325,000, and equity for $430,000. The equity portion was split between share capital of $130,000 and retained earnings of $300,000.

The cost of capital for these three sources of financing is as follows:

- Equity 12.0%
- Short-term borrowings 8.0%
- Long-term borrowings 7.0%

Questions

1. Calculate Ingram Corporation's EVA.
2. Comment on the EVA. How could EVA be improved?

5 Describe the parts of the average weighted cost of capital: common shares, retained earnings, preferred shares, and long-term borrowings.

EXERCISE 5: COST OF CAPITAL

Daniel and Evelyn are considering buying a house valued at $250,000. They have combined savings of $20,000, and the bank approved a $200,000 first mortgage. Another financial institution agreed to provide them with a $20,000 second mortgage. Also, Daniel has just won $10,000 from a lottery. If Daniel and Evelyn invested their money in guaranteed certificates, they would be able to earn 4%. The interest rates offered by the bank are 6% for the first mortgage and 7% for the second.

Question

Calculate Daniel and Evelyn's cost of capital.

EXERCISE 6: COST OF CAPITAL AND RETURN ON INVESTMENT

One of the capital expenditure projects included in a company's capital budget was a $10 million investment for the construction of a new manufacturing facility in South America. The preliminary information provided by the financial analysis department of the company indicated that the project would earn an 8% return on investment. The treasurer met several investors who showed an interest in the project and were prepared to provide the following:

Common shares	$ 3,500,000
Retained earnings	500,000
Preferred shares	1,000,000
Bonds	5,000,000
Total	$10,000,000

The cost of capital for each source of financing is as follows:

- Common shares 12.0%
- Retained earnings 11.0%
- Bonds 7.5%
- Preferred shares 10.0%

The company's corporate income tax rate is 45%.

The members of the management committee were reviewing all projects in the capital budget. When they examined the $10 million manufacturing facility, several showed some concern about the project's viability and were unsure whether it should be approved.

Question

Ignoring flotation costs or brokers' fees, calculate the cost of capital for raising the $10 million. Should the management committee approve this project? Why?

EXERCISE 7: COST OF CAPITAL (PUBLIC COMPANY)

The CEO of an electronics business was contemplating going public. Assume that the prospectus shows an expansion plan that would cost $20 million, and the CEO wants to raise funds from the following sources:

a) $8 million from common shares. Each share would be sold for $15 and yield $2 in dividends. The flotation costs would be 10%.
b) $1 million through the company's retained earnings.
c) $1 million from preferred shares. The expected selling price would be $10, and the flotation costs would be $0.50 per share. Annual dividends of $1 per share would be paid to the preferred shareholders.
d) $8 million from a mortgage at a cost of 5%.
e) $2 million from a second mortgage at a cost of 7%.

The corporate tax rate is 48%, and the prospectus showed the growth rate to be 5% per year.

Question

Calculate the company's cost of capital.

EXERCISE 8: COST OF CAPITAL AND CAPITAL PROJECT

Silverado Inc. is contemplating spending $25 million to expand its mining operation, a project that is considered to have a reasonable amount of risk. Based on some initial analysis, the project would expand the operation's production output by 18% and provide a 15% return on investment.

Before deciding whether to proceed with the venture, the CEO asked the treasurer to determine where the financing would come from and how much each source will cost. The following are the findings of the treasurer:

a) $11 million will be funded from common shares. Each share will be sold for $50, yielding $4 in dividends. The flotation costs will be 10%.
b) $3 million will be provided from internal sources (retained earnings).
c) $1 million will be generated from preferred shares. The expected selling price is $100, and the flotation costs will be $5 per share. An amount of $10 in annual dividends per share will be paid to the preferred shareholders.
d) $4 million will be funded by the selling of bond A and $6 million by the selling of Bond B. The cost of Bond A is estimated at 6% and the cost of Bond B at 8%.

The company's corporate tax rate is 47%. The treasurer expects the common shares to continue to grow at a rate of 5% per year.

Questions

1. Calculate the company's cost of capital.
2. Should the CEO approve the expansion program? Why?

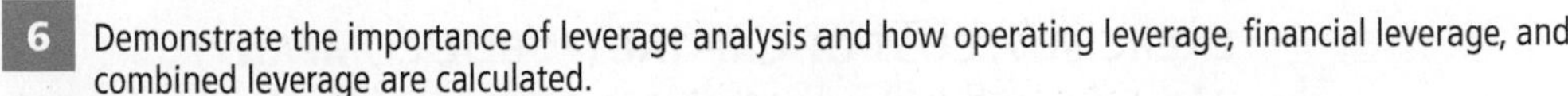
6 Demonstrate the importance of leverage analysis and how operating leverage, financial leverage, and combined leverage are calculated.

EXERCISE 9: LEVERAGE CALCULATIONS

Use the following information to calculate the company's operating leverage, financial leverage, and combined leverage:

Sales volume	100,000 units
Price per unit	$ 11.30
Variable costs (per unit)	$ 8.30
Fixed costs	$100,000
Interest	$ 25,000
Corporate income tax rate	40%

EXERCISE 10: LEVERAGE CALCULATIONS

Using the data in Exercise 9, assume that the company wants to make its plant more automated and is able to reduce the variable costs to $7.30 per unit, increase the fixed costs by $100,000 (i.e., to $200,000), and increase the finance costs from $25,000 to $35,000.

Question

Calculate the new operating leverage, financial leverage, and combined leverage.

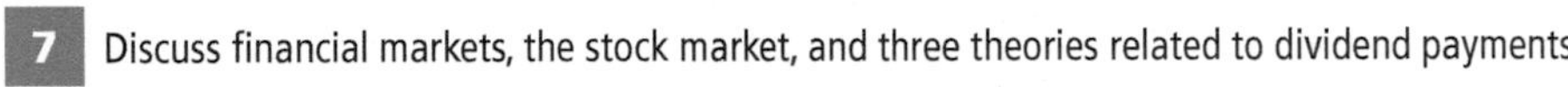
7 Discuss financial markets, the stock market, and three theories related to dividend payments.

EXERCISE 11: PUBLIC COMPANY'S FINANCIAL RATIOS

In 2014, Pirex Ltd. earned $6 million in profit for the year. The company had 2.3 million shares outstanding and paid $3.0 million in dividends. The market price for each share was $15.00.

Questions

Calculate the following:

a) The company's EPS
b) The company's dividends per share
c) The company's dividend yield
d) The company's P/E ratio
e) The payout ratio

Cases

CASE 1: SHARCO SYSTEMS INC.

Sharco Systems Inc., a manufacturer of auto parts, wants to make inroads in the European and Asian markets. Sharco's executives know it will be difficult because of the strongly entrenched existing competitors in those markets. However, the company executives believe that if they formulate effective business goals and strategies and raise the resources required to implement their plans, they could become viable competitors in these markets.

The company's statement of income and statement of financial position are presented below. As shown, in 2014, the company earned $176 million in profit for the year on assets of $2.0 billion.

Sharco Systems Inc.
Statement of Income
For the year ended December 31, 2014
(in $ millions)

Revenue	2,500
Cost of sales	(1,610)
Gross profit	890
Expenses	
Distribution costs	(260)
Administrative expenses	(120)
Depreciation	(100)
Finance costs	(90)
Total expenses	(570)
Profit before taxes	320
Income tax expense	(144)
Profit for the year	176

The before-tax cost of financing the equity and debt as shown on the statement of financial position is as follows:

Bank loans	8.0%
Current portion of long-term borrowings	7.0%
Mortgage	6.0%
Debentures	7.0%
Equity	12.0%

Sharco Systems Inc.
Statement of Financial Position
As at December 31, 2014
(in $ millions)

Assets		
Non-current assets		
Property, plant, and equipment (at cost)	1,800	
Less: accumulated depreciation	(500)	
Total non-current assets		1,300
Current assets		
Inventories	290	
Trade receivables	350	
Prepaid expenses	10	
Cash and cash equivalents	50	
Total current assets		700
Total assets		2,000
Equity		
Common shares	135	
Retained earnings	750	
Preferred shares	15	
Total equity		900
Liabilities		
Long-term borrowings		
Mortgage	500	
Debentures	300	
Total long-term borrowings		800
Current liabilities		
Trade and other payables	60	
Bank loans	100	
Income taxes payable	130	
Current portion of long-term borrowings	10	
Total current liabilities		300
Total liabilities		1,100
Total equity and liabilities		2,000

The company had to prepare a prospectus to raise $350 million from the following sources:

	In millions
Common shares	$100
Retained earnings*	70
Preferred shares	30
Long-term borrowings	150
Total	$350

* Although retained earnings are not funds raised from the general public, it is shown here for the purpose of calculating the cost of capital.

These funds would be used almost exclusively to expand their operations in Europe and Asia, which would generate a return of 22% on the company's investments. The company's vice-president of finance provided the following information:

- Common share dividend yield is estimated at 7% and growth rate during the past five years has been 6%. (This rate is expected to continue.)
- Internal funding from retained earnings is estimated at $70 million.
- Preferred shares would be sold at $75 and bear a 10% yield.
- Cost of new debt is expected to be 10%.

Questions

1. Calculate the following:
   a. Sharco's before- and after-tax cost of financing for 2014
   b. Sharco's before- and after-tax ROA for 2014 and compare them with your answers to Question 1a
   c. Sharco's economic value added for 2014
   d. The company's cost of capital to raise funds from the following:
   - Common shares only
   - Preferred shares only
   - Long-term borrowings only
   - All sources (WACC)
2. Should Sharco go ahead with the project?

FINANCIAL SPREADSHEETS: EXCEL®

Template 13 of the financial statement analysis component of the financial planning spreadsheets accompanying this text can be used to calculate the economic value added. The EVA is the incremental profit after taxes that a company earns after paying the cost of borrowed capital. There are three templates related to this chapter: Template 3 calculates the operate leverage for three different volume levels. This template helps to determine whether a company, for example, should modernize a plant or not. Templates 4 and 5 calculate the cost of capital for privately owned businesses and for publicly owned companies.

wrangler/Shutterstock RF

CHAPTER 10

[TIME-VALUE-OF-MONEY CONCEPT]

Learning Objectives

After reading this chapter, you should be able to

1. Define time value of money, inflation, and risk.
2. Explain the financial tools used to solve time-value-of-money problems.
3. Differentiate between future values of single sums and future values of annuities.
4. Distinguish between present values of single sums and present values of annuities.
5. Make capital investment decisions by using time-value-of-money tools.

OPENING CASE

From Interest Tables to Financial Spreadsheets

The Millers are examining several investment options. Even though they want to invest money in CompuTech Inc., they also want to make sure that they will invest enough in RRSPs for retirement and in educational funds for their two children, Vincent and Takara. To evaluate their needs, the Millers knew that they had to learn the language of banking and investment and understand compounding and discounting. They realized that investing money in RRSPs and educational funds today means time alone will help their investments grow. They wanted to learn how to use interest tables, financial calculators, and financial spreadsheets to make *time-value-of-money* calculations.

The Millers also realized that to communicate knowledgeably with bankers, insurance agents, and financial advisers, they had to understand such financial concepts as *compounding*. For example, if the Millers deposited $1,000 in the bank today for one year at 5%, time is the only factor that would increase their investment to $1,050. Similarly, if Len Miller wanted a $100,000 life insurance policy, the insurance agent would determine the premiums he would have to pay each year for a certain number of years (depending on average age expectancy). Financial advisers who tell clients how much they need to save each year in different investments, such as RRSPs or guaranteed investment certificates (GICs), must have a good understanding of these time-value-of-money concepts.

Bankers, insurance agents, and financial advisers are also familiar with *discounting*. For example, if the Millers want to have $60,000 for each child by the time each turns 20, they know that the amount they would have to invest today would be less than $60,000.

The Millers know that the time-value-of-money concept is important for their personal financing and for business decisions. In business, however, the focus is on discounting. Because insurance companies pay death benefits in the future, the future values of the premium payments have to be compounded (future value) or brought into the future for comparison purposes (death benefit and all premium payments). Conversely, businesses make different calculations. Because business investments are made today (purchase of assets, opening of a new retail store, or the expansion of an existing one), all cash receipts earned in the future are discounted to find their present value. They are then compared with the initial investment to determine whether the investment is worth it.

THIS CHAPTER WILL SHOW LEN AND JOAN HOW TO

- Use interest tables, financial calculators, and financial spreadsheets.
- Apply time-value-of-money concepts to make personal and business decisions.

Chapter Overview

DON'T COUNT YOUR CASH BEFORE IT'S DISCOUNTED!

This is the first chapter dealing with investing decisions. Chapter 11 deals with capital budgeting decisions such as the purchase of equipment or machinery; construction, modernization, or expansion of a plant; and research and development. These kinds of decisions involve outflows of cash (disbursements), which take place during the year a decision is made, and inflows of cash (receipts), which are generated years after the initial funds are disbursed. To make effective decisions in capital budgeting, it is important to understand why money has a time value. This chapter deals with five topics:

- *The meaning of time value of money, inflation, and risk.* Time value of money will be explained and contrasted with inflation and with risk.
- *Tools for solving time-value-of-money problems.* Practical tools that can be used to make time-value-of-money decisions include (1) algebraic notations that explain the financial equations used in calculating future and present value amounts; (2) the interest tables in Appendix B at the end of this book; (3) financial calculators and spreadsheets used to make time-value-of-money calculations; and (4) the timeline concept, which shows graphically when cash is disbursed or received over time (months or years).
- *Future values.* We'll explain how to use interest tables, financial calculators, and financial spreadsheets to calculate the future value of a single sum and the future value of an annuity.
- *Present values.* How to use interest tables, financial calculators, and financial spreadsheets to calculate the present value of a single sum and the present value of an annuity will be explained.
- *Using interest tables to make decisions.* We'll look at several examples on how interest tables can be used for personal and business decisions about compounding, discounting, and calculating annuities. It also provides a brief introduction to the use of interest tables to make business decisions (covered in detail in Chapter 11) and explains how to link the time value of money to capital investment decision-making tools, such as the internal rate of return (IRR) and the net present value (NPV) methods (Chapter 11).

Time Value of Money, Inflation, and Risk

1 Define time value of money, inflation, and risk.

This section deals with three distinct but related concepts: (1) time value of money, (2) the relationship between time value of money and inflation, and (3) the connection between time value of money and risk.

MEANING OF TIME VALUE OF MONEY

Money has a time value because of the existence of interest. For example, if you have a choice between receiving $100 today or $103 a year from now, which option should you take? If money is worth 3% (the interest rate), it does not matter which option you select. You could invest the $100 in a term deposit, which would give you 3% interest and increase your initial $100 to $103 one year from now. Time is the factor that would have earned $3 or 3% for you. Conversely, we can say that the $103 you would receive one year from now equals today's $100. The fact that there is a *cost* (interest) to borrowing money, whether provided by shareholders or lenders, confirms the fact that money has a **time value**.

Time value of money
The rate at which the value of money is traded off as a function of time.

This illustration confirms that a dollar earned today is worth more tomorrow (compounded). And a dollar earned tomorrow is worth less today (discounted). In capital budgeting, if a company invests money in a long-term-producing asset and wants to calculate its return on investment, the company must take into account the element of time. The reason is simple: The company invests cash today in exchange for cash that it will earn in future years. To respect the time-value-of-money notion, all monies, whether spent today or earned next year or five years from now, must be placed on an equal footing. That is why it is important to understand the basic math involved in interest, compounding, and discounting.

People often believe that money has a time value because of inflation or risk. These three concepts are totally distinct.

TIME VALUE OF MONEY AND INFLATION

Inflation
The rise in prices during periods of prosperity.

Inflation, which is a general increase in price in periods of prosperity, is also considered when capital decisions are made. For example, if you invest $1,000 in a term deposit bearing a 4% interest rate when inflation is 3%, next year's purchasing power of the $1,040 would be reduced to $1,010. Time value of money and inflation should not be confused, particularly in capital investment decisions, because they are two distinct and separate calculations.

Let's examine a capital asset that generates a multi-year cash flow. The revenues and expenses generated by the investment during the life of the asset include two elements: (1) the revenues that are calculated on the basis of the expected volume increases, and (2) the anticipated increase in unit selling price, which should include inflation. Expenses also take into consideration increases in wages and the costs of material, utilities, and so on, caused by inflation. The difference between the projected revenues and projected expenses is the profit for the year, which includes inflation. Once the revenue and expense projections (which include inflation) are calculated, the time-value-of-money calculation of the future cash flows (compounding or discounting) begins. Look ahead to Problem-Solving Example 10.6 to see this calculation.

Problem-Solving Example 10.1

Projected Profit for the Year and Cash Flow

With the following information, calculate the company's yearly (1) profit and (2) cash flow for 2013, 2014, 2015, and 2016. The income statement accounts for 2013 are as follows: revenue ($500,000), cost of sales ($300,000), other expenses ($130,000), straight-line depreciation ($15,000), and income tax rate (30%). The annual inflation rates for revenue, cost of sales, and other expenses for the three years are 4%, 5%, and 6%, respectively.

Solution

Projected Statements of Income

	2013	2014	2015	2016
Revenue (4%)	$ 500,000	$ 520,000	$ 540,800	$ 562,432
Cost of sales (5%)	(300,000)	(315,000)	(330,750)	(347,288)
Gross profit	200,000	205,000	210,050	215,144
Other expenses (6%)	(130,000)	(137,800)	(146,068)	(154,832)
Depreciation	(15,000)	(15,000)	(15,000)	(15,000)
Total expenses	(145,000)	(152,800)	(161,068)	(169,832)
Profit before taxes	55,000	52,200	48,982	45,312
Income tax expense	(16,500)	(15,660)	(14,695)	(13,594)
(1) Profit for the year	38,500	36,540	34,287	31,718
Add back depreciation	15,000	15,000	15,000	15,000
(2) Cash flow	$ 53,500	$ 51,540	$ 49,287	$ 46,718

Self-Test Exercise 10.1

Cash Flow Forecast of a Photo Centre

Several months after opening up their retail store, Len and Joan were thinking about adding a new department—a photo centre. They felt that it was a profitable business, with a markup of about 50%. The cost of the equipment would be $150,000, and the first-year revenue is estimated at $125,000. The five-year revenue forecast shows a 20% annual increase (including 3% for inflation). Operating expenses have different growth patterns. The $25,000 for salaries will increase by 8% (including 3% for inflation), and the $50,000 for materials shows a 15% increase (including 3% for inflation). The equipment is depreciated over 10 years (straight-line), and CompuTech's income tax rate is 35%. With this information, calculate the company's yearly profit and cash flow forecast for the five-year period.

Answers to the Self-Test Exercises can be found at www.bergeron7e.nelson.com.

TIME VALUE OF MONEY AND RISK

Time value of money and risk are also connected, however, the nature of the investment (risk) makes a difference. We would expect to earn more on a high-risk investment (such as in a high-tech businesses) versus a low-risk investment (Canada Savings Bonds). If a company invests $100,000 in a low-risk capital asset that will generate a one-time inflow of cash of $10,000 next year (the original $100,000 plus a profit of $10,000 equals a 10% return), should the asset be purchased? The business may borrow $100,000 for, say, 6% to purchase the $100,000 capital asset. In this case, the purchase could be justified because the return (10%) exceeds the 6% cost of capital. The company would make a 4% return after the cost of borrowing the funds. However, the decision might change if the investment was in a high-risk project where management is looking for 20% instead of 10%. In that case, the purchase could be rejected.

Risk The expectation (probability) that something will happen in the future.

It is important to consider risk when making capital investment decisions. A $1,000 investment in Canada Savings Bonds with a 3% interest rate bears little risk. **Risk** represents the expectation (probability) that something will happen in the future. The chance of recovering the $1,000 amount and the interest is guaranteed. However, if $1,000 is invested in an untried product, risk is the most important factor. Because of risk, the investor would be comfortable with the 3% interest rate for the Canada Savings Bonds but would probably want to earn, say, a 25% return on a new and untested high-tech product.

In the News 10.1 shows that even though inflation and interest rates are two distinct concepts, they are closely linked.

In The News 10.1

HOW INFLATION INFLUENCES INTEREST RATES

While differences exist between interest rates, inflation, and risk, they are all bound together. As we discussed, inflation is a rise in the prices of goods and services. When that happens, consumers' dollars buy fewer goods and services. It is much like a reduction in take-home pay and in the "real" value of money. Inflation discourages investment (personal and business) and saving. To keep the rate of inflation low and stable, the Bank of Canada controls monetary policy by setting interest rates. When interest rates are low, people invest in durable goods and spend more on consumer goods. The reverse takes place when interest rates are high.

In March 2012, the annual inflation rate fell to 1.9% from 2.6% in February. While the Bank of Canada targets a 2.0% inflation rate, the Bank made it clear that it was prepared to start raising interest rates because of the increased underlying inflationary pressures. Higher interest rates can increase the cost of capital and thus lower investments in capital assets.

Source: "Inflation rate hits 18-month low, to 1.9% for March." *Globe and Mail*. Retrieved from http://www.theglobeandmail.com/report-on-business/economy/inflation-rate-hits-18-month-low-to-19-for-march/article2408676/, accessed April 21, 2012. For more information about Bank of Canada interest rates, visit www.bankofcanada.ca/rates/interest-rates/.

Tools for Solving Time-Value-of-Money Problems

2 Explain the financial tools used to solve time-value-of-money problems.

Several tools are available to solve time-value-of-money problems: algebraic formulas, interest tables, financial calculators and spreadsheets, and the timeline concept.

ALGEBRAIC FORMULAS

We discuss algebraic formulas for three reasons: first, to show how the interest tables presented in Appendix B at the end of this book are calculated; second, to explain the parts of the financial equations used to calculate future and present value amounts; and third, to introduce the keystrokes used with financial calculators and spreadsheets to solve time-value-of-money problems. It is not necessary to understand the roots of these formulas, but it is important to learn how interest tables are used to calculate the future value of a sum received today and the present value of a sum received in the future.

Algebraic equations use lowercase letters to stand for percentage rates and time, and capital letters normally stand for money or dollar amounts. For instance, the letter *i* stands for interest rates, *n* for number or periods (months or years), *PV* for present value amounts, *FV* for future value amounts, and *PMT* for constant stream of cash payments. The important symbols and letters to remember are as follows:

P	The principal, which is the amount available today. This is expressed in dollars.
PV	The present value of a sum. This is also expressed in dollars.
FV	The future value of a sum. This is also expressed in dollars.
i	The rate of interest. This can be expressed on an annual, semi-annual, quarterly, or monthly basis.
n	The number of periods over which funds are borrowed. This is expressed in months or years.
PMT	This is a constant stream of funds to be received or spent over a number of periods. This is commonly referred to as an annuity. This equal flow of funds is expressed in dollars.
A	The present value of a constant stream of funds to be received or spent over a number of periods. It is the present value of an annuity. This figure is expressed in dollars.
S	The future sum of a stream of funds to be received or spent over a number of periods. It is the future value of an annuity and is expressed in dollars.
k	An interest rate required to obtain a targeted rate of return.
T	The tax rate.

These symbols are used in algebraic formulas to calculate the following:

- Future value of a single sum (compounding)
- Future value of a stream of sums (compounding)
- Present value of a single sum (discounting)
- Present value of a stream of sums (discounting)

INTEREST TABLES

Interest tables can be used to calculate the following:

- Future (compounding) and present (discounting) values of a single sum of money received or paid out at a given time
- Constant flow of sums of money (an annuity) received or paid out over a given time

Why Four Interest Tables?

Interest tables
Calculated factors used for computing future or present values of single sums and annuities.

The four interest tables listed in Table 10.1 are presented in Appendix B at the end of the text. **Interest tables** present calculated factors used for computing future or present values of single sums and annuities. It is important to understand their function before using them. The *columns* show the interest rates while the *rows* show the years.

Compounding uses Tables A and C. To find the future value of a single sum, use Table A in Appendix B; to find the future value of an annuity, use Table C in Appendix B. For capital budgeting, financial analysts use discount tables—Tables B and D. To calculate the present value of a single sum, use Table B in Appendix B; to find the present value of an annuity, use Table D in Appendix B.

How Interest Tables Came About

Interest tables have been around for more than 80 years. These tables were not developed by bankers or accountants but by actuaries working for insurance companies. The top part of Table 10.2 shows how they used these tables. Suppose someone bought a $30,000 life insurance policy. If that person's expected remaining lifespan was 20 years, he or she would likely pay about $1,000 a year for those 20 years. The insurance companies would then invest each $1,000 payment at, say, 6%. These sums have a future value of $36,786 in 20 years, which is found by multiplying $1,000 by the factor 36.786. This factor is listed in Table C in Appendix B, at the intersection of column 6% (interest rate) and row 20 (years). In 20 years, when the $30,000 amount is paid out (cash outflow), the insurance company would have a surplus of $6,786, which is referred to as the *net future value* (*NFV*).

In the 1950s, the industrial community decided to use the time-value-of-money idea as a capital budgeting tool. Industrial managers said that if the time value of

Table 10.1 Using Interest Tables

These two tables are mostly used in capital budgeting. ↓

	To Compound	To Discount
Single sum	Table A	Table B
Annuity	Table C	Table D

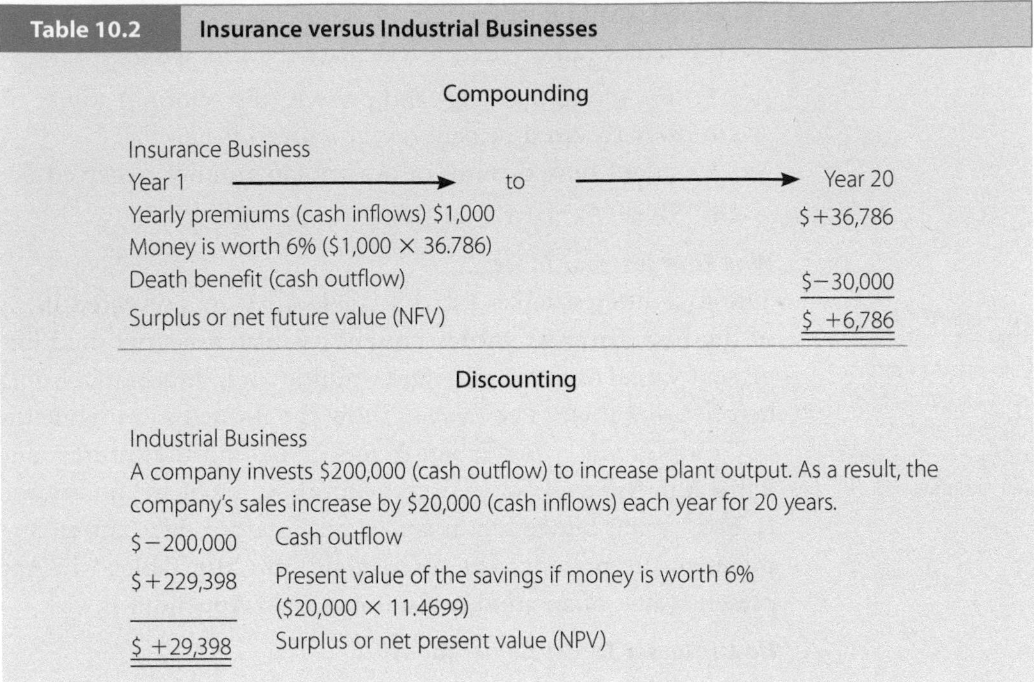

Table 10.2 Insurance versus Industrial Businesses

Compounding

Insurance Business		
Year 1 →	to	→ Year 20
Yearly premiums (cash inflows) $1,000		$+36,786
Money is worth 6% ($1,000 × 36.786)		
Death benefit (cash outflow)		$−30,000
Surplus or net future value (NFV)		$ +6,786

Discounting

Industrial Business

A company invests $200,000 (cash outflow) to increase plant output. As a result, the company's sales increase by $20,000 (cash inflows) each year for 20 years.

$−200,000	Cash outflow
$+229,398	Present value of the savings if money is worth 6% ($20,000 × 11.4699)
$ +29,398	Surplus or net present value (NPV)

money was good for insurance companies, it would also be good for industrial companies, as both have cash outflows and cash inflows. However, there is one major difference: the timing of making the cash disbursements or outflows. In insurance companies, the cash outflow (payment) is made later, that is, in 20 years. In industrial companies, the cash outflow is made at the beginning, and that is why cash receipts have to be discounted (to compare them to the initial investment) instead of bringing them into the future.

The lower portion of Table 10.2 illustrates that the $200,000 expansion project that earns $20,000 a year over the next 20 years gives a $229,398 present value. It is arrived at by multiplying the $20,000 amount by the factor 11.4699, which is drawn from Table D in Appendix B at the intersection of column 6% (interest rate) and row 20 (years). Using a 6% discount factor, the company generates a $29,398 surplus, which is referred to as the *net present value* (*NPV*).

FINANCIAL CALCULATORS AND SPREADSHEETS

Fortunately, financial calculators and spreadsheets can remove the chore of making endless calculations to find solutions to time-value-of-money problems.

Financial Calculators

For compounding and discounting calculations, financial calculators work in the same way as interest tables. For every problem, several variables are known and calculators have a key function for each variable. Of all the variables, one is not known. Inputting the amount for each variable and pressing the key function "Compute" provides the answer. The important function keys set up in financial calculators and their meaning are as follows:

n	Number of periods
i/y	Interest rate per year
PV	Present value
FV	Future value
PMT	Payment

For example, to calculate the future value of a five-year $1,000 annuity bearing a 5% interest rate, you do the following:

Enter 5 years (n).
Enter the $1,000 amount ($PMT$).
Enter the 5% interest rate (i/y).
Press Compute (FV).

The financial calculator displays $5,525.63, made up of $5,000 (that is, the $1,000 five-year annuity) and $525.63 in interest.

Financial Spreadsheets

Financial spreadsheets, such as Excel®, can also be used to solve time-value-of-money problems. To use an Excel® spreadsheet, click Insert on the toolbar, choose Function, and then click Financial in the function category. This will give you many financial calculation options, such as FV, IRR, NPER, PMT, and NPV. Click future value (FV) and click OK. Enter the same information in the dialogue box (see Table 10.3) that we used to calculate the future value of the $1,000 five-year annuity bearing a 5% interest rate. Click OK and $5,525.63 is displayed. Note: these instructions are for Excel® 2003. Your version of Excel® may require different keystrokes. For example, in Excel® 2007, click the Formula tab, click Insert Function, and choose Financial in the drop-down list box.

TIMELINE ILLUSTRATIONS

Timeline
A graphic illustration of time-value-of-money problems.

The last tool we'll discuss is the **timeline**, which is a graphic illustration of time-value-of-money problems. The timelines in Figure 10.1 have several common characteristics. They are divided into time periods (in these cases, into years, although they could be months or quarters). These periods are marked on the horizontal lines.

The timelines all begin at time 0, which is the present, and add periods or years to the right. In these examples, time 1 is the end of the first period, time 2 the end of the second, and so on. The horizontal lines identify aspects of the problems (e.g., amounts, targeted interest rates). In most cases, there is no need to draw timelines, but they are useful tools for understanding the more complicated time-value-of-money problems. A timeline will be used in this chapter to explain some time-value-of-money problems.

Figure 10.1 shows four timelines: two dealing with future values (FV) and two with present values (PV). The first example, future value of a single sum (a), shows

Table 10.3 Excel® Financial Spreadsheets

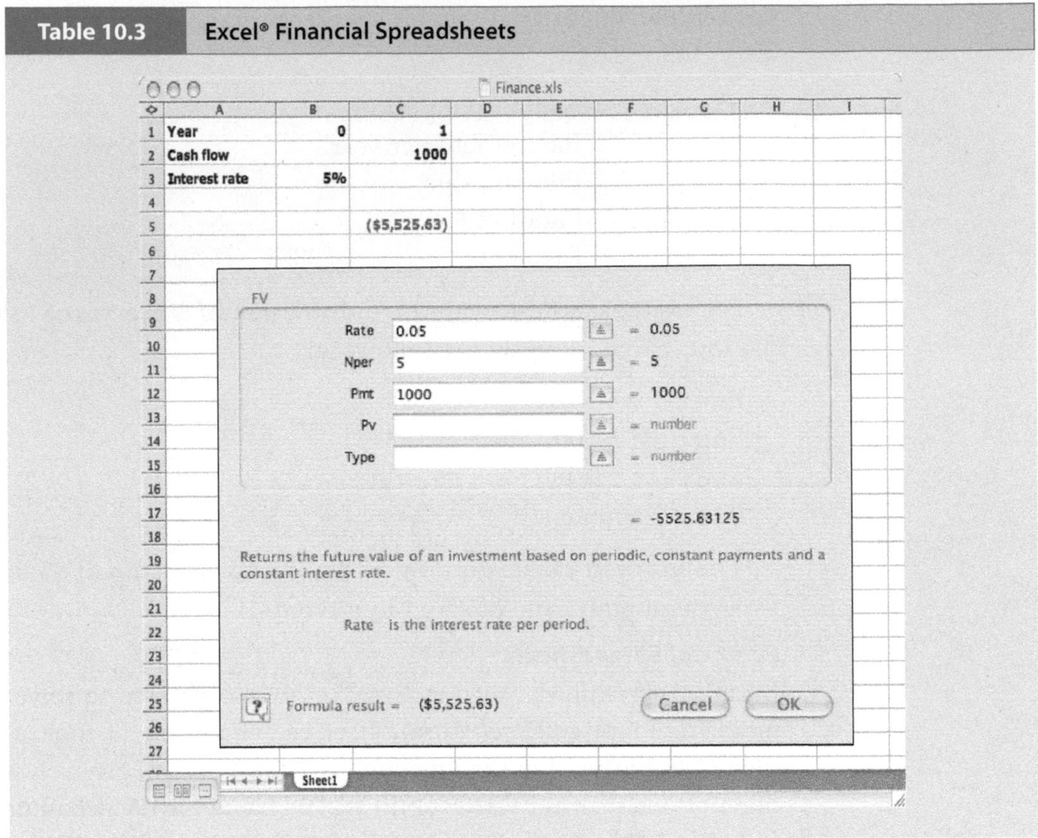

that a $1,000 amount received now will increase to $1,050 ($1,000 × 1.050, with the factor drawn from Table A in Appendix B) by the beginning of year 1. The second example (b) shows what the future value of $1,000 amounts received at the beginning of each year are worth at the beginning of year five. These factors are also drawn from Table A. Each year has a different factor showing the number of years over which the interest accumulates. The third illustration (c) shows that the value of $1,000 received at the beginning of year one is worth $952 ($1,000 × 0.952, a factor drawn from Table B in Appendix B) today. The last example (d) shows how much individual amounts received over five years are worth today. These five factors are also drawn from Table B.

Simple interest
Interest paid on the principal only.

Future Values

3 Differentiate between future values of single sums and future values of annuities.

In this section, we'll show how to calculate the future values of single sums and annuities. First, let's look at the difference between simple and compound interest.

SIMPLE AND COMPOUND INTEREST

Interest can be paid in two ways. First, it can be paid by means of simple interest, which is the easiest form. **Simple interest** is calculated only on the original amount,

Figure 10.1 **Time-Value-of-Money Timelines**

(a) Future value of a single sum

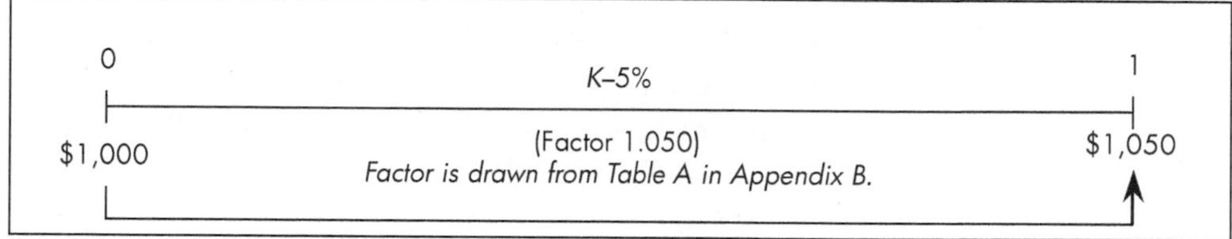

(b) Future value of identical amounts (annuity)

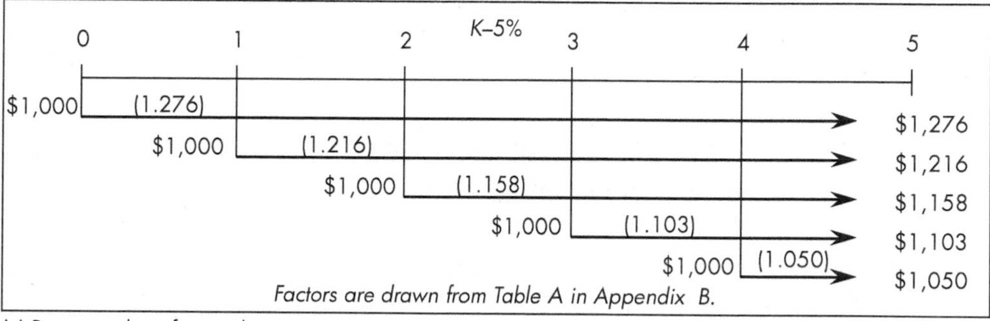

(c) Present value of a single sum

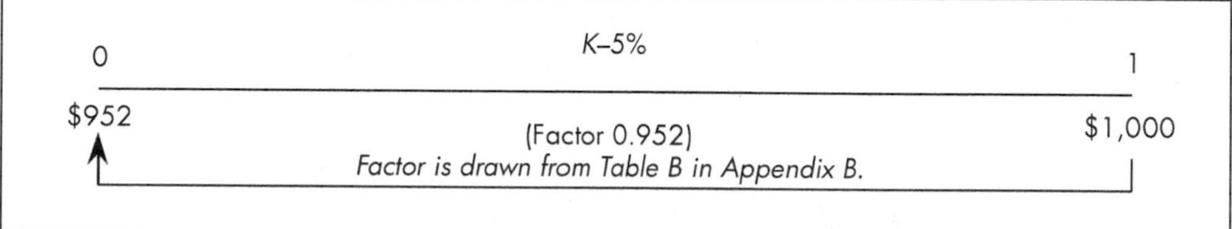

(d) Present value of identical amounts (annuity)

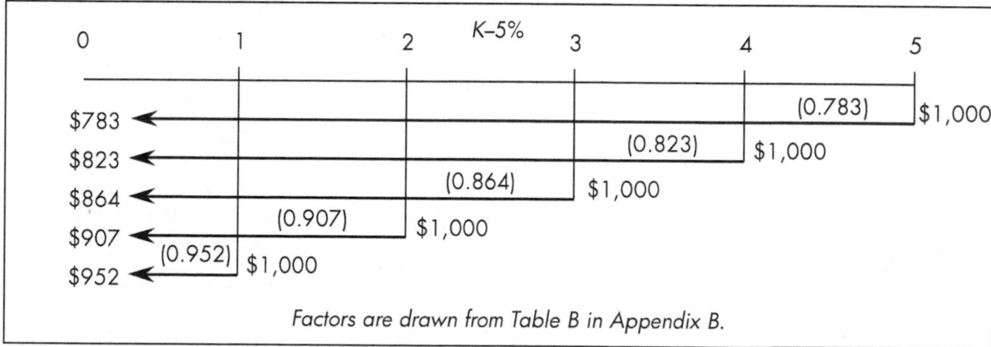

or the principal. When funds are borrowed, interest is charged; when funds are invested, interest is paid. For example, if you invested $1,000 at a rate of 10% for, say, three years, you would earn $300 in interest.

Simple interest is not, however, the conventional way that interest is paid or earned. Usually, when money is deposited in a bank, interest is paid on both the original amount (the principal) and the balance, which increases in each succeeding period when the interest is added. This form of interest is called **compound interest.**

Compound interest
Interest paid on the principal and the previously earned interest.

Figure 10.2 illustrates the difference between simple interest and compound interest. The value of a $1,000 investment (principal) at 10% using simple interest increases by $100 increments. If the investment is made at the beginning of year 1, the $1,000 amount would increase to $1,100 by the end of the first year. Simple interest would make the investment grow to $1,200 by the end of year 2 and $1,300 by the end of year 3. Using compound interest, the value of the investment would grow to $1,100 by the end of the first year, $1,210 by the end of the second year, and $1,331 by the end of year 3. The compounding effect adds an extra $31 by the end of the third year, because in the second year, 10% (or $10) is also earned on the $100 in interest earned during the first year; in the third year, an additional 10% (or $21) is earned on the interest earned during the first and second years (10% of $210).

FUTURE VALUE OF A SINGLE SUM

We said earlier in this chapter that money has a time value because of the existence of interest. This means that if you invest $1,000 today at 10%, you will collect $1,100 at the same date next year. If you keep your original amount invested for an indefinite time, interest will continue to accumulate, and your $1,000 will grow year after year. This future amount is referred to as the **future value (FV)** of a single sum.

Future value (FV)
The amount to which a payment or series of payments will grow by a given date when compounded by interest.

Let's examine the future value at the end of three years of $1,000 invested today at 10%. Table 10.4 shows that at the end of the first year, the investor earns $100 and the ending amount is $1,100. During the second year, $110 in interest will be earned

Figure 10.2 Simple and Compound Interest

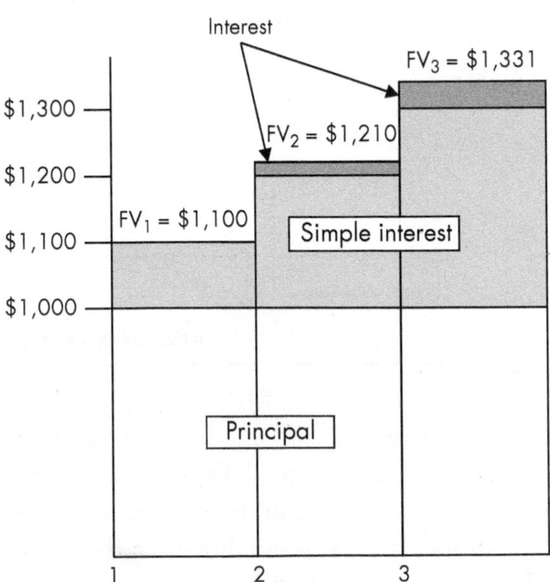

($100 on the original $1,000 and $10 on the $100 interest earned during the first year). The balance at the end of the second year is $1,210. The same arithmetic is done for calculating the interest earned during the third year; the value at the end of that period is $1,331. Figure 10.2 and Table 10.4 show the effect of compounding the future value of a single sum.

An investor does not have to go through these calculations to determine the future value of an investment; he or she can use an interest table instead. Table A in Appendix B at the end of the book contains future value factors for single sums for interest rates from 1% to 36% for a 25-year period. By looking down the 10% column, you can readily see that the future value of $1,000 at the end of the third year is $1,331 ($1,000 × 1.331), the same amount that was calculated in Table 10.4.

The algebraic equation used to calculate the future value of a single sum is as follows:

$$FV_n = P(1 + i)^n$$

$$FV_3 = \$1{,}000\ (1.10)^3$$

$$= \$1{,}000\ (1.331)$$

$$= \$1{,}331$$

The Rule of 72

Rule of 72
A calculation that shows the approximate number of years it takes for an investment to double when compounded annually.

A quick and easy way to calculate the approximate number of years it takes for an investment to double when compounded annually at a particular rate of interest is called the **rule of 72.** To find the answer, divide 72 by the interest rate of the invested principal. For example, an investment at 10% interest compounded annually will double in 7.2 years:

$$\frac{72}{10\ (\%)} = 7.2\ \text{(approximate number of years)}$$

To check this answer, look at Table A in Appendix B at the end of the book. Look down the 10% interest column to see that the $1.00 amount reaches $2.00 between year 7 (1.949) and year 8 (2.144).

Table 10.4 Calculating the Future Value of a Single Sum

Year	Beginning Amount	Interest Rate	Amount of Interest	Ending Amount
1	$1,000	0.10	$100	$1,100
2	1,100	0.10	110	1,210
3	1,210	0.10	121	1,331

Problem-Solving Example 10.2

Future Value of a Single Sum

Calculate the future values of the following investments: GIC ($100,000 at 4% for 10 years), mutual funds ($200,000 at 6% for 15 years), and stocks ($150,000 at 10% for 5 years). What are the total value and the interest/gain at the end of their respective investment periods?

Solution

Total value at end of the investment period is $869,050 and the interest/gain is $419,050.

				Value	Interest/Gain
GIC	1.480	× $100,000	=	$148,000	$ 48,000
Mutual funds	2.397	× $200,000	=	$479,400	279,400
Stocks	1.611	× 150,000	=	241,650	91,650
Total		$450,000	=	$869,050	$419,050

Self-Test Exercise 10.2

Future Value of a Single Sum

Joan Miller has just inherited $30,000 and wants to invest it. She is trying to choose between GICs, safe mutual funds, or in stock options that are more risky. Based on her analysis, the historical performance for each type of investment is 5%, 9%, and 12%, respectively. If there are no withdrawals, how much would Joan have at the end of 20 years for each choice?

Answers to the Self-Test Exercises can be found at www.bergeron7e.nelson.com.

FUTURE VALUE OF AN ANNUITY

Annuity
A series of payments (or receipts) of a fixed amount for a specified number of years.

So far, we have talked about the growth values of single sums. However, some investors invest money on a yearly basis and generate a flow of funds over many years. A series of periodic income payments of equal amounts is referred to as an **annuity**. A mortgage repayment, family allowances, RRSPs, whole-life insurance premiums, and even salaries and wages are considered annuities. In capital budgeting, if a company modernizes its plant at a cost of $100,000 and produces a fixed yearly $25,000 savings, that would also be considered an annuity.

Because investors and capital budgeting decisions deal with multi-year cash flows, it is important to understand how to calculate the future growth and the present value of annuities. Let's calculate the future growth of a five-year, $1,000 yearly annuity bearing 10% interest. There are two ways to do this calculation. First, we can use the compound interest from Table A in Appendix B and calculate the growth of each $1,000 individually. Table 10.5 shows that the sum of all future receipts is $6,105,

Table 10.5 Calculating the Future Value of an Annuity

Year	Amount Received	Interest Factor	Interest	Future Sum
1	$1,000	1.464	$ 464	$1,464
2	1,000	1.331	331	1,331
3	1,000	1.210	210	1,210
4	1,000	1.100	100	1,100
5	1,000	0.000	—	1,000
Total	$5,000		$1,105	$6,105

made up of $5,000 in investment and $1,105 in interest. The calculation assumes that the annuity is paid at the end of each period—that is, on December 31—starting at the end of year 1. In five years, the $1,000 amount will grow to $1,464. Because the fifth payment is received on December 31 of the last year, this receipt does not produce any interest.

This is a complicated way to calculate the future value of an annuity.

The second approach is to use an annuity table; refer to Table C in Appendix B at the end of the book. By looking down the 10% interest rate column to year five, we find factor 6.105. If we multiply this factor by the $1,000 fixed annuity, we get $6,105. This is a much easier way to calculate future values. The algebraic formula used to calculate the future value of an annuity is as follows:

$$
\begin{aligned}
S &= PMT\left[\frac{(1+i)^n - 1}{i}\right] \\
&= \$1{,}000\ (6.105) \\
&= \$6{,}105
\end{aligned}
$$

Problem-Solving Example 10.3

Future Value of an Annuity

Would you prefer to (1) receive $70,000 today and invest it for 10 years, or (2) receive a $10,000 annuity over 10 years? Both options earn 6% a year.

Solution

The annuity is more favourable by $6,440.

(1)	Single sum (Table A)	$70,000	×	1.791	=	$125,370
(2)	Annuity (Table C)	$10,000	×	13.181	=	$131,810
	Difference					$ 6,440

Self-Test Exercise 10.3

Future Value of an Annuity

Joan Miller was given a choice on her \$30,000 inheritance between receiving (1) the full payment today or (2) a \$3,000 annuity for the next 20 years and a lump sum of \$10,000 at the end of the 20th year. If Joan can earn 9%, which option is the most attractive?

Answers to the Self-Test Exercises can be found at www.bergeron7e.nelson.com.

Present Values

4 Distinguish between present values of single sums and present values of annuities.

We now turn our attention to calculating the present values of single sums and annuities and calculating the present values of an uneven series of amounts.

PRESENT VALUE OF A SINGLE SUM

Present value (PV) The value today of a future payment or stream of payments, discounted at an appropriate rate.

The opposite of compounding is discounting. You have learned that compounding means that when money is invested today, it appreciates in value because compound interest is added. The opposite takes place when money is to be received in the future; in this case, the future amount is worth less today. It is called the **present value (PV)**, defined as the value today of a future payment or stream of payments, discounted at an appropriate rate. In our previous example of \$1,000 and an interest rate of 10%, both amounts, \$1,000 today and \$1,331 (\$1,000 × 1.331) in year 3, have equal values today. This, therefore, supports the argument that the \$1,331 to be received three years from now has a \$1,000 value today. Because discounting is the opposite of compounding, we reverse the compound algebraic equation as follows:

$$PV = FV\left[\frac{1}{(1+i)^n}\right]$$

$$= \$1{,}000\left[\frac{1}{(1+0.10)^3}\right]$$

$$= \$1{,}000\left[\frac{1}{1.331}\right]$$

$$= \$1{,}000\ (0.75131)$$

$$= \$751.31$$

This means that if \$1,000 will be received three years from now at 10%, it is worth \$751.31 today; or, to reverse the process, if you invest \$751.31 today at a 10% interest rate, it would appreciate to \$1,000 in three years (\$751.31 × 1.331).

Like the compound interest calculation, the calculation for the present value of a promised future sum is time consuming. Instead, we can use present value tables.

Table B in Appendix B at the end of the book contains present value factors for interest rates for a single sum from 1% to 36% for a 25-year period. Looking at the appropriate interest column (10%) and at year 3, we find factor 0.75131. This means that by multiplying the promised $1,000 future sum by 0.75131, we get $751.31 as the present value.

In the News 10.2 shows that low interest rates can cap borrowing costs, encourage individuals to buy big-ticket items, and persuade businesses to invest in capital projects.

In the News 10.2

LOWERING INTEREST RATES CAN FUEL THE ECONOMY

There is one way to regulate the intensity of a fire: by feeding it with an adequate supply of gasoline, an oxidizing agent. This is precisely one of the roles of the Bank of Canada. The Bank's monetary policy increases or decreases the interest rate to support a well-functioning Canadian economy. A stable economy (1) allows Canadians to make spending and investment decisions with confidence, (2) encourages longer-term investments in the economy, and (3) sustains job creation and improves productivity. It can create real improvements in Canada's standard of living.

The current governor of the Bank of Canada, Mark Carney, has been trying to keep the economy moving in a positive direction since the start of the recession. He helped bring the interest rate down to the lowest possible level, 0.25%, during the financial crisis and promised to keep it there (conditions permitting) until 2012. This was a key factor for driving the Canadian economy back to growth. Now the word is out: With economic conditions improving, the Bank of Canada is strongly considering increasing today's low interest rates. Many economists are advising Canadians to have an escape plan if rates begin to rise. They should not be complacent about their ability to afford higher rates; most families and businesses don't have enough of a financial cushion to absorb higher interest costs on loans or mortgages.

Source: "Start planning your rising interest rate escape plan." *Globe and Mail*. Retrieved from http://www.theglobeandmail.com/globe-investor/personal-finance/rob-carrick/start-planning-your-rising-interest-rate-escape-plan/article2404905/, accessed April 21, 2012.

Problem-Solving Example 10.4

Present Value of a Single Sum

Hannah is six years old and Eva is four. How much would Hannah and Eva's parents need to invest today (a lump-sum investment) in an educational fund if they want $40,000 for each child by the time she is 20 years old? Assume they are able to earn 6% on their investments.

Solution

The parents would have to invest $33,438 in total now to realize $40,000 for each child when she is 20 years old.

	No. of Years	Future Values		PV Factors		Lump Sum Amount
Hannah	14 years	$40,000	×	0.44230	=	$17,692
Eva	16 years	$40,000	×	0.39365	=	$15,746
Total		$80,000				$33,438

Self-Test Exercise 10.4

Present Value of a Single Sum

The Millers would like to have a $30,000 education fund for their son Vincent, who is now three years old, and the same amount for their daughter, Takara, who has just turned one. The Millers expect that their children will start university when they are 20 years of age. How much will the Millers have to invest today (in one lump sum) if the registered education savings plan guarantees a 7% annual interest rate free from any income tax?

Answers to the Self-Test Exercises can be found at www.bergeron7e.nelson.com.

PRESENT VALUE OF AN ANNUITY

Discounting
The process of finding the present value of a series of future cash flows.

Calculating the present value of an annuity is the reverse of compounding an annuity. Compounding gives the future growth of a series of fixed receipts or payments; **discounting** gives the present value of a series of receipts or payments. Let us figure out the present value of a $1,000 received every year for five years, with a 10% interest rate. This calculation can also be done two ways. First, we can multiply yearly receipts by their interest factors, referring to Table 10.6 and calculating the present value of each amount.

However, we can skip this long process and use Table D in Appendix B at the end of the book. It contains present value factors for interest rates for an annuity from 1% to 36% for a 25-year period. Looking down the 10% interest column to the line for year five, we find factor 3.7908. The more simplified approach is, therefore, to multiply this factor by $1,000, giving us $3,791 ($1 rounding difference).

The algebraic formula used to calculate the present value of an annuity is as follows:

$$A = PMT\left[\frac{1-(1+i)^{-n}}{i}\right]$$

Table 10.6 Calculating the Present Value of an Annuity

Year	Amount Received	Interest Factor	Present Value
1	$1,000	0.9091	$ 909
2	1,000	0.8264	826
3	1,000	0.7513	751
4	1,000	0.6830	683
5	1,000	0.6209	621
Total	$5,000		$3,790

Using our example,

$$A = \$1{,}000 \left[\frac{1 - (1 + 0.1)^{-5}}{0.1}\right]$$

$$= \$1{,}000 \left[\frac{1 - 0.62092}{0.1}\right]$$

$$= \$1{,}000\ (3.7908)$$

$$= \$3{,}791$$

We now have two interest factors to keep track of: the compound interest factor and the present value factor. In the former case, factors are used to make a sum grow (compound), while in the latter case, factors are used to depreciate (discount) a sum expected to be received in the future.

Figure 10.3 shows the impact that 10%, 20%, and 30% compound and discount factors have on $1,000 over 12 years. For example, on the left side of the figure, a $1,000 investment at 10% grows to $3,138 in 12 years, while the same investment grows to $23,298 at 30%. The right side of the figure shows that $1,000 received 12 years from now is worth $319 today at 10%, and only $43 at 30%.

Figure 10.3 Graphic Illustration of the Compounding and Discounting Process

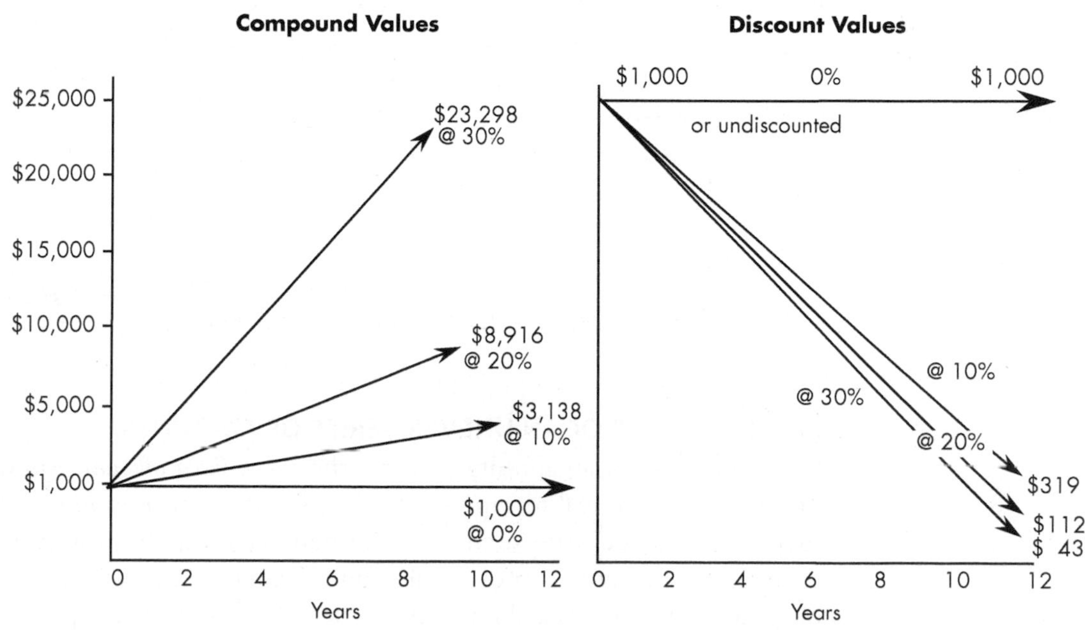

Problem-Solving Example 10.5

Present Value of an Annuity

Komar wants to invest $350,000 in a capital project. His projected statement of income shows that he will be earning a fixed yearly cash flow of $40,000 over a 20-year period. Calculate (1) the present value of the annual cash inflows using a 10% interest rate, (2) the difference between the discounted cash inflows and the cash outflow, (3) how much Komar would have to receive each year to make the inflows equal to the outflow.

Solution

(1) Present value of the annual cash inflows:

$$\$40{,}000 \times 8.5136 = \$340{,}544$$

(2) Difference between the cash outflow and the discounted cash inflows:

$$\$340{,}544 - \$350{,}000 = -\$9{,}456$$

(3) Amount he would have to receive each year to make both amounts equal.

$$\$350{,}000 \div 8.5136 = \$41{,}111$$

Self-Test Exercise 10.5

Present and Future Values of an Annuity

Len has just won $100,000 at a casino. If money is worth 10%, would it be better for Len to receive the full amount now or $15,000 each year for the next 10 years?

Questions

1. What is the value of each amount 10 years from now?
2. What is today's present value of each amount?
3. How much would Len have to receive each year to be equivalent to receiving $100,000 today?
4. If Len received $15,000 each year instead of the $100,000 amount, what would the effective interest rate or the internal rate of return (IRR) be?

Answers to the Self-Test Exercises can be found at www.bergeron7e.nelson.com.

PRESENT VALUE OF AN UNEVEN SERIES OF AMOUNTS

Our definition of an annuity includes the term *fixed amount*. Annuities are made up of constant and equal receipts or payments, but often, amounts received from investments vary. To evaluate such an investment or a capital project, you must calculate each receipt or payment individually (unless you have a financial calculator, spreadsheet, or software to calculate the present values of the future receipts).

Table 10.7 **Calculating the Present Value of Uneven Amounts**

Year	Receipts	Discount Factor	Present Value*
1	$ 200	0.8929	$ 179
2	500	0.7972	399
3	400	0.7118	285
4	600	0.6355	381
5	200	0.5674	113
Total	$1,900		$1,357

* Values have been rounded to the nearest dollar.

To illustrate the process of calculating uneven flows of receipts, assume that you are investing $1,500 that will produce an inflow of funds of $200 in the first year, $500 in the second, $400 in the third, $600 in the fourth, and $200 in the fifth. You want to make a 12% return on your investment. The discounted-value calculations of the future receipts in Table 10.7 show that the investment is not desirable. The discounted value of the future receipts, $1,357, is less than the $1,500 initial outflow.

This time, we'll change the $200 receipt in the fifth year for a $200 annuity received over six years (from year 5 to year 10). We'll need a slightly different procedure to calculate the present value. As shown in Table 10.8, the present value of the receipts for years 1, 2, 3, and 4 are the same as those calculated in Table 10.7. However, because the last $200 receipt is an annuity, we can use a shortcut. In the first step, the $200 receipts from years 5 to 10 (for a total of six years) have to be discounted to year 4, which gives $822.28. In the second step, the $822.28 has to be discounted to year 0, which gives $522.56. The calculation process shown in Table 10.8 is illustrated in Figure 10.4. In total, the discounted value of the receipts amounts to $1,765.76, which is more than the original outflow. Therefore, in this case, the investment is desirable.

Table 10.8 **Procedure for Calculating an Uneven Series of Amounts**

A.	PV of $200 in year 1 (0.8929)	=	$ 178.58
	PV of $500 in year 2 (0.7972)	=	398.60
	PV of $400 in year 3 (0.7118)	=	284.72
	PV of $600 in year 4 (0.6355)	=	381.30
	PV of $200 in years 5 to 10		
B.	Step 1: $200 × 4.1114 = $822.28		
	Step 2: $822.28 × 0.6355	=	522.56
C.	PV of total receipts	=	$1,765.76

Figure 10.4 Illustration of the Present Value Calculations from Table 10.8

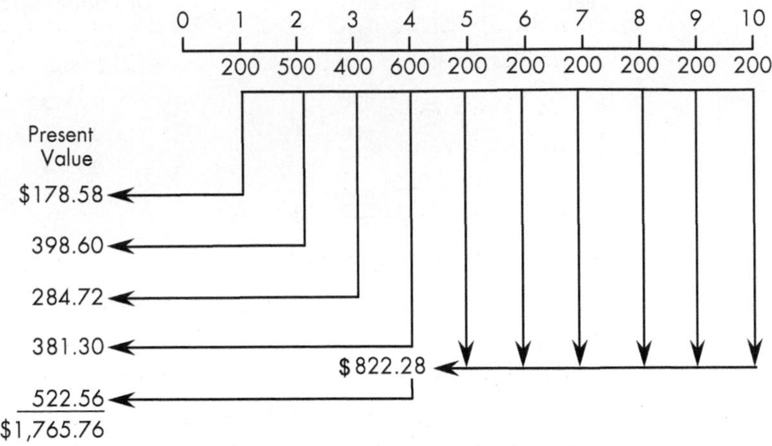

Problem-Solving Example 10.6

Present Value of Uneven Cash Flows

Use the cash flow forecast from Problem-Solving Example 10.1 to calculate the present value of the future cash inflows. Assume the cost of capital is 8% and that 2013 is considered year 1.

Solution

Total present value is $167,188.

Years	Cash Flow	Discount Factors	Present Values
2013	$ 53,500	0.92593	$ 49,537
2014	$ 51,540	0.85734	$ 44,187
2015	$ 49,287	0.79383	$ 39,125
2016	$ 46,718	0.73503	$ 34,339
Total	$201,045		$167,188

Self-Test Exercise 10.6

Present Value of Uneven Sums

Use the cash flow forecast from Self-Test Exercise 10.1 to calculate the photo centre's present value. Assume that the company's cost of capital is 10%.

Answers to the Self-Test Exercises can be found at www.bergeron7e.nelson.com.

Solving Time-Value-of-Money Investment Problems

5 Make capital investment decisions by using time-value-of-money tools.

Let's now examine how interest tables can help individuals and managers evaluate investment opportunities. In the rest of this chapter, we look at the meaning of time-value yardsticks for the following investment and capital budgeting techniques:

- The future value (FV)
- The net future value (NFV)
- The present value (PV)
- The net present value (NPV)
- The internal rate of return (IRR)

To describe how these techniques are used, we will use an example of a $100,000 lottery and determine how much a winner should receive each year over 10 years to make the annuity equal to the lump sum. Investment decisions deal with two key concepts: time and cash (see Figure 10.5). Time is important because when managers invest money today, they expect to earn money from these investments over an extended number of years. For example, when a company invests $100,000 to modernize a plant that has a 10-year lifespan, that initial cash outflow must be compared with all the future cash inflows that will be generated through the savings. There is no question that a $100,000 investment that generates $50,000 in savings over three years (for a total of $150,000) would be more financially attractive than one that generates $15,000 a year over 10 years (also for a total of $150,000).

Cash outflow
Cash disbursement for the purchase of investments, such as mutual funds or capital assets.

Cash inflow
The receipt of money (interest or profit for the year plus depreciation) generated by an investment or a project.

The second critical element is cash. If someone invests money in mutual funds or a company invests money in equipment, machinery, or research and development, it invests cash. Such an investment is commonly referred to as a **cash outflow** or cash disbursement. The investors or the managers will want to compare cash invested with cash generated by the investment. The cash that an investment generates is commonly referred to as **cash inflow** or cash receipts. The common denominator that ties a project together is cash. Therefore, in businesses, when preparing a project's projected

Figure 10.5 Investment Decisions

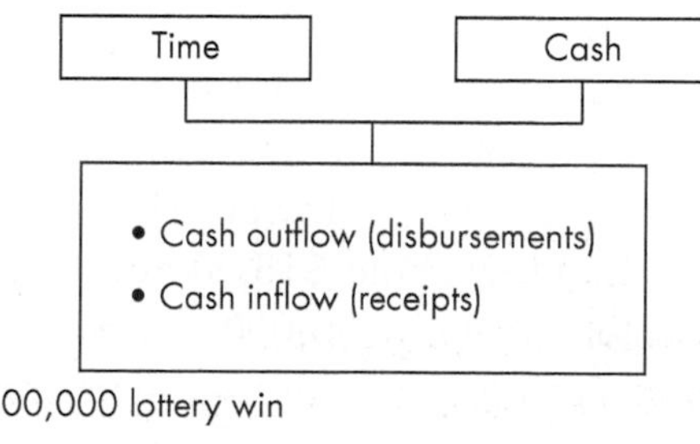

statement of income, the profit for the year shown at the bottom of the statement of income must be converted into cash (e.g., by adding back depreciation) because time-value yardsticks use cash, not profit for the year, to judge a project's desirability. To make capital budgeting decisions meaningful, we must compare apples (cash outflow) with apples (cash inflow).

In the News 10.3 shows that interest tables, financial calculators, or financial spreadsheets are vital tools for making RRSP and RRIF decisions.

In The News 10.3

FINANCIAL CALCULATORS: IMPORTANT TOOLS FOR ANNUITY DECISIONS

Anyone interested in investing in a registered retirement savings plan (RRSP) and eventually converting it into a registered retirement income fund (RRIF) has no choice but to use interest tables, a financial calculator, or a financial spreadsheet. People need to know how much money to put aside each month or year into a savings account, GICs, bonds, or mutual funds during the next 20, 30, or even 40 years, and they need to know how much they'll need during their retirement. Many factors are involved in the calculation: maximum contributions, timing of contributions, claiming of the contribution tax credit, the assets allowed, and the eventual conversion.

Thousands of Canadians make these calculations every year, but less money is being invested than in the past. The percentage of disposable income to invest in RRSPs after paying for housing and other costs is tumbling. In 2012, it fell to 2.9% from a high of 5% in 1997. Some economists predict it could fall as low as 2% by 2017.

Source: "RRSP contributions to decline to levels not seen since 1970s: RBC." *Financial Post*. Retrieved from http://business.financialpost.com/2012/02/23/rrsp-contributions-to-decline-to-levels-not-seen-since-1970s-rbc/ Accessed April 21, 2012.

The following illustrates the significance of time and cash in investment decisions. Assume that you have won the $100,000 lottery and are given the following options:

- Option 1: Receive the $100,000 lump-sum amount today.
- Option 2: Receive $10,000 each year during the next 10 years (also for a total of $100,000).

There is no question that you will go for the first option. In both options, we are dealing with cash and with time. It would be absurd to accept the $10,000 arrangement despite the fact that the total receipts equal $100,000. The fact that you could invest the $100,000 in mutual funds at, say, 10% would make option 1 more economically attractive. However, if you were offered $12,000 a year instead, would you go for it? How about $15,000 or $20,000? How about $25,000 during the next six years (for a total $150,000) instead of only $100,000? Different time factors and amounts call for an analysis to determine the best option.

The same applies in capital budgeting. If you were to invest $100,000 in a capital project that has a 10-year lifespan, how much should that project generate in cash to make it economically attractive? The following sections answer these questions.

FUTURE VALUE AND NET FUTURE VALUE

Question 1: Should the lottery winner accept the $100,000 lump-sum payment or $15,000 a year for the next 10 years?

Question 2: Should the manufacturing manager invest $100,000 to save $15,000 a year for the next 10 years?

For question 1, assume that the lottery winner can invest money in mutual funds at 10%. The future values of both amounts are calculated as follows:

$100,000	×	2.594	(Table A)	=	$259,400	(FV)
$ 15,000	×	15.937	(Table C)	=	$239,055	(FV)
Net future value					$ 20,345	(NFV)

If the $100,000 were invested now in mutual funds at 10%, over the next 10 years, this amount would grow (because of time) to more ($259,400) than if the $15,000 were invested in mutual funds each year ($239,055). These amounts are referred to as future value (FV). By the 10th year, the lump-sum payment would give an extra $20,345, commonly referred to as the **net future value (NFV)**. Individually, both amounts are referred to as the future value, and the difference between both future amounts is referred to as the NFV.

Net future value (NFV)
The future value of the projected compounded cash inflows, less the projected future value of the cash outflow.

PRESENT VALUE AND NET PRESENT VALUE

You could also decide which option to choose by comparing the discounted amounts, which gives a difference of $7,831 in favour of the lump-sum payment.

	−$100,000			
Present value	+$ 92,169	(PV)	=	or $15,000 × 6.1446 (Table D)
	−$ 7,831	(NPV)	=	Net present value

Whether you bring both sums into the future (10th year) or the present, the decision is the same (although the numbers are different)—go for the $100,000 lump-sum payment.

If a business invests $100,000 (cash outflow) to modernize the plant and save $15,000 (cash inflow) a year, the economics would not justify the investment. As shown above, the discounted $15,000 (or $150,000 over the 10 years) gives a present value (PV) of only $92,169. Using the 10% discount rate, the difference between the outflow and the inflow is –$7,831, which is referred to as the **net present value (NPV)**. Whenever there is a negative NPV, the return on the investment is less than the rate used to discount the future cash receipts, which in this case happens to be less than 10%. When the NPV is positive, it means that the return on the investment is more than the rate used to discount the future receipts.

Net present value (NPV)
The present value of the future cash flow of an investment less the initial cash outflow.

Problem-Solving Example 10.7

Net Present Value and Net Future Value

Use the cash flow forecast in Problem-Solving Example 10.1 to calculate the company's (1) net present value and (2) net future value. Assume the cost of capital is 8% and the investment in capital assets is $150,000.

Solution

In both calculations, the NPV and NFV are positive.

(1) A financial calculator shows the net present value is +$17,188.

Cash outflow	−$150,000	
Cash inflow	+ 167,188	(see Problem-Solving Example 10.6)
Net present value	+$ 17,188	

(2) Net future value is +$23,545.

Years	Cash Flows	Compound Factors	Future Values
0 (2012)	−$150,000	1.360	−$204,000
1 (2013)	53,500	1.260	67,410
2 (2014)	51,540	1.166	60,096
3 (2015)	49,287	1.080	53,230
4 (2016)	46,718	1.000	46,718
Net future value			+$ 23,454

Self-Test Exercise 10.7

Net Present Value and Net Future Value

Use the cash flow forecast from Self-Test Exercise 10.1 to calculate the photo centre's NPV and NFV. Assume that the company's cost of capital is 10%.

Answers to the Self-Test Exercises can be found at www.bergeron7e.nelson.com.

INTERNAL RATE OF RETURN

If both amounts were to have the same value, the lottery winner would have to receive $16,275 each year for the next 10 years. This $16,275 amount is calculated by dividing the $100,000 amount by the factor found in Table D in Appendix B under column 10%, row year 10 (6.1446). Only then are both numbers the same; that is, the lump-sum amount is equal to the present value of the $16,275 annual receipts—the NPV is 0.

Here is how the calculation is done (ignore rounding).

	−$100,000		
Present value	+$100,000	=	or $16,275 × 6.1446 (Table D)
	$ 0	=	NPV

For the business, if management wants a 10% return on the $100,000, plant efficiencies would also have to generate $16,275 each year. If the savings are more than this, the plant would generate more than 10%; if they are less, the return would be less. When the interest rate makes the discounted future receipts ($100,000) equal the original investment ($100,000), it is referred to as the internal rate of return. The **internal rate of return (IRR)** can be defined as the interest rate that equates the cost of an investment (cash outflow) to the present value of the expected returns from the investment (cash inflow).

Internal rate of return (IRR)
The interest rate that equates the cost of an investment (cash outflow) to the present value of the expected returns from the investment (cash inflow).

In this case, because 10% makes the future savings equal to $100,000 (the NPV equals 0), the IRR is 10%. If the savings were more than $16,275, the plant generated a higher return. For example, if the plant were to generate $18,429 savings per year during the next 10 years, the IRR would be 13%, because it is this rate that makes the NPV equal to 0.

	−$100,000		
Present value	+$100,000	=	or $18,429 × 5.4262 (Table D)
	$ 0	=	NPV

Conversely, if the annual receipts were less than $16,275, then the IRR would be less. In the case of the manufacturing plant, the annual savings are $15,000. This means that the IRR would be less than 10% (8.1%), which is found by looking at Table D in Appendix B, under the column 8% at row year 10, where we find factor 6.7101.

	−$100,000		
Present value	+$100,652	=	or $15,000 × 6.7101 (Table D)
	+$ 652	=	NPV

The 8% figure gives a positive $652 NPV, which means that the project generates 8% plus $652. If we were to convert this number to a percentage, the answer would be 0.144%. If Table D had a factor for 6.6667, then the PV would have been exactly $100,000, and the NPV would be exactly 0.

Problem-Solving Example 10.8

Internal Rate of Return

Using the cash flow forecast from Problem-Solving Example 10.7, calculate the project's internal rate of return.

(continued)

Problem-Solving Example 10.8 (continued)

Solution

Using the discount rate of 13%, the net present value is positive by $522. A financial calculator shows that the project gives a 13.17% internal rate of return.

Years	Cash Flows	PV Factors (13%)	Present Values
0 (2012)	−$150,000	1.0000	−$150,000
1 (2013)	53,500	0.8850	47,348
2 (2014)	51,540	0.7831	40,361
3 (2015)	49,287	0.6931	34,161
4 (2016)	46,718	0.6133	28,652
Net future value			+$ 522

Self-Test Exercise 10.8

Internal Rate of Return

Use the cash flow forecast from Self-Test Exercise 10.1 to calculate the photo centre's IRR.

Answers to the Self-Test Exercises can be found at www.bergeron7e.nelson.com.

Accounting Rates of Return Can Be Misleading

Table 10.9 shows that when using traditional accounting methods to calculate the return on this project, we would divide the $15,000 by the $100,000 asset and get a 15% return (ROA). If a time-value-of-money yardstick were used, such as the IRR, the investment would give only 8.1%. In this case, the company would be losing 1.9% (after financing) each year during the next 10 years instead of making a net 5.0%.

Table 10.9 Accounting Rate of Return versus the IRR

Calculating the accounting rate of return by using ROA

$$\frac{Receipts}{Assets} = \frac{\$15,000}{\$100,000} = 15\%$$

Statement of Financial Position

ROA	15.0%	Cost of capital 10.0%
IRR	8.1%	

This simple illustration shows that using accounting rates of return in capital budgeting decisions can be misleading. As you will discover in the next chapter, there are different ways of calculating the accounting rates of return, but they are not the most reliable capital budgeting yardsticks. Time-value benchmarks are more reliable for measuring the desirability of capital projects and can be compared more accurately to the cost of capital.

USING INTEREST TABLES IN CAPITAL BUDGETING

To calculate the financial returns by using time-value-of-money yardsticks, you need to know four things:

- Investment amount (cash outflow or disbursement)
- Annual cash inflows (receipts)
- Expected lifespan of the project
- Cost of capital (or the return that management wants to make on the investment)

Let's use one more example to calculate the NPV and the IRR of a capital project by using interest tables. The left side of Table 10.10(a) shows a company that invests $25,000 in a new capital asset and obtains $1,000 in savings each year during the next 25 years. If management wants to make 10%, the present value of the $1,000 receipts gives $9,077. Here, the NPV is a negative $15,923. This means that the IRR is negative.

If management wants to earn 10%, how much should the project generate each year over the life of the asset? The right side of Table 10.10(a) shows that the savings should be $2,754. This annual savings discounted at 10% gives a present value of $25,000, or an NPV of 0. The IRR would be 10% because it is the discount rate that makes the cash inflow equal to the cash outflow.

Table 10.10(a) Investing in a Capital Project

1. A company invests $25,000 in a project. 2. It generates $1,000 in savings each year. 3. The expected life of the project is 25 years. 4. Cost of capital is 10%.		How much must the company save each year to make 10% on the project?	
1. Investment	– $25,000	– $25,000	Investment
2. Annual savings: $1,000			Savings per year: $2,754
3. Total savings: $25,000			Total savings: $68,850
4. Present value of savings (9.0770 × $1,000)	+ $ 9,077	+ $25,000	Present value of the savings (9.0770 × $2,754)
Net present value	– $15,923	0	Net present value

Now, if management wants to earn 16% (instead of 10%), the annual savings would have to be $4,100. As shown in Table 10.10(b), this annual savings gives a $25,000 present value. In this case, because 16% makes the outflow equal to the inflow, this rate would be the IRR.

Now, let's put things in perspective with Table 10.10(c). Assuming that the treasurer of a company raises $25,000 at a cost of 10% (cost of capital on the right side of the Statement of Financial Position) and repays $2,754 a year during the next 25 years, while managers invest this sum (left side of the Statement of Financial Position) in an asset that earns $4,100 or 16% percent per year, the company would make 6% after paying the financing charges, for a net of $1,346 per year.

Table 10.10(b) Investing in a Capital Project

A company wants to make 16% on the $25,000 project.
How much must the project generate in savings or cash each year?

1. Investment	– $25,000
2. Annual savings: $4,100	
3. Total savings: $102,500	
4. Present value of savings (6.0971 × $4,100)	+ $25,000
Net present value	0

Table 10.10(c) Investing in a Capital Project

Statement of Financial Position	
Asset $25,000	Loan of 10%
Saves $4,100	Repayment $2,754
Gives 16% per year	Cost of capital 10%

After financing, the company makes 6% or $1,346 per year

Chapter Summary

1 Define time value of money, inflation, and risk.

Money has a time value because of the existence of interest. Because of interest, a dollar earned today would be worth more tomorrow (compounding). Conversely, a dollar earned tomorrow would be worth less today (discounting). In capital budgeting, *inflation* rates, like price or cost increases, are included in financial projections. Once the projected statements of income are completed, the time-value-of-money concept is used to discount all future cash inflows to the present. *Risk* has to do with uncertainties related to a project. The more uncertain the variables are that affect a capital project, such as the cost of the equipment, market condition, and competition, the more risky the project. If a project is highly risky, managers will use a high discount rate to calculate the net present value of a project and determine the IRR.

2 Explain the financial tools used to solve time-value-of-money problems.

The tools used to calculate time-value of-money problems are financial equations, interest tables, financial calculators, and financial spreadsheets. The timeline concept shows graphically when cash is disbursed or received over a period of time (months or years).

3 Differentiate between future values of single sums and future values of annuities.

Appendix B at the end of this book presents four interest tables. Tables A and C deal with compounding. If you want to find the future value of a single sum, use Table A. If you want to calculate the future value of an annuity, use Table C.

4 Distinguish between present values of single sums and present values of annuities.

In capital budgeting, financial analysts use discounting tables, included as Tables B and D in Appendix B at the end of this book. If you want to calculate the present value of a single sum, use Table B. If you want to find the present value of an annuity, use Table D. Four elements must be taken into consideration in investment decisions: cash outflows (investments), cash inflows (receipts earned from the project), expected life of the project, and cost of capital raised that will be used to finance the project.

5 Make capital investment decisions by using time-value-of-money tools.

Understanding compound and discount value concepts is important for comprehending many topics in finance and for improving the quality of capital budgeting decisions. It is essential to know how to use compound and discount tables. For example, if a business invests \$100,000 in a capital project and earns \$40,000 over the following five years, the present value (if the cost of capital is 10%) of the \$200,000 would be \$151,632 (\$40,000 × 3.7908). The NPV would be +\$51,632, or the difference between the \$100,000 cash outflow and the \$151,632 present value of the future cash inflows. The IRR would be 28.65%, which is the interest rate used to discount all future cash inflows so that the present value equals the cash outflow.

Key Terms

Annuity p. 436
Cash inflow p. 445
Cash outflow p. 445
Compound interest p. 434
Discounting p. 440
Future value (FV) p. 434
Inflation p. 425
Interest tables p. 429
Internal rate of return (IRR) p. 449
Net future value (NFV) p. 447

Review Questions

1 Define time value of money, inflation, and risk.

1. Explain why money has a time value.
2. What is the difference between time value of money and inflation?
3. What differentiates time value of money and risk?
4. What is the difference between profit for the year and cash flows?

2 Explain the financial tools used to solve time-value-of-money problems.

5. What do the symbols *PMT*, *A*, and *S* mean?
6. How did interest tables come about?
7. Give the full names of the four interest tables.

3 Differentiate between future values of single sums and future values of annuities.

8. Explain the rule of 72.
9. What is the difference between simple interest and compound interest?
10. What is an annuity?

4 Distinguish between present values of single sums and present values of annuities.

11. What is the meaning of present value (PV)?
12. What is the meaning of net present value (NPV)?

5 Make capital investment decisions by using time-value-of-money tools.

13. Why are cash and time critical elements in investment decisions?
14. Within the capital budgeting framework, give a few examples to explain the difference between cash inflows and cash outflows.
15. What is the meaning of net future value (NFV)?
16. What do we mean by internal rate of return (IRR)?
17. Why is time value more important in gauging capital decisions than the traditional accounting methods?
18. How can the internal rate of return help managers gauge the economic value added of investment decisions when compared with cost of capital?

Learning Exercises

1 Define time value of money, inflation, and risk.

EXERCISE 1: PROJECTED STATEMENTS OF INCOME (INFLATION)

Evelyn Kent's projected statement of income for 2013 is as follows:

In dollars		
Revenue		600,000
Cost of sales		(400,000)
Gross profit		200,000
Administration expenses	(50,000)	
Distribution expenses	(75,000)	
Depreciation	(25,000)	
Total expenses		(150,000)
Profit before taxes		50,000
Income tax expense		(15,000)
Profit for the year		35,000

Prepare Evelyn Kent's projected statements of income for 2014, 2015, and 2016 based on the following annual inflation rates: revenue (3%), cost of sales (2.5%), administrative expenses (2.0%), and distribution costs (3.0%). The income tax rate is 30%.

EXERCISE 2: COMPOUND INTEREST CALCULATIONS OF A SINGLE SUM

If you invest $10,000 at 8%, how much will your investment be worth at the end of the following time periods?

a) 5 years
b) 10 years
c) 15 years

2 Explain the financial tools used to solve time-value-of-money problems.

EXERCISE 3: COMPOUND INTEREST CALCULATION (TWO OPTIONS)

If you receive an inheritance and have two payment options, would you prefer $85,000 now or payments made at the beginning of each year in the following way?

Year 1	$20,000
Year 2	$25,000
Year 3	$15,000
Year 4	$10,000
Year 5	$25,000

Calculate the future value of both options by the end of the fifth year if you can get 8% on your investment.

EXERCISE 4: FUTURE VALUES AND PRESENT VALUES

With an 8% interest rate, calculate the (1) net future value and (2) net present value with the following five-year cash flow projections.

Years	Cash Flow
0	$150,000
1	40,000
2	50,000
3	55,000
4	60,000
5	70,000

3 Differentiate between future values of single sums and future values of annuities.

EXERCISE 5: FUTURE VALUE OF A SINGLE SUM VERSUS AN ANNUITY

You have a choice between receiving (1) a $50,000 payment today, and (2) a $7,500 annuity for the next 10 years and a lump-sum amount of $20,000 at the end of the 10th year. If money is worth 10%, which option is the most attractive?

4 Distinguish between present values of single sums and present values of annuities.

EXERCISE 6: PRESENT VALUES AND FUTURE VALUES

Suppose you were offered the following options: a 10-year annuity of $10,000 at the end of each year or a $60,000 lump-sum payment today. If you want to make 10%, which option would you prefer? To answer this question, calculate the present value of both options and the future value of both options.

EXERCISE 7: FUTURE VALUES

Su Mei's parents want to put enough money aside for her education by the time she goes to university 10 years from now. If they invest the amounts listed below at the beginning of each year, how much will Su Mei's education fund have grown by the end of the fifth year and tenth year? Assume that Su Mei's parents earn 7% on their investment.

Year 1	$5,000
Year 2	$6,000
Year 3	$7,000
Year 4	$8,000
Year 5	$9,000

EXERCISE 8: USING TABLE B

If you were to sell a new car, and the terms of the agreement were that you received $5,000 as a down payment and three payments of $10,000 each year for the next three years, what would be the real purchase price of the car if the interest rate were 5%?

EXERCISE 9: FUTURE VALUES

How much would you be willing to pay for an investment fund that is expected to generate $1,000 at the end of two years, $1,500 at the end of three years, and $2,000 at the end of four years if you wanted to earn 16% annual interest on your investment?

5 Make capital investment decisions by using time-value-of-money tools.

EXERCISE 10: FUTURE VALUES AND PRESENT VALUES

If money is worth 12%, would you prefer receiving $200,000 now or $30,000 each year for the next 10 years?

Questions

1. What is the value of each amount 10 years from now?
2. What is today's present value of each amount?
3. How much would you have to receive each year to be equivalent to receiving $200,000 today?
4. If you receive $30,000 each year instead of the $200,000 amount, what is the effective interest rate or the IRR (internal of return)?

EXERCISE 11: PRESENT VALUE, NET PRESENT VALUE, AND INTERNAL RATE OF RETURN

Two young entrepreneurs want to invest $150,000 in a restaurant. Their business plan shows that the restaurant will generate $40,000 in cash from year one to year five and $50,000 from year 6 to year 10. They want to earn at least 20%. Use this information to calculate (a) the present value, (b) the net present value, and (c) the internal rate of return.

EXERCISE 12: PRESENT VALUE, NET PRESENT VALUE, AND IRR, CALCULATIONS OF UNEVEN CASH FLOWS

You plan to invest $150,000 in a retail business. The projected 10-year cash flows are as follows:

Year 1	$20,000
Year 2	$21,000
Year 3	$22,000
Year 4	$24,000
Year 5	$30,000
Year 6	$35,000
Year 7	$40,000
Year 8	$45,000
Year 9	$50,000
Year 10	$55,000

In the 10th year, the business will be sold for $100,000. The cost of capital is 12%. Use this information to calculate the following for the project:

a) Present value
b) Net present value
c) Internal rate of return

Time-Value-of-Money Calculations Using a Financial Calculator

Use a financial calculator or spreadsheet to do the following calculations. For each, calculate the net present value, the net future value, and the internal rate of return.

EXERCISE 13: NET PRESENT VALUE, NET FUTURE VALUE, AND IRR

Year 0	Cash outflow	$1,000,000
Years 1 to 10	Cash inflow	$ 175,000
Interest rate	10%	

EXERCISE 14: NET PRESENT VALUE, NET FUTURE VALUE, AND IRR

Year 0	Cash outflow	$200,000
Years 1 to 30	Cash inflow	$ 20,000
Interest rate	8%	

EXERCISE 15: NET PRESENT VALUE, NET FUTURE VALUE, AND IRR

Year 0	Cash outflow	$100,000
Year 1	Cash outflow	$300,000
Years 2 to 16	Cash inflow	$ 50,000
Interest rate	6%	

EXERCISE 16: NET PRESENT VALUE, NET FUTURE VALUE, AND IRR

Year 0	Cash outflow	$200,000
Year 1	Cash outflow	$300,000
Year 1	Cash inflow	$100,000
Year 2	Cash outflow	$100,000
Years 3 to 12	Cash inflow	$110,000
Interest rate	7%	

EXERCISE 17: NET PRESENT VALUE, NET FUTURE VALUE, AND IRR

Year 0	Cash outflow	$400,000
Year 1	Cash outflow	$100,000
Year 1	Cash inflow	$125,000
Year 2	Cash inflow	$125,000
Year 3	Cash inflow	$130,000
Year 4	Cash inflow	$135,000
Year 5	Cash inflow	$140,000
Year 6	Cash inflow	$145,000
Year 7	Cash inflow	$150,000
Year 8	Cash inflow	$155,000
Year 9	Cash inflow	$160,000
Year 10	Cash inflow	$170,000
Interest rate	10%	

EXERCISE 18: NET PRESENT VALUE, NET FUTURE VALUE, AND IRR

Year 0	Cash outflow	$1,500,000
Years 1 to 10	Cash inflow	$ 350,000
Year 11	Cash inflow	$ 500,000
Interest rate	6%	

EXERCISE 19: NET PRESENT VALUE, NET FUTURE VALUE, AND IRR

Year 0	Cash outflow	$250,000
Years 1 to 10	Cash inflow	$ 35,000
Years 11 to 20	Cash inflow	$ 40,000
Interest rate	8%	

EXERCISE 20: NET PRESENT VALUE, NET FUTURE VALUE, AND IRR

Year 0	Cash outflow	$390,000
Years 1 to 10	Cash inflow	$ 40,000
Interest rate	20%	

EXERCISE 21: NET PRESENT VALUE, NET FUTURE VALUE, AND IRR

Year 0	Cash outflow	$4,000,000
Years 1 to 10	Cash inflow	$ 450,000
Years 11 to 20	Cash inflow	$ 600,000
Interest rate	10%	

EXERCISE 22: NET PRESENT VALUE, NET FUTURE VALUE, AND IRR

Year 0	Cash outflow	$350,000
Year 1	Cash outflow	$250,000
Year 2	Cash outflow	$200,000
Year 3	Cash inflow	$700,000
Year 4	Cash inflow	$800,000
Year 5	Cash inflow	$900,000
Interest rate	12%	

Cases

CASE 1: THE FARM PURCHASE

Jan Schmidt is 45 years old and has the option of buying a farm for $500,000 or investing his money in an equity fund that has earned 14% over the past seven years. Discussion with a few investment analysts has led him to believe that this fund's performance could continue over the next 20 years.

If Jan buys the farm, it would generate $75,000 each year over the next 20 years. In 20 years, based on real estate information, the farm would be worth approximately $2 million.

Questions

1. If Jan wants to make the same return on his investment as on the equity fund, should he buy the farm? Why or why not?
2. What is the farm's net present value with and without the sale of the farm (using 10% as the discount rate)?
3. What is the farm's internal rate of return?

CASE 2: ED'S BOWLING ALLEY

In 2013, Ed intends to invest $1,500,000 in a bowling alley. After two years of operation, he plans to invest an extra $450,000 in the business by opening a restaurant. In 10 years, Ed anticipates selling the business for $3 million. Ed's cost of capital will be 11%. Ed would like to earn at least a 20% internal rate of return.

Ed can also lease a bowling alley that is located in a different city. The yearly cash flow from operations is estimated at $200,000 (net after the lease payment) for the next 10 years. Ed would also like to make 20% on this investment.

Questions

1. Is purchasing the bowling alley and restaurant a good investment? To answer this question, calculate the following:
   - The net present value by using the cost of capital
   - The internal rate of return

Ed predicts that the business will generate the following cash flows:

Year	Amount	
0	−$1,500,000	
1	+200,000	
2	−450,000	(restaurant purchase)
2	+250,000	
3	+300,000	
4	+350,000	
5	+400,000	
6	+450,000	
7	+500,000	
8	+525,000	
9	+550,000	
10	+575,000	
10	+$3,000,000	(sale of business)

2. Is leasing the bowling alley a good decision?
3. If Ed can only do one or the other, should he purchase or lease? Why?

CASE 3: PALMTECH INC.

PalmTech Inc. is considering developing a software program that requires an initial investment of $450,000. The owners have put together a financial plan covering the company's additional investments in research and development. During the third year, the company expects to inject an additional $100,000 in research and development and another $50,000 in year five.

During the first five years, the company expects to generate $100,000 per year in cash flow. However, it expects to increase its yearly cash inflows to $150,000 between years six and 10, $200,000 between years 11 and 15, and $250,000 between years 16 and 20. In the 20th year, if the owners were to sell the business, they would expect to get $600,000.

The weighted average cost of capital is 8%, but the company owners expect to earn 20%. Use this information to calculate the project's net present value based on the company's weighted average cost of capital and the expected return on the investment. What is the project's internal rate of return? Should the owners proceed with the development of their software program? Why?

FINANCIAL SPREADSHEETS: EXCEL®

As we discussed, Excel® spreadsheets are excellent tools for solving time-value-of-money problems. The spreadsheet can do many time-value-of-money calculations, such as the FV, the IRR, and the NPV. Template 6 of the Decision-Making Tools spreadsheets is also an excellent tool to calculate the financial desirability of capital projects. This template will be explained in more detail in Chapter 11.

CHAPTER 11

[CAPITAL BUDGETING]

Learning Objectives

After reading this chapter, you should be able to

1 Explain the importance of capital projects.

2 Differentiate between compulsory investments and opportunity investments.

3 Explain the capital budgeting process.

4 Comment on the key elements used to judge capital projects.

5 Evaluate capital investment decisions by using time-value-of-money yardsticks.

6 Assess capital investments by measuring risk.

7 Explain what can stop a capital project from being approved.

OPENING CASE

Pinning Down the Real Return of a Capital Project

By the end of 2014, the Millers were looking at several ways to expand their retail operations. The most likely option, one that was in line with their longer-term objective, was opening a new retail outlet. Now that they had several years of experience in the retail business and had enough cash, they were ready to move ahead.

The Millers estimated that it would cost around $350,000 to open their new retail store. Because they intended to lease a building for 10 years, the investment would be mainly in leasehold assets, the purchase of office equipment, and working capital. During the first year of operations, the Millers expected to invest $100,000 in working capital. During the second year, they expected to invest an additional $75,000 in working capital for a total of $175,000.

The following summarizes the Millers' capital investment for their new retail store:

Time 0	Capital assets		$350,000
Year 1	Working capital	$100,000	
Year 2	Working capital	75,000	175,000
Total capital employed			$525,000

At the end of the 10-year lease, if the business kept growing, the Millers could either expand the store or move to a larger building. If they instead decided to sell their business (inventories, leasehold assets, goodwill, and so on), they estimated the sale price at $900,000.

CompuTech's weighted average cost of capital is 11%. This is based on funds that could be raised from lenders and shareholders.

The Millers hired a market research firm to determine how much revenue the new store could generate. They used that information to prepare the new store's projected financial statements and will include them in the business plan to be presented to potential investors. The estimated cash inflows the new store will generate are as follows:

Year	Cash Inflows
1	$75,000
2	80,000
3	100,000
4	125,000
5	140,000
6–10	150,000

The new store's cash inflows during the first year are estimated at $75,000, with gradual increases between years 1 and 6. Starting in year 6, the Millers estimate that the cash inflows will remain constant through year 10. If these financial projections hold true, the Millers' investment would create a positive $516,046 net present value, using the 11% weighted average cost of capital, and produce a 25.5% internal rate of return. (Self-Test Exercise 11.10 deals with the calculation.)

THIS CHAPTER WILL SHOW LEN AND JOAN HOW TO

- Analyze capital expenditure projects by using such capital budgeting elements as cash outflows and cash inflows.
- Comment on the key elements used to judge capital projects.
- Use time-value-of-money financial yardsticks to evaluate capital projects.

Chapter Overview

EVALUATING AND PRIORITIZING CAPITAL PROJECTS

Managers are continually faced with two broad types of decisions: operating decisions (ongoing) and capital expenditure decisions (strategic). Capital expenditure decisions have to be analyzed to determine whether they make sense financially, to see how they fit within an organization's overall strategic plans, and to be ranked in order of importance. This is our second chapter dealing with investing decisions. It examines seven topics:

- *Importance of capital investment decisions.* We will compare the characteristics and importance of capital investments with those of expense investments.
- *Capital expenditure portfolio.* We will differentiate between compulsory investments (those made to respond to a need, legislation, or employee demands) and opportunity investments (those that are strategic and have far-reaching implications).
- *Capital budgeting process.* We will look at the steps involved in the capital budgeting process, which include establishing corporate priorities and strategies; planning for capital expenditure projects; ranking projects through capital budgeting methods (priorities, operations, and return/risk); comparing the project's return to the weighted average cost of capital; determining the hurdle rate; and approving and implementing projects.
- *Key capital budgeting elements.* We'll explore the key capital budgeting elements, such as the investments in capital assets, net working capital, and normal capital additions (cash outflows); profit for the year, depreciation or capital cost allowance, and the residual value of assets (cash inflows); the economic life of the project; and sunk costs.
- *Time-value-of-money yardsticks.* We will explain the different time-value-of-money yardsticks commonly used to evaluate and rank capital expenditure projects. They include the accounting methods, the payback method, the net-present-value method, the internal rate of return, and the profitability index.
- *Sophisticated time-value-of-money yardsticks.* You'll learn about more sophisticated time-value-of-money yardsticks commonly used to measure the risk in capital projects, namely, sensitivity analysis and risk analysis.

- *Rejections of capital projects.* We will look at the reasons that some capital projects are not approved. These include a lack of cash and failing to meet the hurdle rate.

Why Capital Projects Are Important

1 Explain the importance of capital projects.

Capital budgeting is the process of planning, evaluating, and choosing capital expenditure projects that generate benefits (returns, profits, savings) over an extended number of years. Capital budgeting decisions are critical to the financial future of a company because they are irreversible, usually require a significant amount of financial resources, and can alter the future success of a business for many years. Capital projects may call for the development of a new product, a major expansion of an existing product line, the launch of a new product line, the construction of a new facility, or a significant change in direction to take advantage of opportunities.

Capital investment A project that requires extensive financial resources (cash outflows) to generate a return (cash inflows) over the long term.

Expense investment A fully tax-deductible cost that should increase profits in the short term.

A **capital investment** (expenditure or cash disbursement) may be defined as a project that requires extensive financial resources (cash outflows) in return for an expected flow of financial benefits (cash inflows) to be earned over many years. A capital investment differs from an **expense investment** in that the latter generates benefits for a short period (less than one year). For example, the construction of a new plant costing $30 million (cash outflow) with an economic or physical lifespan of 20 years, generating a $3 million cash inflow each year, is a capital investment. A $20,000 advertising cost that boosts profit during the current operating year is an expense investment. Table 11.1 compares capital investments and expense investments.

Capital investments are important for a number of reasons. First, because new funds may need to be raised, they can significantly change a company's capital structure. Second, long-term return on a company's assets and shareholders' yield can be highly influenced by the mix of projects undertaken. It takes only one ill-conceived capital investment decision to reduce a company's profit performance and return (often for many years) and, with it, management's credibility. Third, the future cash position of

Table 11.1 Characteristics of Capital Investments and Expense Investments

	Capital Investments	Expense Investments
Size of cash outlay	Large	Small
Nature of commitment	Durable	Impermanent
Accounting treatment	Capitalized	Expensed
Cash turnover	Recurrent and spread over many years	One time and immediate
Financial impact of commitment	Significant	Minimal
Effect on financial structure	Minimal to sizeable	None

a company can be affected significantly, a vital consideration for a firm that is committed to meeting fixed-debt obligations, paying dividends, and experiencing growth (which usually means undertaking more capital investments). Fourth, once committed, a project often cannot be revised or can be revised only at a substantial cost.

Capital Investment Portfolio

2 Differentiate between compulsory investments and opportunity investments.

Companies invest in capital projects for many reasons. A firm wanting to improve its financial performance could invest in cost-reduction programs or research and development, expand a manufacturing operation, replace obsolete equipment, install computer equipment, build a warehouse, or even buy an ongoing business. Each project varies significantly with respect to cash outlay, risk, profit levels, and time horizon. Capital projects can fall into several major categories:

- Necessary investments to reduce operating costs
- Replacement investments to replace worn-out equipment
- Market investments to improve the distribution network
- Expansion investments to increase sales volume, profit, and cash flows in existing product lines
- Research and development investments to develop new products and new manufacturing or processing technologies
- Product improvement investments to sustain the life cycle of a product
- Strategic investments to alter a business's mainstream activity

These types of capital projects can be grouped under two main categories: compulsory investments, which are essential to sustain the life of a business, and opportunity investments, which are discretionary and made only if management believes they will improve the firm's long-term prosperity. Table 11.2 compares these two types of capital investments.

Table 11.2 Comparing Compulsory and Opportunity Investments

	Compulsory Investments	Opportunity Investments
Effects	Maintain operating efficiencies	Increase momentum of the firm
Response	To a need	To an opportunity
Benefits	Immediate	Long-term
Risk	Negligible	High
Management involvement	Low level	Top level
Implications	Legislative, employee safety, and satisfaction	Economic returns, share of market
Analytical techniques	Simple calculation	Mathematical models

COMPULSORY INVESTMENTS

Compulsory investments Investments in capital assets to respond to a need, legislation, or employee demands and that do not require in-depth analysis.

Generally, **compulsory investments** are made for one of three reasons: contingency, legislative, and cosmetic. Contingency-related investments respond to a *need*. For example, a manufacturing department may have to increase its operating capacity to meet an expanded market need. Or a production manager may request that a producing asset be replaced to maintain an acceptable level of operating efficiency. In short, these types of investments prevent a company's rate of return from deteriorating. The second type of compulsory investment is dictated by *legislation*. For instance, the government may force businesses to invest in machinery to reduce pollution, in equipment to meet regulatory quality control standards, or in assets that improve employee safety. The third type of investment is for *cosmetic* reasons. These include expenditures for office furniture; for protecting existing company assets (e.g., fences, warehouses) from fire, theft, and so on; for improving the company image; and for making employees happier (e.g., cafeteria, sports facilities).

These types of capital expenditures do not require in-depth analysis. Because the investments have to be made, all that has to be done is to include the required capital amounts in the company's annual capital budget and to record them when the funds are disbursed. The major requirement in this process is to ensure that the firm obtains the best possible assets for the best possible price. The impact from such investments on profit (minor expansion or modernization programs) can be measured with relative accuracy.

OPPORTUNITY INVESTMENTS

Opportunity investments Strategic investments made in capital assets that usually have far-reaching financial implications.

Opportunity investments are complex and require sophisticated analysis, state-of-the art decision-making tools, and sound managerial judgment. Examples of these investments include launching a new product line, constructing a new plant, or substantially increasing manufacturing output to capture new markets. These capital projects are usually considerable and have far-reaching financial implications. The risk is enormous: If the venture fails, management's reputation suffers, and there will likely be a heavy cash drain from existing operations—or even worse, bankruptcy may result. These types of investments, however, can improve a company's competitive capability and profitability beyond current levels of performance.

Before the company commits to such investments, the first step is to accurately appraise the investment's chances of success. Because the investment's financial return depends on internal and external environmental forces, the appraisal demands an analysis of all aspects of the capital venture. Figure 11.1 illustrates the impact that opportunity investments can have on a company's future. The vertical axis shows the return on investment; the horizontal axis represents the improvement profile of the return position against that of the industry over an extended number of years.

The main reason for injecting funds into capital assets is to improve a company's return on investment—either to close the "return gap" with that of the industry or to improve further the company's financial position. For example, Figure 11.1 shows

Figure 11.1 **Growth Gap Analysis**

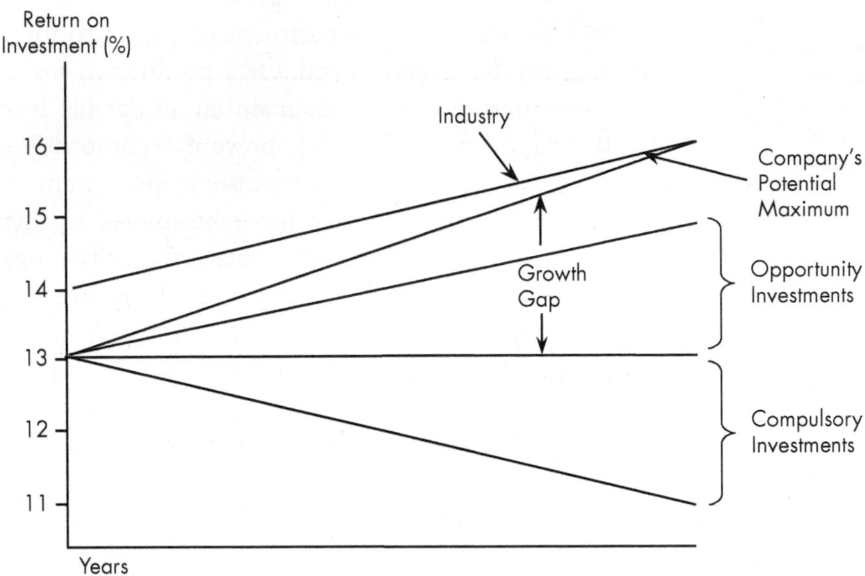

that the company's return on investment may be 13%, compared with the industry's 14%. If nothing is done (e.g., improving the productivity of its existing capital assets, injecting funds into new equipment, or doing research and development on new product lines), over the long term, the company's return may drop to 11% while the industry's climbs to 16%—the gap widens from 1% to 5%. If the company plows funds into compulsory investments, it can hold its position at 13%, and the gap with industry will be only 3%. With additional financial resources, the firm may make opportunity investments, thus reducing the gap further. But because of resource constraints, the firm may still not match the industry's growth. If, however, the firm is not financially bound, it could grow to a 16% level and reach its full potential and match the industry's growth.

The Capital Budgeting Process

3 Explain the capital budgeting process.

Figure 11.2 outlines the steps involved in capital budgeting. The first step is to establish corporate priorities and strategic and operational goals within the external general and industry environments (opportunities and threats) and internal environment (strengths and weaknesses). The future can never be predicted with certainty, but with the information available and modern risk-analysis techniques, it is possible to deal successfully with the uncertainty. It is within this framework that the company's mission statement, strategic goals, and plans are created.

The second step is to prepare the business plan and the evaluation of the capital expenditure projects. Capital projects affect a business in different ways, such as by

Figure 11.2 Capital Budgeting Framework

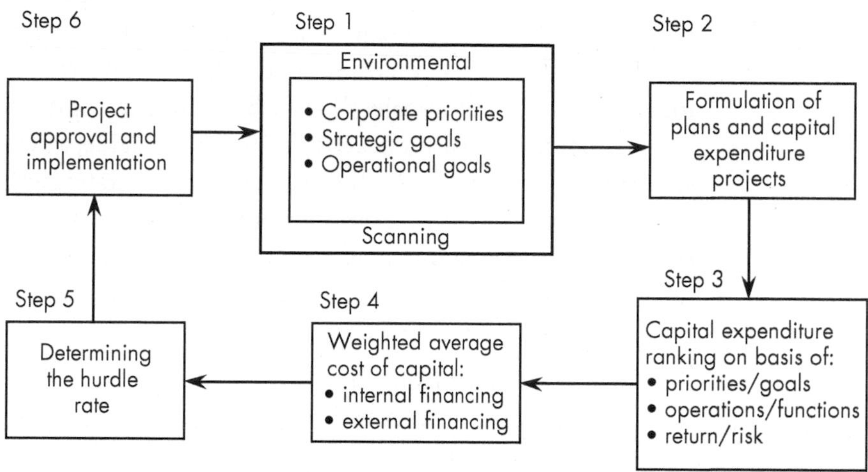

improving operating efficiencies and increasing market share. Management must therefore identify, select, and implement the best projects, that is, those that will help the business achieve its strategic goals.

The third step is to rank the capital projects on the basis of the corporate priorities and goals, business needs (functional units), and returns:

- *Priorities and goals.* Most companies have priorities and a hierarchy of goals. Capital projects are ranked according to how they will meet these overall priorities and strategic goals. (Are they to increase market share, improve manufacturing efficiencies, or diversify operations?)
- *Operations/functions.* Capital projects must be ranked within their respective business units, operations, or functions (e.g., marketing, research, manufacturing, distribution).
- *Return/risk.* Because a healthy return is the ultimate goal of any business, opportunity investments should be judged largely on this basis. However, there is a direct connection between risk and return. The higher the risk, particularly opportunity investments, the higher the expected return.

The fourth step is to explore the cost of alternative sources of capital. Funds are obtained either internally (e.g., through profit for the year and depreciation) or externally (e.g., from shareholders and lenders). If internal funds are to be used, management must decide what types of projects it intends to launch several years before the funds are committed, so that the cash can be set aside. External funds are generally obtained from long-term borrowings or share capital. As discussed in Chapter 9, while equity and liability can be structured in a number of ways, it is critical to find the optimum financial structure: the one that combines the lowest cost with the least amount of risk.

Hurdle rate
The capital budgeting rate used to rank capital projects according to their cost of capital.

The fifth step is to determine the **hurdle rate**, the level of return that each project should generate to be accepted (high risk, medium risk, and low risk). The hurdle rate reflects the cost of capital and an adjustment for the project's risk. For example, if a company's weighted average cost of capital is 10% and the business is dealing with a medium-risk project, management will probably require a 20% return, which will include 10% for the project's risk. Because the capital needed to finance an investment portfolio usually exceeds the funds available, a firm needs financial criteria for selecting projects with the best returns. Hurdle rates, which can be used for that purpose, are determined in a number of ways, such as a company's weighted average cost of capital for financing new projects, long-term borrowing rates, ongoing internal rate of return, or even a figure chosen arbitrarily by top management. Hurdle rates are influenced by the following:

- Level of capital funds needed
- Reputation of the company or management
- Capital structure
- Type of issues to be offered
- Nature of projects (e.g., risk)
- Nature of industry

Once the hurdle rate has been agreed on and projects have been ranked on the basis of objectives, operations, and return, all that remains is the last step: approving and implementing the projects.

4 Comment on the key elements used to judge capital projects.

The Capital Budgeting Elements

You'll need to understand a few basic capital budgeting concepts before looking at the time-value-of-money techniques used to judge the economic appeal of capital projects. This section reviews the key elements used in capital project evaluation: cash outflows, cash inflows, economic or physical lifespan, and sunk costs.

CASH OUTFLOWS

When management decides to invest funds in a capital project, the decision affects outflows of cash in terms of the initial cash outflows (capital assets), working capital (inventories and trade receivables), and normal capital additions (future investments in capital assets).

Initial Investment in Capital Assets

When a decision is made to proceed with a capital project, such as the purchase of equipment, initial cash outflows are recorded. Cash outflows could also take place over several years. For instance, a new plant could be constructed over three years, with cash outflows taking place over that same span. Irrespective of the accounting treatment, all initial cash disbursements must be considered cash outflows. For example, a firm may invest $10 million to modernize a plant; from an accounting perspective, part of that amount, say, $200,000, could be expensed the year the outflows take place, while the remaining $9.8 million is capitalized and depreciated over 10 years. However, for a capital budgeting evaluation, all outflows must be shown as disbursements in the year the money is spent.

Note that the financing of a project need not be taken into account in the evaluation. A company may finance 50% of the $10 million capital outlay, but regardless of the amount to be received from external sources, the evaluation should assume that the company uses its own cash or its equivalent. Finance costs should not be considered an expense and thus should not be included in the projected statements of income. The intent of capital budgeting is (1) to gauge the economic returns of each capital project (stand-alone projects), (2) to compare each competing project with the others, and (3) to compare the return (i.e., IRR) with the weighted average cost of capital (refer back to the lower portion of Figure 9.2).

Working Capital

Another cash outflow to consider is working capital. Some projects, such as modernization, replacement of obsolete equipment, or installation of antipollution equipment, may not require additional working capital. However, other projects, such as the construction of a new plant or the expansion of an existing one, may increase revenue and working capital. The working capital spending usually takes place when the project comes on-stream, that is, when it starts to generate revenue, which usually takes place during the first and second year of operation. Increases in net working capital can take place several years after the launch of the new plant. These additions to working capital should therefore be included as cash outflows in the evaluation of the project.

Normal Capital Additions

Some capital projects may need additional capital expenditures for repairs and parts after the initial capital investment. These expenditures should be included as cash outflows when evaluating the capital project.

CASH INFLOWS

A capital project usually generates cash inflows during its entire physical life. These inflows of cash originate from several sources: profit for the year, non-cash expenses, and residual value.

Profit for the Year

A new project will generate additional cash because of increased revenue (see Table 11.3) or produce savings resulting from more efficient operations.

Non-Cash Expenses

Because capital cost allowance, or CCA (equivalent to depreciation expense), is not a cash outflow and is used solely for income tax relief, the operating profit figure does not reflect the true cash inflow. The calculation of the profit for the year and cash inflow is shown in Table 11.3. Because capital projects deal with cash flow and not profit, the amount used in the project evaluation is $77,500 (cash), not $27,500 (profit for the year).

Table 11.3 **Profit for the Year versus Cash Inflow**

	Profit and Cash Inflow
Operating profit (other cash expenses)*	$100,000
Capital cost allowance	(50,000)
Profit before taxes	50,000
Income tax expense (45%)	(22,500)
Profit for the year	27,500
Add back capital cost allowance	50,000
Cash inflow	$ 77,500

* Could include incremental profit resulting from increased revenue, and excludes depreciation expense.

Residual Value

Residual value
The value from the sale of an asset or a business at the end of its physical life.

Because money has a time value, it is important to anticipate not only the future cash inflows of a project, generated by additional revenue or savings, but also the sale of the assets at their **residual value** at the end of their life. Estimating the residual value of an asset can be done in a number of ways:

- Engineers can examine similar facilities and, based on historical experience, estimate the future residual value of the asset.
- Accountants can calculate the depreciated book value of the assets and determine the residual value of the newly acquired assets.
- Suppliers of equipment and machinery can also provide valuable assistance in estimating residual values.

Residual values can have a significant impact on the return calculation. We look at the impact of the present value of residual assets in the next section.

In the News 11.1 gives an example about two critical capital budgeting elements—investments in capital assets (purchase of a refinery or cash outflow) and the savings (cash inflows) that must be synchronized to maximize profitability over the long term.

In The News 11.1

BACKWARD INTEGRATION CAN CUT COSTS AND INCREASE CASH FLOWS

One way to cut costs and increase cash flow is through backward integration, which is controlling your own supply of products you need to run your business. Delta Air Lines used this strategy in the early part of 2012 when it bought a Pennsylvania oil refinery from ConocoPhillips. Delta Air Lines, a major world airline with headquarters in Atlanta, Georgia, and approximately 80,000 employees, operates more than 4,000 flights every day and moves about 88 million passengers a year. It spends a lot of cash on fuel!

(continued)

In The News 11.1 (continued)

Delta decided to cut fuel costs, which had reached $12 billion in 2011, by spending $150 million to buy a refinery. This refinery is expected to provide 80% of Delta's fuel in the United States while also giving it control of its own supply. Delta Air Lines believes there will be enough savings in fuel costs (cash inflows) to offset the cost of the refinery (cash outflow) and generate a positive return on their investment (IRR).

Source: "Delta buys refinery to cut fuel costs." *Globe and Mail*. Retrieved from http://www.theglobeandmail.com/globe-investor/deltabuys-refinery-to-cut-fuel-costs/article2418364/, accessed April 30, 2012. For more information about Delta Airline visit www.delta .com/about_delta/corporate_information/index.jsp.

ECONOMIC OR PHYSICAL LIFE OF A PROJECT

Economic life
The number of years that a capital asset or an investment opportunity will last.

A capital investment (cash outflow) is made in exchange for future profit (cash inflows). Because the **economic life** of a project plays a key role in the financial return of a project, this aspect of the analysis should be done carefully. For example, in one instance, engineers, suppliers, or accountants may determine that a piece of equipment (e.g., a vehicle) will last five years; in another instance (e.g., a plant), they may estimate 25 years. The longer the physical life of the project, the longer the cash inflows will be generated, and the more beneficial the financial return will be. For example, Table D in Appendix B at the end of the book shows that the present value of a five-year $10,000 annuity bearing a 10% interest rate is $37,908 ($10,000 × 3.7908), while the present value of a 25-year $10,000 annuity with the same interest rate is $90,770 ($10,000 × 9.0770).

The physical lifespan of a project is also important for calculating the present value of the residual value of the asset. The time span and the interest rate also affect the financial return of a project. Table 11.4 shows the present values of an asset that has a residual value of $1,000, with varying discount rates and economic lives.

Table 11.4 Present Values of $1,000 Residual Value

	Economic Life (Years)				
Discount Rates (%)	5	10	15	20	25
5	784	614	481	377	295
10	621	386	239	149	92
15	497	247	123	61	30
20	402	162	65	26	10
25	328	107	35	12	4
30	269	73	20	5	1

SUNK COSTS

Sunk costs Investment costs incurred before deciding whether or not to proceed with a capital project.

Sunk costs are funds that have already been spent on a project before the decision to proceed with it has been made. For instance, a firm may hire engineers to study whether it should invest huge sums of money in a project; the engineering costs may amount to $300,000. Whether the engineers recommend going ahead with the capital project or not, the engineering fees are considered sunk costs and are not included when calculating the financial return of the project. Whether the decision is positive or negative, the $300,000 will still have been spent.

Evaluating Capital Expenditure Projects

5 Evaluate capital investment decisions by using time-value-of-money yardsticks.

The purpose of capital budgeting is to make decisions that will maximize a company's investments. Capital budgeting forces management to answer two basic questions: Which projects from which departments should be approved? How many projects should be approved?

Capital budgeting gives management a way to rank investment proposals in order of priorities, strategic and economic importance, and return on investment.

Rate of return is probably the most widely used guide to capital investments. The purchase of securities, acquisition of new assets, investment in product development, modernization, expansion, or construction of a new plant all have one common trait—they generate profit (or cash inflows) in return for cash spent (or cash outflows). The rate of return can, therefore, be regarded as the relationship between cash committed and cash generated. This relationship is expressed as a ratio or percentage.

In this section, we'll cover five types of capital budgeting methods:

- Accounting methods
- Payback method
- Net present value (NPV)
- Internal rate of return (IRR) or discounted cash flow (DCF)
- Profitability index (PI)

We'll analyze each method in terms of (1) what they are, (2) what they do, (3) how they work, and (4) the arguments for and against them.

ACCOUNTING METHODS

Accounting methods Calculations of the book value rate of return by using data from financial statements.

What they are. The **accounting methods**, also referred to as the *traditional yardsticks*, *financial statement methods*, *accountant's methods*, and *book value rate of return*, use data from financial statements to show the economic results of a capital investment.

What they do. The accounting methods give a rate of return of a capital project at a particular time (year) based on the profit for the year and a book investment.

How they work. To find the rate of return calculation based on these yardsticks, divide the profit for the year by an appropriate investment base. It can be calculated in one of the following ways: (1) return based on annual profit for the year divided by capital assets, (2) return based on annual profit for the year divided by capital employed, (3) return based on average profit divided by capital assets, (4) return based on average profit divided by capital employed, (5) return based on annual profit divided by average capital assets, (6) return based on annual profit divided by average capital employed, (7) return based on annual profit divided by depreciated assets, and (8) return based on annual profit divided by depreciated capital employed.

By using the assumptions shown below, Table 11.5 lists the different rates of return using each of the eight accounting methods for years 1 to 5 for this capital project. The important point is this: When someone says, "My project gives a 17.5% return," make sure you ask how that return was calculated.

Original investment		$1,500,000	capital assets
		500,000	working capital
		$2,000,000	total capital employed
Salvage value		nil	
Life of the project		5 years	
Depreciation		20% per year (straight-line)	
Profit	Year 1	$ 50,000	
	Year 2	$ 90,000	
	Year 3	$150,000	
	Year 4	$200,000	
	Year 5	$250,000	

If a large corporation used the accounting rates of return method during the capital budgeting process, the capital investment analysis department would usually issue written guidelines telling all departments or divisions how to make the calculations.

Arguments for accounting methods:

- They are simple to use and easy to calculate.
- The audit is simple because the information relates to accounting data.
- The emphasis is on profit for the year rather than on cash flow.

Table 11.5 Return on Investment Using Different Accounting Methods

Methods of Calculation	1	2	3	4	5	6	7	8
Year 1	3.3	2.5	9.9	7.4	6.7	4.0	4.2	2.9
Year 2	6.0	4.5	9.9	7.4	12.0	7.2	10.0	6.4
Year 3	10.0	7.5	9.9	7.4	20.0	12.0	25.0	13.6
Year 4	13.3	10.0	9.9	7.4	26.7	16.0	66.7	25.0
Year 5	16.7	12.5	9.9	7.4	33.3	20.0	100.0+	50.0

Arguments against accounting methods:

- They do not take into account that money has a time value.
- They do not provide a "true" rate of return, which is essentially the earning rate of the dollars in use. The average book return method usually understates the rate of return, while the annual return method overstates it.
- The returns focus only on the specific year, while a project usually has a longer lifespan.
- It is meaningless to compare an accounting rate of return with other rates offered on bonds, loans, or any other figures quoted on the financial markets.
- The methods assume that a capital project will last for the depreciated life, when in fact this is generally not true.
- Because the time pattern of profit varies across projects, it is difficult to make effective comparisons between them.

PAYBACK METHOD

Payback method
The number of years required for a capital investment to generate enough cash inflows to cover the initial cash outflow.

What it is. The **payback method** (also known as the *cash recovery period*, *payoff method*, or *payout method*) measures the time it takes for the cash outflow of a project to be recovered by the anticipated cash inflows; in other words, it measures how soon the initial funds used are earned back by the project.

What it does. This technique measures *time risk* and not *risk conditions.* It is helpful in the project-selection process and gives a valid measure of the expected risk. The longer it takes for the initial investment to be recovered, the greater the risk. This is critical for a company in an industry in which product obsolescence is a factor and in which abrupt technological changes occur. A firm in a relatively stable industry will be more likely to accept projects with longer payback periods. Payback can be considered an indicator of profitability. Projects that have a short payback period should have higher earnings in the short run. However, because this method favours immediate cash inflows, it may sacrifice future cash growth.

How it works. The math used to calculate traditional payback period is simple:

$$P = \frac{I}{NCF}$$

where the original investment (I) is divided by the net cash inflow (NCF). Note, however, that this formula works only when cash inflow is equally distributed annually or when the irregular annual cash inflow is averaged out. Let's look at an example: a business that invests $1.5 million in a venture that generates an annual cash inflow of $500,000 during its physical life will have a three-year payback period:

$$\textbf{Payback} = \frac{\$1,500,000}{\$500,000} = 3.0 \textbf{ years}$$

The traditional payback method (shown on the previous page), the payback reciprocal, and the discounted payback are three methods used for calculating the economic desirability of a project.

Traditional Payback Method

When cash inflow is irregular, the calculation of the traditional payback period is done in the following way:

Years	Annual Net Cash Flows	Cumulative Cash Flows	
0	$(200,000)	$(200,000)	
1	25,000	(175,000)	
2	70,000	(105,000)	
3	80,000	(25,000)	← Payback
4	90,000	65,000	
5	100,000	165,000	
Total cash inflows	$ 365,000		

The payback period takes place between years 3 and 4 as cash flow turns positive during the fourth year. In most cases, cumulative cash flow will not equal zero at a specific year, but at some point in that year, as it does here. This requires dividing the remaining cumulative negative net cash flow for the third year, amounting to $25,000, by the positive net cash flow for the fourth year of $90,000. This gives a fraction of a year of 0.278 ($25,000 ÷ $90,000). The payback period therefore is 3.278 years.

Payback Reciprocal

Payback reciprocal A capital budgeting technique that gives a rough estimate of the return on investment of a capital project.

Another way of calculating the payback is by finding the **payback reciprocal**, which gives a very rough estimate of the return on investment. The calculation of the reciprocal is done in two steps. First, the average net cash inflows generated by the project are calculated. In this case, the project generates an average net cash inflow of $73,000 ($365,000 ÷ 5 years).

Second, the average net cash inflows are divided by the initial cash outflow:

$$P = \frac{\$73,000}{\$200,000} = 36.5\%$$

Discounted payback period The number of years needed for a capital investment to generate enough discounted cash inflows to cover the initial cash outflow.

Discounted Payback Method

During the early 1980s, because of high interest rates (around 20%), more businesses were taking the time value of money into consideration when calculating the payback period. Those companies used the **discounted payback period** by calculating the present value of future cash inflows to find the number of years it takes for the initial cash outflow to be recovered. Using a discount factor of, say, 15% to calculate the present value of the future stream of funds, the *discounted payback period* in our example is 4.28 years:

Year	Annual Net Cash Flows	Discount Factors	Present Values	Cumulative Present Values
0	$(200,000)	1.00000	$(200,000)	$(200,000)
1	25,000	0.86957	21,739	(178,261)
2	70,000	0.75614	52,930	(125,331)
3	80,000	0.65752	52,602	(72,729)
4	90,000	0.57175	51,458	(21,271) ←
5	100,000	0.49718	49,718	28,447

Arguments for the payback method:

- Because it is simple to use, it may be used as a crude screening device. Before the company begins extensive, complicated, and costly feasibility studies, this quick calculation can easily distinguish between profitable and unprofitable projects.
- A firm to which technological innovations are important would likely use this method. In this type of business, management would want to be reasonably assured that the cost of a venture could be recovered before newer products or manufacturing processes are introduced. Management may have no alternative but to start capital projects that generate high initial cash inflows and recover their costs within a short time.
- A growth business that relies heavily on internal cash may find payback a useful method. Management of businesses in need of cash may want to trade longer-term yield for short-term cash. A rapidly growing firm that opts for dynamic projects would find this method appropriate.
- Payback focuses on factors that are more visible. Even under dynamic environmental conditions, a firm with good intelligence reports and forecasting techniques can, within reasonable limits, determine a project's initial cash outlays and cash inflows, at least up to the payback point. Time-value-of-money yardsticks, such as the internal rate of return (covered briefly in Chapter 10 and discussed in more detail later in this chapter), must incorporate into the calculation the more distant and unpredictable cash inflows (total physical life of the assets), which, in many circumstances, are merely calculated guesses.

Arguments against the payback method:

- This technique fails to measure the *true economic worth* of a capital expenditure project because it focuses only on cash flow earned before the payback point, and it ignores the project's total physical lifespan. The payback methods emphasize liquidity and not return. The issue is whether a firm should invest to recover its cash as quickly as possible or base the decision on return? In other words, should management inject funds into a project that offers a short payback at the expense of lucrative cash inflows earned beyond the payback point?

- The opponents of this method say that it does not adequately compare the worth of projects, because it can encourage the use of capital funds for less efficient projects rather than highly efficient ones. For example, a capital-intensive project with high initial cash outflows and start-up expenses and a 20-year physical life may show a long payback period. Conversely, a labour-intensive project with minimal initial cash outlays but substantially higher labour and operating costs over its physical life may show a shorter payback and probably a shorter physical lifespan. Because of a shorter payback, the less efficient (or labour-intensive) project may be accepted instead of the capital-intensive project that could very well be more efficient.
- It does not take into consideration the timing of the flow of cash before the payback point. Although the payback method is geared to measure liquidity, it fails to do this job properly. Consider the following hypothetical example. Two projects with initial cash outflows of $1.6 million may show a four-year payback period.

	Cash Flows in $000s		
Year	Project A	Project B	Difference
0	$(1,600)	$(1,600)	—
1	400	200	$200
2	400	200	200
3	400	600	(200)
4	400	600	(200)
Net cash flow	0	0	
Payback period	4 years	4 years	

Project A shows a superior cash flow profile because it produces $400,000 more by the end of the second year. These funds can be reinvested. Also, if both projects cease to operate at the end of the second year, the firm would get back 50% of the original outlays in project A and only 25% in project B. (This method is called the bailout payback period.)

Problem-Solving Example 11.1

Traditional Payback Period

A company wants to invest $500,000 in a new facility. The project will generate $120,000 in cash each year over the next 10 years. Calculate the project's payback period by using the traditional approach.

Solution

The payback is 4.17 years.

$500,000 ÷ $120,000 = 4.17 years

Self-Test Exercise 11.1

Traditional Payback Period

The Millers are considering a $200,000 expansion for their existing retail outlet. The expansion would generate $35,000 in cash each year over the next 10 years. Calculate CompuTech's payback period.

Answers to the Self-Test Exercises can be found at www.bergeron7e.nelson.com.

Problem-Solving Example 11.2

Payback Reciprocal

Use the information in Problem-Solving Example 11.1, and assume that the company was able to sell the project for $500,000 in year 10. Calculate the project's return on investment by using the payback reciprocal method.

Solution

Return on investment is 34%.

Yearly cash flows	$120,000 × 10 years	= $1,200,000
Residual value		500,000
Total cash inflows		$1,700,000
Average yearly cash inflows	$1,700,000 ÷ 10	= $ 170,000

Return on investment: $170,000 ÷ $500,000 = 34%

Self-Test Exercise 11.2

Payback Reciprocal

A retailer is interested in selling a retail business to the Millers for $1 million. This includes all physical assets, the working capital, and goodwill. The Millers estimate, based on the company's historical financial statements, that the annual cash inflows would be around $195,000. Calculate the project's payback reciprocal.

Answers to the Self-Test Exercises can be found at www.bergeron7e.nelson.com.

NET PRESENT VALUE METHOD (NPV)

What it is. The net present value technique measures the difference between the sum of all cash inflows and the cash outflows discounted at a predetermined interest rate, which sometimes reflects the company's weighted average cost of capital or the hurdle rate.

What it does. This method helps to establish whether a project will bring returns that are higher than the cost of borrowing funds to undertake it. The rationale is relatively straightforward. If the net present value of a project, discounted at the company's weighted average cost of capital, is positive, the project may be acceptable. If the resulting net amount is negative, it would be rejected. This method is also useful for making realistic comparisons between projects. Because a common denominator (discount factor) is used in the calculation, it is easy to identify those projects that generate the most favourable results.

How it works. Calculating the net present value of a project takes three steps: (1) determine the projected cash flows, (2) determine the expected weighted average cost of capital, and (3) compute the net present value. Using our example from the payback calculation earlier, the present value of the $200,000 investment with a 15% discount rate is $228,447 in discounted cash inflows and a net present value of $28,447.

Year	Net Cash Flows	Discount Factors	Net Present Value
0	$(200,000)	1.00000	$(200,000)
1	25,000	0.86957	21,739
2	70,000	0.75614	52,930
3	80,000	0.65752	52,602
4	90,000	0.57175	51,458
5	100,000	0.49718	49,718
Net present value (NPV)			$ 28,447

Arguments for net present value:

- It is easy to use.
- It examines the total physical life of the assets.
- It helps management choose between different projects.

Arguments against net present value:

- The time-value-of-money concept is more difficult to grasp than other accounting methods, such as return on assets.
- It is difficult to determine which cost of capital should be used to find the present value: Short term or long term? Current weighted average cost of capital or next year's? Current rate of return or the short- or medium-term rate? The hurdle rate?
- The net present value method does not measure the risk of a project. It is difficult to determine whether a project offers enough benefits in relation to its potential hazards. Saying that a project gives a $28,447 net present value when discounted at 15% is meaningless when evaluating the risk of a capital project.

Problem-Solving Example 11.3

Net Present Value

Use the information in Problem-Solving Examples 11.1 and 11.2 to calculate the project's net present value, with the assumption that the cost of capital is 9%.

Solution

Net present value is $480,118.

Cash outflow (time 0)		$(500,000)
Cash inflows (years 1 to 9)	$120,000 × 5.9952 = $719,424	
Cash inflow (year 10)	$620,000 × 0.42241 = 261,894	
Total cash discounted cash inflows		981,318
Net present value		$ 481,318

Self-Test Exercise 11.3

Net Present Value

Using the information in Self-Test Exercise 11.1, and assuming that CompuTech's weighted average cost of capital is 8%, calculate the project's net present value.

Answers to the Self-Test Exercises can be found at www.bergeron7e.nelson.com.

Problem-Solving Example 11.4

Net Present Value Using Different Discount Rates

Use the information in Problem-Solving Examples 11.1 and 11.2 to calculate the project's net present value by using the following discount rates: 18%, 20%, 22%, 24%, and 26%.

Solution

By using a financial calculator, the net present values are as follows:

NPV at 18%	=	$134,823
NPV at 20%	=	$ 83,849
NPV at 22%	=	$ 39,232
NPV at 24%	=	0
NPV at 26%	=	$ (34,648)

Self-Test Exercise 11.4

Net Present Value: Purchase of Existing Business

Use the information in Self-Test Exercise 11.2, and assume that the Millers want to make 20% on their investment and would like to sell the retail store for $4 million in the 20th year. Calculate the company's net present value, and calculate the net present values by using the following discount rates: 18%, 19%, 20%, 21%, and 22%.

Answers to the Self-Test Exercises can be found at www.bergeron7e.nelson.com.

INTERNAL RATE OF RETURN

What it is. The *internal rate of return,* also known as the *discounted cash flow (DCF) rate of return, true yield,* or *investors' method,* can be described as the specific discount rate used to discount all future cash inflows so that their present value equals the initial cash outflows. The financial community has used this discounting mechanism for decades to calculate insurance premiums and bond yields. Later, the industrial community adopted it to evaluate capital projects.

What it does. It shows the economic merits of several projects and compares their returns with other financial indicators, such as the weighted average cost of capital and the company's aggregate rate of return.

How it works. The internal rate of return is found by trial and error (if a financial calculator or a spreadsheet is not available). Once the total annual cash flows are estimated, the net present value of the cash inflows and outflows is found by using a reasonable interest rate. The totals are then compared. If the present value of the cash inflows is lower than the cash outflows, the procedure is repeated, this time using a lower interest rate. If, however, the present value of the cash inflows is higher than the cash outflows, a higher interest rate is used. The process continues until the total net cash flow equals zero. The required calculation for our earlier example follows:

Year	Undiscounted Cash Flows	At 18% Factor	PV	At 20% Factor	PV	At 22% Factor	PV
0	$(200,000)	1.00000	$(200,000)	1.00000	$(200,000)	1.00000	$(200,000)
1	25,000	0.84746	21,187	0.83333	20,833	0.81967	20,492
2	70,000	0.71818	50,273	0.69444	48,611	0.67186	47,030
3	80,000	0.60863	48,690	0.57870	46,296	0.55071	44,057
4	90,000	0.51579	46,421	0.48225	43,403	0.45140	40,626
5	100,000	0.43711	43,711	0.40188	40,188	0.37000	37,000
NPV			$ 10,282		$ (669)		$ (10,795)

The 20% interest rate equalizes (closely enough) the cash flows. (By using a financial calculator or a spreadsheet, we get exactly 19.87%.) The internal rate of return on this investment is therefore 20%. Trial-and-error calculations would have to be done if the net difference is more significant.

If the cash outflow takes place at time 0, and all cash inflows are constant each year of the project, it is easy to figure out the internal rate of return. For example, a $200,000 initial cash outflow and a $70,000 annual cash inflow give a 22% internal rate of return. To arrive at this, we first divide $200,000 by $70,000, which gives a factor of 2.8571. We then use the present value of an annuity of $1 in Table D in Appendix B, and look across year 5 to find the value closest to the internal rate of return of 2.8571. The present value factor of 2.8571 lies between 22% (2.8636) and 23% (2.8035). In this case, the IRR is 22.11%.

Arguments for internal rate of return:

- It focuses attention on the entire economic life of an investment. It deals with cash flows and ignores accounting allocations.
- It considers the fact that money has a time value.
- It lets a company compare the return of one project with the cost of capital (look back to Figure 9.2).
- It makes comparisons between projects easier.

Arguments against internal rate of return:

- This method covers activities that take place during the entire lifespan of a project. While this may be considered a strong point, it could also be a drawback. How can we predict internal and external environmental conditions 10, 15, and 20 years ahead?
- It ignores potential "cash throw-offs"—that is, should a company assess the financial desirability of a project in a vacuum, or should it include the added profit produced by the cash generated by the project? For example, when a project generates $25,000 during the first year of operation, should the interest earned on this money be taken into account when calculating the return of the project?
- The technique is relatively difficult to grasp. Operating managers understand ratios, such as the division of profit for the year by the project's investment; however, the internal rate of return calculation is more than simple arithmetic. Such concepts as cash flows, time span, discounting, and present value—all essential parts of the internal rate of return calculation—are used.
- This method poses some difficulty for determining the true financial benefits of a project because the investment return is expressed in a percentage or a ratio. For instance, a company's capital expenditure budget may contain several projects of $100,000, with internal rates of return around 25%. Other important projects near $1 million with a 20% internal rate of return may be weeded out because of the comparatively

low factor yield. The absolute present-value sums are not evident. Put simply, you can invest $100 at 30% and $10,000 at 25% for one year and, although the return on the first project is highly attractive, the amount earned is only $30. In the second case, the yield is lower; however, the amount earned is $2,500. This cash throw-off can be reinvested in other projects that will generate additional profit or cash.

- It assumes that the cash flows can be reinvested at the calculated rate of return.

Problem-Solving Example 11.5

Internal Rate of Return

Use the information in Problem-Solving Examples 11.1 and 11.2 to calculate the project's internal rate of return.

Solution

The internal rate of return is 24%.

Cash outflow (time 0)			$(500,000)
Cash inflows (years 1 to 9)	$120,000 × 3.5655 =	$427,860	
Cash inflow (year 10)	$620,000 × 0.11635 =	72,137	
Total cash discounted cash inflows			499,997
Net present value			$ (3)

Self-Test Exercise 11.5

Internal Rate of Return

Use the information in Self-Test Exercise 11.1 to calculate the project's internal rate of return.

Answers to the Self-Test Exercises can be found at www.bergeron7e.nelson.com.

Problem-Solving Example 11.6

Internal Rate of Return

Use the information in Problem-Solving Examples 11.1 and 11.2 (*but* assume that the residual value of the project is zero) to calculate the project's internal rate of return.

(continued)

Problem-Solving Example 11.6 (continued)

Solution

The present value factors in the interest tables give a positive $3,100 NPV at 20%. When using a financial calculator, the project's internal rate of return drops to 20.18% (from 24.0%).

Cash outflow (time 0)		$(500,000)
Cash inflows (years 1 to 10)		
Using the 20% discount factor	$120,000 × 4.1925 =	$ 503,100
Net present value		$ 3,100

Self-Test Exercise 11.6

Internal Rate of Return

Use the information in Self-Test Exercises 11.2 and 11.4 to calculate the project's internal rate of return.

Answers to the Self-Test Exercises can be found at www.bergeron7e.nelson.com.

In the News 11.2 illustrates how an effective pricing strategy can help revenue, profitability, cash flow, and return.

In The News 11.2

CASH FLOW INJECTION STARTS AT THE TOP

Knowing how to price your products affects the top line on the statement of income and is also an effective way to increase cash inflows. A company can price its product so high that it discourages people from becoming loyal customers or fails to attract new ones. Or it can price them so low that its operating costs are not covered. gShift knew how to price its products well.

In 2010, gShift Labs, located in Barrie, Ontario, was one of Canada's hottest innovative companies. The company wanted to change the way people search for information through its Web Presence Optimizer software. The software provides business intelligence to marketing professionals and agencies to help improve their positioning results over time.

The company's co-founder and CEO, Krista LaRiviere, indicated that when she introduced her first product on the market (a search engine optimizer), she went through a detailed analytical process to determine how to price it. The product's price would have to be high enough to cover costs and low enough to entice customers to try it. Her pricing strategy worked well and it helped increase sales, gross margin, and the bottom line. She was able to cover both her operating costs and her initial investment in research and development while also generating a positive cash flow.

Source: "How does a new business price its first product?" *Globe and Mail.* Retrieved from http://www.theglobeandmail.com/reporton-business/small-business/sb-money/cash-flow/how-does-a-new-business-price-its-first-product/article2407650/, accessed May 3, 2012. For more information about gShift Labs, visit www.gshiftlabs.com.

PROFITABILITY INDEX

Profitability index (PI)
The ratio of the present value of cash inflows to the present value of the cash outflows, discounted at a predetermined rate of interest.

What it is. The **profitability index (PI)**, also known as the *present value index* or the *benefit-cost ratio,* is the ratio of the present value of cash inflows to the present value of the cash outflows, discounted at a predetermined rate of interest.

What it does. This method helps to rank capital projects by the ratio of the net present value for each dollar to the cash outflow, and to select the projects with the highest index until the budget is depleted.

How it works. We'll use our earlier example in which the initial cash outlay is \$200,000, the cost of capital is 15%, the life of the project is five years, and the cash inflows are as follows:

Year	Cash Inflows	PV Using Discount Rate of 15%
1	\$ 25,000	\$ 21,739
2	70,000	52,930
3	80,000	52,602
4	90,000	51,457
5	\$100,000	49,718
PV		\$228,446

The present value of the future cash inflows is \$228,446. The PI is calculated as follows:

$$\frac{\$228,446}{\$200,000} = 1.142$$

If the index is greater than 1.0, it means that the inflow of cash discounted at a predetermined discount factor (e.g., weighted average cost of capital) is more than the outflow of cash. If it is less than 1.0, it means that the cash inflows from the project are less than the cash used. For example, if 15% was used to calculate the PI of all projects shown in Table 11.6, it means that projects A to E generate 15% or more, and projects F to K, less than 15%.

This method helps to rank capital projects in a logical way because it looks at projects both in relation to budget constraints and in terms of which ones offer the highest total net present value. Look again at Table 11.6. Let's say that a company has \$1.7 million to invest. As shown in the table, the company has 11 projects under review (A to K), each with specific cash outflows and corresponding net present values and profitability indexes. The company will give the green light to projects A to E for a total cash outlay of \$1.7 million. This means that projects F to K would not be approved (unless they are compulsory investments). The aggregate PI for all approved projects is 1.36 (\$2,310,000 ÷ \$1,700,000).

Arguments for and against the profitability index:

The arguments for and against the profitability index are the same as those for and against the net present value method, with one exception: the NPV expresses results in absolute dollars, while the PI method expresses results in relative terms, that is, as an index.

Table 11.6 Capital Rationing and the Profitability Index

Projects		Cash Outflows	PV	PI	Aggregate PI
A		$300,000	$510,000	1.7	
B		200,000	320,000	1.6	
C	$1,700,000	600,000	840,000	1.4	1.36
D		400,000	440,000	1.1	
E		200,000	200,000	1.0	
F		200,000	160,000	0.8	
G		250,000	175,000	0.7	
H		150,000	60,000	0.4	
I		90,000	27,000	0.3	
J		300,000	60,000	0.2	
K		200,000	0	0	

Problem-Solving Example 11.7

Profitability Index

Use the information in Problem-Solving Example 11.3 to calculate the project's profitability index.

Solution

The PI index is 1.96.

Discount rate at 9%		
Cash inflows (years 1 to 9)	$120,000 × 5.9952 =	$719,424
Cash inflow (year 10)	$620,000 × 0.42241 =	261,894
Total cash discounted cash inflows		$981,318
$981,318 ÷ $500,000 = 1.96		

Self-Test Exercise 11.7

Profitability Index: Expansion

Use the information in Self-Test Exercises 11.1 and 11.3 to calculate the profitability index.

Answers to the Self-Test Exercises can be found at www.bergeron7e.nelson.com.

Problem-Solving Example 11.8

Profitability Index

Use the information in Problem-Solving Example 11.3 (assume that the project's cost of capital is 10% and the residual value is zero) to calculate the profitability index.

Solution

The PI index is 1.47.

Discount rate at 10%
Cash inflows (years 1 to 10) $120,000 × 6.1446 = $737,352
$737,352 ÷ $500,000 = 1.47

Self-Test Exercise 11.8

Profitability Index: Purchase of Existing Business

Use the information in Self-Test Exercises 11.2 and 11.4 to calculate the profitability index.

Answers to the Self-Test Exercises can be found at www.bergeron7e.nelson.com.

Problem-Solving Example 11.9

Buy versus Lease Option

Two partners are interested in starting their own business. They have two options. The first option is to build their own facility for $5 million. The new business would generate $1.2 million per year for 10 years. At the end of the 11th year, they believe that the business would be worth $7.0 million and would sell it. The second option is to lease an existing but smaller building that would generate a net yearly cash inflow of $700,000 for 10 years. The cost of capital is 10%, but management would like to earn a 20% return on their investment. Which option is the most economically attractive?

Solution

The purchase option is more favourable for two reasons. First, the NPV at a 10% discount factor is superior ($4.8 million versus $4.3 million), and it generates a 24.39% internal rate of return. Management's hurdle rate is 20%.

Purchase option			
Cash outflow			$(5,000,000)
Yearly cash inflows	$1,200,000 × 6.1446 =	$7,373,520	
Sale of business	$7,000,000 × 0.35049 =	2,453,430	9,826,950
Net present value			$ 4,826,950

(continued)

Problem-Solving Example 11.9 (continued)

The internal rate of return is 24.39%

Lease option

Lease cost ($700,000 × 6.1446)	$4,301,220

The internal rate of return cannot be calculated for the leasing option since there is no cash outflow.

Self-Test Exercise 11.9

Buy versus Lease Option

The Millers are considering two options: to buy or to lease another retail outlet.

Option 1: Purchase

Year		
0	Cost	$900,000
1	Additional cost	100,000
1	Cash flow from operations	150,000
2	Cash flow from operations	300,000
3	Cash flow from operations	400,000
4	Cash flow from operations	500,000
5	Cash flow from operations	600,000
5	Cash flow from sale of business	1,000,000

Option 2: Lease

With the lease option, the Millers would generate a net $70,000 annual cash inflow.

Questions

If the Millers want to make 30%, should they buy or lease the retail store? To answer this question, calculate the following:

1. Net present value
2. Internal rate of return

Answers to the Self-Test Exercises can be found at www.bergeron7e.nelson.com.

Problem-Solving Example 11.10

Project Analysis

A company is interested in investing in a capital project: initial cost ($10 million), annual cash inflows ($3 million), project's lifespan (20 years), residual value ($0), cost of capital (10%), and hurdle rate (25%). With this information, calculate the following: (1) net present value, (2) payback period, (3) internal rate of return, and (4) profitability index. Should the owners go forward with the project?

Solution

Management should go ahead with the project: (1) it produces a positive NPV using the cost of capital, (2) the payback period is only 3.3 years, (3) the IRR (29.84%) is more than the hurdle rate (25%), and (4) the profitability index is positive (2.5).

1. Net present value calculation (10% discount rate)

Cash outflow		$(10,000,000)
Cash inflow	$3,000,000 × 8.5136 =	25,540,800
Net present value		$ 15,540,800

2. Payback period

$10,000,000 ÷ $3,000,000 = 3.3 years

3. Internal rate of return (using the 30% discount factor)

Cash outflow		$(10,000,000)
Cash inflow	($3,000,000 × 3.3158) =	9,947,400
Net present value		$ (52,600)

By using a financial calculator, the IRR is 29.84%.

4. Profitability index (using the 10% discount rate)

$25,540,800 ÷ $10,000,000 = 2.55

Self-Test Exercise 11.10

Project Analysis

After looking at several options, including those described in Self-Test Exercise 11.9, the Millers became more interested in opening a new retail outlet. The investment in the new outlet is estimated at $350,000, and an additional $175,000 in working capital (inventories and trade receivables) is to be spent over the first two years of operations. The economic life of the project is estimated at 10 years, with a resale value of $900,000. The weighted average cost of capital is estimated at 11%, and the Millers would like to have a 20% IRR. CompuTech's second retail store will generate the following cash flows during a 10-year period:

(continued)

Self-Test Exercise 11.10 (continued)

Year	Cash Inflows	Cash Outflows
0		$350,000
1	$75,000	100,000
2	80,000	75,000
3	100,000	
4	125,000	
5	140,000	
6–10	150,000	
10	900,000	

Questions

1. **What is CompuTech's NPV using 11% and 20% weighted average cost of capital?**
2. **What is the retail store's payback period?**
3. **What is CompuTech's IRR?**
4. **What is the PI?**
5. **Should the Millers go ahead with the opening?**

Answers to the Self-Test Exercises can be found at www.bergeron7e.nelson.com.

Capital Budgeting Techniques That Deal with Risk

6 Assess capital investments by measuring risk.

We noted earlier that time-value-of-money yardstick results are based on a project's total physical lifespan. This implies the need to deal with the future and use some assumptions to calculate the best estimates. The weakness in this approach is its vulnerability to change. No one can predict with certainty future conditions, such as those related to economic, political, social, and technological factors, and, more specifically, elements affecting the industry, such as prices, competitors' aggressiveness, level of investment by competitors, research and development, and labour costs. The internal rate of return is based on the assumption that *all* predictions will come true: that the price over the next five years will be x, that the cost of materials and wages will be y and z, and so on. Thus, there are many chances for estimates to be wrong. For example, a 15.6% internal rate of return may increase or decrease because of a change or several changes in the planning assumptions.

More sophisticated capital budgeting techniques have been developed to help decision makers to deal with probabilities or possibilities. These yardsticks can identify a range of results based on patterns of variations, rather than using one single set of factors to generate the best possible result (such as the one used to calculate the internal rate of return).

Two techniques used for dealing with a range of results are sensitivity analysis and risk analysis.

SENSITIVITY ANALYSIS

Sensitivity analysis involves identifying profitability variations caused by one or more changes related to key elements of a project. These could include the purchase of land, buildings, and equipment; sales volume; unit selling price; cost of material or labour; length of the physical life of the assets; and even a change in the tax rate. To illustrate, the internal rate of return of the project mentioned earlier was 20% based on one set of estimates. If selling prices vary by 10%, construction costs by 5%, and sales volume by 10%, the changes (individually) on the base case would be as follows:

Factors	% Variation in Factor	Internal Rate of Return
Base case	—	20.0%
Selling price	−10%	16.3%
Cost of construction	+5%	18.8%
Sales volume	−10%	17.5%

These factors may vary either individually or in combination. It is important to note that sensitivity checks consider the probability of individual factors. This method simply shows how much the base internal rate of return will change as a result of one or more changes related to a project.

RISK ANALYSIS

Risk analysis
The process of assigning probabilities to the individual estimates in a capital project's base case.

Risk analysis is the process of assigning probabilities to the individual estimates that make up the base case. We stated earlier that judging investment proposals has one weakness—the element of uncertainty. Those preparing the estimates to be included in the IRR calculation must know how much uncertainty their estimates have.

Managers can use past experience to judge the degree of error in their estimates. The risk-analysis method will produce a full range of return outcomes, from the most pessimistic to the most optimistic. Weighing the uncertainty factor, therefore, is an important part of the evaluation process. The sales manager, the production manager, the financial analyst, the plant engineer, the cost accountant, the purchasing agent, and others can all provide their estimates about how likely possible outcomes are in the selling price, cost of labour, cost of machinery, cost of raw material, and so on. Their input can be illustrated as follows:

Sales volume (in units)	100,000	200,000	300,000	400,000
Probabilities	5%	15%	65%	15%
Selling price	$ 1.50	$ 1.70	$ 1.90	$ 2.10
Probabilities	5%	15%	70%	10%
Cost of labour	$ 0.75	$ 0.80	$ 0.85	$ 0.90
Probabilities	10%	15%	60%	15%
Project cost	$200,000	$250,000	$300,000	$350,000
Probabilities	5%	10%	75%	10%
Life of project (in years)	10	11	12	13
Probabilities	5%	10%	80%	5%

The probabilities shown under each variable (volume, price, etc.) are provided by managers based on their experience or their calculated estimates.

The results of the risk analysis calculations could read as follows:

IRR Range (%)	Number of Occurrences	% of Total	% Cumulative
5–8	4	0.4	0.4
8–11	30	3.0	3.4
11–14	133	13.3	16.7
14–17	323	32.3	49.0
17–20	283	28.3	77.3
20–23	167	16.7	94.0
23–26	43	4.3	98.3
26–29	17	1.7	100.0
Total	1,000	100.0	

The first row in the table shows that there are 4 chances out of 1,000 that the project's internal rate of return will fall between 5% and 8%, 30 chances out of 1,000 that it will fall between 8% and 11%, and so on. The report also shows the following:

Minimum rate of return: 5.3%
Maximum rate of return: 29.3%
Mean: 18.1%

Probability

68.3% that the return will fall between 15.6% and 22.0%.
95.5% that the return will fall between 9.0% and 23.9%.
99.7% that the return will fall between 5.9% and 29.0%.

This example indicates that of the 1,000 internal rate of return outcomes (an arbitrary number chosen by the financial analysts), the most pessimistic estimates predict a financial return of 5.3%, while the most optimistic estimates predict a 29.3% return. Within these two extremes lies a full range of outcomes to help judge the risk of a project.

In the News 11.3 gives an example of how merging two distinct but complementary projects can trigger cash flow and profitability.

In The News 11.3

TRIGGERING CASH FLOWS THROUGH ALLIANCE

Sometimes, the belief that 2 + 2 = 5 can work miracles. It did for Vancouver-based Gemcom Software International, a privately held company founded in 1985. The company developed geology and mine planning software that attracted the attention of Dassault Systemes of France. Dassault made an all-cash $360 million friendly acquisition of the company and its 360 employees, serving 4,000 mining sector customers in 130 countries.

The software merger will potentially create more sales and profit than if they were to operate independently. Gemcom's president and CEO Rick Moignard noted that the deal would allow Gemcom to expand the scope of its software by incorporating Dassault's 3D platform. Moignard said, "That platform contains an unbelievable number of tools and components that are used in other industries such as automotive, such as aerospace, that have very strong applicability directly into the mining area. Our job is to take that leading-edge technology and bring it into the mining sector; the process will accelerate the infusion of cash."

Source: "B.C.'s Gemcom subject of friendly $360-million takeover." *Vancouver Sun*. Retrieved from http://www.vancouversun.com/business/Gemcom+subject+friendly+million+takeover/6526240/story.html, accessed May 3, 2012. For more information about Gemcom Software International, visit www.gemcomsoftware.com.

Capital Expenditure Constraints

7 Explain what can stop a capital project from being approved.

A business will reject a capital project for two reasons: cash insufficiency and the hurdle rate (which determines the extent to which projects are financially worthwhile).

CASH INSUFFICIENCY

Before overloading a business with too much debt (a cheaper source than equity), management will calculate the appropriate debt-to-total-capitalization ratio. The risk factor largely determines this best capital mix. If a firm adds too much debt to its capital structure, future fixed charges will increase, affecting the firm's cash position. Firms need to know whether the capital project will generate enough cash to meet the proposed fixed commitments or whether there will be a **cash insufficiency**.

Cash insufficiency The state of not enough cash being generated by a capital project to pay for fixed charges.

HURDLE RATE

The hurdle rate or the weighted average cost of capital can be used to rank the financial desirability of capital projects. Capital budgeting is the process of finding the break-even point between the yield of a capital project and the weighted average cost of capital. The wider the spread between the aggregate yield or IRR of the projects and the weighted average cost of capital, the better it is for the shareholders.

To find this break-even point, the aggregate IRR (the IRR of all projects together) must be known. It is also essential to identify the sources and weighted average cost of the capital needed to finance all capital projects (e.g., internal financing, such as retained earnings, and external financing, such as bond or share issues).

The capital project selection system is often referred to as the capital rationing process, meaning that only the most viable projects—that is, those that exceed the hurdle rate (or the weighted average cost of capital, or WACC)—would be approved. Figure 11.3 presents this process. The company's total for requested capital projects is $7 million, made up of 10 capital projects (A to J) and several other minor projects grouped under K (see the axis line at the bottom of the figure and the cumulative costs column in the box in the figure). Project A costs $1.0 million and generates a 25% IRR. Project B, which also costs $1.0 million, produces a 20% IRR. The cumulative IRR for these two projects is 22.5%. Projects C-D-E, which cost $2.0 million, return 16.0%, for a cumulative 19.6% IRR. The cumulative IRR for all projects—that is, $7.0 million—is 10% (see under column cumulative IRR in the enclosed box and project K on the horizontal line). If management decides to set the project's hurdle rate or the WACC at 15% (the broken line in the figure), projects G to K could be rejected. It is at that point that projects A to F give a cumulative 15% IRR

Figure 11.3 **Capital Rationing Process**

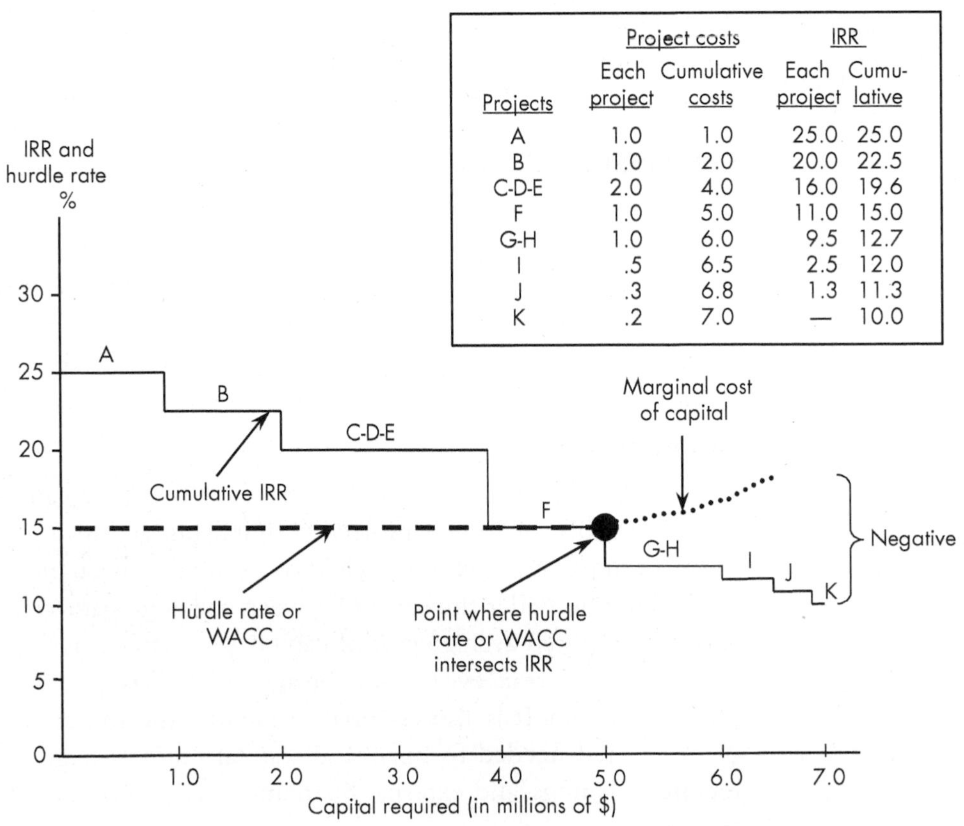

Projects	Project costs: Each project	Project costs: Cumulative costs	IRR: Each project	IRR: Cumulative
A	1.0	1.0	25.0	25.0
B	1.0	2.0	20.0	22.5
C-D-E	2.0	4.0	16.0	19.6
F	1.0	5.0	11.0	15.0
G-H	1.0	6.0	9.5	12.7
I	.5	6.5	2.5	12.0
J	.3	6.8	1.3	11.3
K	.2	7.0	—	10.0

and meet the company's hurdle rate. If the company wants to raise more money (above the $5.0 million) to approve more projects, the company's hurdle rate would be raised because the company's marginal cost of capital would also be raised (dotted line). However, the cumulative IRR for the additional projects would create a negative spread between the hurdle rate and the cumulative IRR.

Chapter Summary

1 Explain the importance of capital projects.

Capital projects are critical because they can easily alter the financial future of a business. They are irreversible and usually require significant financial resources.

2 Differentiate between compulsory investments and opportunity investments.

Capital projects fall into two groups: *compulsory investments*, which should be done in order to sustain the life of a business, and *opportunity investments*, which can be done to make the business grow.

3 Explain the capital budgeting process.

The capital budgeting process has six key steps: (1) setting corporate priorities and strategic goals, (2) creating the plans and capital expenditure projects, (3) ranking projects by using capital budgeting methods (priorities, operations, and return/risk), (4) calculating the weighted average cost of capital, (5) determining the hurdle rate, and (6) approving and implementing projects.

4 Comment on the key elements used to judge capital projects.

Capital budgeting elements include *cash outflows*, such as the initial cash outlays, net working capital, and normal capital additions; *cash inflows*, which include profit, non-cash expenses, such as depreciation, and the residual value; the economic life of a project; and sunk costs.

5 Evaluate capital investment decisions by using time-value-of-money yardsticks.

Many techniques are used for evaluating and ranking capital projects. We looked at five of them: the accounting methods, the payback method, the net-present-value method, the internal rate of return, and the profitability index. There are arguments for and against using each method.

6 Assess capital investments by measuring risk.

More sophisticated methods are used to evaluate risk: sensitivity analysis and risk analysis.

7 Explain what can stop a capital project from being approved.

A business will reject capital budget submissions for two reasons: lack of cash and the hurdle rate.

Key Terms

Accounting methods p. 474
Capital investment p. 465
Cash insufficiency p. 495
Compulsory investments p. 467
Discounted payback period p. 477
Economic life p. 473
Expense investment p. 465
Hurdle rate p. 470
Opportunity investments p. 467
Payback method p. 476
Payback reciprocal p. 477
Profitability index (PI) p. 487
Residual value p. 472
Risk analysis p. 493
Sunk costs p. 474

Review Questions

1 Explain the importance of capital projects.

1. Why are capital projects critical?
2. Differentiate between a capital investment and an expense investment.

2 Differentiate between compulsory investments and opportunity investments.

3. What are compulsory investments? Give several examples.
4. What are opportunity investments? Give several examples.

3 Explain the capital budgeting process.

5. What are the critical steps involved in the capital budgeting process?

4 Comment on the key elements used to judge capital projects.

6. What items are usually included in the initial cash outflow?
7. Why is working capital part of cash payouts in a capital investment, and what is its makeup?
8. Use an example to show how you would calculate the cash inflows by using the profit for the year.
9. Why is capital cost allowance used instead of depreciation expense in capital budgeting?
10. What do we mean by residual value?
11. What do we mean by the economic life of a project?

5 Evaluate capital investment decisions by using time-value-of-money yardsticks.

12. Why are accounting methods not reliable yardsticks for measuring the economic desirability of capital projects?
13. Differentiate between time risk and risk conditions.
14. What are the arguments for and against the payback method?
15. What does the net present value measure?
16. What are the arguments for using the net-present-value method of calculating the economic viability of capital projects?

17. How is the internal rate of return calculated?
18. How is the profitability index calculated?

6 Assess capital investments by measuring risk.

19. What is sensitivity analysis?
20. What is risk analysis?

7 Explain what can stop a capital project from being approved.

21. What factors can prevent a business from going ahead with a capital project?
22. "Capital budgets are neither absolute limits on investment nor automatically affected by project ranking on purely quantitative grounds." Do you agree or disagree with this statement? Explain.
23. Why does the weighted average cost of capital affect investment capability and risk tolerance?

Learning Exercises

4 Comment on the key elements used to judge capital projects.

EXERCISE 1: PROFIT FOR THE YEAR AND CASH FLOW

With the following information, calculate the project's (1) profit for the year, and (2) cash flow: operating profit ($200,000); capital cost allowance ($50,000); other expenses ($100,000); and income tax rate (40%).

EXERCISE 2: CASH INFLOWS AND CASH OUTFLOWS

With the following capital budgeting elements, identify the cash outflows and cash inflows that you would use to judge the attractiveness of a project by using the time-value-of-money yardsticks: capital assets ($1.5 million), working capital in year 1 ($500,000) and year 2 ($200,000), salaries ($140,000), working capital loan ($190,000), residual value at the end of the 11th year ($1 million), profit for the years 1 to 10 ($300,000), mortgage ($1.1 million), non-cash expense ($50,000), revenue ($300,000), and sunk costs ($100,000). The project's lifespan is 10 years and the cost of capital is 8%.

5 Evaluate capital investment decisions by using time-value-of-money yardsticks.

EXERCISE 3: TIME-VALUE-OF-MONEY YARDSTICKS

XYZ Inc. wants to invest $1 million in a capital project that would generate $300,000 in savings each year. The physical life of the project is 10 years, and the cost of capital is 10%. Using the above information, calculate the following:

1. Payback period
2. Net present value
3. Internal rate of return
4. Profitability index

EXERCISE 4: TIME-VALUE-OF-MONEY YARDSTICKS

You have some cash and the opportunity to buy a small retail store downtown for $700,000. This price includes all physical assets in the retail store and the inventories. You also have the option of buying $700,000 of mutual funds that pay 14% interest. The annual cash flow from the retail store operations is expected to be $115,000. In 20 years you plan to retire, and you feel that the store will be sold then for $2 million. If you wanted to make the same return on your investment as you would with the investment securities, would you buy the retail store?

To answer this question, calculate the following:

1. Payback period
2. Net present value
3. Internal rate of return
4. Profitability index

EXERCISE 5: TIME-VALUE-OF-MONEY YARDSTICKS

With the following capital budgeting elements, identify the cash outflows and cash inflows that you would use to judge the project by using the time-value-of-money yardsticks. Also, calculate the project's (1) net present value, (2) internal rate of return, (3) payback period, and (4) profitability index. Capital assets ($2.5 million), capital additions in year 1 ($300,000), working capital in year 1 ($600,000) and year 2 ($300,000), salaries ($140,000), working capital loan ($190,000), residual value at the end of the 11th year ($2 million), profit for the year ($400,000), mortgage ($1.1 million), non-cash expense ($60,000), revenue ($300,000), and sunk costs ($100,000). The project's lifespan is 10 years and the cost of capital is 8%.

EXERCISE 6: LEASING VERSUS BUYING

You have two options: to buy or to lease a video store.

Option 1: Purchase

Year		
0	Cost	$300,000
1	Additional cost	80,000
1	Cash flow from operations	45,000
2	Cash flow from operations	70,000
3	Cash flow from operations	90,000
4	Cash flow from operations	105,000
5	Cash flow from operations	140,000
6	Cash flow from operations	160,000
7	Cash flow from operations	165,000
8	Cash flow from operations	170,000
9	Cash flow from operations	175,000
10	Cash flow from operations	180,000
11	Cash flow from sale of business	400,000

If you want to make 25% on your money, should you buy the video store? To answer this question, calculate the following:

1. Net present value
2. Internal rate of return

Option 2: Leasing

You can lease a video store in another town. The net yearly cash flow from operations after deducting lease payments is estimated at $45,000 (net) from year 1 to year 10.

1. If you want to make 25% on your investment, should you lease the video store?
2. Which of the two options would you choose?

EXERCISE 7: CALCULATING THE NPV AND THE IRR

Aaron Manufacturing Inc. intends to invest $70,000 in a modernization capital project that will generate the following cash inflows during eight years:

Year	
1	$12,000
2	17,000
3	18,000
4	23,000
5	15,000
6	11,000
7	9,000
8	8,000

Questions

1. Calculate the NPV at 12% and 18%.
2. Calculate the internal rate of return of the capital project.
3. If the annual cash flow were an even $15,000 per year for eight years, what would be the NPV at 12% and 18%?
4. What level of annual cash flow would be required to obtain a 20% IRR?
5. How would the results of (1) and (2) change if there was a capital recovery of $40,000 at the end of year 8?

EXERCISE 8: DECIDING BETWEEN TWO OPTIONS

Luster Electronics Company is analyzing two capital projects, project A and project B. Each has an initial capital cost of $12,000, and the weighted average cost of capital for both projects is 12%. The projected annual cash flows are as follows:

Year	Project A	Project B
0	($12,000)	($12,000)
1	7,000	5,000
2	4,000	3,500
3	3,500	3,000
4	3,000	2,500
5	2,300	2,000
6	2,000	1,500

Questions

1. For each project, calculate the following:
   - Payback period
   - Net present value
   - Internal rate of return
   - Profitability index (using the 12% discount rate)
2. Which project or projects should be accepted if the two are independent?
3. Which project should be accepted if the two are mutually exclusive (that is, you can choose only one)?

EXERCISE 9: CALCULATING THE PV, THE NPV, THE IRR, AND THE PI

Smith Manufacturing is subject to a 45% income tax rate and a 12% hurdle rate. Management is considering buying a new finishing machine that is expected to cost $200,000 and reduce materials waste by $60,000 a year. The machine is expected to have a 10-year lifespan and will have a zero salvage value. For the purpose of this analysis, straight-line depreciation should be used instead of the CCA.

Questions

1. Calculate the cash flows.
2. Calculate the present value, the net present value, the internal rate of return, and the profitability index.

6 Assess capital investments by measuring risk.

EXERCISE 10: SENSITIVITY ANALYSIS

With the following information, calculate the project's (1) net present value, and (2) internal rate of return:

Base case

Time 0	Capital assets	$2,500,000
Year 1	Working capital	500,000
Year 1 to 20	Cash inflows	500,000

Cost of capital is 6%.

Sensitivity analysis

Calculate, for each of the following, the NPV, IRR, and payback period if

(a) capital assets are increased by 10%.
(b) working capital is increased by 5%
(c) cash inflows are increased by 5%.
(d) capital assets are increased by 20% and cash inflows by 15%.
(e) both working capital and cash inflows are decreased by 10%.
(f) cost of capital is increased to 8%.

Cases

CASE 1: EXCEL PRODUCTS LTD.

One of Excel Products Ltd.'s strategies is to invest in new product lines. This involves periodic investments in research and development, plant, equipment, and working capital. This year, the company invested $4 million in a research and development project to develop a new product.

The managers are unsure whether they should invest an additional $9 million in capital assets to launch a new product line. The economic life of the project is expected to be 12 years, and straight-line depreciation will be taken over the project's lifespan. At the end of the life of the project, it is expected that company will sell the equipment and machinery for $2 million.

Working capital will also be invested over the first three years: $2 million during the first year, $1 million during the second, and $500,000 during the third; $2.9 million of that amount is expected to be recovered at the end of the 12-year period.

The company estimates that profit before depreciation, promotional expenses, and income taxes will be $3 million a year during the first five years, $4 million per year for the following five years, and $5 million during the last two years.

The company's income tax rate is 46%, and its cost of capital is 10%. For this analysis, the depreciation expense will be used as the CCA tax deduction.

Questions

Use the above information to calculate the following for the project:

1. Net present value
2. Internal rate of return
3. Profitability index

CASE 2: KOPLAYE INSTRUMENTS INC.

Note: Use the financial spreadsheet (Template 6: Project Analysis) to do this calculation.

The board of directors of Koplaye Instruments Inc. is considering investing more than $5.8 million in the construction of a new plant to produce widgets for export. Although several members of the board have reservations about the project, many feel that the company has made a wise decision.

The treasurer of the company has been able to raise funds from different sources and says that the company's cost of capital would be 11%.

The board members feel that the project is not too risky and that a 15% hurdle rate would be acceptable.

The engineers of the company present the following information and estimate the life of the project to be 10 years.

	Costs (in 000s)	CCA
Land	$ 600	
Buildings	2,000	5%
Machinery/equipment	2,500	20%
Research and development	500	20%
Other assets	200	10%
Total assets	$5,800	

The marketing department indicates that there would be $300,000 invested in working capital in year 1, $250,000 in year 2, and $200,000 in year 3.

The controller provides the details of the project's projected revenue and cost data.

Year	Revenue (in $000s)	Cost of Sales (in $000s)	Other Expenses (in $000s)
1	$5,000	$2,000	$700
2	5,500	2,200	700
3	6,000	2,400	750
4	6,500	2,600	800
5	7,000	2,800	800
6	7,500	3,000	850
7	8,000	3,200	900
8	8,000	3,200	900
9	8,000	3,200	900
10	8,500	3,400	950

The company's controller estimates that $600,000 of the working capital will be recovered at the end of the project. The engineers estimate that the capital assets will be sold at the end of year 10 for $2 million. The company's income tax rate is 46%.

Questions

With the above information, calculate the following for the project:

1. Annual cash flow forecast during the 10-year period by using the actual CCA rates
2. Payback period
3. Net present value using the cost of capital and the hurdle rate
4. Internal rate of return
5. Profitability index

FINANCIAL SPREADSHEETS: EXCEL®

Template 6 (capital project analysis) of the financial statement analysis section of the financial spreadsheets accompanying this text can calculate the net present value, the internal rate of return, the profitability index, and the payback period. Unlike financial calculators and other spreadsheets, this tool can calculate the annual capital cost allowance for different capital assets, which makes the project's cash flows more accurate and, ultimately, the time-value-of-money financial calculations more exact.

CHAPTER 12

[BUSINESS VALUATION]

Learning Objectives

After reading this chapter, you should be able to

1 Differentiate between market value and book value.

2 Discuss valuation models.

3 Comment on what it means to scan the environment.

4 Explain how to document planning assumptions.

5 Show how to restate the statement of income and the statement of financial position.

6 Present ways to price an ongoing business.

7 Calculate the market value of publicly traded companies.

8 Determine the investment return on capital projects from an investor's perspective.

OPENING CASE

Selling an Ongoing Business at Its True Market Worth

After three years of operations, CompuTech Inc. was doing extremely well in meeting its financial goals. The Millers were now moving their business into another phase of its development, that of opening several retail stores. The retail concept they had used was popular with customers, and the earnings generated by CompuTech were better than those of competing firms.

The Millers had two options for growth. First, they could grow slowly by opening a retail outlet, say, every 2 years over the next 10 years by using internally generated cash flows and loans from conventional lenders. Second, they could approach a risk capital investor to invest in their business. This option would help them grow faster: the Millers would be able to open five retail outlets in 2016 and more the year after. However, this strategy would require equity participation in CompuTech Inc. by a venture capitalist; the Millers would have to share business ownership.

They discussed this option with their advisers Bill Murray and May Ogaki, and both agreed that this course of action was a viable one. Bill made the following points:

> Risk capital investors are very demanding and need a high return on their investment. The investment proposal will have to be complete and demonstrate clearly several key points. First, these investors want to see evidence that the investment opportunity can generate a return commensurate with the risk—usually 25% to 40% compounded and adjusted for inflation. Second, they want a good management team. Because most risk capital investors claim that management is the single most important aspect of a business opportunity, they regard the reputation and quality of the team as key. Third, they will be looking for an exit strategy and options to realize their investment. Because these types of investors usually want to cash in their shares three to seven years after making their investment, they want to know that you will have thought about how to make this happen. This may require going public or selling their shares to another buyer. They might even want you to buy back the shares. Fourth, these investors will want to monitor and control their investment by having a voice on your board of directors, suggesting who should sit on your board and its composition, receiving monthly financial statements, having a say in hiring key managers, and so on.

May Ogaki added the following points about the strategy for approaching private investors:

> These types of private investors often reject investment opportunities because entrepreneurs do not understand the needs, requirements, and specialization of a particular investor. If you approach the wrong investor, you run the risk of being rejected. The best approach to contacting private investors is to ensure that they will be able to provide the amount of capital

you need. Be certain that they are familiar with the industry that you are in and, most important, that they are located in your region. This is particularly important if they want to take an active part in your business. Another key criterion when selecting a private investor is to pick one who is a leader in the investment community and able to give you sound business advice. This type of deal should provide benefits to both sides: you offer a good investment opportunity in terms of a return, and the investor offers the capital you need to realize your dream.

The Millers realized that the investment proposal or business plan would have to be convincing if they were to attract venture capital funds. The proposal would have to clearly provide information about financing needs, financial requirements, investment potential, and management capabilities.

THIS CHAPTER WILL SHOW LEN AND JOAN HOW TO

- Attract private investors to invest in their business.
- Calculate the return on investment that private investors could earn from their investment.

Chapter Overview

EVALUATING THE CONDITIONS AND POTENTIAL OF AN ONGOING BUSINESS

Throughout the text, we have talked about book value: what a business owns and owes, or the value of a business's assets and liabilities. We haven't yet mentioned the market value of a business: how much it would be worth if it were sold as an ongoing business. This is the third and final chapter dealing with investing decisions, and we examine the six steps involved when pricing an ongoing business, under eight topics (see Figure 12.1):

- *Market value versus book value.* We will first look at the difference between book value and market value, and differentiate between price-level accounting and current-value accounting.

Figure 12.1 **Process for Pricing an Ongoing Business**

1. Recognize the difference between
2. Examine the valuation models
3. Scanning the environment
4. Documenting the planning assumptions
5. Restating the financial statements
6. Market value of an ongoing business

Book value
Market value
Which one is most suitable?
General
Industry
• Past
• Present
• Future
Statement of income
Statement of financial position
Price-tagging the business

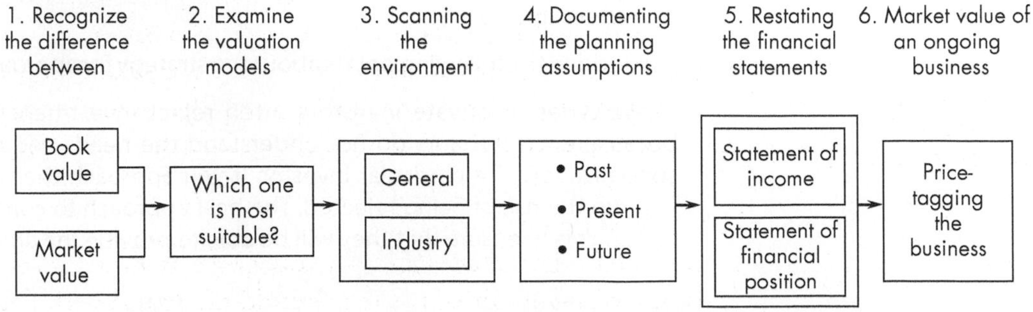

- *Valuation methods.* We will then examine the valuation methods organizations and investors use to determine the value of ongoing businesses: the liquidation value, the replacement value, the collateral value, the assessed value, and the economic value.
- *Scanning the environment.* Next, we will explain what it means to scan the environment, a method used during the planning process to pin down planning assumptions.
- *Planning assumptions.* We then look at the process of making the planning assumptions needed to prepare the projected financial statements.
- *Projected financial statements.* We'll see how various components of the statement of income (revenue, cost of sales, etc.) and statement of financial position (non-current assets, inventories, trade receivables, etc.) can be restated, based on planning assumptions, to determine the real worth of a business.
- *Privately owned business.* We will then turn to four methods used to value a privately owned ongoing business: asset valuation, net present value, industry multipliers, and price-earnings multiple.
- *Publicly traded company.* We'll also look at how to calculate the value of publicly traded companies.
- *Investors' perspective.* The last topic details how investors, in particular venture capitalists, calculate the return on their investment.

Market Value versus Book Value

1 Differentiate between market value and book value.

Book value
The accounting value of an asset (the original cost minus total depreciation to date) shown on the financial statements as a firm's assets.

Market value
The price at which an item, a business, or an asset can be sold.

To many individuals, it may not make much sense to report information on financial statements that does not reflect the "true" or "real" market value of assets. For example, Table 12.1 presents a statement of financial position for a Toronto house that was purchased in 1970. About 40 years later, the $40,000 house, after allowing for depreciation, would have a $15,000 value on the books. The "real value" of the house, however (shown in the bottom half of the table), could be near $500,000. If the owner wants to borrow, say, $200,000, the owner's statement of financial position would look ridiculous (upper half of the table) because the liability side of the statement of financial position would be $185,000 more than the book value of the house. In this example, the **book value** is the accounting value of an asset (the original cost minus the accumulated depreciation). This is shown on the statement of financial position as net book value or net capital assets. However, if the market value of the house were shown on the statement of financial position, the owner's financial structure would be more appropriate. In this case, the **market value** is the price at which an item, a business, or an asset can be sold. The owner could have done different things with the $200,000 mortgage money, such as the following:

- Deposited in a bank account
- Renovated the house
- Purchased other assets, such as a cottage, a car, or a trailer
- Took a year-long first-class trip around the world with family members

Table 12.1 Book Value versus Market Value

Statement of Financial Position (based on book value, ignoring cash proceeds from mortgage)			
House			
Original cost	$40,000		
Depreciation	(25,000)		
Net book value	$15,000	New mortgage	$200,000
Statement of Financial Position (based on market value)			
House			
Market value	$500,000	New mortgage	$200,000

If the homeowner picked the fourth option, the trip, that mortgage money would have simply been spent and not shown on the asset side of the statement of financial position. The statement of financial position would then have shown $15,000 on the asset side and $200,000 on the liability side, similar to Table 12.1.

Because of the difference between book values and market values, some individuals challenge the validity of traditional accounting practices and ask the following question: Do financial statements prepared according to traditional accounting principles present fairly the financial position of a company in a period of inflation? Many would say no. For this reason, over the past decades, accountants have attempted to present information on financial statements in a more sensible way. They have come up with two suggestions: price-level accounting and current-value accounting.

Price-level accounting
An accounting method used to restate assets on financial statements in terms of current purchasing power (inflation).

Current-value accounting
An accounting method used to restate assets on financial statements in terms of what they would be worth if purchased today.

In **price-level accounting**, the numbers on financial statements are restated in terms of current purchasing power. Thus, if an asset, such as a building, were purchased five years ago for $1,000,000 when yearly inflation was 4%, the value of the building would be reported now as $1,217,000.

Current-value accounting is based on what it would currently cost a business to acquire an asset with the same capability or capacity as the one it currently owns. In the previous example, if the asset were to be purchased today at a cost of, say, $1,200,000, that would be the value of the existing asset reported on the statement of financial position.

Refer back to the example of Eastman Technologies Inc.'s 2013 statement of financial position in Table 2.4. It shows the owners' equity to be $555,000. This is the book value and it is based on the original or historical purchase price of all assets, adjusted for depreciation (total $1,800,000), less the amount of money owed to lenders ($1,245,000).

If Eastman's owners were to sell their business for book value, they would sell the assets for what they are worth on the books, transfer the liabilities to the new owners, and ask for a $555,000 cheque. However, the company could be worth more than $555,000 for two reasons. First, Eastman's assets listed on the statement of financial position are historically based. This means that if the company purchased a piece of machinery in 2009 for $100,000, the transaction is an objective measure of the asset's value, which is shown on the company's statement of financial position. However, this 2009 value may not have much relevance today. In fact, the asset could be worth more (particularly if it was land).

Second, the assets of the company could generate excellent earnings. These earnings are not reflected in the statement of financial position. However, if the earnings produce a 20% or 25% annual return, anyone wanting to sell such a business would certainly take the high level of earnings of these assets into consideration.

Some may argue that accountants should ignore the purchase price of capital assets and use a more meaningful current value in financial statements. The problem with this is that for many assets, objective current values do not exist. Therefore, accountants have opted for objective historical cost values over subjective estimates of current value.

Also, the Government of Canada would have serious reservations about having company officials re-appraising capital assets at higher than historical values. The reason is simple: the original $100,000 used to calculate the capital cost allowance would be increased and consequently reduce the amount of income tax that the company would pay to the government. Furthermore, what government organization would be responsible for policing whether assets shown on statements of financial position reflect the true market value? Finally, statements of financial position would have to be adjusted each year to reflect inflation or the changing prices of the capital assets. How would these changes be reflected on the liability and equity side of the statement of financial position?

To solve the valuation problem, the Canadian Institute of Chartered Accountants recommended that all Canadian enterprises whose securities are publicly traded disclose in their annual reports, whenever appropriate, information about the effects of changing prices. In other words, if the value of a building is shown in the books at $600,000 (after depreciation) and the market value is $1,200,000, the annual report would comment on this difference through a footnote. The International Financial Reporting Standards that came into effect in Canada in January 2011 now allow for property revaluation gains (or losses) in the statement of comprehensive income.

Problem-Solving Example 12.1

Book Value

If a company showed $3,000,000 in total assets and $2,000,000 in total liabilities in its statement of financial position, what would the company's book value be?

Solution

The company's book value is $1,000,000:

(continued)

Problem-Solving Example 12.1 (continued)

Total assets	$3,000,000
Total liabilities	2,000,000
Equity (book value)	$1,000,000

Self-Test Exercise 12.1

Book Value

Use CompuTech Inc.'s 2015 statement of financial position in Appendix A to calculate the company's book value.

Answers to the Self-Test Exercises can be found at www.bergeron7e.nelson.com.

Valuation Models

2 Discuss valuation models.

Different models can be used to value businesses. So far, we have talked about book value and market value. In Chapters 10 and 11, we examined the present value and the discounted cash flow methods to determine the value of an investment in capital assets (i.e., NPV and IRR). The time-value-of-money approach can also be used for business valuation. Depending on the reason for valuing a business, organizations use different approaches.

In his book *Techniques of Financial Analysis*,[1] Erich Helfert identifies several valuation models. First is the *economic value*, which has to do with the ability of an asset to produce after-tax cash flows. For example, a person who invests $100,000 in Canada Savings Bonds does so to earn future cash receipts in the form of interest payments. However, the person may invest $100,000 in a capital asset to save money through increased productivity or for increased revenue. The investor would therefore compare the worth of the future receipts (cash inflows) to the original investment (cash outflows). The economic value approach is a future-oriented concept based on the principles of trade-off and risk. For example, the investor might be prepared to accept a 3% return on the virtually risk-free Canada Savings Bonds investment or 25% in a revenue-generating business venture that is riskier. Risk is the price tag on the sought-after economic return. The economic value concept therefore looks at future cash flow expectations and the relative risk associated with the investment.

1. Erich A. Helfert, *Techniques of Financial Analysis*, 11th edition, Boston: Irwin/McGraw-Hill, 2002.

The second approach is based on *market value*, the worth of an asset traded on the market between a buyer and a seller. The stock market is a classic example of market value. At any point, some buyers would be prepared to buy (and others to sell) a share for what each party believes it is worth. By using this approach, the buyer and the seller are able to arrive at a mutually acceptable value for the commodity. A consensus is built between the two parties, and the value of a commodity is therefore subject to individual preferences and the psychological climate at the time of the transaction.

Both the economic value method and the market value approach deal with theoretical values, based exclusively on estimates. Unless the commodity is actually transferred between two parties, the market value is considered hypothetical. Consequently, we can establish a minimum and a maximum value of a commodity on a particular date.

We have already mentioned the third approach, the *book value* method. This method deals with the worth of an asset as recorded on the statement of financial position, based on generally accepted accounting principles.

Liquidation value
The worth of an asset if sold under duress.

The **liquidation value** shows the worth of specific assets when sold separately. Liquidation means that a business must sell an asset under duress to get cash. The liquidation value does not reflect the real worth of an asset or a business. In most cases, it is substantially below the economic value, the market value, and even the book value of an asset.

In the News 12.1 highlights the steps involved when a business must sell its assets under duress during the liquidation process.

In The News 12.1

CANADIAN BUSINESS ICON LIQUIDATES ASSETS UNDER PRESSURE

After celebrating more than 100 years of growth and lucrative profits, in 1995 Nortel decided, as part of a strategic move, to dominate the burgeoning global market for public and private networks. A company that employed more than 94,500 people worldwide, with market capitalization of $398 billion in September 2000, filed for protection from creditors on January 14, 2009—a sad ending for a much-celebrated Canadian business icon.

In early 2012, mediation began on how to distribute Nortel Networks Ltd.'s $9 billion worth of assets. Ontario Chief Justice Warren Winkler is responsible for settling the scores of creditor claims coming from around the world. The business lines that are on the chopping block include intellectual property from 20 countries. Those looking for a piece of the assets include Nortel pensioners, former employees with disabilities, bondholders, trade creditors, and governments. The proceedings, the most complicated of their kind in history, according to Mr. Winkler, will be held in Canada, the United States, and Britain.

Source: "Mediation begins on $9-billion of Nortel assets." *Globe and Mail*. Retrieved from http://www.theglobeandmail.com/reporton-business/9-billion-nortel-bankruptcy-mediation-begins/article2412502/, accessed November 22, 2012. To learn more about Nortel's story, visit www.allaboutnortel.com.

Problem-Solving Example 12.2

Liquidation Value

Use Eastman Technologies Inc.'s 2013 statement of financial position from Table 2.4 to calculate the company's liquidation value with the following assumptions: non-current assets are valued at 40%, inventories at 35%, and trade receivables at 45%.

Solution

Eastman's liquidation value is negative by $471,700:

	2013	Liquidation Value	%
Total non-current assets	$1,200,000	$ 480,000	40%
Current assets			
Inventories	218,000	76,300	35%
Trade receivables	300,000	135,000	45%
Other	82,000	82,000	
Total current assets	600,000	293,300	
Total assets	1,800,000	773,300	
Total liabilities	1,245,000	1,245,000	
Equity (liquidation value)	$ 555,000	$(471,700)	

Self-Test Exercise 12.2

Liquidation Value

Use CompuTech Inc.'s 2015 statement of financial position (see Appendix A at the end of this book) and the following assumptions to calculate the company's liquidation value. By liquidating the assets, the Millers would probably obtain the following:

- 30% for the non-current assets
- 50% for inventories
- 70% of trade receivables

Would the Millers have enough money to pay all their creditors? If the Millers' business cannot cover all its liabilities, what will they have to do?

Answers to the Self-Test Exercises can be found at www.bergeron7e.nelson.com.

Replacement value The cost of acquiring a new asset to replace an existing asset with the same functional utility.

The **replacement value** or reproduction value is the cost of replacing an existing capital asset with an identical asset. This is a good approach for measuring the worth of an ongoing business because it is based on engineering estimates and judgments. However, this approach is flawed because it does not consider the real worth of the management team, the reputation of the business, the strength of the organization, and the value of its products. Furthermore, it is difficult to equate the value of assets of an ongoing plant with so-called "equivalent assets." For example, what appears to be a duplicate asset may, in fact, have a higher or lower rate of productivity. With time, most physical assets are subject to some technological and physical wear and tear.

Collateral value
An assessment by lenders of the value of an asset taken as a guarantee for credit.

To secure their loans or other types of credit, lenders use the **collateral value** approach. This method is based on the premise that the credit amount given to a business will match the identified asset. Generally, to allow for a margin of safety, lenders will set a lower value than what the asset is worth in the market.

Assessed value
A valuation method used by municipal governments for determining property taxes.

Municipal governments use the **assessed value** approach for property taxation. The rules used to determine the assessed value vary widely between municipalities and do not necessarily reflect market values. The prime purpose of the assessed value is to levy taxes. Such values have little connection with other market values.

Economic value
A valuation method used to determine the ability of an asset to generate cash.

Economic value is the price placed on an ongoing business. For example, you will certainly pay more for a retail store that is operating (ongoing) than for the physical assets of a similar business that is on the brink of declaring bankruptcy. For the ongoing business, you would have to pay for the goodwill, which includes the customers, reputation, patents, employees, image, and so on. This approach compares the cash outflows to future cash inflows. Later in this chapter, we will explore how to calculate values of ongoing businesses through time-value-of-money yardsticks, such as the internal rate of return and the net present value approach.

Let's look at the steps involved in putting a price tag on an ongoing business. They include scanning the environment, documenting the planning assumptions, and restating the financial statements.

Scanning the Environment

3 Comment on what it means to scan the environment.

Scanning the environment
A method used during the planning process to pin down planning assumptions.

An important step involved in the valuation process is looking at the nature of the industry in which a business operates and the competition it faces. This is commonly referred to as **scanning the environment** (look back to step 3 in Figure 12.1). If the business operates in a volatile and competitive environment, this affects its viability and profitability. Its risk is higher and the cash and earnings generated by the business may be more difficult to predict.

Scanning the environment means creating planning assumptions on which the value of the business will be based. Here, we are talking about assessing the general and industry environments and creating planning assumptions that could be expressed in quantitative and qualitative terms. *Quantitative factors,* such as the GNP, labour rates, market demand, supply capability, imports, unemployment rate, and prevailing interest rates, help to show the conditions under which the business operates and to prepare the detailed operating plans related to marketing, manufacturing, research and development, engineering, and production.

Qualitative factors examine additional important elements, such as government regulations and controls, labour activities, consumer preferences, and so on. The general environment includes economic, political, social/ethical, technological, and international conditions. Industry conditions include such factors as the profile of customers, the number and power of suppliers, the competitive climate (rivalry among competing sellers), the threat of substitute products, the potential entry of new competitors, and growth patterns. The goal of scanning the environment is to identify the *opportunities* and *threats* facing the business and the *strengths* and *weaknesses* within the various operating departments and divisions of a company.

Planning assumptions were covered in some detail in Chapter 7. Look back to the section called "Planning Assumptions."

Documenting the Planning Assumptions

4 Explain how to document planning assumptions.

The next step is to document the planning assumptions (or premises) that will help prepare the projected financial statements (step 4 in Figure 12.1). Investors will want to examine a company's past performance, determine whether the existing resources will be adequate to realize the new owners' plans, and look at the company's projected financial statements (i.e., statement of income and statement of financial position); these statements will be discussed later in this chapter.

PAST PERFORMANCE

Looking at the track record of a business (for, say, the previous four or five years) is always important for investors. A healthy past performance supports the decision to purchase. A company's track record can be measured in terms of overall performance, operating performance, and market performance.

Overall performance The ratios used to measure how well a business is deploying its resources.

Operating performance A method for measuring the efficiency and effectiveness of management at the operating level (e.g., marketing, production).

Market performance A method used for measuring the efficiency and effectiveness of management within the industry in which the business operates.

Overall performance is a measure of how a company has used its resources in the past. Useful ratios to measure overall performance may be grouped under two headings: those measuring financial conditions, such as current ratio, acid test ratio, and debt ratios; and those measuring profitability, such as return on revenue, return on assets, and return on equity.

Operating performance is a measure of managerial and technical competence. This is important in determining the extent to which the existing management team is able to make the business profitable. Relevant information on managerial performance relates to the major organizational functions. For example, under marketing are product acceptability, distribution efficiencies, and sales performance; under manufacturing are operating expenses, cost of raw material, use of plant capacity, capital assets turnover, inventory turnover, and trade receivables turnover; and under human resources are labour turnover, quality of the workforce, and general working conditions.

Market performance is a measure of a firm's position within its industry. Did it lose, maintain, or improve its market position? Was it able to manage its business under adverse environmental or industry conditions? How? Why? By how much? A number of firms compile industry data against which historical company performance can be compared. For example, Dun & Bradstreet Canada, Standard & Poor's, and several commercial banks disclose, through written reports or websites, industry ratios based on financial and tax statistics. Dun & Bradstreet Canada provides its Canadian Industry Norms and Key Business Ratios, comprehensive and essential financial data on company and industry key ratios related to solvency, efficiency, and profitability. Also, Standard & Poor's Compustat Services provides online information related to industry and company financial performance. Look back at Table 4.8 for examples of this type of information.

PRESENT PERFORMANCE

If a business is purchased, owners will analyze the company's strengths and weaknesses, and determine what needs to be done to carry out any new strategic and operational plans. They will also figure out how to fix any problems or deficiencies. If, for instance, market share and profitability have been declining steadily, the new investors may try to reverse this trend by introducing new products, modifying some existing products, and changing production processes to eliminate waste and inefficiencies.

The purchase of a business may call for a change in direction and how resources are used. Therefore, the analysis of present capability focuses on the following questions: Can the resources be extended? By how much? What new resources must be added to make the business more profitable? How will existing and new resources be integrated? Is there a need to redefine the company's mission, goals, and priorities? The new owners may have to plan in detail the new business's capabilities in the following areas:

- Human resources (technical and managerial)
- Financial resources
- Machinery, equipment, and facilities
- Sources of raw material (suppliers)
- Know-how (techniques, programs, systems)
- Internal relations (employees)
- External relations (union, image, financial community, community relations, government relations, associations)
- Organizational structure

FUTURE CASH NEEDS AND PROFITABILITY

Analyzing future cash needs and profitability is the most time-consuming and demanding part. It is difficult because, unlike analyzing past performance and diagnosing operating function problems (e.g., marketing, production, research and development), looking into the future involves establishing a series of assumptions underlying the purchase decision. The point of the analysis is not only to justify the purchase but also to determine how much the business is really worth and what is required to make the business achieve its strategic, operational, and financial goals.

Restating the Financial Statements

5 Show how to restate the statement of income and the statement of financial position.

The key documents investors examine when buying a business are its statement of income and its statement of financial position. On the statement of financial position, investors look at the book value of a company's assets and how much the business owes to creditors on these assets. By examining each item, investors can put a price tag on each asset to determine how much it is actually worth, or its market value.

However, looking at the statement of financial position is not enough. The investor will also examine the statement of income to determine the company's existing and, most important, its potential earning power. The true value of a business is directly related to its ability to generate earnings, and the statement of income is the best way to arrive at this number. However, the earnings that the existing owners are able to generate may be different from what the new owners will be able to realize. Therefore, as with the statement of financial position, the new owners must assess the individual part of the statement of income to determine, for example, if more revenue can be generated and if improvements in operating efficiencies could improve the bottom line. Each expense account on the statement of income is examined for cost savings through economy, downsizing, and increased productivity.

Financial ratios are used to analyze financial statements to assess a company's liquidity, debt/coverage, asset management, and profitability performance. Typical questions that investors ask include the following:

- Have these financial statements been audited?
- Is the business carrying too much debt?
- What is the real worth of the physical assets?
- Is the company profitable?
- Are the operating costs reasonable? Inflated? Out of line?
- Is the business carrying too much in trade receivables compared with sales revenue? Too much inventory compared with cost of sales? What is the real worth of these assets?
- How much is the reputation of the business worth?

After looking at a company's financial statements, the investors will create planning assumptions for each item in the financial statements to help produce the projected statements of income and statements of financial position.

Let's now examine how each element shown on the statement of income and the statement of financial position can be restated to determine the real worth of a business.

RESTATING THE STATEMENT OF INCOME

Looking at only one year's statement of income does not give enough information to measure a company's operating performance. The company's historical financial and operating performance must be analyzed closely. Several years are used to determine how consistent a company is in generating revenue and earnings, and how each cost element has performed in the past. Specific things to look for are the following:

- Has revenue been increasing?
- Have the operating expenses, such as cost of sales, distribution costs, and administrative expenses, been consistent from year to year?
- If we were to buy this company, would we be able to increase revenue? Reduce costs? If so, how would we be able to achieve such improvements?

Let's assume that an investor wants to purchase Eastman Technologies Inc. The investor would want to analyze the company's existing statement of income and restate the numbers. Eastman Technologies Inc.'s 2013 actual statement of income and 2014 restated statement are shown in Table 12.2. Comments related to the more important segments of the statement of income follow. Typical questions related to accounts on the statement of income that can help in creating planning assumptions are listed under the heading Projected Statement of Income Planning Assumptions in Chapter 7.

Table 12.2 **Restating the Statement of Income**

	Actual: 2013		Buyer's Restated Estimates: 2014	
Revenue	$2,500,000	1.00	$4,000,000	1.00
Cost of sales	(1,900,000)	(0.76)	(2,400,000)	(0.60)
Gross profit	**600,000**	0.24	**1,600,000**	0.40
Other income	20,000	0.01	32,000	0.01
Distribution costs:				
Sales salaries	(140,000)	(0.06)	(245,000)	(0.06)
Advertising expenses	(20,000)	(0.01)	(85,000)	(0.02)
Total distribution costs	**(160,000)**	(0.07)	**(330,000)**	(0.08)
Administrative expenses:				
Office salaries	(170,000)	(0.07)	(190,000)	(0.05)
Rent	(20,000)	(0.01)	(30,000)	(0.01)
Depreciation	(40,000)	(0.01)	(150,000)	(0.03)
Total administrative expenses	**(230,000)**	(0.09)	**(370,000)**	(0.09)
Finance costs	(35,000)	(0.01)	(194,000)	(0.06)
Total other income and costs	(405,000)	(0.16)	(862,000)	(0.22)
Profit before taxes	195,000	0.08	738,000	0.18
Income tax expense	(97,500)	(0.04)	(369,000)	(0.09)
Profit for the year	$ 97,500	0.04	$ 369,000	0.09

Revenue

In 2013, Eastman Technologies Inc. had sales of $2,500,000, and the new owners estimate $4,000,000 in 2014, a 60% increase. The new owner's marketing plan would determine how this growth will be realized. The so-called "marketing variables," which include selling, advertising, promotion, distribution, product, market finance, and market definition, have a direct influence on that all-important figure in the restated statements of income: revenue. Miscalculating the number of units to be sold and the selling price could severely affect profitability.

Cost of Sales

Based on a marketing plan, each expense item in the expense accounts on the statement of income is examined carefully. For example, even though the cost of sales shows one figure, the new buyers would want to examine the many different costs that are included in the $1,900,000 to determine whether efficiencies can be obtained through purchasing, freight, and manufacturing. Most expenses are incurred at the manufacturing level, through plant expenses, manufacturing costs, maintenance, raw material purchases, insurance, inventory costs, utilities, and wastage.

This plan focuses on efficiencies and shows production at competitive prices. Manufacturing's goal is to make a product that meets the needs of marketing (its selling agent) at the best possible price. The total manufacturing concept should include the most modern techniques, equipment use, material handling, storage, inventory control, traffic, record keeping, and costing.

Calculating the break-even points for several future years of operation could highlight the relationship between revenue and costs (fixed and variable) and is considered a valid yardstick to determine level of risk. Several sensitivity checks can estimate the margin of safety for a price or volume drop, or an increase in operating expenses with no corresponding change in selling price.

As shown in Table 12.2, vertical analysis helps to determine the extent to which the new owners would be able to improve manufacturing efficiencies. Under the present owners, cost of sales as a percentage of revenue is 76% (or $0.76 for each $1.00 worth of revenue), and the new owners would show a $0.16 improvement, down to 60% (or $0.60 for each dollar's worth of revenue). Because of this exceptional improvement in cost of sales, the gross profit would jump from 24% to 40%.

Distribution Costs

The assumptions related to distribution costs can be covered in the marketing plan and reflect the planning assumptions related to sales and advertising. As shown in Table 12.2, distribution costs will be increased by 106%, reflecting the emphasis that the new owners place on selling their products and services. Distribution costs as a percentage of revenue increase slightly from 7% to 8%.

Administrative Expenses

Administrative expenses include office salaries, rent, and depreciation. There is a 61% increase in these expenses, which is equivalent to the revenue increase. Because of this, total administrative expenses as a percentage of sales are maintained at 9%. Individually, office salaries increased by 12%, rental charges by 50%, and depreciation expense by 275%; the last increase is due to the significant increase in capital assets.

Total other income and costs, which include other income, distribution costs, administrative expenses, and finance costs, increased by 113%; as a percentage of revenue, they increased from 16% to 22%. Because of the significant improvements in revenue and cost of sales, profit before taxes increases by 278%; as a percentage of revenue, it improves from 8% to 18%.

Bottom Line

As a result of the changes in the revenue and expense accounts, profit for the year reaches $369,000, which represents a 278% increase. As a percentage of revenue, profit for the year increases from 4% to 9%. This means that in 2014, for every $1.00 of revenue, the company will make $0.09 in profit, compared with $0.04 in 2013.

The acquisition of the business by the new owners will therefore make the business more profitable. The new owners are expected to earn $369,000 in profit and $519,000 ($369,000 + $150,000) in cash flow (profit for the year plus depreciation).

Now that we know the potential earning power of the business, the next question is this: Based on the statement of income projections, how much is the business worth? Restating the statement of financial position will give us this information.

RESTATING THE STATEMENT OF FINANCIAL POSITION

Table 12.3 shows Eastman Technologies Inc.'s statement of financial position of the present owners and the buyer's estimated value of individual asset and liability accounts. The buyer's estimated market value represents the new owner's projected statement of financial position. For this reason, items such as non-current assets, inventories, trade receivables, and retained earnings reflect what the investors would really buy from the present owners and how these assets would be financed. Let's look at the parts of the statement of financial position. Typical questions related to individual accounts appearing on the statement of financial position that can help formulate planning assumptions are listed under the heading Projected Statement of Financial Position Planning Assumptions in Chapter 7.

Property, Plant, and Equipment

Property, plant, and equipment (also called capital assets or fixed assets), which include land, buildings, equipment, and machinery, are valued at $3,000,000, for an increase of 150% over the book value of the seller's assets ($1,200,000). Presumably, both the investor and the seller asked their respective real estate agents (to appraise the land value) and engineers (to evaluate the value of the machinery and equipment) to estimate the market value of the assets shown on the statement of financial position. Because we are dealing with the opening statement of financial position for the new company in 2014, there is no accumulated depreciation. At the end of the first fiscal year, however, this account would show a depreciation amount (drawn from the statement of income) for the use of the property, plant, and equipment assets.

Table 12.3 **Restating the Statement of Financial Position**

Eastman Technologies Inc.
Statement of Financial Position
As at December 31
Actual and Buyer's Restated Estimates

	Actual: 2013		Buyer's Restated Estimates: 2014	
Assets				
Non-current assets				
Property, plant, and equipment	$1,340,000	0.75	$3,000,000	0.77
Accumulated depreciation	(140,000)	(0.08)	—	0.00
	1,200,000	0.67	3,000,000	0.77
Goodwill	—	—	400,000	0.10
Total non-current assets	1,200,000	0.67	3,400,000	0.87
Current assets				
Inventories	218,000	0.12	170,000	0.04
Trade receivables	300,000	0.17	250,000	0.06
Prepaid expenses	60,000	0.03	60,000	0.02
Cash and cash equivalents	22,000	0.01	22,000	0.01
Total current assets	600,000	0.33	502,000	0.13
Total assets	$1,800,000	1.00	$3,902,000	1.00
Equity and liabilities				
Equity				
Share capital	$ 300,000	0.17	$1,457,000	0.37
Contributed surplus	—	—	—	—
Retained earnings	255,000	0.14	—	—
Total other comprehensive income/(loss)	—	—	—	—
Total equity	555,000	0.31	1,457,000	0.37
Non-current liabilities				
Long-term borrowings	800,000	0.44	2,000,000	0.51
Current liabilities				
Trade and other payables	195,000	0.12	195,000	0.05
Short-term borrowings	150,000	0.08	150,000	0.04
Accrued expenses	20,000	0.01	20,000	0.01
Taxes payable	80,000	0.04	80,000	0.02
Total current liabilities	445,000	0.25	445,000	0.12
Total liabilities	1,245,000	0.69	2,445,000	0.63
Total equity and liabilities	$1,800,000	1.00	$3,902,000	1.00

Note: Shaded amounts are items taken into consideration in the purchase of the business.

Goodwill

Goodwill is a special asset that appears on a statement of financial position when a business is purchased. It represents the value of the reputation, faithful customers, and good name of the existing company. It is the excess paid for a business over the fair market value of the assets less the liabilities just before the purchase. In the case of Eastman, the new owners might pay $400,000 for the name and reputation.

Current Assets

Based on the market value, the worth of the current assets is estimated at $502,000. The value of both prepaid expenses ($60,000) and cash and cash equivalents ($22,000) shows their actual worth. Based on a detailed audit of the company's inventories and trade receivables accounts, they have been reduced to $170,000 and $250,000, respectively.

Share Capital

Share capital is the cash that the buyers would have to put up to buy the business. An amount of $1,457,000 would be invested in the business by the new owners, which represents 37% of the total equity and liabilities.

Long-Term Borrowings

As shown in Table 12.3, the buyers will borrow $2,000,000 to purchase some of the assets of the business.

Current Liabilities

All items reported under current liabilities are brought forward from the seller's statement of financial position to the new owner's opening statement of financial position. In Table 12.3, current liabilities are $445,000, or 12% of the company's total equity and liabilities.

Pricing an Ongoing Business

6 Present ways to price an ongoing business.

Now that we have created the projected statement of income and opening statement of financial position, we can determine how much the business is worth as a going concern. The going-concern value relates to the ability of an asset to produce after-tax cash flows. The investor would therefore compare the worth of the future receipts (cash inflows) with the original investment (cash outflows). The going-concern value approach is a future-oriented concept based on the principles of trade-off and risk.

Four techniques will be used to make that calculation: asset valuation, net present value, industry multipliers, and price-earnings multiple.

Asset valuation
A method used to restate the numbers appearing on financial statements.

ASSET VALUATION

The **asset valuation** method looks at the buyer's restated statement of financial position (Table 12.3) and selects the items that the buyer is interested in purchasing. These items are shown in Table 12.4. The only assets that are of interest to the new owners are property, plant, and equipment; goodwill; inventories; and trade receivables. Property, plant, and equipment include such assets as land, buildings, equipment, machinery, and tools. These assets would be listed in detail at book price and market price. The value of these assets is $3 million. The other asset that the buyer will purchase is the goodwill. This is valued at $400,000.

The other item that the buyer will probably keep is trade and other payables ($195,000) because they are used to finance current assets, such as inventories ($170,000) and trade receivables ($250,000). Based on the reappraised value, the buyer will purchase the seller's net working capital for $225,000 (that is, $170,000 + $250,000 − $195,000).

Table 12.4 shows that the seller is asking $3,625,000 for the business. Based on the projected statement of income, is the business worth the asking price? The potential buyers could invest $3,625,000 in investment securities at 10% a year (before tax) and earn $362,500 a year. If they buy the business instead, they should expect superior earnings because of the risk factor.

NET PRESENT VALUE METHOD

The net present value method is based on the time-value-of-money concept and takes into account cash inflows and cash outflows. This topic was covered in Chapters 10 and 11. The net present value is calculated by taking into account both the weighted average cost of capital and the hurdle rate (see Table 12.5). The seller's asking price is $3,625,000. This is the amount of cash that the buyer would have to pay and includes non-current assets, goodwill, and working capital (see Table 12.4).

The next step is to determine the amount of cash that would be generated over the life of the project. From the buyer's statement of income shown in Table 12.2, the cash inflow is estimated at $519,000. This is made up of the profit for the year of $369,000 plus depreciation of $150,000. If we assume that the owner will want to keep the business for 10 years, after which he or she will want to sell it for, say, $6,000,000, the net present value of the purchase, using a 10% discount rate, gives a

Table 12.4 Cost of the Business

Property, plant, and equipment	$3,000,000
Goodwill	400,000
Total non-current assets	3,400,000
Inventories	170,000
Trade receivables	250,000
Total current assets	420,000
Less: trade and other payables	195,000
Net working capital	225,000
Purchase price	$3,625,000

Table 12.5 NPV Based on the Weighted Cost of Capital and the Hurdle Rate

(in $)	Cost of Capital 10%	Hurdle Rate (NPV) 20%	Hurdle Rate (Purchase Price) 20%
Purchase price (outflows)	(3,625,000)	(3,625,000)	(3,144,968)
Cash inflows			
Cost of capital 519,000 × 6.1446	3,189,047		
Hurdle rate 519,000 × 4.1925		2,175,908	2,175,908
Sale of business			
Cost of capital 6,000,000 × 0.38554	2,313,240		
Hurdle rate 6,000,000 × 0.16151	—	969,060	969,060
Net present value	1,877,287	(480,032)	0

positive $1,877,287. This means that the buyer would earn 10% on the investment plus $1,877,287 over the 10 years.

If the weighted average cost of capital were used as the rate for approving the purchase, the buyer would certainly buy the business. However, because of the risk involved, if the buyer's hurdle rate on the investment is 20%, the net present value would be $480,032 short. In this case, the buyer would earn less than the expected 20%. The buyer would probably not buy the business for the $3,625,000 asking price. If the buyer insists on making a 20% return, a counteroffer of $3,144,968 ($3,625,000 − $480,032) could be made—which would make the cash outflow equal to the cash inflows. At that price, the IRR would be 20%. Conversely, if the buyer still purchases the business for the $3,625,000 asking price, an internal rate of return of only 17.2% would be made.

In the News 12.2 shows how cash flow projections based on even vague planning assumptions can satisfy investors in research and development projects.

In The News 12.2

WILL R&D INVESTMENT IN A NEW KEYBOARD MAKE A DIFFERENCE?

Research In Motion (RIM), the Canadian multinational telecommunications company headquartered in Waterloo, Ontario, is doing everything it can to maintain its competitive stamina in the smartphone arena. The company is planning to introduce a new keyboard for its BlackBerry 10 operating system.

(continued)

In The News 12.2 (continued)

This time, the new phones will include models with and without keyboards. It's now the "battle of the keyboards" and RIM hopes to make a difference with its "trapezoid-parallelogram-shaped keys." Supposedly, it will make it easier for users to type and to be more accurate. A considerable amount of money was spent on research and development, with the hope that it will generate more sales and more cash, and in the process, positively influence return on investment. But will the future projected incoming cash flows compensate for the R&D cash outflows?

Submitted in January 2009, it took three years (May 2012) for RIM to be granted a patent from the United States Patent and Trademark Office for its newly designed angular keyboard. The troubled company, with sales of $19 billion and a net income of $3.4 billion in 2011 is now battling other smartphone makers, such as Apple's iPhone and Google's Android operating systems, which use electronic visual display, that is, the touchscreen.

Source: "Do BlackBerry typers dream of trapezoid keys?" *Globe and Mail.* Retrieved from http://www.theglobeandmail.com/news/technology/mobile-technology/do-blackberry-typers-dream-of-trapezoid-keys/article2427706/, accessed May 10, 2012. For updates about RIM, visit www.rim.com.

INDUSTRY MULTIPLIERS

Industry multipliers Standards used to determine the value or worth of a business.

Another approach to putting a price tag on a business is the use of **industry multipliers**, standards used to determine the value or worth of a business. Here, the buyer or seller would refer to a list of multipliers for the industry. The method calculates the value of a business by using an industry average sales figure as a multiplier. For example, a seller of a business with annual sales of $300,000 may set the multiplier at 0.40 to obtain a sales price of $120,000 (e.g., $300,000 × 0.40 = $120,000). Such numbers as monthly gross sales, monthly gross sales plus inventory, or after-tax profits of comparable businesses in the industry can be used for the calculation.

In his book *Buying a Business*,[2] Richard Snowden lists the multipliers of many industries. Here are three examples:

Retail businesses	0.75 to 1.5 × annual net profit + inventory + equipment
Fast food (non-franchise)	0.5 to 0.7 × monthly gross sales + inventory
Food distributors	1 to 1.5 × annual net profit + inventory + equipment

The argument against this method is simply that it's not the top line that counts but the bottom line. However, these multipliers can be used as a complementary tool, such as the NPV to obtain a rough estimate of an asking price.

Because of a wide variation in gross revenue from year to year, it may be wise to calculate the asking price by using the company's last three or four years' statements of income. For example, the buyer may want to average out the last three years' gross revenue to calculate the asking price.

2. Richard W. Snowden, *Buying a Business*, New York: AMACOM, 1994, p. 151.

PRICE-EARNINGS MULTIPLE

In the case of Eastman Technologies Inc., a price-earnings multiple can also be used to determine the value of the company. A price-earnings multiple is the inverse of a capitalization rate. For example, if the investors want to use an 11% capitalization rate, the price-earnings multiple will be 9.1 (100 ÷ 11%). If they want to use 13%, the price-earnings multiple will be 7.7 (100 ÷ 13%). To determine the company's market value by using the price-earnings multiple, the investor would therefore have to determine the appropriate capitalization rate and multiply this rate by maintainable after-tax cash flows, which in the case of Eastman is $519,000 ($369,000 + $150,000). If the investors want to use a 13% capitalization, the value of the business would be $3,996,300 ($519,000 × 7.7).

7 Calculate the market value of publicly traded companies.

Market Value of Publicly Traded Companies

To calculate the value of publicly traded companies, analysts multiply the number of outstanding common shares by the share price on the last day that the shares were traded on the stock market.

Let's assume that Eastman Technologies Inc. is a publicly traded company and has 30,000 shares outstanding. With a $555,000 net worth, that means that the book value of each share outstanding would be $18.50 ($555,000 ÷ 30,000). However, if the shares were traded at, say, $25.00, the market value of the company, or the equity portion of the statement of financial position, would be $750,000 ($25.00 × 30,000). In this case, the ratio of the market value to the book value would be 1.35 times ($25.00 ÷ $18.50).

Problem-Solving Example 12.3

Common Share Valuation

Use the information contained in the following statement of financial position to calculate the company's (1) book value of the shares, (2) market value of the shares, and (3) ratio of the market value to the book value. The company issued 300,000 shares and they are currently trading at $22.00.

Non-current assets	$2,000,000	Capital shares	$2,000,000
Current assets	4,000,000	Retained earnings	2,000,000
		Total equity	4,000,000
		Total liabilities	2,000,000
Total assets	$6,000,000	Total equity and liabilities	$6,000,000

Solution

1. Book value: $4,000,000 ($13.33 × 300,000)
2. Market value: $6,600,000 ($22.00 × 300,000)
3. Ratio: 1.65 ($6,600,000 ÷ $4,000,000)

Self-Test Exercise 12.3

Common Share Valuation

The shareholders of CompuTech Inc., Len and Joan Miller, want to go public and are considering selling shares. CompuTech's statement of financial position for 2015 is as follows:

CompuTech Inc.
Statement of Financial Position
As at December 31, 2015

Non-current assets	$402,000	Share capital	$170,000
Current assets	235,000	Retained earnings	135,000
		Total equity	305,000
		Long-term borrowings	200,000
		Current liabilities	132,000
		Total liabilities	332,000
Total assets	$637,000	Total equity and liabilities	$637,000

Assume that CompuTech Inc. has 20,000 shares outstanding, which are currently trading at $35.50.

Questions

1. **What is the book value of the shares?**
2. **What is the market value of the shares?**
3. **What is the ratio of the market value to the book value?**

Answers to the Self-Test Exercises can be found at www.bergeron7e.nelson.com.

Return on Investment from an Investor's Perspective

8 Determine the investment return on capital projects from an investor's perspective.

Finding the value of an ongoing business for investors, such as venture capitalists, by using the time-value-of-money approach can be done for several investors at the same time. For example, if several investors were interested in buying Eastman Technologies Inc., the return on investment for the portion of the investment made by each investor would be calculated. In this example, however, we are assuming that one investor (owner/manager) is interested in buying Eastman.

Calculating the return on investment based on this time-value-of-money yardstick has four steps. Let's assume that the investor wants to buy Eastman Technologies Inc. for $3.4 million in 2013. The amount consists of capital assets and goodwill. An additional $225,000 will be invested in working capital during 2014, the first year of operations. We'll use the financial statements presented in Tables 12.2 and 12.3 in the four-step calculation as follows:

Step 1: The yearly after-tax cash flow
Step 2: The projected residual value

Step 3: The estimated market value
Step 4: The investor's before- and after-tax return (IRR)

STEP 1: THE YEARLY AFTER-TAX CASH FLOW

The first step for calculating Eastman Technologies Inc.'s market value is to determine its after-tax cash flow forecast for 2014 to 2018. Table 12.6 shows that Eastman's after-tax cash flow from operations increases from \$519,000 (statement of income is drawn from Table 12.2) to \$1,408,000 by 2018. During those five years, Eastman will continue to invest in capital assets and in working capital. Investments in capital assets will be \$100,000 a year, while incremental working capital changes each year (e.g., \$225,000 in 2014 and \$50,000 in 2018). The lower portion of Table 12.6 shows how the increases in the working capital accounts were calculated and includes inventories, trade receivables, and trade and other payables.

After adding the investment in capital assets and working capital to the after-tax cash flow from operations, Eastman moves a negative cash flow of \$3.4 million in 2013 (end-of-year investment) to a positive cash flow of \$1,258,000 in 2018. This discretionary after-tax cash flow for each year in the forecast period is then discounted to its present value by using an acceptable discount rate, in this case, 20% (which is the hurdle rate). (See the discount factors in Appendix B at the end of the book that were used to calculate the present value amount between 2014 and 2018.) The 20% discount factor reflects the risk associated with the nature of Eastman's operations. As shown, the projected cash flows lose more value (because of discounting) as we reach the end of the forecast period. For example, the cash flow generated during the second year of the forecast (2015) is discounted for two years only, while cash flow for the fifth year (2018) is discounted for five years. The cumulative net present value of the cash flows for the six years (2013–2018) is negative in the amount of \$1,449,000 (−\$3,400,000 + \$1,951,000).

Table 12.6 **Eastman Technologies Inc.'s After-Tax Cash Flows**

(in \$000s)	2013 Actual	2014 Forecast	2015 Forecast	2016 Forecast	2017 Forecast	2018 Forecast
Revenue		4,000	4,700	5,800	6,700	7,700
Cost of sales		(2,400)	(2,800)	(3,500)	(4,200)	(4,600)
Gross profit		1,600	1,900	2,300	2,500	3,100
Other income		32	30	28	30	30
Distribution costs		(330)	(360)	(380)	(400)	(420)
Administrative expenses		(370)	(400)	(410)	(420)	(440)

(continued)

Table 12.6 Eastman Technologies Inc.'s After-Tax Cash Flows (continued)

Finance costs		(194)	(270)	(288)	(300)	(300)
Total other income and costs		(862)	(1,000)	1,050	(1,090)	(1,130)
Profit before taxes		738	900	1,250	1,410	1,970
Income tax expense		(369)	(405)	(563)	(645)	(887)
Profit for the year		369	495	687	765	1,083
Add back: depreciation		150	200	250	300	325
Cash flow from operations		**519**	**695**	**937**	**1,065**	**1,408**
Capital assets	(3,400)	(100)	(100)	(100)	(100)	(100)
Incremental working capital	—	(225)	(45)	(60)	(30)	(50)
Total additional investment	(3,400)	(325)	(145)	(160)	(130)	(150)
Cash flow with additional investments		194	550	777	935	1,258
Discount factor (20%)	0.0000	0.8333	0.69444	0.57870	0.48225	0.40188
Annual discounted cash flows	**(3,400)**	**162**	**382**	**450**	**451**	**506**
Net present value for the five years	**(1,449)**					
Incremental working capital						
Inventories		(170)	(200)	(240)	(260)	(300)
Trade receivables		(250)	(300)	(350)	(400)	(450)
Total		(420)	(500)	(590)	(660)	(750)
Less: Trade and other payables		195	230	260	300	340
Net increase in working capital for the year		(225)	(270)	(330)	(360)	(410)
Previous year's working capital			225	270	330	360
Incremental working capital			(45)	(60)	(30)	(50)

Problem-Solving Example 12.4

Cumulative Cash Flows and Net Present Values

Use 6% as a company's weighted average cost of capital and the cash flow estimates below to calculate the following values:

1. The yearly present values
2. The cumulative present values

In 000s	Year 1	Year 2	Year 3	Year 4	Year 5
Projected profit for the year	$300	$350	$400	$450	$500
Projected capital cost allowance	30	35	40	45	50
Projected incremental investments in working capital	$ 3.0	$ 2.0	$ 2.0	$ 1.0	$ 1.0

(continued)

Problem-Solving Example 12.4 (continued)

Solution

In 000s	Year 1	Year 2	Year 3	Year 4	Year 5
Projected profit for the year	$ 300	$ 350	$ 400	$ 450	$ 500
Projected capital cost allowance	30	35	40	45	50
After-tax cash flow	330	385	440	495	550
Projected incremental investments in working capital	(3)	(2)	(2)	(1)	(1)
Net cash flows	327	383	438	494	549
Discount rates (6%)	0.94340	0.89000	0.83962	0.79209	0.74726
Present values	308.5	340.9	367.8	391.3	410.2
Cumulative present values	308.5	649.4	1,017.2	1,408.5	1,818.7

Self-Test Exercise 12.4

Cumulative Cash Flows and Net Present Values

Use 11% as CompuTech's weighted average cost of capital and the estimates shown below to calculate the following values for one of the company's retail stores:

1. The yearly present values
2. The cumulative present values

(in $000s)	Year 1	Year 2	Year 3	Year 4	Year 5
Projected profit for the year	80	90	100	110	120
Projected capital cost allowance	6	8	9	10	11
Projected incremental investments in working capital	2	3	2	1	1

Answers to the Self-Test Exercises can be found at www.bergeron7e.nelson.com.

STEP 2: THE PROJECTED RESIDUAL VALUE

At the end of the forecast period (for Eastman, in 2018), Eastman will likely remain viable and continue to generate cash flows. The residual value is the estimated present value of the after-tax cash flows expected to be earned throughout the company's lifespan. As shown below, the residual value calculation includes the calculation of the maintainable cash flow from operations beyond 2018 and the capitalization calculation.

Maintainable cash flow from operations. The cash flows before income tax for the last year of the forecast period are representative of the maintainable cash flows. Eastman's cash flow from operations is $1,408,000, which is drawn from Table 12.6.

Income tax expense and an estimate of annual ongoing capital spending (future average annual spending on equipment and other capital assets) are deducted to find the maintainable after-tax cash flow. Capital spending for each year after 2018 is estimated at $100,000. This amount will be spent to maintain the business at revenue levels equal to the last year of the forecast (2018). There will be a $50,000 yearly increase in working capital accounts. It is assumed here that Eastman will remain at the 2018 level of operations, generating a steady yearly cash flow from operations of $1,258,000.

	2018 Forecast
Cash flow from operations	$1,408,000
Sustainable spending in capital assets	(100,000)
Incremental working capital	(50,000)
Total additional investments	(150,000)
Net cash flow	$1,258,000

Capitalization rate. The next step in calculating the residual value is determining the capitalization rate. Using capitalization is the same as discounting a maintainable cash flow continually. The residual value is calculated by dividing the maintainable after-tax cash flow of $1,258,000 by an acceptable rate of return. The capitalization rate used for Eastman is reduced by 2% (from the 20% rate used in Table 12.6) to 18%. This difference between the discount rate used in the table and the capitalization rate is adjusted for inflation, growth, and risk. Eastman's residual value is $6,989,000.

Cash flow with incremental investments	$1,258,000
Divided by capitalization rate (20% less 2%)	18%
Residual value	$6,989,000

The last step in estimating Eastman's residual value is to calculate the present value of the $6,989,000 to be received in 2018 to the end of 2013 (the year of the investment by the new investor). By using the same 20% discount rate as the one used in Table 12.6, the present value of the residual value would be $2,809,000:

Residual value	$6,989,000
Present value factor at 20%	0.40188
Present value of the residual value	$2,809,000

Problem-Solving Example 12.5

Capitalization Rate

The following are accounts shown on a company's statement of income: revenue ($400,000), income tax expense ($30,000), distribution costs ($65,000), cost of sales ($210,000) administrative expenses ($50,000), finance costs ($15,000), and depreciation ($40,000, included in distribution costs and administrative expenses).

Questions

1. Calculate the value of the business as a going concern by using the following capitalization rates: 10% and 20%.
2. Use a 20% discount rate to calculate the present value of the business if it has a 15-year lifespan.
3. If an investor were to invest $150,000 in the business, how much cash should the business generate each year during a 15-year period if the investor wants to earn 20%?

Solution

1. Capitalization at 10% is $700,000, and at 20%, $350,000.
2. Value is $327,285.
3. Cash flow required is $32,082.

Statement of Income

Revenue		$400,000
Cost of sales		(210,000)
Gross profit		190,000
Distribution costs	$(65,000)	
Administrative expenses	(50,000)	
Finance costs	(15,000)	
Total expenses		(130,000)
Profit before taxes		60,000
Income tax expense		(30,000)
Profit for the year		30,000
Add back depreciation		40,000
Cash flow		$ 70,000

1. Capitalization calculation:

After-Tax Cash Flow		Capitalization Rate		Going Concern Value
$70,000	÷	10%	=	$700,000
$70,000	÷	20%	=	$350,000

(continued)

Problem-Solving Example 12.5 (continued)

2. Present value of the business:

Cash Flow	No. of Years	Discount Rate	Discount Factor	Present Value
$70,000	15	20%	4.6755	$327,285

3. Cash inflows that the business must generate each year if the investor wants to earn 20%:

Investment		Discount Factor		Annual Cash Flow
$150,000	÷	4.6755	=	$32,082

Self-Test Exercise 12.5

Capitalization Rate

Use the following information to calculate the after-tax cash flow from CompuTech Inc.'s operations.

Accounts	Amounts
Revenue	$800,000
Income tax expense	42,000
Distribution costs	135,000
Cost of sales	406,000
Administrative expenses	110,000
Finance costs	30,000

Depreciation of $80,000 is included in distribution costs and administrative expenses.

Questions

1. Calculate the value of the business as a going concern by using the following capitalization rates: 15% and 25%.
2. Use a 30% discount rate to calculate the present value of the business if it had a 15-year lifespan.
3. If an investor were to invest $300,000 in the business, how much cash should the business generate each year during a five-year period if the investor wants to earn 25%?

Answers to the Self-Test Exercises can be found at www.bergeron7e.nelson.com.

STEP 3: THE ESTIMATED MARKET VALUE

This step in the process involves the calculation of Eastman's estimated fair market value. The company's fair market value is estimated at $1,360,000 (shown on the following page), which reflects Eastman's five-year after-tax discounted cash flow of a negative $1,449,000 (drawn from Table 12.6) and its estimated positive residual value of $2,809,000 that was calculated in step 2.

Present value of cash flow from operations	$(1,449,000)	(step 1)
Plus present value of the residual value	2,809,000	(step 2)
Estimated fair market value	$ 1,360,000	

STEP 4: THE INVESTOR'S BEFORE- AND AFTER-TAX RETURN (IRR)

The last step involves the calculation of the investor's return on investment on a before- and after-tax basis. The buyer invests $3,400,000 (shown below) by the end of 2013 (excluding the $225,000 amount in working capital, an amount that will be invested in 2014). The business generates an after-tax cash flow from operations (with additional investments) of $1,258,000 by the year 2018 (see Table 12.6). It is assumed that the investor will want to sell the business at a future date at a certain price. The total value at the time of the sale is determined by multiplying the maintainable after-tax cash flow of $1,258,000 by a multiple. The multiple is equal to the inverse of a capitalization rate. In this case, a 12.5% capitalization rate is used, which is equal to an eight times earnings multiple.

By using the eight times multiple, the value at the time of selling the business is estimated at $10,064,000 (shown in the table below). The investor will have a 100% ownership in the business. By using a 24.2% discount rate, we find that the present value of the $10,064,000 is equivalent to the $3,400,000 investment. This discount rate would therefore be considered the investor's before-tax internal rate of return (IRR).

(in $000s)	2013	2014	2015	2016	2017	2018
Before-tax rate of return						
Initial investment	(3,400)					
Total value at exit						
After-tax cash flow						1,258
Multiple						8.0
Total value at time of selling						10,064
Initial investment	(3,400)					
Total cash flows	(3,400)					10,064
Before-tax return (IRR)	*24.2%*					

Similar calculations would have to be done to find the investor's IRR on an after-tax basis (shown on the following page). The investor would receive $10,064,000 at the time of selling. The original $3,400,000 investment is then deducted from the cash proceeds, which would leave the investor with a capital gain on the investment of $6,664,000. If the investor's taxable portion is estimated at 75%, the tax payable would be $2,499,000. If the investor is in the 50% tax bracket, an after-tax amount of $7,565,000 would be received. By using a 17.3% discount rate, we find that the present value of the $7,565,000 is equivalent to the $3,400,000 investment made by the investor. The discount rate would therefore be considered the investor's after-tax IRR. This discount rate chosen is the rate of return the buyer requires to take on the risk associated with meeting the forecast cash flow.

(in $000s)	
After-tax rate of return	
Proceeds received on exit	10,064
Initial investment	(3,400)
Capital gains on investment	6,664
Taxable portion (say, 75%)	(4,998)
Investor's tax payable (50%)	2,499
Gross proceeds received on exit	10,064
Investor's tax payable	(2,499)
Net after-tax proceeds to investor	7,565

	2013	2014	2015	2016	2017	2018
After-tax rate of return						
Initial investment	($3,400)					
Total value at exit						
Total value at time of selling						$7,565
Initial investment	($3,400)					
Total cash flows	($3,400)					$7,565
After-tax return (IRR)	*17.3%*					

Problem-Solving Example 12.6

Business Valuation Using the Discounted Cash Flow Method

Several partners want to invest in a capital project. Because of the size of the investment, they want to approach a venture capitalist and ask for $150,000 in equity participation, representing 30% of the total equity investment.

The following shows the partners' financial projections:

Year	Cash Flow from Operations	Investment in Capital Assets	Investment in Working Capital
0	—	$500,000	—
1	$300,000	200,000	$100,000
2	400,000	200,000	100,000
3	600,000	200,000	100,000
4	700,000	100,000	50,000
5	800,000	50,000	25,000
6	950,000	—	—

(continued)

Problem-Solving Example 12.6 (continued)

A 15% discount rate will be used to calculate the present value of the project's cash flow and the capitalization rate. The investor indicated that (1) he wanted to make an exit at the end of six years, and that (2) the project should be worth at least five times its last year's cash flow.

Questions

1. What is the project's net present value?
2. What is the project's internal rate of return using only the six-year projections?
3. What is the project's present value of the residual value?
4. What is the company's fair market value?
5. What is the investor's internal rate of return on his investment?

Solutions

1. Using a 15% discount rate, the project's net present value is $858,498; year 0 (–$500,000); year 1 ($0); year 2 ($100,000); year 3 ($300,000); year 4 ($550,000); year 5 ($725,000); year 6 ($950,000).
2. The project's internal rate of return is 44.02%.
3. The project's present value of the residual value is $2,738,090.

   Using the company's sixth year cash flow of $950,000 and the 15% capitalization rate, the present value of the residual value of $6,333,333 amounts to $2,738,090 ($6,333,333 × 0.43233) when discounted at 15% for a six-year period.
4. The company's fair market value is $3,596,588

Present value of the six-year forecast	$ 858,498
Present value of the residual value	2,738,090
Fair market value	$3,596,588

5. The investor's internal rate of return on his investment is

Sixth year projection	$ 950,000
Multiple factor	× 5
Value	$4,750,000
30% share	$1,425,000

Using a 45.53% discount factor, the present value of the $1,425,000 is $150,000, which equals the initial $150,000 investment.

Self-Test Exercise 12.6

Business Valuation Using the Discounted Cash Flow Method

The Millers are looking at the possibility of opening three new retail stores for CompuTech Inc. Len will be approaching a risk capital investor, Oscar Eden, asking for $200,000 in equity participation. This amount is 20% of the company's equity share.

(continued)

Self-Test Exercise 12.6 (continued)

When the Millers had their first meeting with Oscar, he presented the following financial projections:

Year	Cash Flow from Operations	Investments	Working Capital
0	—	$200,000	—
1	$200,000	200,000	$100,000
2	300,000	300,000	100,000
3	500,000	300,000	50,000
4	600,000	50,000	25,000
5	900,000	50,000	25,000

During the conversation, Len and Oscar agreed that 15% should be used as a discount rate to calculate the present value of the company's cash flow and as a capitalization rate. Oscar stated that he hoped that at the end of five years, when he would make his exit, the company would be worth at least five times its last year's cash flow.

Questions

1. What is CompuTech's net present value?
2. What is CompuTech's internal rate of return using only the five-year projections?
3. What is CompuTech's present value of the residual value?
4. What is CompuTech's fair market value?
5. What is Oscar Eden's internal rate of return on his investment?

Answers to the Self-Test Exercises can be found at www.bergeron7e.nelson.com.

In the News 12.3 provides an example of a company that went through an initial public offering (IPO) setting trade volume records.

In The News 12.3

A $16 BILLION DOLLAR PRICE TAG!

Who could have imagined that a social networking service and website business, started by students on a university campus in 2004, would have gone public with a $16 billion price tag eight years later. It happened on May 18, 2012, when Facebook Inc. priced its initial public offering (IPO) or stock market launch (which is the first sale of stock by a company to the public with the intent of raising expansion capital and becoming publicly traded). More than 576 million shares, selling for around $38, changed hands on that first day, setting a trading volume record for U.S. market debuts.

In February 2004, Mark Zuckerberg and a few fellow Harvard students launched the social networking service. Initially, the website's membership was limited by the founders to Harvard students; they later expanded it to other colleges in the Boston area and Stanford University. Today, Facebook Inc., with headquarters in Menlo Park, California, provides social networking services on a multilingual worldwide basis, serving 901 million users (as of April 2012). In 2011, the company generated $3.7 billion in revenue with only 3,200 employees.

(continued)

In The News 12.3 (continued)

This IPO made quite a number of individuals instant millionaires and even billionaires: Bono, the lead singer of U2, earned $1.5 billion in shares, possibly making him the richest musician on the planet. How is it possible for such a company to raise such overwhelming interest in the investment community? It is the number one social network in the world and has the ability to raise billions of dollars in advertising and, more importantly, still thrive.

Source: Olivia Oran and Alistair Barr, "Facebook prices IPO at $38 a share." *Globe and Mail.* Retrieved from http://www.theglobeandmail.com/globe-investor/facebook-prices-ipo-at-38-a-share/article2436013/?utm_medium=Feeds%3A%20RSS%2FAtom&utm_source=Report%20On%20Business&utm_content=2436013, accessed May 17, 2012; and Alexei Oreskovic, "Facebook debut falls short." May 19, 2012, *Ottawa Citizen*, p. H1.

Chapter Summary

1 Differentiate between market value and book value.

The *book value* of a business is what a business is worth on the books—that is, the difference between total assets and total liabilities. *Market value* is what a business is worth to a buyer as an ongoing entity. Because financial statements do not necessarily reflect the true market value of a business, accountants have attempted to resolve this issue through price-level accounting and current value accounting.

2 Discuss valuation models.

Valuation models include economic value, market value, book value, liquidation value, replacement value, collateral value, assessed value, and going concern value.

3 Comment on what it means to scan the environment.

When buying a business, it is important to scan the environment and note the planning assumptions to create a projected statement of income and projected statement of financial position.

4 Explain how to document planning assumptions.

Documenting the planning assumptions means examining a company's past performance, determining whether the existing resources will be enough to realize the new owner's plans, and looking at the restated company's projected statement of income and statement of financial position.

5 Show how to restate the statement of income and the statement of financial position.

Potential owners should restate the statement of income and statement of financial position to show what they see in terms of revenue, cost of sales, operating expenses, and statement of financial position accounts (assets, equity, and liabilities).

6 Present ways to price an ongoing business.

Pricing a business can be done through the *asset valuation method*, which is the difference between the market value of the assets of an ongoing business and its liabilities; the *net present value method*, which considers cash outflows (purchase price of the business), cash inflows (profit for the year plus depreciation), and the potential resale value of the business at a later date; *industry multipliers*, which are a percentage of the revenue, and price-earnings multiple which is the inverse of a capitalization rate.

7 Calculate the market value of publicly traded companies.

We calculate the value of publicly traded companies by multiplying the number of common shares issued and the share market price.

8 Determine the investment return on capital projects from an investor's perspective.

Four steps are involved in calculating an investor's return on investment when buying an ongoing business: (1) determine the yearly after-tax cash flows, (2) project the business's residual value, (3) estimate the business's market value, and (4) calculate the investor's before- and after-tax return (IRR).

Key Terms

Assessed value p. 515
Asset valuation p. 523
Book value p. 509
Collateral value p. 515
Current-value accounting p. 510
Economic value p. 515
Industry multipliers p. 526
Liquidation value p. 513
Market performance p. 516
Market value p. 509
Operating performance p. 516
Overall performance p. 516
Price-level accounting p. 510
Replacement value p. 514
Scanning the environment p. 515

Review Questions

1 Differentiate between market value and book value.

1. Differentiate between market value and book value.
2. What do we mean by price-level accounting?
3. What do we mean by current-value accounting?

2 Discuss valuation models.

4. Identify the most commonly used valuation models.
5. Explain the following valuation models:
   - Market value
   - Liquidation value
   - Collateral value
   - Assessed value

3 Comment on what it means to scan the environment.

6. Why is it important for buyers of a business to scan the environment?

4 Explain how to document planning assumptions.

7. What are planning assumptions? Why are they important?
8. What do buyers look for when they assess the past performance of a business?

9. What financial ratios are useful for appraising a business?

5 Show how to restate the statement of income and the statement of financial position.

10. How would you restate the statement of income of a business?
11. How would you restate the statement of financial position of a business?
12. What is goodwill?

6 Present ways to price an ongoing business.

13. What do we mean by asset valuation?
14. How can the net present value method help buyers figure out the worth of a business?
15. What are industry multipliers? What are their primary weaknesses?

7 Calculate the market value of publicly traded companies.

16. What technique is used to price the market value of publicly traded companies?

8 Determine the investment return on capital projects from an investor's perspective.

17. What do we mean by maintainable cash flows?
18. What is a residual value?
19. Discuss the meaning of estimated fair market value.
20. What do we mean by capitalization rate and price-earnings multiple?
21. Are the methods and techniques used for valuing a small business the same as those for a large business? Why?
22. Valuation techniques are essentially assessment tools that try to quantify the available objective data. Yet such quantification will always be subjective in part. Explain.
23. Why is it that valuing a business for sale or purchase is one of the most complex tasks an analyst can undertake?

Learning Exercises

1 Differentiate between market value and book value.

EXERCISE 1: BOOK VALUE AND LIQUIDATION VALUE

John Hepworth, the sole proprietor of John's Variety, is having some difficulty with his retail store. He's concerned about the possibility of having to close it. He knows that the value of his business as an ongoing entity is not worth much because of the minimal level of profit that his store has shown over the past two years.

He's now thinking seriously about getting out of the business by liquidating his assets and paying his creditors in full. His bank manager informed him that if he liquidates his assets, he would probably get 60% for his non-current assets, no more than 40% for his inventories, and 65% of the trade receivables amount shown on his statement of financial position as at December 31, 2013.

John was hoping to obtain at least $50,000 after liquidation. With the information below, prepare the following:

- John's statement of financial position as at December 31, 2013.
- John's revised statement of financial position if he were to liquidate his business.

Accounts	Amounts
Revenue	$3,000,000
Inventories	200,000
Share capital	150,000
Accumulated depreciation	200,000
Distribution costs	130,000
Cash	10,000
Marketable securities	50,000
Retained earnings	385,000
Trade and other payables	150,000
Accrued expenses	50,000
Taxes payable	25,000
Other current assets	25,000
Long-term borrowings	350,000
Non-current assets (at cost)	900,000
Trade receivables	300,000
Short-term borrowings	175,000

Questions

1. What is John's book value?
2. What is John's liquidation value?
3. Will John have enough money to pay all his creditors?
4. If John's business cannot cover all his liabilities, what will he have to do?

5 Show how to restate the statement of income and the statement of financial position.

EXERCISE 2: PLANNING ASSUMPTIONS

With the following accounts included in Brown Inc.'s financial statements and assumptions, restate the company's statement of income and statement of financial position.

Statement of income: revenue of $3,000,000 will increase by 7%; cost of sales, as a percentage of revenue will decrease from 50% to 45%; distribution costs of $600,000 will increase by 10%, and administrative expenses of $500,000 will be 15% of revenue; the $100,000 of other expenses will increase by 10%; and income tax expense will go from 40% to 42%.

Statement of financial position: non-current assets of $2,000,000 will grow by 10%; inventories currently at 5 times will improve to 5.5 times; both trade receivables at

$200,000 and other current assets at $100,000 will grow by 10%; equity remains unchanged at $1,100,000; current liabilities will grow from $500,000 to $600,000, and long-term liabilities is $1,000,000.

6 Present ways to price an ongoing business.

EXERCISE 3: VALUATION OF A BUSINESS (CAPITALIZATION RATE AND NPV)

With the following information, calculate the after-tax cash flows from operations.

Accounts	Amounts
Revenue	$3,000,000
Finance costs	100,000
Income tax expense	175,000
Cost of sales	1,800,000
Distribution costs	400,000
Administrative expenses	300,000

Depreciation expense of $100,000 is included in distribution costs and depreciation expense of $200,000 is included in cost of sales.

Questions

1. Calculate the value of the business as a going concern by using the following capitalization rates: 10%, 20%, 30%, and 40%.
2. Use a 20% discount rate to calculate the present value of the business if it had a five-year lifespan and a ten-year lifespan.
3. If an investor were to invest $400,000 in the business, how much cash should the business generate each year during a 10-year period if the investor wants to earn 30%?

EXERCISE 4: BOOK VALUE AND MARKET VALUE (PUBLIC COMPANY)

The shareholders of Zimtex Electronics Inc. are considering selling their shares. The company's statement of financial position is as follows:

Zimtex Electronics Inc.
Statement of Financial Position
(in $)

Non-current assets	800,000	Share capital	200,000
Current assets	300,000	Retained earnings	350,000
		Total equity	550,000
		Long-term borrowings	400,000
		Current liabilities	150,000
		Total liabilities	550,000
Total assets	1,100,000	Total equity and liabilities	1,100,000

The company has 25,000 shares outstanding, which are currently trading at $42.50.

Questions

1. What is the book value of the shares?
2. What is the market value of the shares?
3. What is the ratio of the market value to the book value?

7 Calculate the market value of publicly traded companies.

EXERCISE 5: ANNUAL AND CUMULATIVE PRESENT VALUES

Use 10% as the company's weighted average cost of capital and the estimates shown below to calculate the following values for a manufacturing plant:

1. The yearly present values
2. The cumulative net present values

In millions	Year 1	Year 2	Year 3	Year 4	Year 5
Projected profit for the year	$3.0	$3.4	$3.9	$4.3	$4.8
Projected capital cost allowance	$1.1	$1.2	$1.3	$1.4	$1.5
Projected incremental investment in working capital	$0.6	$0.5	$0.6	$1.0	$0.5

8 Determine the investment return on capital projects from an investor's perspective

EXERCISE 6: PRICING A BUSINESS

Kenisha Johnson, CEO of Eastern Electronics Inc., is looking at the possibility of marketing a new product line. Kenisha will be approaching a risk capital investor, Manon Miller, asking for $500,000 in equity participation. This is 30% of the company's equity share.

When Kenisha had her first meeting with Manon, she presented the following financial projections:

Year	Cash Flows from Operations	Investments	Working Capital
0	—	$100,000	—
1	$300,000	800,000	$300,000
2	500,000	300,000	200,000
3	800,000	200,000	100,000
4	900,000	100,000	50,000
5	1,300,000	100,000	50,000

During the conversation, both agreed that 20% should be used as a discount rate to calculate the present value of the company's cash flows and as a capitalization rate. Manon said that she hoped that at the end of five years, when she would make her exit, the company would be worth at least six times its last year's cash flows.

Questions

1. What is the company's net present value?
2. What is the company's internal rate of return using only the five-year projections?
3. What is the company's present value of the residual value?
4. What is the company's fair market value?
5. What is Manon Miller's internal rate of return on her investment?

Cases

CASE 1: LEWIN FOODS INC.

Helen Campbell and several business friends are considering buying Lewin Foods Inc., a privately owned company. Helen has just received the financial statements from the present owner and is trying to calculate the bid that should be made to the owners of the company.

Helen realized that the financial statements were not providing enough information to make a decision. So she hired several real estate agents, engineers, and accountants to help her determine the value of the land, machinery, equipment, and working capital.

Lewin Foods Inc.'s statement of income and statement of financial position are as follows:

Lewin Foods Inc.
Statement of Income
For the year ended December 31, 2013
(in $)

Revenue		5,600,000
Cost of sales		(3,400,000)
Gross profit		2,200,000
Distribution costs	(750,000)	
Administrative expenses	(440,000)	
Depreciation	(100,000)	
Finance costs	(35,000)	
Total expenses		(1,325,000)
Profit before taxes		875,000
Income tax expense (41.94 %)		(367,000)
Profit for the year		508,000

Although the company is generating $508,000 in profit and $608,000 in cash flow, Helen and her team believe they could increase revenue substantially and reduce costs. After much deliberation, the management team estimates that it could increase the profit for the year to $850,000 and cash flow to $975,000.

Lewin Foods Inc.
Statement of Financial Position
As at December 31, 2013
(in $)

Assets		
Non-current assets (at cost)	3,000,000	
Accumulated depreciation	(1,200,000)	
Non-current assets (net)		1,800,000
Current assets		
Inventories	1,200,000	
Trade receivables	765,000	
Prepaid expenses	60,000	
Cash	200,000	
Total current assets		2,225,000
Total assets		4,025,000
Equity and liabilities		
Equity		
Share capital	300,000	
Retained earnings	1,425,000	
Total equity		1,725,000
Liabilities		
Non-current liabilities		
Mortgage	500,000	
Long-term borrowings	600,000	
Total non-current liabilities		1,100,000
Current liabilities		
Trade and other payables	600,000	
Notes payable	400,000	
Taxes payable	200,000	
Total current liabilities		1,200,000
Total liabilities		2,300,000
Total equity and liabilities		4,025,000

The consultants and auditors reported to Helen that the trade receivables are worth $650,000, or about 85% of what is currently shown on the company's statement of financial position. The value of the inventories, however, is not as good. The auditors indicated that only $800,000 would be worth buying, which represents 67% of what is shown on Lewin's statement of financial position. Helen is prepared to take over all of the trade and other payables.

The estimates regarding the property, plant, and equipment assets are as follows:

Land	$ 200,000
Buildings	800,000
Equipment	1,400,000
Machinery	600,000
Total	$3,000,000

During his conversation with Helen, Daniel Lewin, owner of Lewin Foods Inc., indicated that an amount of $700,000 in goodwill would have to be included in the selling price.

Because of the risk, Helen and her partners feel that they should earn at least a 25% internal rate of return on the business. The partners would be prepared to keep the business for 15 years and hope to sell it for $8 million.

Funds raised to purchase the business would come from various sources at a cost of 12%.

Questions

1. Would you buy the business?
2. If so, how much would you offer Daniel Lewin if you wanted to make a 25% internal rate of return?

CASE 2: NATIONAL PHOTOCELL INC.

In early 2013, Bill MacMillan, one of the shareholders of National Photocell Inc., was completing a proposal for the expansion of his research-oriented business into a commercial supplier of photochemical equipment.

MacMillan felt his proposal was sound. However, he was concerned that the business might have difficulty raising funds, as the project would require a high level of financial support, particularly from high-risk capital investors.

Only a few firms, all with their own specialized production, were in the photochemical equipment industry. There was little direct product competition, and many opportunities existed for new product innovations. Companies in the industry were typically small, with sales generally less than $3 million per year. MacMillan's revenue forecast is shown on the statements of income (see Illustration 1). Revenue jumps from $1.0 million in 2014 to $8.0 million by 2019. The forecast period also shows that the net cash flows will have substantial increases from $70,000 in 2014 to $667,000 in 2019. However, National Photocell expects to show a negative net cash flow in 2015 of $536,000.

MacMillan felt that the company would require $1.5 million in financing to set up production, marketing, and training of personnel and for equipment purchases. Investment in capital assets for production start-up would take place in 2014 and continue in 2015. Other funds would be used for working capital, with the heaviest investment in inventories and trade receivables, which would also be required in 2014.

MacMillan felt that traditional lenders would be willing to finance about $500,000 of the new financial needs. This would help with the purchase of the capital assets and some working capital. The remaining $1.0 million would be raised from equity. About 60% of the new equity capital would be provided by existing shareholders and 40% by private investors. The statements of financial position (Illustration 2) show that the inflow of funds from the sale of the common shares would take place in 2014.

National Photocell Inc. would operate on a three-year cycle: high growth during the first two years, consolidation and planning for future growth during the third year. Marketing efforts will focus on North America for the first two years and then shift to Europe.

MacMillan was of the opinion that these financial needs and financing requirements were very accurate and realistic. Nevertheless, he felt that he would have to prepare a very effective and comprehensive investment proposal to attract one or two investors. He fully understood that risk capital investors are interested in ventures that offer the following:

- A good business opportunity, one that generates a high return
- An excellent management team
- A feasible exit strategy
- The ability to monitor and control their investment

MacMillan was prepared to explain to potential investors how National Photocell could meet their needs. The most important factor would be the potential return the investors expect to earn when they exit the business. MacMillan knew that the investors would want to exit their investment by 2019. He also knew that the business had to demonstrate a superior return. The investors must earn a return between 30% and 40%.

ILLUSTRATION 1
National Photocell Inc.
Projected Statements of Income
For the period ended December 31

(in $000s)	2014	2015	2016	2017	2018	2019
Revenue	1,000	2,500	3,500	5,000	7,000	8,000
Cost of sales	(700)	(1,750)	(2,380)	(3,350)	(4,620)	(5,200)
Gross profit	300	750	1,120	1,650	2,380	2,800
Expenses						
Distribution costs	(100)	(250)	(420)	(650)	(910)	(1,040)
Administrative expenses	(56)	(140)	(214)	(301)	(462)	(520)
Finance costs	(30)	(125)	(110)	(105)	(105)	(95)
Total expenses	(186)	(515)	(744)	(1,056)	(1,477)	(1,655)
Profit before taxes	114	235	376	594	903	1,145
Income tax expense	(34)	(71)	(132)	(220)	(361)	(458)
Profit for the year	80	164	244	374	542	687
Add back depreciation	50	100	110	120	125	130
Cash flow from operations	130	264	354	494	667	817
Investments in capital assets	(40)	(600)	(200)	(200)	(200)	(100)
Incremental working capital	(20)	(200)	(100)	(100)	(100)	(50)
Subtotal	(60)	(800)	(300)	(300)	(300)	(150)
Net cash flows	70	(536)	54	194	367	667

ILLUSTRATION 2
National Photocell Inc.
Protected Statements of Financial Position
As at December 31

(in $000s)	2014	2015	2016	2017	2018	2019
Assets						
Non-current assets (cost)	2,800	3,400	3,600	3,800	4,000	4,100
Accumulated depreciation	(300)	(400)	(510)	(630)	(755)	(885)
Non-current assets (net)	2,500	3,000	3,090	3,170	3,245	3,215
Current assets						
Inventories	170	430	644	803	1,200	1,407
Trade receivables	150	380	500	750	965	1,250
Prepaid expenses	50	55	75	80	105	120
Cash	20	25	40	100	250	650
Total current assets	390	890	1,259	1,733	2,520	3,427
Total assets	2,890	3,890	4,349	4,903	5,765	6,642
Equity						
Share capital	1,400	1,400	1,400	1,400	1,400	1,400
Retained earnings	150	315	559	933	1,475	2,162
Total equity	1,550	1,715	1,959	2,333	2,875	3,562
Liabilities						
Current liabilities						
Trade and other payables	75	150	170	190	200	240
Short-term borrowings	100	400	400	350	450	500
Accrued expenses	30	80	70	80	90	90
Taxes payable	35	45	50	50	50	50
Total current liabilities	240	675	690	670	790	880
Long-term borrowings	1,100	1,500	1,700	1,900	2,100	2,200
Total liabilities	1,340	2,175	2,390	2,570	2,890	3,080
Total equity and liabilities	2,890	3,890	4,349	4,903	5,765	6,642

On the basis of the following assumptions, answer the questions below:

- The discount rate used to calculate the net present value is 20%.
- The capitalization rate to calculate the capitalized value of National Photocell is 18%.
- The times-multiple ratio to calculate the total value at exit in 2019 is 8.5.
- The taxable portion of the capital gain on investment is 75%.
- The company's income tax rate is 50%.

Questions

1. What will the company's book value be by 2019?
2. What is the company's net present value from 2015 to 2019?
3. What is the company's capitalized value?
4. What is the company's fair market value?
5. What is the company's internal rate of return during the five-year period (2015–2019)?

6. What is the company's internal rate of return using the estimated fair market value?
7. What is the risk capital investor's internal rate of return on the investment on a before-tax basis? On an after-tax basis?
8. Give your overall impression about the company's financial projections by using the liquidity ratios, the debt/coverage ratios, the asset-management ratios, and the profitability ratios.
9. Do you think that the risk capital investors will be interested in this venture? Why or why not?

[APPENDIX A]

CompuTech Inc. Financial Statements

STATEMENTS OF INCOME
STATEMENTS OF COMPREHENSIVE INCOME
STATEMENTS OF CHANGES IN EQUITY
STATEMENTS OF FINANCIAL POSITION
(FOR THE YEARS 2013 TO 2015)

CompuTech Inc.
Statements of Income
For the years ended December 31
(in thousands of $)

	2015	2014	2013
Revenue	**800**	**420**	**350**
Cost of sales	(406)	(209)	(177)
Gross profit	**394**	**211**	**173**
Other income	5	5	5
Distribution costs			
Salaries	(80)	(60)	(50)
Commissions	(5)	(3)	(2)
Travelling	(5)	(3)	(2)
Advertising	(10)	(5)	(3)
Depreciation/amortization	(40)	(20)	(20)
Total distribution costs	(140)	(91)	(77)
Administrative expenses			
Salaries	(60)	(38)	(30)
Leasing	(10)	(7)	(5)
Depreciation/amortization	(40)	(20)	(18)
Total administrative expenses	(110)	(65)	(53)
Finance costs	(30)	(14)	(10)
Total other income/expenses	**(275)**	**(165)**	**(135)**
Profit before taxes	119	46	38
Income tax expense	(42)	(13)	(13)
Profit for the year	**77**	**33**	**25**

CompuTech Inc.
Statements of Comprehensive Income
For the years ended December 31
(in thousands of $)

	2015	2014	2013
Profit for the year	**77**	**33**	**25**
Other comprehensive income/(loss)			
Exchange differences on translating foreign operations	—	—	—
Cash flow hedges	—	—	—
Gains on property revaluation	—	—	—
Other comprehensive income/(loss) for the year, net of tax	—	—	—
Total comprehensive income for the year	77	33	25

CompuTech Inc.
Statements of Changes in Equity
For the years ended December 31
(in thousands of $)

	2015	2014	2013
Common shares			
Balance at beginning of year	100	100	100
Common shares issued	70	—	—
Dividend reinvestment and share purchase plan	—	—	—
Shares issued on exercise of stock options	—	—	—
Balance at end of year	170	100	100
Retained earnings			
Balance at beginning of year	58	25	0
Profit for the year	77	33	25
	135	58	25
Dividends	—	—	—
Balance at end of year	135	58	25
Contributed surplus			
Balance at beginning of year	—	—	—
Stock-based compensation	—	—	—
Options exercised	—	—	—
Balance at end of year	—	—	—
Total shareholders' equity	305	158	125

CompuTech Inc.
Statements of Financial Position
As at December 31
(in thousands of $)

	2015	2014	2013
Assets			
Non-current assets			
Property, plant, and equipment	560	210	170
Goodwill	—	—	—
Other intangible assets	—	—	—
Accumulated depreciation/amortization	(158)	(78)	(38)
Total non-current assets	402	132	132
Current assets			
Inventories	110	65	50
Trade receivables	90	45	35
Prepaid expenses	10	5	5
Cash and cash equivalents	25	21	15
Total current assets	235	136	105
Total assets	637	268	237
Equity and liabilities			
Equity			
Share capital	170	100	100
Retained earnings	135	58	25
Contributed surplus	—	—	—
Total equity	**305**	**158**	**125**
Liabilities			
Non-current liabilities			
Long-term borrowings	200	50	60
Current liabilities			
Trade and other payables	47	20	17
Short-term borrowings	75	35	30
Current portion of long-term borrowings	10	5	5
Total current liabilities	132	60	52
Total liabilities	332	110	112
Total equity and liabilities	637	268	237

[APPENDIX B]

Interest Tables

TABLE A: FUTURE VALUE INTEREST FACTOR (FVIF)

($1 at i% per period for n periods)

$$FVIF = (1 + i)^n$$

Year	1%	2%	3%	4%	5%	6%	7%	8%
1	1.010	1.020	1.030	1.040	1.050	1.060	1.070	1.080
2	1.020	1.040	1.061	1.082	1.103	1.124	1.145	1.166
3	1.030	1.061	1.093	1.125	1.158	1.191	1.225	1.260
4	1.041	1.082	1.126	1.170	1.216	1.262	1.311	1.360
5	1.051	1.104	1.159	1.217	1.276	1.338	1.403	1.469
6	1.062	1.126	1.194	1.265	1.340	1.419	1.501	1.587
7	1.072	1.149	1.230	1.316	1.407	1.504	1.606	1.714
8	1.083	1.172	1.267	1.369	1.477	1.594	1.718	1.851
9	1.094	1.195	1.305	1.423	1.551	1.689	1.838	1.999
10	1.105	1.219	1.344	1.480	1.629	1.791	1.967	2.159
11	1.116	1.243	1.384	1.539	1.710	1.898	2.105	2.332
12	1.127	1.268	1.426	1.601	1.796	2.012	2.252	2.518
13	1.138	1.294	1.469	1.665	1.886	2.133	2.410	2.720
14	1.149	1.319	1.513	1.732	1.980	2.261	2.579	2.937
15	1.161	1.346	1.558	1.801	2.079	2.397	2.759	3.172
16	1.173	1.373	1.605	1.873	2.183	2.540	2.952	3.426
17	1.184	1.400	1.653	1.948	2.292	2.693	3.159	3.700
18	1.196	1.428	1.702	2.026	2.407	2.854	3.380	3.996
19	1.208	1.457	1.754	2.107	2.527	3.026	3.617	4.316
20	1.220	1.486	1.806	2.191	2.653	3.207	3.870	4.661
21	1.232	1.516	1.860	2.279	2.786	3.400	4.141	5.034
22	1.245	1.546	1.916	2.370	2.925	3.604	4.430	5.437
23	1.257	1.577	1.974	2.465	3.072	3.820	4.741	5.871
24	1.270	1.608	2.033	2.563	3.225	4.049	5.072	6.341
25	1.282	1.641	2.094	2.666	3.386	4.292	5.427	6.848

Year	9%	10%	11%	12%	14%	16%	18%	20%
1	1.090	1.100	1.110	1.120	1.140	1.160	1.180	1.200
2	1.188	1.210	1.232	1.254	1.300	1.346	1.392	1.440
3	1.295	1.331	1.368	1.405	1.482	1.561	1.643	1.728
4	1.412	1.464	1.518	1.574	1.689	1.811	1.939	2.074
5	1.539	1.611	1.685	1.762	1.925	2.100	2.288	2.488
6	1.677	1.772	1.870	1.974	2.195	2.436	2.700	2.986
7	1.828	1.949	2.076	2.211	2.502	2.826	3.185	3.583
8	1.993	2.144	2.305	2.476	2.853	3.278	3.759	4.300
9	2.172	2.358	2.558	2.773	3.252	3.803	4.435	5.160
10	2.367	2.594	2.839	3.106	3.707	4.411	5.234	6.192
11	2.580	2.853	3.152	3.479	4.226	5.117	6.176	7.430
12	2.813	3.138	3.498	3.896	4.818	5.936	7.288	8.916
13	3.066	3.452	3.883	4.363	5.492	6.886	8.599	10.699
14	3.342	3.798	4.310	4.887	6.261	7.988	10.147	12.839
15	3.642	4.177	4.785	5.474	7.138	9.266	11.974	15.407
16	3.970	4.595	5.311	6.130	8.137	10.748	14.129	18.488
17	4.328	5.054	5.895	6.866	9.276	12.468	16.672	22.186
18	4.717	5.560	6.544	7.690	10.575	14.463	19.673	26.623
19	5.142	6.116	7.263	8.613	12.056	16.777	23.214	31.948
20	5.604	6.728	8.062	9.646	13.744	19.461	27.393	38.338
21	6.109	7.400	8.949	10.804	15.668	22.575	32.324	46.005
22	6.659	8.140	9.934	12.100	17.861	26.186	38.142	55.206
23	7.258	8.954	11.026	13.552	20.362	30.376	45.008	66.247
24	7.911	9.850	12.239	15.179	23.212	35.236	53.109	79.497
25	8.623	10.835	13.586	17.000	26.462	40.874	62.669	95.396

Year	22%	24%	26%	28%	30%	32%	34%	36%
1	1.220	1.240	1.260	1.280	1.300	1.320	1.340	1.360
2	1.488	1.538	1.588	1.638	1.690	1.742	1.796	1.850
3	1.816	1.907	2.000	2.097	2.197	2.300	2.406	2.515
4	2.215	2.364	2.520	2.684	2.856	3.036	3.036	3.421
5	2.703	2.932	3.176	3.436	3.713	4.007	4.320	4.653
6	3.297	3.635	4.002	4.398	4.827	5.290	5.789	6.328
7	4.023	4.508	5.042	5.630	6.275	6.983	7.758	8.605
8	4.908	5.590	6.353	7.206	8.157	9.217	10.395	11.703
9	5.987	6.931	8.005	9.223	10.605	12.167	13.930	15.917
10	7.305	8.594	10.086	11.806	13.786	16.060	18.666	21.647
11	8.912	10.657	12.708	15.112	17.922	21.199	25.012	29.439
12	10.872	13.215	16.012	19.343	23.298	27.983	33.516	40.038
13	13.264	16.386	20.175	24.759	30.288	36.937	44.912	54.451
14	16.182	20.319	25.421	31.691	39.374	48.757	60.182	74.053
15	19.742	25.196	32.030	40.565	51.186	64.359	80.644	100.713
16	24.086	31.243	40.358	51.923	66.542	84.954	108.063	136.969
17	29.384	38.741	50.851	66.461	86.504	112.139	144.804	186.278
18	35.849	48.039	64.072	85.071	112.455	148.024	194.038	253.338
19	43.736	59.568	80.731	108.890	146.192	195.391	260.011	344.540
20	53.358	73.864	101.721	139.380	190.049	257.916	348.414	468.574
21	65.096	91.592	128.169	178.406	247.064	340.450	466.875	637.261
22	79.418	113.574	161.492	228.360	321.184	449.394	625.613	866.675
23	96.890	140.831	203.480	292.300	417.539	593.200	838.321	1178.680
24	118.205	174.631	256.385	374.144	542.800	783.024	1123.350	1603.000
25	144.210	216.542	323.045	478.905	705.640	1033.590	1505.290	2180.080

TABLE B: PRESENT VALUE INTEREST FACTOR (PVIF)

(\$1 at i% per period for n periods)

$$PVIF = \frac{1}{(1 + i)^n}$$

N	1%	2%	3%	4%	5%	6%	7%	8%
1	0.99010	0.98039	0.97087	0.96154	0.95238	0.94340	0.93458	0.92593
2	0.98030	0.96117	0.94260	0.92456	0.90703	0.89000	0.87344	0.85734
3	0.97059	0.94232	0.91514	0.88900	0.86384	0.83962	0.81630	0.79383
4	0.96098	0.92385	0.88849	0.85480	0.82270	0.79209	0.76290	0.73503
5	0.95147	0.90573	0.86261	0.82193	0.78353	0.74726	0.71299	0.68058
6	0.94204	0.88797	0.83748	0.79031	0.74622	0.70496	0.66634	0.63017
7	0.93272	0.87056	0.81309	0.75992	0.71068	0.66506	0.62275	0.58349
8	0.92348	0.85349	0.78941	0.73069	0.67684	0.62741	0.58201	0.54027
9	0.91434	0.83675	0.76642	0.70259	0.64461	0.59190	0.54393	0.50025
10	0.90529	0.82035	0.74409	0.67556	0.61391	0.55839	0.50835	0.46319
11	0.89632	0.80426	0.72242	0.64958	0.58468	0.52679	0.47509	0.42888
12	0.88745	0.78849	0.70138	0.62460	0.55684	0.49697	0.44401	0.39711
13	0.87866	0.77303	0.68095	0.60057	0.53032	0.46884	0.41496	0.36770
14	0.86996	0.75787	0.66112	0.57747	0.50507	0.44230	0.38782	0.34046
15	0.86135	0.74301	0.64186	0.55526	0.48102	0.41726	0.36245	0.31524
16	0.85282	0.72845	0.62317	0.53391	0.45811	0.39365	0.33873	0.29189
17	0.84438	0.71416	0.60502	0.51337	0.43630	0.37136	0.31657	0.27027
18	0.83602	0.70016	0.58739	0.49363	0.41552	0.35034	0.29586	0.25025
19	0.82774	0.68643	0.57029	0.47464	0.39573	0.33051	0.27651	0.23171
20	0.81954	0.67297	0.55367	0.45639	0.37689	0.31180	0.25842	0.21455
21	0.81143	0.65978	0.53755	0.43883	0.35894	0.29415	0.24151	0.19866
22	0.80340	0.64684	0.52189	0.42195	0.34185	0.27750	0.22571	0.18394
23	0.79544	0.63416	0.50669	0.40573	0.32557	0.26180	0.21095	0.17031
24	0.78757	0.62172	0.49193	0.39012	0.31007	0.24698	0.19715	0.15770
25	0.77977	0.60953	0.47760	0.37512	0.29530	0.23300	0.18425	0.14602

N	9%	10%	11%	12%	13%	14%	15%	16%
1	0.91743	0.90909	0.90090	0.89286	0.88496	0.87719	0.86957	0.86207
2	0.84168	0.82645	0.81162	0.79719	0.78315	0.76947	0.75614	0.74316
3	0.77218	0.75131	0.73119	0.71178	0.69305	0.67497	0.65752	0.64066
4	0.70843	0.68301	0.65873	0.63552	0.61332	0.59208	0.57175	0.55229
5	0.64993	0.62092	0.59345	0.56743	0.54276	0.51937	0.49718	0.47611
6	0.59627	0.56447	0.53464	0.50663	0.48032	0.45559	0.43233	0.41044
7	0.54703	0.51316	0.48166	0.45235	0.42506	0.39964	0.37594	0.35383
8	0.50187	0.46651	0.43393	0.40388	0.37616	0.35056	0.32690	0.30503
9	0.46043	0.42410	0.39092	0.36061	0.33288	0.30751	0.28426	0.26295
10	0.42241	0.38554	0.35218	0.32197	0.29459	0.26974	0.24718	0.22668
11	0.38753	0.35049	0.31728	0.28748	0.26070	0.23662	0.21494	0.19542
12	0.35553	0.31863	0.28584	0.25667	0.23071	0.20756	0.18691	0.16846
13	0.32618	0.28966	0.25751	0.22917	0.20416	0.18207	0.16253	0.14523
14	0.29925	0.26333	0.23199	0.20462	0.18068	0.15971	0.14133	0.12520
15	0.27454	0.23939	0.20900	0.18270	0.15989	0.14010	0.12289	0.10793
16	0.25187	0.21763	0.18829	0.16312	0.14150	0.12289	0.10686	0.09304
17	0.23107	0.19784	0.16963	0.14564	0.12522	0.10780	0.09293	0.08021
18	0.21199	0.17986	0.15282	0.13004	0.11081	0.09456	0.08080	0.06914
19	0.19449	0.16351	0.13768	0.11611	0.09806	0.08295	0.07026	0.05961
20	0.17843	0.14864	0.12403	0.10367	0.08678	0.07276	0.06110	0.05139
21	0.16370	0.13513	0.11174	0.09256	0.07680	0.06383	0.05313	0.04430
22	0.15018	0.12285	0.10067	0.08264	0.06796	0.05599	0.04620	0.03819
23	0.13778	0.11168	0.09069	0.07379	0.06014	0.04911	0.04017	0.03292
24	0.12640	0.10153	0.08170	0.06588	0.05322	0.04308	0.03493	0.02838
25	0.11597	0.09230	0.07361	0.05882	0.04710	0.03779	0.03038	0.02447

N	17%	18%	19%	20%	21%	22%	23%	24%
1	0.85470	0.84746	0.84034	0.83333	0.82645	0.81967	0.81301	0.80645
2	0.73051	0.71818	0.70616	0.69444	0.68301	0.67186	0.66098	0.65036
3	0.62437	0.60863	0.59342	0.57870	0.56447	0.55071	0.53738	0.52449
4	0.53365	0.51579	0.49867	0.48225	0.46651	0.45140	0.43690	0.42297
5	0.45611	0.43711	0.41905	0.40188	0.38554	0.37000	0.35520	0.34111
6	0.38984	0.37043	0.35214	0.33490	0.31863	0.30328	0.28878	0.27509
7	0.33320	0.31392	0.29592	0.27908	0.26333	0.24859	0.23478	0.22184
8	0.28478	0.26604	0.24867	0.23257	0.21763	0.20376	0.19088	0.17891
9	0.24340	0.22546	0.20897	0.19381	0.17986	0.16702	0.15519	0.14428
10	0.20804	0.19106	0.17560	0.16151	0.14864	0.13690	0.12617	0.11635
11	0.17781	0.16192	0.14756	0.13459	0.12285	0.11221	0.10258	0.09383
12	0.15197	0.13722	0.12400	0.11216	0.10153	0.09198	0.08339	0.07567
13	0.12989	0.11629	0.10420	0.09346	0.08391	0.07539	0.06780	0.06103
14	0.11102	0.09855	0.08757	0.07789	0.06934	0.06180	0.05512	0.04921
15	0.09489	0.08352	0.07359	0.06491	0.05731	0.05065	0.04481	0.03969
16	0.08110	0.07078	0.06184	0.05409	0.04736	0.04152	0.03643	0.03201
17	0.06932	0.05998	0.05196	0.04507	0.03914	0.03403	0.02962	0.02581
18	0.05925	0.05083	0.04367	0.03756	0.03235	0.02789	0.02408	0.02082
19	0.05064	0.04308	0.03669	0.03130	0.02673	0.02286	0.01958	0.01679
20	0.04328	0.03651	0.03084	0.02608	0.02209	0.01874	0.01592	0.01354
21	0.03699	0.03094	0.02591	0.02174	0.01826	0.01536	0.01294	0.01092
22	0.03162	0.02622	0.02178	0.01811	0.01509	0.01259	0.01052	0.00880
23	0.02702	0.02222	0.01830	0.01509	0.01247	0.01032	0.00855	0.00710
24	0.02310	0.01883	0.01538	0.01258	0.01031	0.00846	0.00695	0.00573
25	0.01974	0.01596	0.01292	0.01048	0.00852	0.00693	0.00565	0.00462

N	25%	26%	27%	28%	29%	30%	31%	32%
1	0.80000	0.79365	0.78740	0.78125	0.77519	0.76923	0.76336	0.75758
2	0.64000	0.62988	0.62000	0.61035	0.60093	0.59172	0.58272	0.57392
3	0.51200	0.49991	0.48819	0.47684	0.46583	0.45517	0.44482	0.43479
4	0.40960	0.39675	0.38440	0.37253	0.36111	0.35013	0.33956	0.32939
5	0.32768	0.31488	0.30268	0.29104	0.27993	0.26933	0.25920	0.24953
6	0.26214	0.24991	0.23833	0.22737	0.21700	0.20718	0.19787	0.18904
7	0.20972	0.19834	0.18766	0.17764	0.16822	0.15937	0.15104	0.14321
8	0.16777	0.15741	0.14776	0.13878	0.13040	0.12259	0.11530	0.10849
9	0.13422	0.12493	0.11635	0.10842	0.10109	0.09430	0.08802	0.08219
10	0.10737	0.09915	0.09161	0.08470	0.07836	0.07254	0.06719	0.06227
11	0.08590	0.07869	0.07214	0.06617	0.06075	0.05580	0.05129	0.04717
12	0.06872	0.06245	0.05680	0.05170	0.04709	0.04292	0.03915	0.03574
13	0.05498	0.04957	0.04472	0.04039	0.03650	0.03302	0.02989	0.02707
14	0.04398	0.03934	0.03522	0.03155	0.02830	0.02540	0.02281	0.02051
15	0.03518	0.03122	0.02773	0.02465	0.02194	0.01954	0.01742	0.01554
16	0.02815	0.02478	0.02183	0.01926	0.01700	0.01503	0.01329	0.01177
17	0.02252	0.01967	0.01719	0.01505	0.01318	0.01156	0.01015	0.00892
18	0.01801	0.01561	0.01354	0.01175	0.01022	0.00889	0.00775	0.00676
19	0.01441	0.01239	0.01066	0.00918	0.00792	0.00684	0.00591	0.00512
20	0.01153	0.00983	0.00839	0.00717	0.00614	0.00526	0.00451	0.00388
21	0.00922	0.00780	0.00661	0.00561	0.00476	0.00405	0.00345	0.00294
22	0.00738	0.00619	0.00520	0.00438	0.00369	0.00311	0.00263	0.00223
23	0.00590	0.00491	0.00410	0.00342	0.00286	0.00239	0.00201	0.00169
24	0.00472	0.00390	0.00323	0.00267	0.00222	0.00184	0.00153	0.00128
25	0.00378	0.00310	0.00254	0.00209	0.00172	0.00142	0.00117	0.00097

TABLE C: FUTURE VALUE INTEREST FACTOR OF AN ANNUITY (FVIFA)

($1 per period at i% per period for n periods)

$$FVIFA = \frac{(1 + i)^n - 1}{i}$$

N	1%	2%	3%	4%	5%	6%	7%	8%
1	1.000	1.000	1.000	1.000	1.000	1.000	1.000	1.000
2	2.010	2.020	2.030	2.040	2.050	2.060	2.070	2.080
3	3.030	3.060	3.091	3.122	3.153	3.184	3.215	3.246
4	4.060	4.122	4.184	4.246	4.310	4.375	4.440	4.506
5	5.101	5.204	5.309	5.416	5.526	5.637	5.751	5.867
6	6.152	6.308	6.468	6.633	6.802	6.975	7.153	7.336
7	7.214	7.434	7.662	7.898	8.142	8.394	8.654	8.923
8	8.286	8.583	8.892	9.214	9.549	9.897	10.260	10.637
9	9.369	9.755	10.159	10.583	11.027	11.491	11.978	12.488
10	10.462	10.950	11.464	12.006	12.578	13.181	13.817	14.487
11	11.567	12.169	12.808	13.486	14.207	14.972	15.784	16.646
12	12.683	13.412	14.192	15.026	15.917	16.870	17.889	18.977
13	13.809	14.680	15.618	16.627	17.713	18.882	20.141	21.495
14	14.947	15.974	17.086	18.292	19.599	21.015	22.551	24.215
15	16.097	17.293	18.599	20.024	21.579	23.276	25.129	27.152
16	17.258	18.639	20.157	21.825	23.658	25.673	27.888	30.324
17	18.430	20.012	21.762	23.698	25.840	28.213	30.840	33.750
18	19.615	21.412	23.414	25.645	28.132	30.906	33.999	37.450
19	20.811	22.841	25.117	27.671	30.539	33.760	37.379	41.446
20	22.019	24.297	26.870	29.778	33.066	36.786	40.996	45.762
21	23.239	25.783	28.677	31.969	35.719	39.993	44.865	50.423
22	24.472	27.299	30.537	34.248	38.505	43.392	49.006	55.457
23	25.716	28.845	32.453	36.618	41.430	46.996	53.436	60.893
24	26.974	30.422	34.427	39.083	44.502	50.816	58.177	66.765
25	28.243	32.030	36.459	41.646	47.727	54.864	63.249	73.106

N	9%	10%	11%	12%	14%	16%	18%	20%
1	1.000	1.000	1.000	1.000	1.000	1.000	1.000	1.000
2	2.090	2.100	2.110	2.120	2.140	2.160	2.180	2.200
3	3.278	3.310	3.342	3.374	3.440	3.506	3.572	3.640
4	4.573	4.641	4.710	4.779	4.921	5.066	5.215	5.368
5	5.985	6.105	6.228	6.353	6.610	6.877	7.154	7.442
6	7.523	7.716	7.913	8.115	8.536	8.977	9.442	9.930
7	9.200	9.487	9.783	10.089	10.731	11.414	12.142	12.916
8	11.029	11.436	11.859	12.300	13.233	14.240	15.327	16.499
9	13.021	13.580	14.164	14.776	16.085	17.519	19.086	20.799
10	15.193	15.937	16.722	17.549	19.337	21.322	23.521	25.959
11	17.560	18.531	19.561	20.655	23.045	25.733	28.755	32.150
12	20.141	21.384	22.713	24.133	27.271	30.850	34.931	39.581
13	22.953	24.523	26.212	28.029	32.089	36.786	42.219	48.497
14	26.019	27.975	30.095	32.393	37.581	43.672	50.818	59.196
15	29.361	31.773	34.405	37.280	43.842	51.660	60.965	72.035
16	33.003	35.950	39.190	42.753	50.980	60.925	72.939	87.442
17	36.974	40.545	44.501	48.884	59.118	71.673	87.068	105.931
18	41.301	45.599	50.396	55.750	68.394	84.141	103.740	128.117
19	46.019	51.159	56.940	63.440	78.969	98.603	123.413	154.740
20	51.160	57.275	64.203	72.052	91.025	115.380	146.628	186.688
21	56.765	64.003	72.265	81.699	104.768	134.840	174.021	225.026
22	62.873	71.403	81.214	92.503	120.436	157.415	206.345	271.031
23	69.532	79.543	91.148	104.603	138.297	183.601	244.487	326.237
24	76.790	88.497	102.174	118.155	158.659	213.977	289.494	392.404
25	84.701	98.347	114.413	133.334	181.871	249.214	342.603	471.981

N	22%	24%	26%	28%	30%	32%	34%	36%
1	1.000	1.000	1.000	1.000	1.000	1.000	1.000	1.000
2	2.220	2.240	2.260	2.280	2.300	2.320	2.340	2.360
3	3.708	3.778	3.848	3.918	3.990	4.062	4.136	4.210
4	5.524	5.684	5.848	6.016	6.187	6.362	6.542	6.725
5	7.740	8.048	8.368	8.700	9.043	9.398	9.766	10.146
6	10.442	10.980	11.544	12.136	12.756	13.406	14.086	14.799
7	13.740	14.615	15.546	16.534	17.583	18.696	19.876	21.126
8	17.762	19.123	20.588	22.163	23.858	25.678	27.633	29.732
9	22.670	24.713	26.940	29.369	32.015	34.895	38.029	41.435
10	28.657	31.643	34.945	38.593	42.620	47.062	51.958	57.352
11	35.962	40.238	45.031	50.399	56.405	63.122	70.624	78.998
12	44.874	50.895	57.739	65.510	74.327	84.321	95.637	108.438
13	55.746	64.110	73.751	84.853	97.625	112.303	129.153	148.475
14	69.010	80.496	93.926	109.612	127.912	149.240	174.065	202.926
15	85.192	100.815	119.347	141.303	167.286	197.997	234.247	276.979
16	104.935	126.011	151.377	181.868	218.472	262.356	314.891	377.692
17	129.020	157.253	191.735	233.791	285.014	347.310	422.954	514.661
18	158.405	195.994	242.586	300.252	371.518	459.449	567.758	700.939
19	194.254	244.033	306.658	385.323	483.973	607.473	761.796	954.278
20	237.989	303.601	387.389	494.213	630.165	802.864	1021.810	1298.820
21	291.347	377.465	489.110	633.592	820.214	1060.780	1370.220	1767.390
22	356.444	469.057	617.278	811.998	1067.280	1401.230	1837.100	2404.650
23	435.861	582.630	778.771	1040.360	1388.460	1850.620	2462.710	3271.330
24	532.751	723.461	982.251	1332.660	1806.000	2443.820	3301.030	4450.010
25	650.956	898.092	1238.640	1706.800	2348.800	3226.850	4424.380	6053.010

TABLE D: PRESENT VALUE INTEREST FACTOR OF AN ANNUITY (PVIFA)

(\$1 per period at *i*% per period for *n* periods)

$$PVIFA = \frac{1 - \frac{1}{(1+i)^n}}{i}$$

Year	1%	2%	3%	4%	5%	6%	7%	8%
1	0.9901	0.9804	0.9709	0.9615	0.9524	0.9434	0.9346	0.9259
2	1.9704	1.9416	1.9135	1.8861	1.8594	1.8334	1.8080	1.7833
3	2.9410	2.8839	2.8286	2.7751	2..7232	2.6730	2.6243	2.5771
4	3.9020	3.8077	3.7171	3.6299	3.5459	3.4651	3.3872	3.3121
5	4.8535	4.7134	4.5797	4.4518	4.3295	4.2123	4.1002	3.9927
6	5.7955	5.6014	5.4172	5.2421	5.0757	4.9173	4.7665	4.6229
7	6.7282	6.4720	6.2302	6.0020	5.7863	5.5824	5.3893	5.2064
8	7.6517	7.3254	7.0196	6.7327	6.4632	6.2098	5.9713	5.7466
9	8.5661	8.1622	7.7861	7.4353	7.1078	6.8017	6.5152	6.2469
10	9.4714	8.9825	8.5302	8.1109	7.7217	7.3601	7.0236	6.7101
11	10.3677	9.7868	9.2526	8.7604	8.3064	7.8868	7.4987	7.1389
12	11.2552	10.5753	9.9539	9.3850	8.8632	8.3838	7.9427	7.5361
13	12.1338	11.3483	10.6349	9.9856	9.3935	8.8527	8.3576	7.9038
14	13.0038	12.1062	11.2960	10.5631	9.8986	9.2950	8.7454	8.2442
15	13.8651	12.8492	11.9379	11.1183	10.3796	9.7122	9.1079	8.5595
16	14.7180	13.5777	12.5610	11.6522	10.8377	10.1059	9.4466	8.8514
17	15.5624	14.2918	13.1660	12.1656	11.2740	10.4772	9.7632	9.1216
18	16.3984	14.9920	13.7534	12.6592	11.6895	10.8276	10.0591	9.3719
19	17.2261	15.6784	14.3237	13.1339	12.0853	11.1581	10.3356	9.6036
20	18.0457	16.3514	14.8774	13.5903	12.4622	11.4699	10.5940	9.8181
21	18.8571	17.0111	15.4149	14.0291	12.8211	11.7640	10.8355	10.0168
22	19.6605	17.6580	15.9368	14.4511	13.1630	12.0416	11.0612	10.2007
23	20.4559	18.2921	16.4435	14.8568	13.4885	12.3033	11.2722	10.3710
24	21.2435	18.9139	16.9355	15.2469	13.7986	12.5503	11.4693	10.5287
25	22.0233	19.5234	17.4131	15.6220	14.0939	12.7833	11.6536	10.6748

Year	9%	10%	11%	12%	13%	14%	15%	16%
1	0.9174	0.9091	0.9009	0.8929	0.8850	0.8772	0.8696	0.8621
2	1.7591	1.7355	1.7125	1.6901	1.6681	1.6467	1.6257	1.6052
3	2.5313	2.4868	2.4437	2.4018	2.3612	2.3216	2.2832	2.2459
4	3.2397	3.1699	3.1024	3.0373	2.9745	2.9137	2.8550	2.7982
5	3.8896	3.7908	3.6959	3.6048	3.5172	3.4331	3.3522	3.2743
6	4.4859	4.3553	4.2305	4.1114	3.9976	3.8887	3.7845	3.6847
7	5.0329	4.8684	4.7122	4.5638	4.4226	4.2883	4.1604	4.0386
8	5.5348	5.3349	5.1461	4.9676	4.7988	4.6389	4.4873	4.3436
9	5.9952	5.7590	5.5370	5.3282	5.1317	4.9464	4.7716	4.6065
10	6.4176	6.1446	5.8892	5.6502	5.4262	5.2161	5.0188	4.8332
11	6.8052	6.4951	6.2065	5.9377	5.6869	5.4527	5.2337	5.0286
12	7.1607	6.8137	6.4924	6.1944	5.9176	5.6603	5.4206	5.1971
13	7.4869	7.1034	6.7499	6.4235	6.1218	5.8424	5.5831	5.3423
14	7.7861	7.3667	6.9819	6.6282	6.3025	6.0021	5.7245	5.4675
15	8.0607	7.6061	7.1909	6.8109	6.4624	6.1422	5.8474	5.5755
16	8.3125	7.8237	7.3792	6.9740	6.6039	6.2651	5.9542	5.6685
17	8.5436	8.0215	7.5488	7.1196	6.7291	6.3729	6.0472	5.7487
18	8.7556	8.2014	7.7016	7.2497	6.8399	6.4674	6.1280	5.8178
19	8.9501	8.3649	7.8393	7.3658	6.9380	6.5504	6.1982	5.8775
20	9.1285	8.5136	7.9633	7.4694	7.0248	6.6231	6.2593	5.9288
21	9.2922	8.6487	8.0751	7.5620	7.1016	6.6870	6.3125	5.9731
22	9.4424	8.7715	8.1757	7.6446	7.1695	6.7429	6.3587	6.0113
23	9.5802	8.8832	8.2664	7.7184	7.2297	6.7921	6.3988	6.0442
24	9.7066	8.9847	8.3481	7.7843	7.2829	6.8351	6.4338	6.0726
25	9.8226	9.0770	8.4217	7.8431	7.3300	6.8729	6.4641	6.0971

Year	17%	18%	19%	20%	21%	22%	23%	24%
1	0.8547	0.8475	0.8403	0.8333	0.8264	0.8197	0.8130	0.8065
2	1.5852	1.5656	1.5465	1.5278	1.5095	1.4915	1.4740	1.4568
3	2.2096	2.1743	2.1399	2.1065	2.0739	2.0422	2.0114	1.9813
4	2.7432	2.6901	2.6386	2.5887	2.5404	2.4936	2.4483	2.4043
5	3.1993	3.1272	3.0576	2.9906	2.9260	2.8636	2.8035	2.7454
6	3.5892	3.4976	3.4098	3.3255	3.2446	3.1669	3.0923	3.0205
7	3.9224	3.8115	3.7057	3.6046	3.5079	3.4155	3.3270	3.2423
8	4.2072	4.0776	3.9544	3.8372	3.7256	3.6193	3.5179	3.4212
9	4.4506	4.3030	4.1633	4.0310	3.9054	3.7863	3.6731	3.5655
10	4.6586	4.4941	4.3389	4.1925	4.0541	3.9232	3.7993	3.6819
11	4.8364	4.6560	4.4865	4.3271	4.1769	4.0354	3.9018	3.7757
12	4.9884	4.7932	4.6105	4.4392	4.2785	4.1274	3.9852	3.8514
13	5.1183	4.9095	4.7147	4.5327	4.3624	4.2028	4.0530	3.9124
14	5.2293	5.0081	4.8023	4.6106	4.4317	4.2646	4.1082	3.9616
15	5.3242	5.0916	4.8759	4.6755	4.4890	4.3152	4.1530	4.0013
16	5.4053	5.1624	4.9377	4.7296	4.5364	4.3567	4.1894	4.0333
17	5.4746	5.2223	4.9897	4.7746	4.5755	4.3908	4.2190	4.0591
18	5.5339	5.2732	5.0333	4.8122	4.6079	4.4187	4.2431	4.0799
19	5.5845	5.3162	5.0700	4.8435	4.6346	4.4415	4.2627	4.0967
20	5.6278	5.3527	5.1009	4.8696	4.6567	4.4603	4.2786	4.1103
21	5.6648	5.3837	5.1268	4.8913	4.6750	4.4756	4.2916	4.1212
22	5.6964	5.4099	5.1486	4.9094	4.6900	4.4882	4.3021	4.1300
23	5.7234	5.4321	5.1668	4.9245	4.7025	4.4985	4.3106	4.1371
24	5.7465	5.4509	5.1822	4.9371	4.7128	4.5070	4.3176	4.1428
25	5.7662	5.4669	5.1951	4.9476	4.7213	4.5139	4.3232	4.1474

Year	25%	26%	27%	28%	29%	30%	31%	32%
1	0.8000	0.7937	0.7874	0.7813	0.7752	0.7692	0.7634	0.7576
2	1.4400	1.4235	1.4074	1.3916	1.3761	1.3609	1.3461	1.3315
3	1.9520	1.9234	1.8956	1.8684	1.8420	1.8161	1.7909	1.7663
4	2.3616	2.3202	2.2800	2.2410	2.2031	2.1662	2.1305	2.0957
5	2.6893	2.6351	2.5827	2.5320	2.4830	2.4356	2.3897	2.3452
6	2.9514	2.8850	2.8210	2.7594	2.7000	2.6427	2.5875	2.5342
7	3.1611	3.0833	3.0087	2.9370	2.8682	2.8021	2.7386	2.6775
8	3.3289	3.2407	3.1564	3.0758	2.9986	2.9247	2.8539	2.7860
9	3.4631	3.3657	3.2728	3.1842	3.0997	3.0190	2.9419	2.8681
10	3.5705	3.4648	3.3644	3.2689	3.1781	3.0915	3.0091	2.9304
11	3.6564	3.5435	3.4365	3.3351	3.2388	3.1473	3.0604	2.9776
12	3.7251	3.6060	3.4933	3.3868	3.2859	3.1903	3.0995	3.0133
13	3.7801	3.6555	3.6381	3.4272	3.3224	3.2233	3.1294	3.0404
14	3.8241	3.6949	3.5733	3.4587	3.3507	3.2487	3.1522	3.0609
15	3.8593	3.7261	3.6010	3.4834	3.3726	3.2682	3.1696	3.0764
16	3.8874	3.7509	3.6228	3.5026	3.3896	3.2832	3.1829	3.0882
17	3.9099	3.7705	3.6400	3.5177	3.4028	3.2948	3.1931	3.0971
18	3.9279	3.7861	3.6536	3.5294	3.4130	3.3037	3.2008	3.1039
19	3.9424	3.7985	3.6642	3.5386	3.4210	3.3105	3.2067	3.1090
20	3.9539	3.8083	3.6726	3.5458	3.4271	3.3158	3.2112	3.1129
21	3.9631	3.8161	3.6792	3.5514	3.4319	3.3198	3.2147	3.1158
22	3.9705	3.8223	3.6844	3.5558	3.4356	3.3230	3.2173	3.1180
23	3.9764	3.8273	3.6885	3.5592	3.4384	3.3254	3.2193	3.1197
24	3.9811	3.8312	3.6918	3.5619	3.4406	3.3272	3.2209	3.1210
25	3.9849	3.8342	3.6943	3.5640	3.4423	3.3286	3.2220	3.1220

[GLOSSARY]

A

Accounting The process of recording and summarizing business transactions on a company's financial statements. p. 45

Accounting equation Assets = Equity + Liabilities or Assets − Liabilities = Equity p. 39

Accounting methods Calculations of the book value rate of return by using data from financial statements. p. 474

Accrual method An accounting method that considers sales when made and costs when incurred, regardless of when the transaction takes place. p. 47

Accrued liability What a company owes for services it has received and not yet paid or an expense that has been incurred but not recorded. p. 65

Adjustment in non-cash working capital accounts The cash flow provided (or used) by working capital accounts, such as trade receivables, inventories, and trade and other payables. p. 100

Administrative expenses Expenses that are not directly related to producing and selling goods or services. p. 50

Aging of accounts receivable A report showing how long trade receivables have been outstanding; it gives the percentage of receivables past due for one month, two months, or other periods. p. 241

Angel investors High-net-worth individuals looking for investment opportunities. p. 334

Annual report A report issued annually by corporations to their shareholders that contains the financial statements and management's opinion of the company's past year's operations and prospects for the future. p. 67

Annuity A series of payments (or receipts) of a fixed amount for a specified number of years. p. 436

Assessed value A valuation method used by municipal governments for determining property taxes. p. 515

Asset valuation A method used to restate the numbers appearing on financial statements. p. 523

Asset-based financing A form of short-term risk capital financing. p. 352

Asset-management ratios Measures to evaluate how efficiently managers use the assets of a business. p. 142

Assets Resources that a business owns to produce goods and services (e.g., buildings, equipment, trade receivables, inventories). p. 58

Auditor's report A report prepared by an independent accounting firm that is presented to a company's shareholders. p. 67

Average collection period (ACP) How many days it takes for customers to pay their bills. p. 143

B

Balanced Scorecard A management system that can translate an organization's mission, vision, and strategies into measurable targets and action plans. p. 279

Benchmarking The process of searching for the best practices by comparing your own business to a competitor's excellent performance. p. 152

Benchmarks Excellent industry norms to which a business's own financial ratios can be compared. p. 152

Bond A long-term loan (10 to 30 years) that can be secured or unsecured. p. 340

Book value The accounting value of an asset (the original cost minus total depreciation to date) shown on the financial statements as a firm's assets. p. 509

Bookkeeping The activity that involves collecting, classifying, and reporting accounting transactions. p. 39

Bookkeeping and accounting cycle The steps involved in processing financial transactions for preparing financial statements. p. 40

Break-even chart A graphic that shows the effect of change in both revenue and costs on profit. p. 190

Break-even point The level of production at which revenues equal total costs. p. 186

Break-even wedge A tool that helps managers to determine the best way of structuring operating costs (fixed versus variable). p. 203

Budgeting The process by which management allocates corporate resources, evaluates financial outcomes, and sets systems to control operational and financial performance. p. 277

Business plan A document that gives a complete picture about an organization's goals, plans, operating activities, financial needs, and financing requirements. p. 288

Business risk The uncertainty built into projecting the level of revenue and EBIT. p. 327

C

Capital assets turnover ratio A measure of how intensively a firm's capital assets are used to generate revenue. p. 144

Capital budget A budget that shows how much will be spent to buy capital assets. p. 287

Capital cost allowance (CCA) A tax deduction that Canadian tax laws allow a business to claim for the loss in value of non-current assets through wear and tear or obsolescence. p. 59

Capital investment A project that requires extensive financial resources (cash outflows) to generate a return (cash inflows) over the long term. p. 465

Capital structure The permanent or long-term financing sources used to buy non-current assets. p. 376

Cash Cash holdings and short-term deposits. p. 244

Cash break-even point The number of units or revenue that must be reached to cover total cash fixed costs (total fixed costs less depreciation/amortization). p. 194

Cash budget A treasury function that determines the cash flow of a business at the microlevel to control the level of liquidity. p. 98

Cash conversion cycle The movement of cash through working capital accounts, such as inventories, trade receivables, and trade and other payables. p. 224

Cash conversion efficiency (CCE) A measure of how quickly a business converts revenue to cash flow. p. 223

Cash flows Cash that is obtained (cash provided) and allocated (cash used). p. 88

Cash inflow guidelines A cash inflow takes place when there is a decrease in an asset account or an increase in an equity or liability account. p. 94

Cash inflows The money (interest or profit for the year plus depreciation) generated by an investment or a project; these include profit for the year, proceeds from sale of non-current assets, proceeds from sale of investment securities, and loans or new equity. p. 445

Cash insufficiency The state of not enough cash being generated by a capital project to pay for fixed charges. p. 495

Cash method An accounting method that records business transactions when cash is received or disbursed. p. 47

Cash outflow guidelines A cash outflow takes place when there is an increase in an asset account or a decrease in an equity or liability account. p. 94

Cash outflows Cash disbursements for the purchase of investments, such as mutual funds or capital assets; these include a loss from operation, the purchase of non-current assets, and the purchase of investment securities. p. 445

Characteristics of long-term financing sources Payout, risk, voting rights, cost of capital, tax cost, and cost of issue; these characteristics should be considered when raising funds from long-term sources. p. 385

Chart of accounts A set of categories by which accounting transactions are recorded. p. 39

Chartered bank An institution that provides short-term loans, such as seasonal loans, operating loans, or working capital loans. p. 346

Chief executive officer (CEO) The person who plays a major role in the complete management process and is responsible for creating and implementing strategic plans. p. 10

Chief financial officer (CFO) The person in charge of the finance function and responsible for all accounting functions and external activities. p. 10

Collateral value An assessment by lenders of the value of an asset taken as a guarantee for credit. p. 515

Combined leverage A financial technique used to calculate both operating and financial leverage. p. 399

Committed fixed costs Costs that must be paid to operate a business. p. 205

Complementary budgets Budgets that complement operating budgets, presenting data differently and in more detail. p. 281

Compound interest Interest paid on the principal and the previously earned interest. p. 434

Comprehensive budget A set of projected financial statements, such as the statement of income, the statement of financial position, and the statement of cash flows. p. 287

Compulsory investments Investments in capital assets to respond to a need, legislation, or employee demands and that do not require in-depth analysis. p. 467

Conditional sales contract An agreement between a buyer and a seller for the purchase of an asset (e.g., a truck) by installments. p. 340

Confirming institution An organization that finances inventories. p. 354

Consecutive statements of financial position Two statements of financial position occurring in succession between two periods or in logical sequence; comparing them helps to determine whether a change in each account is a cash inflow or a cash outflow. p. 94

Contribution margin The difference between revenues and variable costs. p. 186

Controllable costs Costs that operating managers are accountable for. p. 206

Controller The person responsible for establishing the accounting and financial reporting policies and procedures. p. 11

Corporate culture A shared system of values and beliefs within an organization. p. 27

Cost of capital The cost of borrowing money from different sources (shareholders or lenders) to finance a business. p. 374

Cost of common shares Dividends paid to shareholders, flotation costs, and growth rate. p. 388

Cost of debt Finance costs less income tax expense. p. 391

Cost of financing Effective after-tax cost of raising funds from different sources (lenders and shareholders). p. 20

Cost of preferred shares Fixed dividends paid to shareholders and the flotation costs. p. 390

Cost of retained earnings Dividends and growth rate. p. 390

Cost of sales The cost incurred in making or producing goods that are sold. p. 50

Cost–volume–profit analysis A tool for analyzing how volume, price, product mix, and product costs relate to one another. p. 182

Credit Accounting entries recorded on the right side of an account. p. 40

Credit insurance policy Insurance to cover losses when a firm's trade receivables that become uncollectible. p. 243

Credit policy A decision about the extent of credit that should be extended to customers. p. 239

Credit terms The conditions under which credit is extended, especially how quickly the customer is expected to pay the account. p. 235

Credit-scoring system A system used to determine the creditworthiness of potential customers. p. 237

Cs of credit Factors that investors look at to judge a business's creditworthiness: character, collateral, capacity, capital, circumstances, and coverage. p. 330

Current assets Assets, such as inventories and trade receivables, expected to be turned into cash, usually in one year or less. p. 61

Current liabilities Debts that a business must pay within one year (i.e., trade and other payables). p. 65

Current ratio A test of general business liquidity. p. 136

Current-value accounting An accounting method used to restate assets on financial statements in terms of what they would be worth if purchased today. p. 510

D

Days of working capital (DWC) The number of DWC a business holds to meet average daily sales requirements. p. 223

Debit Accounting entries recorded on the left side of an account. p. 40

Debt/coverage ratios Measures of the capital structure of a business and its debt-paying ability. p. 138

Debt-to-equity ratio A measure of the proportion of debt and of equity used to finance all assets. p. 139

Debt-to-total-assets ratio A measure of how much debt a business used to finance all assets. p. 138

Depreciation An allocation of the cost of a non-current asset against revenue over the asset's life and an estimated decrease in the value of non-current assets through wear and tear or obsolescence. p. 51

Direct costs Materials and labour expenses that are directly incurred when making a product. p. 206

Discounted payback period The number of years needed for a capital investment to generate enough discounted cash inflows to cover the initial cash outflow. p. 477

Discounting The process of finding the present value of a series of future cash flows. p. 440

Discretionary fixed costs Costs that can be controlled by managers. p. 205

Distribution costs Money spent by a business to promote, sell, and distribute its goods and services. p. 50

Dividend aversion theory A theory suggesting that investors may prefer future capital gains to current dividends because of lower tax rates on capital gains. p. 408

Dividend irrelevance theory A theory suggesting that investors are indifferent to the payment of dividends because the value of lower dividends now is offset by growth-created value in the future. p. 407

Dividend payout ratio The proportion of earnings that a business pays out in dividends. p. 408

Dividend preference theory A theory suggesting that investors prefer instant cash to uncertain future benefits. p. 407

Double-entry bookkeeping A system for posting financial transactions so that the accounting equation remains in balance. p. 39

DuPont financial system The presentation of financial ratios in a logical way to measure ROA. p. 159

E

Earnings before interest charges and taxes The profit before taxes and finance costs shown on the statement of income. p. 139

Earnings per share (EPS) A measure of how much profit is available to each outstanding share. p. 150

Economic life The number of years that a capital asset or an investment opportunity will last. p. 473

Economic ordering quantity (EOQ) A method that determines the best quantity of goods to order each time. p. 231

Economic value A valuation method used to determine the ability of an asset to generate cash. p. 515

Economic value added (EVA) A tool that measures the wealth a company creates for its investors. p. 382

Economy The process for determining the type of resources (human and materials) that should be acquired (the least costly option) and how they should be processed. p. 267

Effectiveness indicators Measures of the goal-related accomplishments of an organization; effectiveness means doing the right things. p. 268

Efficiency The relationship between profit (outputs) generated and assets employed (inputs). p. 13

Efficiency indicators Measures of how well resources (inputs) are brought together to achieve results (outputs); efficiency means doing things right. p. 268

Electronic funds transfer (EFT) A means of transferring funds between customer and supplier by using the Internet or any other electronic medium. p. 246

Equity Funds provided by shareholders, that is, share capital, contributed surplus, retained earnings, and total other comprehensive income/(loss). p. 62

Expense investment A fully tax-deductible cost that should increase profits in the short term. p. 465

External financing Cash obtained from investors (long-term lenders and shareholders). p. 17

External sources Funds provided by investors (shareholders and lenders). p. 325

F

Factoring Selling trade receivables to a financial institution. p. 352

Feedback controls A system that helps to focus on variations of past performance. p. 304

Financial benchmarks Financial performance ratios calculated by using dollar amounts on the statement of income and statement of financial position to find areas of excellent financial performance. p. 153

Financial health score (Z-score) An analysis in which five measures are weighted to give an overall score for the financial health of a business. p. 298

Financial lease An agreement to lease a specific asset for a specified period. p. 355

Financial leverage A financial technique used to determine the most favourable capital structure (equity versus debt). p. 399

Financial management The activities involved in raising money and buying assets to obtain the highest possible return. p. 7

Financial markets Organizations and procedures involved in the buying and selling of financial assets. p. 403

Financial needs The items for which a business needs money. p. 321

Financial ratio A comparison of relationship between numbers on financial statements. p. 122

Financial risk The way that a business is financed (debt versus share capital). p. 327

Financial statements Financial reports, which include the two-statement report called the statement of income and the statement of comprehensive income, the statement of changes in equity, the statement of financial condition, and the statement of cash flows. p. 44

Financial structure The way a company's assets are financed by the entire right side of the statement of financial position (long-term and short-term financing). p. 376

Financing activities The portion of the statement of cash flows that shows how much cash was provided (or used) from external sources (e.g., proceeds from the issue of shares or borrowings, repaying long-term debt, or payment of dividends). p. 103

Financing decisions Decisions related to borrowing from long-term lenders and shareholders. p. 20

Financing requirements Who will provide the money (shareholders and lenders) to finance a business and in what form (e.g., mortgage, working capital loan). p. 322

Fixed costs Costs that remain constant at varying levels of production. p. 182

Fixed-charges coverage ratio A measures of the extent to which a business can pay all its fixed charges (e.g., interest charges, leases). p. 141

Flexible or variable budgets The budgets prepared by managers in the manufacturing or production department. p. 278

Float The amount of funds tied up in cheques that have been written but are still in process and have not yet been collected. p. 246

Future income taxes payable Future tax liability resulting from the difference between depreciation and CCA. p. 63

Future value (FV) The amount to which a payment or series of payments will grow by a given date when compounded by interest. p. 434

G

Goal of working capital management Accelerating the cash flow cycle after sales have been made. p. 222

Governance The process by which decisions are implemented (or not implemented). p. 26

Government financing Funds obtained (directly or indirectly) from government or government institutions to finance a business. p. 336

Gross profit The difference between revenue and cost of sales. p. 23

H

Hard financial benchmarks Financial targets that can be applied to any business or industry to measure financial performance. p. 153

Holding costs The costs associated with storing goods in inventories (e.g., insurance, rent). p. 231

Horizontal analysis A method of analysis that shows the percentage change of accounts on two consecutive financial statements. p. 131

Hurdle rate The capital budgeting rate used to rank capital projects according to their cost of capital. p. 470

I

Income tax A percentage of taxable income paid to the provincial or territorial and federal governments based on taxable income less certain tax deductions. p. 53

Income tax expense The total amount of taxes due to federal and provincial or territorial governments on the taxable income earned by the business during the current fiscal accounting period. p. 53

Indemnification policy Insurance that a business takes against a catastrophic loss in cash. p. 243

Indirect costs Costs that are necessary in production but that cannot be clearly allocated to specific products or services. p. 207

Industry multipliers Standards used to determine the value or worth of a business. p. 526

Inflation The rise in prices during periods of prosperity. p. 425

Initial public offering (IPO) The securities of a company newly established as a public one, offered to the general public for the first time. p. 405

Instrument risk The quality of security available to satisfy investors. p. 327

Intangible assets Assets that cannot be seen, touched, or physically measured and are included in the non-current asset section of the statement of financial position. p. 59

Interest tables Calculated factors used for computing future or present values of single sums and annuities. p. 429

Interim financing A loan made to a business to help finance a capital project, such as the construction of a new plant, until regular financing is obtained. p. 351

Internal financing Cash provided from retained earnings, depreciation/amortization, and a reduction in working capital accounts. p. 16

Internal rate of return (IRR) The interest rate that equates the cost of an investment (cash outflow) to the present value of the expected returns from the investment (cash inflow). p. 449

Internal sources Funds generated by a business (e.g., profit for the year, depreciation/amortization). p. 325

International Accounting Standards Board (IASB) Organization that develops, in the public interest, a single set of high-quality, understandable, and enforceable global standards that require transparent and comparable information in general-purpose financial statements. p. 28

International Financial Reporting Standards (IFRS) Accounting standards issued by the IASB. p. 27

Inventory The monetary value a company places on the material it has purchased or goods it has manufactured. p. 61

Inventory replenishment The decision of when to order goods from supplier. p. 233

Inventory turnover The number of times a year a company turns over its inventories. p. 143

Investing activities The portion of the statement of cash flows that shows how much cash was provided (or used) to buy or sell non-current assets (e.g., purchase or proceeds from the sale of a building). p. 104

Investing decisions Decisions related to the acquisition of non-current assets. p. 19

Investment securities Short-term deposits, such as treasury bills and bank deposits. p. 247

J

Journalizing The process of recording, electronically or manually, transactions in a journal (e.g., sales journal, salaries journal). p. 41

Journals (books of original entry) The books used to record accounting transactions in chronological order. p. 41

Just-in-time inventory management An inventory management technique that obtains supplier materials just when they are needed. p. 231

L

Ledger (books of final entry) Books that show all amounts debited and credited in individual accounts (e.g., trade receivables, revenue, inventories, and salaries), including a running balance. p. 41

Lessee One who pays to use an asset without owning it. p. 355

Lessor One who lends an asset to someone (lessee). p. 355

Leverage A technique used to find the most suitable operating and financial structure to amplify financial performance. p. 374

Liabilities The debts of a business. p. 63

Line of credit A formal written agreement between a bank and a borrower regarding a loan. p. 348

Liquidation value The worth of an asset if sold under duress. p. 513

Liquidity The ability of a firm to meet its short-term financial commitments. p. 14

Liquidity ratios Measures of a firm's ability to meet its cash obligations. p. 136

Listed company A company that is listed and traded on an organized stock exchange. p. 405

Long-term loan A loan to finance capital assets for a long period (more than five years). p. 338

M

Marginal cost of capital (MCC) The increased average cost from having obtained new funds at higher rates than previously. p. 392

Market performance A method used for measuring the efficiency and effectiveness of management within the industry in which the business operates. p. 516

Market value The price at which an item, a business, or an asset can be sold. p. 509

Market-value ratios Measurements of how investors react to a company's market performance. p. 150

Material requirements planning (MRP) A method of scheduling that coordinates and the use of resources in production. p. 230

Miscellaneous assets Assets, such as bonds and shares, purchased from other businesses. p. 60

Mortgage A loan obtained against which specific real property is used as collateral (e.g., a building). p. 341

N

Net future value (NFV) The future value of the projected compounded cash inflows, less the projected future value of the cash outflow. p. 447

Net present value (NPV) The present value of the future cash flow of an investment less the initial cash outflow. p. 447

Net working capital The difference between current assets and current liabilities. p. 221

Non-controllable costs Costs that are not under the direct control of operating managers. p. 206

Non-current assets Statement of financial position accounts, such as land, buildings, equipment, and machinery. p. 19

Non-current liabilities Debts that are not due for at least one year. p. 63

Not-for-profit organizations Organizations that operate exclusively for social, educational, professional, religious, health, charitable, or any other NFP purpose. p. 70

O

Operating activities The portion of the statement of cash flows that shows how much cash was provided by the business itself (e.g., profit for the year, depreciation/amortization, and adjustments in non-cash working capital accounts). p. 100

Operating budgets The budgets prepared by operating managers. p. 277

Operating cycle The number of days inventories and trade receivables take (in days) to be converted into cash. p. 226

Operating decisions Decisions related to accounts appearing on the statement of financial position (current assets and current liabilities) and the statement of income (e.g., revenue, cost of sales, distribution costs). p. 23

Operating lease A lease that is cancellable by the lessee at any time upon due notice. p. 355

Operating leverage A financial technique that determines to what extent fixed costs should be used relative to variable costs. p. 397

Operating managers The people in charge of organizational units, such as marketing, manufacturing, and human resources, and responsible for making operating and investing decisions. p. 11

Operating performance A method for measuring the efficiency and effectiveness of management at the operating level (e.g., marketing, production). p. 516

Operating section Section of the statement of income that shows a company's gross profit and profit before taxes. p. 49

Opportunity cost The income sacrificed by not pursuing the next best investment alternative. p. 390

Opportunity investments Strategic investments made in capital assets that usually have far-reaching financial implications. p. 467

Ordering costs The costs associated with buying goods (e.g., receiving, inspecting, and accounting). p. 231

Other income Revenue that is not directly related to the central operations of a business. p. 50

Overall performance The ratios used to measure how well a business is deploying its resources. p. 516

Overhead budgets The budgets prepared by managers responsible for staff units, such as human resources, finance, or legal departments. p. 278

Owners' section The section of the statement of income that shows the amount of money left for shareholders (i.e., profit for the year). p. 53

P

Payback method The number of years required for a capital investment to generate enough cash inflows to cover the initial cash outflow. p. 476

Payback reciprocal A capital budgeting technique that gives a rough estimate of the return on investment of a capital project. p. 477

Performance indicator A measurement used to evaluate organizational performance. p. 267

Performance standards Benchmarks against which performance is measured. p. 267

Planning The process of creating goals and outlining action plans to meet those goals. p. 265

Planning assumptions Boundaries on which priorities, goals, plans, budgets, and financial projections are based. p. 272

Post office box A location to which customers send their cheques, which are then transferred to the seller's bank account. p. 247

Posting The process of transferring recorded transactions from the journals to the appropriate ledger accounts (e.g., revenue, trade receivables). p. 41

Prepaid expenses Payments made for services that have not yet been received. p. 62

Present value (PV) The value today of a future payment or stream of payments, discounted at an appropriate rate. p. 438

Preventive controls A system that helps to guide actions toward intended results. p. 303

Price/earnings ratio (P/E) A measure of how much investors are willing to pay per dollar of reported profits. p. 150

Price-level accounting An accounting method used to restate assets on financial statements in terms of current purchasing power (inflation). p. 510

Prime rate The interest rate that banks charge to their most creditworthy customers. p. 348

Privately held company A business that can sell shares to a small group of people but not to the general public. p. 405

Productivity A measure of performance in how resources are used. p. 125

Profit before taxes The difference between gross profit and costs related to distribution and administration. p. 24

Profit break-even point The number of units or revenue that must be reached to cover total costs and meet a profit goal. p. 195

Profit for the year The difference between profit before taxes and income tax expense. p. 24

Profit margin The profit before tax, after adjusting for non-operating accounts, such as other income and finance costs. p. 147

Profit margin on revenue A measure of the operating efficiency of a business. p. 147

Profitability index (PI) The ratio of the present value of cash inflows to the present value of the cash outflows, discounted at a predetermined rate of interest. p. 487

Profitability ratios Measures of the overall efficiency and effectiveness of a business. p. 147

Profit-volume (PV) ratio The contribution margin expressed on a per-unit basis. p. 187

Projected financial statements Expected results of some assumed events that are part of financial projections (e.g., statement of income, statement of financial position, and the statement of cash flows). p. 291

Property, plant, and equipment The types of assets that are considered permanent and are used over an extended time, that is, many years (previously called capital assets or fixed assets). p. 58

Prospectus A document that discloses the details of a security and the underlying business to prospective investors. p. 332

Prosperity The ability of a firm to grow (i.e., revenue, profit, and equity). p. 15

Publicly traded company A business that can sell securities broadly, after a prospectus is approved by the securities commission. p. 405

Q

Quick ratio A measure of the relationship between the more liquid current assets and all current liabilities. p. 137

R

Ratio analysis A method to help readers of financial statements to assess the financial structure and performance of a business. p. 124

Regional banks Banks where customers pay their accounts and the money is transferred to the seller's bank account. p. 247

Relevant costs Cost alternatives that managers can choose from to operate a business. p. 189

Relevant range Costs (fixed and variable) that apply to a certain level of production. p. 189

Replacement value The cost of acquiring a new asset to replace an existing asset with the same functional utility. p. 514

Residual value The value from the sale of an asset or a business at the end of its physical life. p. 472

Retained earnings The profit generated by the business that the owners have not claimed in dividends. p. 62

Return on equity A measure of the yield shareholders earn on their investment. p. 148

Return An adequate cash and profit to finance a company's growth. p. 126

Return on revenue A measure of a company's overall ability to generate profit from each revenue dollar. p. 148

Return on total assets A measure of the performance of assets used in a business. p. 148

Revenue What a business earns from the sale of its products and services. p. 50

Revenue break-even point The revenue that must be reached to cover total costs. p. 193

Revolving credit The maximum amount of a loan a bank agrees to provide a business (borrower). p. 351

Risk The expectation (probability) that something will happen in the future. p. 427

Risk analysis The process of assigning probabilities to the individual estimates in a capital project's base case. p. 493

Risk capital investors Individuals or institutions that provide money to finance a business that entails relatively high risk; these investors seek a high potential return. p. 333

Rule of 72 A calculation that shows the approximate number of years it takes for an investment to double when compounded annually. p. 435

S

Sale and leaseback An arrangement to sell an asset to a lessor and then lease it back. p. 356

Sales budgets The budgets prepared by managers in the sales or marketing department. p. 277

Scanning the environment A method used during the planning process to pin down planning assumptions. p. 515

Screening controls A system that helps to monitor performance while work is being performed. p. 304

Secured loan A loan that the borrower guarantees by pledging some assets. p. 352

Self-liquidating loan Funds used to finance temporary or fluctuating variations in working capital accounts (e.g., inventories, trade receivables). p. 351

Self-regulated financial benchmarks Financial targets that are determined by a business's own policies and practices and other financial measures. p. 153

Semi-variable costs Costs that change disproportionately with changes in output levels. p. 183

Sensitivity analysis A technique that shows to what extent a change in one variable (e.g., selling price, fixed costs) affects the break-even point. p. 196

Share capital Amount of money that is put into the business by the shareholders. p. 62

Shareholders The owners of a business (common and preferred shareholders). p. 333

Short-term financing Financing for less than one year (e.g., trade credit, line of credit). p. 345

Simple interest Interest paid on the principal only. p. 432

Soft financial benchmarks Most financial benchmarks fall in this category and should be used with some degree of caution. p. 153

Solvency The ability to service or pay all debts (short and long term). p. 125

Stability Relationship between debt and equity. p. 15

Statement of cash flows A financial statement that shows where funds come from (cash inflows) and where they went (cash outflows). p. 46

Statement of changes in equity A statement that represents the interest of the shareholders of a business, showing the cumulative net results in equity with respect to share capital, contributed surplus, retained earnings, and accumulated other comprehensive income/(loss) for the period. p. 46

Statement of comprehensive income A financial statement that shows items of income and expense that are not in the statement of income. p. 46

Statement of financial position A financial statement that shows a "snapshot" of a company's financial condition (assets, equity, and liabilities). p. 46

Statement of income A financial statement that shows a summary of revenue and costs for a specified period. p. 46

Stock market A network of exchanges, brokers, and investors that trade securities. p. 404

Strategic business unit (SBU) A unit within a multi-business company. p. 265

Subordinated debt A loan that is risky, for which investors charge higher interest rates. p. 343

Sunk costs Investment costs incurred before deciding whether or not to proceed with a capital project. p. 474

Supplier credit Financing from suppliers (trade payables). p. 345

Sustainable growth rate The rate of increase in revenue a company can attain without depleting financial resources, borrowing excessively, or issuing new stock. p. 296

SWOT analysis An acronym for a method of identifying a company's strengths, weaknesses, opportunities, and threats. p. 271

T

Term loan A loan made to buy capital assets. p. 338

Time value of money The rate at which the value of money is traded off as a function of time. p. 425

Timeline A graphic illustration of time-value-of-money problems. p. 431

Times-interest-earned ratio (TIE) A measure of a business's ability to pay the interest charges on debt. p. 139

Total assets turnover ratio A measure of how intensively a firm's total assets are used to generate revenue. p. 144

Total comprehensive income/(loss) Transactions and other events (e.g., asset revaluation) that affect the equity account. p. 46

Total quality management A management approach in which everyone in an organization is responsible for creating customer satisfaction. p. 7

Trade and other payables Money owed to suppliers of goods or services that were purchased on credit. p. 65

Trade receivables Money owed to the company by its customers for the purchase of goods or services. p. 61

Transparency The extent to which business processes and related information resources, assets, and outcomes are visible and open to inspection by stakeholders. p. 24

Treasurer The person responsible for raising funds and regulating the flow of funds. p. 11

Trend analysis Analyzing a company's performance over a number of years. p. 157

Trial balance A statement that ensures that the general ledger is in balance (debit transactions equal credit transactions). p. 41

Types of inventories Raw materials, work-in-process, and finished goods. p. 230

U

Unit break-even point The number of units that must be sold to cover total costs. p. 193

V

Variable costs Costs that fluctuate directly with changes in volume of production. p. 182

Venture capital Risk capital supplied to small companies by wealthy individuals (angels), partnerships, or corporations, usually in return for an equity position in the firm. p. 335

Vertical analysis Listing (1) all numbers on the statement of financial position as percentages of total assets, and (2) all numbers on the statement of income as percentages of revenue. p. 128

W

Weighted average cost of capital Composite weighted after-tax cost of raising funds from long-term investors (bonds, mortgages, common shares, preferred shares). p. 21

Weighted average cost of financing The proportion of the cost of each amount financed in a company's financial structure. p. 376

Working capital accounts Statement of financial position accounts, such as inventories, trade receivables, and cash (current assets), and trade and other payables and short-term borrowings (current liabilities). p. 23

Working capital loans Short-term loans made to finance working capital accounts (e.g., inventories, trade receivables). p. 250

Working capital management Managing individual current asset and current liability accounts to ensure proper interrelationships among them. p. 222

Z

Zero-based budgeting The process of preparing a budget by using decisions packages and the assumption that a new organizational unit will be started. p. 279

[INDEX]

D

G

L

M

N

O

P

T

U

V

W

Y

Z